BIG TOWN BIG TIME

A NEW YORK EPIC: 1898-1998

JAY MAEDER, Series Editor

DAILY NEWS BOOKS

DAILY NEWS

1999

BIG TOWN BIG TIME

A NEW YORK EPIC: 1898-1998

Library of Congress
Catalog Card Number: 98-89001
ISBN: 1-58261-028-2

JAY MAEDER, Series Editor

ROBERT SHIELDS, Series Designer

LES GOODSTEIN, Executive Producer

IRA ELLENTHAL, Assistant Executive Producer

Production and Design Assistance by Sports Publishing Inc.
www.SportsPublishingInc.com

BIG TOWN BIG TIME

ACKNOWLEDGMENTS

A project the size and scope of BIG TOWN/BIG TIME would not have come together without the support of a small group of ardent corporate sponsors. All of New York joins us as we extend our heartfelt gratitude to our Platinum Partners: P.C. Richard, Sleepy's, the Brooklyn Campus of Long Island University, Con Edison, Chase, Heineken and Empire Blue Cross/Blue Shield.

LES GOODSTEIN

Associate Publisher
New York Daily News

EDITOR'S NOTE

This volume collects a newspaper series called BIG TOWN/BIG TIME that appeared in the New York Daily News from February to December 1998 and was the newspaper's contribution to a year-long civic celebration of the modern City of New York's 100th anniversary.

Several new chapters that were not part of the original series have been added to the book. Several original series chapters have been dropped. Several pieces have been rewritten since their initial publication.

JAY MAEDER

Series Editor
New York Daily News
December 1998

BIG TOWN BIG TIME

A NEW YORK EPIC: 1898-1998

GRAND CENTRAL STATION

BIG TOWN BIG TIME™

A NEW YORK EPIC: 1898-1998

TABLE OF CONTENTS

BIG TOWN BIG TIME™

A NEW YORK EPIC: 1898-1998

BIG TOWN BIG TIME

BIG TOWN BIG TIME™

A NEW YORK EPIC: 1898-1998

BIG TOWN BIG TIME

A NEW YORK EPIC: 1898-1998

Great forces at the beginning of the 17th century were re-forming history, and they were impelling men of character to occupy new fields of endeavor and discovery . . . Henry Hudson was the normal product of a great epoch. Neither before nor since his time could any man have conceived a project at once so reasonable and so unreasonable, so dependent upon sober logic and upon baseless fable, upon newly awakened knowledge and old superstition, as that which urged him to strive again and again to penetrate the barriers of an unknown West for a pathway to the impossible East.

— Edgar Mayhew Bacon,
"Henry Hudson: His Times And His Voyages," 1907

A VERY GOOD LAND TO FALL IN WITH

Henry Hudson And The Great River

By JAY MAEDER
Daily News Staff Writer

The legends of the red man would hold that one day there appeared before the fishers what first seemed to be an immense supernatural bird on the horizon. Then, as it drew closer, they saw that it was a wigwam floating on the water. There was much consternation. Higher counsels concluded that the gods had sent a great ark, and upon the shore did the deer-skinned natives gather in wonder to behold the visitors and offer them tobacco and dried fruit.

And indeed, what sailed in to greet them was nothing less than half the moon.

SOMEWHERE there was a great polar sea, a passage from Europe to the fabulous riches of the Orient, and through the grand age of merchants and mariners there had been many captains, sailing under many flags, who had spent their lives searching for it. In the year 1609, the Englishman Henry Hudson was just another of them.

Twice already Hudson's explorations had found nothing but walls of Greenland ice; twice he had gone home a failure. Now London had no further use for him. Amsterdam, on the other hand, was prepared to receive him more cordially, and Henry Hudson changed masters. On the fourth day of April, under contract to the empire-building Dutch East India Co., he sailed for a third time.

And, but for a crew of shivering malcontents who rose up in mutiny when Hudson yet again hit the frozen seas somewhere off Norway and forced him to change course toward warmer climes away from the fogs and floes, The Great River That Runs Two Ways would have taken its modern name from some other sailor at some other point in the glorious forward-flowing accident called history.

But Henry Hudson's time had come. Westward went the tiny, flat-bottomed Halve Maene with her grumbling hands, across the ocean to, by mid-July, somewhere off Maine. Southward then did Hudson proceed to Chesapeake Bay; there, not desiring to intrude nearer to the fledgling settlements of English Virginia, he turned about and plied northward again up the coast of the New World.

On Aug. 28, he passed the lower capes of Delaware Bay and saw the shores of what would later be called Cape May. Briefly he set his crew to work groping for channels through the sandbars, then decided that this shallow basin was probably not the entrance to the passage he sought and again stood north. And on Sept. 2, the

men of the little Half Moon noted that the flat and sandy New Jersey shore was climbing into highlands.

"It is a very good land to fall in with, and a pleasant land to see," recorded First Mate Robert Juet.

"At three of the clock in the afternoon we came to three great rivers."

HISTORIANS of a later day would debate exactly where the Half Moon was in the first week of September in the year 1609. The "three great rivers" might have been the Raritan, the Narrows and Rockaway Inlet; Henry Hudson might have come to anchor off Coney Island, or off Staten Island, or off New Jersey, or somewhere else. Chronicled by Juet is the first visit to the vessel, on Sept. 4, by the canoes of "very civil" Indians bearing gifts, and then Hudson's reciprocal courtesy call, the following day, to their village on the shore — and then, on Sept. 6, the skirmish between a less-friendly neighboring tribe and several of Hudson's thuggish crewmen, an incident that left one sailor dead and the natives suddenly suspicious of the fine ark that the gods had sent them.

Through the Narrows and into the

Upper Bay proceeded the Half Moon. On Sept. 12, Henry Hudson entered the ocean-flooded river to which he would give his name. He first anchored off what would someday be Manhattan's W. 42nd St.; two evenings later he was at Spuyten Duyvil; then he was sailing through the majestic Highlands. Any serious expectation he might still have harbored that he had at last found the great passage to China was now waning. Late in September, near Albany, he turned back.

The chronicles reflect that the Half Moon continued to trade amiably enough with the Indians of the shore on her journeys both upriver and down again — until Oct. 1, when, perhaps somewhere near Peekskill, the fragile peace fell apart.

"The people of the mountains came aboard us wondering at our ship and weapons," wrote Juet. *"We bought some small skins of them for trifles. This afternoon, one canoe kept hanging under our stern with one man in it, which we could not keep from thence, which got up by our rudder to the cabin window, and stole my pillow and two shirts. . . . Our master's mate shot at him and struck him in the breast; and killed him. Whereupon all the rest fled away. . . . Then one of them that*

swamme got hold of our boat. But our cook took a sword and cut off one of his hands, and he was drowned.

"By that time it was dark. So we anchored in four fathoms water and rode well. At break of day we weighed. . . . Then came one of the savages with many other, thinking to betray us. But we, perceiving their intent, suffered none of them to enter our ship. Whereupon two canoes full of men with their bows and arrows shot after our stern: in recompense whereof we discharged six muskets and killed two or three of them. Then above an hundred of them came to a point of land to shoot at us. There I shot a falcon at them and killed two of them.

"Yet they manned off another canoe with nine or 10 men, which came to meet us. So I shot it through and killed one of them. Then our men with their muskets killed three or four more."

In a hail of arrows did the Half Moon make her way back to the mouth of the extraordinary river she had entered just a month earlier, and from there, on Oct. 4, she set out for home.

"By 12 of the clock we were clear of the inlet," wrote Juet of the uneventful moment that concluded the adventure. *"Then we took in our boat and set our mainsail, and sprit sail and our topsails, and steered away east southeast, and southeast by east, off into the main sea."*

HENRY HUDSON never saw his river again. After reporting back to the Dutch East India Co., he returned to English employ and in April 1610 set out a fourth time to find the lost Arctic sea. Aboard the ship Discoverer, his crew remained as mutinously surly as ever; late in June 1611, deep in Hudson's Bay, they finally settled matters by putting him over the side and cheering as his forlorn little shallop disappeared forever into the fog.

But by now, the merchant princes of Amsterdam had taken excited note of the river and its possibilities. France might have done the same in 1524, after the Florentine navigator Giovanni da Verrazano first discovered the river, but King Francois I had other things to think about; Spain might have done so in 1526, but her explorer Esteban Gomez had been so little impressed with his find that he just shrugged and sailed away. In the accident that is history, this moment now belonged to the Dutch. In another dozen years there would be a permanent settlement here in this very good land. Someday it would be the capital of the world.

BIG TOWN BIG TIME™

PRELUDE

THE GROWINGEST PLACE EVER

Early Manhattan

The city, about 1850.

By BILL BELL and JAY MAEDER
Daily News Staff Writers

It might have become New France, had King Francis paid more attention to the 1524 report of his hired Florentine explorer Verrazano. It might have become New Spain, had the sailor Gomez been more than fleetingly interested in the place.

Instead, once the canny Dutch merchants who had dispatched Henry Hudson to the land across the sea grasped its wealth in furs, the place at the mouth of Hudson's great river became New Netherland. And in May 1623 — three years after the Mayflower landed the Pilgrims in Massachusetts — the first permanent European inhabitants of New Netherland arrived aboard a Dutch vessel named the New Amsterdam.

There were about 100 of them, French-speaking Protestant men, women and children who were fleeing Catholic persecution in Spanish-ruled Belgium and who had agreed to establish trading outposts for the lately organized Dutch West India Co. Most went up Hudson's river to the new Fort Orange at once, but eight settled on Governors Island. Some months later they were joined by 45 comrades and 103 head of livestock, and they all moved to the southern tip of nearby Manhattan, and called their settlement New Amsterdam. By May 1626, when the colony's first director-general, Peter Minuit, traded local Indian leaders 60 guilders' worth of tools and dry goods for more or less legal title to Manhattan Island, the population was about 200.

Blessed with rich timber, fish and fur resources and a splendid natural port, the Dutch outpost bustled. Soon there were permanent homes, a church and a rudimentary street system dominated by the Breede Wegh, or Broad Way. By 1638 there was a ferry across the East River to a settlement called Breuckelen.

There were also wars with previously hospitable Indians, touched off by Minuit's bumbling successor, Willem Kieft, who in the winter of 1643 ignored the pleas of Algonquian tribes seeking Dutch protection from their traditional enemies the Iroquois — and instead had his troops massacre them. Enraged, the Algonquian tribes killed scores of farm families throughout the region and burned their homes and villages.

In turn, New Amsterdam's defenders killed more than 1,200 Indians before a shaky peace treaty was signed. Kieft was followed by peg-legged Peter Stuyvesant, who continued to grapple with Indian troubles — notably 1655's so-called Peach War, ignited when an angry farmer shot dead an Indian woman who had taken a peach from his orchard — but who also was credited with turning the struggling, shabby colony into a genuinely thriving community.

For all that, New Amsterdam was proving to be less successful a company town than the merchants of Holland desired. The Dutch West India Co. was far more interested in the West Indies anyway, and soon pieces of its American settlement were being sold off to eager private buyers. Another problem for the Dutch was that there were never very many of them here in the first place; the first census in 1656 recorded just 1,000 inhabitants. That meant they were greatly outnumbered by the neighboring English. Warships, inevitably, arrived from London one day in August 1664.

The invasion was bloodless; the Duke of York demanded surrender and got it at once. Thereafter — save for a fleeting moment a few years later, when the Dutch futilely sought to reclaim the place — the town would forever be called New York.

More commercially successful in English hands, the city quickly began to rival Boston and Philadelphia in mercantile importance, and by 1760 it numbered 20,000. A good many New Yorkers, though, were just as unhappy with their new English masters as they had been with the Dutch. While the well-to-do landlord and merchant classes were mostly loyal to the crown, the city was also a rebel stronghold, and revolutionary sentiment simmered here years before the seminal Battle of Lexington in Massachusetts in 1775.

When the brave new Declaration of Independence was read aloud on the steps of City Hall the following year, cheering crowds toppled a statue of King George. British troops invaded Manhattan on Sept. 15, routed Gen. George Washington's ragtag Continental Army and burned a quarter of the city to the ground.

New York remained occupied until November 1783, when the Redcoats were finally driven out — along with thousands of Tory locals who fled elsewhere in disgrace, immediately halving the population. In ruins physically and economically, it began at once to rebuild itself; briefly it became the capital of the new federal government.

In just a single generation it became America's largest city, with nearly 100,000 residents by 1810. "The growingest place ever," someone said admiringly. With the opening of the Erie Canal in 1825 and the inauguration of regular packet service to Liverpool, great maritime and manufacturing fortunes were now being made overnight; New York still extended no farther north than Houston St., but it was already positioning itself to become a world capital.

By midcentury, that northern boundary was 42nd St., and waves of newcomers — mostly Irish and German immigrants, but also many New Englanders — had swelled the population to 800,000. Many thousands more were still coming, and in 1886 there arose from the harbor a majestic lady lifting a torch of welcome to the millions more yet to land in the fabulous melting pot. With great growth came great constructions: an astonishing bridge to Brooklyn, elevated trains that fast transformed distant farmlands into city streets, a grand central railroad hub, a powerful political machine that ruled the town and regularly plundered it.

By the 1890s New York was bursting at its seams, already annexing portions of the Bronx, still seeking more room. A defining moment was at hand: The time had come for Manhattan and its neighbors to consolidate into one giant, golden city.

BIG TOWN BIG TIME™

PRELUDE

SECOND CITY

Early Brooklyn

By DENNIS WEPMAN
Special To The News

Having settled New Amsterdam in lower Manhattan, the Dutch West India Co. in 1635 cast its eyes eastward to the neighboring island and began buying up parcels of land from the local Indian tribes. There, the Dutch governors established five farming towns: Breuckelen; New Amersfoort; New Utrecht; Vlache Bos, or Flat Bush, and Boswijk, or Bushwick. A sixth town, Gravesend, was settled by Englishmen. A thriving ferry service carried farmers and their produce to the Manhattan markets across the river. Life was pastoral and uneventful, and things stayed about the same even after the English took over in 1664. The English tried to rename the place Brookland, but that never caught on. Otherwise, they continued to treat it as a rural suburb where they got their meat and milk and vegetables, and so life went on for another hundred years.

By 1776, there were still fewer than 4,000 people in Kings County. In August of that year the British invaded Brooklyn, forcing the tiny American Army to flee to the tip of Brooklyn Heights, where George Washington and his troops narrowly escaped in rowboats. Some 15,000 Redcoats poured into Brooklyn, soon reinforced by 5,000 Hessians; the Battle of Brooklyn that followed was a disaster for the American patriots, and so were the next seven years, as the British occupation force remained. It is estimated that 12,000 American captives died in misery aboard British prison ships moored off the Brooklyn coast.

Like Manhattan across the river, Kings County flourished commercially after the Revolution; by 1835 the population was more than 30,000, and 20 years later the City of Brooklyn, which had absorbed the villages of Williamsburgh and Bushwick, was home to more than 200,000. No longer a rural suburb, it was suddenly the third most populous city in America, after New York and Philadelphia — and the great influx of immigrants was only beginning.

In they flooded from Germany and Ireland, seeking work and finding it — at the Navy Yard, which

When the great bridge opened in 1883, Brooklyn became an integral part of New York — whether it liked it or not. And many proud Brooklynites didn't.

those who worked in Manhattan. That appeal increased particularly after the introduction of steam-powered ferry service in 1814. The Nassau, Robert Fulton's boat, provided fast and safe passage between the two cities for 3 cents, as increasingly their destinies became linked.

But it was the bridge that really established the connection. Spanning the East River had been discussed since the turn of the century — indeed, Brooklyn had a Bridge St. long before it had a Brooklyn Bridge — but it wasn't until 1857 that the idea of actually building a bridge was taken seriously. That year German engineer John Roebling proposed constructing a bridge twice as long as any in existence. The severe winter of 1866, when the river froze and ferry traffic stopped dead, decided the matter. Work began three years later on Roebling's astonishing project — 1,595 feet in length, the longest suspension bridge in the world, the engineering feat of the century. The job took 14 years and 26 lives, including Roebling's; his son Washington was crippled by the work and supervised the last of it from a wheelchair in his Brooklyn Heights home. When the bridge opened in 1883, there were 13 ferry lines on the river, making 1,200 crossings daily; most were gone a few years later. Brooklyn was now an integral part of New York — whether it liked it or not.

And many Brooklynites didn't. Brooklyn was a proud city, none too eager to join its larger and more prosperous neighbor when the amalgamation of the boroughs was proposed. But, in fact, it was expanding too fast for its own economy; it badly needed money for schools and hospitals and roads. When the vote finally came, consolidation of the nation's first and third largest cities passed by fewer than 300 votes.

Brooklyn mourned its loss of sovereignty but gained much by being included in New York's budget, its mass transit network and its fine water system. And it was now, in 1898, part of something larger and more splendid than either city had been alone. Wrote a poet consolingly:
*This is not death,
but a second creation.*

had opened in 1801 where the prison boats had been anchored, and in the thousands of factories, foundries, machine shops, shipyards and refineries that by 1880 had made Brooklyn the nation's fourth-largest industrial center. There were iron, rope, glass, paint, petroleum and other chemicals; there were clocks; there was gin and beer.

Housing was cheap, and residing in Brooklyn was always attractive to

By DICK SHERIDAN
Daily News Staff Writer

The early founders of New Netherland concentrated chiefly on their trading post at the southern tip of Manhattan and on the Brooklyn shoreline, where they established a few farms, and they left the neighboring natives pretty much to themselves for a time. But the sandy loam and oak forests of Queens could not long escape the notice of the white men eager to raise crops and log timber.

A few hardy souls tried to farm what is now Astoria in the 1630s but were driven away by Indians. Meanwhile, Englishmen from the colonies to the north were moving west along the spine of Long Island, and they established the first Queens settlement at Maspeth in 1642. Indians attacked that village the following year, and the English fled as well. Dutch authorities under Gov. Willem Kieft began to fight back. Over the next few years there were sporadic wars and peace treaties. Finally the Indians signed dozens of deeds formally giving up claims to their territories.

Meanwhile, more English settlers continued to move in. Quakers established Vlissingen in 1645, and other new arrivals — moving farther inland from Maspeth to build more easily defensible villages — settled Middleburgh in 1652 and Rustdorp in 1656.

Relations between the English colonists and their Dutch governors were never cordial, and, in Queens, the 1664 Dutch surrender of their New Netherland territories to London was a welcome development. Administration of the former Dutch colonies was reorganized in 1683, and 10 counties were established. One was Queens County, which then included Nassau and was named for the Portuguese princess Catherine of Braganza, wife of King Charles II.

The inhabitants of the newly created Queens County lived principally on family farms that surrounded the tiny villages of Newtown, the former Dutch Middleburgh; Flushing, the Anglicized Vlissingen; and Jamaica, where Rustdorp previously stood. For many years they led quiet lives, mostly raising specialty crops for

Lutheran Cemetery in Middle Village, 1852.

ACROSS THE RIVER AND INTO THE TREES

Early Queens

local markets and for export (the Newtown Pippin apple became a favorite item in London). But the serenity of the farms was shattered by the Revolutionary War.

Save for the inhabitants of Newtown, most locals took the side of King George, and the British billeted their troops in Queens. The honor had a heavy price: The British commandeered homes and fields, chopped down wood lots and even fence posts for firewood and confiscated grain, vegetables and meat. By the end of the war in 1783, Queens was broke. When the British gave up the fight and went home, many of their Queens friends also left, emigrating to Nova Scotia and Newfoundland.

Like its sister counties — and as Manhattan exploded into a primary commercial center — Queens began to experience spurts of growth in the early 19th century. By the

1830s, wealthy New Yorkers were finding that bucolic Queens made for a convenient escape from the ever more crowded and sometimes unhealthy conditions of their own tiny island of Manhattan. In the summer of 1833 a seaside hotel called the Marine Pavilion opened in Far Rockaway — where the 4-mile-long sand barrier of the Rockaway peninsula joined the mainland of Long Island — to serve well-heeled refugees from the big city's cholera outbreak.

Then, in 1847, Queens gained its most visible industry. Manhattan city fathers forbade conversion of additional land into cemeteries, and Manhattanites looked across the East River for the land they needed to bury their dead. The State Rural Cemetery Act suddenly provided for immense new commercial burial sites, and Queens' wide-open spaces drew their gaze.

Calvary, Cypress Hills and Evergreen cemeteries were organized in 1848, and many more followed, along with flourishing new floral and coffin businesses.

At the same time, starvation in Ireland and political upheaval in central Europe were sending floods of immigrants to America. Thousands of Irish settled in Astoria, Flushing and Jamaica; thousands more Germans, after bursting the seams of Brooklyn, spilled into Queens as well. Middle Village, solidly English in 1840, was entirely German 20 years later.

Along with the Irish and Germans, another breed began filling Queens during the 1850s: land developers.

Long Island City was incorporated in 1870, and a series of new villages began to appear on the map. New industry and jobs followed. John Locke, a tinware manufacturer, came to Whitestone in 1853. French immigrant Florian Grosjean

opened his tinware factory in Woodhaven the following year, while Conrad Poppenhusen, a German immigrant, moved his hard rubber plant from Brooklyn to College Point. After the Civil War, William Steinway moved his family's piano factory to Astoria, constructing a community of homes and shops for his workers.

The wave of development continued into the 1890s. By then, most areas of the county had been populated, and many of the amenities of urban life had arrived.

With the infrastructure of a budding municipal lifestyle in place, the legal artifice would follow. On Nov. 6, 1894, residents of Queens, with those of the other counties, cast their ballots on the question of consolidation into a Greater New York. On Jan. 1, 1898, the historic towns and villages of Queens disappeared into the new city.

The bridge at Spuyten Duyvil.

PRELUDE

MAINLAND ROAD

The Early Bronx

By DENNIS WEPMAN
Special to The News

New York City's only foothold on the U.S. mainland, the Bronx started out strictly as a real-estate speculation, bought in 1639 from the Indians by the Dutch West India Co. in case the population of New Amsterdam should ever overflow Manhattan. Which it did.

But the Dutch never dominated the area. Its first settler was a Scandinavian sea captain named Jonas Bronck, who bought 500 acres in 1641 and set up as a tobacco grower. The area was associated with wealth and style from the beginning: Bronck owned the largest library in the Dutch colony, and one impressed visitor to his mansion wrote of him that he "used silver on his table and had tablecloths . . . and possessed as many as six linen shirts."

It wasn't to last. Though Bronck's river (now, of course, the Bronx River) gave its name to the whole borough, Jonas died in 1643 and his books, tablecloths and linen shirts disappeared along with his servants. By then the region was swept with Indian troubles, and the Dutch did little to solve things. Two English settlers who also had set up housekeeping on the mainland came to grief: Anne Hutchinson and her family, who had come to Long Island Sound in flight from religious persecution in Massachusetts, were slaughtered in an Indian raid, and John Throckmorton, who had settled 35 families on the southern peninsula later known as Throgs Neck, was driven away to New Jersey. In 1646, Adriaen van den Donck, New Netherland's first lawyer, moved 50 families into his huge estate extending from Spuyten Duyvil Creek through Riverdale to Yonkers, but that settlement was wiped out by Indians as well. It wasn't a promising beginning for the Bronx.

But new settlements nevertheless kept cropping up, and the Bronx was prospering by 1664, when the English took New Amsterdam and made it New York. In 1693, New York merchant Frederick Philipse thought it worth building a toll bridge across Spuyten Duyvil Creek to link Manhattan to the mainland, and thence to Boston by the old Post Road. By 1700 there were two bustling towns — Eastchester and Westchester — and the four great manors of Pelham, Fordham, Philipseburgh and Morrisania.

The region saw considerable action during the Revolutionary War, none of it very effective for the Americans. British troops landed at Throgs Neck in October 1776 and, despite tireless rebel raids, occupied the Bronx until 1783. In January 1777 a small party of patriots dragged a cannon to the top of a hill near the Bronx River and fired on the Redcoats, but without much success.

Following the war, the Bronx experienced rapid growth and its ties with New York City tightened. Philipse's bridge had closed in 1759, but new ones were built to serve the growing community of New Yorkers there. Many immigrants arrived in the 1840s, from famine-ravaged Ireland and politically unsettled Germany. The great landed families — the Pells of Pelham, the Morrises of Morrisania, the Philipses of Philipseburgh — were broken up, but new ones emerged, and new fortunes were made. Pierre Lorillard, founder of the tobacco fortune Jonas Bronck didn't live to make, was the first man ever called a millionaire — a term coined for his obituary when he died in the Bronx in 1843. Jordan Mott, inventor of an improved coal stove, built a foundry on the Harlem River and founded his own town, Mott Haven, in 1848.

Rich New Yorkers built elegant summer homes in the Bronx, just as the Dutch had predicted. The fashionable track at Jerome Park was credited with retrieving the once-noble sport of horse racing from the lowlifes into whose hands it had slipped and making it respectable again in 1866. Spacious, 310-acre Woodlawn Cemetery, which had opened for business the year before, became a favorite place of New Yorkers seeking pleasant burial grounds for themselves.

Large sections of land were bought for parks — almost a quarter of the total area, the most of any borough — and the last of the hemlock forest was preserved as part of the New York Botanical Garden. In the 1890s, as the city moved northward, New York University moved from cramped lower Manhattan to a large, airy campus near Fordham Road, and work began on the broad, tree-lined Grand Concourse, one of the most elegant thoroughfares in the city.

As transit facilities increased between the Bronx and New York, the advantages of integrating Manhattan and the surrounding areas into one metropolis seemed more and more obvious to some; Brooklyn and Queens, with their scattered villages, were not so sure, but the Bronx welcomed consolidation. By the 1860s Morrisania was already renumbering its streets as an extension of those in Manhattan, and consolidation took its first step in 1874 when the western Bronx villages of Morrisania, Kingsbridge and West Farms were annexed — nearly doubling the city's area and extending it from the Battery to Yonkers. Three townships east of the Bronx River — including the thriving villages of Throgs Neck, Unionport, Olinville, Williamsbridge, Wakefield, Eastchester and part of Pelham — joined up in 1895, adding another 14,000 acres and 17,000 people to the city. Greater New York was on its way.

> As transit facilities increased between the Bronx and New York, the advantages of consolidating into one metropolis seemed more and more obvious.

Cornelius Vanderbilt and his ferry-boat, around 1810.

PRELUDE

ANOTHER COUNTRY

Early Staten Island

By JAY MAEDER
Daily News Staff Writer

THE DUTCH tried several times to settle the great Staaten Eyelandt that stood harbor guard at the gateway of New Netherland, but the Indians always sent them packing back to Manhattan, and it wasn't until 1661 that a community called Oude Dorp was effectively established. By the time the purchase of the island was concluded in 1670, tribal leaders had become part of the new English at least three times already. It finally went for guns and axes and other goods worth more than twice what Peter Minuit had paid for Manhattan. Staten Islanders have always been very proud of their relative worth on the real estate market.

Also by that time, New Netherland wasn't New Netherland anymore anyway, and Staten Island had become part of the new English regime's Yorkshire, which also included Westchester and Long Island. Geographically, though, New Jersey insisted it had the rightful claim, and the island's ownership was disputed by rival governors until, according to the island legend, the Duke of York decreed that anything that could be circumnavigated in less than 24 hours belonged to New York. The legend has it that it fell to a Capt. Christopher Billopp to undertake the decisive sailing, that he made it with a few minutes to spare, and that, accordingly, he is the reason Staten Island is not part of Jersey today.

Not that Staten Islanders ever had much to do

with the rest of New York. A ferociously independent breed, they might as well have been living on their own continent for years after Billopp settled the boundary matter. With a flourishing shipping economy of their own, for starters, they never particularly needed Manhattan's seaport, and for generations they went their own way in their idyllic land of oyster beds and huckleberry fields and tiny shore villages. For generations, their island remained sparsely populated — just the way they liked it. There were still fewer than 3,000 residents by the summer of 1776, when Sir William Howe landed with 30,000 British troops and prepared to invade Long Island and Manhattan.

A focal point of the American Revolution, Staten Island was not only the Redcoats' staging area but also the scene of the celebrated summit that would have averted the war had only Benjamin Franklin and John Adams been softer touches. Meeting with Howe's brother, Admiral Richard Howe, at Capt. Billopp's landmark family home in Tottenville, patriots Franklin and Adams intractably rebuffed all British compromise offers. The Continental Congress, they noted, was already in session. The admiral said he regretted he was not at liberty to recognize the Americans as legitimate public officials.

"Your lordship may consider me in what light you please, except that of a British subject," Adams replied famously — and that was the end of the Staten Island peace conference.

After the war, the island returned to rural ways for 100 more years or so, largely untouched by the increasing hurly-burly all around. Ferry service to Manhattan did become a commercial

necessity, of course — among the pioneer ferrymen was a young Cornelius Vanderbilt, who started building his fortune around 1810 by carrying passengers for 18 cents a head — and, by reason of the ferries and the Staten Island stagecoaches, crossing the island was for a time the fastest way to get to Philadelphia. More villages developed hither and thither as a result, but urban civilization remained decades away. So offended were Staten Islanders by attempts to install newfangled gas lighting that the gas company had to disguise its tanks as a church.

Modern times eventually began to arrive, initially because the island was discovered by the rich and the social, who built lavish homes, grand hotels, yacht clubs, country clubs, hunting preserves and assorted splendid playgrounds. America's first tennis courts were introduced at the Staten Island Cricket and Baseball Club by a sporting-minded member of the old Outerbridge family. Then, in the 1880s, a developer named Erastus Wiman began to carve out cheap residential subdivisions, and the middle classes started flocking in with their large families and small down payments. The rich moved elsewhere, and such was the state of things in the mid-1890s, when islanders were asked to consider if they wished to consolidate into the proposed Greater New York.

They did, largely because they were promised municipalization of the ferry, which was owned by the Baltimore & Ohio Railroad. In January 1898, they became part of the big city. Many of them, upon further reflection, have been trying to secede ever since.

GREAT EXPECTATIONS

The Imperial City, 1898

By OWEN MORITZ and JAY MAEDER
Daily News Staff Writers

SHORTLY AFTER 10 a.m. on the first day of 1898, the final mayor of old New York arrived at City Hall to hand his office over to the first mayor of the newly consolidated Greater New York and discovered that Tammany Hall had already moved in. On William Strong's desk sat a large Tammany Tiger made of flowers. The windows were wide open, and the winter gusts were blowing away the last whiffs of Strong's noble, and accordingly brief, reform administration.

"Going to freeze me out, eh?" Strong murmured. "Well, I can stand it two hours longer."

At the stroke of noon, old New York and Long Island City and the City of Brooklyn and some three dozen other municipalities ceased to exist. The ceremonies were perfunctory; Tammany's puppet mayor Robert Anderson Van Wyck pointedly snubbed Strong, Brooklyn Mayor Frederick Wurster and Long Island City Mayor Patrick (Battle Axe) Gleason, then sat down and got to work. In his first official act, he fired every one of the three former cities' department heads.

The metropolis was the work of two men: one a visionary idealist who sought to build a mighty monument, the other a professional politician who schemed to wrest power from New York's Tammany Hall masters. The first man succeeded. The second failed. On New Year's Day 1898, after three years of lying low, Tammany was running things again.

LIMITLESS WERE the possibilities of the fabulous invention called Greater New York, overnight a city of 360 square miles and 3.3 million souls. The newspapers boomed with the day's great expectations: Soon there would be a subway system, and new bridges across the East, North and Harlem rivers, and tunnels to New Jersey and Long Island, and a new aqueduct, and a public library and zoological gardens and an ocean parkway. And surely now would the seaport regain its eminence. This was a most pressing matter. Amid daily calls for the immediate deepening of the East Channel and improvements to dock facilities was the new city born.

It was concern for the port that had led Andrew Haswell Green to first propose consolidation 30 years earlier. Green had saved New York's ruined finances in the 1870s after the fall of the legendarily larcenous Tammany boss William Marcy Tweed; he had been a key player in the creation of Central Park, the Museum of Natural History and the forthcoming New York Public Library; through all these public-spirited years he had argued for an "imperial city," one unified governmental instrument that would, chiefly among other things, centralize the port's administration and insure continued commercial importance.

Notwithstanding the staunch support of New York's mercantile leaders, Green got nowhere at all with the idea — until the early 1890s, when, in the legislative corridors of the Albany he controlled utterly and absolutely, Republican State Sen. Thomas Platt looked upon Green's proposal for a supercity and saw that it was good.

The implications were clear to GOP boss Platt: The multitudes of a much larger New York might easily outnumber the Manhattan immigrants who were forever throwing their votes to Tammany's Democrats. Elated by the prospect of an unbroken string of Republican mayors, Platt immediately began oiling the legislative machinery to make Greater New York happen.

Local voters would have to ratify the plan, of course, and they debated it for several years. Manhattan was wildly in favor, and the Bronx was already quite happily being annexed to Manhattan anyway. Long Island City and most other Queens communities were eager to tap into Manhattan's

"*The New Instrument Tammany Will Play On,*" New York Herald, Dec. 20, 1897.

tax base and water supply. Staten Island liked the idea of cheap ferry transportation. In November 1894, the citizens voted yea.

Brooklyn was another story. Brooklyn was itself a major city, proud of its bedrock middle-class values, wary of patently less-civilized Manhattan, unwilling to suffer subsumption. But overexpanded Brooklyn was so deeply in debt that consolidation was really its only hope. The vote passed by just two-tenths of one per cent, and resentments long ran deep: In April 1896, when Boss Platt's Legislature signed consolidation into law, Brooklynites rioted in the streets.

Meanwhile, presiding over business in his "Amen Corner" at Manhattan's elegant Fifth Avenue Hotel, Boss Platt had miscalculated the long-term strength of the separate reform movement that had driven Tammany Hall out of New York's political equation in 1894. The now-revitalized Tammany's new candidate, Van Wyck, won handily when voters in November 1897 were called upon to elect Greater New York's first mayor. On New Year's Eve, Van Wyck nodding at his side, Tammany chieftain Richard Croker installed himself comfortably at the Murray Hill Hotel and began receiving a long line of favor seekers. It seemed there was not a Republican mayor after all.

ON GOVERNORS Island on New Year's Eve, soldiers fired a 100-gun salute to the shining new city. In Union Square, 100,000 New Yorkers paraded under the finest display of fireworks the city had seen since the 1858 celebration of the laying of the Atlantic Cable had accidentally set City Hall afire. A team of spooked horses trampled a crowd of merrymakers. There were numerous severe injuries.

In Brooklyn, Mayor Wurster and other heartsick citizens solemnly gathered to wake the extinguished City of Churches. Hymns were sung. Brooklyn was now destined to be no more than a residential section of New York City, Wurster acknowledged. But there would be many more paved streets, he added hopefully. Also, it was noted, the merger did mean that Brooklyn men could now get a barber's shave on Sunday without having to cross the river.

In Long Island City, Battle Axe Gleason fumed. Not for nothing was Paddy Gleason called Battle Axe: The undisputed king of his turf was a man who literally chopped down new construction that did not meet with his personal approval, and he had been a formidable early champion of consolidation. Somehow he had it in his head that he was the man who would be Greater New York's first mayor. Having delivered Long Island City, he had now found out otherwise.

"They have taken my ship away from me, but I am still captain!" he thundered, warning that his private army of policemen and firefighters would never stand for their city's disappearance. No violence would be necessary, he promised: "I will not be surprised," he said, "if we should suddenly learn that, legally and constitutionally, no election for such a city as Greater New York was ever held!" On New Year's Eve, steadfastly clutching at straws, Mayor Gleason matter-of-factly approved Long Island City's budget for the following year.

AT THE STROKE of noon on New Year's Day, Greater New York effectively became synonymous with Greater Tammany Hall. "*The sun will rise this morning,*" the Tribune had written, "*upon the greatest experiment in municipal government that the world has ever known.*"

CHAPTER 2

STARS AND STRIPES FOREVER
War Movies, 1898

**By JONATHAN LEWIN
and JAY MAEDER**
Daily News Staff Writers

JADED NEW Yorkers, wouldn't you know, were tired of Thomas Edison's amazing moving pictures by February 1898 already, and Edison's kinetographs and vitascopes might have disappeared into the maw of oblivion there and then — along with, for example, his amazing voice-activated flywheel, which never quite found a market — had it not been for the wonderful, star-spangled Spanish-American War.

Not that it was much of a war, as wars went, only a few months long and fundamentally pointless in any case, but it was the first war Americans had been treated to in more than 30 years and they loved it with all their hearts. Roaring crowds marched on Fifth Ave., waving flags and beating drums, and night after night they mobbed the elegant Eden Musee showplace on W. 23rd St. to watch the riveting war films so freshly delivered from the Cuban front that the whiff of gunsmoke was still upon them. Whatever else the Spanish-American War did or did not accomplish, it made William Randolph Hearst America's most powerful newspaper magnate, it made a public hero out of an ebullient man named Theodore Roosevelt — and overnight it transformed New York City's fledgling, faltering motion picture industry into a vital social institution.

Evening after evening at the Eden Musee as the primitive films flickered away did the crowds hiss the wicked Spanish butchers, clutch their breasts at the desperate plight of the gentle, liberty-loving Cubans and proudly salute the grand old red, white and blue. They didn't care a bit that Teddy Roosevelt's hell-for-leather charge up San Juan Hill had been filmed in New Jersey, or that the doomed Spanish battleships of Manila Bay had been exploded and sunk in a tank on an E. 14th St. rooftop.

THOMAS EDISON, having electrified America's cities, had turned his attention to movies in 1888. At his laboratories in West Orange, N.J., he had built the world's first indoor studio, a tar-papered 50-foot box he called Black Maria, and in 1893 had begun shooting half-minute variety entertainments starring the day's most popular performers: dancers, jugglers, strongmen, acrobats, anything that, well, moved. Subsequently it had occurred to him to send out his camera crews to shoot street scenes: elevated trains, bicycle parades, Coney Island thrill rides. At 1155 Broadway in April 1894, he opened the world's first kinetoscope parlor, where customers fed nickels into individual viewing boxes and peered at the jittery marvels through tiny windows. This they did with great enthusiasm for a season or two, then got bored. Edison now decided it was time to invent the public theater experience: On April 23, 1896, the nation's first projection films premiered at Koster & Bial's Music Hall at Broadway and 34th St.

Within two years, though, even this novelty was wearing thin. The moving picture camera might have been the wonder of the age to its developers — Edison assistant William Kennedy Laurie Dickson reverently pronounced it "the crown and flower of 19th-century magic" — but not to theater audiences. Eventually the vaudeville houses took to placing films at the end of programs, serving as "chasers" to get the people out.

Then, on Feb. 15, 1898, the U.S. battleship Maine blew up in Havana Harbor.

Actually, it seemed clear to many that the blast might well have been an accident. But Hearst and his New York Journal had been noisily demanding war for months and suddenly President William McKinley had little choice but to call upon Congress to declare one. Edison got straight to work, dispatching his cameramen to Florida and Cuba to shoot such films as "The Wreck of the Maine" and "Funeral of Nine of the Victims" and "Cuban Refugees Going to Breakfast." Immediately seven reenergized Manhattan theaters were headlining Edison's pictures and those of his two main rivals, Vitagraph and Biograph. By May the Eden Musee was showing nothing but war movies — eventually nearly 200 of them — to the Old Glory-saluting crowds. In short order the filmmakers were finding it necessary to shoot the war locally to keep up with the demand.

The actual fracas was over by August, but the movie men kept on shooting it anyway, staging combat heroics in and around the city for months thereafter, and the crowds kept cheering. Edison in particular was growing fond of faking his footage anyway. After McKinley was shot in 1901, Edison quickly produced "Execution of Czolgosz," a lurid re-creation of the assassin's punishment (initially he considered reenacting McKinley's killing as well, but he was talked out of it). And his 1902 sensation "Firemen Fighting the Flames at Paterson," ostensibly presenting scenes of a great New Jersey fire, was really footage of firefighters putting out a stable blaze on Central Park West. Dickson, for his part, left Edison's employ and went off to Africa to shoot the Boer War and pioneer the legitimate newsreel.

IT WASN'T LONG before the New York movie men realized they could just as easily make up their own yarns as reenact events of the day, and so arose the "story film." Edison's director Edwin S. Porter made history in 1903 with his thrilling Jersey-shot "The Great Train Robbery," at 12 minutes in length the longest movie to date. Featuring gun battles aboard a speeding train — and including a hair-raising scene in which a bandit fired directly at the audience — it wowed crowds everywhere it played. By the end of 1904, story films dominated a flourishing industry.

Edison got out of the film business just a few years later — after his unsuccessful attempts to monopolize it via a series of patent claims drove his competitors away to California, where they invented Hollywood — and that was the end of New York City as film making's epicenter. But by then the Wizard of Menlo Park had invented — along with the light bulb and the phonograph — the enduring national pastime of going to the movies.

CORBIS-BETTMANN

CHAPTER 3

YOUSE AN' YER NOBLE SCRAP

On Strike With The Newsboy Legion, 1899

By DAVID NASAW

Special to The News

Suddenly, in July 1899, the city's largest papers were in trouble. "The newsboys' strike has grown into a menacing affair," the managing editor of Joseph Pulitzer's New York World memoed his boss. "Practically all the boys in New York and adjacent towns have quit selling. . . . The advertisers have abandoned the papers. . . . It is really a very extraordinary demonstration."

Indeed it was. The New York City newsies had formed their own union and gone out on strike against the World and William Randolph Hearst's New York Journal. A confederation of children was challenging the two most powerful publishers in the nation.

In 1899, the newsies were in the enviable position of being virtually irreplaceable. As people began to live farther from their jobs and ride home instead of walk, the boys became the papers' major distributors. The event that led to their strike was the wholesale price increase — from 5 to 6 cents per 10 papers — that the Journal and the World had instituted the year before, at the height of the Spanish-American War circulation boom. As long as the boys were making money hawking war extras, they did not protest: They sold each paper for a penny, and though they got nothing back on the papers they could not sell, returns were low. By the summer of 1899, however, as the news grew tamer and the headlines shrank, they began to feel the pinch. And it was apparent that the temporary increase would become permanent unless they did something about it.

The first reported actions took place in Long Island City, where the newsies discovered that a

Journal deliveryman had been cheating them with short bundles. On July 18, they tipped over his wagon, ran off with his papers and chased him out of town. Flush with success, the boys demanded a price rollback and notified their suppliers they would no longer buy the Hearst or Pulitzer papers. Word traveled swiftly to the downtown Manhattan newsies; in City Hall Park on July 19, they organized their union and announced a strike.

It was a propitious moment for a strike. The Brooklyn streetcar operators were already out and, as one 11-year-old newsie observed, "de cops is all busy!" On July 22, 100 club-wielding boys rallied in Newspaper Row to greet the World and Journal wagons. Police scattered them, but at Columbus Circle the drivers met a mob of nearly 500 more howling lads who pelted them with fruit and seized their papers. In Brooklyn, Yonkers, Jersey City and other distribution points, the scenario was much the same. The mighty Hearst and Pulitzer were under siege by an army of urchins with names like Boots McAleenan, Kid Blink, Young Mush, Crutchy Morris, Racetrack Higgins and Bob the Indian.

"Hold out, my gallant kids!" Brooklyn newsie chief Spot Conlon cheered on his Manhattan comrades. "An' tomorrer I meself, at de head of t'ree tousand noble hearts from Brooklyn, will be over here t' help youse win yer noble scrap fer freedom an' fair play!"

The Journal and World did not at first take the strike very seriously. Their opponents were, after all, only children. It was not until the advertisers began requesting "allowance on their bills on account of the strike" that the publishers realized the gravity of the situation. The boys were substantially cutting circulation, in the city and across the rivers, and within days the strike was spreading to Troy,

Rochester, New Haven, Fall River, Mass., and Providence, R.I. The publishers, at last fully aware that matters were serious, called in favors from politicians and police captains. Hearst's Journal, which had been running editorials condemning the police for their actions in other strikes, quickly reversed itself. The papers tried hiring Bowery bums to replace the strikers — but the boys went into the flophouses to explain their cases, and as one bum declared: "Every one of us has decided to stick by the newsboys! We won't sell no papers!"

The boys were well aware of the value of public support. At a mass meeting at New Irving Hall on Broome St., 5,000 newsies from all over the city showed up to proclaim their solidarity, and songs were sung and speeches made through speakers played to the larger public. "Ain't that 10 cents worth as much to us as it is to Hearst and Pulitzer who are millionaires?" demanded Kid Blink. "Well, I guess it is. If they can't spare it, how can we? I'm trying to figure how 10 cents on 100 papers can mean more to a millionaire than it does to newsboys, an' I can't see it!" Meanwhile, the strikers were making a chivalrous point of declining to apply the customary water-splashing treatment to newsstand owners who happened to be women. "A feller don't soak a lady," Kid Blink explained.

The strike held together for the rest of that week and the next. At the World, the press run was reduced from 360,000 to 125,000. "It really is remarkable the success these boys have had," the managing editor admitted.

The publishers conceded defeat. The price would remain where it was, but the World and Journal would henceforth take back unsold papers at a full refund. The boys agreed. On Aug. 2 they began to sell the banned papers again.

The union itself did not survive. Had the publishers formally negotiated, it might have been strengthened or at least given something to do. But the publishers ignored the union; when they decided to compromise with the boys, they simply spread the word, and the agreement was accepted without formal vote.

And so the New York newsboys' union turned out to be ephemeral. But for two weeks in the summer of 1899, the children who joined together to do battle with Pulitzer and Hearst proved, to the delight of some and the astonishment of practically everyone, that they could organize, and win, a strike.

Adapted from "Children of the City: At Work and at Play," originally published by Doubleday/Anchor and © David Nasaw. Reprinted by arrangement with the Virginia Barber Literary Agency Inc.

By JAY MAEDER
Daily News Staff Writers

WELL, OF COURSE it wasn't *really* the turn of the century, was it? The great French astronomer Flammarion was beside himself with exasperation; for weeks he had been pelting the world's capitals with communiques, learnedly explaining again and again that there could be no true *fin de siecle* for another full year yet, astronomically speaking.

Still, it didn't feel like 1899 anymore, did it? The Vatican had declared 1900 a Holy Year. At St. Patrick's Cathedral, Archbishop Corrigan presided over a solemn pontifical midnight Mass beneath a great vaulted ceiling festooned with evergreen. Downtown, the bells of Trinity, Grace and St. Andrew's pealed joyously, and Watch Night services were held at 100 other churches through the city. Thousands of revelers swept up Broadway from the Battery, honking on tin trumpets; the Tenderloin roared with fish-horns and rattles; every steamboat in the harbor blasted its whistles for 10 minutes, as indeed did every factory and every locomotive, anything with a head of steam, and midnight came in a mighty din of gladness and thanksgiving. A minute later, Miss Annie Waddilove of Jersey City married Mr. William J. Witt of W. 115th St., the beaming first bride of a fine new age.

"You might have believed it was the new century after all," commented the New York World on New Year's morning.

"Poets, perhaps, reckon otherwise than astronomers," conceded Flammarion.

SPLENDID OUTLOOK, the papers shouted. **FUTURE FULL OF PROMISE. NATION SHOULD LEAD IN WEALTH AND COMMERCE, AND NEW YORK BE SUPREME CITY. POSSIBILITIES ARE BEYOND COMPUTING.** It was a moment of boundless poetry. America in 1700 had been a land of 300,000 souls, in 1800, of 5.3 million; today, her people numbered 86 million, fully a quarter of those millions arrived to these shores just in the last 10 years alone. Greater New York was exactly two years old — "the metropolis of a nation," boasted the city's chief financial officer, Bird Coler, "whose tremendous resources are in the infancy of development."

It had been an avalanche of thrillingly improbable times as successive generations came and went. In the previous 100 years the stagecoach had given way to the streetcar, the candle to the incandescent bulb, the pony rider to the telegraph. If the three single most revolutionary developments of the 19th century, as scholars generally agreed, had been the first passenger railway train (in England, in September 1825), the initial laying of the first submarine cable (from Ireland, in August 1857) and the opening of the Suez Canal (in Egypt, in November 1869) — where on the great list would sit steamboats, sewing machines, friction matches, penny postage . . . ?

The rush of things had defied ready comprehension. Medicine had witnessed the appearances of anesthesia, the X-ray, bacteriology to such a degree that newly knowledgeable health inspectors at Ellis Island had already been able to stop what might easily have been deadly invasions of yellow fever and bubonic plague. Samuel Morse's telegraph now girdled the Earth ("Whether the telephone will ever rival its elder brother in the transmission of long-distance messages is still a mere matter of speculation," mused the New York Herald).

CHAPTER 4

ROOTY TOOT TOOT

Jan. 1, 1900

Nikola Tesla's astonishing dynamo, an unthinkably cheap and efficient means of converting mechanical to electrical energy, had recently enabled engineers to harness Niagara Falls and with it light cities. The United States led the world in the production of foodstuffs, textiles, coal and iron. Horseless carriages were beginning to sputter through America's streets. A few dreamers appeared to be imagining quite seriously that it was possible to build a flying machine.

In New York, the old 42nd St. reservoir had been dismantled; arising now in its place was the greatest library on Earth, sure to be unrivaled by even the British Museum or the Bibliotheque Nationale. Probably the world's tallest office building, fully 20 stories, was going up at Broad St. and Exchange Place. The Williamsburg Bridge was half completed; a third East River bridge was in the planning; so was a mighty cantilever span across the Hudson at 59th St. Tunnels would connect everything else to everything else, and ground soon would be broken for the fabulous underground railway system, and there would be a great ocean parkway to the glittering beaches ...

The indomitable nation had survived a wrenching civil war, the terrible assassinations of two Presidents, a godless crusade to debase the currency; all was well. Surely the new century would see nothing but triumph after triumph. "Its victories are to be moral," said Edward Everett Hale. "By the end of the 20th century, war will be relegated to the past." Elsewhere on the high road, other philosophers were serenely confident that in another 100 years man would no longer need such a thing as money.

OVERFLOW CROWDS *at St. Patrick's jostled one another to get into the services; there were many bruises. Hundreds upon hundreds of the poverty-stricken sought food and warmth from the Salvation Army and the Department of Charities. Fire had struck the Manhattan Electric Light Co. plant a few days earlier, and large sections of the East Side between 14th and 42nd Sts. were still blacked out, and thousands of modern households in the nation's greatest city welcomed in the new year by candlelight.*

By CLEM RICHARDSON
Daily News Staff Writer

NEW YORK CITY greeted the new century with its arms akimbo and its chest stuck out, the biggest town in a thriving nation that was steadily finding its footing 35 years after a bloody civil war threatened to tear it in two.

There was fighting in the world — the English were battling the godless Boers in South Africa, and missionaries were lost and feared dead in China — but it was someone else's problem. Meanwhile, it was a fine time to be a New Yorker, even for Negroes — at least compared with what was happening down South, where sharecropping was the new slavery and where black men were beaten or lynched just for suggesting that they might drop their rented plows and head up the freedom road.

Negroes had lived in the city since Peter Stuyvesant's time, free men after 1827, but their numbers were never significant. Of nearly 2 million Manhattan residents in 1900, about 35,000 were colored, about the same number as New York's French, and most of them lived in the West Village and the tenements of Chelsea, Hell's Kitchen and parts of the upper West Side — anywhere a landlord could be found who would rent to colored.

Thirty-seven years after white mobs lynched 11 colored men during the notorious Draft Riots, frictions between the races were few. Chief among them were the rubs between Irish and colored, who often found themselves competing for low-end jobs. By 1900, many coloreds had settled into such service trades as catering and barbering. Many Irish, meanwhile, were policemen.

But real racial unpleasantness was a Southern thing, and New York's papers clucked in 1900 when race riots broke out in Newport, Va., and New Orleans.

Then to New York came the hot summer night of Sunday the 12th of August. **NEGRO HUNT BY 10,000 PERSONS ON BROADWAY!** screamed Monday's editions of The World. **EXCITED CREWS IN WEST SIDE STREETS SAVAGELY ATTACK ALL THE COLORED MEN AND WOMEN IN SIGHT TO AVENGE THE MURDER OF POLICEMAN THORPE! DRAGGED FROM STREET CARS AND BEATEN!**

THINGS HAD BEGUN about 9 p.m., when Police Officer Robert Thorpe, in plainclothes, tried to arrest drunken Mary Eno of 241 W. 44th St. When her common-law husband, Arthur Harris, sought to intervene, Thorpe knocked him down. Whereupon Harris pulled a knife and stabbed him three times in the chest. The policeman died. Harris fled.

It still might have been a quiet night had not another Negro, one Spenser Walters, later walked past the dead Thorpe's Tenderloin home, outside of which several dozen cops were gathered.

Two white women shrieked that Walters had a gun, whereupon he was beaten senseless and dragged off to the stationhouse. Word spread — and shortly young white toughs were assembling on every streetcorner for a mile along Eighth Ave., by some accounts more than 10,000 of them. And then they were on the move, rolling loudly down into the Negro blocks of Chelsea and

New York Daily Tribune, Aug. 19, 1900

CHAPTER 5

A SORT OF HUMAN NATURE

The Tinderbox, 1900

Hell's Kitchen, looking for someone to hurt.

LUCKY WAS THE Negro who saw them coming and was able to get inside and barricade the door. Many who didn't were chased down in the street and set upon.

One man was pursued into the Metropole Hotel at 42nd and Broadway, where the staff gathered at the door and fought the mob back. One was caught at the corner of Seventh and 39th and nearly killed before cops dragged him out of the mob and to the safety of the precinct house. One fled into the Marlborough Hotel, sprinting straight through a banquet honoring the chief of the Fire Department.

"I have seen Negroes lynched in the South and men strung up in the West, but never such an outbreak of fury as took place on Broadway," a white man, Charles Boyd, told reporters.

Many whites risked mob frenzy to help. A scolding woman singlehandedly shamed away a crowd that had pounced on two black newsboys; a Salvation Army captain hovered over a Negro chased from Times Square to Bryant Park and dared anyone to touch him. Businesses

throughout the neighborhood hid their colored help in their basements.

Police, who had turned out reserves from Harlem to Battery Park to deal with the rioters, estimated that at least 200 blacks were assaulted between 23rd and 42nd Sts. from Sixth to Ninth Aves. — including a man who would have been hanged from a lamppost if the rope had held.

It was also true, though, that no few of the injuries were inflicted by police officers themselves. At the W. 37th St. stationhouse, cops refrained from beating their captives only because crowds of reporters were present. Outside, Police Chief Big Bill Devery was heard to exhort his troops: "Use your judgment, but use your clubs!"

Many Negroes tried to buy pistols the next day. Police ordered shopkeepers not to sell them any.

THE WHITE mobs were back the next night, as many as 30,000 people — "a bunch of loafers looking for excitement," said one magistrate. Pickings were slim, since most Negroes knew to stay inside.

They came back again and again, for four nights straight, defying a police curfew, until cops finally barred whites from congregating in Chelsea and enforced the edict with clubs.

AS RIOTS WENT, the numbers were not so bad. No one had died. The number of injured seemed to be about 200, though many more were assumed to have treated themselves privately at home. Twenty-three blacks had been arrested on various charges, only four whites.

But the episode was a major embarrassment for the city. Southern papers seized the opportunity to note that Northern whites were not so benign after all. "The race riots in New York," chortled the editor of the New Orleans Times-Democrat, "seem to me from this distance to be much the same as those recently in New Orleans, due to that race prejudice, which is a sort of human nature, and to the labor competition of white and black felt only among the poorer classes, who are the principal actors in these troubles."

In New York, the incident resulted in a large rift between black citizens and the Police Department. "Were it not for the assistance of the police, there would not have been one half of the disturbance," the Rev. P.L. Coyter declared from the pulpit of Zion M.E. Church on Sunday next. "The conduct of these uniformed bullies cannot be too strongly censured."

Fed up and frightened, many Negroes moved out of Hell's Kitchen, pushing beyond a rim of Negro tenements above 110th St. into the old Dutch neighborhood called Harlem.

Arthur Harris, arrested at his mother's house in Washington, was sentenced to life in prison.

Cars were just a fad for the rich, people snapped. Petitions were circulated to ban them from the roads. Citizens shot out tires. Kids threw rocks.

CHAPTER 6

WILD HORSES

At The Auto Show, 1900

By JON KALISH
Special to The News

NEW YORK CITY had seen its first automobile five years earlier, when the ever-spectacular Diamond Jim Brady took his new Woods electric brougham out for a crowd-stopping spin down Fifth Ave. And it already had seen its first auto-related fatality, on Sept. 13, 1899, when a Mr. Henry Bliss stepped off a Central Park West streetcar into the path of someone's limo. And by now a small experimental fleet of electric taxis was working the town, carrying their fares more or less quite reliably when their batteries weren't dead. ("In time, cab riding will be a positive pleasure," said Scientific American.)

But in November 1900 there were still no more than 500 horseless carriages in all New York State, and mostly they remained nothing but amusing novelties, playthings of the rich and idle. That's who turned out, resplendent in their gowns and tuxedos, when the Automobile Club of America staged its first National Automobile Show at Madison Square Garden, Vanderbilts and Rockefellers and Astors and Morgans and Bostwicks and Van Rensselaers and automotive enthusiasts of that stripe. There were 60,000 of them in all during the week-long festivities, an attendance still rather less than that of the average society horse show. In the United States in November 1900 there were about 8,000 autos, and about 18 million horses.

It was believed that things were changing. "The automobile is here to stay," ventured the New York Sun. "It is rapidly being developed to the point where it will be

absolutely free from any danger and easily manipulated by anyone." Certainly it never would become as popular as the bicycle; for starters, the rock-bottom-cheapest machine to be found cost nearly $300, a sum unimaginable by the average $5-a-week working man, and most cost considerably more than that. But everyone in high society would surely own one. John Jacob Astor himself had motored into Manhattan in his flashy 12-horsepower French racer, making the 90-mile trip downriver in a bone-rattling five hours, and he was quite the talk of the show.

So were the pioneer automakers Charles Duryea and Alexander Winton. Both men were known to New Yorkers already; Duryea, of Springfield, Mass., had won the nation's second auto race, held in the city, in 1896, and Winton had actually driven one of his cars the 800 unpaved miles from Cleveland to New York in 1898. They, along with racer Andrew Riker — who

seven months earlier had set a speed record at Springfield, L.I., covering 50 miles in two hours and three minutes — spent the week drafting the by-laws of the first automakers' trade association. Standards were far from settled. Manufacturers had no clear idea yet whether steering mechanisms belonged on the right side or the left. Most cars had four wheels, but some had three. Steamers and electrics were the popular favorites, but the new gasoline-powered buggies seemed to be gaining market share.

Some 300 machines from some 40 manufacturers — surreys, stanhopes, phaetons, runabouts, commercial delivery wagons — were on display on the Garden floor. Demonstration models went around and around a planked oval track throughout the week. On the Garden roof, a 200-foot inclined ramp that simulated a steep country road let competitors show off their climbing and braking capabilities. Much admired was the elegant, white-enameled, rose-upholstered bridal carriage with footman's perch. Notable as well was the 12-horse military steamer that carried four soldiers and 10,000 rounds of ammunition and was guaranteed to cross 100 miles of warfront in 12 hours.

Several vehicles came with an extra seat for the onboard mechanic their manufacturers assumed the well-equipped motor hobbyist would always want to keep handy. "An automobile is an engine and needs an engineer," said one man. "In England, all the machines are made to carry a man. Here,

where we try to educate everyone up to the point of managing an auto, we are always in trouble. A steam engine, a gas motor or an electric engine is not a kid-glove proposition."

TEN YEARS LATER there would be nearly 300,000 automobiles in the United States, and there would be speed limits, and licensing and registration requirements, and the beginnings of a profoundly new national way of life beyond the ken of those attending the auto show at Madison Square Garden in November 1900. For the time being, as terrified horses reared at every sight of the unnatural carriage that somehow pulled itself, there would be petitions to ban the thing from public streets; anti-auto zealots would spread broken glass on roadways or shoot out the tires of passing machines; kids would throw rocks.

Some quarters were more far-seeing than others. Scientific American, for example, recognized early that the automobile was going to be a boon to the public health, because there would be fewer horses excreting in the streets, and to the general civility as well, because rubber-tired motorcars ran much more quietly than steel-wheeled wagons. "The noise and clatter which makes conversation almost impossible on many streets of New York will be done away with, for horseless vehicles of all kinds are always noiseless or nearly so," said the magazine. It conceded: "The bells of the new vehicles will be somewhat annoying at first."

THAT DAMNED COWBOY

Teddy Roosevelt, 1901

By JAY MAEDER
Daily News Staff Writer

BOSS TOM PLATT of Albany had not, as things turned out, been sufficiently powerful to wrest Greater New York away from the Tammany Tiger in 1897. But three years later he could still, by God, make a man vice president. And Gov. Theodore Roosevelt of the State of New York didn't even want the job.

Roosevelt was not without national aspirations, but really he had wanted to stay on as governor for another term. This Boss Platt could not allow. Electing the rough-riding hero of San Juan Hill to the governorship had been a fine political idea in 1898, but Roosevelt, alas, had swiftly proved himself to be no warm friend of the banking and insurance interests that kept Boss Platt boss, and the time had come to remove him from state affairs. The master of the New York Republican machine addressed this matter with his customary efficiency. In Philadelphia in the summer of 1900, by Platt-orchestrated acclamation, Roosevelt joined the reelection ticket of President William McKinley, rather baffled by the turn of events. "I am glad we had our way!" Boss Platt announced to the papers, then modestly corrected himself: "The people, I mean, had their way."

Now, in a presidential reception line at the Pan-American Exposition in Buffalo, at 4:07 p.m. on Sept. 6, 1901, a man with a gun was about to reshape the American 20th century.

So harmless-looking was the assassin that one Secret Service man actually gave him a friendly clap on the shoulder at exactly the instant he leaped forward to fire at McKinley point-blank. Young Leon Czolgosz was a silly Cleveland millworker who fancied himself an anarchist. "I done my duty!" he cried as horrified mobs fell upon him with their fists. McKinley did not initially seem to be in grave danger. *Resting Comfortably*, the papers reported. *Will Recover.* When he died eight days later, his vice president was camping in the Adirondacks; forest rangers had to track Roosevelt down in the middle of the night. Rushed to Buffalo, a stunned Theodore Roosevelt raised his right hand and, at age 42, became the 26th President of the United States.

And now the Republican Party was stuck with a reformer in the White House. National chief Mark Hanna couldn't believe it. "That damned cowboy," he groaned.

THE NATION'S ONLY New York City-born chief executive, Teddy Roosevelt came to the presidency as a patrician with a social conscience. He had been reared in the rarefied worlds of Park Ave. and Long Island's Oyster Bay, but he also had been a two-fisted Dakota rancher who slept beneath the stars, and he had been New York's incorruptible police commissioner in the mid-1890s, a national legend who personally patrolled Manhattan's fleshpots in the wee hours and scolded any officer he found discharging duty less than satisfactorily.

And he had became close to two crusading newspaper reporters, Jacob Riis of the Sun and Lincoln Steffens of the Mail, who covered the squalor of the city's

slums and the desperate lives of their poor, and whose stories had only sharpened his aristocrat's keen sense of public responsibility to the less privileged classes.

He would be President for seven cyclonic years, the living embodiment of everything that was energetic about the new century. He was the first President to ride in an automobile. He built the Panama Canal. He created the Departments of Commerce and Labor. As commander-in-chief, he created the world's second most powerful navy and with its gunboats policed the planet, then became the first American to win the Nobel Peace Prize.

As a consumer advocate, he forced unfamiliar ethical standards upon food producers; as a champion of the working man, he triggered a crisis of conservatism by openly siding with striking coal miners; as an implacable foe of predatory Big Business, he prosecuted the Rockefellers and Morgans and Harrimans of the land and gleefully dismantled their monopolies. As a social revolutionary, he antagonized the entire white South when he invited Booker T. Washington of Alabama to dine at the White House.

When he stood for election in 1904, he was given the largest popular majority ever won by any candidate.

Roosevelt's was a presidency of enormous merriment as well; he laughed heartily and often, and his ebullient good cheer overwhelmed everything in its path. Cabinet officers and diplomats visiting his big Victorian home atop Sagamore Hill on Cold Spring Harbor grew accustomed to the fact that the President of the United States wouldn't think twice about interrupting a crucial conference to go romp with his children in the duck pond. Sober-sided old Secretary of State John Hay called him "more fun than a goat." Explained one British envoy to his startled colleagues: "You must always remember the President is about six."

His legacies would include both a great stone face watching forever over the land from a Western mountaintop and a small cuddly toy loved by the whole world. The toy was born about a year into Roosevelt's first term, when, in the course of a Mississippi hunting holiday, he declined to shoot a young bear. That story made headlines across the country and inspired one Morris Michtom of Brooklyn to fashion a stuffed cloth cub, put it in the window of his candy shop and call it a "Teddy Bear." Michtom went on to found the Ideal Toy Co.; his little teddies have been warming the slumbers of millions of tykes ever since.

It was a time of chest-thumping patriotism, of self-reliance and common sense, of rectitude and virtue and high good spirits. Years later, citizens would remember that never again had there been a moment when things were so palpably fine, so fundamentally and mythologically American, as in the America presided over by Theodore Roosevelt of New York City.

'**T**HERE IS NO ROOM *in this country for hyphenated Americanism," the old cowpoke said in 1915, addressing the Knights of Columbus in New York. "The one absolutely certain way of bringing this nation to ruin, of preventing all possibility of its continuing to be a nation at all, would be to permit it to become a tangle of squabbling nationalities."*

By JAY MAEDER
Daily News Staff Writer

SINCE ANTIQUITY, the political history of New York has never been anything but cycles of corruption and reform, and then more corruption and then more reform, and the professional politician has usually understood these cyclical matters and presciently divined the appropriate moment to lay himself low and await the more propitious day.

In 1894, for example, Boss Richard Croker of Tammany Hall found it desirable to leave not only the city but the country for three full years. Upon his return, he immediately elected his own mayor and went back to business as usual. Reformers were like hornets, Tammany sages liked to observe: They sting you once or twice and then they go away.

Now, on Election Night in November 1901, Croker sat with his sachems in the Tammany wigwam on E. 14th St., a cigar clutched grimly in his teeth, sheaves of returns piling up on the table before him. He said nothing. This time all was lost. This time there would be no coming back.

ONCE UPON A TIME, Tammany Hall had been purely a nest of thieves, for years presided over by the ravenous William Marcy Tweed, a man who plundered the city's coffers so openly that after a while it just seemed to be the natural order of things. By 1870, indeed, Tweed had engineered a new City Charter that effectively made it legal to steal.

Even so, the $250,000 Chambers St. courthouse that somehow ended up costing $12.5 million finally seemed a bit much. "Well, what are you going to do about it?" Boss Tweed shrugged when the press confronted him with evidences of massive fraud. He seemed genuinely surprised when he actually went off to prison.

Subsequently, under Tweed's more businesslike successor, Honest John Kelly, the Tammany banditry became much less crude. If Tammany, through its attentiveness to the daily needs of New York's immigrant swarms, controlled the ballot box, and if Tammany, through its patronage apparatus, controlled the city's contracts and franchises, then the clever fellow had no pressing need to dip his snout into the public trough at all, at least on any brazenly regular basis, for many were the opportunities to invest wisely.

Richard Croker — for example — happened to enjoy the friendship of financiers and railroad barons and other gentlemen who insisted upon presenting him with stock; in 1890 and 1891 he was able to drop nearly $1 million on his prize stable of champion racehorses alone.

County Cork-born Croker had come to New York as a child, grown up with the brawling Fourth Ave. Tunnel Gang and then, like so many ambitious Irish lads, sought to improve himself by joining Boss Tweed's Fire Department. Fast did he find himself useful to a Tammany organization always on the lookout for such a promising young fellow as himself: Dick Croker was very good at voting many times over for a given Tammany candidate, and he was very good at breaking the bones

"FOR MY OWN POCKET ALL THE TIME"

Puck Oct. 23/01.

CHAPTER 8

STING LIKE A HORNET

Boss Croker's Last Stand, 1901

of citizens who seemed to want to cast their votes for anyone else.

In short order he became an alderman, then coroner, then the personal protege of Honest John, who named him fire commissioner. When Honest John died in 1886, it was Croker who succeeded him, merely by sitting down in his chair and asking what anyone was going to do about it.

They called him The Master of the City, and this he indisputably was. His Tammany Hall was the very model of administrative efficiency: "I go down to the City Hall every day and go through the departments and see what is going on," Croker explained once, "and if I find anyone at fault I take them to task." Recalcitrant district leaders were summoned to his office, slammed into the walls for a while and then sent away more agreeable to his wishes. And all ran smoothly until the Rev. Charles Parkhurst of Madison Square Presbyterian Church took it upon himself to blow the lid off Tammany's thoroughly crooked Police Department and the many brothels, opium dens and gambling houses from which its captains collected fair tribute.

"Feeding day and night on the city's quivering vitals!" Parkhurst shrieked from his pulpit. "A lying, perjured, rum-soaked and libidinous lot!" The noisy preacher soon brought down a state investigative committee, and through all 1894 New Yorkers heard one shocking revelation after another. Not since Boss Tweed's great fall two decades earlier had Tammany endured such a pious bunch of do-gooders.

As the voters cleaned house and

reform Mayor William Strong and Police Commissioner Theodore Roosevelt swept into town, Boss Croker quietly sailed for England.

In late 1897, sniffing splendid new patronage possibilities in a consolidated New York City twice as big as the one he had left, he came home. The people of New York, of course, were sick of Good Government by now; Strong and Roosevelt might have given them new parks and schools, but they'd also closed the saloons on Sunday. *"Well! Well! Well! Reform has gone to hell!"* the crowds whooped on Election Night as Croker's man Robert Anderson Van Wyck won the mayorship. Three years earlier, the legislative investigators had publicly branded one Big Bill Devery the city's single most rotten cop; Van Wyck now named Devery chief of police. And soon the town was roaring again, and the good Rev. Parkhurst was forgotten.

And all ran smoothly again. Until the scorching summer of 1900, when the unspeakable Charles Morse was inspired to double the price of ice overnight.

ICEMAN MORSE couldn't believe his good luck. Temperatures were soaring. And his American Ice Co. was New York's sole supplier of one of everyday life's most essential commodities.

In the blistering heat wave, Morse's shameful gouge instantly doomed the poor to misery. The public health suffered at once; great shouts of revulsion went up across the city. Inquiries followed, and it was disclosed that one of the reasons Ice King Morse held his

monopoly was that both Boss Croker and Mayor Van Wyck held handsome chunks of American Ice Co. stock.

New Yorkers were not entirely unaccustomed to having their pockets picked, and as often as not they didn't even mind all that much, but this was outrageous. Tammany Hall had been the common people's most trusted friend. Now Tammany had ruthlessly betrayed them, letting them broil in their wretched slums, letting them sicken their children with spoiled meat.

In the wake of the Ice Trust scandals, another band of Fusion reformers rallied around the unimpeachably honorable Seth Low, formerly a graft-battling mayor of Brooklyn, more recently the president of Columbia University. The cornered Croker, with Van Wyck's reelection out of the question, now feebly fielded an obscure candidate named Edward Shephard.

And now it was election night in November 1901, and Boss Croker silently chewed his cigar as the returns came in.

Finally he stood. "It would seem that Shephard is beaten," he said.

He put on his coat. "Tammany Hall will be here when we are all gone," he said.

And then he walked out into the night, and The Master of the City never set foot in Tammany Hall again.

BOSS RICHARD CROKER *was succeeded by Boss Charles Murphy, who two years later put Seth Low out of office and installed his man, George McClellan, as mayor.*

FARKLEMPT

The Kosher Beef Riots, 1902

By MARA BOVSUN
Special To The News

ONE WARM MAY DAY in 1902, the frugal housewives of the lower East Side discovered that the price of kosher beef had suddenly soared from 12 to 18 cents a pound. Just crazy this made them.

"The Revolution of the Women" is what the New York papers dubbed what followed, and it went on for weeks — an uprising that spread from tenement to tenement, from street to street, from lower Manhattan to Brooklyn, Harlem and the Bronx and then on to Newark and Boston. Before it was over, tens of thousands of otherwise perfectly nice Jewish ladies had rampaged through the city, smashing windows, wrecking stores, overturning pushcarts, belting cops and smacking anyone who got in their way with shoes, dishes, broomsticks, bricks and big slabs of raw liver.

The butchers blamed the price hike on the Beef Trust, a powerful conglomerate of wholesalers. But the women didn't buy that story.

They formed picket lines outside each of the 600 butcher shops in their ghetto and pushcart neighborhoods, first trying to persuade other Jews not to eat beef until the prices dropped. Then they resorted to force.

At 8 a.m. on May 15, a woman ignored the boycotters outside Jacob Kalinski's butcher shop on Cherry St., went inside and bought a chunk of chuck. When she came out, 30 angry picketers pounced upon her, ripped her package from her hands and flung it through Kalinski's window.

Then they stormed the shop, grabbed up every piece of meat in the place and dumped the lot in the gutter outside. Kalinski barricaded himself and his family in their apartment behind the store and huddled there in terror until the ladies' fury was spent. Meanwhile, the offending shopper was chased to the end of the block and pummeled some more. She finally escaped, sans her wig and several pieces of clothing.

The same scene was played out across the lower East Side all through the day — woe to any shopper who bought a cut of meat. Even buying a chicken wasn't safe. A Mrs. Abraham Schwartz of Norfolk St. was chased home by a howling mob that plucked her bird away from her at her doorstep and tossed it from hand to hand. One unfortunate man attempting to make it safely home with a wrapped hen broke his collarbone when he was shoved down cellar steps on Eldridge St.

More than 500 policemen were called to block streets as the rioting spread. "From windows came all manner of missiles raining on helmets and heads," reported the New York Herald, "and then the police used their clubs left and right." Wrote the Sun: "A woman in a Cherry Hill mob held a nursing

"The Power of Women," *Jewish Daily Forward, May 24, 1902; Courtesy of The Forward Association*

baby in one arm; with her free hand she threw a plate that knocked a cop's helmet off."

That night, boycott organizer Sarah Edelson held a rally at New Irving Hall on Essex St. As many as 20,000 people showed up. The police came out in force — and the crowds blew up, swarming through Broome, Orchard and Ludlow Sts., wrecking every kosher butcher shop in their path, piling up mountains of meat in the streets and setting them afire. The women's families joined in behind them, and, wrote The New York Times, all night long "the streets were black with noisy, excited people: the women urging the men, the children throwing things at the police."

Hundreds of women were arrested and dragged kicking and screaming to jail, sometimes with children in their arms. Children themselves — such as the two little girls who tackled a bluecoat, bowled him over into the gutter and tore off his sleeve — were swept away in patrol wagons, too. Hordes of other children chased after the police wagons, shrieking for their mothers. A large crowd of men — husbands,

brothers, other kin — ringed the Essex Market Police Court and cried for the women's release; stick-swinging cops chased them away.

The Great Kosher Beef Riots had only just begun.

WITHIN A WEEK, the boycott leaders were turning on one another; Sarah Edelson had a falling-out with a Mrs. Caroline Schatzburg, who formed a group, the Ladies' Anti-Beef Trust Association, over Mrs. Edelson's objections, and the street rowdiness went on by itself as the two women fought each other for dominance. Presently, the menfolk of the lower East Side found it necessary to step in and, as the newspaper Yiddishes Tageblat put it, "bring order to the great struggle for meat." The men organized their own group, the Allied Conference for Cheap Kosher Meat, and, in time-honored fashion, instructed the women to sit down and be quiet.

For the disorders were not building excellent public relations for the city's immigrant communities. The New York World called the women "a pack of

wolves"; The Times denounced them as "a dangerous class. . . . They do not understand the duties or the rights of Americans. They have no inbred or acquired respect for law and order as the basis of the life of the society into which they have come." Explained a Mrs. Rebecca Ablowitz to the magistrate before whom she had been hauled: "If all we did was to weep at home, nobody would notice it, so we have to do something to help ourselves." Explained the magistrate back: "You aren't allowed to riot in the streets."

By mid-June, the relatively calmer leadership of the allied conference managed to have beef prices rolled back, and the women returned to their kitchens, not to be heard from again.

BUT SEEDS OF *political awareness had been planted, and little spriglets were growing, and surely among the passionate leaders of the great garment industry strikes and other social actions of a later day were those who in May 1902 had been children, watching their mothers fight for food for the table.*

*New York Herald,
Dec. 21, 1902*

CHAPTER 10

THE GENERAL AND THE LADY

Incident at Grant's Tomb, 1902

By JONATHAN LEWIN
Daily News Staff Writer

POLICE TOLD the curious crowds at the Jersey City train station they didn't know who it was being delivered by the somber funeral train. The coffin was loaded onto an Army transport tug and borne up the Hudson to a dock at 129th St. in Manhattan. From there, as 400 officers held back the throngs, the dark procession made its way several blocks south to the largest mausoleum in the United States.

Twenty-five elderly Civil War veterans stood watch as, for the first time, electric lights illuminated two red granite sarcophagi. A derrick lifted the 5-ton lid of one of them just enough to let the coffin be slipped inside.

It was Dec. 20, 1902, and Julia Dent Grant was joining her husband at last.

More than 1,000 New Yorkers stood vigil in the cold rain outside the private services the next day. Seventeen years after Ulysses S. Grant's death, and 37 years after his acceptance of Robert E. Lee's surrender at Appomattox, there remained enormous reverence and affection for the great Union general — and for his ever loyal and supportive wife, if not for whom there would never have been a Grant's Tomb in New York at all.

WHEN GRANT SETTLED in New York in 1879, following an unfortunate presidency that had left many public officials wealthy but Grant himself quite poor, generous friends made it possible for him to live in a manner befitting a man who, despite everything,

remained the nation's grandest living hero. Five years later, dying of throat cancer, he was using his remaining strength to complete his memoirs, hoping to provide dependable income for Julia after he was gone. New Yorkers admired his brave, painful struggle, regularly saluting his E. 65th St. home when they passed.

He died on July 23, 1885, just days after finishing his book. Hundreds of thousands turned out to pay their respects as his funeral procession wound 7 miles through the streets of Manhattan. Even the defeated South still respected Grant because of his willingness to let Lee surrender with dignity, and two former Confederate generals were among the pallbearers.

Still, Grant was not, after all, a native New Yorker — he had lived in the city for just six years — and many questioned why he should be interred here. Civil War veterans' groups and many members of Congress thought Arlington National Cemetery was far more appropriate. Grant himself, so far as that went, would have preferred burial at West Point.

But he wanted Julia to be buried

with him when her time came, and that was not possible at West Point. New York got the nod only because Julia insisted that the general's dying wish be honored, and Mayor William Grace pledged that the city would so honor it.

Personally, Julia was not all that keen on Riverside Park. She liked Central Park better, or Union Square. The Riverside Park site was finally accepted, since it was on a hilltop, easily viewable from the Hudson River, and since also the increasingly elegant neighborhood was slated to include such majesties as Columbia University and the Cathedral Church of St. John the Divine.

In any case, the Grant Monument Association's ambitious million-dollar fund-raising drive was getting nowhere. Reflecting its disdain for America's great metropolis, much of the heartland simply refused to contribute. Five full years after Grant's death, the fund-raisers were far short of their goal, a tomb design had not even been selected and the general was still reposing in a temporary vault. In Congress, sentiments mounted afresh to transplant him to Arlington and be done with it, and it took the emphatic Julia to block that movement as well.

Finally, in 1892, the presidency of the Monument Association fell to Gen. Horace Porter, one of Grant's former staff officers, and Porter made it his mission to make New Yorkers civically ashamed of themselves. He cited "the humiliating spectacle of the remains of the most illustrious soldier of his age" lying unburied. "New York, chosen by him as his home, has not yet provided a

tomb to give shelter to his ashes," Porter chided. So challenged, 90,000 people came up with $650,000.

Briefly there was trouble with the initially chosen site, where construction would have disrupted a small marker dedicated to a 5-year-old boy named Saint Claire Pollock, who had died in 1797. Local parents defiantly ringed the child's shrine, and finally Grant's Tomb was relocated 100 yards to the southeast.

On April 27, 1897, John Duncan's stately Roman-style monument was formally dedicated. Sixty thousand soldiers marched. A naval flotilla coursed up the river. A million spectators watched. The pomp and pageantry was unequaled in the city's history and, it was said, perhaps the nation's.

JULIA DENT GRANT had been one of the earliest public Presidential wives — "First Lady" was not yet a popularly familiar term — and she continued to be well-known to Americans in the years after the general died. The successful publication of his memoirs did in fact make her financially comfortable, and she spent her last years active in Susan B. Anthony's women's suffrage movement and, during the Spanish-American War, the Women's National War Relief Association. Upon her death she was quite genuinely mourned.

By December 1902, when she was laid to rest alongside her husband, a half-million Americans were visiting Grant's Tomb every year. A century later there is less remembrance, but the two of them sleep there still — the only U.S. President buried in New York City, and his lady.

A NEW YORK EPIC: 1898-1998

Photo-illustration re-creates the Park Ave. shooting; New York World, Nov. 14, 1903

CHAPTER 11

SINS OF THE FATHER

The Murder Of Andrew Haswell Green, 1903

By JAY MAEDER
Daily News Staff Writer

ANDREW HASWELL GREEN, on the last day of his long and virtuous life, Friday the 13th of November 1903, went as usual to his lower Broadway office. At the stroke of 1 p.m., he put on his hat and topcoat, bade his associates a good afternoon and boarded a Fourth Ave. car for his final ride home. At 1:30, the old man doddered up the steps of the Park Ave. tunnel, emerged on 40th St. and made his last stroll across the avenue to the gate of his brownstone at No. 91. There he stepped for the last time into his vestibule and came face to face with a neatly dressed black man who had quietly stalked him for a week.

Witnesses to the confrontation included an arriving housekeeper, a nearby cab driver and a passing deliveryman, and all three reported to police identical accounts of Andrew Haswell Green's last instants on Earth:

"Why do you back that woman to slander me?" Green's visitor demanded.

"Go away," said Green. "I don't know you."

"Yes, you do," replied Cornelius Williams. "I met you in 1895 in 53rd St."

"You did not," retorted Green. "I don't know you, I tell you, and you must go away from here."

"Yes, you do know me," Williams insisted. "You backed this woman to slander me. Now you've got to take the consequences."

And with that, Williams pulled a heavy revolver and fired five shots, and the Father of Greater New York, age 83, crumpled dead to his flagstones.

Williams made no attempt to flee; gun pocketed, he stood calmly over Green's body until two policemen led him to the 35th St. stationhouse. There, expressionless, he answered every question thrown at him by police and press. "He deserved it," the killer declared. "Thank God he's dead."

Why? Why in God's name had a furnace tender wanted to kill good Andrew Green? The city reeled at the story Williams spun.

NINETEENTH-CENTURY New York had known few men more towering than Andrew Green, and many were the testaments to his life and works: Central Park, Riverside Park, the new Public Library, the Zoological Society, the American Museum of Natural History — indeed, the consolidated city itself, born of his vision and tireless 30-year crusade. "He loved New York as Dante loved Florence," remarked The World upon his death. "For many years to come, New York will be a more beautiful, a more healthful and a more commodious city than if he had not lived in it."

Massachusetts-born Green had come to the city as a young clerk in the 1830s, then, upon becoming Samuel Tilden's protege and law partner, embarked upon a life-long career of public service: president of the Board of Education at first, then president of the Central Park Commission; it was Green who commissioned Calvert Vaux as park landscaper. With Tilden, he was instrumental in ridding the city of the corrupt Tammany boss William Tweed; subsequently, as city controller, he personally restored the municipal credit that Tweed had demolished. He was among the forces that merged the Tilden, Astor and Lenox libraries into what would become the New York Public Library. And in 1890, two decades after he first proposed consolidating New York and Brooklyn into a single "imperial city," he was named chairman of the commission that oversaw the creation of the new city and drafted its Charter.

A distinguished elder statesman in his twilight years, the Father of Greater New York lived to become critical of some of what he had wrought. Writing to the New York Herald two months before he died, Green commented: "A grave mistake was made in dividing the city into boroughs. This unfortunate step was succeeded by one infinitely worse — namely, that of erecting a separate district government in each borough, thus rendering simplicity and unity of administration impossible."

Active to the last, he was, on the day he met his murderer, working to eliminate horsecars and street railways in favor of "electrical conveyances moving over smooth, noiseless pavements."

PROSECUTORS INSTANTLY branded Cornelius Williams "obviously deranged." A boardinghouse keeper named Bessie Davis, Williams said, had ruined his good name with vicious lies, and for eight years he had been searching for her in order to cut her tongue out of her head. But Davis, he explained, was under Andrew Green's protection, and therefore it was necessary to kill Green. "I did it to save my character," he maintained. Officials agreed that the yarn was absurd: Surely such a man as Andrew Green could never have known this Davis woman.

To the degree that the average citizen, on the other hand, might have found Williams' story not necessarily all *that* implausible, the titillation increased when the newspapers discovered that humble Bessie Davis, formerly of 132 W. 53rd St., was now a bejewelled woman called Hannah Elias, who lived in a mansion on Central Park West and kept a Chinese cook, a Japanese butler, an English coachman and an exquisite art collection. Her neighbors surmised her to be some sort of exiled African princess. Some were sure there had been a child that had died several years earlier.

Obliged to call the exotic Mrs. Elias in for questioning, the district attorney did so, then quickly announced that there was not a shred of evidence linking her to Andrew Green.

And then, as the great man was buried and the most eminent citizens of New York gave him their eulogies, the story abruptly disappeared from the public prints.

Little more was heard until April, when Cornelius Williams was quietly adjudged paranoiac and dispatched to the state hospital for the criminally insane.

And thereafter all Andrew Haswell Green's secrets, if he had any, would lay cold with him in his grave.

BIG TOWN BIG TIME™

A NEW YORK EPIC: 1898-1998

By JAY MAEDER
Daily News Staff Writer

CONEY ISLAND had been discovered, never mind Henry Hudson, by the rich yachtsman swells of the earlier 19th century, and after the Civil War it turned into a popular beach resort brimming with hotels, music halls, bathhouses, bordellos, hot dog stands and boardwalk hustles. The 5-mile playground was long presided over by Boss John McKane, a man as powerful on his own turf as were the Tammany bosses Tweed, Kelly and Croker on theirs. But by the early 1890s, Brooklyn had annexed the island and Boss McKane was on his way to prison and there was plenty of room for fresh ideas. George Tilyou had several.

The first of them climbed 250 feet into the sky and carried passengers round and round and round as they screamed with joy and held one another tight. It was called a Ferris wheel. George Tilyou beheld this wonder at the Columbian Exposition in Chicago in 1893 and could not believe his eyes. He was looking at the future. Until that moment just a Surf Ave. theater operator, he immediately put up a Ferris wheel of his own on the Coney beach and he immediately got rich.

Next, noting attendance at the three big local horse tracks — Sheepshead, Gravesend and Brighton Beach — Tilyou decided that perhaps the fun seekers might enjoy wooden nags built to ride on rails. When he opened his Steeplechase Park on 15 acres of land between 16th and 19th Sts. in 1897, his showpiece Steeplechase Horses instantly joined the world's

CHAPTER 12

SHINE ON BRIGHTLY

Old Coney Island, 1904

top attractions.

By 1901, when Tilyou brought in fellow impresarios Fred Thompson and Skip Dundy — whose breathtaking Trip to the Moon cyclorama had been a sensation at the Pan-American Exposition in Buffalo — he was the father of the modern amusement park, and his Steeplechase, awash in the glow of electric lights in the oceanfront evenings, was famous around the globe.

If he had not exactly invented Coney Island itself, in a few short years he had personally made it a glittering magic kingdom on the sea, the City of Shining Lights. Boss McKane was dead now. Amusements-wise, Boss McKane had been pretty much just a whorehouse man. It was hard to know what he would have made of Ferris wheels.

ENTIRELY PRACTICAL showman that he was, Tilyou did not mind a bit when his partners Thompson and Dundy ran out on him and in the summer of 1903 opened their own Luna Park a few blocks up Surf Ave. Admittedly, the new rival was some

humdinger of a place, easily the more dazzling of the two spreads: If Steeplechase had tens of thousands of light bulbs, Luna Park had *hundreds* of thousands. Still, there were plenty of customers for everyone, and Tilyou recognized that Luna Park would draw only bigger crowds in these merriest of times.

Then, just a year after that, Brooklyn developer William Reynolds opened a third grand park on Surf Ave., Dreamland by name, and Reynolds had fully a *million* lights.

There were five railroads serving Coney Island on Saturday the 14th of May in 1904, and on that day they delivered 250,000 New Yorkers to the festivities attending the widely anticipated first day of the new summer season. All agreed they could scarcely recognize the place.

Steeplechase was offering many fresh thrills — the Earthquake Stairway, the Barrel of Love, the Whichaway — and Tilyou had built a 1,300-foot pier to accommodate the excursion-boat crowds. Luna Park was twice as big as it had been the previous summer;

covering 16 full acres of it was a replication of the city of Delhi, full of cobra charmers and dancing girls and jeweled camels and mirrored elephants. Military bombardments were being staged in the new Naval Spectatorium, and beyond the lagoons in the Babylonian Hanging Gardens were now 10,000 trees and 25,000 potted plants. At the astonishing new Dreamland, a great tower ascended seemingly all the way to the clouds, and a mighty volcano erupted into fire and smoke, and then rivers of lava destroyed old Pompeii.

All up and down Surf Ave. there were spires and minarets. Everywhere there were jugglers and acrobats, and chariots and boxing bears, and marching bands and parachutists, and troops of performing Eskimos and dwarfs, and when the sun went down the electric lights came up and you could see Coney Island for miles and miles. And this is the way things would stay always. In May 1904, none of this was ever going to end.

DREAMLAND BURNED to the *ground in 1911. Luna Park burned to the ground 33 years later.*

Steeplechase Park had already burned to the ground in 1907, actually, but George Tilyou swiftly rebuilt it and in the meantime charged visitors 10 cents a head to come in and look at the rubble.

As late as 1940, Coney Island one blistering summer day recorded 3.3 million visitors, or approximately half the population of New York City.

CHAPTER 13

BUILT LIKE A BONFIRE

General Slocum, 1904

By JAY MAEDER
Daily News Staff Writer

THEY WERE EARTH'S *Purest Children, Young And Fair.* Proudly wearing their Sunday school best, hundreds of them together boarded an East River excursion boat one sunny picnic morning in June 1904 — and together they perished, in a screaming horror that remains to this day the single worst disaster New York City has ever known.

The final toll of the General Slocum fire has never been fixed: 1,021 dead at least, perhaps 1,031, perhaps 30 more than that, and that number counts only those who were roasted or drowned in 30 awful minutes. Later, dozens of survivors committed suicide in their desolation; more yet were led vacant-eyed to mental wards. In the end, an entire neighborhood — a lively, laughing, gracious, prosperous, bustling lower East Side community called Weiss Garten — disappeared forever.

The "white garden" had taken its name from the clean white fences enclosing the Tompkins Square sector of the great German colony that had years earlier arisen between Houston and E. 14th Sts. on the riverfront. Germans had been in New York from the very beginning; old Peter Minuit himself had been a German. By 1904, there were three quarters of a million of them scattered about the city, fully a third of the metropolitan population, and the Weiss Garten, an enclave of the larger German community known since the 1840s as Kleindeutschland, was its spiritual center. At the very heart of the garden, on Sixth St. between First and Second Aves., was that which gave the hearty émigrés their affirmation and sustenance, the red-brick St. Mark's Evangelical Lutheran Church, a house of worship almost mystically revered in the old country as the first place any voyager would seek out upon arrival in the New World.

For a German child in early-century New York, the annual church picnic was the first of summer's sweet pleasures. At 9 o'clock on the morning of Wednesday, June 15, they gathered excitedly at the Third St. pier, the children and their mothers and aunts and grandmothers, perhaps 1,350 in all, and by 9:30 they were bound for Locust Grove on Huntington Bay for a day of Christian frolic. They were to be home, weary and elated, by nightfall. In less than an hour, most of them would be dead.

> *From the first instant someone smelled smoke, somewhere in the treacherous whirlpools of Hell Gate, there was never a hope for her.*

In those steamboat days, the General Slocum was one of the river's most colorfully familiar sights. Named for a Civil War officer who had gone on to Congress, she was a wonderful three-deck side paddler, and on this perfect picnic morning she was gaily pennanted and carried a merry oompah band that was already playing "Ein Fest Burg Ist Unser Gott" as she set out.

But she was a deathtrap, nothing but tinder and fresh paint and crumbling life preservers and the cheapest fire hose her owners could buy. She had not been inspected for years. Her crew had never known a fire drill. From the first instant someone smelled smoke, somewhere in the treacherous whirlpools of Hell Gate, there was never a hope for her.

Hundreds watched horrified from shore as the burning steamer continued upriver; why on earth was she not instantly putting into any one of the dozens of wharves between 125th and 135th Sts.? But elderly Capt. William Van Schaick had already determined to beach his boat on North Brother Island off 149th St., and there he remained steadfastly bound as the long minutes passed — and the General Slocum plowed full speed ahead directly into a brisk wind that sent great walls of oil-fed flames whipping from stacks to stern.

There was no escape for the picnickers. They died where they stood in the roaring flames. They died in the merciless currents into which they flung themselves. The terrible river ran thick with their bodies for days. Many were found locked in one another's arms.

Long lines of hearses jammed the black-creped streets of the lower East Side, and Kleindeutschland wailed with funerals. On Friday the 17th, there were hundreds of services at 37 churches — 114 at St. Mark's Evangelical Lutheran alone. Then there were hundreds more on Saturday and Sunday.

"Built like a bonfire and certain to burn like one," snapped one newspaper of the General Slocum as the official inquiries got under way. But in fact there was little illegal about the Slocum; she was no more or less shoddy than any other working rivercraft. There were multiple criminal indictments — of her owners, of her crew, of federal steamboat inspectors — but in the end only old Capt. Van Schaick was convicted of negligence. Crippled and blinded in the accident, he served several years in Sing Sing; President William Howard Taft pardoned him at Christmas 1912, and he spent the rest of his life insisting that he had done everything he could to save his passengers.

In the wake of the Slocum disaster, maritime safety standards were considerably tightened. That was one of the doomed ship's legacies.

Another was the end of Kleindeutschland. Devastated, stripped forever of its gaiety, it fell swiftly apart as its mourning residents turned their backs on the place forever and fled uptown to Yorkville, to Astoria in Queens and to Brooklyn and the Bronx, surrendering their historic neighborhood to fast-incoming new waves of Russians and Poles. Never again in New York would there be so vibrant and close-knit a German Protestant community. All that remains is a small monument in Tompkins Square — *They Were Earth's Purest Children, Young And Fair* — in testimony to a perfect picnic morning long ago when laughter all at once turned to screams.

By JAY MAEDER
Daily News Staff Writer

THERE MIGHT HAVE been a New York subway 30 years or so before there was one, had it not been for the dependably rapacious Boss Tweed, who had put his money on surface rail and did not care to entertain other propositions. On the other hand, considering that electricity hadn't particularly come along yet anyway, it would have been a very bad subway. In this particular case, Boss Tweed probably saved the city a lot of infrastructural grief, and it is probably the case that the engineering professions are in his debt.

Still, it was certainly true that traffic-choked, street-bogged New York opened its underground railroad not a minute too soon. In 1904, the city remained the same bedlam of slow-moving, desperately overcrowded streetcars and elevated trains it had been for decades. The fine new subway was going to fix all this; instead, of course, for four long, nightmarish years its construction had only made everything far worse — disrupted every aspect of the city's daily life, gutted its major thoroughfare like a fish, stopped commerce in its tracks, shattered the windows of respectable homes and businesses with its ceaseless blastings, muddied the skirts of ladies seeking only to cross their own streets.

But now it was Thursday the 27th of October, and the subway system was finished at last, at least from City Hall up to Broadway and 145th St., and the city was draped with flags and bunting, and mobs of New Yorkers backed up for blocks at the stations as they waited to board. It was said that the new marvel could clip along at 40 mph. It was said that it could deliver them from their homes to their work places and back in mere minutes.

GETTING AROUND in the city had never been one of those cogently well-planned things. Once upon a time, if you wanted to go somewhere and you didn't have your own carriage, you just walked. In 1829, discerning the need, an enterprising gentleman named Abraham Brower invented public transportation with a couple of stagecoach-like vehicles called omnibuses, that initially carried passengers up Broadway as far as Bleecker St. for a shilling a head. By 1835 their drivers were notorious maniacs who would run down old ladies for laughs, and the fast-spreading omnibus lines would continue to terrify decent New Yorkers out of their wits for generations to come.

Meanwhile, there arrived the

CHAPTER 14

NOTES FROM THE UNDERGROUND

The Subway, 1904

miracle of street rails: The New York & Harlem Railroad launched the first horse-drawn railway system in 1832, initially up the Bowery from Prince to 14th St. By the Civil War, there were more than a dozen horse railway lines and nearly 700 omnibuses in the streets, as well as carriages and wagons and hordes of pedestrians, and everything regularly collided with everything else, there being no such things as traffic lanes or traffic lights yet.

Amid this havoc, subways were being discussed by serious public men as soon as London opened the

world's first system in 1863, but Boss Tweed's powerful Tammany Hall effortlessly killed at least one early proposal. Thus was Alfred Ely Beach pressed to keep the construction of his own remarkable private enterprise a complete secret until the day he opened for business.

Beach, publisher of Scientific American magazine and a leading technological visionary, had hit upon the idea of moving a cylindrical car by compressed air, blowing it through a tube and then sucking it back again with a gigantic fan. Tunneling

clandestinely by night as Tweed's City Hall remained clueless upstairs, Beach finished his Beach Pneumatic Railway in 1870, and it was, as he had anticipated, so great a public sensation that there wasn't much Tweed could do about it by then.

On the other hand, it was a perfectly ridiculous subway. Compressed air worked fine, but that was because Beach's line was just a block long, running under Broadway between Warren and Murray Sts., and it never would have huffed and puffed anyone to Brooklyn and back; 19th century technological idealism, bless its heart, didn't know that yet. Noble but essentially useless, Beach's 300-foot experiment folded after a year or two.

By two decades later, when municipal underground possibilities were explored anew, electric railway systems had become not only possible but plainly desirable. Since Beach's day there had arisen the city's elevated steam trains, great lurching, noisy, unpleasant beasts that forever burped cinders and ash onto Second, Third, Sixth and Ninth Aves. beneath them and occasionally set whole blocks afire. Everybody hated the els, but it still took the entire 1890s before the subway contracts got through the political jungles of three mayoral administrations.

As 1899 turned to 1900, it remained uncertain that the subway would ever be built. Finally, that spring, financier August Belmont's Interborough Rapid Transit Co. broke ground, and an army of immigrant laborers led by Chief Engineer William Barclay Parsons went straightaway to work with picks and shovels and dynamite and began disemboweling the town.

FOUR YEARS LATER, on Oct. 27, 1904, at half past two in the afternoon, Mayor George McClellan took the controls of the VIP train waiting below City Hall and commenced the IRT's official first run. McClellan was supposed to drive for only the first few ceremonial minutes, but he loved the work so much that he refused to give the train up. "This is my train!" he bellowed, gleefully goosing the throttle as IRT officials quaked and blanched and sputtered. They didn't get the controls away from him until 103rd St.

Up from City Hall clattered the city's first subway, to the Grand Central Depot at 42nd St., then west to what had recently been renamed Times Square, then north again up Broadway. The express run to 145th St. took 26 minutes; the local run back to City Hall took 41. The top-hatted dignitaries spent the rest of the afternoon riding back and forth as the crowds above them clamored for the IRT's public debut.

That came at 7 p.m., and as many as 150,000 New Yorkers streamed into the kiosks and down onto the white-tiled platforms that first night. On Sunday the 30th, nearly a million tried to ride; more than half of them had to be turned away. Within days, rush-hour straphanging was a firmly established New York City institution, as if the trains had been running forever.

CORBIS-BETTMAN

CHAPTER 15

CROSSROADS

The Birth Of Times Square, 1904

By OWEN MORITZ, HOWARD KISSEL and JAY MAEDER
Daily News Staff Writers

EVENTUALLY IT WOULD be said of Times Square that if you stood there long enough you would meet everyone you had ever known, but that observation was made much later, when it was pretty much true. Long before that, the Civil War-era Gov. Horatio Seymour had predicted that Broadway at 42nd St. someday would witness "more people than ever migrated through any other avenue of travel on the globe," and at the time it was hard to know what he was envisioning of this barren, mud-slopped crossroads at the northern extreme of civilized Old New York.

If by the latter years of the 19th century this address was no longer quite at the ends of the Earth, it remained a place of the lower refinements. William K. Vanderbilt had taken over most of the area in the early 1880s and settled his American Horse Exchange there, and by day Long Acre Square, as it came to be known, bustled with traders and stablehands and blacksmiths and harness makers. At night it went dark and empty, save for a hotel or two, save for a beer garden, save for wayward Tenderloin strays.

As the century turned, there were three more or less simultaneous new developments. The city's gaily lighted Rialto district was moving up Broadway from Herald Square. The first leg of the new subway system was under construction. And one of the city's larger newspapers was relocating. Convergence occurred. On the last day of 1904, Times Square was officially born.

NEW YORK HAD been a theater city as early as the late 1600s, lively with amateur programs; the first documented professional production arrived in 1750, when an English company presented "Richard III," and that led to a small explosion of theaters in lower Manhattan, centered on Beekman and John Sts. As the years passed and popular tastes broadened, melodramas and minstrel shows joined Shakespeare as box-office draws, and in 1866 the American musical theater was accidentally born when a French ballet troupe, stranded when the theater into which it had been booked burned down, was persuaded to flesh out the scene changes in an altogether unrelated production called "The Black Crook." And through the 1800s the Rialto, like the city itself, kept wending further and further up the spine called Broadway; once-central Union Square, by the end of the century, was left with little but vaudeville and freak shows.

In 1883, a group of patrons who had found themselves of insufficient social stature to secure boxes at the Academy of Music on 14th St. built the Metropolitan Opera House on Broadway at then-comparatively remote 40th St., bringing a whiff of class to the lower reaches of the malodorous horse district. At that point several theaters began to appear in the neighborhood as well: in 1888, the Broadway, at 41st St.; in 1893, the Empire, at 40th St., the Knickerbocker, at 38th St. and the American on, quite extraordinarily, faraway 42nd St. itself.

Then, in November 1895, showman Oscar Hammerstein, who theretofore had been running the Manhattan Opera House down on 34th St., did an amazing thing: He pushed beyond 42nd St., all the way to 44th, and opened a palatial $3 million theater called the Olympia.

Hammerstein at that moment became the founding father of what was not yet called Times Square, and the Gay White Way, gaslit since the 1820s, electrically illumed only recently, followed him to the new theater district he had created. Over the next few years, Hammerstein and other impresarios opened numerous new houses in the square and its environs: the Victoria, the New Amsterdam, the Republic, the Lyric, the Lyceum. Hotels arrived. So did elegant *apres-theater* restaurants.

Directly beneath all this flowering, meanwhile, soon to open the neighborhood to New York's millions, a subway station was being built.

AND IT WOULD have been called the Long Acre Square Station but for the fact that in April 1904 the city formally renamed the square Times Square.

This was because a wonderful new pink granite building was going up in the heart of the place, the Times Tower, the forthcoming home of The New York Times now that Adolph Ochs had decided to move his increasingly important sheet uptown from old Newspaper Row. At 375 feet tall the city's second-biggest building, the Times Tower towered over everything around it long before it was even finished, plainly destined to be the very emblem of its domain. **TIMES SQUARE IS THE NAME OF CITY'S NEW CENTRE,** headlined The Times, not unreasonably pleased with itself. Down in Herald Square, the Herald was less enthralled; for years to come the Herald would continue to refer to Times Square as Long Acre Square.

To everyone else it would be Times Square forever, carved into the firmament the night of Dec. 31, 1904, when Adolph Ochs hosted the square's first public New Year's Eve celebration and inaugurated what would become one of the city's defining traditions: As 1904 turned to 1905, amid the flash and thunder of a great fireworks display, as rockets hurtled into the sky and bombs exploded in the night, as tens of thousands of revelers cheered, a lighted ball dropped slowly down the side of Times Tower and welcomed in the new morning.

And thereafter Times Square was, in fact, the center of New York life and the crossroads of the whole world, a mythical place O. Henry was soon calling "Baghdad on the Subway," only a few short years after it had been home to nothing much more than a bunch of horses.

By JAY MAEDER
Daily News Staff Writer

MANY WERE those who felt in 1901 that William Randolph Hearst's scabrous New York Journal was directly responsible for the murder of President William McKinley — for one thing, there had been a famous editorial that openly called upon McKinley to die — and suddenly Hearst was a much-despised and distrusted man, denounced as a scoundrel, hanged in effigy. Mildly abashed, Hearst got on with things nevertheless. There was work to do. He had decided to be President himself.

To be sure, there would, for appearances' sake, have to be a couple of preliminary stops on the road to the White House. One of these was Congress, election to which he won in 1902, although, what with one thing and another, his candidacy killed 18 more people.

Another, as things turned out, was the mayorship of New York City. And in November 1905, quite astonishingly, he apparently won that as well, snatching the race from the grim sachems of Tammany Hall and genuinely winning the thing. He really would have been mayor of the town. Were it not for the thousands of ballots that went straight into the river.

WILLIE HEARST had exhibited no particular political aspirations when, in 1895, he left his thriving San Francisco Examiner to his lieutenants and came East. In those days it had been only the lovely prospect of commanding a New York paper that seemed to amuse the young millionaire. The Times was for sale, but not to him, and James Gordon Bennett's Herald wasn't available either (asked his price, Bennett wired back: **HERALD THREE CENTS DAILY, FIVE CENTS SUNDAY**), and Hearst had to settle for a gasping rag called the Journal & Advertiser. Which, by century's end, via bluster and showmanship and a brilliantly unerring grasp of the baser popular tastes, Hearst had made over into the city's largest and most influential sheet.

Aside from starting the Spanish-American War all by himself, Hearst was also hell on banks and railroads, and in the public-spirited glow of his many journalistic triumphs he had in 1900 been persuaded to let his name be floated as a Democratic vice presidential prospect. This had come to nothing. But he had liked the taste of it.

A problem besetting his newfound political ambitions was that he had railed for years against the boundless venalities of Tammany Hall, the city's all-powerful Democratic organization. Hearst was not an impractical soul. In 1902, determining as a practical matter that perhaps it was not such a repellent thing to be a Tammany Democrat after all, he cut a deal with Boss Croker's newly installed successor, Silent Charlie Murphy, and graciously accepting nomination by the good people of Manhattan's 11th Ward to serve them in the United States House of Representatives.

His subsequent election was a foregone

CORBIS-BETTMAN

CHAPTER 16
GOOD CITIZENSHIP
Hearst For Mayor, 1905

conclusion — this was, after all, the 11th Ward — and on Nov. 4 he rented most of Madison Square for a gala celebration. It was an unfortunate night. There were improperly stored fireworks. There were three mighty explosions. Twelve citizens died on the spot and six more succumbed later. Hearst would be settling damage claims for decades to come. On the other hand, he was on his way to Washington.

BUT IF CONGRESSMAN Hearst was perhaps not the most attentive congressman that Washington had ever seen, it remained the case that he owned influential newspapers not only in New York and San Francisco but also by now in Chicago and Boston and Los Angeles, and his several minor public initiatives were so warmly reported by these organs that in the summer of 1904 he almost won the Democratic presidential nomination.

By now obsessed with the presidency, Hearst looked toward a strong 1908 run. There were two useful stepping stone offices he might seek at this point. One was the New York State governorship, but that wasn't available until 1906. Meanwhile, New York Mayor George McClellan would be standing for reelection.

Mayor McClellan, however, remained in Tammany's good graces, and Boss Murphy was not inclined to remove him. So rebuffed, Hearst in 1905 formed his own party, the Tammany-savaging

Municipal Owners' League, and in October he consented to run as its mayoral candidate.

This was a big laugh, so Tammany thought at first. But Hearst had deep pockets, and his noisy campaign bowled the city over. Quite improbably, he overnight became a good-government reform hero, promising to imprison Murphy, pledging city ownership of the streetcars and utilities. Thousands of workingmen turned out to cheer him at every appearance, chant the strange campaign song (*"Hoist! Hoist! He is not the woist!"*) and literally lift him to their shoulders. Murphy was horrified. Hearst's marginal third party was conceivably about to demolish the Tammany slate.

ALL THROUGH Election Day, gangs of goons stormed polling places across the city, beat up poll workers, wrecked ballot boxes. "It looks close," someone suggested to Murphy at the Tammany wigwam at 9 p.m. "I don't care," Murphy shrugged. "We win." The final tally gave Hearst 225,000 votes to McClellan's 228,000. Few doubted that Hearst had had at least 50,000 votes quite baldly stolen from him.

A judge ordered police to deliver 6,000 ballot boxes to the Bureau of Elections for a recount, but Tammany's elections commissioner refused to accept them. They sat on the sidewalks, seals broken, ballots flying in the breeze. Tammany, meanwhile, printed up thousands of new ballots and threw them to McClellan. The whole town was dumbstruck by the naked thievery. For the first and last time, even Hearst's publishing rivals rose up to champion the rights of their odious colleague.

"We do not suppose that anybody in the city of New York, George B. McClellan himself included, thinks that McClellan was elected Mayor on Tuesday," snapped the Press.

"There is a very deep-seated feeling in this town that Tuesday's election was not immaculate," agreed the Sun.

"Mr. Hearst is fairly within his rights when he decides to make a contest," said the Tribune.

"If William Randolph Hearst received in Tuesday's election one single vote more than McClellan," said even Hearst's arch-competitor The World, doubtless choking on its own words, "then Mr. Hearst should be seated. It is not in question now who is best suited for the Mayor's duty."

In the wake of the blatantly crooked election, there were many arrests and prosecutions, and ultimately the election laws were reformed. But, for now, in the New York City of 1905, McClellan remained mayor and Silent Charlie Murphy remained boss.

Again Hearst got past things. There was nothing to do now but go after the governorship. Warily he and Murphy regarded each other once more, and warily they resumed the courtship rituals that would bind them together for years yet.

HEARST WAS NOT *elected governor in 1906 or President in 1908, but he remained a formidable Democratic Party power broker into the 1920s, and he outlived Charles Murphy by 27 years.*

By JAY MAEDER
Daily News Staff Writer

SUMMER HAD PASSED, and the crowds at the New York Zoological Park were thinning, but the Monkey House was always a popular attraction, and many visitors were there this Saturday morning to watch Dohong the orangutan pedal his tricycle around his cage. Sharing Dohong's habitat today was a newcomer, a tiny fellow who wore trousers and a jacket and sat quietly weaving straw, and sometimes looked up to bare the teeth he had filed into sharp points.

A woman gasped. "Is that a *man?*" she said.

Another spectator turned away uneasily. "Something about it that I don't like," he murmured.

It was Sept. 8, 1906, and Ota Benga had come to New York.

"The human being caged was the little black man, Ota Benga, whom Prof. S.P. Verner, the explorer, recently brought to this country from the jungles of Central Africa," The New York Times reported the next day. *"Prof. Verner lately handed him over to the New York Zoological Society for care and keeping.*

"It is probably a good thing that Benga doesn't think very deeply."

SAMUEL PHILLIPS VERNER was part missionary, part circus man, part legitimate anthropologist, part quack; in the 1890s he had befriended and lived among the natives of the Belgian Congo, and he had returned to America with wildlife for the Central Park Zoo and artifacts for the Smithsonian Institution. He also had brought back two young black men and enrolled them in school in Tuskegee, Ala. One of them died there, alas, trampled to death in a riot that broke out during a Booker T. Washington lecture. The other, in 1904, returned to Africa with Verner to help him round up a collection of pygmies for display at the St. Louis World's Fair.

One of these was Ota Benga, whom Verner found miserably enslaved by a cannibal tribe and whose freedom he purchased. Saved from the pot, he was only too happy to travel to America with his new friend — and, when the World's Fair engagement was concluded, he was the sole member of Verner's bushman troupe who decided he did not wish to go home again.

Ota Benga was one of the bigger stars of the anthropology-themed World's Fair, in whose University of Man exhibit were assembled specimen aboriginals of many lands: Hottentots, Zulus, Eskimos, Filipinos, Japanese primitives, the old Apache chief Geronimo himself. None were captives; they were in show business. Like the mercenary Geronimo, Ota Benga fast learned to expect a few tossed coins in return for his work as a professional pygmy — dancing, weaving, baring his teeth, snarling. He was one of the grand prize winners at fair's end. Traveling thereafter with Verner, he got used to hotels and streetcars and baseball games, and he liked to wear white duck suits.

Official Bronx Zoo Portrait; Courtesy New York Zoological Society

CHAPTER 17

THE LITTLE MAN IN THE ZOO

Ota Benga, 1906

He knew about 100 words of English, and he was quite the gent by the summer of 1906, when Verner brought him to New York.

THE BRONX ZOO, when it opened in November 1899 with a collection of 843 beasts, birds and reptiles, was immediately the world's largest. Organized by wealthy sportsmen led by Theodore Roosevelt and underwritten by benefactors with such names as Morgan, Dodge, Whitney, Schuyler and Morris, the park was one of New York City's great crown jewels. "Not to be in the New York Zoological Society," sniffed one tony magazine, "is not to be in society."

Park director William Temple Hornaday, formerly of the National Zoo in Washington, had said from the beginning that, anthropologically speaking, he did not find it inappropriate to regard human beings as display specimens. Initially it had been his hope to build an American Indian reservation on the buffalo range.

In September 1906, Samuel Phillips Verner brought him Ota Benga instead.

BUSHMAN SHARES A CAGE WITH BRONX PARK APES, the headline blared, and on Sunday the 9th many thousands of New Yorkers packed the zoo to goggle at the pygmy with the pointed teeth. The sign above his enclosure read: **THE AFRICAN PYGMY. "OTA BENGA." AGE 23 YEARS. HEIGHT 4 FEET 11 INCHES. WEIGHT 103 POUNDS. . . . EXHIBITED EACH AFTERNOON DURING SEPTEMBER.** Someone had given Ota Benga a pair of shoes to wear this day. "He seemed to like the shoes very much," noted The Times.

Immediately there was tumult. The Colored Baptist Ministers' Conference, angrily led by the Rev. R.S. MacArthur of Calvary Baptist, denounced Hornaday and the zoo. "The person responsible for this exhibition degrades himself as much as he does the African," snapped MacArthur. Added J.H. Gordon, superintendent of the Howard Colored Orphan Asylum in Brooklyn: "Our race, we think, is depressed enough without exhibiting one of us with the apes."

Hornaday never quite grasped the objections. "We are taking excellent care of the little fellow," he protested. "He has one of the best rooms in the primate house."

The public uproar mounted as the days went by. "Absolutely shameful disgrace," fumed The Journal — "in bad taste, offensive to honest men and unworthy of New York City's government." The exhibit, agreed The Times, was "tactless" at the very least. After two weeks, Hornaday gave up his pygmy. By the end of the month, Ota Benga was a resident of the Orphan Asylum — "free," declared Gordon, "of the witchcraft of the white men."

Still a celebrity, he went automobiling with Gordon, attended the circus. He was taught the alphabet, table manners, how to wear a watch on a chain. He regularly attended Sunday school, though it seemed to puzzle him.

After a time it was learned that Ota Benga was, in fact, being kept segregated from the asylum's orphans. He was, after all, an African pygmy.

"He eats with the cooks in the kitchen," Gordon told reporters. "He can smoke if he chooses."

OTA BENGA *disappeared from public view, and in 1910 he quietly left New York for Virginia, where he went to work in a tobacco factory. In July 1916, he committed suicide.*

"He was one of the most determined little fellows that ever breathed," mourned Verner, "A brave, shrewd little man who preferred to match himself against civilization rather than be a slave."

A NEW YORK EPIC: 1898-1998

CHAPTER 18

MARY, MARY, WHAT DO YOU CARRY?

The Cook, 1907

By DENNIS WEPMAN
Special to The News

TYPHOID FEVER was a serious problem at the turn of the century; in 1900 it killed 35,000 Americans. And in August 1906, when six people suddenly came down sick in the Oyster Bay household of banker Charles Henry Warren, public health officials rushed in at once.

They found the water uncontaminated, and at that point there wasn't much they could do but let the disease run its course and hope it didn't spread. But the man who had rented the house to the Warrens feared he wouldn't be able to rent it the next summer if he didn't clear up the mystery. He hired George Soper, a sanitary engineer with a gift for medical detective work, to investigate.

Soper went at it methodically. He inspected the drainage and tested the milk the family drank and the clams they ate — and drew a blank. Then he began checking the servants and came up with a clue: The Warrens had hired a new cook on Aug. 4. That was about three weeks before the first symptoms of typhoid had appeared in the household — exactly the incubation period for the disease.

His suspicions grew when he learned that she had disappeared soon after the sickness broke out. All anyone knew about her was her name — Mary Mallon.

New York American, June 30, 1909

Soper went to work to trace Mallon's background, starting with the agency that had sent her to the Warrens. When he compiled a list of her previous employers, a sinister pattern emerged: Almost every family she had cooked for had come down with typhoid shortly after her arrival, and she always left as soon as the fever appeared. But she never seemed to get sick herself.

The sanitary engineer had an answer for that. New European research suggested the idea — a crucial one for the emerging science of bacteriology — that a person can carry a disease without showing any symptoms, breeding the germs but apparently immune to them. Soper was convinced Mary Mallon was such a person.

In March 1907, he tracked her to her latest job, a house on Park Ave., and found that typhoid had been reported there, too. Mary was in the kitchen when he called. He confronted her, tried to explain that she probably was the cause of the sickness and asked her to submit to tests.

Mary was furious. She'd never been sick a day in her life, she shouted. When he persisted, she grabbed a fork and ran him out of the house.

Soper went straight to the Board of Health.

Mary was "a living culture" of typhoid, he argued, "a proved menace to the community." Dr. S. Josephine Baker decided to follow up the case herself and paid Mary a visit. She, too, was chased away.

The next day Baker came back with two interns and three policemen. Mary opened the door — then fled in terror. The police searched for hours before they tracked her to the house next door. There, one of the officers noticed a bit of cloth sticking out of a closet door behind some ashcans. When they forced the door, Mary came out kicking and screaming curses.

It was all the men could do to get her into the waiting ambulance, and Baker had to sit atop her the whole trip to the hospital. "Like being in a cage with an angry lion," she told the papers.

MARY MALLON'S TESTS proved Soper right: She was full of typhoid bacteria. Doctors tried to convince her to undergo treatment, but she refused. Finally, they sent her to a hospital for contagious diseases on North Brother Island off the Bronx. There she stayed, sullen and uncooperative, for nearly three years. She never admitted she was a carrier, and apparently never really believed it.

She soon became a celebrity. The papers called her "Typhoid Mary." Children chanted, "Mary, Mary, what do you carry?" as they skipped rope. But she had sympathizers as well: Many felt she had been unjustly deprived of her liberty. Then, in 1910, she promised never to work as a cook again, and health officials released her.

But cooking was all she knew. She merely changed her name — and went back to work, in hotels and restaurants and private homes.

Her past caught up with her in 1915, when there was an outbreak of typhoid at the Sloane maternity hospital. She was a staff cook there, calling herself Mary Brown. She was captured by police in Long Island — carrying a bowl of gelatin to a friend — and sent back to North Brother Island. There she spent the remaining 23 years of her life, deemed "a special guest" of the City of New York. She was given a cottage and a job as a laboratory technician, but, bitter and unrepentant, she refused all friendships and dined alone the rest of her days.

THE CASE OF Typhoid Mary became a symbol of the conflict between the individual's right to freedom and society's right to public health.

The first fully documented typhoid carrier in the United States, Mary was far from the worst; other registered carriers were known to be responsible for far more cases, and they weren't locked up for life for it. Some considered her a martyr, discriminated against because she was a woman or because she was Irish.

But she was a typhoid carrier. Had she stayed out of other people's kitchens, she probably would have been left in peace. Her ferocious independence was her undoing. "Liberty," Soper said, "is an impossible privilege to allow her."

Culver Pictures

Above, creamy-complexioned Anna. Left, on stage with the 1907 Ziegfeld Girls.

CHAPTER 19

PLAY WIZ ME

Flo And Anna And The Follies Of 1907

By JAY MAEDER
Daily News Staff Writer

BACK HOME in Chicago, the ambitious young showman had launched his career by managing a troupe of dancing ducks, and he had done all right with the ducks until the do-gooders discovered that the reason they danced so well was that there were gas jets heating the floor.

After that, he unveiled a plain tank of water and bade customers come behold his amazing invisible fish, and even the country boys didn't swallow that one. Had he not then met Eugene Sandow, The World's Strongest Man, it is not inconceivable that Florenz Ziegfeld might have stayed in Chicago all his days.

Eugene Sandow was pretty strong, all right. Eugene Sandow could lift grand pianos. Eugene Sandow was quite the sight to see, particularly after his new manager Ziegfeld cannily decided that Eugene should wear not much besides fig leaves and a coat of oil as he grunted and bulged and popped. This was a business decision that regularly brought the ladies to flutters and swoons at the Columbian Exposition of 1893 and through the national tours that followed, and Eugene and Ziegfeld quickly made each other rich. Still, Ziegfeld was thinking, there had to be something more to life than managing a guy who lifted pianos.

In London, Florenz Ziegfeld found Anna Held.

Anna was 23, a tiny Paris-born Polish girl with big goo-goo eyes, and she had been a cabaret star in most of Europe's capitals before she was 16,

knocking them dead with her fetching signature tune:

Won't you come and play wiz me
I have such a nice little way wiz me

Ziegfeld died and went to heaven on the spot. Here was the ticket. Anna happened to be married at the time to some sort of mysterious South American, but Ziegfeld took care of that *tout de suite* and brought her straightaway to New York, where, in September 1896, he starred her in a show called "The Parlor Match" and reinvented himself as a Broadway producer.

Anna slaughtered the town. Anna was about the naughtiest little thing anybody had ever seen. Sometimes she flashed her ankles. Sometimes, for God's sake, she bared her shoulders.

FLO ZIEGFELD and Anna Held were Broadway royalty for 10 years. They lived extravagantly at the Ansonia Hotel as Anna starred in hit after hit — "Papa's Wife," "The French Maid," "The Parisian Model," other such confections tailored to her particular gifts — and they traveled the world with the dozens of trunks that Flo always packed and the personal orchestra without which Anna never went anywhere. From time to

time, she would find it necessary to take another milk bath.

Flo had early on invented the story that Anna bathed daily in milk like some kind of ancient queen — women around the globe took up milk baths as a result of this — and thereafter, whenever public interest in Anna's career seemed to be waning, he would summon a few reporters to come watch the lady splash in her tub. "Zee milk, she preserve zee creamy complexion!" Anna would chirp, and that would get her back in the papers again. And so things glittered on and on.

At this same time, two theater-management factions were at grim war with one another. Under the ruthless Abe Erlanger and Mark Klaw, the Theatrical Syndicate was a fearsome monopoly that controlled every aspect of contracts and bookings; meanwhile, three brothers named Shubert had arrived in town from Syracuse with plans to break the syndicate's stranglehold and establish a trust of their own. In 1906, it was Florenz Ziegfeld's great good fortune that both groups badly wanted Anna Held.

BUT BY THE time Klaw & Erlanger opened the groundbreaking Parisian-style revue that would put Flo's name in lights forever, the showman and his star were barely speaking. There had been an unpleasant incident: In Cleveland, someone stole nearly $300,000 worth of cash and gems from Anna. A nationwide search for

the thieves proved inconclusive, and after a while Anna developed suspicions that Flo was himself the culprit. Whether that was true or not, the two of them were now rent asunder.

So it was that Florenz Ziegfeld's historic first Follies opened at the rooftop Jardin de Paris with 50 dancers billed as The Anna Held Girls — but with no Anna. It was July 1907, and while the showgirl was a not altogether unknown concept, Broadway had never imagined such a racy assemblage as Ziegfeld presented on this night. At one shocking point, a girl called Annabelle Whitford actually showed off her bloomers.

MODESTLY SUCCESSFUL at the outset, Ziegfeld's Follies got hotter later in the season when thrush Nora Bayes joined the cast; a year later, Nora would become a large star with a hit Follies tune called "Shine On Harvest Moon." Thereafter, Ziegfeld would become famous for making the careers of many show business greats: Al Jolson, W.C. Fields, Fanny Brice, Eddie Cantor, Will Rogers, Jimmy Durante and Gypsy Rose Lee were all Ziegfeld graduates, and Follies dancers included Irene Dunne, Paulette Goddard, Eleanor Powell, Gilda Gray and Marion Davies. Over the years, his shows would earn more than $100 million.

ANNA HELD died in 1918, washed up. Florenz Ziegfeld died in 1932, stone broke.

By PETER GRANT

Daily News Staff Writer

JOHN PIERPONT MORGAN was by now 70 years old, semi-retired, long a Wall Street legend — founder of J.P. Morgan & Co., underwriter of U.S. Steel, patron of one of the world's largest private art collections. As the Panic of 1907 began to shake the foundations of global finance, his greatest moment was yet to come.

During two dramatic weeks in October, the great financier singlehandedly put down the calamity. By himself he prevented the stock market from crashing. By himself he saved banks from failing. By himself he restored public confidence in The Street.

He did it all through simple force of personality. Overpowered by Morgan's formidable physical presence, steely eyes and commanding voice, some of the biggest names in finance and industry bowed to his will.

At one critical moment, as the New York Stock Exchange teetered near collapse for lack of capital, he instantly raised $25 million to keep it open. At another, he kept several of the nation's top bankers all but prisoners in the library of his home at Madison Ave. and 36th St. — refusing to let them leave until they hammered out a deal to save key trust companies.

"People believed in him," George Perkins, a Morgan partner, later explained to a congressional committee.

THE SPECTACULAR rescue crowned a storied career that mirrored New York City's rise as a financial powerhouse. J.P. Morgan became a Wall Street titan not only because he was brilliant and breathed fire — but also because he had the good fortune to live during gilded times that rewarded those traits with riches.

When Morgan was born in Hartford in 1837, New York was still struggling with Philadelphia for supremacy as the nation's business capital. The New York Stock Exchange, then just two decades old, listed no industrial companies. Fewer than 10,000 shares traded a day.

But as Morgan grew into a powerful financier, so did New York grow into the unchallenged center of capitalism.

With the opening of the Erie Canal in 1825, New York had become the young nation's most important seaport, gateway to the Great Lakes and the boundless West. With such access to the waterways, the city spawned America's largest exporting and trade businesses. The merchants who ran those companies went on to become leading stock traders and financiers, flourishing particularly in the mid-19th century as railroads began tapping into Wall Street capital to surge westward.

The railroads drove the national destiny, setting the stage of the upcoming Industrial Age. In New York, they created a new generation of millionaire robber barons: Andrew Carnegie, Jay Gould, "Commodore" Cornelius Vanderbilt.

Morgan flourished in this new world of unlimited opportunity. Born into a wealthy family that had made its fortune financing the cotton trade, he showed at an early age a genius for mathematics, a love of business and a willingness to take high-stakes risks. After graduating from schools in England, Switzerland and Germany, he got his first Wall Street job in 1857 as a junior accountant. Five years later he founded his own firm.

His timing was perfect. Wall St. was booming in the 1860s, the Civil War having created an insatiable demand for goods and capital. Financiers like Morgan made fortunes by filling that demand. By the time he was 27 years old, Morgan was making more than $53,000 a year — about 53 times what the average skilled worker then earned.

That was only the beginning. After the war, Morgan emerged as the key player in the booming but chaotic railroad industry; believing that bigger was always better, he engineered the mergers of numerous competing roads. His bank, meanwhile, renamed J.P. Morgan & Co. in 1895,

CULVER PICTURES

CHAPTER 20

THE GIANT

J.P. Morgan And The Panic Of 1907

became the principal financier for the huge corporations that were transforming the U.S. into an industrial dreadnought: American Telephone and Telegraph, General Electric, International Harvester and — America's first billion-dollar company — U.S. Steel.

As the new century dawned, Morgan was the city's first business celebrity, a larger-than-life man whose houses and steam yachts and lavish parties became symbols of the opulent day. But far more important to Morgan than riches was his power to direct the growth of America's burgeoning economy, well on its way to becoming the mightiest in the world. On several occasions he used his enormous influence to rescue the financial system from crises: In 1895 he organized a group of financiers to resupply the Treasury's depleted gold reserve.

With that power, of course, came controversy: Morgan's railroad interests were among President Theodore Roosevelt's primary trust-busting targets. But in October 1907, when the threatened failure of a chain of banks triggered

the Panic, Morgan was the only man who could lead the effort to restore public confidence and prevent a massive bank run that could have toppled the nation's entire financial system.

Attending an Episcopal convention in Virginia at the time, Morgan returned at once to New York, and for the next two weeks he cajoled, lobbied and browbeat leaders of finance and industry to step forward with their money and influence to save institutions facing imminent collapse. By putting out one fire after another, he doused the Panic. His actions also helped set the stage six years later for the creation of the Federal Reserve, the country's first central bank, designed to prevent such panics from occurring in the future.

THERE WOULD BE, of course, future panics. But there would be no more J.P. Morgans to contain them. The Panic of 1907 marked the last time in history that one individual wielded so much power. Never again would any one man be bigger than The Street.

CHAPTER 21

WRETCHED REFUSE OF YOUR TEEMING SHORE

Strangers In A Strange Land, 1907

By LENORE SKENAZY
Daily News Staff Writer

THE LARGEST MIGRATION of human beings in the history of the world. That's what happened in 1907, as a record 1.3 million immigrants streamed into America through Ellis Island.

Glimpsing the Statue of Liberty after two or three weeks at sea, some cheered, some cried, some prayed, some fainted. At last they had reached The Golden Door, as Emma Lazarus dubbed America in her poem on the base of that famous statue:

Give me your tired, your poor, your huddled masses
Yearning to breathe free
The wretched refuse of your teeming shore.

Most were, in fact, pretty wretched. The few arrivals who looked well-off were waved through by respectful Ellis Island officials. Everyone else was herded into the Great Hall, then sent upstairs for processing, including the hideous eye exam.

This consisted of a medical examiner poking a buttonhook under each immigrant's eyelid and flipping it inside-out to check for trachoma, a contagious disease that could result in blindness. Unfortunately, lax sanitary conditions meant that the contaminated buttonhooks probably spread more disease than they ever arrested.

Meantime, officials at the top of the stairs closely observed everyone as they climbed. People who wheezed, stumbled or appeared infirm got their coats marked with chalk: X for mental disorder, K for hernia, SC for scalp disease.

One Russian family of eight, the Sopirovs, watched their 4-year-old Natasha receive an "X." She was merely deaf, but the official assumed she was mentally incompetent — grounds for a one-way ticket home.

Suddenly the Sopirovs were faced with a horrible choice: Return with Natasha to Russia — and the poverty and danger they'd just escaped — or send her home to relatives.

They chose the latter, and they never saw Natasha again.

WITH STEAMSHIP tickets running an astronomical $30 to $40 each, this was not a trip anyone could undertake lightly. It often took immigrants years to save enough for the voyage.

These gutsy newcomers arrived with little:

> *One Jewish housewife arrived lugging a giant jug of chicken fat. She'd heard none was available in New York.*

Perhaps a couple of comforters, some photos of left-behind loved ones and a few household items deemed (correctly or not) necessary. One Jewish housewife arrived lugging a giant jug of chicken fat. She'd heard none was available in New York.

Unlike earlier waves of immigrants who'd come to America from Northern Europe, Asia and, unwillingly, Africa, by 1907 the vast majority of arrivals hailed from southern and Eastern Europe.

The Italians, for the most part, were escaping poverty. Often it was the young men who came here — Birds of Passage, they were called, intending to work for a few years, save money and return home. Actually, only about a third of them went back.

The Jews of Eastern Europe and Russia, meantime, were escaping not only poverty but pogroms — widespread, government-sanctioned anti-Semitic massacres. Stampeding into town on their horses, soldiers would lash and trample anyone Jewish, even babies, burning their homes and slashing their throats. Not surprisingly, these immigrants had no intention of ever going home.

What made these groups different from their 19th century predecessors was the fact that the majority chose not to head out West once they arrived, but instead to settle in the great cosmopolitan melting pot of New York.

Too poor to buy land, too unschooled to join a profession, too desperate to turn down any employment, most of 1907's immigrants had to find work within days of their arrival. They took jobs building bridges, sewing corsets, stuffing sausages, laying bricks. The city needed all the cheap labor it could get.

And "cheap" was the word. These jobs paid so little that laborers could not afford to live anywhere but the most squalid tenements of the Lower East Side. By 1905 the density of the poorest parts of New York was 1,000 people per acre. That meant you shared your home with boarders, you slept on a plank between two chairs and you caught whatever flu or diphtheria was going around.

Naturally, immigrants tended to cluster in neighborhoods already populated by others from their home country, even their hometown. They lent a hand with everything from finding work to buying burial plots. They read newspapers in their native languages and ate the foods they were familiar with. Italians popularized tomatoes and peppers in America; Jews brought the bagel and pastrami. Since landlords often offered one month's free rent, most families moved yearly. Lives were in constant turmoil.

Luckily, community centers where students of any age could learn English, local customs and even domestic skills like cooking and sewing sprang up to aid the immigrants. These were called settlement houses, and their goal was the same as that of the immigrants: Americanization.

FOR NO MATTER how proud these new arrivals were of the language, land and lives they left behind, they were prouder yet to have reached The Golden Door. Behind it lay star-spangled America, and they wanted nothing more than to start becoming American.

CRAZY HEART

The Playboy And The Showgirl, 1908

By WENDELL JAMIESON
Daily News Staff Writer

ALREADY IT WAS The Trial Of The Century, and the century was only a few years old.

In the first week of 1908, Harry Thaw, millionaire playboy, heir to a vast Pittsburgh railway fortune, loving husband of showgirl Evelyn Nesbit, was back in court to answer to a crime that had riveted the nation for two years: the murder of Stanford White, the renowned architect whose elaborate Beaux-Arts buildings captured the optimism and brashness of the young city.

Every citizen knew every detail of the killing by heart: On a balmy evening in June 1906, Thaw had shot White three times in the head during a party on the palm-ringed roof of Madison Square Garden, one of the architect's grandest creations. The music stopped. Glasses of iced champagne crashed to the floor. Gibson Girls and men in tuxedos ducked for cover. White, his face blackened by powder burns, slumped forward to the table. His famous brains were all around.

Thaw lowered his weapon and calmly returned to the table he shared with his friends and young wife.

"I have probably saved your life," he informed her.

Then he surrendered to a startled fireman, the only semi-official person around.

Crazed jealousy had pulled the trigger, and scarcely anyone at the roof garden who had just enjoyed the premiere of a musical called "Mlle. Champagne" had any doubts about that.

The eccentric and wildly excessive White was well known to have been Nesbit's lover both before and after she met Thaw. Even after he married the girl, Thaw was obsessed by the dissolute architect, a cad he believed had drugged, seduced and ruined Nesbit before she was 16. That June night, Thaw could no longer contain his rage.

He had gone on trial once, in January 1907, and New Yorkers hung on every lurid detail as Nesbit — 22, porcelain-skinned, delicately featured, exquisitely lovely — recounted the life she had once lived with White. She described his mirrored boudoir, her naked rides atop a red velvet swing pushed so excitedly by her patron that her bare toes brushed a Japanese parasol hung from the ceiling. It seemed after a time that she was the one on trial. Thousands of citizens jammed the streets to get any glimpse of the scandalous lady.

The jury came back hung — and now, a year later, Thaw was back in Manhattan State Supreme Court for a retrial. This time he pleaded insanity.

HARRY THAW'S second trial would set the stage for a century of debate over the insanity defense and about the ability of the rich to escape justice by using their wealth to buy the best lawyers and psychologists.

Jury selection went on for an unheard-of week. Nesbit spent every day in court, reading the faces of prospective panelists and sharing her opinions with the press. Again she was the focus of the city's attention, far more so than defendant Thaw. When the show finally got under way, the crime itself was never disputed and barely discussed.

As Thaw sat glassy-eyed in his chair, defense lawyer Martin Littleton told jurors how the grief-stricken playboy had tried to poison himself in Paris when Nesbit first told him of her sordid past with the married, philandering White. Other witnesses described outbursts in Rome and Monte Carlo, treatment for insanity in London and, just two months before the shooting, a screaming fit aboard a Chicago-to-New York train.

On Jan. 20, Evelyn Nesbit took the stand and, once again, spilled out her shocking stories.

Daily News photo-illustration by Jim Willis

Threesome: Late White, jailed Thaw, ruined Nesbit.

Thaw, the papers reported, trembled and moaned as he relived the events that had plainly driven him quite desperately looney. And, with every bit of testimony, Thaw-paid alienists took the stand to explain to the jury how each incident had affected his mind.

Littleton's defense worked. On Feb. 1, after deliberating for 25 hours, jurors found the gibbering Thaw not guilty by reason of insanity. Thaw stumbled to his feet, and Justice Victor Dowling ordered the crazy prisoner to be held at Matteawan State Prison for the Criminally Insane.

Outside court, Thaw grandly informed reporters: "I am perfectly sane. But I am going to Matteawan on the advice of my counsel.

"Counsel," he said, "will proceed in the matter of my release as soon as they can get together the proofs that will present that I am at present sane."

Joined by his wife and two attorneys, Thaw had dinner, then was taken to Grand Central Terminal — which White had designed — and boarded an upstate train.

HARRY THAW *was indeed declared sane and released, but not until 1915. Save for occasional dustups with the law, he lived out the rest of his life a free man.*

After divorcing Thaw, the beauteous Nesbit spent the next 60 years fading away. She would pop up in the papers from time to time, detailing for new generations a scandal from another era that seemed, with each passing year, a little less shocking. Stanford White was the lucky one, she said; he had died, and she had lived on.

A NEW YORK EPIC: 1898-1998

CHAPTER 23

"WE WANT SOMETHING TO SAY"

Suffragettes, 1908

By DENNIS WEPMAN
Special to The News

WOMEN WERE demanding their civil rights in New York State long before the idea swept the rest of the country. The grievances were sometimes small. In January 1908, for example, the New York City Board of Aldermen enacted an ordinance prohibiting women from smoking in public, and, though the mayor later vetoed it, one woman spent a night in jail for defying the new law. But the right to puff on a cigaret was the least of the demands. Women wanted equality in marriage, education and employment. They wanted legal control over their property and their children. Above all, they wanted the vote.

That idea had crystallized in 1848 in upstate Seneca Falls, where activists Lucretia Mott and Elizabeth Cady Stanton gathered some 300 revolutionaries to call for a Declaration of Independence for women. The community was appalled. A local paper called the convention "the most shocking and unnatural incident ever recorded in the history of humanity." The editorial warned that the right to vote would "degrade from their high sphere and noble destiny women of all respectable and noble classes and prove a monstrous injury to mankind."

Agitation for reform nevertheless continued. Sixty years after the shocking and unnatural incident in Seneca Falls, things reached a head in New York City. On Dec. 31, 1907, suffragettes officially launched their American campaign at a meeting outside the Metropolitan Life Building and got a turnout of several hundred, mostly amused, males. "You don't know the importance of the ballot!" one speaker declared. "Yes, we do!" the crowd cried back. Shouted one livid gent: "The place for the women is in the home and to cook the dinners!" But at day's end, many of the men signed a petition asking the federal government for voting rights for women. "We have been wanting a long time to talk to the men, and that is why we are here," said one pleased rally organizer.

Things rolled on. On Jan. 28, the Woman's Progressive Suffrage Union announced plans for the nation's first suffrage parade. The police commissioner found a reason not to issue a permit, but a union spokeswoman said calmly: "Our plans are not altered at all." And indeed they weren't. On Feb. 16, a brave little band of 23 women wearing yellow suffragette sashes and buttons marched from their tiny office off Union Square to the Manhattan Trade School on E. 23rd St. for a public meeting. A dozen policemen tried to break it up, but the enthusiastic crowds were more than they could handle.

The march was a great success. The speakers presented their grievances and demanded "self-sovereignty" for women, an end to "the absolute tyranny of men," equal pay for equal work and "the pivotal right, the one that underlies all other rights," the right to vote. One rally leader stated the case in verse:

> *For the long work day,*
> *For the taxes we pay,*
> *For the laws we obey,*
> *We want something to say.*

The audience applauded, and the collection plate netted $100.

Eleven days later the activists didn't fare so well. An open-air meeting on Wall St. was hooted into silence. The mob cheered derisively at everything, drowning out the suffragettes. It even cheered when one speaker said, "Let all those that are jackasses cheer." A shower of hard rolls, apple cores and wet sponges finally sent the women packing. The same thing happened in Harlem in April. There, a police

CORBIS-BETTMAN

reserve had to be called out to keep order.

There was organized opposition as well. Manufacturers' associations, labor unions and chambers of commerce fought the suffrage movement fiercely, abetted by friends in the press. "Women are born smugglers," opined The New York Times. "How would they vote at an election involving tariff issues?"

And many anti-suffrage groups enlisted influential women to speak out against the movement. The New York-based Association Opposed to the Extension of Suffrage to Women had the wife of U.S. Secretary of State Elihu Root as an officer and included prominent journalist Ida Tarbell on its executive committee. The Ladies' Home Journal campaigned vigorously against the suffragettes.

Such big names lent weight to the notion that respectable women didn't really want the vote.

But some still did, and they would keep marching — in growing numbers. Working women would organize major strikes against textile and clothing manufacturers in New York and inspire similar actions nationwide. Suffrage rallies and torchlight processions would become almost weekly events in the city, particularly on the lower East Side. In October 1915, thousands of women would parade up Fifth Ave. Women had something to say, and nothing would stop their saying it.

In 1920, 12 years after a determined little group defied a police ban and marched from Union Square to E. 23rd St., they would get the constitutional amendment they wanted.

THE BONEHEAD

Very Bad Day At The Polo Grounds, 1908

By VIC ZIEGEL
Daily News Staff Writer

SECONDS AFTER the winning run that gave the New York Giants a dramatic 2-1 victory over the Chicago Cubs, the fans came pouring out of the bleachers onto the field. Either they wanted to congratulate their Giants or they wanted to break their arms.

The Giants didn't wait around to find out. They raced for the safety of their clubhouse in the Polo Grounds' right center field. Fastest among them was Fred Merkle, the club's 19-year-old first baseman.

It was Sept. 23, 1908, and the win had just put New York a full game ahead of the Cubs in a tight three-way National League pennant race. That is, it *would* have been the winning run — had only Chicago's second baseman not noticed what immediately went into the history books as Merkle's Boner.

BLUNDER COSTS GIANTS VICTORY, The New York Times headlined the next morning. **MERKLE RUSHES OFF BASE LINE BEFORE WINNING RUN IS SCORED. CONFUSION ON BALL FIELD. CROWD BREAKS UP GAME. UMPIRE DECLARES IT A TIE.**

Fred Merkle remained in the big leagues for another 18 years. Through every one of them, and for long after that, no one ever let him forget the tag: *Bonehead Merkle. The Man Who Cost The Giants The Pennant.*

THE GIANTS were the only New York team to take seriously that 1908 season. The Highlanders, not yet known as the Yankees, were only six years old, and they were on their way to losing 103 games. The Dodgers, of Brooklyn, would lose 101.

Pitcher Christy Mathewson was the Giants' biggest star, and he was emerging as America's first sports hero in a day when most ballplayers were viewed as dumb country bumpkins. Matty had been his class president at Bucknell, and he was a checkers champion who also excelled at chess and bridge. Big Six, they called him, because he was a 6-footer, taller than most. He never wore his Giants uniform on Sunday; he had promised his parents he wouldn't play on the Sabbath.

Merkle, meanwhile, was only a rookie, a part-time player. But the regular first baseman, Fred Tenney, had been sidelined by a backache. On the day he became immortal, Merkle was starting his first game of the year.

The Cubs, in town for a four-game series, had beaten the Giants in a doubleheader the day before, tightening the race. On Sept. 23, there were 30,000 fans inside the Polo Grounds, and more were perched on Coogan's Bluff, the hill behind the home plate stands. Many more yet had stationed themselves behind the outfield rope.

The Giants had once played in a polo field on Fifth Ave. between 110th and 112th Sts. But then the city had decided it needed a traffic

circle there, and the club moved north, to property on the west side of Eighth Ave. The new stadium resembled an open-ended bathtub. The first base foul line went toward 157th St., the third base line toward 159th. Centerfield was more than 450 feet long, but the foul lines were laughably short, 279 to left, 257 to right. Another bizarre touch: Fans wound their way from Coogan's Bluff to the grandstand seats, making the Polo Grounds the only park that made you climb down to reach the upper deck.

This day, the fans were treated to a remarkable game. Matty was opposed by Chicago lefthander Jack Pfiester, who, on the strength of his record, was known as Jack the Giant Killer.

The Cubs scored first, when Joe Tinker's fifth inning flyball, misplayed by rightfielder Mike Donlin, became an inside-the-park home run. ("This boy Donlin should have been sent home without his supper, if this boy was our boy," recorded The Times.)

The Giants tied the game at one in the sixth on an error, a sacrifice bunt and Donlin's single, and at the bottom of the ninth they were batting. With two out and Moose McCormick on first, Merkle sliced Pfiester's pitch for a single to right, sending McCormick to third.

When the next hitter, Al Bridwell, rapped the first pitch into center field, McCormick trotted home. The game was over: Giants 2, Cubs 1.

But Merkle had made a small mistake. He had left the baseline before he touched second base.

Johnny Evers, Chicago's second baseman, realized this at once. And he screamed for the outfielder to throw him the ball.

THERE HAS BEEN some dispute as to whether the ball that showed up in Evers' hand was the one that Bridwell actually hit. But Evers claimed it was, and he put his foot on second base, arguing that it was a forceout, the third out, and that the run shouldn't count.

The senior umpire, Hank O'Day, decided to think things over before announcing a decision. Meanwhile, the game couldn't continue: There were fans shaking their fists all over the field.

At 10 p.m., O'Day ruled in favor of the Cubs. The game, he said, was a tie.

The season ended two weeks later with the Cubs and Giants in a tie for first place. There was a one-game playoff at the Polo Grounds, and the Giants lost it, Three-Finger Mordecai Brown outdueling Matty.

"We were robbed of the pennant, and you can't say Merkle did that," contended Giants manager John McGraw.

But Merkle was forever the focus of the defeat. For a time, "to merkle" was part of the language, meaning "to fail to arrive."

The Giants forgave Merkle. He never forgave himself. "I suppose when I die," he grumbled, "they'll put on my tombstone *Here Lies Bonehead Merkle.*"

WELL, IT WASN'T as bad as all that. But in 1950 — 42 years after that Cubs game, and 24 years after he left baseball — Fred Merkle went back to the Polo Grounds for an old-timers' game, and cries of "Bonehead!" met his ears.

"I *wish* folks would forget that," he sighed.

Compliments of Piedmont Cigarettes

By JAY MAEDER
Daily News Staff Writer

AFTER A TIME it became just a matter of course for the more established southern Italian hoodlums to walk their newly arrived countrymen to a point near Police Headquarters and point out to them the short, squat, derby-hatted detective, so that in the future they might recognize him on sight and accord him wide berth. Petrosino was his name, Joseph Petrosino, and he was out to get every one of them. He was fearless, Petrosino was; he would stomp into a basement and collar two desperate killers at a time and march both of them off to the electric chair by the scruffs of their necks, and the room could be full of armed men and nobody would dream of drawing on him. Of Joseph Petrosino it was most wise to beware.

It wasn't merely that he was a cop. With Petrosino, the sworn duty was a matter of private honor. Giuseppe Petrosino had been born in Salerno, and he had come to the New World as a youth, and he had shined shoes and he had sold newspapers and he had gone to school and bettered himself, and then he had become New York's first Italian policeman, a man deeply trusted by the city's immigrant families, a man looked up to by children in the street.

And now, every day, he had to watch as the cheapest dregs of Naples and Sicily got off the boat and scuttled into the corners of the murderous Italian underworld, thieves and cut-throats and bone crushers come to prey upon their own kind, come now from the old country's *mafia* and *Camorra* to make all the city think that Italians were nothing but unwashed criminal rodents.

He was personally affronted by this. He was mortified. It was not now just a job, ridding his America of such vermin. Giuseppe Petrosino had been shamed.

THERE HAD BEEN fewer than 20,000 Italians in New York when Petrosino arrived on these shores in the mid-1870s; by 1909 there were more than half a million, most of them deplorably crushed together in the tenements of the lower East Side and East Harlem, and they lived every day of their lives fearing that somehow they would come to the attention of the terrible Black Hand.

Whatever its medieval origins, the Black Hand in turn-of-the-century New York was largely the invention of the city's first Italian crime family, a brutish collection of relatives, step-relatives and relatives-in-law variously named Morello and Terranova. Associated with them was the frightful Ignazio Saietta, known to all as Lupo the Wolf. Lupo was an importer of lemons and olive oil. He was also New York's leading professional Black Hand terrorist, the man who rained unceasing misery upon thousands of hardworking peddlers and shopkeepers from whom he regularly demanded tribute.

The Black Hand arithmetic was straightforward: A man paid, or a man died. First a man's store might be bombed. Or his tongue might be slit. Or his wife and daughters might get their fingers cut off. But in the end, a man, if he remained obstinate, would surely die. Lupo and the Morellos were headquartered at a dismal

Joseph Petrosino, center, and the NYPD Italian Squad, top. Left, Lupo The Wolf of East Harlem. Right, Don Vito Cascio Ferro of Palermo (courtesy William Balsamo Collection).

Photo-illustration by
Jim Willis/Daily News

CHAPTER 25

PAY OR DIE

Lieutenant Petrosino And The Black Hand, 1909

stable on E. 107th St. near First Ave., and it has never been known how many dozens of souls perished shrieking on Lupo's meat hooks. Throughout the city's Little Italys, a man would cross himself at the merest mention of Lupo's dark name.

Most often, to be sure, things did not end in Lupo's stable. The simple arrival of a Black Hand letter — or even a whisper that one might be forthcoming — was usually enough to unbutton a man's pocket. Accordingly there arose many unofficial Black Hand enterprises, run by freelancers who might demand $1,000 and happily settle for $50. Indeed, it was not unknown for an otherwise legitimate businessman to fall back on a Black Hand letter if he were pressed for cash.

In any case, seldom did complaints come to police. Aside from threats of physical harm, there was *omerta*, the Old World code of silence: A man of honor, particularly a poor immigrant of little standing and few English skills in the City of New York, did not take his troubles to the authorities.

For this reason was Joseph Petrosino a police officer. Appointed a patrolman in 1883, personally promoted to detective-sergeant in 1895 by Police Commissioner Theodore Roosevelt, Petrosino in 1905 had been named a lieutenant and given command of the new Italian Squad, a unit established specifically to address the Black Hand menace. In four years Petrosino and his men had sent more than 500 animals to prison. For all his wrathful determination, Petrosino never succeeded in getting the goods on Lupo himself, but he had broken the Brooklyn rule of Camorra chieftain Enrico Alfano and he had driven back to Sicily the would-be mafia boss Vito Cascio Ferro, and it was said that the Italian Squad had cut Black Hand crime in half.

Now, in early 1909, Lt. Joseph Petrosino, NYPD, boarded a ship and carried his private war back to Italy.

PROBABLY IT WAS the case that he never had a chance. Friends came forward after he died to report that Petrosino had confided to them his premonitions that he would not be coming home again. He was 48 years old, recently married, father of an infant daughter. He sailed anyway.

In his bags was a list of names. Italian authorities, he knew, had long been emptying their jails of *mafiosi* and *Camorristas*, giving them phony passports, putting them aboard boats to New York, washing their hands of them. If he could dig into local records and find criminal histories, he could deport these men — and spare New York generations of trouble.

He was traveling as Guglielmo de Simone, a merchant, but he was made before he ever left Rome and he apparently well knew it. Spurning the pleas of consular officials that he accept a bodyguard, Petrosino traveled on to Sicily to begin his work. On Feb. 21, he arrived in Palermo — where Vito Cascio Ferro now reigned as a man of respect, the city's constabulary and judiciary at his beck and call.

Don Vito let Petrosino work quietly for several weeks.

Then, on the rainy Friday night of March 12, after spending the day in courthouse records in a nearby village, the detective returned to Palermo, dined at a small cafe and then began to walk back to his hotel. Outside the Garibaldi Garden in the Piazza Marina, he was accosted and shot four times. He went down returning fire. Don Vito had many witnesses who swore to his presence elsewhere at the time of the murder, but it has always been assumed that of course Don Vito was the man who personally pulled the trigger.

GIUSEPPE PETROSINO came home to New York a month later. In the streets of the lower East Side, a quarter-million sobbing Italians turned out to salute the passing coffin of the policeman who had freed so many of them from their Black Hand predators and made them all prouder Americans.

It remains incalculable how dramatically different the history of New York City might have been had he lived to bring his list of deportable names back to the department.

LUPO THE WOLF *went to prison for counterfeiting in 1910. Don Vito Cascio Ferro ran afoul of Benito Mussolini in the 1920s and also went to prison. During World War II, fleeing an Allied bomber attack, his jailers accidentally left him behind in his cell, where, at age 86, he starved to death.*

Lt. Joseph Petrosino, the only New York police officer ever killed in the line of duty outside the U.S., is buried in Calvary Cemetery in Woodside, Queens.

By JAY MAEDER
Daily News Staff Writer

EPOCHS PASSED, continents drifted, man lurched blinking and scratching from the bogs, and he trembled sore afraid before the streaks of light splashed across the night skies. Man, as was his custom, gravely attributed practically everything to his gods; obviously it was not for nothing that the baffling incandescences always appeared at exactly those thunderous moments when kings died and empires fell and plagues rode the land like nightmares. From this did man construct still another of his interminable mythologies: The skies, lo, were amok with damnation.

This was nothing to fiddle with in the dawntimes of the intellect. Today it is only dimly possible to grasp what a revolutionary thing it was when, in the early 18th century, not at all very long after man had reluctantly decided that perhaps he was traveling in some lovely puzzled circle around the blazing sun after all, Edmond Halley of Oxford University peered into the imponderable and reckoned that comets were actually quite predictable things. Indeed, overturning several extant systems of thought, the Great Comet of 1682 returned on schedule in 1758 exactly as Halley promised it would, faithfully shooting out of some far place where some ancient heart beats like clockwork.

And indeed this was the same Dreaded Wanderer that had harbingered Noah's Flood in 2349 B.C. And the fall of Sodom and Gomorrah in 1900 B.C. And the defeat of King Harold at the Battle of Hastings in 1066 A.D. And the conquest of Asia by Genghis Khan in 1222. And the fall of Belgrade to the Turks in 1456.

In the year 1910 A.D., few but the astronomers knew that the terrible silver scimitar gleaming like sorcery across the timeless night was nothing but frozen hydrogen and helium and ammonia gases. In the year 1910, it was not entirely immoderate to harbor small suspicions that perhaps the ancient prophets had been on to something. In the year 1910, the great fearsome stripe of unspeakable skyfire could still cow down the creature man and sculpt his notions of Heaven and Earth and move him to cut desperate deals with his gods. Behold the creature man, contriving meaning and reason from shining paths of nothing.

THE LAST TIME Halley's Comet had come to visit, true enough, about half of New York had burned down. That was in 1835. The old folks were still talking about that.

Worse yet, in the spring of 1910, some of the astronomers were saying now that the comet's tail was full of deadly cyanogen gas and that Planet Earth was going to hurtle straight into this brew like a cannonball. This probably meant that the skies would curdle and the seas would boil and

CHAPTER 26

DOOMSDAY

When Halley's Comet Came To Town, 1910

CORBIS-BETTMANN

every living soul would smother. It was calculated that the world would end sometime between 10:20 p.m. and midnight on Wednesday the 18th of May.

And, true to old Ptolemy's observation that comets bring with them "disturbed conditions," dark events were recorded as April folded into May and Halley's Comet burned malevolently overhead:

Strange black rains fell on Bermuda. Huge meteors crashed into Mexico and California and set forests aflame. A monster earthquake wrecked Costa Rica. Hailstorms and heat waves simultaneously beset much of Europe. Chicken farmers all over the world began to report the hatchings of two-headed chicks. In Maine, 12 of the polar explorer Robert Peary's 14 sled dogs inexplicably dropped dead.

And on May 6, King Edward VII of England suddenly took ill and died.

Two days later, in Bermuda, Fort Hamilton's soldiers fired a 101-gun salute to the dead monarch; at 3:52 a.m., at the very instant the 101st shot was fired, Halley's Comet flared up and the entire sky turned blood red. This was a clear

enough warning, said the seers, that there would surely come a devastating world war during the reign of newly crowned King George.

In New York City, street vendors hawked anti-comet pills. Concerned public officials urged citizens to wear helmets as protection against showers of debris. Householders boarded up their windows and stuffed blankets into their doorjambs to block the toxic fumes.

WEDNESDAY night the 18th of May was clear and bright, to the degree that, actually, the comet was never visible at all. This was a disappointment to the revelers gathered on the roofs of the city's smart hotels and to the crowds of skywatchers assembled in Central Park and along Riverside Drive. To the hundreds of thousands of superstitious immigrants crammed into the lower East Side, it was just further evidence that they were all going to die like bugs at the beckoning of the unseen.

Ten thousand men refused to go to work that day, choosing instead to spend their last moments praying with their families. Churches overflowed with the terrified. Wailing mobs marched through Mulberry Park by torchlight. On Elizabeth St., two mandolinists played hymns as the crowds around them fell weeping to their knees. Fully 20,000 persons gathered on the Williamsburg Bridge to huddle together and await the end.

From a Grand St. rooftop, a couple of pranksters tied a lamp to a balloon and sent it aloft, and screaming panic broke out on the bridge as the evil apparition sailed toward Brooklyn. Amid the din, one small boy was seen to be dubious. "Ain't it low?" he inquired.

Midnight came and went, and it seemed that the world had not ended after all, and most everyone started to call it a night. Cops finally cleared out Central Park and Columbus Circle at 3 a.m. and told the recalcitrant to go home.

In Brooklyn, a 16-year-old schoolgirl attending a rooftop comet party had fallen four floors to her death. In Carleton Hills, N.J., a 40-year-old maiden lady had suffered a nervous collapse and been led away to an asylum, babbling that she would follow the comet wherever it went.

HALLEY'S COMET reappeared on schedule in 1986: The space shuttle Challenger blew up, Ferdinand Marcos of the Philippines and Jean-Claude Duvalier of Haiti were driven from their countries, the first U.S. government-approved genetically altered virus was released into the environment and the New York Mets won the World Series. The comet is due back in 2061.

By JAY MAEDER
Daily News Staff Writer

LIKE ROBERT FULTON, who built a steamboat and then concluded that the Hudson River was his alone, Orville and Wilbur Wright built a flying machine and then decided that they personally owned the sky. Their endless patent suits against men who built and flew aeroplanes better than they did effectively established the Brothers Wright as rather considerable impediments to the early development of aviation in America.

In the spring of 1910, for example, manufacturer Glenn Curtiss was under court order to pay the Wrights stiff royalties on every aeroplane he sold. The crippling litigation had already cost him a lucrative Army contract and it promised to go on forever. Curtiss was at this point the toast of Europe, the world's foremost flier, and still he had to spend half his time wrangling in court. He may very well have never even attempted his sensational, history-making Hudson River flight had he not badly needed the $10,000 prize money to cover indemnities that the Wrights had forced upon him.

Flying from Albany to New York was unthinkable, out of the question; no man could do that. Curtiss almost didn't. Battered by winds high above the Hudson, plunging like a stone in the Highlands downdrafts, Curtiss gulped as his oil pressure finally dropped to nothing and his motor coughed blue smoke. He came down just inside the city limits, barely clearing a creek bank. He had won the prize only technically.

Eighteen thrilling minutes after he fixed his oil line and took off again, he won it publicly, emphatically and eternally. It was the stroke of noon, Sunday the 29th of May, and hundreds of thousands of people screamed from both sides of the Hudson and every boat on the river blasted its whistle as Curtiss circled the Statue of Liberty and triumphantly touched down on Governors Island, a legend forever.

MOTORCYCLE RACER Glenn Curtiss had been the fastest man in the world since 1904. At one point he had hit nearly 140 mph. Having set land records no one would break for years yet, he had then teamed up with pioneer dirigiblist Capt. Thomas Scott Baldwin and started building motors for Baldwin's airships. By 1907 he was partnered with Alexander Graham Bell, who, his telephone work long behind him, had emerged as a leading aviation patron. Together they formed the landmark Aerial Experiment Association, sometimes headquartered at Bell's estate in Nova Scotia and sometimes at the Curtiss shops in Hammondsport, in the heart of central New York's pastoral Finger Lakes.

Orville and Wilbur Wright had been flying since December 1903, but their work was done secretively and their names were largely unknown to the public until five years later. By that time Hammondsport was long accustomed to the sight of the AEA

CORBIS-BETTMANN

Departing Inwood, bound for Governors Island

CHAPTER 27

REACH FOR THE SKY

Glenn Curtiss And The Hudson Flier, 1910

machines buzzing the shores of lovely Keuka Lake. On July 4, 1908, Curtiss won the first Scientific American Trophy when he publicly flew his June Bug a full kilometer. On July 17, 1909, he won the trophy a second time by taking his Golden Flier nearly 25 miles around a course at Hempstead Plains, L.I., the nation's first exhibition flight. A month after that, he was on his way to France to compete in the first Grand International Aviation Tournament.

The Wrights had charmed Europe some months earlier with a series of exhibitions, but 31-year-old Glenn Curtiss, the sole American entrant in *La Grande Semaine d'Aviation* at Rheims, took the continent by storm. Hitting a record 47 mph, his Rheims Racer outflew French ace Louis Bleriot, the man who had flown the English Channel, and captured the meet's grand prize. After that, Curtiss went on to Italy and took the Brescia tournament's grand prize as well.

When America's champion aviator returned home, lawyers were waiting. The Wright brothers were moving to put him out of the flying business.

ENJOINED FROM building aeroplanes for sale, Curtiss won a court order that let him continue to make exhibition flights. In late September 1909, along with Wilbur Wright, he was in New York to perform at the city's great Hudson-Fulton Celebration, marking the 300th anniversary of Henry Hudson's arrival and more or less the 100th anniversary of Robert Fulton's boat.

It was a bad week for Curtiss, a good one for Wright. The weather was never to Curtiss' liking, and finally he elected not to go aloft at all. Wright, meanwhile, treated the town to a spectacular 33-minute joyride from Governors Island up the river to Grant's Tomb and back. Red-faced, Curtiss left New York in mid-festival, the newspapers barking at his heels. He had just lost a big one to the Wrights.

BUT EVEN THE Wrights wouldn't have any part of The New York World's $10,000 call for a flight between Albany and New York. Even with two stops permitted, it just couldn't be done.

Disregarding this matter of fact, Curtiss built a 50-horsepower machine, christened it the Hudson Flier and, a few minutes after 7 a.m. on May 29, 1910 — after delaying the flight for three days to await favorable winds — he left Van Rensselaer's Island, climbed to 1,000 feet and headed south as a special New York Central train carrying dignitaries and reporters and Curtiss' wife followed him downriver.

The initial hop was uneventful. He made Hudson by 7:35 and Rhinecliff by 8:06, and at 8:24, as townsfolk and boatmen waved and cheered, he touched down near Poughkeepsie to refuel. An hour later he was back in the air — and, at 9:45, the treacherous winds blowing around Storm King Mountain nearly killed him. Down he plunged, righting himself and regaining control just 50 feet off the water, and after that he mostly kept to about 200 feet. At 10:20, over

Tarrytown, he sighted the Metropolitan Tower on the distant Manhattan skyline.

But by now his oil was vanishing. At 10:35, nervously circling over Spuyten Duyvil, he spotted a meadow at Inwood and made a hair-raising emergency landing. He was inside the city limits. He had covered 137 miles in 152 minutes, averaging nearly 55 mph. And he had won $10,000 and, for the third time, the Scientific American Trophy.

At 11:42 he lifted off again, bound for Governors Island and immortality.

"I could see crowds everywhere," he wrote later. *"New York can turn out a million people probably quicker than any other place on Earth. Every craft on the river turned on its siren, and faint sounds of the clamor reached me even above the roar of my motor. It seemed but a moment until the Statue of Liberty came into view."*

WRIGHT LAWSUITS *would continue to pester Curtiss for years, but his standing was now unassailable and he soon became a major defense contractor, supplying seaplanes to the Navy and the famous Curtiss Jenny to the Army.*

His 1910 Hudson flight ranks to this day in the history of aviation romance alongside Charles Lindbergh's 1927 Atlantic crossing and Alan Shepard's 1961 journey to the edge of space. For all that, the record was broken just two weeks later, when Curtiss sidekick Charles Hamilton flew from New York to Philadelphia, had lunch and then flew back.

By JAY MAEDER
Daily News Staff Writer

PRICKLY, GRUMPY, scornful of even the small pretenses toward social and political niceties — this was William Gaynor, and even with the full weight of Boss Murphy's Tammany Hall behind him, it was hard to see how this man could possibly have been elected mayor of the City of New York.

On the campaign trail, he treated voters like imbeciles; on the dais, he heaped insults on fellow dignitaries. "A worse man than Judge Gaynor might have been chosen," mused the Sun, "but it would have entailed a good deal of trouble to find him."

Yet he was somehow an endearing old soul, and New Yorkers took him to their hearts, and he wasn't by any means a bad mayor; he might even have become an important one. Instead, it was William Gaynor's destiny one summer morning in 1910 to cross paths with a disgruntled city employee and to take his place in history as the only New York mayor ever gunned down in office.

THINGS HAD COME to such a pass in the city by the fall of 1909 that Silent Charlie Murphy deemed it necessary to field an honest man for mayor. Thus did Tammany reach out for Judge Gaynor, who had been sitting irreproachably, if unremarkably, on the state Supreme Court bench since 1893 and against whom no man could realistically utter a word. This was a crapshoot for Silent Charlie. Gaynor was a good Democrat, but certainly no Tammany bootlick. It remained to be seen exactly what Tammany was going to get.

What Tammany got was the single most ferociously independent man that had ever darkened its dreams. If the wigwam's sachems had entertained any notions that Gaynor could be worked with, His Honor swiftly disabused them of these. Addressing a roomful of district supervisors early in his mayorship, Gaynor looked around him incuriously and said: "So this is Tammany Hall. But where is the tiger which they say is going to swallow me up?"

There were a few uneasy chuckles, but things only got worse. "If there happens to be any swallowing up," the mayor continued, "it is not at all unlikely that I may be on the outside of the tiger."

The sachems turned pale, here realizing that they had elected a man who was probably not in their pockets. As indeed he was not. Gaynor gave Tammany nothing, ever, and he reveled in sweeping out city offices and appointing fresh men to the desks. Particularly did he intend to clean up Tammany's police department. "People have become so accustomed to the older order of things," he groused, "that they do not seem to appreciate the fact that a policeman has no right to use his club unless his life is in danger."

Neither, on the other hand, was Gaynor much of a bleeding-heart, and such professional reformers as the good Rev. Charles Parkhurst were shown the door every bit as fast as men of lesser piety. Tammany might be full of rascals, he observed, but Parkhurst "lives at the northwest

Instant of impact. Photograph by William Warnecke, New York World.

CHAPTER 28

'SAY GOODBYE TO THE PEOPLE'

The Day The Mayor Was Shot, 1910

corner of the Milky Way."

Reflected the Evening Post as time went by: "Even those who had thought that his peculiarities would militate against an efficient administration had to admit that the very simplicity that showed up at times so awkwardly on the stump was a valuable adjunct in cutting away red tape and achieving the reforms that he had in mind."

"I suppose that they really are honest in saying they don't understand me," said Gaynor of his critics. "We must try and be charitable anyway."

After a while, New Yorkers realized that they sort of loved their peevish, wise, grandfatherly mayor. An utterly unpretentious man, he regularly walked 3½ miles to work from his Brooklyn home, and he became a familiar morning sight on the bridge. Ladies and children would gaily wave at him; gentlemen would tip their hats. Sometimes Gaynor would grunt and nod.

ABOARD THE KAISER Wilhelm Der Grosse at the great liner's Hoboken pier, shortly after 8 a.m. on Tuesday the 9th of August 1910, Gaynor was making a few grumbling goodbyes as wellwishers gathered on the forward promenade deck to see him off on a brief European holiday. Gaynor was 62 years old, he had been in office for eight tumultuous months and, he had confessed to City Hall reporters the night before, he was tired.

In the crowd was angry James Gallagher, formerly a New York Department of Docks watchman, discharged for incompetence three weeks earlier. Gallagher had repeatedly petitioned the city for reinstatement; he had written directly to Gaynor. In his pocket was a crumpled letter from the mayor's secretary: *"He can do nothing for you in the matter in which you write."*

New York World photographer Bill Warnecke, assigned to catch a routine shipboard departure, had arrived late, and he was just now setting up his camera as the other newsmen packed up and left. Warnecke pointed exactly as Gallagher lunged forward, gun in hand, and made his picture at the instant the bullet struck Gaynor just under his right ear.

Rushed to St. Mary's Hospital, Gaynor appeared to believe he was a dead man. "Say goodbye to the people," he softly instructed an aide.

'PUBLIC OFFICE is no longer safe," grieved one city official. "Either a man's character or his life may be exacted as the penalty for doing the right thing." Mourned another: "The thought that a public officer may be shot down for doing his duty and doing it well is one that must awaken resentment on the part of everyone."

President William Howard Taft declared himself shocked. Col. Theodore Roosevelt said he was horrified beyond measure. Behind bars, Gallagher remained sullen. "He deprived me of my bread and butter," he snapped.

Gaynor lived, but the bullet was irremovable and he was forevermore in pain, his voice a rasp, his attention flagging; for three more years he mayored fitfully on, seeking without success to municipalize the subway, mostly conducting ever more irascible public feuds with everyone in sight. Not surprisingly denied renomination in 1913 by the Tammany Hall he had so deeply annoyed, he was quickly embraced by a citizen's committee and, on Sept. 4, nominated as an independent. And he might well have been reelected.

But six days later he was dead. Haggard and worn, he had boarded another ship, bound again for Europe. He left behind him a brief message for the newspapers:

"The rentpayers and taxpayers of New York City will not throw the government of their city into the control of a vulgar gang of grafters. Give them the shovel. No king, no clown shall rule this town. That day is gone forever."

At sea, he died quietly in a deck chair, a book in his lap.

"THEY HIT THE PAVEMENT JUST LIKE RAIN"

The Triangle Shirtwaist Factory Fire, 1911

By HENRY LEE
Daily News Staff Writer

EVEN TODAY, in a city calloused by recurring tragedies, the horrible half-hour of flame and choking smoke and falling bodies that erupted on that long-ago Saturday remains burned in New York's collective memory — surviving through the years as the emblem of the never-ending quest for better health and safety conditions in the workplace, to insure that 146 victims did not die in vain.

At 4:43 p.m. on that bright and pleasant March 25, 1911, a fire alarm came in from Washington Place and Greene St. off Washington Square, site of the 10-story Asch Building. At the Triangle Shirtwaist Co., on the top three floors, it was quitting time for almost 700 employes, 600 of them immigrant sewing girls ages 13 to 23.

The blaze spread with terrifying speed. Girl after girl, clothing and hair aflame, hurled herself to eternity. By the time Engine Co. 72 arrived from its quarters a half-dozen blocks away, the street was already full of broken bodies. Coroner Herman Holzhauer fell to his knees on the sidewalk and wept.

"They hit the pavement just like rain," Battalion Chief Edward Worth sadly testified later. "Life nets — what good were life nets! Nobody could hold life nets when those girls came down."

"They came down in twos and threes," said another witness, Frances Perkins. "The firemen kept shouting for them not to jump. But they had no choice. The flames were right behind them."

High above, three men formed a living bridge to a neighboring building so that girls could cross over to safety. One lost his grip; all three fell to their deaths. On the ninth floor, a man helped three girls to a window and let them drop. He embraced a fourth, kissed her lingeringly, dropped her — then followed her in death. Two elevator operators made 20 trips to rescue girls. When they could take no more, many left behind tried to slide down the cables but crashed to the cages far below.

Inside, firemen found a charred mass of 25 bodies in a cloakroom, another 19 behind a locked door.

A sign was posted by the city Buildings Department — 48 hours later — that the loft was unsafe. It did little to mollify the mounting fury over the disaster, as one funeral procession after another wound through the streets, crossing paths. One undertaker conducted eight services simultaneously.

City officials discouraged a single public funeral because they thought hysteria would erupt, but in the drenching rain of April 11, a mourning parade without banners or bands marched on Washington Square from two directions. Police estimated that 400,000 turned out, about a third of them as marchers.

BROWN BROTHERS

FROM THE OUTRAGED public there was one cry: What had happened? Just about everything that could have gone wrong did. The Asch Building itself, built in 1901, was considered a modern fireproof structure, but there was no sprinkler system, and a ninth-floor door had been kept locked to prevent the girls from slipping away with stolen clothing. Fire ladders reached only to the sixth floor, fire hoses only to the seventh.

Triangle owners Max Blanck and Isaac Harris were indicted. Despite testimony that the sewing girls had been locked into their death chamber, both men were acquitted at trial in December.

"This is America?" stunned relatives cried outside the courthouse. "This is justice?"

Blanck and Harris later paid $75 to each of 23 families that had sued them for violation of the fire laws.

But in the long run, the disaster proved crucial to the fortunes of the struggling garment-union movement. Eleven years earlier, 11 cloak makers from New York, Philadelphia and Baltimore had met on the lower East Side to found the International Ladies' Garment Workers' Union. Now the ILGWU drew much public support, and Gov. John Dix and the state Legislature promptly formed a Factory Investigation Commission. The reports that came back from the commission's inspectors made shocking reading, and in the next few years some three dozen laws, ranging from fire regulations to working hours for women and children, were passed.

Frances Perkins, who had watched as the Triangle girls jumped, was able to report on "the greatest battery of bills to prevent disasters and hardships affecting working people . . . the likes of which have never been seen." Perkins later became Franklin D. Roosevelt's secretary of labor. The New Deal itself, she always believed, resulted from the "stirring of conscience" sparked by the Triangle fire.

The late Henry Lee originally wrote this story for the Daily News Magazine of Jan. 22, 1989.

By JAY MAEDER
Daily News Staff Writer

ATOP THE Wanamaker department store in New York in the spring of 1912 was a promotional novelty: a functioning wireless radio station, around which shoppers regularly assembled to watch its crackerjack young operator send and receive telegraph messages, and on Sunday the 14th of April David Sarnoff was at his post as usual, idly monitoring routine traffic. Then a feeble transmission from the ocean liner Olympic, 1,400 miles at sea, sat him bolt upright in his chair.

Titanic ran into iceberg. Sinking fast.

All through the day, all through the night, all through the day after that, Sarnoff sat at his key, the city's reporters gathered at his side, trying to make sense of wildly contradictory garble passed along in fragments from station to station. The mighty ship had gone down like a stone; no, she was unsinkable, of course she remained afloat. A dozen other ships were speeding to her rescue; no, none were needed. The passengers were all quite safe; no, they weren't; yes, they were. Now the great Titanic had gone to the bottom again; now she was under tow to Halifax. Little by little, dispatch by dispatch, the news grew worse.

On Monday night, the Evening Telegram got out a late extra that brought the city its first firm announcement of the unimaginable disaster. The world's largest, most majestic, most utterly indestructible ship had been destroyed on her maiden voyage from Britain to America. She was gone. Apparently there were no more than several hundred survivors. Apparently more than 1,500 souls had perished.

ALREADY ON Monday evening, as the terrible rumors spread through the city and the bulletins posted outside the newspaper offices changed by the hour, frantic men and women were converging on the White Star Line's second-floor offices at 9 Broadway, pleading for answers. There were none. White Star had no official confirmation that anything had happened, office manager P.A.S. Franklin insisted. It was not until ashen-faced Vincent Astor arrived to inquire about his father, the billionaire John Jacob Astor — and was quickly escorted into Franklin's private office, from which 30 minutes later he came out sobbing — that the muttering crowds knew at last. A woman screamed hysterically. A man fainted.

Even all through Tuesday — as the papers reported that 675 sodden survivors were New York-bound aboard the Carpathia, or 715, or 868 — White Star refused to acknowledge that the Titanic had gone down. It was not until that night that confirmation was reluctantly made. Asked by reporters what had happened, Franklin just stared out the window

Culver Pictures

CHAPTER 30

WHEN THE SHIP COMES IN
Waiting For The Carpathia, 1912

and shook his head.

Nearly three full days after they had been taken aboard the Carpathia, the surviving passengers remained mostly unidentified. Their names emerged in trickles, a few at a time, and 40 cops were called to hold back the throngs at Bowling Green as ragged immigrant families and handsomely dressed ladies with footmen anxiously sought assurances that their loved ones still lived.

There was, in fact, almost no communication between New York and the Carpathia. Aboard that vessel, White Star managing director J. Bruce Ismay was strictly enforcing a near-total information freeze; hundreds of inquiries were piling up, unanswered, in the wireless shack — even one from President William Howard Taft, who was desperately trying to learn the fate of his aide, Major Archibald Butt. Taft had sent two Navy ships to meet the Carpathia as she steamed out of the icefields toward New York, and the Carpathia was ignoring their messages as well.

If the President himself could get no word, certainly no information was forthcoming for the wailing woman whose elderly mother had been coming to visit, or the grief-stricken young man who had been expecting his bride-to-be, or the relatives of a couple who had cut short a European holiday to return home for the funeral of a son killed in an auto accident. Tuesday turned agonizingly to Wednesday, and Wednesday to Thursday, and still the Carpathia was silent.

As New York waited, the enterprising Travelers Insurance Co. took out advertisements squarely amid the Titanic columns in the daily papers. *On Sea And Land — At Home And Abroad — Night And Day — Accidents Are Happening! Are You Covered?*

IN A DRIVING RAIN on the night of Thursday the 18th, 30,000 people gathered at Pier 54 off 14th St. to meet the Carpathia as she sailed in from the gloom. Long lines of ambulances and hearses jammed the streets. White Star's Ismay had ordered the Titanic crew members to tell no tales, but as more than 700 of the doomed ship's bedraggled passengers came down the gangplanks, there swiftly unfolded stories of heroism and cowardice and fear and love and death that would endure for all time.

John Jacob Astor had stood philosophically on deck, waving farewell to his wife. Mrs. Isidor Straus had refused to leave her husband's side, choosing to die with him. Archibald Butt had held off at gunpoint a mob of crazed men trying to board lifeboats ahead of women and children. An Englishman named William Stead, author of an 1892 short story called "From the Old World to the New," which posited a crash between a steamship and an iceberg, had refused to believe there was any danger and retired to his stateroom. The captain had bravely gone down with his ship. The band had played on.

On the pier, young immigrant girls searched futilely for family members who had been told they were dead and were not there to meet them. Others, more fortunate, rushed to embrace their waiting relatives. A small boy screamed for his forever lost mother. Two French-speaking tykes, too young to even tell their names, were taken home by a young woman who had watched over them in a lifeboat.

One group of steerage passengers found themselves detained by dock authorities because they had, of course, no papers; they went on their way after an imposing bystander who identified himself as a federal official angrily ordered their release. It was subsequently suggested that the liberator had probably been New York World reporter Herbert Bayard Swope.

Amid reports that J. Bruce Ismay had arranged to transfer to another ship and sail back to England without setting foot in New York at all, two U.S. Senate investigators stormed aboard the Carpathia and served him notice that he was expected to appear before an investigating committee. Treed, Ismay told the press he had left the Titanic on the last remaining lifeboat. Several Carpathia officers replied that actually, it had been one of the first, and that Ismay, upon arriving aboard their vessel, had immediately demanded to be fed.

On Friday, after searching the city's hospitals all night, the bridegroom found his bride, and he married her that afternoon.

Culver Pictures

Taking the sun, Atlantic City.

By MARA BOVSUN
Special To The News

RUMORS SPREAD from the glittering lobster-and-champagne palaces of Times Square to the dressing rooms of the Follies showgirls on Broadway: Diamond Jim Brady was dead.

The rumors were wrong. Diamond Jim wasn't dead. He was merely in Baltimore.

Doctors in New York and Boston had told the legendary Brady there wasn't much they could do to ease his stomach pains. So he had gone to Baltimore's Johns Hopkins Hospital, where it was said a surgeon had a new technique.

Early in April 1912, Dr. Hugh Young got his first stunned look at the sparkling king of the Great White Way. The 56-year-old Brady literally seemed to be nothing but diamonds. There were huge rocks in his tie, in his vest, on his watchchain, in his cuff links, on the head of his cane. The doctor blinked.

Beyond the dazzle, Brady was just another sick patient, beset by diabetes, urinary infections, high blood pressure, heart disease. Not to mention a stomach that had stretched to six times its normal size. "A formidable series of complications," Young decided.

WHAT HAD BROUGHT on these problems was no mystery. Diamond Jim's eating habits were notorious, the living symbol of the dizzying robber-baron prosperity of the early century. Gorging was what the man did, and it became the fashionable way for the wealthy to comport themselves.

No one came close to Diamond Jim. A typical feeding would be two or three dozen large oysters, half a dozen crabs, two bowls of turtle soup, six or seven lobsters, two whole ducks, a steak and half a dozen venison chops. Dessert was a pound or two of chocolates. Everything was washed down with gallons of orange juice.

On one occasion he threw a dinner for 50 to celebrate the success of a friend's racehorse. Guests started eating at 4 p.m. and didn't finish till 9 the next morning. It was estimated that each had downed 10 bottles of champagne, and the bill came to $100,000.

Restaurateur Charles Rector actually sent his son to Paris for two years just to find and bring back the perfect recipe for Sole Marguery, which

CHAPTER 31

SPARKLE PLENTY

The Fabulous Diamond Jim Brady, 1912

Brady had demanded Rector start serving. Working undercover as a dishwasher, the young Rector picked up the recipe by stealing peeks over the shoulder of a fish chef. On the day his boat got back to New York, Diamond Jim was waiting for him on the dock. "Have you got the sauce?" Jim shouted. That night he downed nine portions.

"The best 25 customers I ever had," Rector said fondly.

Everyone wanted to be where Diamond Jim went, wear what he wore and eat what he ate. New York was full of Diamond Jim imitators seeking to set the pace for Gilded Age glamor and gluttony. There was Pearl Jim Murray, a Montana miner who kept his pockets jammed with hundreds of thousands of dollars' worth of pearls. There were the Pittsburgh Millionaires, a group of 30 men who had worked for Andrew Carnegie and got rich when Carnegie sold his business to J.P. Morgan. They all became Brady clones, copying his jewels and his clothes. Brady took them under his wing and gave them fashion tips.

But it was Diamond Jim who was always unquestionably at the center of the scene, spending lavishly, as many as 10 showgirls on his arm at a time. His favorite gal pal was actress Lillian Russell. She could pack away chow pretty

good herself, though she often ordered nothing but bottomless platters of corn on the cob.

But if the good life had made Brady the reigning prince of elegant excess, it also left him with a gigantically swollen prostate that threatened to kill him. Surgeons had been unwilling to operate, fearful of cutting through the layers of lard covering the man's massive frame. But Dr. Young had recently invented a new technique — called Young's Punch — that cleared the blockage in minutes without a single incision.

After the emergency treatment, Young had to rush away to a medical conference in London, and he left his wealthy patient behind to recover at Johns Hopkins, where nurses fought to take care of him because of the diamond rings he gave them for their trouble.

The minute Young and his family arrived in New York, they were met by Brady's secretary, who put them up royally at the Vanderbilt Hotel and gave them the maharajah's tour of Broadway.

By August, Brady was back in New York, at the center of many splendid stories. Some said the doctors had removed his stomach altogether and replaced it with the belly of a pig, or a cow — or, according to one yarn, a deceased man whose widow had agreed to accept $200,000 for her late husband's digestive organs.

Reporters stalked Brady at his W. 86th St. home. One of them brought back an exclusive, if probably spurious, interview with the great man: "They certainly handed me back a newly lined, high-powered, pliant and pleasantly dispositioned stomach! Why, if you roasted a full-size bull moose and just put me in front of it, I guess I could eat the whole thing!"

To the exultation of Rector and his fellow restaurant owners, this appeared to be true. And for five more years, Diamond Jim Brady remained in the world of enormous meals, theatrical first nights and lovely companions.

THINGS CAUGHT UP with him at last in April 1917. He left the bulk of his fortune to doctors at Johns Hopkins and New York Hospital, with the stipulation that they establish a medical institute in the name of James Buchanan Brady.

He had died of angina, ulcers, diabetes and several other things. One disease wouldn't have been enough for him.

CHAPTER 32

SCRAPING THE SKY

The World's Tallest Building, 1913

By OWEN MORITZ
Daily News Staff Writer

STANDING IN City Hall Park, a minister named S. Parkes Cadman dabbed his eyes as he peered across Broadway and heavenward at the world's tallest building.

It was April 24, 1913, the building was the Woolworth Building and, at that precise moment in Washington, President Woodrow Wilson flicked a switch that set 80,000 light bulbs ablaze to dedicate this glorious, richly detailed, 60-story Gothic tower that indeed resembled a cathedral.

And as he stood among jubilant thousands, the Rev. Cadman couldn't contain himself. "It inspires feelings too deep even for tears," said the minister, who promptly anointed the building at 233 Broadway the "Cathedral of Commerce."

Inside the skyscraper's florid 27th-floor banquet hall, no one was more aglow than five-and-dime tycoon Frank Woolworth. Amid pheasant and the clink of champagne glasses, the captains of New York industry toasted a new general of the skyline.

Meanwhile, all the world toasted Woolworth's 792-foot-tall cathedral. Once a postcard arrived from the West Coast, addressed simply to "The Highest Building in the World." Woolworth's reign would last for 17 years — until the 1,046-foot Chrysler Building went up in 1930, itself to be one-upped by the Empire State Building a year after that.

F.W. Woolworth financed his $13.5 million building from his own piggy bank. He had 684 stores in his variety chain, including his flagship at Fifth Ave. between 39th and 40th Sts.

First, though, Woolworth had engineers measure the 50-story Metropolitan Life Tower at 23rd St. and Madison Ave.

That had been back in 1908, when the insurance company's headquarters had still been the world's tallest structure. F.W. greatly admired the building, especially the four-sided clock whose faces were even bigger than those on London's Big Ben.

Then he had called on architect Cass Gilbert to design a building, modeled on London's Houses of Parliament, that would enshrine F.W.'s three great passions — Napoleon, Christianity and commerce — and stand nearly 100 feet taller than the Met Life tower.

What he got was a Gothic masterpiece. A facade of flying buttresses and ornamental gargoyles. Interior walls of golden marble. Tiffany elevator doors. No ceiling less than 11 feet high, and some as high as 20. Woolworth's own suite was modeled after a room in one of Napoleon's palaces, complete with a bronze bust of Bonaparte himself.

Beyond the three-story entrance, laden with mosaics and gold leaf, was a lobby full of heroic sculpture: A marble image of Woolworth counting his nickels, one of

architect Gilbert holding a model of the building, one of the building's structural engineer measuring a girder.

Woolworth had also created an observation deck from which 300,000 visitors a year would enjoy a splendid view of New York Harbor. Too splendid, as it turned out: On the eve of World War II, the Navy ordered the deck closed lest spies use it to track Allied movements, and it never reopened.

Meanwhile, no one knew in 1913, or has ever known since, why the building had no 42nd, 48th or 52nd floors.

SKYSCRAPERS WERE a Chicago invention; that city's great fire of 1871 had led to innovative steel-frame construction. About the same time, elevators were invented. There was now birthed a new era of buildings much taller than their masonry predecessors could ever have been. By the end of the 1870s in New York, there were a number of buildings that climbed 10 stories or more. By 1890, the New York World had put up a building that was 309 feet tall.

Skyscrapers quickly proliferated thereafter, most of them clustered around lower Broadway at first, then moving northward along the city's solid bedrock, Manhattan schist. The 21-story Flatiron Building at Madison Square and the 25-story Times Tower at Times Square both went up in the first few years of the 20th century. After that, barons of American business quickly came to recognize the commercial value of putting their names on structures that towered over the ones next to them. And so along came the 47-story Singer Tower at 149 Broadway, the Met Life Tower at Madison Square — and then Frank Woolworth's grand cathedral.

A few years later, in 1916, the appearance of the Equitable Life Assurance Society headquarters at 120 Broadway put a check on the runaway skyscraping. Equitable had taken a plot of land of just under one acre and built a commercial high-rise of 1.2 million square feet — a floor area nearly 30 times the area of the site. This exploitation of space was too much — here was the entire sun being blotted out by one immense building — and planners, alarmed at the specter of a city in shadows at high noon, moved quickly to curb other buildings of similar bulk. The result was the nation's first comprehensive zoning plan.

No such bad thoughts for the Woolworth Building. As late as 1930, a merchants association voted it the single most impressive thing about New York City — better even than the subway and the Brooklyn Bridge.

POLITICS AS USUAL

Impeaching The Governor, 1913

By JOSEPH McNAMARA
Daily News Writer

WILLIAM SULZER was still only freshly in the New York State governorship when he chose to challenge Boss Charles Murphy of New York City's Tammany Hall, who at the time was threatening to have the Legislature kill all Sulzer's proposals if the governor didn't stop vetoing Tammany bills.

"Political conventions must go!" Sulzer bellowed. "Disgraceful secret alliances between special privileges and crooked politics must cease!"

He was either ethically valorous or vainly stupid, depending on the viewpoint. In the fall of 1913, less than a year after he went to Albany, Sulzer was impeached, the only New York governor ever to be removed from office.

He had been accused of laundering campaign funds. Indeed, he admitted, he had forgotten to declare $9,000, and there were those who were inclined to believe this simple explanation. But he had incurred Tammany's wrath, and that made all the difference.

LAWYER SULZER had once been a good Tammany man himself. In 1889, at age 26, he was elected to the state Assembly on the Tammany ticket and reelected five times to one-year terms. In 1893 he was elected speaker of the Assembly; a year later, after serving as Democratic minority leader, he resigned — but vowed to return to Albany someday as governor.

Back in Manhattan, he was elected to the congressional district of the lower East Side. Serving from 1895 until 1912, he rose to the chairmanship of the House Foreign Affairs Committee and long espoused enlightened social legislation, women's suffrage and direct election of U.S. senators. Though not a Jew, he was a strong champion of the many Eastern European immigrants who poured by the boatload into his district; he took up the cause of Jewry in Congress and denounced the pogroms in Russia. This was a factor in his election to the governorship in 1912, for he split the Jewish vote with philanthropist Oscar Straus, otherwise the strong candidate of Theodore Roosevelt's Bull Moose Party.

Sulzer also carried the support of Tammany in that election, however second-handed; Boss Murphy had preferred another man, but the Democratic State Convention deadlocked, and Sulzer was there to step into the vacuum. Once in Albany, though, Sulzer immediately began refusing obeisance to Murphy. Tammany men were kicked out of some offices. And Tammany men were not appointed to fill others. Boss Murphy was not pleased.

It was time, Sulzer said, for the Legislature to adopt a direct primary for nominating political candidates. And he called the Legislature into special session to enact one.

Instead, the lawmakers, influenced by Murphy, voted to expand the powers of a joint committee set up earlier to investigate the finances of state-supported institutions. The committee was now empowered to probe campaign receipts and spending of candidates for public office. Conveniently, they excluded from the probe senators, assemblymen and mayors.

SULZER, AS IT happened, appeared to be pretty guilty anyway. He had failed to add three checks totaling $9,000 in campaign contributions to the $5,460 he did declare. Purely an oversight, he insisted.

Hearings began in June under the chairmanship of a Tammany senator. On Aug. 11, the committee reported to the Assembly, and eight articles of impeachment were voted two days later. A tribunal consisting of the state Senate and the Court of Appeals convened in September; a month later, this court found Sulzer guilty of perjury and filing a false campaign statement. On Oct. 17, he was removed from office.

"If I had served Mr. Murphy instead of serving the state," Sulzer declaimed, "if I had obeyed Mr. Murphy instead of the dictates of my conscience — Mr. Murphy would never have instituted this impeachment."

The day after his removal, 10,000 staunch supporters gave a reception for the fallen Sulzer in Albany and presented him with a cup inscribed: "A Martyr to the Cause of Good Government."

HE RETURNED a political hero to the lower East Side — whose citizens promptly elected him to the Assembly again and sent him right back to Albany.

This wouldn't do, and Tammany quickly had the district gerrymandered so reelection for Sulzer was now impossible.

Sulzer later ran unsuccessfully for mayor, governor and President. He died in 1941.

"I impeach the criminal conspirators!" he had thundered as he left the governor's mansion in 1913. "Posterity will do me justice. Time sets all things right."

New York Tribune, Nov. 8, 1912

By JAY MAEDER
Daily News Staff Writer

IT WAS NOT one of the lovelier electrocutions Sing Sing ever saw. Charlie Becker was a big man, 6-feet-3, 215 pounds, and the creaking old death house chair just wasn't up to the job. The first jolt blew flames out Charlie's ears; it took two more after that to finally kill him. MURDERED BY GOVERNOR WHITMAN, Charlie's sobbing widow wrote on his tombstone, but the cops made her take it off.

Whitman, as it happened, had previously been the Manhattan DA who had convicted Charlie in the first place. Now, on July 30, 1915, his gubernatorial ambitions satisfied, he found it untaxing to turn a deaf ear to the condemned man's 11th-hour pleas for clemency. "I am sacrificed for my friends," Charlie announced from Death Row. Then he walked his final mile, the first and last New York City police officer ever to suffer execution for taking a few bucks on the side.

WHICH, between November 1911 and June 1912, had come to about $72,000. Shakedowns. Protection. The usual. Lt. Charles Becker ran the police department's Strong-Arm Squad, as it was actually called in those no-nonsense times, and the $2,200-a-year cop had forged profitable understandings with many of his constituents in the city's gaudy midtown Tenderloin district. Among these was a gambler named Herman Rosenthal, who had one day concluded after the bulls raided his W. 45th St. faro joint one too many times that he was not getting his fair money's worth from Charlie and in an intemperate moment gone straight to The New York World. The lurid Page One revelations greatly distressed many parties. Herman's associates all shook their heads. By and by it was not lost on even Herman himself what a foolhardy thing he had done.

Indeed, Herman got his just two days later. He had spent the evening of Monday the 15th of July 1912 getting grilled by crusading DA Whitman, and he had been informed that he was to go before the grand jury to repeat his disclosures. "The trail leads to high places!" Whitman promised reporters. Late that night Rosenthal repaired to the Hotel Metropole at Broadway and 43rd St. to calm his nerves with drink. At 2 a.m. Tuesday he stepped outside and was straightaway gunned down by a team of bushwhackers who then sped away in a waiting car. The sensational public killing put the word "gangster" into the language. It possibly marked the first time a hit squad ever made a getaway

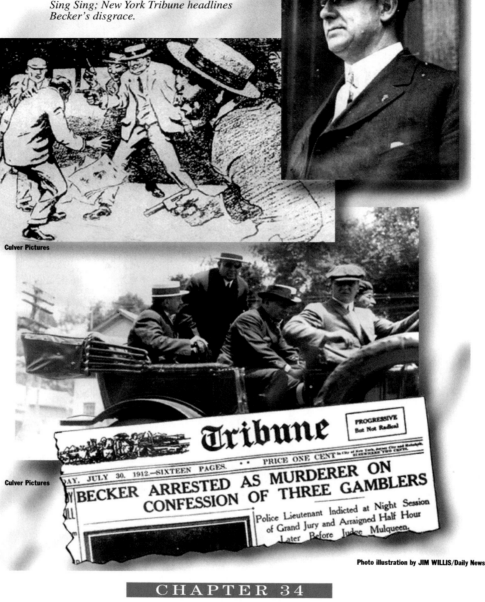

Right, Becker outside court at his second trial. Below, artist's conception of the Rosenthal slaying; Becker (second from left) en route to Sing Sing; New York Tribune headlines Becker's disgrace.

Culver Pictures

Culver Pictures

Tribune PROGRESSIVE But Not Radical
DAY, JULY 30, 1912—SIXTEEN PAGES. ・・ PRICE ONE CENT In the City of New York, Jersey City and Hoboken ELSEWHERE TWO CENTS
BECKER ARRESTED AS MURDERER ON CONFESSION OF THREE GAMBLERS
Police Lieutenant Indicted at Night Session of Grand Jury and Arraigned Half Hour Later Before Judge Mulqueen.

Photo illustration by JIM WILLIS/Daily News

CHAPTER 34

BAD LIEUTENANT

Frying Becker, 1915

by automobile. And it blew the lid off the comfortable so-called System long enjoyed by crooked cops, crooked pols and the underworld in a big-town scandal that would resonate for decades to come.

BECKER'S OWN BAGMAN, a chrome-domed gambler named Jack Rose, quickly turned himself in as a matter of self-preservation and gave up the shooters, four lads known on Broadway as Lefty Louie, Gyp the Blood, Dago Frank and Whitey Lewis. They worked for Bronx racketeer Jack Zelig, whose expanding enterprise down Manhattan's West Side into the Great White Way was a large reason that the Strong-Arm Squad had been formed in the first place, and all agreed that Charlie Becker had personally ponied up $1,000 to shut Herman's big mouth.

Confronted with much evidence — he actually held the mortgage on Rosenthal's

gambling den, for one thing, and then of course there were the nine bank accounts stuffed like ducks with cash — Becker readily admitted to being dirty. But he insisted he'd had nothing to do with the Times Square rubout.

On July 29, when he was arrested at his desk in the Bathgate Ave. stationhouse in the Bronx and marched off to the Tombs, 42-year-old Lt. Charles Becker wore the look of a man who had just realized he was taking a fall.

EIGHTEEN COPS were indicted as the pay-off investigations ran their course. Four inspectors went to prison. Commissioner Rhinelander Waldo was forced to resign. Mayor William Gaynor's otherwise decent administration was left measurably poisoned.

Lt. Becker and the four gunmen were quickly convicted of first-degree murder and sentenced to death. Becker himself, loudly claiming a frameup at the hands of Tammany Hall's powerful state Sen. Big Tim Sullivan, a man who also benefited enormously from Rosenthal's silence, managed to win a retrial on appeal, and the triggermen went to the chair without him. On the eve of his execution, Dago Frank issued a statement clearing Becker of any involvement in Herman's killing.

But presiding Judge Samuel Seabury refused to admit Frank's statement when the lieutenant went to trial a second time. Again the verdict was guilty. Again the sentence was death. Through 1915, as his time drew nigh, Becker spilled ever more colorful insights into the System's daily business. Sullivan had been behind everything, he said, Rosenthal was meant only to have been kidnapped and scared off, the killing was an accident, the shooters had lost their heads, he'd had nothing to do with it anyway. Rackets boss Zelig might have confirmed his yarn. Alas, Zelig had been shot to death while boarding a Second Ave. streetcar.

In the end, Charlie Becker's last hope was clemency from the governor. This was, of course, former DA Whitman, who was now very busily contemplating a presidential nomination and really couldn't be bothered with Charlie anymore.

SIX YEARS LATER *a police inspector named John Dwyer publicly charged that Becker had been "framed, without a shadow of doubt" and called for a state probe of offenses by the Police Department and the district attorney's office against "law, order and our civilization and humanity." Nothing came of this.*

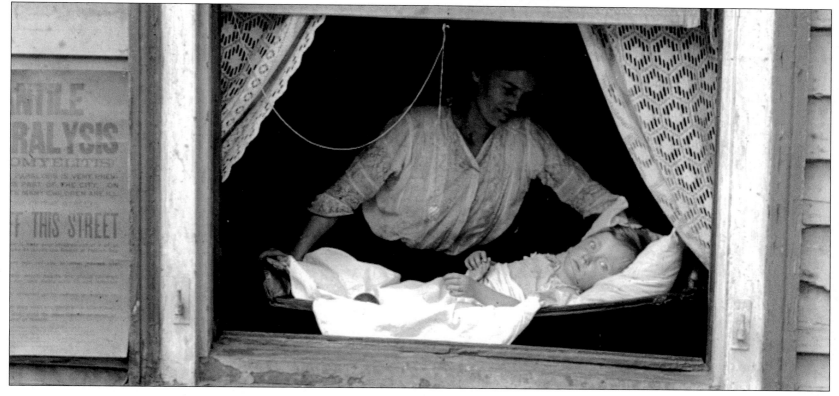

CORBIS-BETTMANN

By DENNIS WEPMAN
Special to The News

THERE HAD BEEN epidemics in New York before — cholera, typhoid and pneumonia all had swept the city — but this was like nothing else. It mainly attacked children, with no apparent source or pattern, and its effects were dreadful. After the first mild symptoms — headache, slight fever — the little ones were suddenly unable to move. Doctors called it poliomyelitis, but most people knew it as infantile paralysis, and the popular term for it was "The Crippler." It was nothing new, but the world's first major epidemic of it occurred in New York City in the summer of 1916, and it struck down thousands.

The public was terrified. No one knew where polio came from, how it spread or what to do about it. Because it first appeared in an Italian neighborhood, the Department of Health initially blamed it on immigrants — but Ellis Island reported no cases. Health Commissioner Haven Emerson accused the people of Brooklyn of leaving their garbage uncovered; the borough, he snapped, had not "developed sufficient pride to keep its own streets clean." The city became obsessed with sanitation. Any book returned to a public library from an infected home was routinely burned. Animals were thought to be carriers, and people were urged to destroy their pets; the city exterminated more than 70,000 cats. Screens, fly swatters and flytraps enjoyed record sales. Giant flytraps were installed in public places.

Quarantine was the only other means the Health Department knew to contain an epidemic. Mayor John Purroy Mitchel declared the city to be in a "state of peril" and greatly extended the powers of health officials to enforce quarantines. Families who could afford it nursed their sick children at home, behind bright red warning signs, as sanitation officers

CHAPTER 35
STATE OF PERIL
Polio, 1916

patrolled outside. The poor had to hide their babies: Three policemen, guns drawn, raided a Brooklyn apartment one day, snatched a 2-year-old from the arms of his aunt and handed him out the window to a surgeon.

Every effort was made to keep children, sick or well, isolated. Emerson urged the city to require everyone under 16 to stay home for two weeks. The proposal wasn't accepted, but trolleys refused to carry kids, theaters refused to admit them and schools, playgrounds and parks were closed.

None of these measures slowed the indiscriminate spread of the disease. Polio democratically crossed social and ethnic lines, appearing in the cleanest and most fashionable neighborhoods as frequently as in the slums.

The rich fled the city. By early July, about 50,000 kids had been taken from New York to the countryside. Soon the suburbs became as panicky as the city. Hoboken, N.J., police were stationed at every point of entry — tube, train, ferry, road — with instructions to turn back every van, car, cart and person laden with furniture. Ferry service from the Bronx was suspended, and railroad companies required a health certificate before they would sell a ticket to anyone under 16. Summer resorts in the Catskills and the Adirondacks closed their doors.

THE PANIC MOUNTED as the grim specter continued to stalk. More than 1,100 cases and 301 deaths were reported in a single week in early August. By October, when the epidemic had finally run its course, more than 9,000 polio cases had been tallied, 2,449 of them fatal. All but a few of the victims were less than 10 years old. Apparently nothing the Health Department did had any effect one way or the other.

Officials continued to regard polio as a bacterial disease spread by poor immigrants with low standards of hygiene, but the scientific evidence showed otherwise. The old models of epidemics spawned by malnutrition, overcrowding and unsanitary conditions didn't work this time. Polio hit native and foreigner, rich and poor, about the same, and it seemed to have nothing to do with dirt, flies, cats or food. If the 1916 epidemic did anything positive, it established that.

On the negative side, since most of the Health Department's explanations were wrong as well as socially biased, the epidemic dealt a severe blow to public faith in scientific authority. It wasn't until the 1940s that the poliomyelitis virus was clearly understood. It wasn't until the 1950s, with Dr. Jonas Salk's polio vaccine, that some of that faith was restored.

CORBIS-BETTMANN

By DENNIS WEPMAN
Special To The News

SHE CLUTCHED ROSES as she sat in Brooklyn's Court of Special Session, a spitfire Irishwoman charged with distributing obscene materials — contraception information. For having opened the nation's first birth-control clinic, she was further charged with "maintaining a public nuisance." The roses were a gift from the grateful mothers of Brooklyn.

Her sister, charged with the same offenses, had just been pardoned by the governor after hunger-striking herself nearly to death in her Blackwells Island cell. Her clinic clerk was being let off with a fine, paid for by an indignant committee of prominent New Yorkers. Now, on Feb. 2, 1917, 40-year-old Margaret Sanger herself stood up in a court of law.

Calmly she admitted authorship of birth-control informational material, the sale of some of which to anti-vice crusader Anthony Comstock had already cost her husband, William, a month in jail and focused world attention on her teachings. Outside the courtroom marched crowds of planned-parenthood supporters, and the panel of three judges decided it didn't care to make Sanger more of a martyr than she already was: It would release her, it said, if she would agree not to violate the law again.

"I cannot promise to obey a law I do not respect," Sanger snapped.

The chief judge rapped his gavel to quiet the cheers from the gallery.

Sanger, he sighed, could have her choice of a fine or 30 days in the workhouse. The defendant insisted on the jail time. Three days later, she started serving it.

HERSELF ONE OF 11 children, little Margaret Higgins had watched her weary mother grow old and spent before her time; years later, as a maternity nurse in the tenements of New York City's lower East Side, Margaret Sanger had seen legions of impoverished women bring unwanted child after unwanted child into lives of hopeless wretchedness — "submerged, untouched classes," she later remembered, "beyond the scope of organized charity or religion." Often these women attempted crude self-abortions; in 1912, nurse Sanger cared for one desperately near-fatal case for weeks, then listened as her patient pleaded with a doctor for protection against further pregnancies. The prescription: "Tell Jake to sleep on the roof."

Six months later, the same woman tried to abort another pregnancy, and this time she died. Sanger abandoned nursing as futile — and took to the battlefront.

These were times of turbulent socialism in New York City, and Sanger in 1914 launched a radical magazine, The Woman Rebel — "No Gods, No Masters" was its motto — and in its firebrand pages she invented the term "birth control." Her detailed descriptions of how to use condoms and diaphragms were, the postmaster general ruled, "lewd, filthy, vile and indecent"; Sanger was quickly indicted for sending the magazine through the mails. Facing 45 years in prison, she left her husband and three small children and fled to Europe.

In her absence, William Sanger went to jail for continuing to sell his wife's writings — and by the time she

Every child a wanted child: Sanger, left, greets supporters outside court.

Planned Parenthood of New York City, Inc.

NO GODS, NO MASTERS

Margaret Sanger Goes To Jail, 1917

returned to the U.S. in January 1916 to face the mails charge, the notion of family planning was emerging as a major social issue. Progressive physicians and clergymen were breaking ranks and siding with Margaret Sanger; a movement was building; the federal government quietly dropped the postal prosecution. In July, she announced her intentions to open a Brooklyn clinic.

She did so in October, on Amboy St. in the Brownsville section, and 10 days later she was arrested. "You're not a woman, you're a dog," she screamed at the policewoman in charge of the raid, and crowds of mothers jeered the officers as Sanger was dragged to a patrol wagon. She spent the night in the Raymond St. jail; out on bail the next day, she immediately reopened the clinic — and was immediately rearrested.

Amid a storm of public condemnation in January 1917,

authorities pursued their case against the troublemaking ex-nurse who championed women's right to their own bodies. Sanger's sister, Ethel Byrne, was being force-fed in her jail cell; influential citizens were protesting the prosecutions; delegations of planned-parenthood supporters were noisily demanding action from Gov. Charles Whitman and the Legislature.

Now, as the world watched, Sanger was put behind bars.

SHE REFUSED to be fingerprinted, proclaiming herself a political prisoner. She also refused a physical examination. The matrons did not insist. They were getting a bad enough press as it was.

Sanger spent her 30 days reading aloud to the 37 women in her cellblock, giving them birth-control advice. The matrons protested that the prostitutes and thieves in their

charge "knew bad enough already," but they couldn't stop her. When her term was up, several guards forcibly sought again to fingerprint her, but she resisted so fiercely they gave up.

Outside the workhouse doors, society women, working mothers and militant feminists had covered the path with flowers, and as Sanger left jail they all broke into a chorus of the "Marseillaise," the French national anthem celebrating the Revolution. At their cell windows, the female prisoners joined in.

SANGER'S LAWYER appealed the case, although she had already served her sentence and never denied her guilt. The Court of Appeals upheld the conviction, but she continued her work undismayed, soon incorporating the Birth Control League of New York City and embarking on a year-long battle with state officials over the production and exhibition of her instructional film "Birth Control." She started another magazine, wrote books. Motherhood, she tirelessly preached, deserved "a higher level than enslavement." Every child, she said, deserved to be a wanted child.

"When motherhood," she wrote, "becomes the fruit of deep yearning, not the result of ignorance or accident, its children will become the foundation of a new race."

IN 1937, *the American Medical Association formally recognized birth control as a legitimate practice. At Margaret Sanger's death in 1966, The Pill was in widespread use.*

AMERICAN SOUNDTRACK

Tin Pan Alley Goes To War, 1917

By DAVID HINCKLEY
Daily News Staff Writer

GEORGE M. COHAN may have lived on a palatial estate in Great Neck, L.I., one of his rewards for 13 years of song-and-dance success on Broadway, but on the morning of April 7, 1917, his newspaper gave him the same news it delivered to Americans everywhere: We had declared war on Germany, and U.S. troops would officially join the war to end all wars.

Being 39 years of age, Cohan did not rush to his recruiting station. But he did feel a patriotic compulsion to do his part, and as he told the story in later years, he soon felt a song a-comin'.

"I read the war headlines and I got to thinking and humming to myself, and for a minute I thought I was going into my dance. Soon I was all finished with the chorus and the verse, and by the time I got to town I had a title."

Cohan's task was rendered somewhat easier by the fact that he was basically rewriting an already existing off-to-battle song called "Johnny Get Your Gun." His new hook line: *"We'll be over / We're coming over / And we won't come back till it's over / Over there."*

Not too long after, Charles King sang it at New York's Hippodrome, during a Red Cross benefit, and "Over There" started its march into history.

Before it was finished, it had been the best-selling recording and sheet music in the country for 17 weeks, inspiring hit versions by everyone from Nora Bayes to Enrico Caruso. Twenty-three years and one world war later, it earned George M. Cohan the congressional Medal of Honor.

Moreover, the success of "Over There" illustrates one of New York's most enduring industries: popular music.

MUSIC COMES FROM everywhere. But by the turn of the century, much of it was being channeled through a mobile entity known as Tin Pan Alley.

Distribution and compensation had always been tricky for songwriters. Stephen Foster, a great writer who was also immensely popular, died penniless at Bellevue Hospital in 1864 at age 37.

What came along later, alas too late for Foster, were affordable instruments and the embryonic phonograph machine. With those two developments, song distribution soon became more systematic, and one of the first fruits was the popular song boom of the Gay '90s, with the likes of "The Band Played On," "After the Ball" and "Bird in a Gilded Cage."

Because inexpensive sheet music exceeded expensive recordings as the primary means of song distribution through the early years of the new century, the heart of the industry became song publishing, which in the 1870s and '80s had centered on the Bowery. As the city's musical theater moved uptown, so did the publishers — first to Union Square around 14th St. and Broadway, and then, in the '90s, to W. 28th St. between Broadway and Fifth Ave.

It was on 28th St. that someone — a freelance writer, some say, while others credit songwriter Monroe Rosenfeld — likened the sound on the street to the clanging of pots and dishes.

Tin Pan Alley. It was perfect. No tin, no pans, no alley. Just like the egg cream, with no eggs and no cream.

Whatever it was called, songwriters and publishers found 20th century America positively dizzy with song, and from Irving Berlin to the Gershwins, most of the great writers stopped off early at Tin Pan Alley.

BY THE TEENS, the public appetite had evolved into a taste for ragtime, albeit in a diluted form like Berlin's 1911 hit "Alexander's Ragtime Band." A new craze was born.

America was also in the mood to dance, and Vernon and Irene Castle became national idols for their graceful way with a fox trot.

Happily, dancing required music, and in 1911 the F.W. Woolworth Co. installed a pipe organ at its flagship store at Fifth Ave. and 40th St. By 1917, Woolworth sold millions of dollars in sheet music a year. Best seller: "I'm Forever Blowing Bubbles," 2.6 million copies.

America was having far too good a time to want it spoiled by a war in Europe, and Tin Pan Alley tried to help national denial by offering tunes like the 1915 hit "I Didn't Raise My Boy to Be a Soldier."

On that April morning in 1917, however, it was clear that peace was no longer an option, and Tin Pan Alley swung four-square behind the war.

There was the occasional poignant note ("Just a Baby's Prayer at Twilight for Her Daddy Over There"), but the dominant tone was belligerence: "America, Here's My Boy," "Hunting the Hun," "Let's All Be Americans Now," "Just Like General Washington Crossed the Delaware, General Pershing Will Cross the Rhine."

Not every song was a call to arms. The day after Armistice Day, the country's best-seller was "Tiger Rag."

Nor did all war songs lack humor ("There'll Be a Hot Time for All the Old Men When the Young Men Go to War") or a conscience ("When the Good Lord Makes a Record of a Hero's Deed, He Draws No Color Line").

All in all, though, the popular music industry was regarded highly enough that the War Industries Board allowed music publishers an exemption from paper rationing. Sheet music was "essential to win the war," ruled the board.

ONCE THAT WAS accomplished, Tin Pan Alley kept rolling. Songwriters started working with jazz in 1917, and by the '20s an explosion in home phonographs and records pushed demand for new songs even higher.

True, record sales often came at the expense of sheet music, and true, some of the music industry would follow the movies to the West Coast. But New York's very own Tin Pan Alley and its successors, like the Brill Building, remain largely uncontested as the primary seedbed for the soundtrack of 20th century America.

CHAPTER 38

AFTER THE FLOOD
The Good Gift Of Water, 1917

The Ashokan Reservoir.

By GEORGE MANNES
Special To The News

FINALLY, NEW YORK had plenty of fresh, clean water for everyone, and all it took was the obliteration of a few upstate towns.

It was Oct. 12, 1917, and Mayor John Purroy Mitchel was formally dedicating the Catskill Aqueduct, a 120-mile engineering marvel — a pipeline from the newly created Ashokan Reservoir that more than doubled the water supply of the thirsty metropolis.

The festivities began at City Hall at noon, with speeches from Mitchel and former Mayor George McClellan, who had launched the Catskill project 10 years earlier to meet the fast-growing city's demands. They continued at the Central Park reservoir at 86th St., where Mitchel turned a handle to debut a glorious fountain — an 80-foot jet of water that the aqueduct had brought down. Finally, at the Sheep Meadow, 15,000 school children and 1,000 Hunter College women commenced a pageant called "The Good Gift of Water."

The great spectacle was to feature dances by Corn, Wheat and Flower Maidens, a singing of "The Star-Spangled Banner" and an appearance by what were billed as "mountain spirits." Unfortunately, the gala celebration of the good gift of water was interrupted by rain, and the maidens and the spirits fled the field in their soaked pink cheesecloths.

It was an ironic moment for a city that had suffered from a water shortage for as long as anyone could remember.

DECENT DRINKING water, in fact, was hard to come by for more than 200 years after Peter Minuit came to Manhattan.

Through the 17th and 18th centuries, New Yorkers relied on rainwater cisterns and public and private wells. Townspeople also drew water from a 48-acre pond called the Collect, located at what is now Foley Square.

But this water was often fouled by dust, privies, cesspools and dead animals. The best available came from what was called the Tea Water spring north of the city, whose population was then concentrated below Canal St. and east of the Collect. Tea Water vendors would fill 130-gallon barrels, then sell water to townspeople by the bucketful.

As the city grew, the water became more obviously hazardous to the public health. Cholera killed 3,500 in 1832, for example. Meanwhile, there wasn't enough of it for firefighting, and great conflagrations destroyed large portions of the city in 1776 and again in 1835.

Several unsuccessful attempts were made at a municipal water system. British engineer Christopher Colles built a reservoir on Broadway between Pearl and White Sts. in 1774 and sought to feed water through mains made of bored logs; the Revolution put an end to this operation. Twenty-five years later, Assemblyman Aaron Burr established the Manhattan Co., sank a well, built a reservoir and installed a 40-mile hollowed-log system of his own. But it never served more than a fraction of the population, and it was widely agreed that the water was terrible anyway. Burr's company subsequently got out of the water business and went into banking instead, becoming Chase Manhattan.

Not until the 1830s, when the population numbered 220,000, did the city begin work on a public system. Rather than sink another well or, as some suggested, draw water from the Bronx River, officials took the advice of civil engineer Col. DeWitt Clinton Jr. and decided to tap the Croton River, more than 40 miles away. Starting in 1837, gangs of Irish immigrants labored to build the Croton system — a dam on the river, an aqueduct to the city, a receiving reservoir where would later sit Central Park's Great Lawn and a distributing reservoir at Fifth Ave. and 42nd St.

The first Croton water started flowing into the city in June 1842. There was a jubilant 5-mile parade in celebration of what was plainly a perpetually inexhaustible water supply — as well as of a new icon dominating New York's landscape and life. For more than 50 years, until it was retired from service and torn down to make way for the New York Public Library, citizens would promenade atop the great stone walls of the four-acre, 24 million-gallon Murray Hill reservoir.

THE CROTON-FED system, which by 1850 included 200 miles of cast-iron pipes, at first supplied nine times more water than anybody thought New York would ever need.

But by 1885 it was already necessary to build a second Croton aqueduct. Then, in 1898, Manhattan and the Bronx and Queens and Brooklyn and Staten Island consolidated into Greater New York; the population was now 10 times what it had been six decades earlier. While Manhattan and the Bronx got Croton water, Queens and Staten Island were relying on wells and Brooklyn drew its water from Long Island. Future planning would have to take the needs of all the boroughs into account.

And so McClellan had initiated construction of the new Catskill system. In 1914, the great Ashokan Reservoir had been completed — with a dam that had flooded over the homes of several thousand upstaters, requiring them to move elsewhere — and now New York City's 6 million were getting a half-billion gallons of water every day.

And plainly, this was going to be plenty of water forever.

THE ASHOKAN RESERVOIR *became inadequate in less than 20 years. It took a Supreme Court battle with the State of New Jersey, but in 1937 the city began a 30-year project to draw water from tributaries of the Delaware River.*

New York's water system currently feeds the city 1.3 billion gallons a day through more than 6,000 miles of pipes, nearly half of which are at least 70 years old.

BIG TOWN BIG TIME

By JAY MAEDER
Daily News Staff Writer

WHO KNEW WHAT the fighting was about? Europe had never done anything but make war for century after century, the English, the French, the Austrians, the Prussians, the Turks, forever grumbling over their incomprehensible sovereignties and suzerainties and pouncing upon any opportunity to pick a fight with anyone. Far across the sea, mud-caked armies had been blowing up the old cities of the old empires since 1914, when some crazed Serb nationalist had shot some visiting Viennese archduke for some reason or another and put all Europe to flame. It wasn't even remotely an American fracas, and America had stayed out of it for nearly three years. In April 1917, when the tides had forced him at last to deliver American boys to the cannons, President Woodrow Wilson was said to have wept.

AND NOW JOHNNY was marching home again, ta ra, ta ra. Johnny had been marching home for months. Johnny had won The War To End All Wars, Johnny had bopped Der Kaiser on der noodle and shown those Boches a thing or two, and now he was demobilized and marching home, and all through 1919 New York City had hosted chest-thumping, bugle-blowing, star-spangled parades for one brave outfit after another. The 8th Trench Mortar Battery. The Sunset Division. The all-black 369th Infantry, famed as the uncommonly valorous "Harlem Hellfighters." The 11th Engineers. The 9th Coast Defense. The 42nd Division. The 77th Division. Finally, late in the summer, the mighty 1st Division was coming home too. First over. Last back. Ta ra. Ta ra.

"The American soldier is the best soldier in the world," said Gen. John Joseph Pershing. "He has no equal, due to the way the American boys are raised. They are taught from infancy that they are the makers of their destiny."

On the morning of Monday the 8th of September, the commander of the American Expeditionary Force sailed into Hoboken's Pier 4, standing ramrod stiff on the bridge of the Leviathan as military seaplanes flew overhead and brass bands played "Home Sweet Home" and guns fired salutes. Black Jack Pershing was the nation's greatest military man since George Washington, hero of Mexico and the Philippines, now the general whose troops had done in six months what the European Allies could not do in 44. Rome, Paris and London had already showered him with victory celebrations; today New York, too, was draped in flags. It was widely expected that Pershing was going to be the sure-thing presidential candidate in 1920. Nobody knew whether he was a Republican or a Democrat, and nobody cared.

A police boat took the general to the Battery. A motorcade carried him first to City Hall to accept the greetings of Mayor John Hylan and Gov. Al Smith and federal dignitaries, then, as confetti and roses cascaded from New York's upper windows, on to receptions and banquets at the Waldorf-Astoria. On Tuesday afternoon in Central Park, 2,000 boy scouts escorted him to the Sheep Meadow, where 50,000 school children were assembled to sing "Over There" and the national

Culver Pictures

CHAPTER 39

NOT SOON FORGET
Soldiers, 1919

anthem. "I wish that every man who went to Europe could be here to see this," Pershing said. Then he kissed the flag and planted a tree.

At 10 Wednesday morning, 8,000 police officers stood at attention along Fifth Ave. from 110th St. down to Washington Square as Black Jack Pershing climbed a police horse called Captain and ordered: "Forward, march!" Down the avenue swept the great parade: Pershing, an honor guard of 3,600 handpicked men from seven divisions, 22,000 regulars from the 1st Division, hundreds of wounded riding trucks, hundreds of women from the Red Cross and various canteen services, tanks, big division guns, mule trains, endless seas of flags.

High overhead, all the way from 110th St. down to 57th, there actually circled an eagle.

THE ILLUSTRATED Daily News, a small paper that had started publishing a few months earlier, invoked Abraham Lincoln's Gettysburg tribute to the nation's fightingmen in its editorial Thursday morning: *The world will little note nor longer remember what*

we say here. It can never forget what they did here.

"The world did not forget," said the Daily News. "Nor can it ever forget the devotion of the men who went overseas to fight for freedom. Long may that memory be kept green!

"We have seen perhaps the last of the great homecomings of the gallant men who so cheerfully risked their lives. But parades will not be necessary to keep alive the thought of them and the gratitude which every American owes to them. But for what they did we should be now menaced with a brutal enemy, powerful enough to destroy our defenses and pitiless enough to loot our land.

"It was the American soldiers who won this war. Don't ever forget that. And don't ever forget to honor Pershing and every man who fought under his command, and to do all you can to see that these men are given not only cheers but practical and visible evidence of their nation's gratitude. For until every man is returned to as good or a better position than that he left, the nation will not have done its duty by them."

NEWS ITEM, Feb. 14, 1921: "Tramping the streets of New York, vainly searching for work, are approximately 17,000 men who less than two years ago made their triumphant entry into America to the accompaniment of hoarse sirens, shrill whistles, the ringing of bells and the fervent shouting of a grateful nation.

"In the lapels of many of these men is the silver button denoting a wound received in action. Yet through some error they are not receiving the compensation that is their due.

"More pitable is the plight of the men — and their number is on the increase daily — who are now giving way to the effects of doses of gas they received two years ago.

"A long and weary process must be experienced before these men can get compensation from the government. Meanwhile, they have no place to go, they have no money with which to pay for food and lodging, with the result that bread lines are growing longer.

"There are from 1,200 to 1,500 new cases being reported every month."

HIDE AND SEEK

Dry Times, 1920

By JAY MAEDER
Daily News Staff Writer

TELL A NEW Yorker not to drink? Why, you might as well have told a New Yorker not to jaywalk. Yet here it was all the same: The Forces of Temperance had somehow had their way out there in the good honest Protestant heartland, flinty farm belt simpletons stewing in their ancient resentments of the wicked libertine city full of sots and harlots and actors and poets and foreigners and who knew what else. Prohibition, groused the sage H.L. Mencken, was "no more than a legal realization of the Methodist's hatred of the civilized man. With all due respect, blah."

Yet here it was. The Anti-Saloon League had been born in 1893 in the cornfields of Ohio. Initially just another bunch of tight-lipped country preachers, 25 years later it was an amazingly sophisticated political action group that had rammed through Congress a constitutional amendment outlawing the manufacture and sale of intoxicating spirits. It took the required 36 states just 13 months to approve the measure; now, on Jan. 16, 1920, it was going to become the law of the land.

The Forces of Temperance couldn't even wait until that date arrived; suddenly, along came something called Wartime Prohibition, which took effect on July 1, 1919. The war had been over for nearly eight months, of course, but the Justice Department explained that the peace treaty had not yet been ratified. On Monday night the 30th of June, New York City witnessed a monumental wake. From gilded cafe to neighborhood pub, drinkers stuck daisies in their lapels, the national symbols of mourning, and set out to drink up their favorite barkeeps' stocks of case goods. Late that afternoon, restaurateurs and hotelmen had received word from Washington that, for now, light wine and 2.75% beer remained acceptable, so no one was completely out of business just yet. Two-seven-five beer was better than no beer, if only marginally.

John Barleycorn, for his part, was no longer permitted to work his depredations.

IN THE BEGINNING it was all just a good-natured game, about like playing hide-and-seek with the truant officer. Of *course* you could still get a belt; all it took was a wink at the barkeep as you called for a glass of sherry or a cup of tea. The city cops weren't much interested in enforcing Wartime Prohibition anyway. Cops didn't like 2.75 beer any more than anybody else did.

But in late August the federals kicked into action, riding through the city in Army trucks, raiding dozens of bars and hotels. That sweep dried things up for a time; still, many establishments chose to stay open, trusting that President Woodrow Wilson would soon annul what one restaurant lawyer, speaking for the many, termed "this unwarranted, absurd and unjustifiable law." On Oct. 27, Wilson did just that. Less than two hours later, the House of Representatives overrode his veto, 176 to 22. In Washington the next afternoon, Internal Revenue Commissioner Daniel Roper telegraphed local agents across the land that vigorous enforcement was to commence forthwith.

Five minutes after the wire was received in New York, 196 agents started fanning out. Thousands of saloons across the city closed their doors at once, 1,800 in Brooklyn alone. On the night of

Oct. 29, two agents invaded a Times Square joint and opened fire, wounding a bartender and a customer who protested he had been sipping only ginger ale.

The fun was over. En masse, in New York City and everywhere else, American citizens said to hell with the law of the land.

EVERYBODY KNEW the recipe for good homebrew: *2 pounds brown sugar, 1 pound raisins, 1 quart corn meal, 3 sliced lemons, 1 yeast cake, 1 gallon water; mix, let stand 30 days, strain.* Everybody knew somebody who knew somebody who could find a bottle of cheap bathtub lightning; maybe it would blind you or kill you, but these were the chances you took. And sometimes you could even lay hands on a bottle of genuine 100-proof bonded whiskey, although it might have a counterfeit tax stamp on it. Obviously the stuff all came from somewhere or another: warehouses, commercial or private stills, maybe Canada. Noted a New York Times reporter, dryly: "Geographies tell us that the St. Lawrence is a long, beautiful river, whose banks are dotted with charming little hamlets."

Fortunately for the drinking classes, the federal government had not seen fit to appropriate sufficient funds for the enforcement machinery; in all America there were just 2,000 revenue agents, most of them making about $25 a week, and the opportunities for self-enrichment were ample. Warned a New York congressman named Fiorello LaGuardia: "In order to enforce Prohibition, it will require a police force of 250,000 men and another force of 250,000 men to police the police." By the time the U.S. formally went dry in January 1920, New York's chief federal Prohibition administrator was already admitting that the illicit production, distribution and consumption of alcohol could never be stopped. For his candor he was removed from his post and replaced by a much sterner man, who several months later concluded the same thing. By May, it was said

that there were more than 30,000 watering holes doing roaring business in the city, probably twice as many as there had been a year earlier. In October, Mayor John Hylan himself was caught attending a booze-drenched dinner at a Sheepshead Bay inn; so unconcerned about this was he that he flatly ignored official demands to appear before a grand jury.

YES, CLEARLY the stuff was coming from somewhere or another. As time went on, it became more difficult not to begin to wonder about the nature of things and what was being wrought upon the land. Late in 1920, a New York stockbroker named Sadler was forced to confess his involvement in a national rum-running ring that paid huge bribes to high-level federal officials in Chicago. "A dirty, slanderous, outrageous lie," fumed Chicago political boss John McLaughlin. Back in New York, meanwhile, on the day after Christmas, Monk Eastman was found shot to death outside the Union Square subway station.

Monk Eastman once had been the city's foremost Jewish gangster, a colorful lad who had reformed, gone off to war and come home a decorated hero. It now appeared that bootlegging's easy profits had lured him back into the life. His killer, it quickly turned out, was a Prohibition agent who had spent Christmas night drinking with him. The agent insisted he had fired in self-defense when Monk got ugly. No one ever believed this.

THOU SHALT NOT!

PROHIBITION

ROLLIN KIRBY

By JAY MAEDER
Daily News Staff Writer

AMERICA'S FIRST piece of air mail, so the story goes, was dispatched from Philadelphia in January 1793, when George Washington handed the French balloonist Jean-Pierre Blanchard a ceremonial letter as Blanchard prepared to go aloft. This was necessarily a to-whom-it-may-concern letter, considering that neither Washington nor Blanchard had any idea where or when the balloon was going to come down. Aside from that, postage stamps hadn't been invented yet anyway, and historians do not always agree on the significance of this event.

More to the point, the nation's first official air mail run was made on Long Island on Sept. 23, 1911, when, as a crowd-wowing air-show stunt, a pilot named Earle Ovington lifted off from Nassau Blvd. in Garden City with a 10-pound sack of properly addressed and postmarked missives bound for Mineola, a few miles away.

At Mineola, Ovington dropped his chugging Bleriot to 16 feet and flung the bundle overboard; it burst apart on impact, scattering cards and letters to the four winds, and the Mineola postmaster had to gallop around fetching them. Several years later, when the United States Post Office Department began seriously laying plans for an airborne mail delivery system, someone decided that it was probably a better idea to land the airplane first and then offload the mailsacks manually.

"The progress being made in the science of aviation encourages the hope that ultimately the regular conveyance of mail by this means may be practicable," said Postmaster General Frank Hitchcock, who had witnessed Ovington's flight and been profoundly impressed. "Such a service, if found feasible, might be established in many districts."

Congress clucked. Why, a fast train could carry the mail from New York to California in four days. Did Hitchcock think a flimsy flying machine could do better than that?

AND SO, what with the war and one thing and another, it was seven years before there were regularly scheduled runs on the first U.S. air mail route, between Belmont Park on Long Island and the Polo Grounds in Washington, D.C., via Philadelphia.

The war wasn't over yet, and the Post Office was using planes and pilots borrowed from the Army when service was inaugurated shortly before noon on May 15, 1918. There were 204 miles between points, and the Post Office was guaranteeing three-hour delivery.

At the Washington field, President Woodrow Wilson and polar explorer Robert Peary and other dignitaries assembled to watch Lt. George Boyle climb into his souped-up Curtiss Jenny. At Belmont, another distinguished crowd applauded as Lt. Torrey Webb readied for take-off. To the great joy of later generations of philatelists, the Post Office had issued special 24-cent stamps for the occasion, and they were misprinted.

Boyle, it turned out, wasn't much of a flier, and he greatly embarrassed his commanders when he accidentally flew off in the wrong direction and then crash-landed in Maryland. Webb, for his part, made it to Philadelphia on schedule and without incident and handed his mail off to Lt. James Edgerton for the Washington leg. Meanwhile, Lt. Paul Culver gave up waiting for Boyle at the Philadelphia stopover, headed for Belmont and in mid-afternoon delivered New York City's first air mail. It was Philadelphia air mail, not Washington air mail, but it was still air mail.

August Belmont's track remained the Air Mail Service's official New York terminus for another year or so, and mail planes became familiar sights as they landed there every afternoon, usually in the middle of the races.

PARTICULARLY after the war ended and legions of ex-Army fliers started signing on with the Post Office, swaggering, scarved-and-goggled, devil-may-care mail pilots fast became darlings of New York nightlife, lightning riders of a modern Pony Express, what-the-hell romantics who lived hard and not infrequently died young. In July 1919, the New York-Cleveland-Chicago route opened up, via a lonely refueling stop at Bellefonte, Pa. "Hell Stretch" was what the pilots called the treacherous run over the Alleghenies, where fogs and gales and blinding rains brought many a luckless ship to grief. Twenty men or so had already perished when, in the late summer of 1920, four more men died flying the mail in a single two-week period.

Federal officialdom was appalled by these mounting fatalities — at precisely the moment ambitious postal officials were pushing for more congressional funding for coast-to-coast service. The trans-continental run had long been envisioned: From New York beyond even Chicago now, to Omaha, to North Platte, to Cheyenne, Salt Lake City, Reno, San Francisco. If the air mail could beat the railroads, its future was assured.

At 7 a.m. on Sept. 8, pilot Randolph Page revved up his DeHaviland at Long Island's Hazelhurst Field, which had replaced Belmont Park as the Post Office's New York operations center, and took the mail to Chicago. There, another man carried it on to Salt Lake City, and from there a third and a fourth went on to Nevada and California.

The epic journey across the Continental Divide, the Medicine Bow Mountains, the desert and the high sierra ended on the afternoon of the 11th, taking 76 daylight hours across the country — a full day faster than the fastest train.

Amid the celebrations, the Post Office announced that very soon the Air Mail Service would start flying by night as well, and would cut that 76 hours in half.

Well, no one had ever flown nights before. There were no radio beacons yet. There were no lighted airfields. And it was almost winter. The men of the Pony Express figured this sounded like their kind of job.

IN FEBRUARY 1921, Air Mail Service fliers made it from New York to California in 36 hours and back in 33. By mid-1923, coast-to-coast was a standard 28 hours.

IN THE CLOUDS FOR UNCLE SAM

Air Mail, 1920

By JAY MAEDER
Daily News Staff Writer

THINGS FELL apart. The center could not hold. Anarchy was loosed upon the world. In the combustible autumn of 1919, scarce was there to be found a New York City working man who was not on strike. Motormen. Longshoremen. Harbor pilots. Railroad boatmen, milk wagon drivers, moving picture projectionists, laundry men, cigar makers, coffee packers. Eighteen separate strikes were in progress in the month of October. The entire Atlantic coast was shut down. Foodstuffs piled up rotting on the piers.

All this was the work of agitators, of course. That was plain to see. Oh, there was no doubt about that. Labor unionists and radicals. Communists, Socialists, Bolsheviks, Wobblies, whatever they were called. It was all one and the same. Reds. Scruffy, bomb-throwing foreigners. In the Pennsylvania coalfields and the Indiana steel mills and the Seattle shipyards, they weren't even bothering to conceal themselves. "Rise against the dogs in uniform, overthrow the puppets!" boomed their broadsides. "We will stand or fall with the Bolsheviks!" cried the Russia-loving Emma Goldman. "Every strike is a small revolution!" thundered International Workers of the World boss Big Bill Haywood. If they didn't like the United States of America, why didn't they just go back where they came from? "The American people will not exchange the solid foundations of their social order for any of these fantastic programs," pledged Secretary of War Newton Baker.

A few months earlier, an alert New York postal clerk had found three dozen bombs awaiting delivery to the likes of John D. Rockefeller and J.P. Morgan. In Washington, Attorney General A. Mitchell Palmer himself narrowly escaped being maimed by a mail bomb that made it to his home. All through the summer there were bloody race riots in New York and two dozen other cities. It was clear, authorities said, that disaffected workers were being inflamed by the Red troublemakers. In Congress there were resolutions to restrict immigration. Deep inside Palmer's Justice Department, a young attorney named John Edgar Hoover was compiling great lists of dangerous aliens and their dupes and stooges.

Across the U.S., authorities struck hard on Saturday night, Nov. 8, 1919. In hotbed New York City alone there were 7,800 known Reds, and police and state troopers rounded up 1,000 of them that first night, smashed their offices, confiscated their books. Only about 25 of these desperados were actually charged with anything, but federal authorities quickly made it known that a mammoth armed revolt had been crushed barely in the nick of time. "The Communist Party has declared a state of war against the United States government," declared Chief U.S. Magistrate William McAdoo. **SECRET CITIZENS OF RUSSIAN SOVIET REPUBLIC**, the newspapers screamed; **LEADERS OF RED ARMY HELD FOR GRAND JURY. NATION TO CRUSH COMMUNISTS. AMERICAN LEGION JOINS NATIONWIDE WAR.** Raids continued, turning up subversive literature here, suspected bomb-making materials there. Three days before Christmas, as New Yorkers jeered from the docks, Emma Goldman and her crony Alexander Berkman and 247 other Red undesirables were put aboard an Army transport dubbed The Bolshevik Ark and shipped back to Europe.

At 9 p.m. on New Year's Day, 1920, Attorney General Palmer directed another mass raid on the Red nests of New York and 32 other cities, and this time nearly 1,700 men and women were picked up in New York and New Jersey. Much to the annoyance of the federals, some of those brought in proved to be actual American citizens who couldn't be deported and seemed to be at least semi-free to espouse any political views they pleased.

ON MAY DAY, 1920, hundreds of soldiers and 11,000 city cops stood guard on the streets and outside the homes of prominent citizens, lest Red assassins start running amok. The demonstrators, though, spent the day quietly protesting the imprisonment of

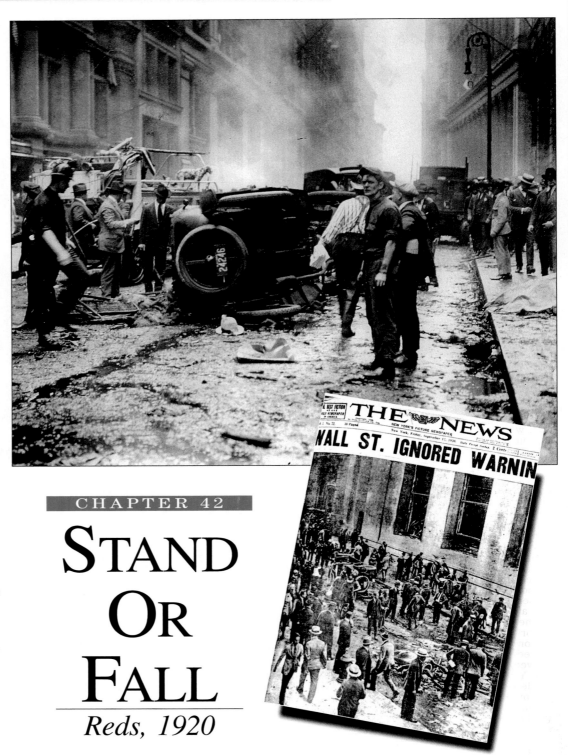

CHAPTER 42

STAND OR FALL

Reds, 1920

Socialist leader Eugene Debs, and there were no discernibly criminal occurrences. Nothing much happened on the Fourth of July, either.

Labor Day was another story. Four thousand Brooklyn Rapid Transit workers were striking again, and they marched through Prospect Park with 60,000 supporters from the Central Labor Union of Brooklyn and Queens, and shots were fired, and policemen were beaten up and a Flatbush Ave. trolley was attacked by a mob. This happened on the same day that 20 Lithuanian radicals were charged in Illinois with conspiring to wreck a train, and hordes of Italian Red Guards seized factories in Milan, Turin and Genoa. It was felt in some quarters that perhaps there was a connection.

Then, on Sept. 16, just 10 days later, Wall Street blew up.

PARTIES UNKNOWN had parked a horse and wagon at Broad and Wall Sts., just outside J.P. Morgan & Co. The wagon was full of explosives and heavy window weights. At one minute past noon a mighty blast rocked

towers, shattered windows, overturned vehicles and flung bodies through the air. Thirty-nine persons were killed, more than 200 injured.

Never for a minute was it believed that the Wall Street horror was anything but a terrorist assault upon American soil by such skulking cowards as had once bombed the Chicago Haymarket, and a national dragnet went out for the fugitives. Suspects were picked up all over the country as the anti-Red hysteria mounted. Police threw up guards around Penn Station and other public buildings. Ellis Island went on alert. No arrests were ever made.

Authorities kept unmasking Red plots all through 1921. **NEW YORK ANARCHISTS REORGANIZED**, the papers said. **REDS OF AMERICA UNITED UNDER ONE HEAD. AGENTS SOWING CLASS HATRED, DISSENSION, SABOTAGE.** One million immigrants continued to arrive in the U.S. every year. At least 15 million more, warned U.S. Immigration Commissioner Frederick Wallis, were certain to come unless Congress did something.

BIG TOWN BIG TIME™

By DICK SHERIDAN
Daily News Staff Writer

'**WE CAN** sit here and talk engineering figures for a year," Al Smith said. "We can draw plans for five years. But if there isn't a healthy, vigorous determination on the part of localities and organizations and people generally in the Port District to make some changes in the old-fashioned, worn-out, dilapidated ways of doing business in this port, the figures would amount to nothing."

The year was 1921. Smith, between terms as New York governor, was one of 12 commissioners of the newly minted Port of New York Authority, an agency he and New Jersey Gov. Walter Edge had created to oversee the operations of 770 miles of waterfront that, by the luck of geography, belonged to two different states and which for years had been administered by dozens of different communities.

New York and New Jersey had agreed as early as 1834 to bear joint responsibility for the splendid waterways they shared, but nothing much had ever come of that pact. In 1898, one of the principal reasons that Greater New York was consolidated had been to bring order to the port's chaos, and nothing much had happened then either. Two decades later it was time at last to look to the future.

The port was the nation's principal gateway for foreign trade, the region's single greatest economic asset. But terminal facilities were not unified, and wasteful routings and rehandlings delayed passengers and goods. Now, finally, New York and New Jersey would address these problems together in a modern, businesslike fashion. On Saturday, April 30, 1921, the nation's first large public authority was signed into being.

As it happened, 125,000 marine workers went out on strike that same weekend, putting half a million other people out of work, tying up 3,600 American ships and paralyzing shipping on both coasts. The new agency began its life as nearly 300 vessels sat idly in the Port of New York.

THE WASTEFUL and uncoordinated operation at the port was the result of 300 years of willy-nilly growth and technological advances and self-centered profiteering in seven bays, four rivers, four estuaries and numerous creeks.

Water trade had formed the underpinning of New York City since the days of the Dutch West India Co. Furs were floated down the Hudson River to Manhattan; European goods sailed in across the Atlantic. Trade was even responsible for adding to the ground on which the burgeoning town stood; when wooden ships burned in their berths, stones and dirt were thrown atop their sunken hulks and new land was formed — and so it was that old lower Manhattan soon doubled in width. Water St., which early on formed the island's eastern shoreline, moved ever inland.

In the years after the Revolutionary War and the withdrawal of the British from the city, the

Big two-sided river: The Hudson docks and Jersey beyond, circa World War I.

CORBIS-BETTMAN

CHAPTER 43

GATEWAY
Port Of Many Ports, 1921

American economy slumped — then boomed. New York thrived. With trade no longer restricted to England, the Empress of China was the first ship to set sail from New York for that Asian land in February 1784.

Wheat was the city's chief export. The price rose from 75 cents a bushel in 1785 to $2.10 in 1800. New York grew rich.

Meanwhile, there had been little planning for the development of the waterfront. So in 1798 the Common Council was authorized by the state Legislature to tidy up the problem and rebuild the docks and wharves from Whitehall Slip to the Fly Market. The big job didn't slow down business a bit — and the bustle only grew after Robert Fulton built his North River Steam Boat in 1807 and the Erie Canal opened in 1825, cutting shipping time from Buffalo and the Great Lakes to the city from 20 days to eight.

The 2-mile stretch of South St. from the Battery to Corlears Hook became famed around the world as "the Street o' Ships," and people strolling its bumpy cobblestones walked under the bowsprits of clipper ships and Liverpool packets.

Though South St. epitomized the waterfront in the public's imagination, other sections of shoreline were developing — in Brooklyn, Staten Island and a number of New Jersey communities. Ferries, scows, barges and lighters scurried across the waters, moving thousands of passengers and tons of goods to and from docks and warehouses and ships.

South St. remained dominant until the last decades of the 1800s, when newer and bigger oceangoing ships requiring deeper waters than

those offered along the East River began steaming up the Hudson and tying up at West Side piers instead.

At the middle of the 19th century, New York's port handled more goods and passengers than all other ports in the nation combined. As the new century arrived, it was the busiest port in the world — and would remain so for another 50 years.

BUT THE constant growth and evolving technologies throughout the 19th century had caused ongoing problems between New York and New Jersey. The two states argued over which should license steamboats on the Hudson, where the boundary line between the two lay in the river and other matters such as waste disposal and the calculation of freight rates and charges.

The disputes came to a head in 1911, when both states named commissions to study the rail freight rates being charged by the 11 privately owned railroads that served the port.

At the suggestion of New Jersey's Gov. Edge and with the blessing of the Interstate Commerce Commission, those two bodies were combined into a single Joint Commission on Port and Harbor Development, which began its work in 1917, just as the U.S. was entering the European War.

Great logistical difficulties arose as tons of materials and thousands of men passed through the port on their way to the war, underscoring the need for change. These woes led the commissioners to recommend the formation of a permanent corporation-style interstate agency to develop and improve the operation of the port.

And so, in April 1921, the new Port of New York Authority became responsible for a 1,500-square-mile Port District that crossed many boundaries — up the Hudson to Tarrytown, westward to Paterson, Newark and Elizabeth, southward to Perth Amboy, eastward to the Connecticut state line.

Its primary goal in the beginning was to resolve the question of freight rates that in 1911 had precipitated the authority's formation. Fearing loss of independence and profits, though, the railroads blocked that move. So far as that went, the Port Authority never achieved a single one of its original goals, which also included a trans-Hudson rail tunnel and a huge rail junction in the Bronx.

But by that time the railroads' power was on the wane as trucks and cars began to play a greater role in commerce. The Port Authority turned its attention to building bridges between Staten Island and New Jersey; the Outerbridge Crossing was named for Eugenius Outerbridge, the agency's first chairman. By the end of the 1920s, the Port Authority had taken custody of the newly opened Holland Tunnel. A few years later it built the George Washington Bridge.

As the years passed, as New Yorkers took to their automobiles and turned their eyes to the road, many of them lost sight of the waters that, shut off by guardian rings of highways, had started it all.

By DENNIS WEPMAN
Special to The News

HE WAS THE most powerful man in Harlem, leader of the greatest black mass movement in American history. At his peak he claimed 4 million followers worldwide. On Jan. 12, 1922, a deputy U.S. marshal and a postal inspector showed up at his W. 129th St. apartment and charged the Emperor of the Kingdom of Africa, Grand Sachem of the African Legion and Knight Commander of the Sublime Order of the Nile with mail fraud.

Marcus Aurelius Garvey — as Marcus Moziah Garvey ambitiously renamed himself at about the time he founded the United Negro Improvement Association in his native Jamaica in 1914 — had initially come to the United States to join Booker T. Washington's great crusade to uplift the black race. Washington, however, died before Garvey arrived, and instead, in 1916, the 29-year-old reformer set up shop in Harlem.

Many thousands of blacks, from the West Indies and the American South, were migrating to New York between 1910 and 1920, particularly during the labor shortages of the war, and the UNIA's message of black unity, pride and economic self-sufficiency quickly took root and flourished among a disaffected and bitter people. "We've got to teach the American Negro blackness," Garvey preached. "Black ideals, black industry, black United States and black religion." By black United States, he meant a territory he personally intended to carve out of West Africa. Into that ancestral homeland he would resettle millions — "Blacks of the entire universe," he cried, "linked up with one determination, that of liberating themselves and freeing the great country of Africa that is ours by right."

At the UNIA's first conference, a 54-article Declaration of Rights proclaimed all the world's blacks Free Citizens of Africa and named Marcus Garvey their Provisional President-General.

"The new Negro desires nationhood," he declared. "We are 400 million people asking for liberty." Garvey's magnetic personality, passionate eloquence and majestic back-to-Africa vision drew thousands of Harlemites to his many rallies, and showy parades brought them cheering to the streets as he passed them in a shiny Packard, fabulously caped and plumed, legions of crisply uniformed dukes and earls and barons and viscounts and princes marching behind him. Within a year, the UNIA had branches in 38 states and six foreign countries. By 1921, Garvey claimed 418 chapters around the globe and another 400 awaiting charters.

Other black leaders were far from impressed. W.E.B. Du Bois of the National Association for the Advancement of Colored People put Garvey's

CHAPTER 44

BLACK STAR

Marcus Garvey, 1922

following at more like 18,000 than 4 million, and publicly branded him an opportunist and a charlatan. Garvey went on tirelessly creating new organizations: the African Communities League, the Universal African Legion, the Order of the Nile, the Black Cross Nurses, the Black Cross Flying Corps. He was publishing the influential newspaper Negro World. He was building a hotel and a chain of restaurants, laundries and grocery markets.

And he was running the Black Star Line. The all-black steamship company had been launched in 1919, 24 vessels that would ship freight between Africa and the rest of the world as well as transport Garvey's flocks to the motherland. "The Black Star Line presents to every black man, woman and child the opportunity to climb the great ladder of industrial and commercial success," Garvey pledged, guaranteeing huge

profits as his followers clamored to buy millions of dollars worth of Black Star stock.

VERY SOON it all came to nothing. The League of Nations, not altogether surprisingly, paid no attention to Garvey's demand that France and England "pack their bags and clear out of Africa" and turn their colonies over to him. Indeed, Liberia, where he hoped to build a base of operations, barred him from entry.

But these were the least of his problems. His penchant for flowing robes, flaming red headgear and grand titles had long dismayed black moderates who considered him an embarrassment; "Marcus Garvey," wrote the NAACP's Du Bois, "is without doubt the most dangerous enemy of the Negro race in America and in the world." Together with Cyril Briggs, chief of the African Black Brotherhood and editor of Crusader magazine, Du Bois organized a campaign against Garvey. The Black Star Line, they reported, had never consisted of more than two or three leaky, boiler-blowing old tubs — and at least one of them appeared to be wholly nonexistent anyway — and they accused Garvey of grossly misrepresenting the firm in his stock sales. The federal government, no little alarmed by Garvey to begin with, was quick to take action.

There was no evidence that Garvey had lined his own pockets, or intended to; but when he went to trial in February 1923, a public inspection of the Black Star books made it plain that he was no businessman. There were clear improprieties, lost receipts, in one instance a $476,000 chunk that simply couldn't be accounted for. "Evidently the American Negroes have no more genius for operating a merchant marine than has Uncle Sam," noted the Morning Telegraph. The fact was that Garvey had lost many thousands of his followers' dollars and run the storied Black Star Line into liquidation, and he was quickly convicted.

Facing five years behind bars, he appealed all the way to the Supreme Court, meanwhile continuing to stage rallies and parades across Harlem, continuing to dream of the great exodus to whatever lands he imagined someone was going to give him. "With Liberia, Abyssinia, Sierra Leone and the French Ivory Coast, we could form the United States of Africa," he was still musing as late as August 1924.

He lost his appeal. In February 1925 he reported to federal prison. Two years later, President Calvin Coolidge, in a tacit acknowledgment that Garvey's prosecution had been to some degree politically motivated, commuted the sentence. The UNIA already had fallen apart, and Garvey left the United States. In 1940, the Emperor of the Kingdom of Africa, Grand Sachem of the African Legion and Knight Commander of the Sublime Order of the Nile died in obscurity in London.

By JAY MAEDER
Daily News Staff Writer

HE WAS THE Bambino, the Babe, the Sultan of Swat, the most amazing slugger baseball had ever seen. He was the New York Yankees' single greatest draw. He was the sole reason little kids still believed in baseball players after the 1919 Chicago series-fixing disgrace. Now, in the spring of 1923, the sports scribes had already written his obituaries. At age 29, it was agreed, George Herman Ruth was washed up.

Once upon a time a fan had literally dropped dead of excitement just watching Babe play. All through unbelievable 1920 and 1921, huge crowds had erupted into bedlam at the sight of him. Then, suddenly, it was all over: Babe Ruth was a bad drunk, a crazy gambler, an out-of-control wild man who got thrown out of games. "A once mighty but now muddled monarch," one of the papers sadly said of him. It was the old story, and New York had seen it many times: Fat life, fat head.

For nearly a year, the two colonels, Jake Ruppert and Til Huston, had been building themselves a new ballpark, the world's largest, across the Harlem River from the Polo Grounds; it was going to seat more than 60,000 fans, and Wednesday the 18th of April was going to be glorious. The Yankees had been exhibitioning through the Deep South for several weeks, and Babe had been notably listless, noncommittal, apparently uninterested in hitting the ball. The sportswriters were all shaking their heads. "The erstwhile homerun king," they called him, as Yankee Stadium readied for Opening Day.

THERE WERE NOT many people New Yorkers had ever loved more than they loved Babe Ruth. By the time the Yankees bought him from the Boston Red Sox for the '20 season he already was a legend, a phenomenal batter who had hit 29 home runs in the 140-game 1919 Boston season. In Yankee pinstripes, Babe the Ball Killer was already at 29 his first three months out.

The Polo Grounds, Monday the 19th of July, 1920: Second game of a Chicago White Sox double header. Fourth inning. Twenty-eight thousand fans leap up screaming as Chicago pitcher Dick Kerr gives up Babe Ruth's 30th home run. Ninth inning. Strike one. Strike two. Kerr fires again, and into the bleachers goes Babe's 31st. Pandemonium. Bedlam.

Actually, New York ended up losing the game to Chicago, but at such an epic moment it was hard to care. "Well, you can't accuse Kerr of failing to treat me pretty decently," the King of Baseball said modestly the next morning. George Herman Ruth had grown up dirt poor, and he was not a pretentious man at all. "Yesterday smashed the record," he acknowledged. "It is particularly satisfying that it was smashed good and plenty." He confided: "I was more nervous over the 30th home run than the 31st. The first was a record-breaker. The second was just a home run, that's all."

Some stat-keepers contended that, in truth, there existed a 40-something homerun record somewhere in the minor leagues. On Sept. 29, though, when the Yankees ended their season in Philadelphia by taking both games of a double header with the Athletics, Babe hit his 54th homer of the season and there was hardly an argument about anything. Babe himself was a little disappointed. He had predicted 55.

He got his 55 the next season — and then, incredibly, four more after that. By now Babe Ruth

CHAPTER 45

AND SOMETIMES CONNECT

The Babe Comes Back, 1923

was the highest-salaried player in baseball, worth every penny of his $1,000 a week. He was the idol of millions, and life got no better than the life the Sultan of Swat was living in the city of New York in the year 1921.

DOWN IT ALL crashed. The Bambino had a very bad '22 season. For starters, he drew a month's suspension for insubordination, and that effectively kept him from setting any new records. Then, in May, he ran amok at the Polo Grounds; enraged at being called out as he sought to stretch a single into a double, he flung a fistful of dirt into an umpire's face and was ordered out of the game — then, loudly booed as he trudged to the dugout, he vaulted into the stands and charged one of the hecklers, who fled for his life as bystanders held the Babe back.

A month later, in Cleveland, he was suspended again after a near-fistfight with another umpire. "There is no player in the American League who can call one of my umpires names like that and conduct himself in such a disgraceful manner on the ballfield and get away with it," ruled League boss Ban Johnson. "I want Babe Ruth to

understand that right now. And he is going to behave himself, or I'll keep him out of the game the rest of the summer." Babe was contrite, but he didn't play good baseball for the rest of the year. In that fall's World Series, the New York Giants spectacularly humiliated him. He finished the season with 35 home runs.

At a banquet at year's end, state Sen. Jimmy Walker publicly pleaded with George Herman Ruth to go on the wagon and clean himself up, and Babe got to his feet and sobbed like a child, pledging to regain the respect of his fans and fellow players.

Early in April 1923, a 19-year-old shopgirl named Delores Dixon cried rape and sued him for $50,000.

The dark headlines and mounting legal difficulties dogged him throughout the spring-training circus season down South. He was well off his game and everyone could see it; in New Orleans the Pelicans made a fool out of him, in Tulsa he whiffed again and again and the locals hissed him. In Jackson, Miss., he didn't play at all, electing instead to address a gathering of high school students. He urged the kids to stay in shape. He warned them against smoking cigarettes. He exhorted them to give everything they had to everything they did.

"I just try my best," Babe Ruth said. "And sometimes I connect squarely."

THE PAPERS PUT Yankee Stadium's Opening Day crowd at 65,000; some observers guessed it was more like 74,000; certainly it was the largest ballpark crowd in history, and at least 15,000 more fans were turned away at the gates. Gov. Al Smith was there to throw out the ball. John Philip Sousa himself had come to lead the Seventh Regiment Band.

Joe Dugan hits a single that brings Bob Shawkey home. New York 1, Boston 0. Third inning. Dugan and Whitey Witt on base. At bat: George Herman Ruth, forlorn has-been.

The crashing homer, long and low into the right field bleachers, just barely clearing the screen, was the Babe's most powerful drive ever. New York 4. Boston managed to pick up a run in the seventh. Otherwise, Yankee Stadium was now officially christened, good and plenty.

Stunningly out of his long slump, Babe Ruth the next day hit a sixth-inning triple that triggered an 8-2 New York triumph over Boston. On Friday the 20th he was the day's big crusher again, coming up with three decisive wallops, including the great slam at the bottom of the ninth — with three balls and two strikes — that brought in two runs and the 4-3 win. On Saturday the 21st, the Yankees beat Boston again, 7-6.

On Sunday in the outfield, Babe muffed a fly that probably resulted directly in the Washington Senators' 4-3 win over the Yankees, the club's first loss in their new park. But that was baseball for you.

A week later, Delores Dixon withdrew her complaint and confessed that she was an extortionist who had never laid eyes on Babe Ruth.

"I am glad that the public knows I am vindicated," the Babe said. "I don't like to have anyone think such harmful things about me."

*L*ater in 1923, the New York Yankees won their first World Series and Babe Ruth was named the American League's most valuable player. In 1925, the sports press declared him washed up again.

Rea Irvin's enduring Eustace Tilley

By DENNIS WEPMAN
Special to the News

WHEN THE SLIM weekly with the mysterious cover hit the newsstands in February 1925, it was not an immediate hit. Priced at 15 cents, The New Yorker sold 15,000 copies. Three weeks later the circulation had dropped to 12,000. By April, it was down to 8,000. The humor magazine that had promoted itself as the ultimate in urban sophistication — "not edited for the old lady in Dubuque" — was apparently not being edited for New Yorkers either.

Creator and editor Harold Ross was a rough-edged Westerner, Colorado-born, Utah-reared, an itinerant newspaper reporter who had gone on to edit the Army paper Stars and Stripes in Paris during the European War. He came to New York when he was discharged, edited the American Legion Weekly for five years, briefly edited the humor magazine Judge, and then turned down an offer from Cosmopolitan in order to start up a magazine of his own. With a provincial's awestruck fascination with the glamor of the metropolis, Ross had developed the idea of a journal that would reflect the jazzy and cynical spirit of New York City in the 1920s — "the color, the tang, the anecdote, and the chat in all the sophisticated circles of New York," as an early ad put it. The New Yorker, Ross declared, would be "a magazine avowedly for a metropolitan audience."

Awkward and brash, with little education and less polish, Ross was anything but a sophisticated metropolitan himself. For a hick, though, he was sure he knew what the metropolitan reader wanted. And, as James Thurber, one of the writers Ross made famous, said of him, he had "a magic gift for surrounding himself with some of the best talent in America, despite his own literary and artistic limitations."

For two years Ross had prowled the city looking for someone to finance the venture. Over lunch at the Algonquin Hotel with a circle of literary friends that included Stars and Stripes alumnus Alexander Woollcott, he finally found a backer in Raoul Fleischmann, whose family

CHAPTER 46

NOT IN UTAH ANYMORE

The New Yorker, 1925

fortune included a bakery chain and a yeast company. Together they formed F-R (for Fleischmann-Ross) Publishing Corp., with $25,000 from F and $20,000 from R.

The talent Ross surrounded himself with and bullied into shape was stellar. His first art director was the popular illustrator Rea Irvin, who created The New Yorker's look, laid out its format, designed its headline typeface and drew the legendary first cover, showing a bored 19th-century dandy examining a butterfly through a monocle. Although the symbolism was a little obscure for a magazine seeking to project an image of vigor and currency, the dandy became a trademark of the journal, if not for the city. Later in the year, humorist Corey Ford wrote a series of advertisements describing an imaginary magazine publisher he called Eustace Tilley, and the name became inseparably attached to Irvin's fop. In time, Ross had his private office telephone listed under Tilley's name.

Under Irvin's direction, The New Yorker was

to revolutionize the visual humor of the era, refining the crude illustrated jokes of Judge, Puck and London's Punch into pointed one-line gag cartoons. The graphic wit of such cartoonists as Gluyas Williams, Peter Arno, George Price, Saul Steinberg, Helen Hokinson and Charles Addams set a standard unmatched elsewhere. The fiction and criticism in the new magazine were no less influential: Woollcott, George S. Kaufman, Robert Benchley, Ogden Nash and Dorothy Parker contributed regularly to the first issues, and shortly Thurber and E.B. White joined the staff to crystallize the breezy, literate editorial style that became the magazine's personal voice.

Stylish as that voice ultimately became, though, it took a little while for Ross to determine what he wanted his magazine to be. Two months after it launched, it was losing $8,000 every week, and Ross and his little band seriously considered giving it up. They cut the budget drastically; in September, Fleischmann hesitantly decided to pump more money into an advertising campaign in the city papers. Then Ross published an article that provided the first glimmer of hope for The New Yorker's survival.

"Why We Go To Cabarets, A Post-Debutante Explains" ran in the Nov. 26 issue, a sharp, sarcastic piece that knocked the boring young men who hung around at deb parties. Written by Ellin Mackay, who was soon to marry Irving Berlin, it struck just the right note of independence for a generation of young women who preferred nightclubs to stuffy Social Register affairs, and it spoke to exactly the market Ross had been looking for. No longer written for Broadway, The New Yorker now found its true audience in the Smart Set on Park and Fifth Aves. Mackay's article attracted the attention of the daily press and made front-page news nationally.

Ross' journal continued to change from issue to issue, under the restless direction of its blustering editor. Like New York itself, it constantly redefined the image of the city it sought to mirror. The path was set; inside 10 years it had 62,000 readers in the city, outselling its rivals Vanity Fair and Vogue by a wide margin. Surprisingly to Ross and Fleischmann, The New Yorker's circulation was far larger outside the city. Intended for Gotham's upper crust, the New Yorker image appealed to people all over the country. Probably even old ladies in Dubuque.

By DAVID HINCKLEY
Daily News Staff Writer

THERE WAS NO indication when John B. Gambling arrived at WOR's New York studio on this chilly winter morning that he would handle anything other than his usual engineering for the three-year-old radio station.

But fate sometimes gets bored with the way things are expected to be, and on this day — some say late February 1925, some say March 8 — the hour for the morning exercise show was approaching and the regular announcer, alas, had a serious case of laryngitis.

So John B. cleared his throat and filled the breach, calling cadence for the exercises that comprised the backbone of a typical morning radio program in the Roaring Twenties.

By the time his hour had lapsed, the British-born Gambling's clear, precise diction had inspired listeners to more pushups than ever before, and he was promptly promoted from probationary engineer to morning host — New York City's first real morning radio personality.

ORIGINALLY DRAWN to the fledgling radio field by tales of David Sarnoff's crucial turn at the telegraph key when the Titanic went down, Gambling was a wireless operator for the Royal Navy in World War I when he caught a glimpse of New York, fell in love and settled in.

Radio was a new frontier on all fronts the morning Gambling suddenly became the exercise man. While the New York area had 10 radio stations as early as 1922, they were all on two wavelengths and had to share time. This arrangement quickly proved unsatisfactory because by the end of 1924, the country was up to 3 million receivers — a number that would grow tenfold in the next decade — and clamoring for more programming on them.

Gambling was among the first to see radio moving way beyond exercise calls. To his own show he added personal chatter, news headlines, a house combo and other elements, making him a morning fixture in the city's radio-equipped households. Concerning the exercises, incidentally, it was said among Gambling's friends that he himself rarely flexed so much as a finger.

But then, that was already the beauty of radio: It didn't matter. On radio, a 4-foot-6 woman with the right voice could be a leggy 6-foot blonde. A couple of middle-age white guys named Gosden and Correll could become Amos and Andy, soon the most popular act in radio history.

And radio itself was about to become the primary in-home entertainment medium of the nation — a medium to crown stars and elect Presidents.

BUT STATION OWNERS still weren't quite sure what to do with their new toy, so they mostly did what everyone else did: a lot of music, a little talking.

On the average day around 1925, owners of a receiving set might hear The Gold Dust Twins singing novelty numbers in Negro dialect on WEAF. They could hear a mystery heartthrob who called himself The Silver-Masked Tenor. The Happiness Boys, Jones and Hare, cracked jokes

KEEP FIT WITH *Gambling's* GYM CLASSES
LOOK FIT WITH *Clemons Clothes*
1409 BROADWAY at 39th STREET
66 NASSAU ST.   152 SIXTH AVE.

Tune in on
WOR
Continuous Every Morning
6:45 SUN TO 8:00
JOHN B. GAMBLING
MUSICAL DIRECTOR

CHAPTER 47

THE BIG BROADCAST

On The Air, 1925

and sang happy songs with punchlines like "How do ya doodle-doodle-doodle-doodle-do?" The Ipana Troubadours played light pop, the Atwater-Kent Hour played serious classics and the Cities Service Concerts played even more serious classics.

The Red-Headed Music Maker, Wendell Hall, regularly came through to sing his signature "It Ain't Gonna Rain No More." The A&P Gypsies played exotic music under the direction of Harry Horlick, who had fled Lenin. Nils Granlund gave melodramatic readings of Kipling poems. Roxy and his Gang on WEAF were primitive pioneers of the ensemble radio cast. The first important radio commentator, H.V. Kaltenborn, was already on his fourth station by 1925 (WJZ, WEAF, WAHG, WOR).

"Coast to Coast on a Bus" featured a large cast of children riding the White Rabbit Bus Line cross-country, listening to hymns, sermons and a heartwarming story. "The Eveready Hour," an

early variety show, delivered into America's living room Will Rogers talking politics and D.W. Griffith talking movies.

CLEARLY, something was in the air. Radio was growing so rapidly in 1925 that the courts still had not sorted out who invented it, or at least who invented which pieces.

Candidates included Nikola Tesla, who demonstrated radio at the 1893 World's Fair in St. Louis; Guglielmo Marconi, who in 1901 was sending wireless messages across the ocean; Reginald Fessenden, who in 1900 was sending voices and music, not just dits and dots, and Lee De Forest, whose transmitter some thought resembled Fessenden's a little too closely.

However wireless technology came together, the government commandeered all of it for the duration of World War I. But after the war it had been put up for grabs, and the first commercial radio stations were born — starting, most say, with KDKA in Pittsburgh.

Westinghouse started selling radio receivers for $10 and was so pleasantly shocked by the popularity of these novelties that it built radio stations to supply programming. Thus was born the first big New York station, WJZ, which launched in October 1921 and soon made the first broadcast of a theatrical production and a running account of a World Series game.

When WOR arrived in 1922, it alternated day and night hours with WJZ.

Meanwhile, AT&T was hurrying to join the game, and by early 1922 it had built WBAY, high atop the AT&T building at 24 Walker St. Unfortunately, when the switch was pulled, the signal was absorbed by the building. So WBAY was moved to 463 West St., where it signed on as WEAF.

WEAF's first innovation was profound: At 5:15 p.m. on Aug. 28, 1922, the Queensboro Corp. pitched apartment houses in Jackson Heights, and radio commercials were born.

Sales were bullish, and so was the radio market into which John B. Gambling stepped. Outfits like Westinghouse also had begun to see the possibility of networks — simultaneously broadcasting in several cities via telephone lines. Ambitious young men like Sarnoff and William Paley were looking around and drinking in the sheer sense of possibility. A mighty business was a-brewin' in the land. Left leg up. Left leg down. Right leg up. Right leg down.

*I*N 1926, the first major radio merger produced the first major network — NBC, which kicked off at 8:05 p.m. Sept. 9 from the Waldorf-Astoria. In 1943, the U.S. Supreme Court ruled that Tesla, not Marconi, had invented radio. WEAF became WRCA, WNBC and WFAN. WOR today is the only station from radio's early days that still has its original call letters and format.

John B. Gambling stopped calling exercises in 1934 but kept hosting the WOR morning show until 1959, when he turned it over to his son John A. Gambling, who turned it over to his son John R. Gambling in 1991. "Rambling with Gambling" continues today, without exercises.

By JAY MAEDER
Daily News Staff Writer

SOMETIMES they could scarcely believe their preposterous disguises themselves. They were both fat, cigar-chomping, middle-aged Jewish guys, and it was one thing to deck themselves out as gravediggers or dockworkers or icemen or undertakers or concert musicians or stout old ladies in babushkas. But they also passed themselves off as elegantly tuxedoed European royals. Federal Prohibition agents Isidore Einstein and Moe Smith somehow even masqueraded as Ivy League college boys. It was said that 250-pound Moe on one occasion managed to transform himself into a beauteous chorus girl.

Izzy and Moe, the New York papers gleefully called the two wildly improbable sleuths through half the Roaring Twenties as day after day their absurd rumhound adventures turned Prohibition into side-splitting low comedy. They were hands down the best revenue agents in the business: Together they seized more than 5 million bottles of illicit booze and made 4,932 arrests, personally accounting for something like a quarter of the federal liquor shutdowns in the city in the five years they were partners. They used to bust 100 joints a week, regularly bringing in throngs of prisoners before breakfast, while their fellow agents were still yawning. Not once was there ever the slightest hint that either had been tempted to accept a crooked nickel.

It always worked pretty much the same way. Izzy and Moe — disguised, as the Brooklyn Eagle put it once, as chunks of ice or breaths of air or unconfirmed rumors — would insinuate themselves into one illegal operation or another and instantly win everyone's complete confidence. Then Izzy would clasp his hands and politely announce: *"Dere's sad news here."* And then he and Moe would arrest the whole room. The phrase swiftly became one of the period's most familiar. Bartenders were known to faint on the spot when they heard those words.

Only mildly less theatrically, sometimes they would just drop into a speakeasy and put down their trombones or whatever ludicrous props they happened to be carrying that day, and then Izzy would say to the bartender: "Heard the latest?" And the bartender would say: "No, what?" And Izzy would say: *"Yer pinched!"* Sometimes they didn't even bother with the props. Sometimes they would just throw their badges down on the bar and Izzy would say: "How about a good stiff drink for a thirsty

U.S. agents Einstein and Smith, in hot pursuit.

RUMHOUNDS
Izzy And Moe, 1925

revenue agent?" And the bartender would laugh out loud and say sure thing, and Izzy and Moe would shout *"Yer pinched!"* and there would be another day's work.

Mostly, though, Izzy and Moe preferred the elaborate to the straightforward. Moe once submerged himself in ice water until he turned blue, whereupon Izzy rushed him into a Coney Island speakeasy and screamed: "A drink before he freezes to death!" And the drink came, and Izzy and Moe sighed. "Dere's sad news here," they agreed. One day they and 10 other agents went into a Van Cortlandt Park joint disguised as a mud-caked football team. "Season's over, set 'em up!" they shouted, and momentarily there was sad news all around.

One night Izzy was such a happy guest inside a German beer garden that his hosts insisted he get up and sing a song, which he did.

"This concludes the evening's entertainment, ladies and gentlemen," Izzy announced at song's end. "The place is pinched."

AUSTRIA-born Izzy Einstein had been a pushcart peddler and a postal clerk until Prohibition came along, at which time he figured revenue agent sounded like a good dodge. "You don't look like an agent," said a dubious federal man when Izzy went downtown to apply for the job. This was true, Izzy acknowledged; this was the point. Anyway, he was fluent in six languages, and the Treasury Department decided maybe he could be useful. Once he had established himself as an overnight success, he asked if his pal Moe Smith could have a job, too. "He doesn't look like an agent either," Izzy explained.

The papers would have loved them anyway, but they turned out to be great cops as well as irresistible little-fat-guy comedians, and if Prohibition agents did not tend to be the most popular people around in general, Izzy and Moe were nonetheless revered around the world during their time together. In the end, it was their own acclaim that was their undoing; they were, of course, mere hired hands getting much larger headlines than their bureaucrat superiors ever saw, and in November 1925 they were both sacked "for the good," their dismissals went, "of the service."

They had offers from vaudeville, radio, the movies. But finally, they both just went to work for an insurance company — "It was good enough for President Coolidge," Izzy observed — and it became not unusual for them to sell policies to people they had once jugged. "If you have arrested 4,900 people, you are running into them here and there," Izzy said.

After a while they were living mostly their own separate lives. In 1932, Izzy published his memoirs, "Prohibition Agent No. 1," and Moe's name was nowhere to be found in it, at Moe's own insistence: He did not particularly think of himself as Prohibition Agent No. 2. There didn't seem to be hard feelings at the time. "The publishers sent me a free copy," Moe said. "Izzy would have sent me a copy too, if I had sent him $2."

But in time they stopped making their occasional public appearances together. "That is whiskey already under the bridge and over the dam," Izzy said in 1935, two years after Prohibition was repealed. "If you know what I mean."

By JAY MAEDER
Daily News Staff Writer

DADDY MET PEACHES at a dance one night in March 1926 and went all goo-goo in about half a minute. He was an aging millionaire real estate baron. She was a chubby schoolgirl, 15 years old. Thirty-eight days later they were married.

This was what was called a May-December situation, the answer to a newspaper editor's most plaintive prayer in those fine days when New York's organs of art and literature included not only the rowdy young Daily News but William Randolph Hearst's Daily Mirror and Bernarr McFadden's spellbindingly lurid Evening Graphic as well. As it happened, both Daddy and his cupcake were shameless publicity mutts anyway, and ultimately it became not possible to escape their storybook saga of concupiscence gained and lost. For 12 months they riveted and repulsed the city and the world. By the time it was all over, millions of words later, even the tabloids were sick of them.

EDWARD WEST BROWNING had been scandal-sheet fodder for several years already. He was a prominent clubman-about-town, and there were headlines aplenty in July 1923 when his wife ran off with a dentist. "Today there is nothing left but ashes of romantic fires!" mourned Browning, always the spectacular cornball. The erstwhile wife's mother told another story. "Edward Browning should be horsewhipped before the eyes of the wide, wide world," mama snapped. "He is the most despicable scoundrel unhung."

Two summers later, Browning decided to adopt a daughter, and he actually advertised in the papers. **WANTED: A PRETTY, REFINED GIRL, ABOUT 14 . . . WILL BE BROUGHT UP AS OWN CHILD AMONG BEAUTIFUL SURROUNDINGS, WITH EVERY DESIRABLE LUXURY, OPPORTUNITY, EDUCATION, TRAVEL, KINDNESS, CARE AND LOVE.** Twelve thousand girls immediately applied for the position, and Browning was regularly photographed sifting through mountains of letters. After due deliberation, he selected one Mary Louise Spas, a 16-year-old from Astoria, Queens, whose parents seemed pleased to sign her over, and he grandly took her around on a shopping spree that filled his Rolls-Royce with 50 dresses, scads of necklaces and bracelets and, as reporters noted, quite a bit of frilly lingerie.

Pretty soon the papers discovered that, actually, Mary Louise was 21 and not exactly a girl scout. Shattered, the tycoon gave up the adoption proceedings, declared himself out of the fairy godfather business and bravely announced that somehow his heart would go on. And in such a state did he drag himself to the Hotel McAlpin to look in on a Phi Lambda Tau social function.

Across the ballroom, in a single blinding instant, he beheld Frances Heenan of W. 157th St.

He called on her the next day with flowers. He brought bon-bons for her mother. They dined. They danced. They giggled and burbled.

In the boudoir: A fanciful visit by the New York Evening Graphic.

CHAPTER 49

DADDY'S LITTLE GIRL

Mr. And Mrs. Browning, 1926

He called her Peaches and she called him Daddy and their romance rocked the town. Day after day he showered her with gifts; night after night the two of them did Broadway in his big blue chauffeured Rolls. If chunky young Frances was perhaps not the keenest-witted little thing who had ever clomped across a dance floor — "hefty of bosom and somewhat open of mouth," as The News politely put it — she certainly adored her Daddy, and Daddy declared himself happier than he had ever been.

Child welfare officials took a dim view of all this, and they were about to haul Daddy into court when he and Cinderella suddenly eloped up the river to Cold Spring and, on April 10, with the written consent of Mrs. Catherine Heenan, became lawfully wedded man and wife.

SHEIK AND SHEBA were never thereafter out of the public eye. Crowds followed them wherever they went; reporters chronicled their $1,000-a-day shopping tours; both supplied the papers with breathless first-person love diaries. "I went forth with all the ardor of youth!" swooned the gazelle. "I feel just like the French maid in one of those plays!" fluttered the bride. All this went on till October, when Peaches and Mother Heenan abruptly emptied their many closets and decamped.

"I was a bird in a gilded cage!"

Peaches wailed. "My life has been made a terror! I have made a grave mistake!" Daddy's tearful front-page pleas for her return accomplished naught; finally, he sued for a separation. She countersued right back, demanding $4,000 a month temporary alimony — "My expenses are huge," she said — and settling for $1,200. When the case went to trial in White Plains in January 1927, howling mobs fought to get into the courtroom.

Readers around the globe hung popeyed on every word as Peaches attested to the horrors she had endured. First there was Daddy's pet African honking gander, a foul-tempered bird that had the run of the house and did nothing but honk, honk, honk all the livelong day. And Daddy was a terrible tightwad, she said, weeping in her $11,000 Russian sable. And he wanted her to call him Bunny. And he liked to wear funny jammies and crawl around barking. Blushing and sobbing, Peaches poured out the salacious particulars of the "bunny games" and "woof-woof games" he had entreated her to play with him. "Mr. Browning tried to make me a party to his unnatural acts," she trembled.

Nightly did sidewalk vendors hawk transcripts of her testimony. Nightly did Daddy leave the courthouse sickly pale, "looking," said The News, "like a great big bunny at bay."

SUGAR PAPA, the papers called him. Mister Bunny. Cinderella Man. The He-Goose Man. The Human Christmas Tree. Seldom had anyone been so mortified in the public prints.

But once on the stand himself, Daddy convincingly detailed a life of unremitting misery. "My wife was never a wife except in name," he said sadly; not only had the girl never once taken off her clothes, he sighed, he had never been so much as kissed. Mother Heenan, he said, had moved into the boudoir right away, kept an eagle eye on things, complained that he snored, soon moved Peaches across the hall. Sometimes the two of them kept him locked inside his own lonely room, he said. "I was merely a drudge," he said. "*Fix* the blinds. *Open* the windows. *Close* the windows. *Keep* the coffee hot.

"Our courts make it too attractive for a girl to do wrong," he said indignantly. "The bigger their lies, the more money they get."

Sympathy for poor Peaches fast waned. The question came down to whether she was an innocent driven to the farthest outlands of depravity or whether Daddy was a silly old mush-head who had fallen into the clutches of a couple of truly venomous gold-diggers. Most everyone bought the latter view. In March, so did the judge, ruling for Daddy and cutting off 16-year-old Mrs. Browning without a cent.

"I still love him," blubbered Peaches as she departed the public stage. "A girl's first love is always the real love of her life."

THERE WAS *never a divorce; several court actions later, Frances Heenan Browning successfully laid claim to a piece of her husband's fortune and, when he died in 1934, she collected enough to keep body and soul together until her own death in 1956.*

By JAY MAEDER
Daily News Staff Writer

SHE HAD BEEN *waiting impatiently, watching the sky and the water, and now the weather seemed fine, and early that morning she plunged heartily into the English Channel, bound for the White Cliffs of Dover.*

But the weather was not fine. The winds whistled in, and things roiled up around her, and every stroke became tortuous. Six hours out, she hit a line squall that whipped the channel into deadly cross-currents. Twelve hours out she was fighting for her life, and those following her in the tugboat became frantic with fear. This thing was no longer possible, they agreed, it was time to stop. They leaned over the side and shouted at her: "Trudy, you must come out!"

She threw a glance over her shoulder and shouted back: "What for?"

THE PAPERS named her Trudy. Her family had always called her Gertie. She was anything but the standard-issue Roaring '20s flapper; Gertrude Ederle was, as the expression had it, a strapping, broad-shouldered girl, big and plain and jolly, modest and guileless and sweet, a butcher's daughter from Amsterdam Ave. whose idea of a good time was helping her mom scrub the floors and polish the stove. At 19, she was the world's best swimmer and had been for several years.

Gertie had taken to the water like a duck when she was a little kid spending her summers at the Ederle family's riverside summer bungalow in Highlands, N.J. Back in the city, she kept trying to paddle around in the 10th Ave. horse troughs, and her old man had to give her a few lickings. She came completely out of nowhere: On Aug. 1, 1922, a total unknown, she entered the Joseph P. Day Cup at Manhattan Beach and swam the 3½-mile race ahead of 51 rivals, including U.S. swim queen Helen Wainwright and British champ Hilda James. Suddenly catapulted into the forefront of world attention, Gertie Ederle of Amsterdam Ave. spent the next couple of years smashing every sprint and middle-distance record in sight, piling up more than two dozen trophies.

There was a slump for a time, and she did not do so well in the 1924 Olympics. In June 1925, though, she became the first woman to complete the classic 21-mile swim from the Battery to Sandy Hook, covering the course in seven hours, 11 minutes, 30 seconds, once again destroying a men's record. Gertie particularly enjoyed doing that.

After that, there was nothing to do but become the first woman to swim the English Channel.

DOZENS OF HOPEFULS had sought to conquer the cold, black, treacherous, 20-mile Strait of Dover; since 1875, only five had succeeded, all men: two Englishmen, two Americans, an Argentine. The channel was swimming's holy grail; William Burgess, for example, had tried 32 times before he finally made it across in 1911. In August 1925, looking at the 16 hour, 33 minute record set by Enrique Tirabocci two years earlier, world champ Gertrude Ederle plunged in.

She didn't make it. Her father, Henry Ederle, lost a $5,000 bet. Nine hours out, she got seasick and trainer Jabez Wolffe ordered her pulled from the water over her kicking, screaming protests; enraged, she sacked Wolffe, a man who had tried and failed 21 times to swim the channel himself, and a year later, when she came back for a second attempt, she was working with Burgess instead.

Years later, even sportswriters would look back and wonder what precisely it was about a

CHAPTER 50

SWIM IT OR DROWN

Gertrude Of America, 1926

young swimmer's challenge of the English Channel that so fired the world's imagination and so endeared the New York City butcher's daughter to so many millions of people. *Well, they were simpler times then,* it was usually concluded; Charles Lindbergh had not yet flown across the Atlantic Ocean; swimming the channel was a nearly mythical thing to do.

Not that Enrique Tirabocci had ever known such glory, of course. In Trudy's case, it helped somewhat that in May 1926 she had signed a contract with and was being financed by the syndicate arm of the New York Daily News and The Chicago Tribune, and accordingly was seldom out of the papers as she trained. When she sailed for Europe in June, News reporter Julia Harpman went with her, and Trudy's every utterance made headlines through the summer.

She was not without competition. On Aug. 3, Clarabelle Barrett of New Rochelle set out from Dover, got lost in fog, was declared missing for a desperate hour or two and finally gave up 2 miles from the French shore. Lillian Cannon of Baltimore was readying herself for an attempt. On Aug. 6, it was Trudy Ederle who made it.

On the beach on the Boulogne side of Cape Gris-Nez, Trudy's handlers coated her in olive oil, lanolin and Vaseline. She wore yellow goggles, a red diving cap and, quite unprecedentedly, a two-piece suit. The careful plan called for her to drift first on a westering spring tide for two hours, then let the north-northeast tide sweep her to midchannel by perhaps three hours later, and then there would be four hours or more of hard swimming.

At 7:05 a.m. on Friday the 6th of August, she entered the water. "Cheerio!" she yelled, and then she was gone.

'WHAT FOR?" she shouted, and the instant Julia Harpman flashed those words back to New York, Trudy became legend, the living symbol of everything indefatigable about America. Dover was only a few more hours away. She chewed another sugarblock and kept fighting through the gales, and she said later she never considered giving up: "After eight hours I knew I would either swim it or drown."

The final 400 yards almost killed her. Screams and flares and searchlights were waiting for her when she stumbled ashore at Kingsdown after 14 hours and 31 minutes in the water. That was more than two hours' better time than Tirabocci's, and it was estimated that she had been forced to swim at least 35 miles. "No man or woman ever made such a swim," Burgess exulted. "It is past human understanding."

Back home, Henry Ederle exulted too; he had bet Lloyd's of London $25,000 against $175,000 that his girl would succeed this time. Proudly announced the Meat Council of New York: "The public will perhaps pardon the retail meat dealers if they rise to remark that Miss Ederle's triumph may be attributed in some measure to the fact that she is the daughter of a butcher and that meats have always been a staple article of food in her diet." At the butcher shop at 110 Amsterdam, Uncle John Ederle joyfully handed out strings of free frankfurters to the whole neighborhood.

TRUDY WAS THE *toast of Europe for several weeks. "Gertrude of America!" they cheered her wherever she went. When she came home in late August, New York gave her a riotous ticker-tape parade and she was swamped with movie, stage, book and marriage offers, and she was barely landed before she suffered a nervous breakdown that ended her career.*

By JAY MAEDER
Daily News Staff Writer

RODOLPHO Guglielmi left his poor village of Castellaneta, landed in the City of New York at Christmas 1913 and found lodgings in a $2-a-week boardinghouse on W. 49th St., just another of the many thousands of Italian lads come to make good in the New World. By day he labored as messenger, dishwasher, grocery clerk. By moonlight he donned his finest suit and made his way to the grand ballrooms, where his smoldering good looks and way with a tango presently improved his position to that of professional dancer and working gigolo. It came to pass that in 1916 there was a little trouble with the law, apparently something involving the white-slave rackets, and he fled to California. There he began to find work in the moving pictures. In August 1926, when at 31 years of age Rodolpho Guglielmi visited New York for the last time, his name was Rudolph Valentino and he was the ruling god of the silver screen.

There had been movie stars already and there had even been heartthrobs, but now Hollywood had confected the great screen lover Signor Rodolpho Alonzo Raffaelo Pierre Filiberto Guglielmo di Valentina d'Antonguolla, directly descended from old Italian nobility, and in "The Four Horsemen of the Apocalypse" and "The Sheik" and "Blood and Sand" post-war audiences beheld a thrillingly magnetic figure at precisely the time they were discovering they had a national libido. The sleek, pantherlike, liquid-eyed Valentino moved Earth and the heavens. *"Lie down, you little fool,"* he commanded a slave girl, and you could hear spinsters falling out of their seats all over the theater. When word first came on Aug. 16 that he had been suddenly struck down by acute gastric ulcers and a ruptured appendix, fans instantly began to gather to stand teary-eyed vigil outside the Polyclinic Hospital across from Madison Square Garden.

Crises came and went as peritonitis set in. For a week the great star was near death, then recovering, then relapsing. At 10 minutes past noon on Monday the 23rd, he died, smiling faintly, it was said, a crucifix pressed to his lips.

Waiting in the wings, hands clasped solemnly, was Frank E. Campbell, the world's foremost mortician, as big a man in the funeral game as Rudolph Valentino was in the movies, and now the undertaker undertook to take Rudolph Valentino under.

FRANK ELLIS CAMPBELL had basically invented the idea of the funeral chapel all by himself. Before Frank E. Campbell came along, you had your funerals in your own private parlors. Frank E.

CHAPTER 51

THE BEAUTIFUL GOLDEN SHORE

Burying Rudolph Valentino, 1926

Campbell changed all that along about 1915, and at Broadway and 66th St. he built a million-dollar palace filled with tapestries and teakwoods and treasures that had once belonged to Napoleon, and pretty soon everybody who was anybody was getting dispatched to the beautiful golden shore from the Campbell establishment. Rudolph Valentino was the biggest client yet, worthy of the extremely exclusive Gold Room up on the second floor, and there to lie in state amid truckloads of wreaths was the fabulous bronze-skinned stiff transported shortly after his admittedly unromantic death from sepsis.

One of the reasons Frank E. Campbell prospered so was that he kept a press agent named Harry Klemfuss on his payroll. Film mogul Joseph Schenck had a stake in this matter too, having sunk a fortune into the just-opened "Son of the Sheik," and Valentino was barely settled in his $10,000 silver coffin before Klemfuss was on the job. Immediately he swept through nearby saloons and flophouses and rounded up dozens of bums to stand in the drizzle outside Campbell's Taj Mahal for a buck apiece. The crowd begat crowds. Even as Tuesday morning's papers were hitting the streets with news of the star's death, mourners were jamming Broadway all the way to Columbus Circle. By early afternoon, more than 10,000 weeping souls were jostling one another for position on line in a driving rain.

Then Klemfuss slipped a few bucks apiece to the janitors of neighboring buildings to start lobbing garbage cans into the thick of the soaked and seething mobs.

The riot lasted all afternoon. Sixty club-swinging cops battered back the shrieking hordes of bereaved as they punched and kicked one another bloody, but they couldn't stop a great wave of citizenry from crashing through Campbell's plate glass window and surging upstairs to pay their respects. The dead man's coffin was quickly sealed as his fans sought to rip locks of hair from his head, and Klemfuss congratulated himself on a swell day's work.

THEN AS NOW, there was nothing like a dead movie star to fire up a newspaper office anyway. At the Evening Graphic, which had a bit hastily announced Valentino's death several times before it actually occurred, there was now the conviction that the whole thing was a hoax. At the Daily Mirror, there were devotionals to the grief of actress Pola Negri, who had declared herself Valentino's current betrothed and was now en route from Los Angeles by train, dramatically fainting at every whistlestop. At the Daily News, assistant managing editor Paul Gallico contrived a theory that Valentino had been murdered and then ran amok with the medical rebuttals (**RUDY POISONED? DOCTORS DENY**).

The sorrow continued to outpour. On Wednesday, 50,000 queued up outside Campbell's and waited for hours to walk past the coffin, at which now were posted what appeared to be four crisply-brownshirted Fascist Guards, ostensibly there at the personal order of Benito Mussolini but actually hired for the occasion by the ingenious Klemfuss. Later there were more headlines when an anti-Fascist regiment stormed the chapel and chased the guards away. Klemfuss had hired them too.

Over the weekend, New Yorkers were distracted somewhat by the ticker-tape parade accorded returning English Channel swimmer Gertrude Ederle, and Rudolph Valentino finally got a little peace and quiet. Unless you counted the much-trumpeted arrival of the fragile Miss Negri, who obligingly fainted several times between the train station and the chapel as photographers snapped away and then collapsed again at bierside, where she had installed an 11-foot-long bank of lilies that spelled out the word POLA.

But on Monday the 30th there were 100,000 mourners lining the streets as services were held at St. Malachy's Church on W. 49th St., only blocks from where young Rodolpho Guglielmi had begun his American journey just a few years before.

BY NOW, Valentino's producers had banged out 200 more prints of "Son of the Sheik," and rushed them into theaters, and business was quite boffo.

By DAVID HINCKLEY
Daily News Staff Writer

THE FIRST TIME Mae West was busted, she got third billing. She made sure that never happened again.

In February 1927, New York was facing a familiar moral crisis: One portion of the citizenry was convinced another portion was having entirely too much of the wrong sort of fun, and it had to be stopped.

The culprit in this case was the theater, which the Society for the Suppression of Vice decried as a snake pit of filth and degeneracy.

And when the Society pointed fingers, public officials took notes. The group had been chartered by the Legislature in 1873 and had had such patrons as John D. Rockefeller and J. Pierpont Morgan. Its long-time leader, Anthony Comstock, had made himself legendary with his efforts to protect the public from such egregious outrages as the painting "September Morn."

Guardian Comstock was succeeded in 1915 by his even more vigilant protege John Sumner, who took on Theodore Dreiser, James Joyce and, in 1922, the Catholic Church, which Sumner felt was corrupting its parishioners with raffles.

Mae West, a 33-year-old showgirl of modest repute, sauntered not unknowingly into this tempest on April 26, 1926, when she opened at the Daly Theater on W. 63rd St. as the star of a self-written production demurely titled "Sex."

She played a hooker with a heart of gold, loyally following the British Navy, yet never finding happiness because she was, well, a hooker. Although the second act featured jazz music, always a lurid sign, the show itself was not particularly explicit, and it had completed an out-of-town warmup in New London, Conn., without incident.

Nor did reviewers on Broadway sound any special alarms. The New York Times thought the show uninteresting, while the Daily News' reviewer wrote: "Most of the 'Sex' appeal falls to the talents of Mae West, a vaudeville actress who somewhat resembles Texas Guinan."

Still, if the content was tame, the timing was ticklish. Six weeks later, on June 6, several citizens' groups demanded that Mayor Jimmy Walker close the show "Bunk of 1926" on grounds of immorality and put "Great Temptations" on notice to clean up.

"Sex" was not on the hit list, nor were most other dramas lighting up the Great White Way, including "Abie's Irish Rose," "Kosher Kitty Kelly," "The Great Gatsby" and the original Marx Brothers production of "The Cocoanuts."

On June 7, District Attorney Joab Banton announced the formation of a "play jury," volunteer citizens who would attend every play and vote on whether it met civic standards of decency. Nine "no" votes, out of 12, would obligate a play to clean up or shut down.

Because cooperation would be voluntary, Banton said, this would keep government off the sticky field of censorship.

Alas, the play jury turned out to be as foolish in practice as it was naive in theory. Critics said it only called attention to wickedness, and there was widespread suspicion that jurors were volunteering less from a sense of civic duty than a desire to see the good stuff for free.

Eight months later, on Feb. 2, 1927, Banton put the play jury out of its misery, or pleasure, and announced that onstage obscenity was now a legal

CHAPTER 52

COMMON NUISANCE

Mae West Goes To Jail, 1927

---

matter. Not coincidentally, Acting Mayor Joseph McKee was now running the town while Walker vacationed, and McKee considered judicial sanction the best remedy.

PRODUCERS QUICKLY formed The Committee of Nine, promising self-censorship. Too little, too late, said McKee.

On Feb. 8, the police tipped off newspapers that raids were imminent on three shows — all of which, incidentally, had been cleared by the play jury: "Sex," by then a huge hit turning a weekly profit of $4,000; "The Virgin Man," with Dorothy Hall, which was barely hanging on before morality groups targeted it, and "The Captive," with Helen Menken, an early lesbian drama.

At 8:35 the next night, the Daly was entered by

what The News described as "three men with square-toed shoes and an air about them that bespoke to the practiced eye long years at police headquarters." After flicking their flashlights, the classic sign of a raid, the officers cut a deal with the manager: The show would finish, and the cops would watch. To get evidence.

The other shows cut the same deal. Around 10:30, Mae, Dorothy and Helen were taken into custody on charges of "contributing to a common nuisance" and "obscene exhibition" and were hauled into night court on W. 54th St. There, Magistrate John Flood Wells set bail at $1,000 each, and Acting Mayor McKee held a press conference to declare the raids "a definite attempt to wipe filth off Broadway" and not a cheap publicity stunt.

The three actresses made bail. In the papers the next day, Hall and Menken were the featured perps, and the producers of all three shows sought restraining orders permitting them to reopen.

"The Captive" never got one, moving out of town to cash in on its notoriety. New York dropped all charges.

"The Virgin Man" reopened long enough for its producers to earn 10-day jail terms. Sentence was suspended for Hall and the cast.

As for "Sex," it reopened through March 20 — and catapulted West to top billing at last.

At her trial in early April before Judge George Donnellan, West's attorney argued that "Sex" was morally instructive. Donnellan didn't see that and strongly suggested a guilty verdict, which the jury returned six hours later. West was fined $500 and sentenced to 10 days at the Welfare Island detention center. She rouged her lips as she sashayed out of court.

At 7 a.m. on April 20, a police Black Maria delivered West to Welfare Island, where she mopped floors, complained that she had to wear cotton stockings, posed for pictures and gave daily interviews.

About the same time, 3,000 miles away, the movie industry buckled under similar pressure and formed the Hays Office to enforce internal decency codes. If censorship was still controversial, it was the wave of the day. So much fun, so little time to stop it.

A YEAR AFTER "Sex," Mae West was busted onstage again in "The Pleasure Man." She closed it down. That same year, she created her most memorable stage character, Diamond Lil, and thus her most memorable character of all — herself, the brassy blonde who said things like, "Between two evils, I always choose the one I've never tried before." She died in 1980 at age 87.

Dorothy Hall died in 1953 at age 47. Helen Menken became president of the American Theater Wing and helped popularize the Tony Awards. When she died in 1966, at age 64, none of her obituaries mentioned "The Captive."

The Society for the Suppression of Vice soldiered on until 1950, dissolving with John Sumner's retirement. When Sumner died in 1971, at 94, he had been deaf and blind for 20 years, serenely unaware of everything that had happened to public morality through the libertine 1960s.

By JAY MAEDER
Daily News Staff Writer

RAYMOND ORTEIG was a distinguished Manhattan hotelier, known to the better classes as Raymond of the Lafayette and to aviators as the patron who had in 1919 put up a $25,000 prize for the first nonstop airplane flight between New York and France. The offer was made ahead of its time; no machine could yet fly the ocean in one hop; it would be seven years before anyone could even think about it. The Frenchman Rene Fonck tried it first, in September 1926, and two crewmen burned to death when his overloaded Sikorsky bi-plane crashed on take-off from Long Island. Four more men would die trying to collect Orteig's jinx money before a spirited young ex-mail pilot from St. Louis would finally get lucky.

It happened that in early May 1927 the trial of husband slayer Ruth Snyder and her Bible-thumping partner in homicide Judd Gray was in its sensational final days, and the fresh flurry of activity out at Curtiss Field was little more than an amusing sideshow. There were three serious teams in the race: in New York, there were Clarence Chamberlin and Lloyd Bertaud, sponsored by aircraft manufacturer Charles Levine, and there were Cmdr. Richard Byrd and Bert Acosta, financed by department store magnate Rodman Wanamaker; in Paris, there were the national heroes Capt. Charles Nungesser and Capt. Francois Coli. Fleetingly there had been another team, but late in April the American Legion-sponsored Navy fliers Lt. Cmdr. Noel Davis and Lt. Stanton Wooster had crashed their bomber during a test flight in Virginia and become the third and fourth to lose their lives.

At Curtiss, Chamberlin's big Bellanca monoplane Columbia was the clear favorite, if only because polar explorer Byrd's triple-engine Fokker, America, was undergoing repairs after a crash. The Bellanca was a splendid ship, and few doubted that here was the plane that would fly the sea, and Chamberlin had been ready to go for weeks. Charles Levine, though, was an impossible eccentric, a backer who sometimes did not appear to be particularly interested in making the flight at all, and he kept ordering delays. Take-off had been announced on several occasions already: Now it would be Thursday, May 5, Chamberlin promised the papers; now it would be Saturday, May 7.

As Byrd fought to get the damaged America back into the running and as Chamberlin pleaded with Levine for the go-ahead, word came from France that Nungesser and Coli had hopped already and were due in New York by Monday afternoon.

Nungesser was a World War ace who had shot down 45 Germans; his fellows called him "the wildest man in the air." One-eyed Coli had been the first man across the Mediterranean. The two gallants were flying a powerful Levasseur bi-plane called White Bird, painted with Nungesser's battle insignia of coffin, candles, skull and crossbones against a crimson heart. They had packed caviar for the trip.

At Le Bourget, they toasted fortune and laughed at the devil. Thousands cheered the honor of France and saw them off. On the Irish coast, farmers waved as the airmen flashed overhead and flew on seaward.

White Bird was never seen again.

AS THE NAVIES of several nations mounted a futile search for the forever-lost French fliers, as New York City somberly called off the gala welcome festivities it had quickly arranged, world attention now was riveted again on Curtiss Field, where Byrd and Chamberlin suddenly found themselves back in the game.

Chamberlin pledged Monday night he would be in the air by dawn if Levine gave the word. On Tuesday, he said take-off was definitely set for the morning of Saturday the 14th. Byrd was noncommittal, finding it unseemly to roar ahead while the fates of Nungesser and Coli remained unclear, but said he might be ready to go on Saturday as well, whereupon Chamberlin immediately announced a Friday departure instead.

Late Thursday afternoon, one Capt. Charles Lindbergh of the Missouri National Guard touched down at Curtiss in a speedy silver Ryan monoplane called Spirit of St. Louis.

THE ARRIVAL OF the unknown dark horse changed the arithmetic at once; here was a brave youth who proposed to fly solo. Lucky Lindy, the papers started calling him, because he had survived several forced parachute jumps, one of them after a midair collision, and he seized the national imagination overnight. It was going to be a frantic three-way race for Paris.

But far at sea the weather was grim, and so it remained, and the three airplanes sat grounded, day after day after day.

At midweek it was clear that Byrd's America was flatly not ready to fly after all, and that left

Clarence Chamberlin and the ship that was almost the first (Charles Levine in cockpit).

CHAPTER 53

RACE WITH THE DEVIL

Across The Atlantic, 1927

Acosta and Byrd.

Coli and Nungesser.

Chamberlin and Lindbergh.

Lindbergh and Chamberlin pacing the floor and watching the skies.

Then, suddenly, in the Columbia camp, there was a quarrel among navigator Bertaud, sponsor Levine and airplane designer G.M. Bellanca, and Bertaud filed suit.

On Thursday, May 19, an injunction was served and the Columbia was padlocked in her hangar.

Late that night the weather cleared.

AT DAWN FRIDAY, *Spirit of St. Louis was fueled and towed from Curtiss to the longer strip at nearby Roosevelt Field. Clarence Chamberlin shook Charles Lindbergh's hand. Then he watched in silence as the little silver plane cleared the treetops at 7:52 a.m.*

The injunction was lifted that afternoon. For an instant, the dazed Chamberlin thought about jumping aboard Columbia, heading for France, somehow overtaking Lindbergh in mid-ocean and. . . .

But of course there was no longer a point. Lindbergh wasn't carrying enough fuel, Chamberlin worried to the papers. The kid couldn't possibly make it.

By JAY MAEDER
Daily News Staff Writer

THE PHENOMENAL institution of the New York City ticker-tape parade was invented by retail executive Grover Whalen, who, on loan from his boss, Rodman Wanamaker, had been the city's official greeter since the mayoral administration of event-phobic John Hylan. It was Whalen who had organized the thunderous civic receptions for the returning World War veterans, for their commander, Gen. John Pershing, for President Woodrow Wilson upon his return from Versailles, for King Albert of Belgium, for the Prince of Wales, for North Pole hero Cmdr. Richard Byrd, for triumphant English Channel swimmer Gertrude Ederle, for Queen Marie of Rumania. Now, in June 1927, Whalen got the biggest job of his life: the homecoming ceremonies for Col. Charles Lindbergh, who several weeks earlier had become the most famous man on Earth before his airplane ever landed in Paris.

Amid the worldwide Lindbergh frenzy there was a bittersweetness for merchant Wanamaker and his friend Byrd. It was long-time aviation patron Wanamaker who had persuaded Byrd to attempt the first nonstop Atlantic Ocean flight in the first place and who had financed the big three-engined Fokker that was to have made the hop. No one, certainly, wished to deny the achievement of the bold young man who had come out of nowhere to snatch Byrd's glory away. Still, all the grand Lindbergh receptions in London and Paris, all the formal presentations of ribbons and medals — all had been planned originally for the great polar explorer.

When Charles Lindbergh flew to New York from Washington on Monday, June 13, some three weeks after he left Roosevelt Field, L.I., and soared into history, he was accompanied by an honor guard of 21 Army planes, one of them graciously flown by the defeated Byrd. In New York, Wanamaker's man Whalen was waiting with the greatest salute to a conquering hero the city had ever witnessed.

ALL WAS deafening bedlam. Boats whistled in the harbor, auto horns blared, nearly 4 million people screamed welcome from the streets and building tops as Lindbergh's motorcade inched through a blinding confetti snowstorm, from the Battery up lower Broadway to City Hall Plaza.

"You can hear the heartbeats of 6 million people," said Mayor Jimmy Walker, pinning a medal on Lindbergh's chest. "And the story they tell is one of pride and one of admiration. As you went over the ocean, you inscribed on the heavens themselves a beautiful rainbow of hope and courage and confidence in mankind. Col. Lindbergh, New York City is yours. I don't give it to you. You won it."

Up Fourth Ave. to the Washington Arch. On to Madison Square for wreath-laying ceremonies at the Eternal Light. Up Fifth Ave. to the Sheep Meadow, where Gov. Al Smith waited to present still more awards. Down and down and down the confetti came, all through the afternoon and into the evening.

"You'll have to provide us with another street-cleaning department," Walker suggested.

Lindbergh, not long on patience with this kind of clamor, smiled grimly throughout. That night he ducked out on several more scheduled ceremonies, leaving an embarrassed Whalen to grope for explanations and apologies. A few days later, he was gone.

BYRD SUCCESSFULLY *flew to Europe shortly thereafter, although he was slower than Lindbergh and didn't make it all the way to Paris. Clarence Chamberlin, the second flier Lindbergh had beaten across the Atlantic, had already salved his self-esteem by flying to Germany, and he was spending several weeks as the toast of Berlin.*

Byrd and Chamberlin sailed back to New York together in July, and Grover Whalen gave them both rousing welcomes.

CHAPTER 54

THE CONQUEROR

Lindbergh Takes New York, 1927

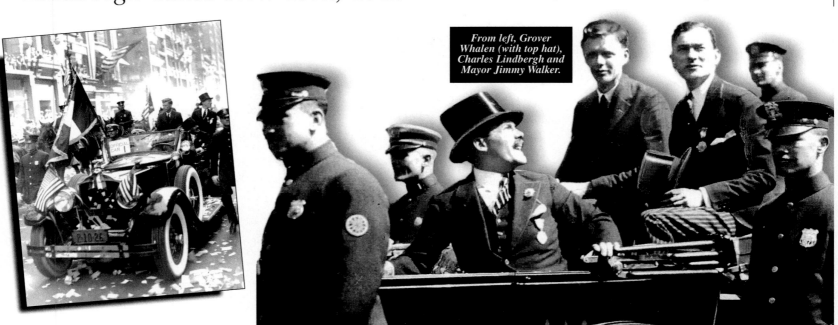

From left, Grover Whalen (with top hat), Charles Lindbergh and Mayor Jimmy Walker.

By BILL BELL
Daily News Staff Writer

WHEN HE realized that he was not likely to die at a ripe old age in bed, surrounded by his loved ones, Frankie Yale of Brooklyn began talking about his funeral.

He wanted to go out, he said, like a big shot.

And on July 5, 1928, he did.

In the presence of two women, each insisting she was Mrs. Frankie Yale, he was delivered to his final resting place in a hearse, followed by 250 automobiles, 38 of them loaded with floral tributes, along a 5-mile route guarded by 100 policemen. More than 15,000 people surrounded the Church of St. Rosalie during a Requiem Mass celebrated by three priests, and flags in the neighborhood were flown at half-mast in final salute. It was the grandest funeral in the history of Brooklyn.

At the time of his death, 35-year-old Frankie Yale — born Frank Ioele and also known as Frankie Uale — had a long rap sheet, an enduring working friendship with Brooklynite-turned-Chicagoan Al Capone and a fearsome reputation in the shakedown and bootlegging rackets. He also owned several legitimate businesses, including a funeral parlor and a cigar company that peddled 5-cent Frankie Yale stogies with his photo on the box, and in Bay Ridge he was known as a philanthropist, a guy who gave generously to the needy and to his parish church. As for himself, he wore 75 diamonds on his belt buckle.

He had been arrested more than a dozen times, including twice on suspicion of murder, and in Chicago cops had picked him up as a suspect in the 1924 shooting murder of Capone's crime rival Dion O'Banion. In fact, it was O'Banion's lavish funeral — attended by 20 judges and featuring music by the Chicago Symphony Orchestra — that got Frankie thinking about his own going-away arrangements. That was some send-off O'Banion had enjoyed, and Frankie wanted one even flashier.

THERE HAD BEEN a couple of close calls for him. Somebody potted him one night in 1925 as he drove home from a Coney Island speakeasy. Somebody threw another slug at him outside a cafe on July 1, 1927. Exactly one year to the day later, attackers hit Frankie again, and this time they got him good.

It happened about 4 p.m., along 44th St. in the Homewood section of Brooklyn. Witnesses said a black sedan carrying four men had pulled up alongside Frankie's shiny new Lincoln. Two shooters opened up with a shotgun and machine gun, and the Lincoln careened up on the sidewalk, knocked down several bushes and crashed into the front porch of a two-story house. By the time detectives arrived, Frankie was slumped over dead, his diamond-studded belt buckle drenched in blood.

Frankie's murder was merely the latest in a series of gangland rubouts, but it made big headlines and led the Bronx district attorney to demand that police do something to end what appeared to be an underworld war. "I have no evidence that there are any gangsters here," said Police Commissioner Joseph Warren, quite straight of face.

Everyone figured that Frank's one-time protege Capone was somehow involved. Although the two men had remained pals of a sort, with a working arrangement in the shipping of booze from New York to the Midwest, there was considerable suspicion on Capone's part that his buddy had mistreated him in several transactions. Moreover, Capone suspected that Yale was involved in the 1927 murder of James (Filesy) De Amato, an important agent in New York who apparently was the man who had informed Al that Frankie was hijacking some of the booze he was supposed to protect.

Two of the men in the second car, which bore Tennessee plates, were later fingered as Capone torpedoes John Scalisi and Albert Anselmi, who subsequently participated in Chicago's St. Valentine's Day Massacre of February 1929. One of the machine guns used in that event, indeed, eventually was identified as the one employed on Frankie Yale.

FRANKIE LAY dressed in evening clothes in his silver coffin, gray buckskin gloves folded on his hands, a rosary wrapped around his fingers. Everybody agreed he looked swell.

Mourners included Mrs. Maria Uale, who had received police permission to bury the deceased after producing a marriage certificate, and Mrs. Luceida Uale, who insisted that she had married him a year earlier.

It turned out that Frankie had divorced Maria without her knowledge to take up with Luceida, widow of a gent who had been blown away in Little Italy. Maria, it was finally decided, was entitled to the estate, which everyone assumed was considerable.

A month later, she learned that actually he had left the grand sum of $7,962, including $2,800 that her lawyer said she couldn't collect because it was in IOUs signed by people who had vanished.

She didn't have to worry about the $165,000 funeral, anyway. Frankie's pals paid for that. Otherwise seeking to make ends meet, she sold Frankie's fabulous belt buckle for $500.

CHAPTER 55

BIG SHOT
Burying Frankie Yale, 1928

By CLEM RICHARDSON
Daily News Staff Writer

YES, HARLEM IN the late 1920s was known largely for its nightlife — a place of countless clubs where Park Ave. swells and rumrunners alike could Charleston with abandon.

And Uptown was the place to be on Saturday night. The giant floor shows and exotic ambiance of places like the Cotton Club, Small's Paradise, Connie's Inn, the Manhattan Casino and the Lenox Ave. Club drew the day's glitterati. Any blindfolded schoolboy with a bean blower could take a random shot through the doorway of the Cotton Club after midnight and be almost sure to pop a Broadway playboy, a rich bootlegger, an actress or a society favorite.

But that was after dark.

By day, the community extending roughly 20 blocks north of 125th St. east of Eighth Ave. was home to some of the greatest intellectual and artistic talents the Negro world had ever produced.

Blacks began moving into the neighborhood above Central Park right after the turn of the century. That movement intensified during World War I, as black laborers abandoned Southern fields and came North in search of factory jobs, and particularly after the Bloody Summer of 1919, when race riots drove black residents out of Chelsea and Hell's Kitchen.

By 1928 there were roughly 300,000 people living in what was known as the Black Belt. Those numbers meant that if it happened among blacks, it happened in Harlem. The black nationalist Marcus Garvey had found his audience here, and it was a required stop for visiting African dignitaries.

Those numbers also meant a strong middle class, as, given the segregated climate of the day, black doctors, dentists, lawyers and morticians settled where they could find customers aplenty.

And so Harlem was the center of the black world 24 hours a day, and there was no place else like it. Where else could you see actress Ethel Waters' house on Strivers Row, or see Paul Robeson or Jack Johnson, or pass bandleaders Fletcher Henderson or Duke Ellington on the

CHAPTER 56

COLORED BUT NOT YET BLACK

Harlem, 1928

street or share a shot with Eubie Blake?

The philosopher W.E.B. DuBois, a founder of the National Association for the Advancement of Colored People, lived in Harlem, as did the writers Jean Toomer, Claude McKay, Countee Cullen and Langston Hughes. Zora Neale Hurston, an author and one of the earliest black feminists, called Harlem home, as did Angelina Grimke, Anne Spencer and Jessie Redmon Fauset.

And the intellectuals at Harlem's cultural core had a lot on their minds. Maybe it was the hard nut of being part of an America that had subdued the Kaiser in a world war but still lynched blacks down South; maybe it was the inspiration of hearing men like Garvey exhort the race to meet its destiny. Colored but not yet black, the collective think tank of the Harlem intelligentsia wrestled with what it meant to be a Negro in America.

"This deep feeling of race is at present the mainspring of Negro life," wrote Alain Locke,

Rhodes scholar and editor of Survey Graphics magazine. "It seems to be the outcome of the reaction to proscription and prejudice: an attempt, fairly successful on the whole, to convert defensive into an offensive position, a handicap into an incentive."

One of the greatest debates among writers was over the use of Negro idiom — whether anything written in black vernacular could be called literature. And the arguments raged just as fiercely as they would again 40 years later, at the height of the civil rights movement.

Writing to The Nation magazine, Hughes ridiculed a man who had told him, "I want to be a poet, not a Negro poet."

"I doubted then that, with his desire to run away spiritually from his race, this boy would ever be a great poet," Hughes said. "But this is the mountain standing in the way of any true Negro art in America — this urge in the race toward whiteness, the desire to pour racial individuality into the mold of American standardization, and to be as little Negro and as much American as possible."

James Weldon Johnson, NAACP secretary and author, wrote to the New York World on the question of "Is the Negro dangerous to white culture and to the white race?"

"This attitude is grounded on assumptions about what makes an American, what is dangerous to an American, what American culture is and who created it," Johnson wrote.

The arguments would rage on long after the Depression brought soup lines and even more crushing poverty Uptown.

Still, the writers and intellectuals of what would come to be known as the Harlem Renaissance set the tone for much of the black literature that came in their wake with wit, anger and penetrating insight into what it was to be a Negro Uptown.

As Melvin B. Tolson wrote in the poem "Harlem":
White cops sure will beat you up, littlest thing you do,
Black cops make Black Boy feel proud, but dey'll beat you too.

By JONATHAN LEWIN
Daily News Staff Writer

TURNING A desolate spit of sand into a public paradise called Jones Beach would have been a very large chore for anyone less determined than the chairman of the State Council of Parks.

But Robert Moses was ready to plant a million new clumps of beach grass, by hand, to stop the wind from blowing away new man-made sand dunes. He was ready to demand millions of dollars at a time when putting public money into recreation was unheard of. And he was ready for a long, bloody siege to win the lands of wealthy Long Islanders who badly wanted to keep the lesser classes of New York City far away from them.

In the end, the powerful citizens Moses antagonized found no friend in Gov. Al Smith when they went before him with their complaints that a new public park such as Jones Beach was sure to be overrun by city rabble.

Smith, born and bred on the lower East Side, reddened.

"Rabble?" he rasped. "That's *me* you're talking about."

When Jones Beach opened on Sunday, Aug. 4, 1929 — and was immediately overrun by city rabble, joyfully taking great gulps of clean ocean air theretofore reserved for their betters — it was at once the crown jewel of a great network of parks, beaches and connecting roads that Robert Moses would continue to build for decades to come.

MOSES, LONG a trusted member of Al Smith's inner circle, had been dreaming about a park system for years. In 1923, he had combined his own plan with other regional plans and presented a skeptical Smith with a state park proposal that would cost a spectacular $15 million. At the time, the only people who considered parks a political priority were social reformers who believed that a taste of nature would be good for the tenement dwellers, and Smith feared that the public would balk at spending such a sum on something so frivolous.

But the huddled masses yearned for the countryside. As assembly-line techniques reduced the average factory work week from 70 hours before the World War to 48 hours by 1929, workers now had the time — and, with the exploding popularity of the automobile, the means — for weekend escapes. Coney Island, though, was like rush hour, and Jersey's beaches were little better.

So the public was quick to embrace the idea

CHAPTER 57

BLOOD AND SAND

Robert Moses Builds Jones Beach, 1929

of new recreational areas. Newspapers lavished praise upon Moses and his grand plan. Parks quickly became something no one could be against. In 1924, Moses got his go-ahead. Now all he had to do was convince the people of Long Island to let him use their land — people who were so eager to discourage visits from city folk that they refused to address their huge mosquito problem, because, as one socialite put it, "I'd rather have the mosquitoes."

Through a combination of charm and threats, Moses convinced small farmers to sell him right-of-way for the new parkways that would ultimately lead to Jones Beach. When the rich were less cooperative, Moses fell back on an obscure law that appeared to give the state arbitrary power to seize property. One estate was appropriated on the spot, and Moses' surveyors began to mark out parkway routes across the front lawns and backyards of others.

Legal fights dragged on for several years as court after court found the property seizures flatly illegal. Ultimately, both press and public saw the combat as one between a dedicated public servant and a bunch of pompous plutocrats. And ultimately Moses won.

Now all he needed was the beach itself.

ALL along Moses had envisioned Jones Beach as a facility unlike any other in the U.S. His plans called for a water tower built as an Art Deco version of the Campanile of St. Mark's in Venice. His bathhouses, each with thousands of lockers, would be built of sandstone and brick in a Neo-Gothic mode of the Art Deco style and they would cost $1 million each. Moses wanted to give people who could otherwise never afford it the chance to feel as if they were on a luxurious ocean liner. Trash cans were designed to resemble ships' funnels, water fountain handles simulated pilot wheels, game areas offered shuffleboard and deck tennis.

Jones Beach would be no cheesy Coney Island, Moses vowed. Save for a theater and two restaurants, private concessions were banned.

Securing the rights to the beach presented several challenges. One of them was that most of it was controlled by Hempstead and Babylon, both of which mounted political objections that Moses found it necessary to overcome. In Babylon, he forced a park referendum that he arranged to win.

Press and public cheered Moses on. In June 1929, Heckscher State Park formally opened; in July, the Southern State Parkway; and finally, on Aug. 4, the Wantagh Causeway, and at the end of the road, Jones Beach.

Opening day speeches by Gov. Franklin Delano Roosevelt and ex-Gov. Smith extolled the value of public parks and noted that some found such huge state projects to be "socialistic." If so, chuckled FDR, "Gov. Smith and I are pretty good socialists."

Twenty-five thousand cars filled with eager beachgoers got a lot of sand that day — indeed, a sandstorm of such force that it chipped the paint off their license plates. But that was fine. By month's end, Jones Beach had tallied 325,000 visitors.

Robert Moses was a hero. It took awhile for a grateful public to notice that the bridges he had built over his parkways were not high enough to accommodate buses. City people were welcome to come to Jones Beach, so long as they had cars.

TO THE DEGREE *that Robert Moses devoured private lands and manipulated elections to gain his ends, it is somewhat fitting that Jones Beach takes its name from Maj. Thomas Jones, a 17th-century pirate.*

In defeating the wealthy and powerful, however, he created one of America's finest beaches. It was merely his first monument. Moses had many things yet to build.

NEW YORK EPIC: 1898-1998

By JAY MAEDER
Daily News Staff Writer

AT LEAST UNTIL the first week of August, it appeared to have been a pretty good year for Joseph Force Crater.

He was 41 years old, a good Tammany Hall Democrat, widely regarded as a comer. Gov. Franklin Roosevelt had recently named him to the state Supreme Court bench. Some felt he was on the fast track to big things, perhaps even the Supreme Court of the United States.

Then he stepped into a New York City taxicab and vanished from the face of the Earth.

Maybe he ended up in the tropics with a sackful of cash and a couple of chorines. Maybe he ended up in small pieces at the bottom of a gravel pit. For the record, the world has never known. Almost certainly it never will. Joseph Force Crater disappeared efficiently, completely and forever. In all New York history, no one has ever gone more impressively missing.

THAT SUMMER OF 1930, he was vacationing in Maine. Court was to convene Aug. 25. A phone call seems to have brought him rushing back to the city Aug. 3. He told his wife he had to attend to some business and that he would return to the Belgrade Lakes bungalow in a few days; this was the wife's story, at any rate. On Wednesday night the 6th he had a leisurely dinner with two acquaintances at a W. 45th St. chophouse. Shortly after 9 p.m., he bade them goodnight, hailed a cab and rode away into oblivion.

On Sept. 3, as an embarrassed Supreme Court continued to find itself one justice short and discreet private inquiries into his whereabouts kept coming up dry, cops were finally notified, and the absent Judge Crater exploded across the headlines.

At first it seemed fairly straightforwardly evident that the judge had taken a fast powder to deal himself out of what was plainly about to become a most distressing corruption scandal. Breaking all around were revelations that judgeships were openly for sale in New York. District Attorney Thomas Crain was tracing payoffs directly to political bosses affiliated with Tammany Hall's Cayuga Democratic Club, of which Crater was president.

Moreover, it was learned, Crater on the day he disappeared had visited his office, packed his valise with private files and then withdrawn more than $5,000 from several bank accounts. Moreover still, flocks of showgirls began to come forward to attest to their palships with the judge. Indeed, one report had him already en route to the West Indies with a comely plaything.

Other reports had him hiding out at a hunting lodge near the Canadian border. This lodge was owned by one Timothy Quillinán, who was district attorney in Troy and who was also the father of one Francis Quillinan, who happened to be a son-in-law of ex-Gov. Al Smith. This younger Quillinan also happened to be the man who had succeeded Crater at Sen. Robert Wagner's prestigious Manhattan law firm after Crater went to the bench. State police denied they were searching the area for Crater. The head of the force was one Maj. John Warner, who happened to be yet another Smith son-in-law.

None of the leads led anywhere. Crain empaneled a grand jury to dig into bankbooks, telephone records and safety deposit boxes, and none of those inquiries led anywhere either. Mrs. Crater flatly refused to answer any questions. Wagner, for his part, moved swiftly to dissociate himself from the judge, who had long been considered Wagner's personal protege. Why, the senator insisted, he hardly knew the man.

THINGS REMAINED baffling into January 1931, when the grand jury was dismissed. Then, on Jan. 21, Crain announced that Mrs. Crater had discovered in her Fifth Ave. apartment three envelopes containing $6,690 in cash, $30,000 worth of insurance policies and what purported to be Judge Crater's last will and testament.

There was some question about the authenticity of this document. Detectives who had already searched the apartment several times swore that the envelopes had not been there before. This apparently suggested that someone had recently slipped them into the place past a 24-hour police guard. It was all very mysterious.

And so it remained until June 1939, when Joseph Force Crater — there having bobbled up from the abyss no shred of him — was declared legally dead.

WHAT HAD become of Judge Crater? There were always dark suspicions that here was a man who knew too much about something or other and had to be silenced; it was whispered by some that shadowy pols had hired gangster Legs Diamond to do the job himself. Another posit was that he was abducted and slain by a criminal gang disappointed with one of his rulings. Another held that he had simply been the random victim of some stickup man who had then dumped his remains with remarkable success.

Meanwhile, over the years, Judge Crater was regularly sighted in the South Seas, the California mountains, the French Foreign Legion.

As late as 1948, investigators still working the case tracked an ex-showgirl to a Long Island mental hospital, convinced she had intimate knowledge of Crater's murder; she was, alas, a babbling lunatic, and she had nothing substantive to offer.

As late as 1964, Westchester authorities bought into the visions of a Dutch clairvoyant and started digging up much of Yonkers in search of Crater's bones.

New York cops closed the books on the case in 1979.

CHAPTER 58
MISSING PERSON
Judge Crater, 1930

DETECTIVE DIVISION CIRCULAR No. 11
SEPTEMBER 17, 1930

POLICE DEPARTMENT
CITY OF NEW YORK

BE SURE TO FILE THIS CIRCULAR FOR REFERENCE

Police Authorities are Requested to Post this Circular for the Information of Police Officers and File a Copy of it for Future Reference.

$5,000.00 REWARD

The CITY of NEW YORK offers $5,000 reward to any person or persons furnishing this Department with information resulting in locating Joseph Force Crater

Any information should be forwarded to the Detective Division of the Police Department of the City of New York, 240 Centre Street, Phone Spring 3100.

JOSEPH FORCE CRATER
JUSTICE OF THE SUPREME COURT, STATE OF NEW YORK

DESCRIPTION—Born in the United States—Age, 41 years; height, 6 feet; weight, 185 pounds; mixed grey hair, originally dark brown, thin at top, parted in middle "slicked" down; complexion, medium dark, considerably tanned; brown eyes; false teeth, upper and lower jaw, good physical and mental condition at time of disappearance. Tip of right index finger somewhat mutilated, due to having been recently crushed.

Wore brown sack coat and trousers, narrow green stripe, no vest; either a Panama or soft brown hat worn at rakish angle, size 6⅝, unusual size for his height and weight. Clothes made by Vroom. Affected colored shirts, size 14 collar, probably bow tie. Wore tortoise-shell glasses for reading. Yellow gold Masonic ring, somewhat worn; may be wearing a yellow gold, square-shaped wrist watch with leather strap.

Phone Spring 3100.

EDWARD P. MULROONEY,
Police Commissioner

By HELEN KENNEDY
Daily News Staff Writer

BEACHCOMBER Daniel Moriarty was sifting through the sands on fashionable Long Beach, L.I., looking for trinkets abandoned by the beautiful people who had sunned themselves the day before.

It was just after dawn on Monday, June 8, 1931. A fog was rolling in, and with the fog came a body.

She came in facedown, rocking slowly in the waves, seaweed tangled in her sand-matted hair. She was 25 and beautiful. She wore a fitted black-and-white print dress with nothing underneath. She was badly bruised. Her name was Starr Faithfull.

She might have stepped from the pages of F. Scott Fitzgerald, a high-society girl who epitomized the age of jazz and bathtub gin, and the mystery of her final hours, the torrid secrets of her wanton flapper life and the desperate sadness that limned her eyes in every glamorous photograph would rivet the public for months.

There would be two explosive diaries detailing sexual adventures dating to her childhood. There would be melodramatic suicide notes, and charges they were forged. There would be broad hints that her death came as no small relief to certain prominent individuals.

"I'm not sorry she's dead," said her 19-year-old sister, Tucker. "She's happier. Everybody's happier."

Nassau County District Attorney Elvin Edwards agreed. "Several people in high places will rest easier with her dead," he said.

"I am playing a dangerous game," the drowned woman had written a friend shortly before she disappeared. *"There is no telling where I'll land."*

SHE WAS barely on the morgue slab before her shocking double life began to spill out. The rich young beauty was a refined product of the finest finishing schools; she was also an out-of-control drunk, a wild-child party girl who snorted ether, gulped barbiturates and didn't always come home every night to the family apartment at 12 St. Luke's Place in Greenwich Village.

She liked to haunt the Cunard docks and crash bon voyage parties aboard outgoing ocean liners. Having sailed Cunard to Europe eight times, she was now, authorities decided, in the habit of trysting with various ships' officers. On May 29, it was established, she had been put off the Franconia, sloshed and crazed and screaming.

CHAPTER 59

DANGEROUS GAME

Starr Faithfull, 1931

"Kill me!" she shrieked as she was wrestled ashore. "Throw me overboard!" Swiftly there arose reports that on Friday, June 5, the day her family saw her last, she had spirited herself aboard the Mauretania, which had sailed that night for the Bahamas.

Her stepfather, industrialist Stanley Faithfull, insisted to police that Starr kept no diary — but detectives found one on Tuesday. And on Wednesday they were in Boston, questioning politically powerful Andrew Peters — 59-year-old former mayor, ex-congressman, President Woodrow Wilson's assistant secretary of the treasury, the man who had seconded Al Smith's presidential nomination in June 1928. He was an old family friend. His wife was Starr's mother's first cousin.

By Friday, Starr's diary — what was printable of it — was all over the headlines. The 40-page bombshell vividly detailed 14 years of drug-addled sexual adventures with at least 19 men, including London aristocrats, Manhattan playboys and, the papers said, a "man of political importance" who had been her "tutor" and who apparently had paid well for the privilege.

In Boston, Peters fumed that he had no knowledge of Starr's demise and warned that he would not see his good name dragged into scandal. But in Nassau County, minutes before Starr's body was to be cremated, Edwards suddenly ordered the proceeding stopped.

That night, police found another diary hidden in Starr's room. The next day, authorities said they were now convinced that she had met her end aboard the Mauretania, perhaps 7 miles at sea, and been put over the rail. On Sunday, after reexamining the body, city toxicologist Dr. Alexander Goettler announced that Starr's liver was full of the good-time drug Veronal — that she had, in essence, gone asleep into the sea.

"Death by drowning," said Edwards, "brought about by someone interested in closing her lips."

Then he made a large point of blasting Stanley Faithfull and Starr's sister Tucker, who had, it seemed to him, been less than fully forthcoming at every stage of the investigation. There was, he said, more to the story yet untold.

A FEW DAYS later, the case took a massive U-turn: Dr. George Jameson Carr, a Cunard ship's surgeon just back from England, produced several letters purportedly mailed to him by Starr in her final hours. "When you receive this letter, I will have committed suicide by drowning," she had written.

Starr had fallen for the doctor when he once helped her with a bad onboard hangover. Her affections were not returned. "You don't become romantic about a girl on whom you used a stomach pump the first time you saw her," Carr explained.

The letters were patently suicidal. Starr had resolved, she wrote, "to end my worthless, disorderly bore of an existence — before I ruin anyone else's life as well. I certainly have made a sordid futureless mess of it all.

"I take dope to forget and drink to try and like people, but it is of no use. Everything is an anti-climax to me now. I want oblivion.

"If there is an afterlife, it would be a dirty trick. But I'm sure 50 million priests are wrong."

This appeared to bring some closure to the matter. Stanley Faithfull loudly insisted that the letters were forgeries and got a handwriting expert to declare them such. Police experts disagreed. And the tawdry tale of the beautiful and the damned came quietly to an end.

BUT IN late July, Stanley Faithfull went back to the papers, charging "shameful official negligence"; Edwards, he said, was "lying down on the job," intimidated by persons "too big and influential for him to tackle." His stepdaughter, he alleged, had been kidnaped and "criminally drowned" by hired assassins. And he produced stunning documents: copies of a $20,000 check from Andrew Peters and a 1927 agreement releasing Peters from liability in the seduction and ruination of Starr Faithfull when she was 11.

In Boston, Peters immediately suffered a nervous collapse as the ghosts of his past rose up to forever destroy his career and social standing. In Nassau County, Edwards declared that he firmly believed Starr to have been murdered but that he had no evidence. "Neither Peters nor anybody else is so highly placed that I won't proceed against them," the district attorney sputtered.

Now the Daily News opened its own investigation and soon asserted that industrialist Faithfull was nearly broke — and that several days before Starr disappeared he had traveled to Boston to seek additional pay-offs from Peters.

Enraged, Faithfull sued The News and several other papers for libel. Late in the year, the courts dismissed his claim.

About that same time, a final inquest into Starr Faithfull's death was held. It was over in 15 minutes, and it reached no conclusion.

"Whatever I decide," said Nassau County Coroner Edward Neu, "it will be only a matter of opinion."

By JONATHAN LEWIN
Daily News Staff Writer

"I knew things were bad when I saw pigeons feeding the people in Central Park."

— Groucho Marx

THE GREAT Depression had thrown millions out of work. Broke, many were now finding themselves on the street. As local shelters became overwhelmed, shantytowns began springing up in parks, in vacant lots, along the rivers. Initially deplored as blights, they became instead symbols of a struggle to maintain dignity and self-reliance in the hardest of times. You sought inspiration where you could find it in those days, even in Hooverville.

Herbert Hoover had become known worldwide as a great humanitarian after he orchestrated post-World War aid to stricken Belgium. Relief stations were called Hoover Kitchens. A new verb was coined — to hoover, meaning to help. But the Depression happened on Hoover's watch, and his name soon acquired quite a different meaning. Now, a homeless man carried his belongings in a Hoover Bag. When he slept on a park bench, the old newspaper he covered himself with was a Hoover Blanket. And when he settled in a shantytown, he had moved into Hooverville.

The President didn't seem to want to acknowledge the grim realities. In December 1930, when the International Apple Shippers Association decided to sell surplus on credit to the jobless for resale at a nickel each and the streets were suddenly filled with shivering apple peddlers, Hoover looked on the bright side. "Many people," he announced, "have left their jobs for the more profitable one of selling apples."

Actually, many of the jobless were so ashamed that they continued to dress in the morning and head out, even when they had nowhere to go. Raised on the work ethic, they blamed themselves for the effects of economic forces well out of their control. They strained to get by without asking for help. They'd buy a cup of coffee, ask for an extra cup of hot water — then mix the water with counter ketchup and make tomato soup.

But, on the street, it was tough to keep up appearances. And without a pressed suit and a clean shirt, a job search was all the more pointless. Social workers believed that it typically took a newly homeless person three days to sink into despair. For one pale widow, it took two. She made the front page of the Daily News when she smashed a glass window at Eighth Ave. and 58th St., then waited patiently to be arrested. "They feed you in jail, don't they?" she observed.

Most of the new homeless ended up in places like the Municipal Lodging House on E. 25th St. near the river. There they got dinner — beef stew most nights, franks and beans Wednesdays and Sundays — then their clothes were deloused and they were issued clean cotton nightgowns. After a hot shower, it was off to try to sleep in a 150-bunk bed dormitory.

In November 1930, 43,280 men found shelter at the Municipal Lodging House. In November 1931, the figure was 111,223. That included 1,777 white-collar workers, including doctors and lawyers.

Meanwhile, good-hearted organizations such as The Salvation Army expanded operations. Those who went to Salvation Army missions usually had to listen to a sermon before dinner. If they wanted a place to stay the night, it helped to claim they'd found salvation.

Sick of the sermons and resentful of the delousings, many shunned the shelters. Alternatives included the many Bowery smoke shops. Smoke was a cloudy mixture of water and impure alcohol, and it was rotgut even by Prohibition standards. But for a couple of drinks at a dime a shot, one could stay in the smoke shop all night.

If that wasn't for you, there was the street. Or there was Hooverville.

THERE WAS little public tolerance for the Depression homeless at first. Several men were arrested in December 1930 when they were found living in a tunnel under the recently drained Central Park Receiving Reservoir. They had set up an area with tables, chairs, red lanterns and chintz curtains; the papers dubbed the place the Little Casino, after the Casino, the fancy park restaurant that served as Mayor Jimmy Walker's unofficial headquarters. But the inhabitants were derided as mere hobos.

By the summer of 1931, though, sympathy was on the rise. When 22 men were arrested for sleeping in the park in July, the judge gave them each $2 from his own pocket. Now press and public began to look beyond the makeshift shacks built of packing boxes, scrap iron and barrel staves. They began to notice the personal touches — linoleum floors and, at Hoover City, at Henry and Clinton Sts. in Brooklyn, vegetable gardens. Some of these shanties, when vacated, could be sold for $50.

And there was discerned a communal spirit. At Unemployed City, a collection of shacks in a vacant lot on West St. between Spring and Charlton, each man was responsible for finding a specific ingredient for that night's stew.

Public support began to grow — especially when the homeless were World War veterans. Companies sent food to a vet encampment at 79th St. and the Hudson River, and the city provided a daily tank of water. When police announced plans to close down one Hooverville amid the garbage dumps of what would become Riverside Park, Walker stayed the order of eviction. Veterans eventually won the right to register their shanties as legal voting addresses.

The best-known Hooverville was the one in the old Reservoir. Known by several names — Hoover Valley, Forgotten Men's Gulch — it actually became a tourist attraction. Ralph Redfield, an out-of-work tightrope walker, regularly performed for visitors.

Hoover continued to maintain that "no one was starving" at a time when an estimated one-fifth of city schoolchildren were malnourished. Walker urged theaters to show only "cheerful films."

But increasingly, the public saw that it was people — not bums, but people just like themselves — who were living in the Hoovervilles. The government found it harder and harder to deny that there was a Depression.

WHEN THE *Central Park Hooverville was torn down in 1933 to make way for the new Great Lawn, the city relocated its inhabitants — to another Hooverville.*

CHAPTER 60

KEEPING UP APPEARANCES

Hooverville, 1931

By JAY MAEDER
Daily News Staff Writer

THIRTY-TWO YEARS later, when mob rat Joe Valachi grandly spilled his guts to Senate racketbusters and provided the first semi-clean insights into the history of organized crime in America, there was at last a glimmering of what had really occurred in New York in April and September of 1931.

In those bloody and bewildering times of perpetual gang warfare, it was not always easy to grasp who was whacking whom for what. Cops had their hands full sorting out the corpses. Joe the Boss was one thing; Joe the Boss was, well, the boss, self-evidently the biggest gangland hit since Frankie Yale in '28. Salvatore Maranzano was another thing. Who knew from Salvatore Maranzano? Salvatore Maranzano was somebody who made the papers for a day or two when he went out and nobody ever heard his name again.

Who could know, in 1931, that the old Italian Mafia was now ceremoniously perished and that the modern mob had just been invented?

GANGSTERS RULED the town in 1931, and there was nothing to be done about it. The district attorney said so himself. The small municipal corruption probe whose launch the previous summer had been punctuated by the mysterious disappearance of state Supreme Court Justice Joseph Crater had by springtime exploded into a spectacular public inquisition, and DA Thomas Crain was suddenly at the heart of it; defending himself against formal charges of incompetence, Crain forlornly testified before Judge Samuel Seabury that the racketeers were out of control, that neither he nor police had any power to curb them. The 1930 homicide rate was through the roof — 421 slayings, up 18% from 1929, at least 66 of them gang rubouts, all of these unsolved. Sometimes it seemed like big black sedans full of machine guns came screeching around corners every night of the week.

As April flowered, bleary-eyed detectives were still fruitlessly working the stale old slaughters of nightspot baron Frankie Marlow, garment boss Little Augie Orgen and lower East Side kingpin Al Wagner, not to mention Frankie Yale, and fresh bodies were piling up all around them. A much-witnessed shootout at Owney Madden's Club Abbey had left some mutt deceased, and of course nobody saw a thing, and the case couldn't be solved even when chief suspect Dutch Schultz himself strolled into the W. 47th St. station and politely volunteered to answer questions. And then gang moll and Broadway blackmail queen Vivi Gordon had turned up garroted in Van Cortlandt Park. It was just one thing after another.

Against the backdrop of this daily mayhem did Giuseppe Masseria, aka Joseph Masseria, aka Joe the Boss, on Wednesday the 15th of April accept the luncheon invitation of his trusted top deputy, Salvatore Lucania, aka Charles Luciano, aka Lucky Luciano, aka Charlie Lucky.

Joe the Boss was a man of great respect, chief of the Unione Sicilione, an old-time Black Hander who had ascended to power after Lupo the Wolf went to prison in 1910. It had been necessary to persuade Lupo's associate Ciro Terranova to remove himself from the line of succession, and then it had been necessary to terminate the careers of several other candidates who were less agreeable, and then Prohibition had come along and offered enterprises more profitable than shaking down street peddlers, and through the 1920s Joe the Boss became at least as powerful in New York as was Alphonse Capone in Chicago. Charlie Lucky ran downtown Manhattan for him, Charlie Lucky was his right arm, and Joe the Boss loved Charlie as a son.

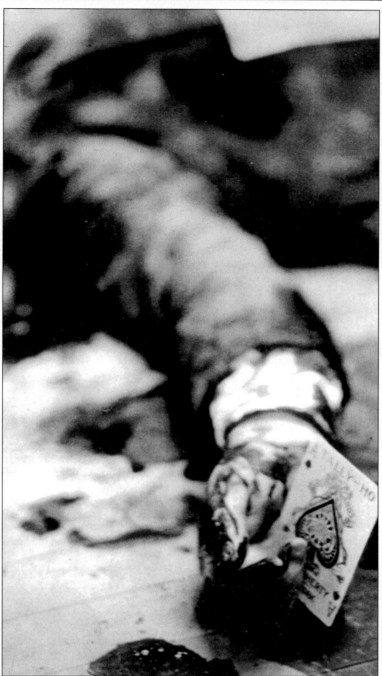

The late Giuseppe Masseria.

Courtesy William Balsamo Collection.

CHAPTER 61

VESPERS
Mob War, 1931

Cards were broken out after a fine meal at the Nuova Villa Tammaro restaurant on W. 15th St. in Coney Island. In midgame, Charlie Lucky excused himself and visited the washroom. Thereupon did assassins surprise Joe the Boss as he mulled his hand. Cops found him holding aces and eights.

The Daily Mirror, for one, noted that Charles Luciano appeared to be a prime beneficiary of Joe's misfortune. Press accounts otherwise bought the official view that the hit had obviously been ordered by Capone in Chicago. "Police believe the Masseria killing will be the start of a gang war that will exceed anything that New York has yet experienced," reported the Daily News. Actually, it was the end of one, not that anyone could have known.

NOT QUITE FIVE months later, on the afternoon of Thursday the 10th of September, four men representing themselves as detectives visited Salvatore Maranzano in his Eagle Building Corp. offices on the ninth floor of the New York Central Building at 230 Park Ave. and stabbed and shot him until such time as he was dead.

Cops found stacks of immigration forms in his desk and figured the previously unknown Maranzano for some kind of player in the alien-smuggling rackets. Actually, they were looking at the body of the man who had vanquished Joe the Boss and then with his own hands created five crime families that would efficiently administer many of New York City's everyday affairs for decades to come. Not that anyone could have known this.

THREE DECADES hence, Joe Valachi and then other songbirds to come would spell out the details of the great Castellammarese War.

It seemed that Salvatore Maranzano had come to New York from the Sicilian village of Castellammare del Golfo with designs on the operations of Joe the Boss, and their rival mobs had battled one another for several years. Dozens of soldiers died in the ceaseless combat, to the point that ambitious young Charles Luciano and such forward-looking fellow up-and-comers as Meyer Lansky, Benjamin Siegel, Vito Genovese, Frank Costello, Tommy Lucchese and Carlo Gambino at length began to wonder why they were working for such a couple of antiquated Old Country fools who didn't understand that this kind of bloodshed was bad for business. Finally Charlie Lucky threw in with Maranzano and took Joe the Boss to lunch.

Even as Giuseppe Masseria went to his grave, the victor Maranzano summoned hundreds of mobsters to a meeting on Washington Ave. in the Bronx, whereat he carved up New York City into parcels and awarded them to designees. Charlie Lucky got Manhattan. Gaetano Gagliano got East Harlem and the Bronx. Brooklyn went to Joseph Profaci, Joseph Bonanno and Vincent Mangano. For a Mustache Pete, Maranzano was not altogether without sound organizational sense.

On the other hand, he named Charlie Lucky his trusted top deputy. To his credit, Maranzano realized very soon that this had not been a brilliant strategic move, and he was arranging to have Charlie whacked when Charlie made his own arrangements first.

On Sept. 10, 1931, Charles Luciano now became the chairman of the board himself. Not that anyone could know.

PRISON AND *deportation would somewhat cramp the chairman before too many more years went by, but he did manage to live to a respectably ripe old age, dropping dead of a heart attack just soon enough that he never had to listen to any of Joe Valachi's stories.*

Charlie Lucky

By JAY MAEDER
Daily News Staff Writer

"Everyone in this life draws bad cards with the good. The great trouble with most of us is that we do not know when to discard quickly."
-Jimmy Walker

BEAU JAMES, they called him, everything New York wanted a mayor to be in the limitlessly roaring 1920s, flashy and smart-ass and Broadway smooth, as charming a sinner as God's chirping angels ever forgave. He presided over big, wide-open times in a big, wide-open town, the perfect embodiment of City Hall in the glorious days of Babe Ruth and Jack Dempsey and Legs Diamond and Duke Ellington and Charles Lindbergh and George Gershwin and Eugene O'Neill and Al Jolson and Texas Guinan and F. Scott Fitzgerald and Amos 'n' Andy, when all the world was a shining place that could never imaginably go dark.

He was an authentically terrible mayor, so far as that went, a showboat butterfly who paid practically no attention to his public duties and who cheerfully permitted his New York to be taken over and shaken down by brigands unmatched since the days of old Boss Tweed. He was not a crook, exactly, just a good Tammany man, not averse to enjoying the friendships of persons seeking this franchise or that, less acutely concerned about holding joint brokerage accounts with such persons than a more attentive soul might have been. Mostly, New Yorkers didn't really care about all this very much, until the time they started to care about it. Over the course of a few hundred years, several New York mayors have taken mighty falls. Jimmy Walker fell hardest.

THE beginning of the end may have been the November 1928 murder of Arnold Rothstein, the underworld czar many suspected had put Walker into office in the first place. Or it may have been the Judge Crater disappearance that in late 1930 turned a small judicial inquiry into a many-tentacled municipal nightmare. Or it may have been something else. There had been plenty of scandals all along. Mayor Walker was not much of a manager. His administration was almost never without smoking guns.

But perhaps the end had begun in April 1924, before he ever came to City Hall, when Tammany chief Charles Murphy died after 22 years in power and the wigwam mutinied against his less able successor, Judge George Olvany. James J. Walker was the Democratic leader of the state Senate, a Tammany loyalist in Albany since 1909, a long-

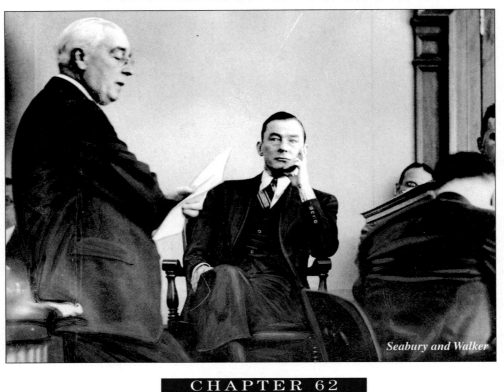

Seabury and Walker

CHAPTER 62

WILL YOU LOVE ME IN DECEMBER?

The End Of Jimmy Walker, 1932

time protege of Gov. Al Smith. Determined to put down an insurrection, Olvany insisted upon running Walker for mayor over the protests of his sachems, who wanted to reelect Honest John Hylan.

So it was that in January 1926 a man who had been a useful legislator but who was manifestly unsuited to be chained to an executive desk came to City Hall. Beau James was in the wrong line of work anyway. He had come to politics only reluctantly; he had wanted to be a songwriter instead; at one point he had actually composed a ditty that proved quite popular, "Will You Love Me in December as You Do in May," and years later orchestras always broke into it wherever he went. Aside from that, his music hall career never took off. So now he was mayor of New York City instead.

This was, of course, the middle of Prohibition, a moment of some general lawlessness in the land, and it was not unusual for such officials as the clerk of courts to consort with felons. Mayor Walker never seemed concerned with these matters. Chiefly, he was interested in making nightly rounds of the clubs and theaters. He was known to skip scheduled meetings with Gov. Franklin Roosevelt because he was doing the town.

Meanwhile, he was openly carousing with showgirl mistress Betty Compton while long-tormented Janet Allen Walker sat home and mourned the wayward man who made her suffer so. From one stand-

point, Allie Walker was something of a municipal embarrassment, a woman who had aged rather less glamorously than had her slick husband; from another, she was the living picture of abandonment, and tongues did cluck. Indeed, it was the untidiness of Walker's private affairs more so than the shambles of his city that distressed his friends and advisers — notably Al Smith, who late in 1929 warned him not to seek a second term or New York would surely someday turn on him.

At this point, in fact, Jimmy Walker could have accepted an offer to become president of the American League. He could have gone to Hollywood, for that matter. He should have.

IN NOVEMBER, he won by a half-million votes, demolishing Fusion challenger Fiorello LaGuardia, whose noisy charges that the city's judges were crooks and the district attorney was a bumbling imbecile had fallen on deaf ears.

A month later — even as District Attorney Joab Banton was somehow failing to convict the man charged with slaying Arnold Rothstein — it was discovered that a magistrate named Albert Vitale had been honored at a Bronx testimonial dinner attended by judges, court officials and a contingent of mobsters led by Ciro Terranova.

Vitale, it happened, was already in disgrace — he had recently admitted once taking a $19,500 loan from

Rothstein — and now bar officials demanded his removal from the bench. The subsequent inquiries turned up the fact that another magistrate, George Ewald, had paid Tammany $10,000 for his seat, whereupon Ewald's old friend Judge Joseph Crater immediately disappeared. Roosevelt, besieged by citizen's committees, asked the appellate court to look into all this. And suddenly an unimpeachably honest Democrat, a retired judge named Samuel Seabury, was heading up the most sensational public inquisition New York had seen since the 1890s.

MAGISTRATES WERE resigning for months as old Judge Seabury turned up the heat, and the probe quickly spread to all city departments. Sheriff Tom Farley was removed after he could not explain how an $8,000-a-year officeholder could bank $400,000 in six years. Numerous other officials got bounced as well. When the beleaguered Police Department dismantled its entire vice squad and sought to build a new one, not a single one of the city's 19,000 cops would volunteer.

Then Seabury uncovered Jimmy Walker's slush funds.

THOUSANDS OF New Yorkers stood in Foley Square to cheer the ebullient, thumbs-up mayor when he showed up at the courthouse Wednesday, May 25, 1932, for what was nothing less than a title fight.

The Daily News called it "a battle between an airplane and a tank." Walker was stylish, flip and funny; the gallery crowds regularly applauded his cracks. But the sober-sided Seabury had a stack of bank-books, letters of credit and other documents. One joint stock account into which Walker had personally not put a dime had paid him $246,692. And he had accepted many gifts, including European vacations and a private railroad car. After two days of grilling, Beau James Walker left the witness box visibly battered. Several days later, New Yorkers booed him at a baseball game.

SEABURY established no criminal wrongdoing, but in June he sent removal charges to Roosevelt on grounds that Walker was simply unfit for office. By late August, it was plain to all observers that Walker would not survive. Ill, pale and shaking, the 50-year-old mayor sought a last-ditch court injunction against Roosevelt — and failed.

At 10:20 p.m. Thursday, Sept. 1, he issued a one-line statement — "*I hereby resign as mayor of the City of New York, said resignation to take effect immediately*" — and slammed his door on reporters. "That's all, boys," he said.

The first New York mayor to quit his office then sailed for Europe with Betty Compton. He left behind him a fatally wounded Tammany Hall and a howling pack of reformers.

By JONATHAN LEWIN
Daily News Staff Writer

"I can't take off and I can't land, but I sure can fly."

— bomber pilot Fiorello LaGuardia, 1918

THE LITTLE Flower always knew he'd make a great New York mayor. By 1933 he'd been waiting years for the job.

As an anti-Tammany liberal Republican, Fiorello LaGuardia attracted national attention in Congress, but he could never build a constituency in his own heavily Democratic town. Now, with Jimmy Walker deposed, civic leaders at last were looking for a fusion candidate with LaGuardia's previously unfashionable reform opinions.

There was only one problem. The one candidate they absolutely refused to consider was Fiorello LaGuardia.

THE FUTURE champion of urban immigrants was born in New York but grew up on Army bases out West; watching corrupt government agents run Indian reservations, he developed a lifelong hatred of hack political appointees. Accordingly, when he entered New York politics, he shunned the Tammany-controlled Democrats and became a Republican.

Soon after being elected the first Italian-American congressman in 1916, he enlisted in the World War as an airman. Upon his return, he was hailed across the country as the "flying congressman," and his continuing interest in aviation eventually would put his name on a city airport.

In 1919 he resigned from Congress to become president of the city's Board of Aldermen, a steppingstone to the mayor's office. But suddenly both his young wife and baby daughter were dying of tuberculosis, and as he tended them conservative Republicans — some wondering if the city was ready for an Italian mayor — gave the 1921 nomination to someone else.

The following year, with his wife and baby dead and his mayoral ambitions derailed, LaGuardia returned to Congress, where he became known as "America's Most Liberal Congressman" — a dubious honor for a Republican in the Roaring '20s. In 1925, he decided against running for mayor, believing that Tammany candidate Jimmy Walker was undefeatable.

But in 1929, after remarrying, LaGuardia was ready for another shot. That fall he secured the Republican nomination and challenged Walker. A week before the election, the stock market crashed — and voters decided to stick with the mayor they knew. LaGuardia lost by the largest margin of any major-party New York mayoral candidate.

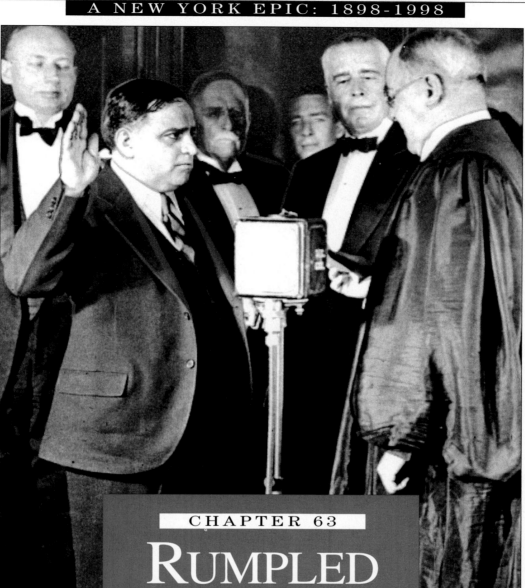

CHAPTER 63

RUMPLED FOREIGNER

LaGuardia, 1933

In 1932, the Franklin Roosevelt landslide finally ushered in a national government sympathetic to LaGuardia's lonely progressive views. Of course, because he was a Republican, that same landslide swept him out of Washington.

IN THOSE DAYS, there was a postelection lame-duck congressional session, and LaGuardia took the opportunity to work with Prof. A.A. Berle, a member of FDR's brain trust, to introduce legislation for the new administration. Berle would prove to be a valuable ally when LaGuardia prepared to make yet another mayoral run that would pit him against his most implacable foe yet — the Goo Goos.

Good Government reformers had been fighting Tammany Hall since the 1890s, indefatigably seeking to replace corrupt pols with men from the better classes. With Walker forced from office and Tammany disgraced, the elitist Goo Goos saw the mayor's office finally within their grasp. They established the Fusion Conference Committee to select a candidate.

Unfortunately for LaGuardia, the last man these aristocrats wanted to support was someone they regarded as a brash, rumpled, working-class, uneducated foreigner. Some of them even preferred Norman Thomas. Thomas might have been a Socialist, but at least he'd gone to Princeton.

The impeccable Judge Samuel Seabury had led the investigation that forced Jimmy Walker's resignation, and he was the Fusion Committee's immediate choice. Seabury, though, concluded he could not run, lest there be appearances that he had chased Walker from office for his own political gain. The reformers approached more than a dozen other choices; each one turned them down. Finally, one said yes — the greatly admired state parks commissioner, Robert Moses.

But if the Fusion Committee was effectively blacklisting LaGuardia, Seabury was equally opposed to Moses, whom he felt was too close to Tammany's Al Smith. Seabury announced that he would never

support Moses — and his influence was such that, for one of the few times in his career, Moses backed down.

With Moses' withdrawal, Berle rushed to assure Seabury that LaGuardia was the right man for the job, and the judge endorsed him. The Fusion Committee was enraged. "If it's LaGuardia or bust, I say bust," snapped committeeman Joseph Price.

But eventually the Goo Goos decided that rallying behind Seabury's choice was the only way to unify the reform movement.

THE DEMOCRATS renominated machine loyalist John O'Brien, who had finished Walker's term. LaGuardia was thrilled to be running against a man who had once praised the famous scientist "Albert Weinstein" before a Jewish audience and had told a Greek-American crowd that he had read the ancient Roman poet Horace in the original Greek.

In September, one of the men who had spurned Fusion's overtures, Joseph McKee, suddenly entered the race as the candidate of the newly created Recovery Party. Now merely making fun of the dim O'Brien was not enough — LaGuardia had to spell out his own platform, featuring slum clearance, public housing, adequate relief and the end of the spoils system for civil servants.

McKee then scandalized the campaign by suggesting that Seabury was anti-Semitic — the judge had been critical of Gov. Herbert Lehman — and demanding that LaGuardia repudiate Seabury's "slander."

In the year Hitler came to power, anti-Semitism was a particularly volatile issue, and LaGuardia was fearful enough of alienating the large Jewish vote that he came close to renouncing Seabury's support. But that move could have splintered the Fusion movement and resulted in his own defeat. Instead, he turned up a Jew-bashing article McKee had written for a Catholic newspaper years earlier.

Catholic Al Smith declined to endorse anyone. Late in October, the Jewish Moses came out for LaGuardia.

On Election Day, LaGuardia got just 40% of the vote. But in a three-way race, that was enough to defeat McKee, who got 28%, and O'Brien, who got 27%. The mayor's office was finally his. And it would remain his for the next 12 years.

ON JAN. 1, 1934, *at a few minutes past midnight, Fiorello LaGuardia was sworn in as mayor in Samuel Seabury's townhouse. It was the first legally wet New Year's Eve in 14 years, but LaGuardia went straight home to bed, as he had a great deal of work ahead of him. In one of his first moves, he made Robert Moses an important member of his administration.*

By DAVID HINCKLEY
Daily News Staff Writer

LIKE MOST entertainment hall magnates, Frank Schiffman was not going to be named Mr. Congeniality.

He was ruthless with competitors and sometimes almost as ruthless with artists, particularly once he had no competitors left.

But under Frank Schiffman's Harlem's Apollo Theatre became the mecca of black show business. If you sang, played, danced or told a joke between the mid-'30s and the mid-'70s, odds are inhumanly high that at some point you did it on the well-worn stage at 253 W. 125th St.

Artists who won the Apollo's Amateur Night contest include Sarah Vaughan, Pearl Bailey, Ruth Brown, King Curtis, Wilson Pickett, Screamin' Jay Hawkins, Frankie Lymon, Dionne Warwick, Gladys Knight, Ella Fitzgerald and Luther Vandross.

The list of artists who simply played the joint starts with Bessie Smith, Billie Holiday, Louis Armstrong, Bill Robinson, Duke Ellington, Cab Calloway, the Nicholas Brothers and Sammy Davis Jr., and goes on from there. Some white guys were regulars, too, like Bunny Berigan and Charlie Barnet, and at the end of the day the Apollo was to entertainment what Yankee Stadium was to baseball and the Louvre was to art. Play there, and you were sitting on top of the world.

The price for the gig was being nice to Mr. Schiffman and accepting Mr. Schiffman's wage scale. On their first visit to the Apollo, the Ink Spots split $160 — total, for the week, seven days, six shows a day.

Schiffman would pay more for headliners, and he also would accommodate performers who had reputations to maintain: He might pay them just $300, but he'd give them a contract that said $1,000 to show their friends. Whatever the deal, he never apologized. Just keeping tickets affordable, he'd say.

Leonard Reed, a dancer and producer who worked for Schiffman, called the man a genius, one of two white people (along with Lew Leslie, who produced Broadway's famed "Blackbirds" stage revues) who understood black show business. On the other hand, Ralph Cooper, who also worked for him and created Amateur Night, called him "a self-ordained great white father of Harlem . . . who ran his theater like a plantation."

Whatever the truth, it is generally agreed that Schiffman was one of the first Harlem theater owners to welcome black patronage

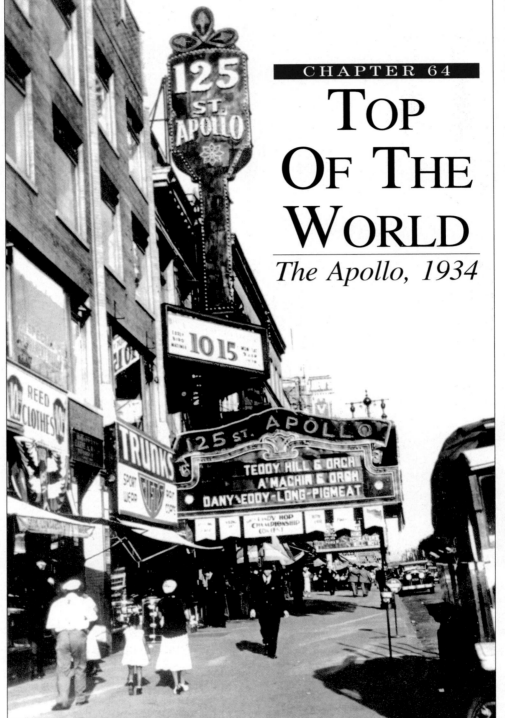

CHAPTER 64

TOP OF THE WORLD

The Apollo, 1934

and to employ blacks. So by and large he co-existed well with the community, which defined the theater by the artists anyhow and saw the Apollo as a proud centerpiece of 125th St.

It didn't start out that way.

THE BUILDING opened around 1913 as Hurtig and Seamon's Music Hall, a dinner club where an orange bitters ran 15 cents and a Tom Collins 30. Until Prohibition, of course. The place also evolved into a burlesque house, featuring stars like George Jessel and Fanny Brice as well as exotically hyped strip shows where women would peel down to white or flesh-colored body stockings.

There was a separate music club in the basement, Joe Wood's Coconut Grove, where it's said Louis Armstrong made his first New York appearance.

Clubs and theaters sprouted like dandelions around Harlem in the post-World War years: the Alhambra, the Lafayette, Connie's Inn, the Cotton Club, the Harlem Opera House, Barron Wilkins', Smalls Paradise. One of the major entrepreneurs in this field was Leo Brecher, and it was he who hired Schiffman, a former school teacher from the lower East Side, as a manager.

Leo liked Frank's no-nonsense style. Leo also liked sitting behind the scenes. So he made Frank his partner. They bought

the Harlem Opera House in 1922 and three years later bought the Lafayette, the crown jewel of theaters at 132nd St. and Seventh Ave.

Soon after this, midtown theaters picked a fight. Tired of seeing discretionary dollars flow uptown, they cut prices and started showing more skin on the stage. This trend accelerated when the Depression hit, as owners scrambled to keep patronage levels up, and sure enough, the moral guardians came knocking. One of Fiorello LaGuardia's solemn pledges in his 1933 mayoral campaign was to clean up burlesque houses.

What he meant was shut them down, and the Lafayette survived mostly because it was one of the

few that did not depend entirely on burlesque. Schiffman's 1925 decision to welcome black patrons had paid off big: By 1933, those patrons had made music shows profitable there.

Less fortunate was Hurtig and Seamon's. When the Little Flower nudged it out of business, owner Sidney Cohen was left holding a $60,000 note. So Cohen, with little to lose, had his manager, Morris Sussman, reopen the place as the Apollo, "The Finest Theater in Harlem."

The bill on opening night, Jan. 26, 1934, included Cooper, Aida Ward, Benny Carter, the Three Rhythm Kings, Norton and Margot, Troy Brown, Mabel Scott, the Three Palmer Brothers and "Sixteen Gorgeous Hot Steppers." Plus a film, "Criminal at Large."

This created a problem for Schiffman. His Lafayette had the name and the muscle, but even though the Apollo struggled at first, it was draining the Lafayette — partly because 125th St. had by now become Harlem's Main Street.

In the summer of '34, Schiffman and Brecher closed the Lafayette and moved their own shows to 125th St. — at their Harlem Opera House, right down the block from the Apollo.

A fierce battle was thus joined, with bidding wars for talent, price wars for tickets and even dueling radio shows — Cooper's original Amateur Night live on WMCA, Schiffman's duplicate on WNEW.

It was a war Sidney Cohen would not win against a pit bull like Frank Schiffman, and in early 1935, Cohen arranged for impresario John Hammond to take over the Apollo. Cohen was on his way to his midtown office to sign the papers when he dropped dead of a heart attack.

On May 13, 1935, Schiffman and Brecher made a deal with Morris Sussman to "merge" the Apollo and the Harlem Opera House. Before the ink was dry, the Harlem Opera House was converted to a movie theater and the Apollo became the only game in town. The sky, from there, was the limit.

FRANK SCHIFFMAN *ran the Apollo until 1961, when his son Bobby took over. Frank died in 1974, age 80, and Bobby closed shop in 1976. The theater has had several owners since then, all of whom have spoken of a desire to return it to its glory days.*

**By HELEN KENNEDY
and JAY MAEDER**
Daily News Staff Writers

REGINALD Claypoole
Vanderbilt, of the
New York and
Newport sporting
Vanderbilts, died in
September 1925 less
monied than you'd have
thought, able to pass along
a $5 million trust fund to
his 19-month-old daughter
but too broke to leave
much else to his bride, a
restless 20-year-old who for
some few years thereafter
found it necessary to fund
her traipsings about
Europe with the $4,000-a-
month income of old
Cornelius Vanderbilt's
small granddaughter.

The late Reggie
Vanderbilt's imperious
sister, arts patroness Mrs.
Harry Payne Whitney, Aunt
Gertrude to the growing
child, did not approve of
the society beauty who had
married into the nation's
richest family and who was
now known around the
globe as The World's Most
Glamorous Widow. For that
matter, neither did young
Widow Vanderbilt's own
mother, Laura Kilpatrick
Morgan, who along with
Aunt Gertrude was left to
rear the little girl as mom
dallied on the Riviera with
counts and princes.

In July 1934, as both
ladies concluded that
Gloria Morgan Vanderbilt
was an unloving and unfit
parent, Mrs.
Whitney quietly
began
Surrogate's
Court
proceedings to
win lawful
guardianship of
her dead
brother's
daughter.

On Friday
afternoon the
21st of
September, little
Gloria Laura
Vanderbilt, age
10, left her
mother's E.
72nd St.
mansion to visit
Central Park
with her nanny
— and was
instantly
spirited to Mrs.
Whitney's
residence at 871
Fifth Ave., where she remained
under lock and key as Gloria
Morgan Vanderbilt, loudly crying
kidnap, went to court to get her
back.

In the midst of the Great
Depression, when strikes and bread
lines sucked the hearts out of
people and hardly anyone had two
nickels to rub together, the savage,
diamond-dripping, high-society
custody battle over the sad little
heiress captivated common folks for
weeks, whisking them away from

CHAPTER 65

MOTHERS AND DAUGHTERS
Poor Little Gloria, 1934

*A Christmas Visit: Gloria, mom
and bodyguard*

their daily hardships into the
drawing rooms and perfumed
boudoirs of the fabulously rich and
the fabulously richer. The front-
page soap opera of Big Gloria and
Little Gloria went on all autumn.
Presently, the rabble began to
figure Little Gloria belonged to
them as much as anyone. "You treat
your ma good, Little Gloria!"
hordes of gawkers shouted
whenever the child entered court.
"Stick to your ma, Little Gloria!"

CONCLUDING THAT
the unfitness
complaints against Big
Gloria warranted review,
Supreme Court Justice John
Carew opened hearings Sept.
28. Little Gloria stared
straight ahead, refusing to
look at her fur-draped
mother as Aunt Gertrude and
Mrs. Morgan began their
testimony that the girl was
chronically nervous, weepy
and difficult as a result of
globe-trotting, pleasure-
seeking Big Gloria's endless
inattentions. In the previous two
years, Aunt Gertrude snapped, mom
and daughter had spent only one
night together. "Little Gloria was
like a poor orphan," added Mrs.
Morgan. "She was not wanted."
Household servants and a physician
agreed that the girl seemed
genuinely terrified of her mother.

The testimony quickly turned
quite lascivious. Nanny Emma
Keislich attested to parades of
dissolute noblemen at Big Gloria's

whirligig all-night parties.
A maid declared that Big
Gloria drank before
breakfast and read erotic
books; in Cannes one
morning, she confided, she
had found Big Gloria
bedding another woman.
The peephole revelations
moved Justice Carew to
blanch and cover his ears.
"Woman, stop!" Carew
commanded the maid. "We
have teeth in the front of
our mouths, you know, so
our tongues won't fall out."

Big Gloria was not
without her supporters.
Her two socialite sisters
showed up to denounce
their mother as a
madwoman. This moved
Mother Morgan to sigh that
she was ashamed of all
three of her daughters.
"This is really the saddest
situation I have ever heard
of," she mourned.
Meanwhile, attempts were
made to blemish Aunt
Gertrude's good character;
the Whitney Museum, Big
Gloria's lawyers noted, was
full of statues and
paintings of nudes.

Most of the public
seemed to side with Big
Gloria. Three hundred
destitute moms from the
tenements of the lower
East Side signed a petition
urging Carew to "give this
mother back her child,"
and the courthouse crowds
regularly chanted "Give
her her baby back!" But
when Big Gloria sought to
visit her girl at Aunt
Gertrude's Wheatley Hills
estate at Old Westbury, L.I.,
Little Gloria flew into
screams and refused to see
her.

In late October, Little
Gloria solemnly appeared
before Carew and said she
wanted to remain with her
Auntie Ger, who was nice
to her and let her have a pony.

IN MID-NOVEMBER, Carew
ended trial and announced that
Gloria Laura Vanderbilt "is not
to have for the future" the life she
had previously known. Little Gloria
was made a ward of the court. Mrs.
Whitney was appointed custodian,
and it was ruled that the child
would continue to make her home
with her five days a week. She
could spend weekends with her
mother.

Big Gloria collapsed sobbing.
"She always did love me, and she
still does," she wept. "That is one
thing that even the Whitney money
can't buy."

GLORIA MORGAN *Vanderbilt
pursued her custody claim
through the courts for several
years, until at last the U.S. Supreme
Court ruled against her. By then the
weekend visits had long stopped.
Mother and daughter were back on
speaking terms by February 1945,
when Gloria Laura Vanderbilt De
Cicco turned 21 and gained control
of her father's millions.*

By JAY MAEDER
Daily News Staff Writer

CHAPTER 66

THE BREAD THIEF

Richard Hauptmann, 1934

YES, HE WAS a criminal. In broken postwar Germany the starving Richard Hauptmann had once stolen a loaf of bread and gone to jail. In 1923 he had slipped out of Kamenz, stowed away on a liner to New York and here disappeared into the city's close-knit German emigre community. When, in 1925, he proposed to a girl named Anna Schoeffler, he reddened with shame as he confessed his old sin. *There was no work,* he told her. *Annie, I had holes in my shoes.* She patted his hand. *This is behind,* she said, *let us never talk about it again.*

He was a carpenter. She worked in a bakery. They pinched and saved and made do. By the year 1934 there was an infant son and the three of them were living comfortably at 1279 E. 222nd St. in the borough of the Bronx.

On Saturday the 15th of September, 35-year-old Richard Hauptmann pulled his Dodge sedan into a Manhattan filling station and paid for 5 gallons of gasoline with a $10 gold certificate. The unusual note aroused the suspicions of the attendant, who noted the Dodge's tag number and took the bill to a nearby bank, where a check of its serial number revealed it to be one of those delivered 2 ½ years earlier by Col. Charles Lindbergh to a mysterious man in a Bronx cemetery as futile ransom for Lindbergh's kidnapped baby son.

Detectives followed Richard Hauptmann for several days. When at last they curbed his car on E. Tremont Ave., he was found to be carrying yet another Lindbergh note. Cops tore apart his house. In the garage, carefully concealed, was $13,760, all of it identifiably Lindbergh money.

By week's end, the prisoner had become Bruno Hauptmann — Richard was his middle name; he had used it all his life; it was only police and prosecutors who ever called him Bruno — and he was the most despised man on Earth. Here at last was the beast who had taken the Lone Eagle's golden son from his crib and with his brutish foreigner's hands crushed out the laughing little life. *Bruno the Baby Killer.* Illegal immigrant. Thief and jailbreaker. Bruno the Hun.

Cops laughed in Anna Hauptmann's frightened face. *He's going to burn,* they promised. At the Greenwich St. police station in Manhattan late Thursday night, mobs hurled curses at the monster's wife. *Hang her!* they screamed. *Kill her!*

Before he was ever indicted, Richard Hauptmann was already on his way to the New Jersey electric chair. It mattered not that, within hours of his arrest, handwriting experts had declared that he was not the author of the Lindbergh ransom notes, that federal fingerprint checks found nothing to link him to the baby's nursery — and that the man at dead center of the long investigation, the elderly Bronx schoolmaster who called himself Jafsie, the one man who had ever met the ostensible kidnapper face-to-face, could not identify him.

JAFSIE WAS Dr. John F. Condon of 2974 Decatur Ave. In March 1932, when the Jersey kidnap of tiny Charles Lindbergh Jr. shocked the world, he had been principal of Public School 12 on Westchester Square, 71 years old, readying for retirement. The kindly old eccentric was well known to readers of the Bronx Home News, which often published his sentimental poetry, and the Home News deemed it worthy of Page One when Condon decided that destiny had chosen him to deal with the kidnapper or kidnappers and publicly volunteered his service. Much to his surprise, someone purporting to have the stolen child contacted him right away. And for weeks thereafter, in a criminal investigation already chaotic with underworld phantoms, mysterious psychics, bogus tipsters and several different ransom gangs, Condon was Lindbergh's personal emissary, communicating with his inside man via the Home News personals. "Jafsie" was secret code, derived from Condon's initials, JFC.

On two occasions Jafsie met with a man code-named "John," once in very dark Woodlawn Cemetery, which was later noted to be just six blocks from Richard Hauptmann's home, and once more in very dark St. Raymond's, when, as Col. Lindbergh himself waited outside in the car, he handed over to John the $50,000 ransom pay-off. The Bronx Home News enjoyed a fine run of scoops over the Manhattan dailies for a time. In May 1932, however, after the unrecognizably decomposed body of an infant was found in the Jersey woods and Lindbergh quickly identified it as that of his missing son, Dr. Condon became marginal to the case and faded back into obscurity.

Now, in September 1934, Condon shook his head and told police he could not be certain that Hauptmann was the man he had met. And Lindbergh, who had heard that man call out "Hey, doctor!" at the St. Raymond's meeting, could not identify Hauptmann's voice.

Pressed by lawmen eager to wrap up the long-unsolved Crime of the Century, they both reversed themselves within days. Bruno Hauptmann and Cemetery John, they were certain, were one and the same. This pretty well sealed matters for Richard Hauptmann, carpenter, of 1279 E. 222nd St., the Bronx.

OH, HE'S GOING to burn, cops chortled at Anna Hauptmann, and Richard was black and blue from the hours of beatings when she visited him in his cell and he whispered to her the story of the snake plant. Three weeks earlier he had been repotting it. He had spilled dirt on the floor. He had gone to the closet for a broom. *And, Annie, there is Isidor's box,* he said. *Annie, do you know what I find is in Isidor's box?*

Isidor Fisch had been a friend of both Hauptmanns. In 1933 he had left a box with them for safekeeping, then sailed for Europe, then died of tuberculosis in Leipzig. The box had been forgotten until Richard repotted the snake plant. There was nearly $14,000 cash in Isidor's box.

Well, certainly Richard had begun to spend it. Isidor Fisch died owing him $7,000. No, he had not troubled to tell Annie about the money. If this seemed a not altogether unreasonable tale to some, authorities had a fine time hooting it down. The "Fisch story," it was branded, and it became a national laughingstock, as if such a thing could really have happened.

Richard held firmly to the Fisch story forever after, even when New Jersey Gov. Harold Hoffman offered to commute his death sentence if he would only renounce it. He was telling the simple truth, he always insisted, looking like a man already dead.

RICHARD HAUPTMANN *was executed in April 1936 for the kidnap and murder of the Lindbergh child. Police and prosecutorial documents that have come to light in the years since have made it abundantly clear that much of the trial evidence against him was fabricated and satisfied many investigators that he almost certainly had nothing to do with the crime.*

By JAY MAEDER
Daily News Staff Writer

HER NAME was Gracie Budd, she was 10 years old and she was delicious.

This her killer made a point of informing the vanished little girl's long-grieving parents, in a letter that arrived at their W. 15th St. home late in November 1934. Gracie had not suffered much, he assured them; she had been strangled quickly, and then she had been chopped into small pieces and roasted, and she had made a fine meal. The killer described his repast in quite some odious detail. Detective William King of Missing Persons immediately postponed his scheduled retirement.

Little Gracie was six years gone. She had briefly made headlines back in June 1928, when Mr. and Mrs. Albert Budd permitted her to go along to a birthday party with a nice old gentleman they had just met and she failed to come home. Frank Howard was the man's name, the Budds told police. He was a prosperous Long Island farmer who had answered 18-year-old Edward Budd's job-wanted classified, and he had offered the lad $15 a week and board, and he had stayed for Sunday dinner in the family's humble basement apartment, and then he had suggested that young Gracie might first enjoy the party at the nearby home of his sister before he and Edward made the trip out to Farmingdale. Gracie had excitedly put on her white confirmation dress for the occasion. "He was such a sweet talker," wept Mrs. Budd.

Cops rounded up various sweet-talking old gentlemen over the next few years and sought to make cases against them. At one point in 1930 they dug up part of Ulster County in search of Gracie's remains. But in time, the case grew as cold as the abyss that had swallowed the child up.

Whatever had been nice old Mr. Howard's twisted need to further torment the Budds these years later, his letter's postmark and other clues led to W. 128th St., where King poked and sniffed and patiently sat stakeout for several weeks until he turned up shriveled, shambling, 65-year-old Albert Fish, a one-time church sexton-turned-itinerant house painter, who readily confessed to Gracie's murder and, on Thursday the 13th of December, led cops to her skull.

"**T**EMPTATION overcame me," Fish explained. He initially intended to take Edward Budd, he confided, but had so stirred at the sight of Gracie that he decided to take her instead. The guileless little girl, once out of the house, had cheerily agreed to a ride in the country rather than a birthday party, and she and kindly Mr. Howard had taken a Ninth Ave. el to Sedgwick Ave., then rode the New York Central into the Westchester County countryside, then strolled along summer-sunny roads to a densely wooded hilltop 75 yards off the Saw Mill River Parkway near

Height 4 Feet
- Last seen wearing white felt hat blue streamer in back.
- Hair dark, straight bobbed.
- Eyes blue
- Complexion sallow. Physical condition anaemic.
- Last seen wearing pink rose here.
- Last seen wearing gray overcoat with fur collar and cuffs and down front of coat.
- Last seen carrying brown pocket book.
- Last seen wearing white silk dress.
- Last seen wearing white silk socks.
- Last seen wearing white shoes.
- Age 10 Years Weight 60 Lbs.

CHAPTER 67

BUCKETS OF BONES
Albert Fish, 1934

Elmsford, where there sat a once-grand but now long-abandoned mansion called Old Wisteria.

Gracie had played outside as Mr. Howard went upstairs and unpacked his saw and cleaver. Then he had stripped naked and called the doomed child indoors. She skipped in carrying a bouquet of wildflowers for him. She got off just a single scream.

Cops plowed through the ghostly old house, ripping up floors, chopping down walls, and swiftly they realized that luckless little Gracie had not been the only visitor to these moldering premises. Everywhere they struck their shovels were bones and bones and bones, ribs, fingers, vertebrae, toes, buckets and buckets of bones. As festive Christmas approached, it became sickeningly evident that what

cops had on their hands in Albert Fish was America's own Fritz Haarman, the Werewolf of Hanover, who in postwar Germany had murdered more than 40 little boys and sold their clothes to ragmen.

Yes, nodded Fish, this was true.

And hardened detectives gagged as the most repellently awful deviant in the annals of criminal psychopathology merrily began to rattle off the particulars of a 40-year child-slaying spree through 33 states.

THERE MUST have been about 100 of them altogether, Fish supposed. He had tortured them, butchered them, plucked them with pliers and bored them out with drills, used them as pincushions, set them afire, gnawed at the roasted chunks of them, drank their blood, buried what was left of them in this lonely orchard and that and then moved along to his next house painting job. The deeply religious old creep was particularly fond of reenacting Abraham's ritual sacrifice of Isaac, although he usually changed the story's ending to suit himself. Cops figured at least some of this had to be imaginative fiction, but there was no way to know; Fish had done his preying mostly on strays and orphans, and many of them never would have been missed. Certainly identification could not be made of all those reposing in Old Wisteria's boneyard.

Not that Albert Fish had no other entertainments. He quite enjoyed visiting physical agonies upon himself as well. He liked to pay children to flog him with switches. He liked to splash himself with alcohol and set himself alight. He liked to stick sharp things into his hindquarters. Doctors who X-rayed the prisoner's groin gulped at the discovery that 29 long needles were buried deep inside his nether regions. He had been carrying them around for years.

"I guess I must be crazy," Fish mused to one reporter. "All three of my wives sort of thought I was."

IF IT SEEMED plain to some that here was about the looniest bug who had ever walked the Earth, psychiatric authorities decided otherwise and ruled him quite sane, if odd, and when the horrible old house painter went to trial in March 1935 it took jurors just a few minutes to condemn him to Sing Sing's electric chair. Fish beamed. In his jail cell he thereafter found regular amusement burning himself with matches. On one occasion he attempted to disembowel himself with a sharpened pork chop bone.

In the end, early in January 1936, he walked the last mile to Old Sparky unprodded, happily babbling that electrocution was sure to be the finest thrill of all and even eagerly adjusting his own ankle straps as his executioners shook their heads and crossed themselves and tried to sit him still.

By JAY MAEDER
Daily News Staff Writer

FROM ITALY'S standpoint, it was true, Italy had been fairly royally chiseled out of any substantive World War spoils. The Allies had promised them the sun and moon and then left Italy with crumbs, Eritrea and Italian Somaliland, nothing but barren desert. Some Roman Empire *that* was. Well, Italy had Albania, too, but of course Albania was worthless. So it was that Benito Mussolini cast Italian eyes again on the ancient cradle of the Kingdom of Abyssinia. Abyssinia was nothing but barren desert either, so far as that went, but at least there was more of it.

Italy was still relatively new to the world stage in the 1930s. Until 1870 Italy had been a medieval collection of poor duchies and poorer principalities, and its early attempts to expand across the Mediterranean into Tunis were contemptuously blocked by the older powers. The Italian armies were not particularly sophisticated, in any case: When in 1896 the dictator Francesco Crispi resolved to make a protectorate of Abyssinia, 8,000 Italian soldiers were slaughtered at Adowa by Abyssinians armed with sticks and spears. Great was this sting. Italy had been just mortified ever since.

Now, in 1935, Mussolini was determined both to avenge the old Adowa humiliation and to stake an emperor's claim at last to Italy's rightful colonial place in the sun. Now the Roman legions were mechanized, bristling with tanks and warplanes, and all the world knew that Italy would storm defenseless Ethiopia the day the September rains stopped. The great powers did not approve, but the slightest diplomatic misstep could easily mean another world war; now Haile Selassie, Ras Tafari, the Lion of Judah, came before the League of Nations to plead for deliverance, and the great powers all went deaf.

On Tuesday, the 1st of October, as Europe watched silently, Caproni bombers blasted Adowa into rubble and columns of troops poured across the border and destroyed the pathetic war-dancing spearmen who rose up to meet them. The sun had not set before the Italo-Ethiopian War came as well to the hundreds of thousands of Italians and the hundreds of thousands of blacks who sought to live together in the City of New York.

REACTION WAS mixed in the Italian communities. "Italy makes war to civilize, just as the old Romans did," said banker Cavaliere Raffaele Prisco. "The Italian people need colonies and must develop Africa," explained newspaper editor Carlo Falbo. Shrugged Times Square barber Federico Fugini: "The war is no concern of us Italians who have come to this country."

Reaction was mixed in the black communities. "The white races stand indicted before the civilized world," scolded Urban League executive director James Hubert. Shrugged porter Walter Anderson: "They can do all the fighting they want to. I guess we all came from Africa some time or other, but that doesn't make an Ethiopian out of me."

If barber Fugini and porter Anderson might have sat down there and then and had a friendly drink, there was no such good will at Public School 178 in Brooklyn, where gangs of black kids and gangs of Italian kids squared off and brawled until school officials took away their sawed-off pool cues. In Harlem, jeering blacks rallied on Lenox Ave., waved the Ethiopian tri-color and vowed to run Italians out of the neighborhood; cops were called out to prevent the destruction of a Jewish-owned grocery that rented stall space to three Italian vendors.

At this very moment, Col. Hubert Julian, the Black Eagle of Harlem, was in Addis Ababa, and it would have been his most glorious hour if he'd only had an airplane.

CHAPTER 68

PLACE IN THE SUN

The Black Eagle, 1935

TRINIDAD-BORN Hubert Fauntleroy Julian had been one of Harlem's most flamboyant figures for years. One of the pioneer black fliers, he had popped up in the early 1920s as black nationalist Marcus Garvey's air minister, and he frequently mesmerized citizens by parachuting, crimson-clad, onto 125th St.

In 1924, three years before Charles Lindbergh flew the Atlantic, Julian announced his intention to make a solo seaplane flight from Harlem to Liberia and back. On the Fourth of July, as 25,000 cheering

Harlemites gathered at the foot of 138th St., the Black Eagle passed the hat around, collected a few hundred dollars, climbed into his plane and, moments later, crashed into Flushing Bay. He had, he explained, developed "pontoon trouble."

Four years later he announced another ocean hop, this one sponsored by the National Association for the Advancement of Aviation Amongst Colored Races, an organization newly formed by a Harlem quack named Geneva Morgan-Johnson, who practiced something called psycho-irradiation, and a white man named Hoffman, who previously had been associated with American Hebrew magazine. Things shortly became acrimonious, and the NAAAACR withdrew its support, pronouncing Julian "not sufficiently outstanding in Harlem aviation circles." Even Julian blinked at that one — "Harlem aviation circles?" he demanded. "I *am* those circles. Who *else* they going to get?" — and he went cross-country seeking to raise private funding. There wasn't any. "An unfortunate apathy curtailed my project," he told the press.

In June 1930, he informed the world that Haile Selassie, Ras Tafari, the Lion of Judah, had appointed him chief of the Ethiopian Air Force.

HE CUT A dazzling figure in Addis Ababa, swaggering about in a splendid colonel's uniform and sending out official Ethiopian military communiques. Ethiopian aviation, he declared, "is in a very advanced state." This was not quite true. Actually, the Ethiopian Air Force consisted of three airplanes, and, late in October, he crashed one of them. It was the Lion of Judah's personal favorite, too. Back to New York sailed the Black Eagle before year's end.

But he remained devoted to Abyssinian causes, and in late 1934 and early 1935, as it became evident that Benito Mussolini had designs on Haile Selassie's kingdom, it was largely Hubert Julian who brought this state of affairs to the attention of American blacks, and the proliferation of Ethiopian flags and relief-fund-raising stations in New York and other cities was very much the result of his impassioned crusading.

In February 1935, he was on his way back to Addis Ababa.

AND AGAIN he cut a dazzling figure, dressed in khakis, swinging a sword, riding a fine white horse. But this time Ras Tafari wasn't about to let him anywhere near an airplane, and the Chicago flier John Robinson was Ethiopia's new air force chief. When the invasion came, it was Johnny Robinson who got the worldwide headlines, bravely flying against Mussolini's airmen.

By December, Julian was back in New York, flying new political colors. "I couldn't stand those lazy people any longer," he sniffed. Ethiopia was a hopelessly barbaric place, he said, and as far as he was concerned the Italians could have their place in the sun. "Ethiopians do not care for the American Negroes," he said. "They do not consider themselves Negroes. American Negroes should face their own problems at home and keep out of international affairs."

He urged Harlem to take down the flags. Ethiopia, he said, "is not worth saving."

As it happened, by now everyone could see that Ethiopia was lost and the relief efforts had pretty much dried up anyway.

When the war ended several months later, Hubert Julian was in Naples, calling himself Col. Huberto Juliano and promising several great trailblazing flights, none of which was ever made.

BACK IN HARLEM *in 1940, the Black Eagle publicly challenged Nazi Luftwaffe chief Hermann Goering to a one-on-one Messerschmitt duel over the English Channel. Goering paid no attention to him.*

CHAPTER 69

DEAD AS SAILING SHIPS

Goodbye To The Trolleys, 1936

By RICHARD E. MOONEY
Special to The News

THE LAST TROLLEY on the Lexington Ave. line left 23rd St. at 9:30 on the morning of Wednesday, March 25, 1936. The route up to Bloomingdale's at 59th St. was lined with flags and bunting. Curious New Yorkers craned to capture the passage. Former Gov. Al Smith and assorted other dignitaries waited — not for the trolley but for the bus behind it. At the appointed moment, with practiced swing, Smith smashed a bottle of wine over the bus' cream-colored prow and christened it the "Lexington-Bloomingdale." Seven days later he would repeat the ceremony when a new crosstown bus line elbowed out an old trolley line on 34th St.

The city's transition from trolleys to buses did not happen all at once. There had been buses on Fifth Ave. as long as there had been trolleys in the rest of the city, since the turn of the century; the merchants and millionaires on Fifth had never wanted any rickety old rattlers disturbing them. A few trolley lines remained in business until the late 1940s. And the last streetcar — the Queensboro Bridge local — was not run out of town until 1957.

But the big switch from rail to rubber began in 1935 and was completed a year later. Most of the city's familiar old streetcars were suddenly gone. It was the first major trolley-to-bus conversion in the United States.

Mayor Fiorello LaGuardia had pronounced trolleys "as dead as sailing ships" in January 1935. He was an aggressive reformer, and transit was one of the things he intended to reform. Trolleys were old-fashioned. Buses were modern.

THE TROLLEY AGE began in the 1890s, when streetcars that were pulled by underground cables replaced streetcars drawn by horses, some on rails laid along old stagecoach routes. In 1901, Broadway got its first electric streetcar, operating on juice from underground power lines because the city would not permit overhead lines. Privately owned, electrically powered trolley systems eventually laced the city. In Manhattan, separate companies operated separate lines up and down the

avenues and on several of the wider crosstown streets. In each of the other boroughs, one or two companies dominated.

By 1920, there were 1,344 miles of track in New York, but ridership was already beginning to taper off. Subways and automobiles were stealing the passengers. The growth of the suburbs spelled more trouble. The trolley tracks didn't reach that far.

Trolleys clearly were going out of style. They had screeching wheels and clanging bells. They lost traction on icy inclines in winter. They were an obstacle to the increasing traffic of cars and trucks. They were, no doubt about it, old-fashioned.

It had not been so long since "rapid transit chased horse-cars off to the scrap heap and the glue factory," observed the American Mercury in 1928. "But already men snicker when they speak of it as rapid."

JIMMY WALKER had promised to rid the city of its trolleys as early as 1925, in his first campaign for the mayoralty. Once elected, he blew it, in a too-friendly deal to franchise a company with no experience but strong ties to Tammany politicians. The deal never came off, and Walker's term was truncated by other mischief. But Tammany still held City Hall. On the eve of LaGuardia's election, the Board of Estimate approved 25-year franchises for five companies, a suspicious 11th-hour prize amid rumors that $300,000 had changed hands.

LaGuardia sought to overturn these contracts, but gave up when they were validated in court and the companies agreed to shorter terms.

General Motors and like-minded collaborators in tires and oil were the primary force behind the wholesale abandonment of trolley systems nationwide. GM, Firestone and Phillips Petroleum, among others, formed National City Lines, which bought up trolley companies and converted them to buses with monopolistic zeal. In New York, GM worked through an interest in the Fifth Avenue Coach Co. and its subsidiaries, which by 1926 controlled most of the trolley business in Manhattan — and which, in 1935 and 1936, then led the way in converting to buses.

The trolley's best chance to survive was the so-called PCC car, a project of the transit industry's Presidents Conference Committee. A cross between a bus and a trolley, the PCC was a streamlined, rubber-cushioned, coachlike thing that ran on electricity, and it was efficient and comfortable. LaGuardia, however, blocked that development. Brooklyn's trolley operator, the Brooklyn-Manhattan Transit Co., or BMT, bought 100 of the new PCCs in 1936 and liked them so much that it considered buying more — but LaGuardia disapproved because he was negotiating for the city to buy the company, which happened in 1940. The original Brooklyn PCCs continued to run on Coney Island and Church and McDonald Aves. until they were scrapped in 1956.

AND SO THE age edged to its end. Early in 1935, the oldest trolley line in the city — on Madison Ave., from Park Row to 135th St. — was one of the first to be converted to buses. A busload of officials headed south from the 135th St. terminal on Feb. 1, and it was an event of such import that a CBS radio reporter broadcast live from the bus.

Buses being faster than trolleys, this one overtook the last southbound at 72nd St. To avoid rubbing it in, the bus slowed to let the trolley lead the way to the end of its run. As a result, the second, third and fourth buses to leave 135th St. at 10-minute intervals backed up behind the first, and they all reached Park Row bunched together. Sixty-three years later, they're still doing that.

By MICHAEL ARONSON
Daily News Writer

CHARLES LUCIANO, boss of all the bosses, king of the Genovese family, founder and ruler of the national Mafia Commission, master of New York City's docks, the Fulton Fish Market and the Feast of San Gennaro, sat fuming in the witness box in Manhattan Supreme Court. Special Prosecutor Thomas E. Dewey had brought him up on, of all things, simple compulsory prostitution, like he was some common pimp. Him. Charlie Lucky. Charged with running hookers. It was embarrassing.

Prostitution was, in fact, among the least of Charlie Lucky's many profitable enterprises. Dewey knew that. But hookers were the witnesses he had. And they were going to send the big boss to prison.

Since Al Capone's conviction in Chicago, most mob prosecutions had relied on dependable income tax evasion charges. But by directly charging Luciano and eight associates with a criminal conspiracy, Dewey was, in the spring of 1936, attempting something new: "trial of a first-rank racketeer," as the Daily News put it, "for the crime of which he is actually suspected."

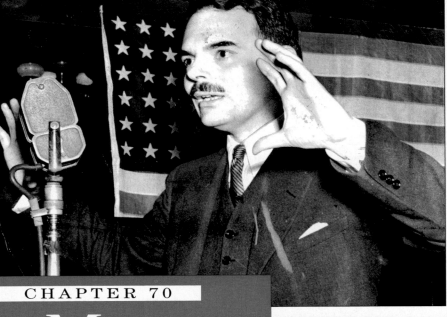

CHAPTER 70
MR. SPECIAL PROSECUTOR
Smashing The Rackets, 1936

Luciano denied any knowledge of prostitution, insisting he was just a gambler and horseplayer. But Dewey had more than 50 witnesses who had overcome their fears of the deadly crimelord and were ready to testify against him — working girls and madams who spent weeks describing Charlie Lucky's illicit play-for-pay empire.

Then, methodically using phone records, police reports and mountains of other documents, Dewey began to link Luciano's affairs with those of fellow mobsters Bugsy Siegel, Louis Lepke and Gurrah Shapiro. He hammered away for five hours. When he was through, Charlie Lucky looked very nervous.

Throughout mobdom and officialdom alike, those who had once laughed off the earnest Tom Dewey as an amusing little Boy Scout were rethinking that view.

DEWEY WAS A Wall Street lawyer when in 1931 his Republican connections got him an appointment, at just 29 years of age, as chief assistant U.S. attorney for Manhattan.

He came to public attention a year later when he indicted mobster Waxey Gordon on tax charges. Waxey was easy. Though he had made millions from his hotels, nightclubs and breweries, Waxey had paid $10.76 in federal income taxes in 1930, and Dewey sent him over for 10 years with little trouble. Arthur Flegenheimer, aka Dutch Schultz, was another matter. Dewey won an indictment against Schultz — but never personally got him into court, because shortly after that he was out of a job. Democrat Franklin Roosevelt had won the White House, and now New York had a new federal prosecutor.

Prohibition was over anyway. The bootleggers and their rackets would soon be a thing of the past. Or so people thought.

TWELVE DRY YEARS had only consolidated and strengthened organized crime. With Prohibition repealed in early 1933, the gangs moved into other enterprises — one of them the policy racket. In the depths of the spirit-sapping Depression, the numbers offered people a chance for a little easy money — a rigged chance, but still a chance.

In 1935, a Manhattan grand jury that had been empaneled to investigate the numbers racketeers began to sense that District Attorney William Dodge — a Tammany Hall man who had been anomalously elected to office amid what was otherwise Fiorello LaGuardia's 1933 reform sweepup at the polls — really didn't wish to probe too deeply. The grand jurors rebelled and went public, calling on Gov. Herbert Lehman to force Dodge to appoint a special prosecutor. They were joined by the city Bar Association — which remembered Dewey and suggested him for the post. On July 29, Special Prosecutor Dewey took his oath of office.

The next night, he gave a radio speech. He would not, he said, go after the "ordinary vice trades" — prostitution, gambling, lottery games; his ambitions were larger. "We are concerned with those predatory vultures who traffic on a wholesale scale in the bodies of women and mere girls for profit," he said. "We are concerned with

professional gamblers who run large, crooked gambling places and lotteries at the expense of the public." He also targeted the extortion rings that made honest businesses pay protection money.

Setting up shop in the Woolworth Building, Dewey recruited a team of prosecutors and investigators. His first target: Dutch Schultz, the one that had got away from him in his federal days. In upstate Malone, the Dutchman had just been acquitted of that old tax charge, and now he was back in the city, defying LaGuardia's order to stay out. And Dewey was openly out to get him.

But Dewey was deprived of the pleasure. In October, as the Dutchman dined in Newark's Palace Chop House, three gunmen dispatched him from this world. Dewey wouldn't know this until several years later, but Schultz had been ordered killed by senior mobsters because he had recklessly vowed to assassinate the special prosecutor, which would have meant big trouble. The mob, in short, had saved Dewey's life.

If Dewey had lost one big catch, he had more fishing to do. He wanted Lepke, he wanted Gurrah, he wanted Charlie Lucky. Shortly, he was striking at the $1 million-a-week loan shark racket, rounding up dozens of usurers in citywide sweeps. Then, in early 1936, he went after the city's prostitution rings, raiding dozens of brothels, on one occasion arresting 77 girls in a single night.

It wasn't the working girls he was after. He wanted their bosses. Using a team of 20 stenographers, the Dewey team grilled a parade of women — and began to turn up references to someone named Charlie.

LUCIANO WAS arrested April 2, as he relaxed in the underworld gambling resort of Hot Springs, Ark., and was extradited back to New York to face grim and unforgiving justice in the person of Tom Dewey.

On June 7, Luciano sat stunned as the blue-ribbon jury found him guilty of 62 counts of compulsory prostitution. Throughout the trial, the New York American observed, "Some strange confidence seemed to support him; some desperate faith that his luck would free him from this temporary inconvenience and set him once again on top of the gangster heap."

Now, handcuffed and headed for the Tombs, Charlie Lucky's luck had run out. It was the most shattering blow the State of New York had ever dealt to its mobsters.

Thomas E. Dewey had only just begun. After the Luciano trial, the special prosecutor empaneled two grand juries and started taking on the rackets industry by industry — garments, restaurants, bakeries, trucking. By the end of 1937 he secured 72 convictions. He suffered just one acquittal.

DEWEY'S SUCCESS as a gangbuster propelled him into the district attorney's office in 1937 and the governor's mansion in 1942.

CHAPTER 71

BLUE WITH DEATH

The Beekman Hill Maniac, 1937

By JAY MAEDER
Daily News Staff Writer

LIKE MANY A modern, free-thinking young woman of the 1930s — like, it often seemed, practically every comely slaying victim in those dependably lurid days — Veronica Gedeon kept both a diary and a Little Black Book.

Clue-wise, the diary wasn't much, nothing but girlish twitterings ("I love him so, but he was not made for me"). The names in the Little Black Book, on the other hand, were fairly interesting, given Ronnie Gedeon's scarlet career as an, as the expression had it, "artist's model," and it was initially felt by detectives that perhaps young Ronnie might have been blackmailing a Broadway sport or two, and her little volume was quite the public sensation for several days until it developed that actually it didn't have anything at all to do with her abrupt departure from this life by reason of strangulation.

After that, police attention turned to Ronnie's own father, a scowling Hungarian who approached the Old Testamentesque in his disapproval of the wayward girl. "She made fools of men!" Father Gedeon shouted as cops grilled him for 33 hours. "You can't treat men like that! She was wild! This rotten American system! Children laugh at their parents and start running wild!" Plainly dad had done her, sleuths now decided. But that didn't pan out either.

Finally, what they stumbled across was a genuine fiend — a tormented artist straight out of the Grand Guignol, a madman against whose depredations New Yorkers kept their doors bolted for weeks, a homicidal lunatic whose commissions of the spectacular Beekman Hill Murders of Easter Sunday 1937 ultimately would result in far-reaching psychiatric reforms in the State of New York.

RONNIE HAD BEEN out late with friends, and she had let herself into the E. 50th St. apartment about 3 on Sunday morning the 28th of March and she had gone straight to her bath, wherein for nearly an hour she had unhurriedly creamed her face and curled her hair and rinsed out her stockings. Her mother was already dead in the bedroom. The strangler was waiting patiently in the dark.

The estranged father, Joseph Gedeon, found the three bodies when he came to visit Sunday afternoon: the model, the mother and the household boarder, a deaf bartender who appeared to have slept through the mayhem and then been stabbed to death as he snored. The savage triple slaying would have been a New York sensation in any case. It was,

of course, also the case that there were many photo studies of the artist's model available.

The papers ran amok with dozens of them, airbrushed as appropriate: Ronnie nude, Ronnie in lingerie, Ronnie the up-and-coming queen of the crime magazines. Ronnie had done a lot of work for the likes of Inside Detective and Headquarters Detective, illustrating such literature as "Party Girl" and "Pretty But Cheap" and "I Am A White Slave," ever the flimsily clad lass getting herself smothered or clubbed or at the very least trussed. As it happened, she had recently flubbed a job for Front Page Detective; called upon to get throttled, she looked, the editor decided, insufficiently terrified and she got fired. But there were plenty of other pix to go around. Cold in her grave, Ronnie was a famous cover girl at last.

It was, in fact, the detective mags that finally brought in the killer. That was three months later.

Cops had already identified their man as 29-year-old Robert Irwin, a sculptor who had once briefly boarded with the Gedeons and been dismissed from the household after developing what were deemed to be unnatural affections for Ronnie's older sister Ethel. Once Irwin's name hit the papers, psychiatrists started coming out of the woodwork; half the shrinks in town knew Irwin, a deranged ex-divinity student who had spent years shuffling in and out of the Bellevue psycho ward and Rockland State Hospital for the Criminally Insane. **SCOUR CITY FOR MANIAC**, the papers screamed. **HUNT ARTIST IN 8 STATES. MAD SCULPTOR HAD MANIA TO STRANGLE. GUARD ETHEL FROM MANIAC**. Millions shivered as cops threw up a national dragnet for the crazed slayer in the greatest criminal manhunt since the Lindbergh kidnapping.

Late in June, a Cleveland hotel employee spotted Irwin in the pages of True Detective and recognized him as the new busboy. Made, the fugitive fled by bus to Chicago, where cops were waiting for him at the depot. The three Beekman Hill deaths had been accidents, he explained. "I only wanted to kill Ethel," he said. "I loved her."

AS A GIFTED student of Lozado Taft, Robert Irwin had once done a conventional bust of President Herbert Hoover and sent it to the White House and gotten back a nice thank-you note. Otherwise his inclinations were idiosyncratic. His women tended to be fanged snakes. At Rockland, where he put in some time after attempting to castrate himself so that he might better sublimate his stirrings to his art, he had done a self-portrait, sculpting himself as a goat with breasts, and the Rockland doctors had liked it so much that they displayed it on the lawn.

What this squirrel was doing loose instantly became the focus of broad official inquiries even as Irwin returned to New York and started spilling his confession. He had intended to cut off Ethel's head and make a death mask, he said, and Mary Gedeon had let him in and they had chatted pleasantly for a while, and then he had learned that Ethel didn't even live at home anymore and this had made him very, very angry. "The room turned blue with death," he remembered. "I got her throat in my hands." Then he had stuffed Mother Gedeon under a bed and gone to the kitchen to fix himself something to eat.

Later, Ronnie had come home. He had thought she was never going to come out of the bathroom. Killing her had been a shame, of course. "I hate to harm anything beautiful," he said. But it had gone efficiently. "Blue death seemed to issue from her." After that, of course, he had to kill the boarder, too.

"There wasn't anything I could do," he insisted. Couldn't anyone understand that?

LATE IN 1938, Robert Irwin was adjudicated nuts and put away in a cage for the rest of his life. By that time there had been mounted state legislative hearings into the nature of the treatment of the disordered. The hospital system came under withering fire, and several top doctors lost their positions for having permitted someone like Irwin his freedom.

By MARA BOVSUN
Special to The News

EVERYBODY knew this was Not A Family Show. The warning was clearly posted on the marquees outside the theater. "Not for your aunt from Dubuque!" winked an ad campaign. Barkers stood outside barking: "Watch! Like a banana, watch her peel! Watch Gypsy Rose Lee take it off, right down to the fruit!"

So this was no secret. What the four brothers Minsky were serving up was burlesque.

Abe, Billy, Herbert and Morton Minsky didn't invent the burleycue. Maybe it dated to Civil War days. Maybe it had roots in the comedy of ancient Greece. By the time the Minskys showed up on Houston St. around 1916, burlesque was already well into its golden age, with the Columbia wheel and several other circuits giving performances around the country.

Nor did the Minskys invent the striptease, which according to legend was unintentionally created when a famous lady trapeze artist snapped her bra while flying through the air in the 1870s.

But once the Minskys got there, burlesque was never the same.

The "impresarios of the epidermis" were the first in the U.S. to put nudie cuties on runways that ran straight into the popeyed, sweaty audience — an innovation swiped from the Folies Bergere of Paris.

They perked up skit titles: "Dress Takes a Holiday," "Anatomy and Cleopatra," "Julius Teaser," "The Sway of All Flesh."

The billed their shows as "The Poor Man's Follies," copying the costumes, the sets, the look of the uptown, upscale girlie revues and offering them at a fraction of the ticket price.

The Minsky name eventually came synonymous with burlesque — hoochie-coochie, bumps and grinds, shimmies, peels and strands of strategically placed beads.

It also meant sock-in-the-kisser comics, putty-nosed, baggy-pants funnymen like Phil Silvers and Abbott and Costello, full of moldy old jokes of the lesser orders:

Costello: I got a new girlfriend from Maine.
Abbott: Oh? Bangor?
Costello: Bang her? I just met her.

Comic: Candy! Bonbons!
Straight man: Do you have nuts?
Comic: No.
Straight man: Do you have dates?
Comic: If I had nuts, I'd have dates.

This stuff was manifestly for theatergoers who liked their comedy fast and loose and their showgirls tall, sexy and unclad, or as close as the law would allow. Sometimes the ladies shimmied and peeled overmuch, and city officials found it necessary to step in and teach them how to live in polite society.

CHAPTER 72
THE OLD OO-LA-LA
Raiding Minsky's, 1937

THE MINSKYS got raided quite a lot. Detectives would often investigate a report of indecent behavior, take careful notes and then order a sweep and haul performers off to jail. It would be alleged that some Parisienne or another "did bare her breasts and cause them to move indecently." There might even be a trial, usually highlighted by a fat cop demonstrating the bump and grind to a judge, then everyone would be acquitted and go to a speakeasy.

Raids only gave the burleycue houses good publicity. A show hot enough for a raid was obviously a must-see. And veteran performers took the pinches in stride. It was said that Gypsy Rose Lee awoke in jail on one occasion, discovered that someone had covered her with a blanket and screamed: "Help! I've been draped!"

And so the shows went merrily on. A pneumatic stripper named Carrie Finnell became famous for twirling tassels in opposite directions. Rose la Rose wore a trick dress that permitted the occasional glimpse of forbidden zones as she sang "Who Will Kiss My Oo-la-la?"

In 1931, the Minskys crossed the line. They moved their growing burlesque empire square into the heart of white-tie-and-tails Broadway.

THE REOPENING of the Republic Theater on 42nd St. near Seventh Ave., for years the home of the hit "Abie's Irish Rose," brought howls of complaints that the Minskys had imported the Bowery and Coney Island to Times Square. The brothers were blamed in full as many less-than-high-class tenants followed them into the area. The two-headed animal museums. The Indian herb doctors. The phrenologists. Hubert's Flea Circus, starring Gypsy Rose Flea. And a wave of other burleycue theaters.

Meanwhile, with radio and movies whittling away at theater audiences — and the rest of the

theater world struggling to survive the Depression — the Minskys flourished by becoming nuder and lewder.

"Cheapest dirt, dirtiest coochers and no talent," grunted Variety. "Just rotten."

Finally, in 1934, reformers turned to the new mayor, Fiorello LaGuardia, and his hand-picked commissioner of licenses, Paul Moss, himself a former producer. Moss immediately declared Minsky's runways a fire hazard and had them ripped out.

The real push came in April 1937, when New York was struck by a series of lurid sex crimes, sparking much burley-bashing right on the eve of license-renewal time.

A parade of good citizens appeared at the license hearings to blast burlesque's offenses against society. Cardinal Hayes sent a personal letter to Commissioner Moss, declaring such entertainments "disgraceful and pernicious."

Cops raided the theaters, dragging near-nude strippers from their dressing rooms. There were 14 burlesque houses in the city, and Moss refused permits to all of them. More than 2,000 girls, stagehands, musicians and ticket sellers were put out on the street.

"Is Moss going to feed us and our families?" blubbered one tearful chorine.

LaGuardia declared "the end of incorporated filth" in New York. Henceforth, the word "burlesque" could not be used in any theater advertising. Neither could the word "Minsky," which of course meant the same thing.

THE THEATERS tried reopening, without the strippers, the G-strings, the dirty jokes — without, in short, the audiences. One cleaned-up variety format called "vaudesque" was tried out, a reverse striptease in which girls started out nearly nude and then put their clothes on.

Well, it just wasn't the same.

By November, the Minskys were closed, broke and out of business. In the city, their day was done.

So the Minsky name went on to flourish in Newark and other such entertainment capitals. A few smaller entrepreneurs managed to stay in business until 1942, when LaGuardia pulled the plug completely. By then, Phil Silvers, Gypsy Rose Lee, Abbott and Costello and the other headliners had moved on to other stages.

By DENNIS WEPMAN
Special to The News

PARADES IN Chinatown were always colorful sights, but the crowd on Nov. 7, 1937, was not a festive one.

On this solemn Sunday, more than 2,000 Chinese men and women marched soberly along Mott and Pell Sts., representing for the first time all the traditionally rivalrous associations that made up the community's complex social structure. Forever in conflict with one another, the many family, professional and political groups of Chinatown had come together at last. There was common cause. Japan was overrunning the homeland.

Indeed, at this very hour, 25,000 Japanese soldiers were encircling Shanghai and the fall of the great city now appeared imminent after 13 weeks of land and air strikes by the invaders. In China, for the first time in thousands of years, an awakened people stood united behind one leader in a desperate war against a foreign aggressor. In New York City, long-fractious Chinatown was now one camp as well.

THE CHINESE had a long, sad history in New York. From an estimated 150 cooks, sailors and candy vendors in 1860, the three-block colony on Mott, Pell and Doyers Sts. grew to more than 3,000 in the 1890s as laborers fleeing anti-Chinese violence in the California gold fields flooded in. There were 27 men to every woman. The Chinese Exclusion Act of 1882 had prohibited wives from entering the U.S. The favored occupation was laundryman. While washing clothes for a living was not particularly a Chinese specialty anywhere in the world, New York's Chinese took it up because the law barred them from doing much of anything else.

By the turn of the century, Chinatown — mysterious of atmosphere, sinister of reputation — was a tourist attraction. Never slow to recognize a profitable market, the Chinese soon began to open restaurants, curio shops and exotic "temples" fragrant with incense. But they remained private and isolated. Family associations supported newcomers with jobs and loans. District organizations settled disputes among people who did not trust American courts. The police seldom ventured into Chinatown. Order, of a sort, was maintained by the tongs.

Originally vigilante groups serving as protection societies for the weaker family associations, the tongs became business and fraternal societies — and bitter enemies. The On Leongs, originally a merchant tong, controlled Mott St. The working-

CHAPTER 73

AWAKE AND STAND

Solidarity In Chinatown, 1937

class Hip Sings considered Pell St. their turf. These and five or six other tongs divided up the business district — and defended their areas with a ferocity that, from 1910 into the 1920s, regularly turned Chinatown into a bloody battlefield.

Truces were declared, seldom respected. The police were helpless. On Sept. 18, 1925, detectives and federal agents arrested 500 Chinese for a shootout only hours after the Hip Sing and On Leong tongs had signed a treaty. The U.S. government called in the Chinese minister of state to make peace, and things quieted down for a while. Finally, the threat of wholesale deportations put a tentative end to the tong wars.

Now, with Japan on the march, hostilities ceased altogether.

IN SUPPORT OF the land of their ancestors, Chinese all over the U.S. contributed to a war fund. In 1937, some $1.5 million was subscribed. San Francisco, the nation's largest Chinese settlement, with a population of 17,000, gave $150,000. New York came up with more than twice that sum. A Chinese Catholic War Relief Association was formed to rally aid for the wounded, and the Methodist churches raised $250,000 for a China Emergency Relief Fund.

Four years before the U.S. went to war with

Japan, the nation had become profoundly China-conscious. Wellesley-educated Mayling Soong Chiang, the fervently nationalistic wife of Generalissimo Chiang Kai-shek, was perhaps the world's most-admired woman, passionately rallying sympathizers to China's cause. The AFL and the CIO voted a boycott on Japanese manufactured goods. Theodore Roosevelt Jr. headed a United Council for Civilian Relief in China. In New York City, the tongs put aside their differences to form the resoundingly named New York Overseas Chinese Anti-Japanese Salvation General Committee for Military Funds. The powerful Chinese Hand Laundry Alliance, recognizing the relation between the survival of the Chinese community in the city and that of the homeland, took for its motto "To Save China, to Save Ourselves."

The November 1937 parade was a public demonstration of unity. Thirty women carried a huge Nationalist Chinese flag to catch coins and paper money thrown by the crowds, and a paper dragon devoured long streamers of bills. When the march ended, Hu Shih, former dean of Peking National University and soon to become China's ambassador to the U.S., addressed 1,500 at the China Theater on Doyers St. and promised that besieged China would "resist to the end."

The new solidarity was even more dramatically displayed six months later, when 12,000 people, very nearly the entire population of Chinatown, turned out for the largest Chinese demonstration ever staged in the U.S. The Chinese Hand Laundry Alliance closed its 1,500 shops to join the 67 organizations represented in the parade. **CHINATOWN'S ANCIENT FOES UNITE**, headlined the papers, marveling that Hip Sings and On Leongs marched side by side after more than 50 years of bitter and bloody internal conflict.

By DAVID HINCKLEY
Daily News Staff Writer

INVITING THE Benny Goodman band to Carnegie Hall in early 1938 had the vaguely sarcastic aura of suggesting that hungry street urchins be served dinner at the Stork Club.

It was all right for them to eat. Did they have to do it *there?*

"Swing" music had been formally identified some 2½ years earlier, thanks largely to Goodman, and the cultural elders of the land felt strongly that its incendiary rhythms and gyrating fans pushed basic propriety, common decency and musical taste pretty much to the limit.

Jitterbugging, the young people called it when they piled out onto the dance floor. *Good heavens, Mabel, they look as if they're possessed.*

The new craze was tolerated, barely, on the assumption that, like flappers and the Charleston, it would soon go away. So there was little sentiment among the city's upper cultural crust that this Goodman person needed to be brought into Carnegie, of all halls.

Carnegie was, after all, the home of the New York Philharmonic, a temple of refinement and high culture. When the place opened in May 1891, Tchaikovsky himself came in to conduct several of his symphonic works, and while not every artist over the next 46 years met that standard, a swing band concert was considered only a small step above square dances and rent parties.

Still, it could not be denied that for a generation raised in the country's longest Depression and now living in the darkening shadow of a world war they knew they could be sent off to fight, this free-spirited music struck a chord.

THE ROOTS OF swing had been kicking around for decades in jazz bands, orchestras and combos led by artists like Fletcher Henderson and Louis Armstrong. But, as often happens in American popular music, it wasn't until it fell into the hands of some white guys who really liked the stuff that it became a certified national phenomenon.

In this case, the carriers included Benny Goodman, who was born tenement-poor in Chicago in 1909 and around age 11 seized on the clarinet as his ticket out. He pursued his music with a monomaniacal intensity that produced stunning performances — and fast drove away many of his musicians, including such legends as Lionel Hampton, Bunny Berigan, Charlie Christian and Teddy Wilson.

One bad note in a show, it was said, and a sideman got "the ray," which was Goodman — even in the middle of his own solo — affixing a cold stare that said someone was about to become history.

Years later, after Goodman finished a good-will tour of the Soviet Union, one band member was asked how it felt. "With Benny," he replied, "it's like playing in Russia every night."

Still, Goodman's bands delivered the music he wanted, and his harvest came home in late

Goodman and Krupa.

CHAPTER 74

THE PRIMITIVE URGE FOR BARBARIC RHYTHM

Benny Goodman At Carnegie Hall, 1938

August 1935, when he opened at the Palomar in L.A. to such large and spirited crowds that word-of-mouth rippled clear across the country. New York crowds were equally adoring the following year at the Paramount, and by the end of 1937, with swing bands popping up everywhere,

Goodman was the king. By then he had one of his best ensembles, with trumpeter Harry James, pianist Teddy Wilson, drummer Gene Krupa and vocalist Martha Tilton.

Like all traveling bands of the time, Goodman's worked and recorded continuously. But it wasn't practice, practice, practice that got them to Carnegie Hall. It was publicist Wynn Nathanson, who saw a good way to get some hot ink. Impresario Sol Hurok bought the idea, and the show was scheduled for Sunday, Jan. 16, 1938, over Goodman's misgivings.

True, Paul Whiteman had won a similar gamble 14 years earlier when he commissioned George Gershwin to unveil the jazz-derived "Rhapsody in Blue" at Aeolian Hall, also previously considered too good for that sort of thing.

But the Aeolian show was presented to a highbrow crowd that included Rachmaninoff and Stokowski. Goodman would be playing to jitterbugging teenagers, and he felt his bets needed enough hedging that at first he considered hiring a comedian to open the show.

On the other hand, the blunt-spoken Goodman had no intention of pretending he was grateful just to be invited to the swells' party. Asked how long an intermission he'd like, he shot back: "I don't know. How long does Toscanini get?"

So it came to pass. As the curtain was rising, Harry James muttered, "I feel like a whore in church."

IF SO, 3,000 happy congregants were primed to offer absolution, as the band swung through Count Basie's "One O'Clock Jump," Duke Ellington's "Blue Reverie," "Body and Soul," "Tiger Rag" and a half-dozen other tunes in a two-hour performance.

Basie, Lester Young, Buck Clayton and several members of the Ellington band sat in at various times, lending star insurance and underscoring the musical relationship between Goodman and the black bands that preceded him.

The audience loved it, though the critics were mixed — still not quite convinced all this was fitting and proper.

"It was the first time the more or less sacred halls of Carnegie have ever echoed to the music of youth, freedom and the primitive urge for barbaric rhythm," wrote the Daily News. "Goodman apparently is one who believes in swing, but one who is also willing to admit that at best it is a bit screwy."

Actually, there's little indication Goodman ever said or thought any such thing. But on the morning of Jan. 17, Carnegie Hall was still standing.

GENE KRUPA *quit Goodman less than a month later, citing personal and musical differences, and within a year the whole band was pretty much dismantled and replaced. The Carnegie Hall concert, recorded almost as an afterthought on a single ceiling microphone, was released in 1950 as a newfangled LP and is now considered a classic. In 1940, Goodman was invited back to Carnegie as a guest clarinetist with the New York Philharmonic.*

By JAY MAEDER
Daily News Staff Writer

HITLER'S TANKS had rolled across Austria a few months earlier. Czechoslovakia was plainly going to be next. And in the late spring of 1938, the New York papers were full of disturbing reports from Germany: **DAWN RAIDS JAIL JEWS. STORM TROOPS BEAT UP JEWS IN BERLIN RIOT. GOEBBELS STIRS JEWISH PURGE.** *"A mob of several hundred civilians tore through the Grenadierstrasse and Dragonerstrasse late this afternoon, pulling Jews out of their shops, punching them and smearing their windows. . . ." "At Buchwald Concentration Camp near Weimar, it was reported 65 Army buses filled with Jews were arriving nightly. . . ."*

In Washington, federal grand juries were indicting the leaders of a nationwide Nazi spy ring. On Long Island, a tavern frequented by Mitchel Field fliers was found to be run by Third Reich agents who were plotting to kidnap

CHAPTER 75

THE HIGHEST OF PRIZES

Louis And Schmeling, 1938

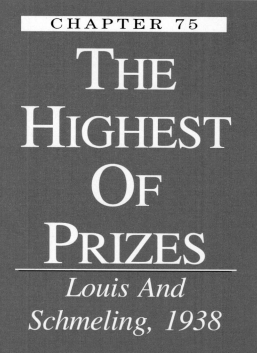

an important colonel. In Manhattan on Wednesday the 22nd of June, a U.S. Senate committee opened hearings into the German-American Bund and the shadowy activities of its Yorkville cadres.

At Yankee Stadium that night, before 80,000 fans and a worldwide radio audience of many millions, world heavyweight champion Joe Louis climbed into the ring and once more looked into the eyes of German challenger Max Schmeling. At stake was the highest of prizes.

JOSEPH LOUIS BARROW, the Brown Bomber, the Dark Destroyer, had come roaring out of the Detroit Golden Gloves in July 1934; after June 1935, when he kayoed Primo Carnera at Yankee Stadium, he was widely recognized as the uncrowned champ, the greatest fighter of his time. On his way to the title, he met Max Schmeling, who had once worn the crown himself and now wanted it back.

It was June 19, 1936. Louis had 27 straight wins behind him, but by now he was accustomed

to the good life, out of shape and careless — "flush on the mush," as they said — and after he took a terrific belt to the chin in the fourth round he never remembered a thing, just kept slogging on dazedly until Schmeling finally demolished him eight rounds later. Now Schmeling was sure to become the first man ever to recapture the heavyweight title. Home in Germany, he was a national hero, glorious living proof of the Nazi doctrine of racial superiority.

Louis was never careless again. Yet there was relatively small comfort when he took the world championship title away from aging Jimmy Braddock in 1937 and became the first black champ since Jack Johnson's dethronement two decades earlier. Some fight circles held that, in purely sporting terms, the ring was no place for ideological debate; mounting international tensions, it was felt — specifically, American Jewish boycotts of Schmeling — had kept the German from getting a fair shot at Braddock himself. Louis, wrote Daily News sports editor Jimmy Powers, hardly a Nazi sympathizer, "is champion only because he fought the arthritic Braddock first. Schmeling knocked out Louis. Schmeling was the rightful No. 1 challenger."

Louis successfully defended his title several times through early 1938 and patiently waited for his rematch with the one man who had defeated him. "I won't feel right till I lick him," Louis said.

THERE REMAINED many political objections to the rematch when Schmeling arrived in the U.S. in May. These were softened somewhat when fight promoters pledged 10% of the million-dollar gate to Jewish refugee relief agencies. Meanwhile, Schmeling's American manager, Joe (Yussel) Jacobs, a man who somewhat uncomfortably found himself required to heil Hitler when in Berlin, assured the world press that Germany's Jews were all quite happy and content.

Schmeling laughed off reports that he was personally doomed to a Third Reich prison camp if he lost this fight to the American black. Nonsense, he said: "Just because Louis is a colored man makes no difference to my people. Sport is sport in Germany, nothing more. Germans are the fairest people in the world."

He was not worried about Louis in any event, Schmeling boasted to reporters at his Adirondacks training camp: "He'll always be afraid of me, down deep inside. He's the kind who always holds a man who has beaten him in some sort of superstitious fear."

At his own camp in Pompton Lakes, N.J., Joe Louis just smiled.

THE FIGHT LASTED 124 seconds. For the last 90 of them, the big German took one of the most savage beatings any fighter had ever taken. Finally, helpless beneath Louis' murderous rain of blows, he screamed and crashed to the mat and went into convulsions as the referee stopped the slaughter. It was five minutes before he could get to his feet. Helped back to his corner, his six-year fight to regain his title finished, his last chance gone, he buried his face in his gloves and sobbed.

Schmeling was hospitalized for a week. At one point he was reported near death. His wife, film comedienne Anny Ondra, stood grim vigil. "I don't think this is a sport any longer," she said quietly.

MAX SCHMELING *was not imprisoned, but there was no official welcome waiting for the crippled fighter when he returned to Berlin on July 9.*

Joe Louis remained world heavyweight champion for another 10 years.

BIG TOWN BIG TIME

By JAY MAEDER
Daily News Staff Writer

ONE OF THE differences between 1938 and the windblown glory days of just a few years earlier was that by 1938 if you wanted to fly your airplane across the Atlantic Ocean you had to ask the government's permission to do it. And in 1938, the government took one look at Douglas Corrigan's beat-up, patched-together, 9-year-old Curtiss Robin and told him no, he couldn't.

Another difference was that by 1938 it was getting a lot tougher to get noticed when you did something amazing. On Saturday the 9th of July, Douglas Corrigan climbed into his beat-up, patched-together, 9-year-old Curtiss Robin and set a new speed record flying nonstop from Long Beach, Calif., to Roosevelt Field, L.I., and hardly anyone paid any attention at all.

Wasn't it just his luck. It seemed that Howard Hughes had impatiently chosen exactly this moment, after months of meticulous preparation, to make his fanfared round-the-world hop. At 4 p.m. Sunday, the dashing multi-millionaire Hollywood producer, daredevil speed king and official flying ambassador of the forthcoming New York World's Fair left his Rockefeller Center offices, drove to Floyd Bennett Field in Brooklyn and piled his three crewmen into his big silver twin-engined Lockheed. At 7:20, as 6,000 well-wishers applauded, Hughes took off for Paris. There was no applause for Douglas Corrigan.

All week long the papers were full of Hughes' adventure. **HUGHES SET FOR MOSCOW FLIGHT. HUGHES SPEEDS ACROSS SIBERIA. HUGHES REFUELS IN ALASKA, HOPS OFF.** At 2:34 p.m. on Thursday the 14th, Hughes realighted at Floyd Bennett, having covered 14,656 miles in three days, 19 hours, 14 minutes and 10 seconds — about half the time it had taken Wiley Post to fly around the world in 1933. Some 25,000 roaring New Yorkers were waiting for him when he landed, and the next day a half-million of them lined Broadway from the Battery to 60th St. as the city gave the unchallenged captain of the clouds its first ticker-tape parade since the Depression had started.

Well, wasn't this just Douglas Corrigan's damn luck.

The fabled Howard Hughes showed up at this black-tie function and that and then excused himself from several others, and the papers all said he had ducked out to go tryst with Katharine Hepburn. Out at Bennett, meanwhile, here was Corrigan, just a greasemonkey with $15 in his pocket, eating fig bars, still wearing the same clothes he'd been wearing all week.

At 5:17 a.m. Sunday, his cross-country record a bust and his petition to fly the Atlantic now denied by the Bureau of Air Commerce not once but twice, Corrigan got into his rickety Robin and

Mayor LaGuardia and New York's main man.

CHAPTER 76
LUCK OF THE IRISH
Wrong Way Corrigan, 1938

headed out, he said, back home to California.

Field mechanics scratched their heads as they watched him go. That was funny, they agreed; why, that fellow had put in 320 gallons of gas and he was a half-ton overweight; why would he do something like that? Another thing that was funny. It looked like he was flying straight northeast, didn't it? Why would he fly northeast? Why, California was in the other direction altogether. Wasn't it?

By Tuesday morning, 31-year-old Douglas Corrigan was front-page news all over the world.

EARLY MONDAY afternoon the 18th, Ireland time, 28 hours and 13 minutes out of Bennett, he had dropped out of the sky and landed his heap at Baldonnel Airport outside of Dublin. "Just in from New York," he announced. "Where am I?"

Officials gaped at the Robin, a machine that really was literally held together by baling wire in several places. He had crossed the ocean in *this*? "Ocean?" he said.

YOU MEAN, he said, that he hadn't flown to California at all? This was *Ireland?* The officials stared at him. "I guess I flew the wrong way," he said. The officials stared at him. "I flew over the clouds all the time," he explained. "I couldn't see what was underneath." The officials stared at him. "I made a mistake," he said. The officials stared at him. "I set the compass wrong," he said. The officials kept staring at him. "I must be a bum navigator," he apologized.

WRONG WAY CORRIGAN was now the fourth person to fly solo from New York across the Atlantic, following Charles Lindbergh, Wiley Post and Amelia Earhart, although he was the first to make what was technically known as an "unannounced" flight and certainly the first to do it without landing papers or passport. Nobody understood how his ancient rattler could possibly have flown anywhere to begin with, much less across the ocean five hours faster than Lindbergh. Questions about the Robin's airworthiness regularly got Corrigan's dander up. "She's good enough to fly around the world," he snorted. "All the motor needs is a bit of grease."

Terrified that the American lunatic might actually take off in the dead of night and try to fly somewhere else, the Irish quickly took his crate into protective custody. Back in the States, meanwhile, the Commerce Department convened to discuss the status of Corrigan's flying license amid mounting suspicions that what it had here was a man who had quite outrageously made an outlaw flight in deliberate defiance of government orders. Corrigan insisted this wasn't true, but the Irish people clapped him on the back wherever he went, and U.S. Minister John Cudahy chuckled as he took the Atlantic flier into his home as his personal guest, and Prime Minister Eamon de Valera couldn't wait to shake his hand.

He remained the toast of Ireland for several weeks, and then he went on to London and dined with U.S. Ambassador Joseph Kennedy, and British Imperial Airways let him fly a four-motored transport, and when Wrong Way Corrigan got back to New York on Aug. 4 Brooklyn gave him a huge parade and Broadway threw a fete twice as big as Howard Hughes'.

"What a new lease on life this fellow has brought to every gag maker," ex-Mayor Jimmy Walker told a screaming crowd of 30,000 at Yankee Stadium.

"One of the grandest wild stunts of all time," said the Daily News, pronouncing Corrigan "a swell egg and an Irish adventurer of the old school."

"Honest, I meant to fly to California," Corrigan kept saying.

The government thought things over and concluded that no useful purpose was to be served by severe punishment of whatever Corrigan's infractions had been. It happened that the Air Commerce director was a man named Denis Mulligan, who handed Corrigan a suspension that came to all of five days and then grinned broadly. "Great day for the Irish," Mulligan said.

DOUGLAS CORRIGAN subsequently made a few bucks selling his story to the big magazines and the movies and then quietly ended up as a California fruit farmer. To his dying day in 1995, he continued to maintain that his flight to Ireland had been purely an accident.

Crate at takeoff.

By JAY MAEDER
Daily News Staff Writer

THE LEDGE was 17 floors above Fifth Ave., barely a foot and a half wide, and the young man who had stepped out onto it at 11:50 on Tuesday morning the 26th of July 1938 clung uncertainly to the ornamental stone fretwork as he stared down into the sweltering summer streets. Just a moment earlier he had been quietly waiting for room service to bring lunch. "I'm going out the window," he had informed his sister, and that's what he did.

A midtown beat cop galloped up to Room 1714 and put his head outside. "What are you doing out there?" the cop demanded. "Come on in."

"Don't you come near me or I'll jump," John Warde replied, clutching the stones.

Now the cop grasped that what he had here was a situation, and he phoned headquarters, and presently radio cars and rescue units were converging on the Hotel Gotham on 55th St., across from the Fifth Ave. Presbyterian Church. By now the lunchtime strollers had spotted the man on the ledge too, and crowds were gaping up at him, and traffic stopped and office workers were at their windows, pointing.

And for the next 10 hours and 48 minutes, thousands of New Yorkers stood vigil as an unknown man lost in despair chain-smoked cigarettes and paced back and forth and weighed matters out on more literally a precipice than most would ever know, all through a hot summer's day and evening on this narrow ledge 17 dizzy floors over oblivion.

JOHNNY WARDE was 26 years old and a heartache to his family, who had watched him sink deeper and deeper into dejection ever since his moody student days at Southampton High. Johnny just couldn't seem to make a success of anything, even killing himself with a knife, for which attempt he had spent several months locked up in a state hospital. Warmhearted family friends, Mr. and Mrs. Patrick Valentine, had taken him in as their chauffeur and tried to cheer him and give him a sense of self-worth, but he remained inconsolable, and just a few days earlier police had stopped him from going off the Pon Quoque Bridge in Hampton Bays, L.I.

Over the weekend the Valentines had taken John and his protective 22-year-old sister, Katherine Bull, on a trip to Chicago, and he had seemed blue. On Tuesday morning, back in New York again, they stopped off for lunch at the Valentines' city residence at the Gotham Hotel before heading back to Southampton, and Katherine gently said something about perhaps seeing another doctor. John took off his jacket and folded it neatly. "I'm going out the window," he said, and he did.

SEVENTEEN FLOORS down, firemen held a useless small net; it was all they could do. Police closed off the streets between Madison and Sixth and 54th and 59th, pushed back the swelling crowds, tried to run off the hawkers selling binoculars. Upstairs, rescuers studied the ledge and assessed the opportunities for lassoing Johnny Warde, or grabbing his ankles, or something, but he was well positioned to keep everyone at bay. "I swear I'll jump," he kept shouting. A priest tried to talk him inside. So did a couple of doctors. A traffic cop named Charles Glasco posed as a friendly bellhop and passed him smokes and talked baseball with him. Johnny liked the Chicago Cubs.

In and out of faints through the long day, sister Katherine perched on the windowsill, legs roped to a bed. "We love you," she wept. "We all love you. Come in and let us love you."

"They'll only send me away again," Johnny observed.

"No," she insisted. "No one's going to hurt you."

"You'd better leave me alone to work this

CHAPTER 77

EVERYONE HAS A PROBLEM

The Jumper, 1938

problem out all by himself," he suggested.

"There are all kinds of problems, Johnny," she pleaded. "Everyone has a problem. You can work it out somewhere else. Please, please come in."

"I'm a rotter," he said.

"You're the best brother in the world," she sobbed, fainting again.

Patrick Valentine gave it a shot. "Come on in and help us eat lunch and then you and I'll go to the ball game," Valentine boomed heartily. "The Cubs are playing here today."

"Who are they playing?" Johnny asked suspiciously.

"The Dodgers," Valentine said.

Johnny stepped back and pulled out another smoke. "I wouldn't care to see the Dodgers," he said.

Evening neared, and there were 20,000 watchers mobbed on the streets, and newsreel crews were positioned on rooftops, and radio announcers were broadcasting the midtown drama live to the world, and Johnny Warde kept smoking and pacing. "Gee, buddy," called Charles Glasco. "You can't stay out there all night."

"Why not?" Johnny asked. "I've got everything I need."

DARKNESS FELL just before 8:20, and now there were searchlights sweeping the hotel as cops brought in a giant Coast Guard cargo net and began to haul it up from the 18th-floor windows. At the same time, a policeman and a fireman were strapping themselves into bo's'n chairs and readying to drop down on either side of the tormented man below. In a few minutes, Johnny Warde saw, he would be effectively trapped.

He took a final drag off his smoke and flung the butt into the wind. It was 10:38.

"**I**'VE MADE UP my mind," he said to no one, and he went off the ledge.

A great roar came up from the street. Katherine Bull screamed; cops held her down as she made a dive for the window herself. "Johnny," she wailed, "I didn't mean it, I didn't mean it."

He went feet first, dropping cleanly to the eighth floor, then he grazed a coping and suddenly he was whirling end over end, and an instant later he bounced off the hotel marquee in a great explosion of glass and smashed facedown into the gutter.

The line of mounted officers couldn't hold back the surging crowds. In the pandemonium, as shrieking souvenir hunters fell to their knees to scoop up fistfuls of the shattered marquee glass, cops rushed to throw Johnny's broken body into the back of an ambulance and speed it away.

"Gee, I thought we were getting to be pals," sighed policeman Glasco.

"But as darkness came on, he seemed changed," Glasco told reporters. "He got like a frightened animal.

"I guess he was just nuts."

FIFTH AVE. *merchants complained that John Warde's 11-hour disruption had cost them hundreds of thousands of dollars worth of business. On the other hand, theater operators soon figured that the newsreel footage was bringing in at least that much in additional grosses, so things worked out.*

By **HENRY LEE**
and **JAY MAEDER**
Daily News Staff Writers

EIGHT P.M., Oct. 30, 1938, just another ho-hum Sunday night at home with the radio.

You chuckle for a minute or two at Edgar Bergen and Charlie McCarthy on the "Chase and Sanborn Hour." You fiddle with the dial. Here's a little dance music from Ramon Raquello's orchestra, live from the Hotel Park Place in New York City.

Flash! Meteor reported landing near Grover's Mill, N.J. . . . 1,500 killed. . . . No, it's not a meteor. . . . It's a flying metallic cylinder!

Live from the scene, radio reporter Carl Phillips is breathlessly announcing horrifying news.

Wait a minute! Something's crawling! I can see peering out of that black hole two luminous disks. . . . Are they eyes? It might be a face. It might be. . . . Good heavens! Something's wiggling out of the shadows like a gray snake.

In America's living rooms, listeners look up from their papers, stir uneasily in their armchairs.

Now it's another one, and another one! They look like tentacles to me. . . . There, I can see the thing's body. It is as large as a bear. . . . it glistens like wet leather. . . .

At police stations, at radio stations, in newspaper city rooms, switchboards light up. The Daily News is suddenly swamped with 1,100 calls.

But that face! It . . . ladies and gentlemen, it's indescribable! I can hardly force myself to keep looking at it, it's so awful.

Entire neighborhoods begin to migrate to their churches. Priests fall to their knees.

The eyes are black and gleam like a serpent. The mouth is kind of V-shaped, with saliva dripping from its rimless lips that seem to quiver and pulsate.

Mobs storm railroad stations and bus terminals. A rumor sweeps the night that President Franklin Roosevelt has taken to the radio, urging the public to hurry northward.

The thing is raising up!
The creatures stream out. . . .

At the NYPD telegraph bureau, 13 operators are overwhelmed by calls and can't keep up with the routine nightly harvest of murder, burglary, assault. Nor can headquarters reach CBS. A radio car is dispatched to the broadcast building on Madison Ave.

Worse to come! Bulletins report that the governor of New Jersey has declared martial law and that military planes have gone aloft.

Those strange beings who landed in the New Jersey farmlands tonight are the vanguard of the invading army from the planet Mars!

They're armed with death rays! They laugh off simple bullets! Over the drone of motors, the reports from the brave aviators can be heard:

. . . Enemy now turns east, crossing Passaic River into Jersey marshes. One of the gigantic creatures is straddling the Pulaski Skyway. Evident objective is New York City. They're pushing down a high-tension power station. . . .

Listeners pray, curse, go into shock. A woman

CHAPTER 78

NO CAUSE FOR ALARM

Mars Attacks, 1938

FAKE RADIO 'WAR' TERRORIZES N.Y.
Scores Flee Homes; 15 in Hospital

Frank R. Paul; Amazing Stories, August 1927

fleeing a midtown hotel tumbles down a flight of stairs and breaks her arm. A dying man leaves his bed in Mount Vernon and disappears into the night.

The machines are close together now, and we are ready to attack! A thousand yards and we'll be over the first one. . . . Eight hundred. . . . Seven hundred. . . . There they go! A giant arm is raised. . . . There's a green flash! They're spraying us with flame!

Radio cars and ambulances scream through city streets.

Two thousand feet! Engines are giving out. No chance to release bomb. Only one thing left to do. Drop on them, planes and all. . . . We're diving. . . .

East Side residents swarm into Park Ave., clutching their belongings. Citizens posted on rooftops report flames in the distance. "We can hear the firing!" a Brooklyn man notifies police.

Poisonous black smoke pouring in from Jersey marshes. Gas masks useless. Urge population to move into open spaces. Automobiles use Routes 7, 23, 24.

"You can't imagine the horror of it!" a Grover's

Mill girl shrieks to police over the phone. "It's hell!"

It is estimated that in the last two hours, 3 million people have moved out along the roads to the north. The Hutchinson River Parkway is still kept open for motor traffic. . . . Avoid bridges to Long Island. . . .

The city Department of Health calls for assistance. Hundreds of doctors and nurses turn out to volunteer. A New York man, in Reno to divorce his wife, immediately starts home to rejoin her.

I've just been handed a bulletin. Cylinders from Mars are falling all over the country. One outside Buffalo . . . another in Chicago . . . St. Louis . . .

From Madison Ave., the radio car reports back to Police Headquarters:

"Station CBS informs us that the broadcast just concluded over that station was a dramatization of a play. No cause for alarm."

"Imaginary affair," broadcasts the New Jersey State Police.

FROM THE CBS "Mercury Theater on the Air," it seems, 23-year-old radio wunderkind Orson Welles has been presenting a Halloween Eve special — a goosed-up, Americanized version of H.G. Wells' 1898 science-fiction shocker "The War of the Worlds." Fledgling writer Howard Koch, who will later script "Casablanca," has done the scenario. The death-ray invasion is fiction. So is reporter Carl Phillips. So is Ramon Raquello's orchestra.

"It's too bad that so many people got excited," murmurs a bewildered Orson Welles.

"How odd," agrees H.G. Wells, reached by a Daily News reporter in London.

CBS is moved to issue a formal statement, pointing out that a this-is-fiction disclaimer had been aired four times during the broadcast, an insurance against just this sort of public calamity.

But the people hadn't really been listening.

In the wake of the uproar, Welles' career is briefly imperiled. Amid calls for strict government radio censorship, the Federal Communications Commission leans hard on broadcasters and CBS piously forswears "the technique of a simulated news broadcast when the circumstances could cause immediate alarm to numbers of listeners."

On the other hand, notes Time magazine, in characteristically kindly fashion, a primary factor in the melee has been "the stupidity of the U.S. radio audience."

And thoughtful public attention is subsequently given to the recollections of Grover's Mill tenant farmer James Wilson, who had been awakened by his wife to listen to the radio reports. "I just looked out the window and saw everything was about the same," Wilson says. "And I went back to sleep."

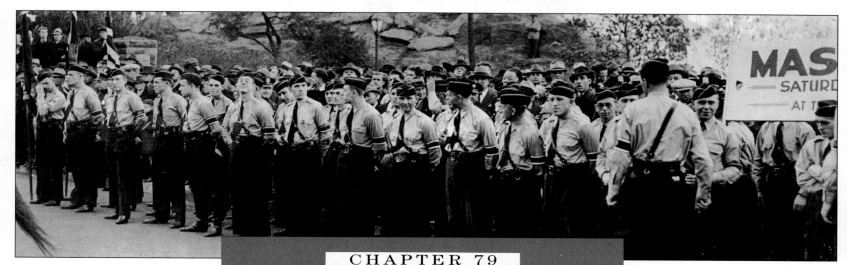

CHAPTER 79

RATZIS

Fritz Kuhn And The Bund, 1939

By JAY MAEDER

Daily News Staff Writer

AS AMERICAN CITIZENS guaranteed freedom of speech and assembly, Fritz Kuhn and his 3,000 brown-shirted storm troopers went unmolested by authorities as they marched into Madison Square Garden on Monday evening the 20th of February 1939 and hung up their swastikas. At Eighth Ave. and 50th St., cops held back the jeering mobs. Mayor Fiorello LaGuardia had made it plain there would be no interference with this lawful gathering.

"It would be a strange thing indeed if I should make any attempt to prevent this meeting just because I don't agree with the sponsors," LaGuardia had announced. "I would then be doing exactly as Adolf Hitler is doing in carrying on his abhorrent form of government."

Eighteen thousand persons roared approval for six hours as the beefy, 42-year-old Fuehrer of the Yorkville-based Amerikadeutscher Volksbund delivered himself of the odious rants that had become familiar to New Yorkers over the past two years. *The Bund is fighting shoulder to shoulder with patriotic Americans to protect America from a race that is not the American race, that is not even a white race . . . The Jews are controlling everything and the white man is thrown out of his job. . . . The Jews are enemies of the United States. . . . All Jews are Communists. . . . Christ was not a Jew . . .*

Melees erupted inside the Garden and out as livid Isidor Greenbaum of Brooklyn vaulted to the stage and charged Adolf Hitler's No. 1 agent in the United States of America. Brownshirts battered him senseless; police rushed in to carry him to safety; on Eighth Ave., the screaming crowds brawled with cops, knocking them off their horses.

Shall America be Jew-ruled? cried Fritz Kuhn.

No, there would be no trampling of the Constitution tonight by Mayor LaGuardia; there would be no abrogation. For in the City of New York, there were more efficient ways to deal with Nazis.

A few days later, the German-American Bund offices at 178 E. 85th St. were hit by city investigators who gathered up all extant records. Many buttons, badges and flags had been openly sold at the Garden rally. It was felt that perhaps the Bundists could be in violation of several municipal business and sales tax laws.

NAZIS IN America. Fritz Kuhn of Jackson Heights, Queens, boasted in the late 1930s that he had a quarter-million followers in 42 states, patriotic Americans all, dedicated to the democratic principles of the Fatherland; in the several pockets of the nation where the Bund flourished, these were citizens who marched beneath both the swastika and the Stars and Stripes. Nobody took them very seriously at first; they were cartoon Nazis, goose-stepping buffoons in armbands and Sam Browne belts. Daily Mirror columnist Walter Winchell regularly laughed them off as "ratzis." They were always deeply offended by that.

Munich-born Fritz Kuhn had been a World War machine-gunner; he had, he claimed, marched with Hitler in the unsuccessful 1923 beer-hall putsch, then fled to Detroit and gone to work for the Ford Motor Co. as a chemical engineer. In January 1936 he became national chief of a group previously known as Friends of New Germany, active in New York since 1933 at such meeting places as the Yorkville Casino and Schwaben Hall in Brooklyn. That summer he traveled to Berlin and was photographed with Hitler. By the end of the year, many disturbed German-American organizations were warning officials that Fritz Kuhn was a dangerous man.

As New York lawyer Julius Hochfelder and Rep. Samuel Dickstein sought to revoke Kuhn's citizenship and deport him, the American Fuehrer left the Midwest and resettled in Queens, arriving in March 1937 as Mayor LaGuardia was denouncing Adolf Hitler as "that brown-shirted fanatic" and getting labeled "that dirty Talmud Jew" by the official Nazi press in return. Kuhn immediately threw himself into this fracas and made headlines by blasting LaGuardia, Dickstein and President Roosevelt as Red dictators. That's why there was a Bund, he said, to protect America from such traitors. "If they don't like us here, they can get out of the country," he sniffed.

And this is what he told Dickstein's House Rules Committee. The Bund, he said, was "an American organization with American ideals" seeking "to open the eyes of the American people to the dangers they are facing." He denied Hochfelder's charge that the U.S. was full of Gestapo agents and that the New York National Guard had already been infiltrated. In October, a federal court threw out Hochfelder's deportation petition.

"This man is bringing pagan philosophies into the country and aims to destroy Catholics and Jews," Hochfelder argued.

"No man has a right to contest the citizenship of another man," said Judge John Clancy. "When did the people of the United States vest you with such authority?"

Vindicated by the American Way, Kuhn began to stage regular Nazi parades through Yorkville and various New Jersey communities. By December, he was claiming 1,000 new Bund members a week. By February 1938, he was leading a drive to prevent American Jews from holding any position in government, finance or education.

THAT SPRING, Kuhn traveled again to Berlin and returned with assurances that Germany's Jews admired Hitler and wanted American Jews to leave them alone. "Thousands of Jews are returning to Germany," he insisted. In May, he presided over the opening of Camp Siegfried in Yaphank, L.I., where 4,000 persons, including an army of children wearing swastikas, heiled Hitler. He was called to testify, first before a state legislative committee, next before the House Un-American Activities Committee in Washington. "I believe in a real democracy," he said. "America hasn't got one now."

But by now, the Veterans of Foreign Wars and other star-spangled outfits were wearying of Kuhn. Hecklers increasingly busted up his rallies around the city, on Long Island and in Jersey. In Union City in October, cops had to save him from enraged demonstrators at a rally celebrating Germany's invasion of the Sudetenland. In February 1939, announcing the Madison Square Garden rally, he demanded police protection, as a citizen.

THE CITY TAX charges were just misdemeanors. District Attorney Thomas Dewey had a better idea; looking over the Bund's books, Dewey found a missing $14,548. In May, as a grand jury handed down a 12-count forgery and grand larceny indictment, Kuhn bolted — and was quickly found in Pennsylvania, brought back and jailed. "Just a common thief," Dewey said.

In early September, in the hours after Germany invaded Poland, vigilant detectives pounced on the free-on-bond Kuhn as he attempted to flee the country.

At trial, his defense was the "principle of leadership," an argument that he had the absolute right to embezzle all the money he pleased. The jury didn't see it. In November, he was convicted.

"Political persecution," fumed the American Fuehrer as he went off to prison.

FRITZ KUHN *finished his sentence in 1943, then was interned as an undesirable alien till war's end. Deported to Germany, he stood trial as a war criminal and went back to jail. He reportedly died in 1951.*

By JONATHAN LEWIN
Daily News Staff Writer

The Fair is a force for peace in the world; for without peace a dream of a better "World of Tomorrow" is but a cruel and mocking illusion.

— **New York World's Fair, 1939 Official Guide Book**

ON FRIDAY the 28th of April 1939, two days before the New York World's Fair was to open on 1,216 acres of former swampland in Flushing, Queens, Adolf Hitler responded to Franklin Delano Roosevelt's pleas for peace by scrapping Germany's naval treaty with Britain and its nonaggression pact with Poland. Still hoping to limit U.S. involvement in any European hostilities, Roosevelt did not utter Hitler's name when he opened the fair before 60,000 spectators packed into the Court of Peace. This international exposition, featuring a record 59 nations, was intended to give Americans an optimistic view of a world still to come — a harmonious place whose peoples would enjoy new consumer products made possible by advancements in technology.

In the year that movie audiences saw the black-and-white world of Kansas explode into the Technicolor world of Oz, the fair offered a streamlined, geometrically elegant vision of the future, conceived by the day's top industrial designers. The fair's twin symbols were the Perisphere, a globe 180 feet in diameter, representing the world, and the Trylon, a triangular pylon 700 feet tall, representing aspiration.

The world's largest cash register, 40 feet high, tallied attendance. A 12-foot-long Remington electric shaver stood next to blown-up photos that made stubble look like logs. Underwood's 14-ton, 18-foot-long typewriter produced letters 3 inches high.

These giant items may not have been particularly futuristic, but the present was amazing enough to fairgoers, many of whom could remember a time before the widespread use of telephones and automobiles. Commercial air travel was still a recent phenomenon. The fair's theme, "Building the World of Tomorrow With the Tools of Today," promised even more wonderful things still ahead.

Television was publicly introduced at the fair, and commercial broadcasting began the day the fair opened — not that there was much programming. More practical to the 1939 fairgoer was AT&T's popular Demonstration Call Room, in which visitors were selected by lot to make long-distance calls to anywhere in the United States.

Along with television, the fair introduced or popularized fluorescent lighting, air conditioning, nylon stockings and the Hammond Novachord, a vacuum-tube keyboard that could synthesize piano, harpsichord, trumpet, guitar and violin. And there was a fax machine that could deliver newspapers into the Living Room of Tomorrow at a rate of 18 minutes per 8-by-12-inch page.

CHAPTER 80

SEEING THE FUTURE
The Fair, 1939

To demonstrate its new X-ray technology, General Electric borrowed an Egyptian sarcophagus from a Chicago museum. Spectators could press a button to see the skeleton inside.

With the memory of the Lindbergh case still fresh, RCA's "Magic Switch" challenged spectators to "Try to Kidnap the Baby." When they placed their hand in a bassinet containing a doll, red lights went on and a bell rang.

Housewives applauded "The Battle of the Centuries," a dishwashing contest between Mrs. Drudge, who used her hands, and Mrs. Modern, who used a Westinghouse electric dishwasher. Other Westinghouse attractions included Elektro, the Moto-Man, a 7-foot robot that could tell jokes and count on its fingers.

The popular Amusements Area offered Billy Rose's Aquacade, a Broadway musical starring Gypsy Rose Lee and topless ladies in the diving tanks of "Dream of Venus," an exhibit designed by Salvador Dali.

Other exhibits were earnestly educational. At Pharmacy Hall, the history of medicine was reenacted by 12-foot puppets. The Metropolitan

Life Pavilion used sculpture and murals to attempt to dramatize life insurance. Borden had more success with its dairy exhibits and its new symbol, Elsie the Cow.

Most popular of all was General Motors' Futurama, which gave spectators an aerial view of a typical utopian community of 1960, featuring $200 teardrop-shaped cars speeding down seven-lane superhighways. The exhibit ended with a life-size 1960 street intersection displaying 1939 GM products. Every spectator received a button that read "I Have Seen the Future."

Utopia also could be glimpsed from above in Democracity, a giant model of an American community of 2039, set inside the Perisphere. With its central work area and spread-out towns connected by landscaped highways, it was a look ahead to something that certainly seemed like utopia to many New Yorkers crowded into 1939 tenements — suburbia.

A different political perspective was offered by a plaque on the Soviet Union's pavilion, which announced that the "victory of socialism" was inevitable. Allies and antagonists alike — save for notably absent Germany — were clustered around the Lagoon of Nations. Murderously at war with China, Japan presented itself as a tranquil friend of America, modeling its pavilion on a Shinto shrine and displaying a replica of the Liberty Bell encrusted with pearls and diamonds. Poland's pavilion celebrated a democratic constitution almost as old as America's. Finland promoted the 1940 Helsinki Olympics.

On the first day of September, Germany invaded Poland, and the World of Tomorrow could no longer keep out the troubles of today. The Polish Pavilion began handing visitors photos of war ruins. In November, the Soviets invaded Finland. There would be no Helsinki Olympics in 1940.

Lower-than-expected attendance made the fair a financial failure in its 1939 season. The following year, admission was lowered from 75 to 50 cents and the educational exhibits were deemphasized. A huge economics exhibit explaining how production, distribution and consumption worked together was replaced by the World of Fashion. The Amusements Area, renamed the Great White Way, was expanded.

The fair got a new slogan: "For Peace and Freedom." The USSR's pavilion was gone, replaced by the American Commons, where patriotic rallies were held. The electric board in the White Owl Pavilion that had shown baseball scores now reported war news. The British Pavilion displayed a captured German parachute.

AFTER THE *fair ended in the fall of 1940, the Trylon and Perisphere were melted down and their 3,000 tons of steel turned over to the military. The World of Tomorrow, the consumerist utopia of suburbia, television, superhighways and the defeat of Mrs. Drudge would have to wait until after the war.*

By JAY MAEDER
Daily News Staff Writer

SOMETHING WAS wrong with him. Everybody could see that. He couldn't run, he couldn't hit. Suddenly his fine athlete's body had just stopped working. "Past his peak," the papers were saying. "Winded." But it was more than just a slump. One day he fell down in the Yankees clubhouse and he had trouble getting up again. Something was wrong with him.

In the 1938 season, Lou Gehrig batted less than .300 for the first time since 1925. Through spring camp in Florida in '39, he could barely move. Teammates watched their fumbling captain in disbelief. Pitchers started taking it easy on him, for fear he couldn't get out of the way of a close one. Nobody really wanted to start grousing out loud that the great Lou Gehrig had lost it, but finally they did, and he couldn't help hearing.

In Yankee Stadium on Sunday the 30th of April, Larruping Lou, No. 4, played his 2,130th consecutive game, against the Washington Senators, and realized he was finished.

"I just can't seem to get going," he told manager Joe McCarthy. "Nobody has to tell me how bad I've been." On May 2, in Detroit's Briggs Stadium, he benched himself.

Babe Dahlgren went in for him that day, and Lou Gehrig clapped him on the back and wished the Yankees' new first baseman the best of everything.

Then he sat down in the dugout and, as those gathered silently around him tried not to see, cried his heart out.

NEW YORK knew him as The Iron Horse, one of life's few great comforting constants, the guy who was always on first base, every time, just as sure as the sun came up in the East in the morning. Since June 1, 1925, when Miller Huggins first threw the college-boy rookie in as a pinch-hitter, Lou Gehrig had durably played in every Yankee game, every single one of them, bad back or broken fingers or not. Modest, self-effacing, good-natured, Gehrig never seemed to mind that the flamboyant Babe Ruth always overshadowed him as the greatest ballplayer of the day. If it was the Babe who was always out doing the big roaring town, it was Lou Gehrig who went home to his wife and played bridge, and there were New Yorkers who appreciated that.

And there were genuine prayers for him when he finally went to the Mayo Clinic in Rochester, Minn., to find out why his body wasn't working anymore.

On June 21, two days after Gehrig's 36th birthday, Yankee President Ed Barrow called in the press and gave them the news.

The Iron Horse, said the terse Mayo statement, *"is suffering from amyotrophic lateral sclerosis. This type of illness involves the motor pathway and cells of the central nervous system and in lay terms is known as a form of chronic poliomyelitis (infantile paralysis).*

"The nature of this trouble makes it such that Mr. Gehrig will be unable to continue his active participation as a baseball player."

Amyotrophic lateral sclerosis? In 1939, it was not entirely clear what that was. Not quite polio, but some kind of slow hardening of the spinal cord. Something that could make powerful muscles atrophy and fail. Something that could stop a big, healthy man cold in his tracks in the prime of his life.

"I don't know any more than you do," Gehrig told reporters.

IT MEANT HE was dying. The bravest of faces was put on things, but everybody knew that Lou Gehrig was going to die.

At Yankee Stadium on Tuesday the 4th of July, between games of a doubleheader with Washington, the Iron Horse hobbled to home plate and, flanked by the Yankees of 1927 and 1939, stood facing newsreel crews and radio microphones and 61,808 screaming fans.

"Fans," he said, when he could bring himself to speak, "for the past two weeks you have been reading about a bad break I got.

LEO O'MEALIA/DAILY NEWS

CHAPTER 81

THE LUCKIEST MAN ON THE FACE OF THE EARTH

Lou Gehrig Day, 1939

"Yet today, I consider myself the luckiest man on the face of the Earth.

"I have been in ballparks for 17 years, and I have never received anything but kindness and encouragement from you fans. Look at these grand men," he said, waving an arm at his teammates. "Which of you wouldn't consider it the highlight of his career just to associate with them for even one day? Sure, I'm lucky. Who wouldn't consider it an honor to have known Jacob Ruppert? Also, the builder of baseball's greatest empire, Ed Barrow? To have spent six years with that wonderful little fellow, Miller

Huggins? Then to have spent the next nine years with that outstanding leader, that smart student of psychology, the best manager in baseball today, Joe McCarthy? Who wouldn't feel honored to have roomed with such a grand guy as Bill Dickey?

"Sure, I'm lucky," he said. "When the New York Giants, a team you would give your right arm to beat, and vice versa, sends you a gift, that's something. When everybody down to the groundskeepers and those boys in white coats remember you with trophies, that's something. When you have a wonderful mother-in-law who takes sides with you in squabbles against her own daughter, that's something. When you have a father and mother who work all their lives so that you can have an education and build your body, it's a blessing. When you have a wife who has been a tower of strength and shown more courage than you dreamed existed, that's the finest I know."

The words were simple, wholly artless, brimming with grace. The entire Stadium was bawling.

"So I close in saying that I might have had a bad break," Lou Gehrig said. "But I have an awful lot to live for."

And that was the last time the Iron Horse took the field. He spent the rest of the season, through the Yankees' fifth consecutive World Series championship, in the dugout, losing weight and turning gray, and he died not quite two years later.

LOU GEHRIG'S *most-consecutive-games record stood unbroken until June 13, 1987, when Sachio Kinugasa of the Toyo Carp played his 2,131st game in Hiroshima, although it took him 23 years to Gehrig's 14.*

By JAY MAEDER
Daily News Staff Writer

IRVING PENN was a short, fat man who was in the sheet music publishing business and had the bad luck to resemble a short, fat man named Philip Orlovsky, who was in the rackets. On Tuesday the 25th of July 1939, the gunmen waiting to whack Philip Orlovsky made an honest mistake.

Accidents happened, but this particular wrong-man murder brought down a lot of clamor, and now the underworld as well as the forces of justice deemed it time to do something about fugitive crime boss Louis Buchalter, aka Louis Lepke. Orlovsky was one of District Attorney Thomas Dewey's witnesses, no few of whom had been getting exterminated lately; now an innocent had died. Suddenly a blue-ribbon grand jury was rounding up everyone Lepke ever knew. "Those other mobsters won't be able to stand the pressure," one detective assessed things. "They'll force Lepke to take the rap to save their own hides, or else we'll find his bullet-riddled carcass some morning."

Holed up in Manhattan for two years while authorities searched as far afield as Palestine and Poland, Lepke divined that this was probably true. There was a difference between being a powerful gang boss no one could refuse to harbor and a hunted animal who was raining down grief on everyone's heads. Lepke was bad for business. He was, as they said in gangland, a hot article. Prison was clearly the safest place for him to be.

So it made good sense to surrender, although certainly not to Dewey, who had enough state charges on him to send him over for hundreds of years, maybe even fry him. What did the federals have? Flight to avoid prosecution for violating the Sherman Anti-Trust Act, that's what. That sounded like maybe a couple of years in the joint. What Lepke needed here was somebody who could set this up.

Walter Winchell of the Daily Mirror, well known to be very tight with the Federal Bureau of Investigation, got the call on Saturday the 5th of August. "Lepke wants to come in," a voice informed him.

"But he's heard so many stories about what will happen to him," the voice continued. "He can't trust anybody. The talk around town is that Lepke would be shot while supposedly escaping."

"I'll tell John Edgar Hoover," Winchell said. "I'm sure he will see to it that Lepke receives his constitutional rights and nobody will cross him."

"Put it on the air," the voice said, and on his network radio broadcast the next night, with Hoover sitting beside him, Winchell mysteriously informed a certain unidentified party, "if you're listening," that a deal was

CHAPTER 82

HOT ARTICLE

Lepke Surrenders To Winchell, 1939

CORBIS-BETTMAN

arrangeable.

There were a couple more calls over the next couple of days, and then they stopped, and this of course was because Lepke was getting to be a hotter article every minute. Even Gurrah Shapiro, his only friend in the world, would have cheerfully blowtorched him to death at this point.

LEPKE AND GURRAH had been pals since they were kids knocking over pushcarts. Strange pair that they were, Lepke the crafty businessman and Gurrah the big stupid bone crusher, they had nonetheless always been side by side in the rackets, working together as rag-trade strikebreakers for Little Augie Orgen and then taking over garments for themselves after Little Augie expired in 1927. It was Lepke who figured out that you could move in on both the manufacturers and the unions simultaneously and strategically stick your own people everywhere in the chain, and this was a very fine arrangement until Tom Dewey got named special prosecutor in the summer of 1935 and the whole house fell down.

Specifically, there was the matter of Billy Snyder. Billy had been a union president who didn't care to have mobster partners, and one night in September 1934 he had rejected a business plan offered over dinner in

an Avenue A restaurant and a dim little thug named Morris Goldis had shot him to death in front of 13 witnesses. Manifestly this job had been done at the behest of Lepke and Gurrah, and Billy Snyder, brave albeit dead, went on to serve as something of a call to arms for Dewey and his racket smashers as they first put away Charles Luciano and then turned their attentions to Charlie Lucky's two apparent successors.

Law-enforcement turf wars being what they were, the federals got to Lepke and Gurrah first, and in the spring of 1937 they both went down on anti-trust counts relating to the fur business. Whereupon, sensing Dewey's hot breath on their necks, they both jumped bond and vanished. Whereupon Dewey, piously invoking Billy Snyder's name at every turn, was elected district attorney of New York County and started making agreeable witnesses out of Morris Goldis and numerous other hired hands.

Gurrah gave himself up in April 1938. Several potentially talkative parties had already been murdered, and word was out that Lepke was quite prepared to silence Gurrah too. In court, the big ox bawled like a baby and went off to the federal pen.

By August 1939, Lepke was obviously on the spot; Dewey was confident he would come in momentarily, the better to stay alive. This was very good, as Dewey was at this moment unofficially launching a 1940 run for the presidency. Nobody bothered to tell him that Lepke was

already reaching out to the FBI, turf wars being what they were.

JOHN EDGAR Hoover recognized Walter Winchell to be a useful publicist, and he put up with quite a lot from him, but he was plenty dubious about this Lepke surrender business, and after two weeks of silence his patience was wearing thin. "This is a lot of bunk, Walter," the FBI chief informed the columnist. "You are being made a fool of and so are we. If you contact those people again, tell them the time limit is up and I will instruct my agents to shoot Lepke on sight."

When, on Wednesday the 22nd of August, a stranger stopped Winchell on Fifth Ave. and reinitiated discussions, Winchell announced that surrender time would be the next day, period. And at 6 p.m. Thursday, as per arrangement, he was waiting at a phone booth.

A caller instructed him to drive to a Yonkers theater. He did. There he got a message to drive back to a Manhattan drugstore. He did. Nursing a Coke at the fountain, he was then joined by a gent who ordered him to park at Madison and 23rd and wait. He did.

Shortly after 10, America's most wanted man climbed into Winchell's car. "Thanks very much," he said.

Hoover, as per arrangement, was waiting alone in a government sedan at Fifth and 28th.

"Mr. Hoover, this is Lepke," said Winchell.

"How do you do," said J. Edgar Hoover.

"Glad to meet you," Lepke grunted. "Let's go."

WALTER WINCHELL, not one to trivialize his triumphs, reproduced in the Daily Mirror the official letter he had no doubt insisted that Hoover cough up. "Without your unselfish and indefatigable assistance, I know that Buchalter would not have surrendered," the G-man wrote. "In rendering this aid you have performed a most patriotic service, not only to your government but to the American people."

The other papers reported that Lepke had turned himself in through "an intermediary."

LOUIS BUCHALTER, *safe behind bars, made no attempt to secure counsel and eagerly looked forward to serving out his soft federal stint until such time as Tom Dewey might no longer be DA. He had misapprehended things, however; the feds gave him 30 years and then handed him off to the state, which efficiently convicted him of murder. In March 1944, quite stunned, Lepke became the only major American crime boss ever to go to the electric chair.*

By JAY MAEDER
Daily News Staff Writer

THE STORY WENT that one day in 1934 the formidable new mayor of the City of New York was flying home from Chicago aboard a TWA DC-2 that landed, as was its practice, at Newark. And everyone got off the plane except Fiorello LaGuardia, who pointed out that his ticket said CHICAGO-NEW YORK and said he wanted to go to New York, not Newark. And the captain politely explained that, well, Newark was where New York flights landed because that's where the airport was. And LaGuardia said again that his ticket damn well said New York and he refused to leave his seat.

And the captain thought this over, and by and by the plane was in the air again, delivering Mayor La-Guardia, its sole passenger, to Floyd Bennett Field in Brooklyn, which could only just barely accommodate a DC-2.

This was, the story went, specifically the reason that five years later New York City had the biggest and best-equipped airport in the nation.

IT IS TRUE, of course, that Fiorello LaGuardia was in any case one of commercial aviation's more indefatigable champions and a great friend and supporter of the various interests that sought to advance it in ever bigger and bolder modern America. Still, it is recorded, he often grumbled that somehow it just wasn't right for New Yorkers to be stuck with an airport that was basically in another state altogether.

Old Floyd Bennett, though, was no more convenient to the city than Newark was, and LaGuardia decided that Governors Island was a fine place for an airport, since soon it would be linked to Manhattan via the long-planned Brooklyn-Battery tunnel. But he could never drum up any federal interest in that idea. Then one day his eye fell upon a peninsula on the Queens shoreline, a dismal strip of badlands called North Beach, separating Flushing Bay from Bowery Bay and scenically overlooking the great Rikers Island garbage dump.

It wasn't pretty, but in 1937 it suddenly had two things going for it. A few minutes away in one direction was the new Triborough Bridge. And a few minutes away in the other was the site of the forthcoming World's Fair.

NORTH BEACH had been developed in the 1880s by piano manufacturer William Steinway, and for some few years it had been a popular shore resort and amusement park. By the end of the 1920s, the Curtiss-Wright Corp. had turned it into a private airfield. North Beach Airport was 20 minutes from the city; sport fliers used it regularly; the Police Department's Aviation Unit was hangared there; so was the Daily News' photo plane. But it certainly couldn't handle commercial airliners. LaGuardia decided he was personally go-

CHAPTER 83

TERMINUS

The Airport, 1939

ing to fix that.

In August 1937, the city bought North Beach Airport from Curtiss-Wright for $1.3 million and immediately began to more than quintuple its 105 acres with 17 million cubic yards of landfill scooped up from Rikers Island's mountains of cinder, ash and refuse. More than 20,000 relief workers from the federal Works Progress Administration worked around the clock for two years. The mayor was determined to finish his pride-and-joy airport by the time the Fair opened April 30, 1939.

He didn't, quite. There were many obstacles to timely completion: For one thing, the price tag swiftly increased from $13 million to $40 million, and the airport was scathed by the cost-conscious as a colossal boondoggle. Building tradesmen branded the WPA workers incompetent wastrels

and insisted that the private sector could have brought the job in for half the cost. Newark officials, meanwhile, lodged protests with civil aviation authorities, seeking to protect their investment in their field. When the Fair opened, there was not yet an airport to serve it.

ON A SPARKLING Sunday the 15th of October, the mayor — "with pardonable pride," he beamed — dedicated his crown jewel before more than a quarter-million New Yorkers. The TWA, American, United and Canadian Colonial lines showed off their gleaming silver ships on the field's six runways; 75 military planes stunted high overhead; the mighty Pan American Atlantic Clipper rode the bay off the Marine Terminal, symbolizing the trans-oceanic service soon to come. As LaGuardia spoke, a young woman paraded before him with a large sign reading NEWARK IS STILL THE WORLD'S GREATEST AIRPORT. Cops hustled her away and told her to go home.

Regularly scheduled service began at 12:01 a.m. on Dec. 2, with the arrival from Chicago of a TWA transport carrying a gentleman named Omero Caton, who previously had been the first person over the Triborough Bridge and through both the Lincoln and Holland tunnels. The first outgoing flight, American's Night Owl to Chicago, left at 1:20, half an hour behind schedule. United, meanwhile, flew in several loads of office files from Newark.

On Nov. 10, North Beach Airport officially went out of existence and became LaGuardia Field. By Christmas, the city was forced to impose parking and observation-deck fees to discourage the tens of thousands of people who were visiting every day just to watch the airplanes take off and land.

THE BUILDING TRADES *may have had a point about WPA labor; within two years the hangars and the airstrips were sinking into the landfill and extensive remedial work became necessary.*

By that time it was plain that LaGuardia Field wasn't big enough anyway, and the mayor began planning the even larger International Airport in Queens.

By JAY MAEDER
Daily News Staff Writer

THE PRESIDENT OF the United States pulled the whistlecord at 10 minutes past noon on Monday the 28th of October 1940, and, as assembled dignitaries applauded the moment, a power shovel bit down into the northeast corner of Hamilton Ave. and Van Brunt St. in Brooklyn and officially began work on the longest underwater tunnel in the world.

Sandhogs would be boring their shafts by February, it was expected, and the whole ambitious $57 million job would be completed by 1944. Along with the new Queens-Midtown Tunnel, set to open in another few weeks, this great tube from lower Manhattan to Brooklyn opened up grand new possibilities to the motoring classes of New York City. Specifically, the Brooklyn-Battery Tunnel was the final link in the great system of circumferential roads that Robert Moses had been planning and building for more than 15 years. West of this link was the West Side Highway; to the east was the recently opened Belt Parkway, 35 unbroken miles between Brooklyn's Owl's Head Park and the Bronx-Whitestone Bridge. This was the last piece of the system.

High above soared a steel-and-concrete ghost, a great, gleaming span to distant Manhattan, the world's most wonderful suspension bridge, a mighty highway in the sky. You could almost see it, this bridge that wasn't there, this monument to defeat, just about the only thing that the imperious Robert Moses never got to build.

THE NOTION OF a Battery-to-Brooklyn tunnel had been around since 1929, when planners noted that the three East River bridges were carrying 150,000 vehicles a day and foresaw more traffic ahead in this fine new age of the automobile.

Envisioned were six lanes between West St. on the Manhattan side and Hamilton Ave. on the Brooklyn side, with a midpoint exit to Governors Island, since something was bound to be built there sooner or later. Beyond the Brooklyn waterfront, of course, surely there would someday be direct routes to Coney Island and the South Shore. It was an exciting project, and it was more or less approved by November 1930.

After that, what with the Depression and one thing and another, the tunnel got stalled for several years. By that time, Robert Moses had built Jones Beach and the Long Island parkways and so on and so forth and, having firmly established himself as a mastermind creator not unlike God, had moved into the city to build the Triborough Bridge and the Grand Central

Parkway and the Henry Hudson Parkway and the Bronx-Whitestone Bridge, and so on and so forth. In the late 1930s Moses was dreaming up several more things. One of them was the Long Island Expressway. Another was the great Circumferential Parkway around Brooklyn and Queens.

The Circumferential — which the newspapers soon renamed the Belt, "circumferential" not being a word that fit comfortably into a headline — was approved by the Board of Estimate in October 1938. The long-dormant tunnel, the piece that would integrate lower Manhattan into

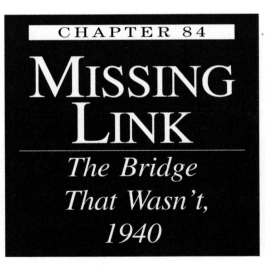

CHAPTER 84

MISSING LINK

The Bridge That Wasn't, 1940

the scheme, would soon follow.

In January 1939, Moses announced that the tunnel was going to be a bridge instead.

BY 1939, Robert Moses had succeeded in making himself accountable to basically no one, and his public works customarily went ahead regardless of what anyone else thought about them. Neither Mayor Fiorello LaGuardia nor the City Council particularly wanted a Brooklyn-Battery bridge, but Moses slammed it past them anyway, and then he slammed it through the Legislature and Gov. Herbert Lehman, and he paid no attention at all to the protests of the Regional Plan Association and horrified civic groups that the Manhattan end of the monster span would obliterate a good chunk of the Battery and its tranquil waterfront esplanades. Work, he declared, would begin by July 1.

Fortunately for the save-the-Battery elements, World War II was looming. On May 18, 1939, the War Department, whose final approval had been regarded as certain, abruptly vetoed the bridge on national-defense grounds: Obviously, it would be a prime target in the event of enemy attack, and its destruction would block the harbor and cripple the vital Brooklyn Navy Yard.

This was a patently ludicrous objection — the navy yard already sat directly between the Manhattan and Williamsburg bridges — and to many noses there wafted the scent of backroom politics. Indeed, the long-memoried recalled that as a young man some years earlier, brusque and peremptory Robert Moses on several occasions had greatly aggrieved Gov. Franklin Roosevelt. In June, LaGuardia met with Roosevelt in Washington and humiliated Moses by publicly apologizing for him and asking that FDR not hold an old grudge against the city. Moses, meanwhile, stormed about charging blatant political sabotage, and the War Department declined to reverse its ruling.

Business groups and some of the papers continued to beat the drums into the fall, trying to keep the bridge alive. "Somebody in Washington dislikes Moses," grunted the Daily News' editorial page. "The fact is that if enemy planes could get over here and sink any of the New York City bridges, the city would be pretty well cooked anyway."

On Oct. 31, Roosevelt personally killed the Brooklyn-Battery Bridge, finally and forever. In March 1940, federal approval was won for a tunnel costing far more.

ROBERT MOSES made no public utterances on the October afternoon that ground was broken for the final link in New York City's arterial highway system. The newspapers did not record that he was even present at the ceremony.

It was Roosevelt who pointedly said the words out loud. "For some time," he genially reminisced, "there was some dispute as to whether we would cross the river between Manhattan and Brooklyn over the water or under the water.

"That was a question that a mere layman couldn't decide," said the President of the United States.

CONSTRUCTION OF *the Brooklyn-Battery Tunnel was interrupted by the war, and it did not open until May 1950 — six years past schedule. Franklin Roosevelt and Fiorello LaGuardia were both dead. Robert Moses endured, more powerful than ever, and he yet had many more things to build.*

By JAY MAEDER
Daily News Staff Writer

CONGRESS HAD been gravely swatting this one around for months. Imposing the first peacetime draft of manpower and industry in American history was not, in an election year, a small matter. On Saturday the 14th of September 1940, the House and the Senate voted yea: More than 16 million males between the ages of 21 and 35 would forthwith register for military conscription for the purpose of providing a reservoir of 5 million trained fighting men for the defense of the United States in the event of war.

That grim likelihood "trembles on the verge of becoming a probability," Army Chief of Staff Gen. George Marshall said on CBS radio minutes after he watched President Franklin Roosevelt sign the draft bill into law on Monday the 16th. "The next six months include the possibility of being the most critical period in the history of the nation. . . . We must be prepared to stand alone." In New York and New Jersey, 19,000 guardsmen of the 27th and 44th divisions immediately went on active duty. In New York City, 1.1 million civilians were ordered to register with their local draft boards Oct. 16 and prepare to surrender a year of their lives to military service — or face prison.

A million New York men. Rich and poor, short and tall, married and single, English-speaking and not, everyone. Deaf, blind, legless — no dispensation. Life imprisonment in Sing Sing — no excuse. Ages 21 to 35, everyone. How were draftees supposed to support their families? Would they get their jobs back when their year was up? There were no answers for these questions yet. Meanwhile, everyone.

RICH AND POOR, short and tall. Cabbies, longshoremen, dandies in tuxedoes. On Wednesday the 16th of October, the city stopped from 7 a.m. to 9 p.m. as 1.1 million of them stood on long lines at 712 registration stations — 355,000 in Brooklyn, 262,000 in Manhattan, etc. — and produced identification. Various shady characters who seemed to have several different names were urged just to choose one they liked and keep the line moving. A Javanese man from Broome St. whose papers said he was 37 insisted that this was in Javanese years and in America he was only 29; the registrars shrugged and signed him up. A 5-foot-1 gent who had been trying unsuccessfully to join the Army since 1933 whistled happily as he finally got his shot.

Roosevelt took to the radio as the men of New York stood on their lines, and his address was broadcast into the streets:

On this day, more than 16 million young Americans are reviving the 300-year-old American custom of the muster.

On this day, we Americans proclaim the vitality of our history, the singleness of our will and the unity of our nation.

We prepare to keep the peace in this new world which free men have built for free men to live in. Calmly, without fear and without hysteria but with clear determination, we are building guns and planes and tanks and ships. We are mobilizing our citizenship.

In the days when our forefathers laid the foundation of our democracy, every American family had to have its gun and know how to use it. Today we live under threats, threats of aggression from abroad, which call again for the same readiness, the same vigilance. Ours must once again be the spirit of those who were prepared to defend as they built, to defend as they worked, to defend as they worshipped. Your act today affirms not only your loyalty to your country but your will to build your future for yourselves.

We of today, with God's help, can bequeath to Americans of tomorrow a nation in which the ways of liberty and justice will survive and be secure. Such a nation must be devoted to the cause of peace. And it is for that cause that America arms itself. It is to that cause that we Americans today devote our national will and our national spirit and our national strength.

At Columbia University, draft resisters mounted a demonstration. But there were just

seven of them, and they were totally ignored.

IN WASHINGTON on Tuesday the 29th of October, a blindfolded Secretary of War Henry Stimson launched the marathon 24-hour lottery by pulling the first of 8,500 numbers from a goldfish bowl. It came up 158. In New York, Chan Chong Yuen, Pell St. laundryman, George Tsatsaronis, owner of a Ninth Ave. coffee shop and Vincent Leibell Jr. of Park Ave., son of a federal judge, began to put their affairs in order in event of imminent call.

That call would not come to every man, of course. In practical terms, the legless and the imprisoned didn't really need to concern themselves, and many more warm bodies, however willing to serve, would not get past military physicals; officials would have to process thousands of men before they would settle on the first batch of 1,917 scheduled for induction in another few weeks. Meanwhile, for those weeks, the fates of those thousands were anybody's crapshoot. Job, school, sweetheart, big plans, big dreams, there was nothing to be done about any of that if Uncle Sam wanted you, and maybe he did and maybe he didn't. Uncle Sam would let you know. For the moment there was

CHAPTER 85

THE MUSTER

Ready For War, 1940

just a great sea of names, mustered from the melting pot of New York City. *Levy. Lizzio. Cavanna. Luzuriaga. McKenna. Potomsky. Rockefeller. Corbett. Becker. McMahon. Quinn.*

IN CHICAGO, a captured German spy was testifying against the army of Third Reich saboteurs already at work in the U.S., and federal agents were swooping down on defense plants across the nation. In 50 minutes on a single November afternoon, 18 persons were killed when three plants in Pennsylvania and New Jersey were wrecked by bombs.

On Monday the 18th of November, 1,917 men found out who they were and started packing their bags. *Sullivan. Posner. Feinberg. Molinari. Paradiso. Eagan. Sherman. Gallo. Greenblatt. Lowe.* Off they went to their local boards to collect their papers. At the nearest armory they took the oath and were inducted. Then they boarded trucks to Camp Dix in New Jersey or Camp Upton at Yaphank, L.I., where they got bedding and boots and haircuts and shots and within three hours became shavetail soldiers.

"Only the strong may continue to live in freedom and peace," said Roosevelt.

Rosenthal. O'Rourke. Summerton. Maguire. Polinsky. Thaler. Adams. Brown. Zito. Douda.

By DAVID HINCKLEY
Daily News Staff Writer

NOBODY WAS much surprised when, in the first inning of the New York Yankees' game against the Chicago White Sox on Thursday the 15th of May 1941, Joe DiMaggio stroked a single.

Then again, nobody paid much attention. DiMaggio was paid to hit, after all, and he hit well. In each of his first five years as a Yankee, he had never hit fewer than 29 home runs or driven in fewer than 125 runs; in 1939 and 1940 he had led the American League in batting, at .381 and .352. He had one of the sweetest swings ever — smooth, compact, controlled. He struck out fewer times than he hit home runs, and he made it all seem as casual as ordering a plate of linguine.

About all the sportswriters noted on May 15, then, was that this hit snapped an unusual three-game slump in which DiMaggio had hit nothing at all. It drove in Phil Rizzuto with the only Yankee run in a 13-1 loss, and beyond that, frankly, there were other things to think about.

These included the conflict in Europe, which with each passing day fewer Americans believed America could avoid joining — although the regular "America's Battle Page" feature in the crustily isolationist Daily News led that day with a piece on "Why the War-Makers Smear Charles Lindbergh." Lucky Lindy, with his colleagues in the America First movement, had been assuring his countrymen it was no skin off their noses if Adolf Hitler overran Europe.

He got no argument on that point from France's new government at Vichy, which publicly announced on May 15 that whatever was good for Germany was good for France. Meanwhile, on this same day, the U.S. and British government announced that they'd given a lot of thought to the week's bizarre solo flight of high German honcho Rudolph Hess into the British Isles, and all they could figure was that the crazy Nazi buzzard must have really thought he could cut a deal for peace with the Brits. They locked him up, of course.

The U.S. also announced that day that it was sending 21 Flying Fortresses to Hawaii in case the Japanese tried anything funny on the other side of the world.

So it was a couple of weeks yet before the sportswriters really began to notice that Joe DiMaggio was on a bit of a hot streak here.

ON TUESDAY the 27th, DiMaggio ran this streak up to 13 games by getting four hits off three Washington Nationals pitchers. Elsewhere in Washington, President Franklin Roosevelt was ordering 1.3 million young men to register for the draft. In London, it was announced that a British Swordfish plane had successfully

CHAPTER 86

THE GOOD OLD SUMMERTIME

War And Peace And DiMaggio At Bat, 1941

put a torpedo into the great German dreadnought Bismarck.

On Monday the 2nd of June, Nazi Luftwaffe chief Herman Goering darkly warned Britain there was "no such thing as an invincible island," as DiMaggio's hitting streak climbed to 19 games. This was the same day that John Rigney of the White Sox, the opposing pitcher back in the third game of Joe's streak, got a notice to report for military induction on June 20.

Three days before he was scheduled to switch uniforms, Rigney faced Joltin' Joe again and almost shut him down. Hitless in his first three at-bats, Joe came up in the seventh and sent a routine grounder to Sox shortstop Luke Appling. As Appling was about to make the play, the ball took a freak hop over his shoulder and bounced into left field.

And this made it 31 games, which was suddenly just 10 games less than the 20th century record of 41 set by George Sisler with the 1922 Browns, and 13 less than the all-time record of 44, set in 1897 by Wee Willie Keeler of the original Baltimore Orioles.

So by now, even those who didn't

particularly follow baseball were aware that something big was happening with Joe DiMaggio.

At the same time on this June 17, the America Firsters were denying reports they would try to shut down Brooklyn Dodger games in protest of Dodger President Larry McPhail's refusal to rent Ebbets Field to Charles Lindbergh for an America First rally.

In Europe, meanwhile, the Germans had just dispatched hundreds of thousands of troops into the Soviet Union to crush their former ally.

EIGHT DAYS LATER, a hit against the Browns put DiMaggio at 38 games. Yankee attendance, which had been averaging 10,000 before Joe's remarkable streak, was now regularly doubling that, and the whole town was counting.

By June 29, Hitler's forces were just 410 miles from Moscow, Minsk had fallen and authorities in Leningrad were drafting women. DiMaggio, by doubling in the opener and singling in the nightcap of a doubleheader against Washington on this day, made it 42 games. Sisler's

record had now fallen, and Joe received prolonged standing ovations from an exceptional crowd of 31,000 at Washington's Griffith Park.

On Wednesday the 2nd of July, against the Red Sox, DiMaggio passed Keeler before a screaming crowd at Yankee Stadium. The record-setting hit was a home run, whose arc the crowd followed with a thunderous roar. It was by now projected that the Yankees would draw a quarter million more fans than they had expected in the 1941 season, solely because of DiMaggio's streak.

He cruised on for 11 more games, reaching 56 with three hits against the Indians on Wednesday, July 16, in Cleveland. He looked good on the 17th, too, when in his first at-bat he smashed a hard ground ball down the third-base line. But Indian third baseman Ken Keltner made a nice play to throw him out, and he didn't come close again that day.

In his final at-bat, he grounded into a double play and the streak was over.

"It was getting to be a strain," DiMaggio admitted after the game. But all things considered, he added, he'd just as soon have kept it going.

THE WORLD STILL had some other concerns on July 17. Japan's cabinet had resigned, and the Army had taken control of the country. The Nazis were closing in on Leningrad. FDR announced that 750,000 more draft registrants would be called to active service.

But none of that dimmed what had over two months been a glorious baseball summer. DiMaggio's streak was already one of the landmark events of 20th century sports. Two hundred miles north, another skinny kid named Ted Williams, of the Boston Red Sox, was on his way to hitting .406, the last time in this century a Major League player would reach that level. A few miles south, in Brooklyn, the Dodgers were about to win their first pennant in 21 years, setting up the first of seven World Series showdowns between the Yankees and themselves.

It wasn't as good as bluebirds over the white cliffs of Dover. But it wasn't bad.

IN NOVEMBER, *Joe DiMaggio was named the American League's most valuable player for 1941. Three weeks later, the Japanese attacked Pearl Harbor. Many ballplayers soon enlisted or were drafted, though Williams and DiMaggio, among others, played the 1942 season. By then, the argument that ballplayers helped maintain homefront morale was losing to the argument that athletes shouldn't be slackers, and despite a legitimately bum knee, DiMaggio enlisted early in 1943. He spent much of his service playing on morale-boosting military baseball teams.*

By JAY MAEDER
Daily News Staff Writer

NOBODY HAD ever been able to pin much on Abe Reles. Fat, pomaded, bejeweled little Abe ran the loanshark rackets in Brownsville and East New York, Brooklyn, and he'd been crippling people for years, everybody knew this, and he led this charmed life: You'd pinch him and he'd just laugh at you, and then sure enough he'd walk out of court for lack of evidence. "Some detective will put a bullet in you," a livid judge had promised him once. "I'll take my chances with any cop," Abe had openly sneered back. By the end of the 1930s, Abe had been arrested 42 times, and he was still running Brownsville and East New York.

Then, on Jan. 1, 1940, a onetime beat cop and county judge named William O'Dwyer took office as Brooklyn's new district attorney and, per a tough campaign pledge, started rounding up every punk in sight. Among them was a minor hood named Duke Maffetore, who happened at the time to fear for his own personal safety and who offered to give up Abe Reles on an old murder in exchange for protection. When Maffetore was finished singing, O'Dwyer announced that he had an airtight case against Reles and was going to fry him.

Reles now divined that he was, in fact, cooked. And he went to O'Dwyer with an offer of his own: He knew a lot more than Maffetore ever dreamed of knowing, and he would spill everything about everyone, in return for, as they said, consideration. O'Dwyer, he promised, would be the most famous crimebuster in America. O'Dwyer liked that. He had already decided he was going to be mayor.

It was reported that fallen rackets boss Gurrah Shapiro, when word reached his prison cell that Abe Reles of Brownsville and East New York had turned state's evidence, immediately suffered a total nervous collapse.

ABE CLEARED UP about three dozen old killings right away. This was a man who genuinely knew where the bodies were, as they said, buried; detectives were digging corpses out of mob boneyards all over the Bronx and Jersey and Sullivan County for weeks. Abe was solving murders cops had never heard of. And he was only starting.

He absolutely delivered on his promise to make DA O'Dwyer a famous man. There was more than just a mob, Reles matter-of-factly confessed, there was a national crime syndicate, the Combination, organized by Charles Luciano and Meyer Lansky and Ben Siegel, and moreover there was an official enforcement arm under the direction of Louis Lepke Buchalter. These enforcers roamed the nation knocking off offenders on assignment, he said; he and his principal partners Martin (Buggsy) Goldstein and Harry (Pittsburgh Phil) Strauss had between them done more than

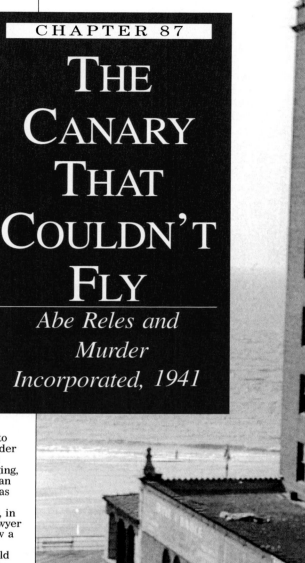

CHAPTER 87

THE CANARY THAT COULDN'T FLY

Abe Reles and Murder Incorporated, 1941

CORBIS BETTMAN

90 guys. Abe's bombshell revelations of a traveling professional hit squad electrified the whole country. The papers dubbed the fearsome outfit Murder Incorporated.

Peter Panto, the crusading Brooklyn longshoreman who had disappeared in 1939 after rallying dockworkers to rise up against the mobsters. Innocent Irving Penn, killed when gunmen mistook him for a key witness against Lepke. Joe Rosen, slain before he could testify against trucking racketeers. Dead man after dead man after dead man; Abe Reles knew about them all.

In May, as Assistant District Attorney Burton Turkus walked him through the eyewitness details in Kings County Court, he described the icepick-and-cleaver dispatch of one Whitey Rudnick and quickly sent his former pals Happy Maione and

Dasher Abbandando to the death house.

"It is an unfortunate thing in the administration of criminal justice that a district attorney at times is obliged to use the testimony of accomplices," scowled Judge Franklin Taylor, visibly disgusted.

IN SEPTEMBER 1940, the star witness left the safe-house comforts of his room at Coney Island's Half Moon Hotel, where he lived behind steel doors guarded around the clock by 18 police officers, and returned to court, where Buggsy Goldstein and Pittsburgh Phil, late of Murder Incorporated, stared at him in disbelief.

The dead man here was one Puggy Feinstein, a gambler who had made the mistake of attempting to move into turf not his own. Puggy had died

very unpleasantly in the living room of Abe's own house on E. 91st St. in Brooklyn. "I was going to move out of there anyhow," Abe said. The thing had been done as his elderly mother-in-law snoozed in the next room, he recounted: "I woke up the old lady and asked her where we kept the rope and the icepick." Afterward, he said, he and Buggsy and Phil had taken Puggy out and set him afire.

"It was a job we did for Albert Anastasia," Abe explained. "Puggy had double-crossed Vincent Mangano."

In one breath, Reles had now fingered Brooklyn's two top bosses, both of them in deep hiding. The remark was allowed to pass. Crimebuster O'Dwyer, some observers had noted, seemed pointedly unwilling to be much interested in waterfront boss Anastasia. Indeed, quite inexplicably, he had earlier shut down a separate probe of the dock rackets.

For now, sending over Buggsy and Phil was a triumph. "You can tell that rat Reles I'll be waiting for him in hell with a pitchfork," Buggsy screamed at reporters as he was put aboard the train to Sing Sing.

And then O'Dwyer went to Washington to get Justice Department permission to try Lepke on state murder charges, and Abe Reles went back to the Half Moon Hotel.

SOMEWHERE BETWEEN 6:45 and 7:10 on the morning of Wednesday the 12th of November 1941, 34-year-old Abe Reles went over his sixth-floor windowsill and immortalized himself as The Canary That Couldn't Fly.

This was one week after William O'Dwyer had failed to be elected mayor of the City of New York. With Fiorello LaGuardia returned to office, the first mayor to serve more than eight years since 1776, O'Dwyer now went back to his DA duties. Lepke, along with two confederates, was on trial for the 1936 murder of Joe Rosen. Reles was a key witness.

But now Reles had splattered himself across the hotel's kitchen roof five floors down. An unsuccessful escape attempt, it was concluded; his bedsheet rope appeared to have broken on him. The rope was only 18 feet long, of course; some observers found that amusing. Several policemen were duly demoted for having been asleep at the switch.

As it turned out, Lepke got convicted without Abe's testimony. There were enough other witnesses to send him to the chair.

As for the many loud calls for the prosecution now of Albert Anastasia, O'Dwyer said there was little he could do about that. Any possible case against Anastasia had just gone out the window. As they said.

WILLIAM O'DWYER *was elected the 100th mayor of New York in 1945. Among his first official acts was naming police Capt. Frank Bals, who had been in charge of the Half Moon security detail, a deputy police commissioner.*

In the early 1960s, gangland elder statesman Charles Luciano asserted that New York policemen had been paid to throw Abe Reles to his death.

By WENDELL JAMIESON
Daily News Staff Writer

FARAWAY BATTLES and blitzes had become grim everyday staples of the papers and radio broadcasts, and on this Sunday afternoon, in the stands of the Polo Grounds in upper Manhattan, the crowds just wanted to cheer the New York Giants and the Brooklyn Dodgers, football teams with followings as loyal as those devoted to their baseball cousins.

The roar of the stands wafted out into a chilly and clear late autumn day. Yes, everyone said war was surely on the horizon. But this was Sunday. It was just 2½ weeks till Christmas.

At 2:26 p.m., Len Sterling of the Mutual Broadcast System interrupted his play-by-play with a bulletin, bringing terse news from a place few had ever heard of.

"The Japanese have attacked Pearl Harbor, Hawaii, by air, President Roosevelt has just announced."

Pearl Harbor . . . Japanese planes . . . sneak attack . . . war.

The crowd hushed, then rustled, and then, as the game continued, young men with military uniforms at home and postings at nearby bases started picking their way through the stands toward the exits.

WAR CAME TO New York on Dec. 7, 1941, as it came to the rest of the nation, in terrifying radio snippets that interrupted football games and Sunday dinners and church. But somehow, in a city of 7½ million, with two battleships under construction at the Brooklyn Navy Yard, with tons of shipping in the harbor, the threat seemed larger, the danger nearer.

Mayor Fiorello LaGuardia got things off to a panicky start by taking to the airwaves from his desk at City Hall and announcing to already alarmed citizens that they were little more than sitting ducks for hordes of enemy agents and swarms of enemy planes.

His voice crackling over five radio stations, LaGuardia warned New Yorkers "not to feel entirely secure because you happen to be on the Atlantic Coast. There is no comfort in that." He wouldn't be surprised, he said, if the city were attacked at any minute.

As the mayor summoned his commissioners to City Hall, scores of cops and FBI agents fanned out across the city to visit members of what was suddenly New York's most hapless minority: Japanese citizens, of whom there were roughly 1,000.

At the Nippon Club on W. 93rd St., raiders rounded up a few workers and hauled them off to the nearest precinct. The Japanese consulate on Fifth Ave. was different; no one was exactly sure if it should be attacked or merely surrounded. Cops milled about aimlessly outside, sniffing the distinct scent of burning papers.

At the Brooklyn Navy Yard, hundreds of workers flooded in as heavy patrols were added around drydocks where the 45,000-ton battlewagons Iowa and Missouri were under construction. The Empire State Building was immediately blacked out.

AS MONDAY morning arrived with war still undeclared, fighter planes from Long Island's Mitchel Field droned down the shoreline and New Yorkers were already lined up at Army, Navy and Marine recruiting stations.

With the new day came a return visit to the Japanese Consulate, the detectives' mission now cleared by Washington: They grabbed what few papers remained and arrested an aide to Consul General Morito Morishima, who had in his possession many photos of the New York skyline.

LaGuardia, who was also chief of the nation's civilian defense program, went to Washington, and City Council President Newbold Morris took over the city in his absence. "Everybody's a soldier now," Morris announced, and everybody was. As the motor corps of the American Women's Voluntary Services drove more than 400 sailors and soldiers to their posts, 110,000 air raid wardens took to rooftops. That night, anti-aircraft guns were rolled into place around the city. By day's end, 700 men had enlisted at the U.S. Navy recruiting station on Church St.; another 1,000 had been turned away.

ON TUESDAY, with the news out of Hawaii and Manila increasingly bad, the war fever sweeping the city reached its frenzied height. That's when the five boroughs and the surrounding counties froze in terror for three long hours, believing they were about to be bombed.

At 11:55 a.m., civil defense officials received word from Washington that hostile planes were two hours out at sea and heading toward New York. An ominously long air raid siren blast, followed by a single short burst, shot over the rooftops of Brooklyn and Queens and echoed through Manhattan's skyscrapers. It was repeated every five minutes.

Thousands stared skyward, waiting for the series of short siren blasts that meant "all clear." It didn't come.

At Mitchel Field, 280 pursuit planes — twin-engine B-25s and cannon-spitting Aircobras — swept aloft. Chemical warfare and machine gun units rolled into place. Houses near the airfield were evacuated. Commercial flights were grounded.

At 12:45 p.m., the radios of police prowl cars announced: "Information received that a squadron

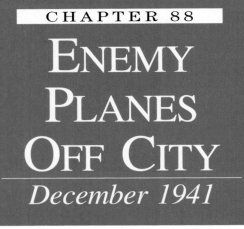

CHAPTER 88

ENEMY PLANES OFF CITY

December 1941

of airplanes is headed toward Long Island, identity unknown at this time."

Forty-five minutes later, there was still no "all clear." Schools ordered a million children home. Minutes later, police radio cars got word the planes were "expected in New York City area within 10 minutes." Inky bundles of afternoon papers announcing **ENEMY PLANES OFF CITY** landed in front of newsstands and candy shops. Office workers spilled into the streets.

The "all clear" finally came at 1:45, and the workers went back to work as their kids enjoyed an early day off.

There had been a misunderstanding. A friendly patrol zooming down the Eastern Seaboard had prompted the erroneous report, which some officials sheepishly contended was a test.

As the fighters dispatched to fight the phantom threat returned to Mitchel Field, a small fire broke out. Word quickly spread that the field was under attack — and again the air-raid warning blasted from every rooftop siren, police radio car and fire truck in the city.

But by now New York had been at war for nearly three days, and there were fewer jitters.

By WENDELL JAMIESON
Daily News Staff Writer

CHAPTER 89

JUMPING SPARK
Normandie, 1942

THE CITY WAS darkened by war, entombed in a frigid winter. And at Pier 88 at the foot of W. 49th St. rode a great gray phantom, a gloomy memory of happier times.

Once she had been the Normandie, pride of the French Line, the sleekest passenger vessel the North Atlantic had ever known. When Germany invaded Poland in September 1939, she had been ordered to remain in New York indefinitely, at a berth specially lengthened and deepened to accommodate the world's largest liner. And there she had sat for two years, manned by a skeleton crew.

Now, with the U.S. in the war, the government had seized her, renamed her the LaFayette and earmarked her for troopship duty. On Christmas Eve 1941, workers began to rip out her elegant insides, gutting the luxe staterooms and deco cafes, putting in spartan bunks and huge mess tables for thousands of soldiers, painting over peacetime colors with camouflage.

On Monday the 9th of February 1942, welder Clement Derrick was removing the last of four light stanchions in the main salon amid bales of burlap bags filled with highly flammable life preservers.

DERRICK WOULD later say he had bumped into a pile of bales as he and his team seared through the stanchion with a blue-hot flame. Sparks rained around them — and one bale flashed alight.

The workers tried to stamp the fire out — flinging flaming preservers aside, quickly spreading the blaze. The fire jumped from one bale to another, from floor to ceiling, from deck to deck.

There was no water pressure for the hoses. The fire extinguishers didn't work. The lights failed, plunging an endless maze of smoke-choked corridors into darkness.

"Get off the ship! Get off the ship!" boomed the loudspeakers.

It took more than 10 minutes for the onboard fire brigade to send out an alarm to the city Fire Department, which responded to Pier 88 with scores of clanging ladder trucks and pumpers. The first unit on the scene was a fireboat, which chugged up the slushy, ice-dotted Hudson from 35th St. and started drenching the smoke-belching ship.

As hundreds of gasping, soot-covered workers scrambled down gangplanks and rope ladders, firefighters fought the panicked exodus to get aboard the monster liner, where they groped through the dark passageways in search of victims and pockets of flame.

The great plume of acrid smoke spread east through the towers of midtown, awakening a city that had listened in frustration to reports of military disasters in the Philippines, Bataan, Wake Island. Now there was a disaster on the West Side.

THOUSANDS OF spectators crammed the streets, and Mayor Fiorello LaGuardia, always the fire buff, bombastically joined his fire commissioner to direct the fight. Civil Defense volunteers in brand-new helmets flocked to the scene, adding to the carnival atmosphere, as the afternoon papers screamed news of the calamity. The smoke reached Nassau County.

The workers who slid down rope ladders and leaped into the Hudson escaped the cauterizing heat only to face jarring cold. Civilian fitter Joseph Cenetola's hands froze to an iron ladder, forcing firefighters to chop him free.

Some 200 men were injured. Astonishingly, there was just one fatality: Frank Trent of Brooklyn, who had been working as a shipboard fire watcher when the first sparks sputtered.

Amid the chaos, more water was poured upon the ship, which began to list ominously away from Pier 88. Watertight doors — shut to block the flames — now trapped the flood on the upper decks. The list increased, snapping with cannonlike blasts the massive hawsers that had lashed the Normandie to the dock.

Now, on the pier, a heated argument broke out. Navy officials wanted to scuttle the liner so it would settle safely into the 40-foot-deep berth right side up, making for an easy salvage job. But fire officials argued against the Navy plan, saying they were confident they could douse the flames quickly. By 9 p.m., as the tide went out and the liner touched bottom, it looked like the battle was won. The flames had died down, leaving only a whisper of smoke.

But the ship was water-logged, perilously top-heavy. Slowly, as the tide came back in, she lifted her hull, and slowly the list increased. Firefighters were ordered off. Rescue ships and fireboats were ordered away. At 2:30 a.m., the blackened Normandie rolled defeatedly over on her side into the ice and the river.

In the morning, she was there for all to see, lying across Pier 88. Half her bridge was out of the river, as were the starboard sides of her stylish funnels and two of her glinting and now useless propellers.

There was immediate talk of sabotage — that the Axis had scored a great victory by sinking what was bound to be one of the fastest and largest troop ships of the war.

But after interviewing workers for a day, District Attorney Frank Hogan put down the rumors. A jumping spark from a torch had done the work of a team of German secret agents, he concluded.

"There is no evidence of sabotage," Hogan said. "Carelessness has served the enemy with equal effectiveness."

THE NORMANDIE *spent the next 18 months on her side — becoming a wartime tourist attraction — before she was righted and broken into scrap.*

It has remained widely believed that in fact she was torched by the New York underworld, making a bid to pressure authorities into freeing mob boss Charles Luciano — who, indeed, left prison after the war and was deported to Italy.

By WENDELL JAMIESON
Daily News Staff Writer

THEY WERE, quite possibly, the worst saboteurs of World War II.

They sloshed ashore in the pre-dawn darkness of Friday, June 12, 1942, on a deserted beach near Amagansett, L.I., carrying $80,000 and boxes of explosives designed to wreak havoc across the U.S.

The arsenal included bombs that looked like pencils, intended to blow off the hands of civilians, and bombs that looked like lumps of coal, meant to be tossed into unguarded piles of the real thing; ideally, these coal bombs would end up in the boilers of American ships and cause horrific blasts. The saboteurs also hoped to destroy the Hell Gate Bridge and key defense factories and cripple the New York City water supply system.

The daring plan had been hatched at the highest levels of the Nazi war machine, calculated to bring the terrors of war to American soil. But it had four things wrong with it — the saboteurs themselves.

GEORGE DASCH, 39, led the team. He had spent 17 aimless years knocking around the U.S. as a waiter. When war broke out in Europe in 1939, he had taken advantage of the Fatherland's offer to return home free of charge and join the military effort.

His three companions had similar backgrounds; they had lived around the U.S. for a time and then snapped up the free ticket home. All four ended up in spy school in Berlin, where they got a crash course in how to blow things up. A single small bomb on an industrial production line, they learned, could stop vital war work for months.

Their training done, Dasch and his comrades visited German-occupied Paris, where they were treated to a final champagne-drenched weekend. Then they boarded U-Boat 202 for the 15-day journey to New York, as another group was dispatched to Florida.

In close quarters aboard the spartan, greasy, cramped submarine, the saboteurs soon discovered that they didn't like one another very much. One was extremely moody. Another was prone to blabbing secrets — a bad trait in a spy. Dasch, increasingly uncomfortable with the mission, started breaking out in cold sweats. His misgivings were not at all soothed when the U-202 was depth-charged and nearly sent to the bottom.

He was very happy when, late on the night of June 11, the submarine nuzzled up to the rural shore of Long Island's East End.

AFTER MIDNIGHT, the four agents clambered through a hatch into rubber rafts, bearing four wooden crates of explosives. They wore German naval uniforms that identified them as combatants entitled to imprisonment in the event of capture — unlike spies, who would face execution.

They paddled ashore, buried their deadly cargo and started changing into civilian clothes.

At this exact moment, 21-year-old Coast Guardsman John Cullen, walking the beach unarmed, happened to stumble across them. What, Cullen inquired, did they think they were doing?

INEXPLICABLY, considering that they were spies, the Germans chose not to kill Cullen on the spot. Instead, Dasch pressed $260 into his palm and instructed him: "Forget you ever saw this."

Cullen was going to do no such thing. Seeing that something worrisome was going on here, the extremely fortunate young sentry walked away, money in hand, and went straight to his headquarters as the Germans finished dressing and headed for the Amagansett railroad station.

Meanwhile, the tide went out, grounding U-202 on a sandbar, conning tower and periscope clearly visible above the surf.

On the beach, Amagansett.

CHAPTER 90

SECRET AGENTS OF THE REICH

Spy Thriller, 1942

After first walking a mile the wrong way, the saboteurs finally made it to the quiet station and hopped the 6:57 to Jamaica, Queens, where they bought new suits and each had a shave.

Then they headed into Manhattan, where they used forged identity papers to check into two hotels: Dasch and Peter Berger at the Governor Clinton, Heinrich Heinck and Richard Quirin at the Martinique on Herald Square.

By this time, Cullen had returned to the beach with a gang of his Coast Guard buddies, who found:

A German submarine immobilized several hundred yards offshore.

A pack of German cigarettes in the sand.

Boxes of explosives and four soggy German naval uniforms.

At this point they called their superiors.

WHEN THE TIDE came in, U-202 slipped away. But the other items remained, and by noon, the barren stretch of beach was teeming with soldiers, FBI agents and Civil Defense crews.

In Manhattan, the spies found themselves in a bustling city a world away from the nightly bombings and severe rationing in Berlin.

According to plan, they were to spend two months scoping targets before returning to Long Island for their bombs. But it was New York. It was almost summer. They bought fancy summer wardrobes and started hitting the nightclubs, and presently they pretty much forgot about their mission.

A few days later, Dasch decided that the plot was doomed and suggested to fellow spy Berger that they give themselves up and seek leniency. Berger, showing all the steely nerve of a cool Nazi killer, quickly agreed that this was a fine idea. Both traveled to Washington, called up the FBI and turned themselves in.

Their two associates were shortly under arrest. So were the four agents who had landed in Florida.

Two weeks after the secret landings in America, the arrests of the eight Germans became front page news. An ingenious espionage plot had been broken, the FBI proudly announced.

Nowhere did the press releases cite the G-men's real contribution to cracking the case: They answered the phone.

AFTER AN *Army trial, six of the saboteurs died in the electric chair. For their help, Dasch and Berger were spared and sentenced to hard labor. Their sentences were commuted after the war. Dasch returned to Germany, where he was hounded out of town after town for having turned in his countrymen.*

Coast Guardsman John Cullen, presented with Legion of Merit.

Flip Corkin and Terry Lee.

Phil Cochran and Milton Caniff

By JAY MAEDER
Daily News Staff Writer

IT WAS June 1943 and the war was practically won and it was swell to be an American. The headlines roared of Allied triumphs, every day on every front: **20 U-BOATS SUNK BY CONVOY. 3 BATTLESHIPS HIT BY FORTS IN ITALY RAID. INVASION HOUR IS SET. YANKS ROUT 80 AXIS PLANES. PANTELLERIA CAPITULATES AS YANKS SMASH NAZI BOMBERS. YANK FLIERS DOWN 77 JAP PLANES IN BIGGEST PACIFIC AIR FIGHT. LAST BOOT ISLE FALLS — WAY OPEN TO SICILY! FDR HAILS VICTORY — IT'S ZERO HOUR SOON!** On Flag Day in Central Park, 30,000 New Yorkers pledged allegiance and bowed their heads as buglers blew taps.

Then they went to the movies and cheered the good guys: Leslie Howard and David Niven in "Spitfire" at the Rivoli, Humphrey Bogart in "Action in the North Atlantic" at the Strand, Robert Taylor in "Bataan" at the Capitol, Tyrone Power in "Crash Dive" at the Paramount. Then they picked up the Daily News and turned to "Terry and the Pirates" to see if air cadet Terry Lee and his fighter pilot buddy Maj. Flip Corkin had found missing Army Nurse Taffy Tucker yet. The French girl Rouge had turned out to be a Japanese agent, and she'd kidnapped Taffy and beaten her up and left her for dead deep in the Chinese interior, and Taffy had been wandering around in an amnesiac daze for weeks now. Flip was kind of sweet on Taffy, and he and Terry were sure going to find her, you could bet on that.

At the Waldorf-Astoria, Army Air Forces Lt. Col. Phil Cochran, enjoying a brief holiday home from North Africa, laughed as he explained to reporters still again — reporters were always asking about this — that no, there wasn't really a Taffy Tucker. Taffy was just somebody Daily News cartoonist Milton Caniff had invented to keep him company in the funny papers. He preferred hatcheck girls, personally, and he couldn't wait for the war to be over so he could spend his evenings at the Copacabana again.

Thirty-three-year-old Phil Cochran in June 1943 was America's best-known flier. One, he was a colorful figure in real life — he commanded a black-sheep P-40 squadron in Tunisia, running a guerrilla air war essentially free of interference from the brass hats, who could never find him, and he was great copy and the war correspondents were always looking in on him — and two, he lived a second life as Flip Corkin in "Terry and the Pirates," and millions of readers followed his adventures every day. Both Cochran and Corkin were all-American tough guys, given to the kind of chest-thumpingly patriotic speeches you liked to listen to in 1943. Sitting in his Waldorf-Astoria suite with New York's reporters, Cochran was the best recruiting poster the Army Air Forces ever had.

"I want to say that our kids, American boys, are just kind of automatically wonderful," Cochran said. "Just through our own way of life they get something that makes them superior fighters. They don't have to be indoctrinated and have it hammered in for months or years. The fighter pilot flies with his heart. The thing that makes him superior in combat is inside him all the time. Our kids have it, and I think it is something they get naturally, something they get just by growing up and living in this country."

The Daily News' editorial page pointed with pride. "The American self-starter system is coming through again," the paper declared.

Back home in Erie, Pa., Mother Cochran beamed too. "I raised my boys to be square shooters," she said.

MILTON CANIFF had known Phil Cochran at Ohio State University. Cochran joined the Army and Caniff came to New York to be a comic strip man. In 1934, drawing "Dickie Dare" for the Associated Press, he got invited by Daily News Publisher Capt. Joseph Patterson to develop a new feature for The News' all-star lineup: "Dick Tracy," "Little Orphan Annie," "Moon Mullins," "The Gumps," "Gasoline Alley," "Smilin' Jack" and the others. "Terry and the Pirates" was kid stuff at first, a yarn about a footloose American youngster in exotic China, mixing it up with cutthroats and bandit queens. After 1937, as Japanese invaders overran the Chinese, the strip became a realistic documentary, and by the early '40s "Terry" was as grimly familiar a war dispatch in America's living rooms as were Edward R. Murrow's radio broadcasts.

In 1941, recognizing that young Terry Lee would soon have to put on a uniform, Caniff looked up Cochran, who was training fighter pilots at Mitchel Field on Long Island, and learned his way around a flight line. Cochran had his boys stage dogfights for the cartoonist. When, in August 1942, Caniff introduced his readers to Flip Corkin, an American officer who trained Chinese air cadets, the aviation sequences were so detailed that you could have learned to fly a P-40 just from following "Terry and the Pirates."

The real Cochran, meanwhile, was in North Africa by now. In June 1943, when he came back to the U.S. to report to the Pentagon on Tunisian operations, he was wearing a Silver Star, a Distinguished Flying Cross, a Croix de Guerre with star and palm and a chestful of other baubles.

'**T**HE FIGHTING heart is what the fighter pilot has to have," Phil Cochran told the reporters at the Waldorf-Astoria. "He must feel vicious, he has to want to fight. He's got to be exhilarated. We want him to go into the fight yelling and bouncing up and down in his seat. The fighting heart has to be inside right at the beginning."

In the spring of 1944, Cochran went to India, formed the First Commando Air Force and led the storied glider raid into the heart of Japanese-held Burma. Terry Lee and Flip Corkin both were in India themselves by now, and Terry was an accomplished flier, regularly shooting down Zeroes all over the Hump. Taffy Tucker had been found, and she was safe and well. There wasn't really a Taffy Tucker, though.

CHAPTER 91

FIGHTING HEART
Flip Corkin, 1943

By JAY MAEDER
Daily News Staff Writer

THE THING about Carlo Tresca was that he looked exactly like what a crazy bomb-throwing radical foreigner was supposed to look like: wild-bearded, wild-eyed, always passionately shaking his fist and thundering away about the oppressed workers. Actually, he was quite a genial fellow, unfailingly polite to the cops who started visiting him regularly in the wake of the 1920 Wall St. explosion. "They are nice boys," he told reporters. "Whenever there is a bomb, they come to me. They ask me what I know, but I never know anything. So we have wine."

He'd been the town revolutionary for four decades, ever since he fled Italy in 1904, an actual practicing political refugee, and the town was really quite fond of the old duck. He'd spent his life on the barricades, striking with the Pennsylvania coal miners and the New Jersey silk workers alongside Big Bill Haywood and Elizabeth Gurley Flynn and the International Workers of the World in those long-ago times; he'd been beaten and shot at and stabbed and kidnapped; he'd been arrested three dozen times and occasionally sent to prison. It was said of Carlo Tresca that he might well have become the most important man in American labor history, had he ever learned to speak better than rudimentary English. Late in his life he was still publishing an earnestly revolutionary newspaper, railing against class principles, doggedly fighting the battles of labor against capital, the trade union against the state. His job, The New Yorker observed of him, was "fanning volcanoes."

In 1943, Tresca was 68 years old; distinguished elder statesman to some, quaint old pterodactyl to some others, a wild-bearded, wild-eyed, firebrand editor enormously proud of the countless enemies he had made in his stormy life. Investigators had absolutely no idea where to start investigating when, at 9:40 p.m. on Monday the 11th of January, on the corner of Fifth Ave. and 15th St., someone slipped up behind Carlo Tresca and fired a bullet into the back of his head.

WHO WERE cops supposed to arrest? To anyone not fluent in revolutionese, Tresca's politics were impenetrable: He had abandoned all party affiliations in 1907 and marched to his own drums since then, sometimes a Leninist, sometimes a Trotskyite, always a rabid anti-Fascist, a life-long foe of Benito Mussolini, with whom he'd had a storied falling-out when they were young men. "Well, Comrade Tresca, I hope America will make you over into a real revolutionary," Mussolini had sneered at him when he left Italy. "I hope, Comrade Mussolini," Tresca had sneered back,

"that you'll quit posing and learn how to fight." Mussolini had put him on an official death list in 1931. Tresca liked to boast about that.

Meanwhile, he was also a noisy anti-Stalinist, energetically crusading to keep Reds out of the unions, and the Communists all hated him too. Chiefly, Tresca was a formal anarchist, meaning he wanted down with pretty much everything. Everybody in the phone book might have been a suspect.

On the last afternoon of his life, Tresca lunched with novelist John Dos Passos; that evening he went to the Fifth Ave. offices of his twice-monthly newspaper, Il Martello (The Hammer), to meet with fellow members of the Mazzini Society. New York in 1943 was not exactly a hotbed of Italian Fascists, but there were pockets of them, and Tresca felt there to be Fascisti elements in the society that warranted purging. But no one showed up for the meeting except his friend Giuseppe Calabi, and after a while the two of them gave up waiting and went out for a glass of wine.

On the blacked-out wartime avenue, Calabi never got a good look at the gunman, who came out of nowhere and then leaped into a

CHAPTER 92

DOWN WITH ANARCHY
Carlo Tresca, 1943

waiting dark sedan and roared away.

Fascists, Communists, who knew? What police had here was a sensational political assassination, a genuine international incident, right here on New York soil.

COPS SOON caught a break. Two hours before Tresca died, a petty Brooklyn hoodlum named Carmine Galante had visited his parole officer down on Centre St. to report that he was gainfully employed as a $25-a-week trucker. The parole officer had believed this not for a minute and had dispatched two men to trail Galante as he left. They lost him when he got into a dark sedan. Unable to follow — with gasoline rationing in effect, their cars had been taken away from them — the state men took down the tag number as Galante disappeared.

And this proved to be the same tag as that on a 1938 Ford found ditched several blocks from the Tresca murder scene. Rounded up, Galante protested that he'd spent the evening at the movies, watching Humphrey Bogart's new "Casablanca." But he couldn't say

what the picture was about, and cops had no doubt that here was their shooter.

Plainly, he was just somebody's hired gun. A little jerk like Carmine Galante wouldn't even know what an anarchist was, much less want to assassinate one. But Galante had no comment. District Attorney Frank Hogan threw him into the jug — and kept him there for eight months, waiting for him to crack. He never did.

Meanwhile, as the Tresca case itself flickered and went cold, it veered, quite accidentally, into another inquiry altogether. And suddenly, in his death, New York City's pet anarchist took the town straight to the door of one of its most explosive political scandals.

DISTRICT ATTORNEY Hogan had put taps on the telephones of hundreds of persons prominent in the city's Italian-American community. He never turned up a lead to Tresca's killing — but late in the summer he recorded a conversation between a city magistrate named Thomas Aurelio, who recently had won nomination to the state Supreme Court bench, and a gentleman named Frank Costello, known by authorities to have a hand in the rackets.

Thanks for everything, Aurelio had said.

It went over perfect, Costello had replied. *When I tell you something is in the bag, you can rest assured.*

I want to assure you of my loyalty for all you have done, Aurelio said. *It's undying.*

I know, Costello said.

On Saturday the 28th of August, Hogan gave this transcript to the papers and wondered aloud why such a man as Aurelio would be so grateful to such a man as Costello.

THE CARLO TRESCA *slaying has never been officially solved. It is widely believed that the hit was ordered from Italy by then-in-exile Vito Genovese purely as a favor to Benito Mussolini.*

By JAY MAEDER
Daily News Staff Writer

ON THURSDAY the 26th of August 1943, three days after Magistrate Thomas Aurelio secured both the Democratic and Republican nominations for a prized seat on the state Supreme Court, the judge happily celebrated his bi-partisan shoo-in with an evening at the theater that was soon interrupted by an urgent telephone call. Michael Kennedy, former congressman and new chief of Tammany Hall, had to see him at once.

Tom, Kennedy announced at the New York Athletic Club 30 minutes later, *I have bad news for you.*

What's the trouble? Aurelio asked.

Did you speak to Frank Costello Tuesday morning?

I did.

Did you know that his wire was tapped and the district attorney has a taped conversation?

Aurelio blinked.

The district attorney will give you until tomorrow night to decline your nomination or he will give the tapped wire to the press at 11 a.m. the next day, Kennedy said. *Did you know Costello was a racketeer?*

No, Mr. Kennedy, said Judge Aurelio. *I did not.*

SO DID Thomas Aurelio tearfully reconstruct the conversation as, in a Manhattan courtroom in late October, Manhattan District Attorney Frank Hogan sought to disbar him from the practice of law in the State of New York.

District Attorney Hogan had a tape, all right — a bombshell that rocked the town, blasted Tammany apart and blew the mask off Frank Costello, shadowy crime boss, king of the slot machines and now, it appeared, a powerful political czar, the puppet master, New York City's big fix. Anti-Tammany leaders were never so jubilant. "Open evidence of gang control of Democratic politics in New York County," whooped state Sen. James Donovan. "One more illustration of the combination between politics and the criminal elements," shouted Mayor Fiorello LaGuardia.

Aurelio, Hogan's tape revealed, had phoned Costello at home the day after he was nominated. *Good morning, Francesco,* the judge had said. *Thanks for everything.*

Congratulations, Costello said. *It went over perfect. When I tell you something is in the bag, you can rest assured.*

It was perfect, Aurelio agreed.

We all will have to get together, you, your missus and myself, and have dinner some night real soon, Costello said.

That would be fine, said Aurelio, *but right now I want to assure you of my loyalty for all you have done. It's undying.*

I know, said Costello.

There was not necessarily a crime here, Hogan said, only an "affront to the electorate and threat to the judiciary." Aurelio was indignant: "I yield to no one in demanding that the integrity of our courts of justice be preserved," he snapped.

A wink for the camera as Aurelio and kids sign register on election day.

CHAPTER 93

IN THE BAG

The Judge And The Fixer, 1943

On Monday, Aug. 30, both political parties repudiated Aurelio's nomination and ducked for cover. "It comes as a great shock to me," sighed Kennedy.

FRANK Costello was, among other things, a successful legitimate businessman — nightclubs, fighters, liquor distributorships etc. — and, save for one minor weapons conviction in 1915, the law had never touched him. The federals had failed to convict him of rum-running in the 1920s, and they had failed to get him for tax fraud.

In 1934, as the crusading LaGuardia rid the town of slot machines — when you saw the mayor and his sledgehammer in the newsreels, those were Frank Costello's machines he was smashing — Costello had quietly relocated to New Orleans, and there he had stayed; accordingly, he was never a target of D.A. Thomas Dewey's racket-busting operations. When he returned to New York in 1940, Charles Luciano and Louis Buchalter were both in

Frank Costello

prison and Vito Genovese had fled to Italy. He was the new boss.

But Costello was a gentleman mobster who kept his name out of the newspapers. He didn't kill people. He bought them. Costello generously contributed to many campaigns. He had hosted lavish banquets at both the Democratic and Republican presidential conventions in 1940; some said he had helped send Franklin Roosevelt to the White House in 1932. Locally, he was the man to see about appointments. Tammany chief Mike Kennedy, for one, owed him his job.

These details emerged during Aurelio's disbarment hearings. The judge had refused to quit the Supreme Court race quietly; when the two parties rescinded their nominations and wiped his name off the ballot, he had mounted a court challenge and won; then he had, quite astutely, resigned his magistracy, thus avoiding removal proceedings. He was still a candidate. The bar association and Hogan now moved to strip him of his ticket. Out of the shadows at last, Frank Costello was among those called to testify.

COSTELLO WAS nothing if not forthcoming. He readily admitted having put his old pal Kennedy in the Tammany leadership, merely by informing supporters of Kennedy's opponent that he would "consider it a nice thing" if they switched their votes; the opponent, indeed, had withdrawn from the race. He acknowledged having leaned on Kennedy several times when his old pal seemed to waver in his support of Judge Aurelio. "I went to Mr. Kennedy and told him I understood he was cooling off," Costello said. "I said, you made a promise and you should live up to it." And Kennedy, he added, had duly done so.

Abe Rosenthal, chief clerk of the Board of Elections and co-leader of Tammany's 8th District — the other co-leader was Aurelio's wife, Aida — testified that he had discussed Aurelio's nomination with Costello on numerous occasions.

And Aurelio acknowledged that he had met with Costello six times and that Costello had informed him, quote: "It's in the bag for you." He had absolutely no idea that Costello was anything but an upright citizen, he insisted. His phone call, he said, was just one of many made to campaign supporters. His profession of undying loyalty, he said, was nothing but "a fulsome expression uttered in the joy, happiness and excitement of the moment."

"A typical fulsome and effusive Italian expression," his lawyer agreed in summation.

ON OCT. 30, the special referee appointed to hear the disbarment case against Thomas Aurelio ruled that the charges were "not proven."

Three days later, voters elected Aurelio to a 14-year Supreme Court term. He had, after all, been personally assured by Costello that he had nothing to worry about.

MICHAEL KENNEDY resigned his Tammany leadership in January 1944. Frank Costello, now regularly in the newspapers, remained the city's top political boss for nearly another decade. In 1945, he elected former Brooklyn District Attorney William O'Dwyer to the mayorship.

At his death in 1973 at age 81, Justice Thomas Aurelio was still sitting on the Supreme Court bench.

By JAY MAEDER
Daily News Staff Writer

ONCE UPON A time there was a little girl named Elizabeth Wehner, who lived in Williamsburg in the Borough of Brooklyn in the City of New York, and then when she was still a very young lady she moved away to Michigan and never came back. The end.

AT LEAST it was the end until August 1943, 30-something years later, when Betty Smith, who didn't live there anymore, took her position in the pantheon as the Borough of Brooklyn's noblest poet since Walt Whitman.

Divorced, rearing two daughters, banging out radio dramas on a playwriting fellowship at the University of North Carolina, Betty Smith was living hand to mouth in 1943. She had trouble making the rent, she owed the dentist and the veterinarian, she was down to her last $100 in the world. But she felt she had to be in New York for the Aug. 19 publication by Harper of her first novel. Originally it had been a one-act play called "Francie Nolan," an affectionate memoir of an early-century Brooklyn girlhood, and over the course of several years she had turned the play into a 1,000-page novel, which Harper had cut in half and agreed to publish under another title, which was "A Tree Grows in Brooklyn." With her last $100 in the world, Betty Smith now bought a bus ticket from Chapel Hill to Manhattan and gamely splurged on an $18-a-night room at the Savoy.

In the morning, she decided to go down for a newspaper herself, because if she had the bellboy bring one up she'd have to tip him 50 cents. And she was thinking she'd grab a bite to eat at the Automat. Then the phone rang.

"Mrs. Smith, there's a whole bunch of photographers down here," reported the front desk. "Something about a book."

THUS DID Betty Smith make the journey from dirt poverty to fame and fortune literally overnight. New York's influential reviewers uniformly fell out of their shoes in awe of her 443-page offering. "Profoundly moving," said The New York Times' Orville Prescott. "Authentic and poignant," agreed the Herald Tribune's Lewis Gannett. The hotel started sending up baskets of flowers to Betty Smith's room. The best dress shops began calling, inquiring if she'd like to try on their creations. Reporters followed her around for days.

"A Tree Grows in Brooklyn" was the tender, courage-awash story of the Nolan family — impossible Johnny, the singing waiter who drank up his tips; patient, suffering Katie, the hardworking janitress who kept home and hearth

together, and ceaselessly pensive daughter Francie, ever buried in library books and dreaming of clean skies somewhere beyond the grime of Williamsburg. The tree in question was an *Ailanthus glandulosa*, the tree of heaven, a Chinese sumac common to every Brooklyn tenement yard — metaphorically

indestructible even when you chopped it down — and the point was that things live and things die and yet life goes on somehow, as it must, and this was precisely the kind of sentimental nonprofundity that has always made readers sniffle and dab their eyes and murmur, "How *true*." Betty Smith's book was immediately a Literary Guild selection, and it sold 300,000 copies in six weeks.

Thereafter did Betty Smith, who lived in North Carolina, make a life-long career as Brooklyn's foremost celebrator, implanting into the national consciousness an indelible image of a Brooklyn that had stopped existing decades earlier. "Little houses with shining, clean windows and wonderful rippled window shades and lace curtains," she would recall for interviewers. "Old stores where they made cigars by hand in the windows, and the pillow shop where they made pillows. . . ."

CHAPTER 94

As The Twig Is Bent

Betty Smith, 1943

'SOME PEOPLE call it the tree of heaven," whispered Francie Nolan, pensively. "It grows in boarded-up lots and out of neglected rubbish-heaps. It grows up out of cellar gratings. It is the only tree that grows out of cement."

Twentieth Century-Fox bought film rights for $55,000 in 1944 and gave the picture to first-time director Elia Kazan. The moviemakers had a great deal of trouble finding an *ailanthus* in Southern California. Finally they chopped one down elsewhere, had the thing brought in and nailed it to the floor of the sound stage, and life went on, as it must.

AT BETTY SMITH'S death at 75 in 1972, "A Tree Grows in Brooklyn" had been through 37 printings and sold 6 million copies. Harper ranked it with "Ben Hur" and "Love Story" as the house's biggest best sellers.

By JAY MAEDER
Daily News Staff Writer

JUSTICE TOM AURELIO's election to the state Supreme Court wasn't the only thing Frank Costello had in his pocket. On Wednesday the 14th of June 1944, he happened to have $27,200 cash in his pocket. And, at 12:55 p.m., he absent-mindedly left it in the back seat of a New York City taxi.

What followed was one of those improbable high-mob-comedy episodes that practicing gangsters are occasionally called upon to endure, even such senior figures as Fancy Frank Costello, gambler, slot machine king and Prime Minister of the Underworld.

Frank Costello personally went down to the city's Lost Property Bureau on Broome St. like any other citizen to put in formal papers for the return of his lost property.

And Mayor Fiorello LaGuardia and Police Commissioner Lewis Valentine, visibly licking their chops at the prospect of beating Frank Costello out of $27,200 that might otherwise worthily benefit the police pension fund, refused to give it back.

Whereupon the Prime Minister of the Underworld actually filed suit against the New York City Police Department and spent the next 2½ years prosecuting his claim.

FORGETFUL FRANK, the papers instantly dubbed him.

Apparently, the two fat envelopes had slipped out of his trousers when he dug up the 60 cents to pay for his ride from the Hotel New Yorker at Eighth Ave. and 34th St. to the Sherry Netherland at Fifth and 59th. Cabby Edward Waters right away spotted the bundle that his well-dressed fare had left behind and, considering that the sport had tossed him a 25-cent tip, jumped out of his car and tried to call him back. But Costello had already disappeared inside the hotel, and about all Waters could do was drive over to the W. 67th St. police stationhouse and dutifully hand the money over to incredulous cops.

It was the custom of Maurice Simmons, the chief of the Lost Property Bureau, to notify the press whenever something halfway interesting turned up in the back of a cab, and he had managed to land himself starring roles in more than a few human-interest features. Now what he had here was $27,200 cash, for God's sake, 271 crisp hundreds and a couple of fifties, and city desks all over town dispatched their reporters to write up this swell yarn he was offering. And then, suddenly and mysteriously, Simmons went stone cold silent, rebuffing all questions, refusing to discuss the matter any further.

Sensing something was up, the newshounds now leaned hard on Valentine, who, on Saturday the 17th of June, unhappily found himself obliged to give up the information that, well, the claimant was Frank Costello.

Costello, 48, was not, after all, just some meathead. He was a criminal kingpin. He was Tammany Hall's ruling puppet master. Fiorello LaGuardia was late in his fourth mayoral term now, crotchety and petty and quite often just a silly old man, but he was still a passionate professional reformer by trade: He was supposed to give back $27,200 to Frank Costello? "What I'm interested in is where did the bum get it and where was he taking it," the mayor snapped. Plainly this was outlaw money, LaGuardia said. Well, the city just happened to have an ordinance stipulating that not only did lost-property claimants have to prove they'd lost the property, they also had to show "lawful title" to it

Empty-handed at the Lost Property Bureau.

CHAPTER 95

PRINCIPLE OF THE THING

Robbing Frank Costello, 1944

as well.

"It's mine!" Costello protested. "I lost it!" He didn't wish to get into the details: Fifteen grand was a collection from a debtor he declined to identify, and the rest of it was a loan from a party he also declined to identify. What was so unusual about carrying $27,200 in cash anyway? he fumed.

"I'm in the real estate business."

"That's a laugh," snorted LaGuardia.

Discerning here that the City of New York fully intended to rob him, Frank Costello now went to state Supreme Court and sued.

Probably he didn't need the money all that desperately. He had just put down $15,000 cash on an elegant 12-room home on Barker's Point Road in Sands Point, L.I., close to the Sands Point Beach Club, and stuffed the place with new furniture. So it wasn't really the $27,200. It was, dammit, the principle of the thing.

FOUR MONTHS LATER, Supreme Court Justice Carroll Walter agreed.

"I cannot tolerate the idea that the Police Department may keep a citizen's property for no better reason than its own innuendo that perhaps the citizen acquired the property in a gambling transaction," Walter said, ordering Costello's money returned forthwith.

This was a hollow victory at best, considering that the federal government by now had slapped liens on the whole notorious pile, alleging income tax delinquencies for the years 1926 through 1930. And things got even hollower a year later, when the city, on appeal, got Walter's decision overturned. Doggedly, the Prime Minister of the Underworld went back to court.

By this time, there was one bright spot. Fiorello LaGuardia, after 12 years in office, was stepping down.

His successor was sure to be the Democrat William O'Dwyer, the one-time Brooklyn district attorney, a man who had vigorously jailed many mobsters while observably leaving the fiefdoms of some others quite intact. O'Dwyer's friendliness with Frank Costello was a large campaign issue in the autumn of 1945, as well as the subject of a blistering grand jury report. None of this prevented his election in November, as it was well known around town that the puppet master Costello had made the necessary arrangements.

In the spring of 1946, when Mayor O'Dwyer declared himself an anti-gambling crusader and launched a crackdown on the city's pinball machines, it was noted that slot machines did not appear to be included in this crackdown.

So Costello had satisfactorily outsurvived LaGuardia. There was that.

But he was still out his $27,200. And these were not otherwise wonderful times. There was a great eruption inside Tammany Hall, as some gang of rebels sought to rid themselves of his political thumb, and once again he was in the newspapers every day. He was unmasked as a secret owner of the Copacabana night club on E. 60th St., and the club, on pain of losing its license, agreed never to allow him inside again.

He was named as a key figure in a basketball gambling scandal. He was branded chief of the Harlem narcotics rackets. He was greatly distressed by all these allegations. He was nothing but a legitimate businessman, he insisted. On the stand, when his lost-property case finally went to trial, he was forced to admit that, well, yes, he had done a little bootlegging once upon a time.

IN THE END, he won. On Thursday the 30th of January 1947, after weeks of trial, jurors deliberated just 53 minutes before they decided that the Prime Minister of the Underworld, seeking redress of a grievance in a court of law, was entitled to get his $27,200 back from the City of New York.

The federal government, following negotiations, settled for $24,233 in back taxes.

Meanwhile, Costello had promised a $3,500 reward to taxi driver Waters. Forgetful Frank came out just about $700 to the good. If you didn't count in the 2½ years of legal fees.

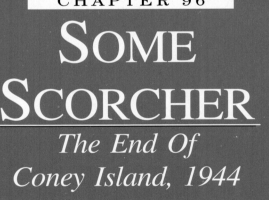

CHAPTER 96

SOME SCORCHER

The End Of Coney Island, 1944

By JAY MAEDER
Daily News Staff Writer

IT WAS **93** degrees out there, the hottest Saturday in your whole life, and you and everybody else just wanted to get to Coney Island. By subway, of course, since at this point that was the only way you could get to Coney. The buses didn't run anymore. And you sure didn't have a tank of gas in the family heap. You could thank the war for that.

You could thank the war for the dimouts, too. Coney Island's millions of light bulbs were gone now, and the ocean went dark every night. For that matter, old Coney was mostly soldiers and sailors these days. And victory-girl bobbysoxers come to chase them. Twelve years old, some of them. The cops shook their heads. Sometimes it seemed like the whole country was going to hell.

You could see the place fading over the years anyway. There had been a few face-lifts here and there; the city had put in miles of sparkling new white beach a couple of years before, and the Silver Streak and the Parachute Jump and some of the other World's Fair thrill rides had been brought in after the fair closed. But old Luna Park had gone bankrupt back around '35 and had since been through several different receivers. A lot of the rides and sideshows were long gone. A lot of the old boardwalk barkers had packed up and slipped away.

But it was still Coney Island. The original Ferris wheel was still here. The Steeplechase Horses were still here. The Mile Sky Chaser and the Tango Palace and the Dragon's Gorge and the gondolas and the minarets were still here, and Paddy Shea and Injun Joe were still colorful fixtures out on Surf Ave. This was still the same place where your own mom and pop had courted and sparked back in the days when things were jake, and now here you were eating custard with your own kids. Things endured.

Saturday the 12th of August 1944. Ninety-three degrees. Some scorcher.

At 3:45 p.m., deep inside the Dragon's Gorge, you smelled smoke.

A million people stood on the beach and watched Luna Park burn down.

THERE HAD BEEN big plans. Just a week before a fellow named Bill Miller had bought the 40-year-old park for $500,000, and he was talking about building it back up and turning it into a showplace again after the war.

Now, in 90 minutes, eight acres went up in thick black smoke. Apparently there had been a short-circuit in a tool room; workmen had tried to put out the fire themselves and didn't think to sound an alarm for more than 10 minutes. Meanwhile, there was a brisk northeast wind, and the park's ancient wooden structures were tinder-dry in the fierce afternoon heat.

Twelve thousand persons scrambled out of Luna Park as workers led the circus dogs and ponies to safety. There was no stopping the blaze. Rides and concessions were going up everywhere, westward to 12th St., north to

Neptune Ave. The 125-foot landmark tower in the center of the park was a great flaming torch. Things were already hopelessly out of control before the 71 fire units responding to the 14-bell alarm got there.

At 4:39, the old tower buckled and crashed to the ground.

As the fire raged on, 14 automobiles in a 12th St. parking lot were destroyed. So were a couple of warehouses. So was the Sea Beach Bridge. So were nearly 20 old wooden trolley cars when sparks showered down on a BMT storage barn at Avenue X and McDonald Ave. half a mile away.

And, finally, so were the Mile Sky Chaser and the Victory Bar and the Boomerang and the Dodgem and the Tilt-A-Whirl and the Mirror Maze and Spook Street and the Rollo-Plane and the Opera House and the Aqua Gal.

And such was the last Saturday afternoon in the life of Luna Park, which never opened its doors again.

STEEPLECHASE remained, a block away, between Surf Ave. and the boardwalk, the last of Coney Island's three storied amusement parks. But the heart had gone out of the old crazy-quilt strip now, and after the war there were never really the same kinds of crowds.

By August 1946, in any case, there was a pressing need for, as it was called at the time, G.I. housing, and for a number of years thereafter the ruins of Luna Park were at the center of various plans for residential projects. For a while, there was talk of building a new ballpark for the Brooklyn Dodgers on the site.

By 1957, what had once been G.I. housing was now called low-income housing, and finally the city Housing Authority broke ground for the Luna Park Houses, which took in their first families in 1961, full of kids who never had the slightest idea what Coney Island had been.

By DAVID HINCKLEY
Daily News Staff Writer

IF THEY HAD to do it over again, the managers of Times Square's Paramount Theater perhaps would not have arranged for Frank Sinatra's fall 1944 engagement to begin on Wednesday the 11th of October, the day before Columbus Day, a date on which occasion his teenage fans were unencumbered by the obligation to attend school, and 30,000 of them headed for the theater, where their sheer mass literally broke down the box office.

Moreover, once the lucky few thousand got inside, they proved so exuberant that the stage band had to strike up "The Star-Spangled Banner" in the futile hope that this might cool them down for a few minutes.

"Sinatramania," cried the papers. Sinatrauma. Swoonatra. Long buried were the rumors that this skinny kid didn't have any real fans at all, just girls who were slipped a few bucks by his savvy press agent to act like they cared.

That might have worked with 30 girls. Not with 30,000.

Whatever it was called and whatever its genesis, all this bubbling excitement caused some concern for the New York City Police Department, which hastily redeployed hundreds of officers from the Columbus Day Parade to monitor squealing bobby-soxers around Seventh Ave. and 43rd St.

Frank Sinatra himself was not wholly displeased by the turnout, as a display of public adoration on this scale can have very helpful implications for a singer so ambitious as himself.

BY OCTOBER 1944, Sinatra was already the kind of sensation unseen since Rudolph Valentino or Bing Crosby and maybe not even then, and he wanted to be even bigger.

A Jersey kid and thus virtually a local boy, he had been a star since the night of Dec. 30, 1942, when, after putting in several years with the Harry James and Tommy Dorsey bands, he appeared at the Paramount as an "extra added attraction" on a bill topped by Benny Goodman and filled out by four other live acts and the patriotic film "Star-Spangled Rhythm," which starred Crosby.

Sinatra, still young and humble, was so thrilled by this big-time engagement that he traveled to Times Square at 7:30 the morning of Dec. 30 to make sure his name was really on the marquee. He was still nervous hours later when Goodman announced to the crowd, "And now, Frank Sinatra."

They answered that with a roar that nearly bowled Goodman over.

"What the hell was *that?*" Goodman said to no one in particular.

CHAPTER 97

BLUE EYES

Sinatra At The Paramount, 1944

By October 1944, America was getting a little closer to answering Goodman's question, though many remained puzzled at exactly how this skinny guy with the oversize bow ties and the wise-guy twinkle in his blue eyes was driving hundreds of thousands of young women into unladylike frenzies.

Whatever caused it, it paid well. Sinatra's first Paramount gig paid him $150 a week. His second time there, in May 1943, it was $3,100. Now, in October '44, it was $25,000 a week.

He was also, inadvertently, the catalyst for an act of massive civil disobedience. When he arrived for rehearsal soon after dawn on opening day, Oct. 11, more than 1,000 girls had been waiting in line since the wee small hours, defying Mayor Fiorello LaGuardia's nighttime curfew for juveniles.

When the doors opened for the first show, 3,600 fans tumbled in and screamed so loudly that Sinatra threatened to leave the stage if they didn't pipe down.

They did, but it soon became evident the Paramount had another problem: lack of turnover. Artists customarily would do a half-dozen shows a day, and the house made its money from re-selling the seats for each show. But these girls weren't leaving.

Most already had cut school, their second defiance of law and order, and they had every intention of staying all day, through the other acts and the movies and all of it.

On Columbus Day, police estimated that before the first show 10,000 fans had queued up, west along 43rd St. from Seventh to Eighth Ave., then up to 44th St. Then another 20,000 began to arrive.

Besides the 700 cops on the street, the Paramount had put in 50 extra ushers, who proved no match for teenage hormones. The ticket booth was pushed in and windows smashed from the sheer crush.

Meanwhile, maids at Sinatra's New York hotel were offered cash for any remnant of his stay — linens, used soap, cigarette ashes. Girls camped outside the small house in Jersey City where he lived with his wife, Nancy, and their daughter.

It was a nuisance, he admitted. But he clearly preferred too much attention to too little — a situation with which he had once been familiar.

ONLY IN FRANK Sinatra's lifetime had his primary audience — teenagers — become a factor in the popular music equation. Through the 1920s, a radio or a phonograph was a major investment, purchased as a living room centerpiece with its programing controlled by the family breadwinner. Therefore, popular music was designed for adults.

But when the Depression hit, record companies introduced budget lines, which opened the market to teenagers, and by 1935 the kids showed their clout by jitterbugging so happily to Goodman's music that they launched the Big Band era.

So when Sinatra went solo in 1942, the teenagers were there.

He had briefly been solo before that, back in the mid-'30s, but though he'd been successful by the standards of a singing waiter in Alpine, N.J., he hadn't really grabbed the kids. This second solo turn, not only did he have to get them, he had to get word of his conquest circulating.

He was working the Mosque in Newark when Bob Weitman, the Paramount's manager, finally went to see him after relentless badgering from press agent Harry Romm. When Weitman arrived, he liked what he saw: Even in a half-empty house, young women seemed to lose all control when Sinatra took the stage.

Weitman gambled that would only get better at the Paramount. Good bet. Sinatra's first run there was extended from one week to four, and when he finished, he had a contract to do the national radio show "Your Hit Parade," plus an RKO movie deal.

He also signed for four weeks at the Riobamba Club, which kept him for 10 and doubled his pay to $1,500 a week. Lines wended around the block, and Down Beat magazine joined the crowd trying to figure out why: "He knows his feminine audience and fires romance — moonlight moods — at them with deadly aim."

Sinatra's new press agent, George Evans, conceded before his death in 1951 that he had indeed planted a few $5 ringers at these gigs, but that frankly he considered it a waste of money, since there were far more screams than he possibly could have afforded to underwrite.

In any case, the October Riot of 1944 made it clear how thoroughly so many observers had miscalculated when they assumed 18 months earlier that Sinatra had "passing fad" tattooed all over his bony forehead. Just because his fans were teenagers, it turned out, didn't mean that in two weeks they'd be back swallowing goldfish.

In fact, by the time Johnny came marching home from the war a year later, solo vocalists like Sinatra were the stars and teenagers like the bobbysoxers increasingly were who they sang for. Much of popular culture would take note of this.

What the hell was that, indeed.

By WENDELL JAMIESON
Daily News Staff Writer

THEY HEARD the engines through the fog, but they didn't even look up from their typewriters at first, thinking the roar would pass overhead and then fade into the swirling gray sky.

But the drone became deafening, filling the offices, rattling glass panes, vibrating coffee cups. So some went to their windows high above midtown, and there, just for an instant, they saw it: a B-25 Mitchell bomber coming straight at them, twin props whirling, nose canopy glinting.

They may have even seen the eyes of the pilot, just a few feet away.

In the cockpit, Lt. Col. William F. Smith Jr. beheld in his final instants a sheer wall of windows and limestone, towering high above his rolling bomber. There was no escape.

The plane plowed into the side of the Empire State Building at 9:49 a.m. on Saturday the 28th of July 1945, straight into the 79th floor, hurtling through the offices of the National Catholic Welfare Council. Those on the streets below gaped as flames billowed up the side of the world's tallest building, lighting the symbol of the city like a torch in the sky.

Then the fog closed in again and there was only a bright orange haze.

COL. SMITH, a veteran of 34 bombing missions, had lifted off an hour earlier from Bedford, Mass., for a routine flight to Newark. With him were co-pilot Christopher Domitvorich and a deadheader, Machinist's Mate Albert Perna, of Brooklyn, hitching a ride home.

En route, Smith decided to land at LaGuardia instead, but the Queens field was fogged in; he was directed back to Newark and told to keep to 1,500 feet over Manhattan, 1,000 feet over Jersey. Either he misunderstood his instructions or he ignored them. Flying over Manhattan, his altitude was just 1,000 feet. That was 250 feet below the Empire State's celebrated but never-used dirigible mooring mast.

Many offices were keeping Saturday hours in these late days of the war. On the streets and at their windows, workers looked skyward and saw an airplane in trouble.

Dipping out of the fog, Smith found himself in a nightmare maze of skyscraper tops. He dodged the New York Central Building and 500 Fifth Ave. as he swerved to the south and tried to gain altitude.

Stanley Lomax, a sports announcer with WOR radio, watched the plane over Fifth Ave. and heard himself scream: "Climb, you damn fool! Climb!"

THE IMPACT tore off the bomber's wings. One engine sliced through the building's north facade and ricocheted into an elevator shaft, piggy-backing on an empty cab and crashing with it into the basement. Pieces of airplane followed, clanking noisily downward.

The second engine cut through the Empire State's outside wall, both sides of an elevator shaft,

CHAPTER 98

INCIDENT ON THE 79TH FLOOR

Empire State Building Airplane Crash, 1945

two firewalls and a partition before shooting out the south side and plummeting afire to the roof of 10 W. 33rd St. Fragments of glass, steel, brick, mortar and human beings sprayed out over midtown.

The bomber's high-octane fuel lit up, instantly incinerating nine young volunteer women in the Catholic offices. Some were found still around the table where they had been putting together care packages for the boys overseas. Others were frozen at the windows. Others were mummified in a hallway where they had sought cover.

Paul Deering, a former reporter handling publicity for the charity, was blasted out the window by the inferno. His charred body was found on a 72nd-floor setback, identifiable only by the old press card in his shirt pocket.

Army Lt. Allen Aiman, 23, a flier home on leave, watched with his wife from the otherwise deserted observation deck as Smith shot out of the fog.

"I saw this plane, and it looked like it was coming right at me, and the ceiling was zero," Aiman told the papers. *"I couldn't believe my eyes."*

The building actually shook at the collision of the 10-ton bomber. But the 102-story Art Deco tower, still largely unoccupied and considered a boondoggle of Depression-era optimism, settled quickly and stood firm.

MANY THOUGHT the nearly defeated Japanese had staged a kamikaze attack on New York.

As news spread that it was one of our own bombers, groping through the fog, the wartime city sprang to action. Don Malony, a 17-year-old Coast Guard hospital apprentice, raced into a drugstore after dodging debris on 34th St. "Give me morphine, hypos, needles, first-aid kits, ointments and distilled water," he shouted to a clerk. "Take anything you need," was the answer. No cash exchanged hands.

In the Empire State's lobby, Malony heard a scream from below, and soon he was struggling to free two young women whose elevator car had plunged into the basement when the B-25 cut the cable.

He stabilized both — smearing a red "M" with lipstick on one woman's forehead to alert medics she'd received morphine — and then started walking . . . and walking . . . and walking. With the elevators filled with firefighters, he trudged up 78 floors to give first aid where it was needed.

Arriving smoke-eaters confronted the highest-up blaze in city history, with 15-foot flames shooting out of the gashed 78th and 79th floors.

They rode the elevators to the 60th floor, then struggled with equipment and hoses up the stairs to the white-hot inferno. Fast behind them were reporters and photographers. And fast behind them was Mayor Fiorello LaGuardia.

Twenty-three fire companies, remarkably, brought the fire under control in 19 minutes, extinguishing it in 40. Fourteen people were dead.

After weeks of inquiries, the blame for the disaster was placed squarely on Smith. Many felt he may have mistaken the East River for the Hudson in the fog and thought he was safely over lowlands New Jersey.

But former flier LaGuardia didn't wait for the official answer. "He had 1,000 feet of altitude," LaGuardia snapped the day after the crash, following a ceremony for Malony and other heroes at City Hall. "Traveling at that rate, 1,000 feet don't last long. This fellow certainly should have been higher."

By WENDELL JAMIESON
Daily News Staff Writer

THERE HAD BEEN two false alarms already, so when rumors flashed at 2 a.m. on Tuesday the 14th of August 1945 that Emperor Hirohito had accepted the Allies' surrender terms, that a murderous world war was over at last, the city wasn't so sure about it.

Those who went to work didn't get much work done. They crowded around radios, they grabbed the afternoon editions of the Journal-American, the World-Telegram, the Sun, the Post and PM. They traded scuttlebutt. They let themselves think about a world without rationing, a world full of new cars and plenty of coffee and sugar, a world in which fathers, brothers and husbands were all home.

And they went to Times Square.

ALL THROUGH the day, the crowds flooded the once neon-lit heart of New York City. Milling, aimless, there were 200,000 of them by early evening, watching the news ticker and grouping around radio trucks blaring the latest: *Japanese envoys have delivered response to Allied surrender demands . . . Awaiting official word . . . Navy off Japanese coast . . . Hostilities still on . . .*

Cops closed Broadway and Seventh Ave. from 34th to 59th Sts. The masses swelled but kept quiet, listening, waiting, hoping.

At 7:01 p.m., the whole world changed.

The WNYC mobile station, thousands pressed around it, announced the bulletin to a roar of cheers that drowned out all but a few key words.

Japan accepts surrender terms.

It was finished. It was done.

The cheer swept up the avenues and along the side streets. It continued, rising and falling, for 20 minutes. Ships whistled in the harbor, along the docks and in the rivers.

Now grinning citizens climbed out of the subways and off the buses and beheld a sight they hadn't seen for several years: All the Broadway theaters blazed with light.

The Army Signal Corps rolled giant searchlights up to the Statue of Liberty replica at Broadway and 43rd St., and the beams threw an 18-story silhouette of the great lady upon the Paramount Building. Revelers mobbed a clanging fire truck. A blizzard of paper rained down from the windows.

And everyone started kissing everyone else, passionately, furiously. Soldiers, sailors, Marines and regular guys in business suits grabbed every female they could find, and the females grabbed back. Old married couples kissed. Young unmarried couples kissed. Couples married to other people kissed. Men and women who had never met before and would never meet again kissed.

"There wasn't a male between 6 and 60 without smudges of lipstick on his face," wrote the Daily News. "There were no strangers in New York yesterday," The Times reported. Some women got some of their clothes ripped off. Some women took off some of their clothes voluntarily. Some 1,200 cops struggled to keep order. Many of them got kissed.

Servicemen now realizing they were not destined to die in a foxhole on some godforsaken Pacific island sought ways to demonstrate their relief. One sailor climbed to the top of a lamppost, waving a flag. Another stood on his head at the bar of the Zanzibar nightclub, his girlfriend serving him champagne from her slipper.

By 10 p.m., more than a million partygoers filled the square — seething, rollicking, screeching, crying, kissing, laughing. By midnight, there were 2 million of

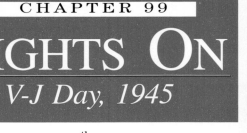

CHAPTER 99

LIGHTS ON
V-J Day, 1945

them.

By 3 a.m., the party started to cool. As the final editions of the papers went to press, 500,000 exhausted, relieved and perhaps to some degree intoxicated persons remained beneath the glare and heat of the reignited lights of Times Square.

Come morning, tons of paper, whisky bottles and articles of clothing were piled high. Around the city, four souls were dead of celebration, nearly 1,000 injured. Two women were hospitalized after being tossed into the air by jubilant sailors who forgot to catch them.

THE FIRST DAY of peace brought more good news: Gas rationing was ended immediately. Canned fruits and vegetables could be purchased without ration points.

At nightfall, the lights of long-dark Times Square fired up again and another roaring party got under way.

But it was a small, intimate affair this time. Only 1.2 million people showed up.

By ELLIOT ROSENBERG
Special to The News

WE ALREADY KNEW that America was the mightiest power on Earth, ever.

But here was the cold gray physical evidence of U.S. Navy invincibility, sailing up the Hudson. It was Saturday the 27th of October 1945. Just eight weeks before, the Japanese Empire had formally surrendered in Tokyo Bay aboard the Missouri. Here was Mighty Mo, the great battleship itself, anchored in mid-Hudson before awed onlookers lining both Manhattan and Jersey shores. Here was the fabled Big E, the carrier Enterprise, veteran of nearly every Pacific action from the Doolittle Raid to Okinawa. Here was the newly commissioned Midway, at 45,000 tons the most potent aircraft carrier ever launched, the warship of the future.

The heavy cruiser Augusta had carried Franklin Roosevelt to the Atlantic Conference off Newfoundland and Harry Truman to Europe for Potsdam. The light cruiser Boise was renowned as the "one-ship task force" of the Pacific. The venerable battleship New York was making its final appearance before retirement, after fighting in both world wars.

Plus the cruisers Helena and Macon, and 15 destroyers and six destroyer escorts, and two attack transports and one submarine chaser and two submarine tenders and 15 submarines — 47 U.S. fighting ships,

stretched nearly 7 miles up the river. Commander-in-Chief Truman, overcoated against the raw chill, formally reviewed the fleet from the deck of a destroyer moving slowly along the lethal gray line as each, in turn, boomed a 21-gun salute. Five million citizens, cramming every waterfront pierhead, Palisades clifftop and riverview roof, stared in wonder at the American armada.

Navy Day, 1945. It was the greatest

CHAPTER 100

WELCOME HOME

Navy Day, 1945

show that ever played the Great Blue Way.

FLEET FEVER had swept the city for weeks as Fast Carrier Force 62 sailed through the Panama Canal and turned northward into the last leg of Operation Broadway. Hoteliers had warned out-of-towners to stay out of town. Retailers were cashing in with small-scale models, $16 for a battleship, $21 for a carrier. On Oct. 16, 101 Navy fighters and torpedo planes flew from the decks of the incoming

Enterprise and zoomed over the Financial District as thousands cheered below. Early the next morning, the great Enterprise made its stately appearance in the harbor. Ship whistles sent up a cry; foghorns blared; a tug blinkered: WELL DONE. . . . WELCOME HOME.

The next day, 7,000 visitors boarded Enterprise at Pier 26, streaming across its huge flight and hangar decks. Other fleet units also accommodated home-fronters eager to sniff around these war-winning hunks of steel. By the weekend, 18,000 New Yorkers were moving up the Big E's gangplank every hour.

Delayed by fog, the Missouri docked Tuesday, receiving a conqueror's welcome as it steamed up the Hudson. It was accorded the maritime equivalent of a presidential suite — Pier 90, at W. 50th St., home berth of the two queens, Elizabeth and Mary. When it opened to the clamoring public the next day, 12th Ave. had to be closed entirely.

SATURDAY. Navy Day. The fleet was ready. Mile after mile of battle-gray men-of-war lined the river where Robert Fulton's Clermont once steamed. Coast Guard picket craft zig-zagged about, keeping sailboats, yachts and tugs away. The Henry Hudson Parkway was bumper-to-bumper by 7 a.m. The West Side Highway was at a standstill. The BMT and IRT lines broke down.

Truman's special train pulled into Penn Station at 10:20. First he was off to the Brooklyn Navy Yard, where

the fleet's newest carrier, the Franklin D. Roosevelt, awaited commissioning. Next, the President motorcaded up lower Broadway to City Hall, escorted by 2,000 sailors, marines, Waves, Seabees, midshipmen and bands playing "Anchors Aweigh." After calling on the mayor, he addressed 80,000 citizens seated on camp chairs in Central Park's Sheep Meadow and 900,000 others sitting on any clump of turf they could find. He spoke of U.S. power, and policy, and hopes. When it was over, a choir sang "America the Beautiful." According to Hooper rating service, 94.6% of all radios in use were tuned in.

Then Truman and the throng headed west to the river. High, darkening cumulus clouds had formed thunderheads — then backed off, perhaps in embarrassment.

Wave after wave of Hellcats and Avengers and Corsairs and Helldivers, 1,200 of them, made their bows in 12-mile ovals overhead. And millions of peacetime New Yorkers looked on, not one doubting that we could lick any bully on our block, or anyone else's.

IT TOOK the Missouri's bluejackets four days to scrub lipstick and crayon marks from bulkheads and to replace the equipment the public had carried off as souvenirs — practically everything not nailed down, as well as hatch covers that were.

"Everything but the anchors and the skipper's hat," one sailor grumbled. Mighty Mo, sighed the big ship's executive officer, "took a worse beating here than she did in combat."

But this was New York. Even a battleship could get mugged.

By RICHARD E. MOONEY
Special to The News

THE 11th-HOUR deal that put the United Nations on a midtown site long covered by East River slums and slaughterhouses came in a frantic rush on Tuesday the 10th of December 1946, just the day before the General Assembly's deadline for decision.

All at once, John D. Rockefeller Jr. had offered to buy the land from developer William Zeckendorf and donate it to the UN. "If this property can be useful to you in meeting the great responsibilities entrusted to you by the people of the world," the old philanthropist told the delegates, "it will be a source of infinite satisfaction to me and my family."

As it happened, the good deed would not only please the famously generous family, it would eliminate a potential rival to Rockefeller Center: Zeckendorf had announced plans to fill the site with a center of his own, with apartments, offices and a new Metropolitan Opera House.

As it also happened, there was some question whether Zeckendorf had sufficient capital for that grand project anyway. Indeed, when he read in the paper over breakfast Dec. 6 that the long UN site search was stalled, he was very quick to offer up his riverfront property in the spirit of public service.

Thus it was that the Metropolitan Opera did not go to First Ave. and the United Nations did not go to Philadelphia.

CHAPTER 101

RIV VU

United Nations, 1946

PRESIDENT FRANKLIN Roosevelt had fancied the Azores. Harry Truman thought delegates should meet around the world and "keep their offices in their hats." Some members favored Geneva, the League of Nations city. But the decision to locate in the U.S. — and thus encourage American participation, the absence of which had been largely the reason the old league had failed — had been made even before the original 51 members wrote the formal UN charter in San Francisco in the summer of 1945.

Now, in a postwar atmosphere charged with noble hopes for a world free of conquerors and jackboots, the fledgling United Nations got down to business in scattered temporary rooms around New York City. The General Assembly settled into the ice rink on the old World's Fair grounds in Queens. The Security Council moved into the gym on Hunter College's Bronx campus, which had been a WAVES training center during the war and was still full of hair dryers.

The noble hopes were soon deflated by Russia's *nyet* at every crucial vote. Meeting at the Henry Hudson Hotel to write rules for future peacekeepers, the military staff committee found itself regularly stymied by Russian objections. Moscow also blocked proposals for atomic weapons control and a census of each nation's armed forces. A new world war, the Cold War, had already begun, and the great global police force still had no permanent headquarters of its own.

The principal candidates were San Francisco, Boston, Philadelphia and the New York area, including Hyde Park and Mount Vernon. But the mayors of Chicago and Denver also were pitching their cities. Martha's Vineyard was an applicant. Even the Black Hills of the Dakotas were suggested.

In New York, Robert Moses, commissioner of parks and much else, was determined to give the UN the World's Fair grounds; the tract was already paid for, and a UN presence there would help justify the cost of the fair. But delegates said no thanks. One Briton likened Flushing Meadows to "the coastal swamps of Southwest Africa."

By February 1946, site selection had focused on Westchester and Fairfield County, Conn. Interest cooled, however, after Greenwich citizens voted 5,505 to 2,019 against anything in their backyard and inspectors visiting the area were pelted with stones.

IN NOVEMBER, the selection committee made a final tour of the main prospects. Washington had indicated no favorite, but on Dec. 3, Truman offered the Presidio, the spectacular military site on San Francisco Bay. Russia said *nyet* — and three days later UN Secretary General Trygve Lie informed Mayor William O'Dwyer that New York was out as well if Flushing was the best the city could do.

It looked like the United Nations would go to Philadelphia.

Enter William Zeckendorf.

For the past year, Zeckendorf had been buying up the slaughterhouses north of 42nd St. between First Ave. and the East River and the surrounding tenements of Turtle Bay, so named because the area had indeed once been a bay, until the 1860s, when it was filled in. Plans already had been drawn up for Zeckendorf's proposed X-City. Now, the developer put down his breakfast paper, called O'Dwyer and offered 17 acres to the UN at, he said, "any price they wish to pay."

Wallace Harrison, a chief architect of Rockefeller Center and the man Zeckendorf had brought in to design X-City, reached Nelson Rockefeller in Mexico City. Rockefeller flew home Sunday, Dec. 8, and convened a family meeting at which his father, John D. Jr., authorized exploration of two possibilities — Zeckendorf's site, or part of the Rockefellers' Pocantico estate near Tarrytown. Harrison hurriedly revamped the X-City drawings — erasing "Metropolitan Opera" and scribbling in "General Assembly," for example — and Nelson Rockefeller got each of his brothers to kick in 1,000 acres of their Pocantico shares.

The UN diplomats turned down Pocantico. It was Turtle Bay or nothing. Late Tuesday night, Nelson phoned John D. to propose offering Zeckendorf $8.5 million.

The father agreed. The son said: "Aw, gee, Pa, that's great!"

Then Harrison was dispatched to find Zeckendorf at the Monte Carlo nightclub. There, Zeckendorf circled the site on Harrison's maps and signed over a 30-day option.

First Ave. was widely known as Blood Alley. The slaughterhouses were so vile that the Tudor City apartments across the avenue had been built without riverview windows. Now, from this rubble, there would arise a mighty monument to peace on Earth.

By JAY MAEDER
Daily News Staff Writer

"When Homer first lost his sight, he used to see visions of beautiful buildings, always in red. He would describe them to me and I would try to paint them just as he directed. Someday, when Homer regains his sight, I will show the paintings to him."
— **Langley Collyer**

THE GHOST MAN of Harlem came out of his spooky old house only very late at night, and the neighbors would see him foraging for rags and junk and scraps of meat in the moonlight. The old hoodoo had lived in the moldering, four-story mansion at Fifth Ave. and 128th St. without telephone or electricity or gas since 1909, and the place was full of rats and pianos and newspapers piled to the ceilings, and the windows were boarded up and the doors were wired shut and the yard was heaped high with bedsprings and broken furniture and old stoves. Some said the Ghost Man was the richest man in New York City.

Already a Harlem legend for decades, the ancient scarecrow Langley Collyer came to larger public attention in 1942, when he stopped making mortgage payments and the Bowery Savings Bank people pounded on his door for weeks. When he finally emerged from the funereal dust, he proved to be a courtly old gentleman, descended from aristocrats who had lived in the Hudson Valley for 300 years; he had a Columbia education; he had once taught Sunday school at Trinity Church downtown; his father had been a Bellevue physician. During the William Howard Taft administration, he and his brother Homer had moved from Murray Hill to Harlem and shut themselves off from the rest of the world. Why? Langley Collyer politely deemed this the brothers' own business, no one else's. "We don't want to be bothered."

Homer was blind and crippled now, and Langley fed him, washed him, read aloud to him from the classics, played him sonatas. Yes, he said, it was true he kept 10 grand pianos: "They all have such different tonal effects." Yes, there were mountains of newspapers, too: "So that when Homer regains his sight he can catch up on the news." No, Homer did not require medical attention: "We are the sons of a doctor. We have a medical library of 15,000 books. Homer eats 100 oranges a week."

And no, they didn't need Con Edison, because they had an old Model T Ford in the house: "I make my own electricity." No, they didn't need a phone: "There is no one I particularly care to talk to." And yes, the doors and windows were all barricaded: "To keep thieves out. I have put boxes all over the house, so that if thieves break in they will trip in the darkness and I will hear them."

The mortgage had slipped his mind, he said; he would attend to it at once. And, refusing to spend a nickel on carfare, he walked from 128th St. to Park Row to meet with a lawyer.

BUT BOWERY SAVINGS did not get paid, and Langley Collyer holed up again and letters collected unfetched on the stoop, and finally the bank began eviction proceedings and sent over a work crew with a court order to clean up the yard.

From an upper window the old hermit screamed down at the shovelers. *You can't take that! You have no right! That's my property! Leave that alone!* Cops smashed through the front door, through the wire netting behind it, through the boxes and barrels and crates stacked upon one another in the foyer; beyond that were endless rolling hills of neck-deep rubble, and the cops gingerly climbed their way across the room until they found Langley Collyer huddled in a clearing he had fashioned in the belly of his fortress.

Silently, he wrote a check for $6,700, paying off

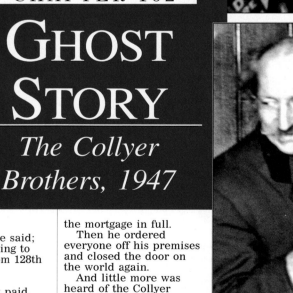

CHAPTER 102

GHOST STORY

The Collyer Brothers, 1947

Langley Collyer

the mortgage in full.

Then he ordered everyone off his premises and closed the door on the world again.

And little more was heard of the Collyer brothers until Saturday the 22nd of March 1947. **ONE COLLYER DEAD,** the headlines said. **SECOND HUNTED IN 5TH AVE. PALACE OF JUNK.**

AN ANONYMOUS phone call had brought the Fire Department rushing to the gloomy old manse. There was no getting in through the front door; firemen went up ladders to the upstairs windows and chopped through solid walls of baby carriages and plaster statues and garden baskets and Christmas trees and picture frames and

chandeliers and bundles of sheet music and dressmakers' dummies and everywhere, everywhere, the stacks of newspapers, every issue of every New York paper since 1918, waiting for the day when Homer Collyer would see again.

The whole place was an impossible maze of warrens and nests and tunnels. Deep inside one of them — crouched on his haunches, head on his knees, hair and beard flowing to the floor — was Homer Collyer, cold and still. Of Langley there was no sign. It was surmised that he was somewhere in the house, hiding.

But everything was booby-trapped. The tunnels were full of trip wires that would bring debris showering down on any intruder. Workers had to cut through the roof and lift out hundreds of tons of junk, floor by floor, before they could even begin to dig for the missing man. They found the 10 grand pianos. They found the Model T Ford. After 18 days they found Langley Collyer, dead for weeks. A rat as big as a rabbit was gnawing at his feet when the flashlights finally landed on him, 10 feet from where Homer had died.

It appeared that he had been delivering dinner to his brother when he triggered one of his own tunnel traps and suffocated. Surely the helpless Homer had heard the great crash and understood what it meant. There was no hope he could have reached a window to cry for help. Slowly, he had starved to death.

Crowds massed daily outside the eerie house as workers continued to pick through it. At one point a black cat appeared on the stoop, and hundreds of spectators fled shrieking.

By DAVID HINCKLEY
Daily News Staff Writer

WHETHER HE WOULD play was no longer an issue. Jack Roosevelt Robinson was in the Brooklyn Dodgers' lineup on Opening Day, Tuesday the 15th of April, 1947, and 25,263 paying fans — about 9,000 short of capacity — were on hand as witnesses.

He was batting second and playing first, where he recorded the opening out of the season. Boston Braves shortstop Dick Culler grounded to third baseman Jack (Spider) Jorgenson, who made the easy throw to Robinson.

If Jackie Robinson had retired on the spot, the color line in baseball was now erased.

BEFORE JACKIE, the last black men to play major league ball were Moses Fleetwood Walker and his brother Welday, for the Toledo Blue Stockings of the American Association, in 1884. Powerful white players, led by Hall of Fame first baseman Cap Anson, arranged for that not to happen again, and for 63 years — longer than the average American lifetime — it did not.

Now, on the green grass of Ebbets Field, the focus shifted to phase two of the question: Could Jackie make it? Sure, he'd been a star running back at UCLA, but could he hit major league pitching?

Not today he couldn't.

Braves starter Johnny Sain, on his way to the second of three consecutive 20-win seasons, gave the 28-year-old rookie nothing. In the first inning, Robinson grounded to third. In the third, routine fly to left. The first time he got a good piece of the ball was in the fifth, when he hit a hard grounder that Culler scooped up to start an inning-ending double play.

In the seventh, with the Dodgers trailing 3-2, Eddie Stanky led off with a walk. Robinson dropped a sacrifice bunt toward first and tore down the inside of the basepath. Braves first baseman Earl Torgeson hurried his throw and hit Robinson's arm, the ball glancing into right field while Stanky took third and Robinson second.

When Pete Reiser followed with a double, Robinson became the winning run in a 5-3 Brooklyn victory.

After the game, in the clubhouse, he shook his head. That ball Culler flagged down, he said, that would have been a hit in Triple-A. And Johnny Sain. Were all the pitchers here that tough?

Nah, Pee Wee Reese told him. Aren't many like Sain.

The Braves came back the next day with Mort Cooper, and Robinson got his first hit: a bunt single in the fifth that bounced off the pitcher's glove. The crowd, a little over 10,000, cheered when the "H" flashed on the scoreboard.

The next day, against the Giants, Robinson went 2 for 4, including his first home run. The day after, he went 3 for 4 with a double,

DODGERS CLUB HOUSE KEEP OUT

CHAPTER 103

PLAYING WITH THE WHITE BOYS

Jackie Robinson, 1947

bringing his batting average to .429 with an on-base percentage over .500.

Yes, it seemed, Jackie Robinson could play with the white boys.

AND HE DID it so smoothly that writers who had debated his and his race's qualifications for years were already turning their eyes elsewhere.

Would Dodger manager Leo Durocher, abruptly suspended by the baseball commissioner for associating with gamblers, be allowed back before his year was up? Who would, meantime, replace him? And how about that Spider Jorgenson? He looked like the answer at third base, eh?

In the stands, Seaman Luican Dambra of Brooklyn called Robinson's arrival "another step toward furthering democracy." Railroad worker Norman Hazzard of New Haven said, "I came out to look at the Negro boy play," which doubtless warmed Dodger owner Branch Rickey's heart, since there was more than slight suspicion that Rickey was not unaware of Jackie's potentially salutary effect on attendance, colored and otherwise.

Rickey was smart enough also to realize the first team to sign black players got first dip into a deep well of fresh talent. With black stars like Robinson, Roy Campanella, Don Newcombe and Joe Black, the Dodgers would win six pennants in 10 years.

But in 1947, Rickey made one miscalculation: He figured that once the initial surprise subsided, Dodger players would all be glad to have a teammate who would help them win.

Maybe, maybe not. On the previous Thursday, when Rickey bought Robinson's contract from the Montreal Royals, sportswriter Dick Young told Daily News readers the players showed "a passive acceptance of the situation."

Even that was progress. A year earlier, when Rickey signed Robinson to play at Montreal, five or six Dodgers formally asked him to keep the big-league team white. These included Dixie Walker, Bobby Bragan, Kirby Higbe, Carl Furillo and, depending on who is telling the story, Eddie Stanky and/or Pee Wee Reese.

Higbe placed Reese in the group, which is interesting because Robinson always said Reese, more than any other player, made him feel like he belonged on the team. The two became friends, and Reese would deflect praise by joking that he was just relieved to find Robinson wasn't taking his shortstop position.

So Robinson had the beachhead, which is not to say he had won the war.

HE SPENT much of 1947 alone. Card games, the universal pastime of ballplayers in the days of intercity train travel, would fold when he passed. The defending champion St. Louis Cardinals threatened to forfeit if he played. The Philadelphia Phillies, led by manager Ben Chapman, picked up where Cap Anson had left off.

But no one who mattered — the Dodgers, baseball or Jackie Robinson — blinked. The National Pastime, a sport that had performed its own ethnic cleansing 63 years before, became the opener for Brown vs. Board of Education and the Civil Rights Act of 1964. Come the second half of the century, the rules would change.

JACKIE ROBINSON hit .297 in 1947 and was voted Major League rookie of the year. Two years later he led the National League in batting. In 1962, his first year of eligibility, he was voted into the Hall of Fame.

By BRIAN MOSS
Daily News Staff Writer

WHEN JOHNNY came marching home again, there were lots of hurrahs, but precious few apartments.

So it was in September 1946 that war veteran Daily Newsman Charles McHarry, who had been living in a hotel room for five months since his discharge from the Army, reported on Everyman's search for a good $75-a-month apartment, not including bribes to doormen and supers.

McHarry figured he could slip somebody $20, but a doorman in the East 50s demanded $75 upfront for the promise of a furnished three-room flat. And the rent would be $125, take it or leave it. McHarry passed. Eventually, a bartender steered him to another place, at just $100, and McHarry quickly accepted.

Most of the city's other conquering heroes — and there were 765,000 of them — weren't so lucky. Many found themselves moving back in with their folks, and sometimes they brought new brides with them, sometimes even babies. Others had to make do with whatever they could find — cheap hotels, rooming houses, somebody's basement. Some 85,000 vets put their names on a list for public housing, of which there wasn't any.

The situation became so desperate that the city set up emergency camps in Canarsie, Brooklyn, and the Soundview section of the Bronx, pitching hundreds of 20-by-48-foot Army surplus Quonset huts. Two soldiers, and their families, lived in each one.

The cause of the housing shortage was obvious. The one-two punch of the Depression and the war meant few new residences were built in or around New York after the early 1930s. The cure was also obvious, decided Mayor William O'Dwyer: 750,000 new apartments. But by the end of 1946, not one of these yet existed.

For a builder and super salesman named William Levitt, just home from the Pacific, postwar New York's dire housing situation dovetailed perfectly with his plans to make himself very rich.

BROOKLYN-BORN LEVITT, the son of a real estate lawyer, had seen the home shortage coming. But he had no intention of building apartments, or building in New York City at all. His vision of the future lay in the sparsely settled

fields of Long Island.

Before the war, Levitt had taken an option on about 1,000 acres of sandy farmland in the hamlet of Island Trees, about 20 miles east of Manhattan. Potato farmers whose fields had been devastated by a wormlike pest called the golden nematode were more than happy to sell.

His new property already flat and clear, Levitt was ready to build. But the houses he envisioned sprouting up from the dusty fields by the Wantagh Parkway were far different from those ever before constructed on Long Island. His were basic, unadorned dwellings: two bedrooms, a bath, living room and kitchen, all built atop a 25-by-30-foot concrete slab. There was no basement. Heat would come from copper tubes filled with running hot water embedded in the slabs.

With an eye toward marketing, Levitt put the kitchen in the front of his houses and equipped them with the latest in gleaming modern appliances. The bedrooms were in the back. An unfinished attic — ripe for turning into extra bedrooms — crowned each home.

Rather than being stick-built, one dwelling at a time, in the conventional way by skilled builders and tradesmen, Levitt's homes could be built en masse, with crews of

CHAPTER 104

AMERICAN DREAM
Burbs, 1947

less-skilled workers doing the same tasks at house after house. Levitt had come up with a one-size-fits-all Model-T home and a method of building it that would make him the Henry Ford of houses.

He still needed cooperation from the local government, whose building code required basements, and the unions, which required that their men be employed on all local construction sites.

But with a little backroom dealing, along with the support of the small Long Island newspaper Newsday, which was eager to add subscribers, Levitt persuaded the Town of Hempstead to change some of its rules. Then he talked the unions into another sweet deal that allowed him, for a relatively small price, to use nonunion labor.

On Tuesday, July 1, 1947, Levitt's houses began rising on the former farmlands, eventually at a rate of more than two dozen a day.

CITY-SLICKER SOLDIERS once might have regarded this neighborhood as the middle of nowhere, but now they had seen the world, and many were not interested in moving back to the suddenly confining neighborhoods they had left a few years before.

In addition, Robert Moses'

parkway projects of the 1920s and 1930s had made Nassau County much more accessible to the automobile than it had seemed before the war. Small-town life — mom, Main St. and apple pie — had come during the war to be idealized as the soul of America. Levitt's little houses were the city boys' opportunity to get a piece of the dream they'd been fighting for.

Lured by ads for rental homes starting at $60 a month — $65 in better locations — ex-soldiers fed up with living with their parents and in-laws lined up to rent the new houses even before they were built. Before long, the houses were being offered for sale, and the vets had the G.I. Bill. Price of the original Cape Cods: $6,990, or $58 a month, nothing down.

Levitt had firm ideas about what life should be like in his Island Trees community. Laundry had to be hung on laundry umbrellas, but never on weekends. Lawns had to be mowed regularly. No fences were permitted. Black families were not initially encouraged.

He planned for shopping, playgrounds and houses of worship — though not for traffic and schools. Those bills would come due in the 1950s and '60s in the form of snarled roadways and sharply higher taxes.

ON THE first day of October, Theodore and Patricia Bladykas and their twin baby daughters moved into their little Levitt home at 67 Bellmore Road, Island Trees' first family. Two months later they had 1,000 neighbors.

Within four years, 17,477 homes had been completed and the population had soared to more than 82,000 people, most of them refugees from Brooklyn and Queens.

Beyond Island Trees, the rest of Nassau County by 1950 had taken in another 50,000 New York veteran families who had migrated out from the city. Most of the men still worked in New York, commuting by train. Many families still had no car, though that would change rapidly.

The new house, everything it represented and everything it would become, grew to be the centerpiece of suburban life. And the houses Levitt built on farmland became the prototype for the booming suburbs — not only in New York, but around the country.

On Dec. 31, 1947, there was one small piece of unfinished business for William Levitt. Island Trees, he decided, was no name for this new community of side-by-side, look-alike Cape Cods. He decided to call it Levittown instead.

By JAY MAEDER
Daily News Staff Writer

"It is well known that gangster-ism, murder and kidnappings are widely practiced in the American criminal world. How, we ask, are the gangster methods used by the American secret police against Soviet citizens different from the bandit methods of American gangsters?"

— Pravda

ON THE OTHER side of the world lay the dark empire, a place of evil incarnate, profoundly committed to the destruction of American ideals. In Washington in the first days of August 1948, Soviet spy Elizabeth Bentley told the House Un-American Activities Committee that a top aide to President Franklin Roosevelt had been her primary contact and ex-Red Whittaker Chambers named one-time State Department official Alger Hiss as his. In New York, the top leaders of the American Communist Party were under indictment for conspiracy to overthrow the government. Pal Joey, some of us were ruefully calling old Joe Stalin these days.

The Daily News' flinty editorial page was by now customarily referring to Uncle Sam as Uncle Sap. "If ever a nation asked for treachery and betrayal, we did," growled the paper. American citizens, added John O'Donnell, The News' man in Washington, were finally about to get "a clear and shocking picture of the betrayal, the traitorous connivance with foreign agents and the selling out of the United States which was winked at by the New Deal of Franklin D. Roosevelt."

At 4:19 p.m. on Thursday the 12th of August, a 52-year-old school teacher named Oksana Stepanova Kasenkina hurled herself from a third-floor window of the Russian Consulate at 7 E. 61st St., preferring death over forcible return to Moscow. Unfortunately for Pal Joey, she lived.

THE CONSULATE had been in the headlines since Saturday the 7th, when Soviet Consul General Jacob Lomakin led a raid on Reed Farm, a Nyack-area refuge for displaced Russians operated by Leo Tolstoy's daughter Alexandra, and physically repossessed Oksana Kasenkina, who had fled there rather than be put aboard a boat back to Russia. Kasenkina had been in New York for three years, teaching chemistry to the consulate's children. She had decided she liked it here. By the time Lomakin got her back to the city, the FBI and the state police had dealt themselves into what under U.S. law plainly appeared to be a criminal abduction.

As Russian claims of diplomatic immunity held authorities at bay, Kasenkina disappeared into the consulate — and for five tense days, 7 E. 61st St. sat at dead center of a dangerous international firestorm.

HUAC denounced Russia as a "foreign power operating its own police force in America." Soviet Ambassador Alexander Panyushkin accused the U.S. of state terrorism. The Soviet news agency

CHAPTER 105

BETTER DEAD THAN RED
Oksana Kasenkina, 1948

Tass railed against the "fascist gangsters" of New York. On 61st St., Lomakin met the press, trotted out a visibly drugged Kasenkina and explained that the woman was very grateful to have been rescued from Countess Alexandra's clutches.

On Wednesday the 11th, state Supreme Court Justice Samuel Dickstein, acting on a suit brought by the citizens group Common Cause, ordered Lomakin to produce Kasenkina in court. A fuming Lomakin threw down Dickstein's writ when it was served and declared that he would not comply.

The next afternoon — as the Soviet government demanded that Washington punish New York

authorities for their interference in a consular matter — Oksana Kasenkina went out her window.

TELEPHONE WIRES broke her fall, probably saving her life. She crashed into the courtyard and lay there, moaning, legs and pelvis shattered, as consular officials rushed out and tried to shoo away reporters camped outside the 7-foot fence. "Leave me alone, leave me alone," she screamed as workers began to drag her broken body inside.

At this point, two New York City policemen, Sgt. Lester Abrahamson and Patrolman Frank Candelas, took it upon themselves to decide they'd had enough of all this.

Over the fence the officers went — and, over the Russians' insistence that they would attend to the critically injured woman themselves, made it plain they intended to call an ambulance and rush her to Roosevelt Hospital.

At Roosevelt, a wall of cops held back the furious diplomats who came to demand that doctors surrender their patient. A sputtering Lomakin lodged protest after protest, but New York refused to budge, particularly after Kasenkina regained consciousness and said she wished to become an American citizen.

For the American propaganda machine, Oksana Kasenkina was a prize catch. She appeared to be genuinely terrified of going home. "They call it paradise," she said in the hospital. "I call it jail."

Observed The News: *"We believe this macabre case will bring home to Americans the really sinister aspects of Red rule far more than days of testimony in Washington.*

"Incidentally," the paper reflected, *"Consul General Lomakin had better not go back to Russia. He has blundered."*

BACK, HOWEVER, he went. As the Kasenkina affair became the lead item on Voice of America broadcasts into the Iron Curtain countries and as HUAC announced that the defector would be a witness once she recovered from her injuries, Ambassador Panyushkin made a formal demand that she be turned over to Soviet authorities, and the State Department formally refused. Shortly after that, Lomakin got the heave-ho. President Harry Truman personally gave him three days to pack up and get out.

In the last days of August 1948, Jacob Lomakin went home to Moscow, Soviet authorities broke consular ties with the U.S. and American diplomats were expelled from Russia.

In Washington, Air Force Chief of Staff Gen. Carl Spaatz proudly announced a new missile capable of carrying an atomic warhead 5,000 miles. At a street fair outside Grand Central Terminal, 50,000 New Yorkers cheered as nuclear scientists ceremoniously split a uranium atom in a blinding flash.

OKSANA KASENKINA *in 1949 published her autobiography, "Leap to Freedom," and briefly enjoyed a career as an anti-Communist heroine. Then, always fearful of Red assassins, she dropped out of sight. She died in 1960 in Miami, where she had been living in a cheap hotel under an assumed name.*

By DAVID HINCKLEY
Daily News Staff Writer

THE NAMES rippled in like waves, reshaping the shores of American culture: Arthur Godfrey, Milton Berle, Ed Sullivan, Douglas Edwards, John Cameron Swayze.

Giants they were, for in 1948 they catapulted television from an American novelty to an American way of life.

With a little help from Jon Gnagy, Dennis James, Argentina Rocca and Howdy Doody.

TELEVISION COULD be traced to 1875, when the American inventor G.R. Carey devised a crude system that used a series of lights to project an image. In 1907, Lee DeForest invented the amplifying tube. In 1923, Vladimir Zworykin invented the iconoscope, or pickup tube. On July 1, 1941, NBC and CBS were given the first two commercial TV licenses, for Channels 1 and 2 in New York, which broadcast nightly sports and entertainment events — not that many New York households had sets on which to watch them.

By 1948, though, Americans owned 190,000 sets, fully a quarter of them in the city. Postwar money was in play here, as American industry shifted from guns to butter. No less important, the broadcast biz realized this toy that had been kicking around for years had become the hottest household item since running water and indoor plumbing.

Americans no longer talked about merely owning a television, they now discussed what they saw on it: the 1947 World Series, or NBC's "Kraft Television Theater," which debuted May 7, 1947, on the bold premise that television could sell cheese by offering serious, movie-quality drama.

At the dawn of 1948, only NBC and DuMont were functioning as networks, and tiny ones at that. DuMont had WABD (Channel 5) in New York and a second station in Washington, a town with fewer than 20 TV sets.

Before the year ended, however, the world changed. Tiny ABC, which had considered it pointless to do anything national without a New York outlet, finally got WABT (Channel 13) and immediately launched a network: a half-dozen stations, all in the East. CBS — which had been futilely hoping the Federal Communications Commission would mandate that all TV signals be transmitted in color — saw the future rushing up like a freight train and jumped in with a network as well.

In the fall of 1948, then, DuMont was on the air six nights a week and its three rivals for seven — all losing millions of dollars but smelling a big pay-off hard around the bend.

WHICH THERE was. "Kraft Television Theater" ushered in the golden age of TV drama — and sent Imperial Cheese sailing off store shelves.

When the makers of Anacin wondered in 1948 if anyone was watching "Mary Kay and Johnny," a DuMont sitcom, they offered a free mirror to the first 200 viewers who sent in comments. They then quietly stashed away an extra 200, to be sure no respondent went mirrorless.

They received 8,960 letters.

So the issue was not demand, which seemed to be creating itself, but supply. How to fill all this air?

CHAPTER 106

TO INFORM, ENRICH, ENLIGHTEN AND LIBERATE

Television, 1948

THE HIGH-MINDED saw television as the ultimate tool to uplift humankind. "The Court of Current Issues," "Teenage Book Club," "Photographic Horizons," "Meet the Press" and fledgling network news programs with Edwards (CBS) and Swayze (NBC), all part of the fall 1948 lineup, reflected the vision of men like Pat Weaver, later president of NBC, who said TV would "inform people, enrich them, enlighten them and liberate them from tribal belief patterns."

Others argued that bread and circuses were the quickest path to the hearts and minds of the masses, and they soon found supporting evidence in NBC's "Texaco Star Theater." It launched June 8, 1948, and rotated hosts for months before settling on vaudeville comic Milton Berle, who would do anything for a laugh. Like wear a dress.

By autumn, Berle's show was such a phenomenon that during his Tuesday night time slot, 8 to 9, it was said that tumbleweeds blew down Broadway.

Also in June, CBS launched "Toast of the Town," a variety show hosted by dour, well-connected Daily News columnist Ed Sullivan. He wore no dresses, but his show, too, was a hit, and in December, CBS gambled that Godfrey, a huge radio star, could cross over to TV. He did, completing the variety-show trifecta of 1948.

New York was the early hub of all this supply and demand. The town had five stations: WABD, WABT, WCBS (Channel 2), WNBT (Channel 4), and the new, independent WPIX (Channel 11). Most signed on around 4 p.m. and passed the time with news features and old movie shorts, particularly Westerns, until a sports event, evening feature or network show came on. They signed off around 11.

This was ample time, it turned out, to begin creating TV stars. Señor Wences, a guest on Berle's first show who became better known later as a Sullivan regular, immediately inspired thousands of viewers to drive their friends crazy with "S'alright!"

A typical menu of Berle guests might be Pearl Bailey, Bill (Bojangles) Robinson, Phil Silvers and Smith and Dale. Sullivan had the June Taylor dancers, and his first guests were Jerry Lewis and Dean Martin and Richard Rodgers and Oscar Hammerstein.

Television had begun borrowing the radio soap opera as early as 1946, with a DuMont serial called "Faraway Hill." In 1948, it began dabbling with the sitcom as well, with "Mary Kay and Johnny" and "The Growing Paynes."

Then there was Jon Gnagy, semi-Bohemian in his goatee and beret. Gnagy hosted "You Are the Artist," part instruction and part history, and while by 1949 he had been deemed too provincial for New York, he left behind thousands of Gnagy artists.

Argentina Rocca was a professional wrestler who worked barefoot and hoisted his sneering foes into the "Argentine Backbreaker," which caused the strongest of men to howl for mercy. In the fall of '48, wrestling fans were served by NBC on Tuesday at St. Nicholas Arena, ABC on Wednesday and DuMont Thursday and Friday from Jamaica Arena. Boxing also got four nights, often with light-hitting middleweights to insure bouts would go the distance and not leave the network with a half-hour of empty air. The enthusiastic Dennis James, who hosted boxing and wrestling on DuMont, was one of the first TV sports commentators to become famous.

Meanwhile, one Bob Smith had persuaded NBC in late December 1947 to take a weekly show called "Puppet Playhouse." In fact, Smith's ensemble was led by a puppet, the perpetually beaming Howdy Doody. By the summer of '48, Howdy and his pals — some human and some plastic, all bobbing along to the show's relentlessly hummable theme — had gone daily and become one of TV's most powerful magnets for the baby boom generation.

New York, with America soon to follow, was suddenly seeing the world in a whole new light. Flickering and blue.

BY 1951, *there were 12 million TV sets in the U.S. By 1955, 70% of America's households had TV. Ed Sullivan remained a national fixture until 1971.*

By JAY MAEDER
Daily News Staff Writer

WHAT WITH a depression and a war and federal quotas, the great waves of the tired, poor and huddled had dried to a trickle, and in the late 1940s there was a full generation of New Yorkers quite unaccustomed to immigrants. It was at this moment that the city suddenly found itself overwhelmed by the largest influx of human beings in 40 years.

They came from the U.S. territory of Puerto Rico — catastrophically overpopulated, desperately impoverished, devastated by decades of sugar company plantationism. All at once there were many thousands of them in the city, where it was said a man might earn in a week what he labored for a year to earn at home. Thus did a new people arrive, as had the forlorn others before them.

But in fact, several things distinguished the *puertorriqueños* from the immigrant hordes of days past. One was that the earlier travelers had come in boom times, when, whatever their other difficulties, employment opportunities abounded; this was no longer the case, and many of the newcomers found here only wretchedness. Another was that many were of color, doomed to suffer greater daily indignities than had most of their predecessors.

Another, on the other hand, was that Puerto Ricans happened to be U.S. citizens already. Which meant that, indignities or not, they were free to travel as they pleased.

And which meant that they could vote.

This was not lost on U.S. Rep. Vito Marcantonio of Manhattan's 18th Congressional District.

VITO MARCANTONIO indignantly denied suggestions that he had personally engineered the postwar Puerto Rican migration purely to pad voter rolls in his district. Still, it was a fact that in November 1946, as his public career seemed otherwise on the wane, *el barrio* had recently grown by nearly 15,000 newly registered voters who managed to return him to Congress by a squeak.

In 1949, as the new arrivals came and came and came, he was running for mayor.

An early protege of Fiorello LaGuardia and LaGuardia's successor in Congress after the Little Flower became mayor in 1934, Harlem-born Marcantonio was a professional leftist reviled in Washington for his faithful adherence to the Red line in every vote. Long disavowed by Republicans and Democrats, he had won several elections as the candidate of the American Labor Party, which he had co-founded in 1936. Nobody but the Daily Worker ever supported him — except for his constituents, and even Marcantonio's critics granted that he worked every weekend on E. 116th

Vito Marcantonio campaigning on E. 111th St.

CHAPTER 107

LAND OF PLENTY
The Barrio Congressman, 1949

St., personally receiving long lines of those in need of succor and comfort.

By 1949, Marcantonio was on the skids. His politics were in disfavor, and he had been damaged by scandal: On Election Day 1946, an opposition pollworker named Joseph Scottoriggio had been beaten to death by a goon squad, and the 80th Congress had tried hard to deny Marcantonio his seat in the wake of the murder. In November 1948, he had needed every one of his voters to get reelected.

And he was going to need even more of them if he hoped to unseat Mayor William O'Dwyer in November 1949.

THE "CALLOUS exploitation" of Puerto Rico's tired, poor and huddled, wrote the Daily Mirror's Jack Lait and Lee Mortimer in 1948, "is one of the dirtiest crimes in the long and shameful record of practical American politics. None knows better than those who have primed and prompted and financed the exodus what they are doing to their victims and what they are doing to the city where they bring them. . . . These poverty-numbed, naive natives are sold a bill. . . . They are told that here fortunes await many and the rest can quickly go on relief. . . . The result is a sullen, disappointed, disillusioned mass of people."

Every day at the Teterboro, N.J., airfield, rattletrap charter planes disgorged impossible numbers of passengers who had paid as little as $20 for the 14-hour, standing-room-only flight from San Juan. By late 1947 there were perhaps a quarter-million Puerto Ricans in New York, and 2,000 more arrived every month.

Those who found work found it chiefly in the needle trades, in restaurant kitchens, in building services. The truth was that thousands more were unemployable — simple fieldworkers woefully unprepared for city life. It was widely believed, not altogether groundlessly, that many were on the public-relief rolls before they ever got off the plane. Many went straight into the miserable squalor of *el barrio*, between E. 97th and 116th Sts. in Marcantonio's district. It was documented that few new arrivals were quickly registered as voters in circumvention of residency requirements.

"An Americanization problem of the first magnitude," fretted a 1947 Board of Education report. New York's Puerto Ricans inhabited "a margin between cultures," the report said, victims of "unrealistic expectations through bald lies" — "the illusion that in New York there is abundant housing and employment for everybody" and that "even if no employment is obtained, the government takes care of the people through relief agencies." The wave of immigration "has reached gigantic proportions. . . . It would appear inevitable that the exodus from the island to the continent will continue and that New York City will be the focal point of this migration."

The city reeled. Welfare bills came to $12 million a year. Hospitals fought near-epidemic levels of tuberculosis and syphilis. Already overcrowded schools lurched under the burden of 35,000 new students.

Profoundly embarrassed by "the Puerto Rican problem" in New York as he partnered with the U.S. in the

Operation Bootstrap program calculated to repair the island's ruined economy, Puerto Rico's newly elected Gov. Luis Muñoz Marin by mid-1949 was pleading with his people to stay home. But Puerto Rico had a million more souls than it could sustain. Nothing was going to stop the great pilgrimage to the land of plenty.

MARCANTONIO had long been a hero of Puerto Rico's nationalist leftists; leaders of the island's Independence Party now assembled in Spanish Harlem to support his mayoral run. At the same time, Muñoz Marin came to town to campaign for O'Dwyer and to beg the city's Puerto Ricans to dissociate themselves from Marcantonio's "Red tinge."

There were other issues in the 1949 mayoral race; O'Dwyer came not without baggage, and Republican challenger Newbold Morris hammered hard at His Honor's all too apparent coziness with mob boss Frank Costello. But O'Dwyer did find it useful to pledge renewed commitment to the Puerto Rican community and to promise that henceforth it would not need "Communist stooges" to represent its interests.

On Election Day, there proved to be insufficient votes to propel Marcantonio into City Hall, and it was observed that Puerto Ricans did not at this time appear to be factors in the body politic.

Assessing matters not unpresciently, one Abelardo Gonzales of E. 108th St., operator of one of the dozens of Harlem travel agencies specializing in the cheap San Juan flights, had this to say:

"A long time back, everybody was beefing about the Irish when they came over. Then they got themselves a mayor and a senator and some congressmen and people quit bothering about them.

"Then came the Jews, and they started kicking about them. They got themselves a governor and some congressmen and they let up on them. Next came the Italians, and they got guys like LaGuardia and they let up on them.

"But us, we got nobody. So they pick on us. But just you wait. After a while we'll get some guys, and they'll let up on us, too. That's the way it goes."

BY NOVEMBER 1950, *a Red tinge was a serious political liability, even in the 18th District, and this time Marcantonio was not reelected. Comeback proceedings ended in August 1954, when he dropped dead in City Hall Park at age 51.*

New York's Puerto Rican population was 610,000 in 1960, 847,000 in 1970.

By JAY MAEDER
Daily News Staff Writer

ON FRIDAY THE 14th of October 1949, Benjamin J. Davis Jr. became the only member of the New York City Council ever to be convicted of conspiring to overthrow the federal government.

The trial had lasted nine raucous months. Eight women and four men had deliberated just seven hours before finding Councilman Davis and 10 other top officials of the American Communist Party guilty as charged.

"Police state!" shouted one of the defendants.

"Frameup!" cried another.

Benjamin Davis said nothing. At 46, he was on his way to prison. His days as a fire-breathing New York pol were over.

GEORGIA-BORN Ben Davis had come up better than many Southern blacks of his generation; son of a Republican national committeeman, he was the product of private academies, Amherst College and Harvard Law School. He had bought into the Red line while labor-lawyering back home down South in the early 1930s, and by 1935 he was in New York, editing a weekly called The Negro Liberator. A year later he was writing for the Daily Worker, and soon he was one of the paper's top executives. In 1939 he made headlines when he personally fired film critic Howard Rushmore for refusing to scathe "Gone With the Wind," a picture Rushmore had rather liked. In 1943, after the city's first black councilman, Adam Clayton Powell Jr., moved on to Congress, Davis' solid pro-labor, anti-Jim Crow credentials handily won him Powell's old Harlem Council seat.

Red was not yet an altogether disreputable public color in 1943; indeed, Davis joined another card-carrying Communist already sitting on the Council, Peter Cacchione of Brooklyn, as well as Laborite Mike Quill of the Bronx. Harlem Rep. Vito Marcantonio was a fevered Laborite as well, and these four men were the axis of leftist militancy in city politics. By 1945, though, Redskys were less glamorous. That fall, Democratic mayoral front-runner William O'Dwyer refused to run on the same ticket with Davis and forced him off the Tammany slate. Harlem turned out for him in huge numbers, and he kept his seat regardless.

But Davis was now beginning to self-destruct. In March 1946, he and Cacchione enraged New Yorkers when they noisily refused to vote for a simple resolution wishing the newly enthroned Francis Cardinal Spellman health, happiness and long life. Later that year, Davis lost a public showdown with O'Dwyer after he warned the mayor that Harlemites would "take things into their own hands" if the city did not immediately provide homes for Negro war veterans.

It was true that thousands of black vets could not find decent postwar housing, but it was also

true that neither could thousands of other people, and O'Dwyer did not appreciate the ultimatum. "If that is an implied threat of violence, and I sincerely hope it is not," the mayor declared, "let me tell you that there will be law and order in the City of New York as long as I am running it." Davis backed off. That fall, when he made a run for the U.S. Senate, he discovered that voters were not in 1946 sending avowed Communists to Washington.

Increasingly, though, he appeared to regard himself as a national instrument. He called President Harry Truman "Little Hitler." He branded members of Congress "stooges." He tried to block the Marshall Plan for European Recovery. "What in God's name do you represent?" a fellow councilman inquired one day.

ON JULY 20, 1948, a federal grand jury indicted 12 of the 13 members of the board of the American Politburo, charging them with "unlawfully conspiring to advocate the overthrow of the government by force and violence." The indictments were not unexpected; the Daily Worker, of whose parent company Davis was now president, had been warning its readers of a "superhoax to dupe the U.S. public," and now the party labeled the Red roundup "the American version of the Reichstag fire" and "an attempt by President Truman to win the election by hook or crook."

Chimed in third-party candidate Henry Wallace: "Another in a series of diversions created for Americans who are complaining about mounting inflation, the stupid bungling in Berlin and other problems. . . . The present situation makes it essential for the administration to create fear through a continued series of crises."

In truth, the government's case rested chiefly on the fact that the defendants had possessed party literature. And the party was not, strictly speaking, illegal. There were perhaps one or two civil liberties issues here.

Not that, in 1948, most Americans much cared. These just weren't good times for Reds. "This is an attack upon the Communist Party," complained the indicted national chairman, William Foster of the Bronx, and he was absolutely right about that.

FOSTER'S CASE was severed from the others, and the remaining 11 defendants — Davis, furriers' union boss Irving Potash of Manhattan, Daily Worker editor John Gates of Queens and various state leaders, including Ohio's Gus Hall — went to trial in Foley Square in January 1949. Davis remained a councilman. The board started holding night meetings to accommodate his trial schedule.

For nine months, demonstrators screamed inside and outside court and in public plazas across the country, and U.S. District Judge Harold Medina patiently endured daily rants from the defendants' attorneys, most of whom he instantly jailed for contempt at the trial's end. Response to the verdicts was as expected. "A vindication of the American system of justice," said Gov. Thomas Dewey. "The first step toward scuttling the Bill of Rights," shrieked Red dowager queen Elizabeth Gurley Flynn. Observed an Army sergeant in Times Square: "They would have been found guilty in nine minutes in the country they would like to see take us over."

Harlem erupted in riots. Harlem's pastors swiftly issued a joint statement, blaming "an army of agitators . . . fomenting strife and discord. . . . The Negro people of Harlem suffer the evil reputation of their actions."

CONVICTED, DAVIS defiantly sought reelection to his Council seat anyway; O'Dwyer and Harlem boss J. Raymond Jones fast rallied Democrats, Republicans and independents around a more moderate black man, Life magazine reporter and Amsterdam News columnist Earl Brown, and on Election Day, Nov. 8, Brown demolished the Red incumbent. On that same day, Laborite Marcantonio failed to take the mayoralty away from O'Dwyer.

Three weeks later, a month before his term was to end, the Council voted unanimously to oust Davis as a felon. The last remaining Communist officeholder in America refused to leave his desk and kept trying to cast votes. "You convicted traitor!" shouted one councilman. "You little crackpot!" Davis shouted back. Finally, everyone just ignored him.

THE PEOPLE of Harlem, announced Councilman Earl Brown, no longer had time for any man who crusaded solely "on a note of martyrdom, heroism and as a persecuted human being. . . . A councilman is not a statesman. He should devote his time to working with and for the people of his district, trying to make the community a respectable, decent place to live."

BENJAMIN DAVIS, *after four years behind bars, became head of the American Communist Party. At his death in August 1964, he was again under indictment.*

Earl Brown sat on the Council for 11 years and later served as chairman of the city's Human Rights Commission.

CHAPTER 108

GUILTY AS CHARGED

The Communist Councilman, 1949

By DAVID HINCKLEY
Daily News Staff Writer

SAY WHAT YOU will about mobsters, they often have very good taste in music.

And thus on Thursday the 15th of December 1949, in the tradition of Owney Madden and his Cotton Club, Morris Levy and several friends opened a nightspot called Birdland, which for the next decade would be known as the Jazz Corner of the World.

True, not everyone called it that. Miles Davis argued that the real creative twinkle was still uptown, at places like Minton's Playhouse on 118th St., where for years the black musicians had come after hours to pick up licks they could dilute enough for white folks to understand and then take them back downtown to make money.

Through the '30s, the boom war years and a few seasons after, "downtown" had meant 52nd St., Swing Street, with its warren of small, smoky clubs. But now the swingers were yielding to the beboppers — the likes of Davis, Thelonious Monk, Dizzy Gillespie, Max Roach and Charlie (Yardbird) Parker.

So now they came to Birdland, named for Parker and conveniently located around the corner, in a basement on Broadway between 52nd and 53rd.

Birdland was divided into three sections: a restaurant, a bar and the bullpen, where those of modest means could pay 75 cents to sit from 8 p.m. until closing time at 4.

On a good night, those six bits bought the best show in town. One evening, Art Tatum was invited onstage during a break in a Parker set. At the time there was heated argument in the jazz world — the terms "jazz world" and "argument" actually being redundant — whether Parker's piano player, Bud Powell, had supplanted Tatum as the premier keyboardist of jazz. The blind Tatum, not unaware of this discussion, made a show of sitting on his left hand before he played two breathtaking pieces using only his right.

Doris Duke and Tennessee Williams hung out at Birdland. So did Jane Russell, Steve Allen and Frank Sinatra. "Symphony Sid" Torin broadcast his radio show nightly from a glass booth at the bottom of the stairs.

It seemed poised to last forever, except all music scenes are magnets for hustlers, and musicians are often eager accomplices in their own self-destruction.

Billie Holiday and Chet Baker lost their cabaret cards — required for club work — over heroin. Powell drank and Davis snorted. But in drug abuse, as in music, the standard was set by Bird.

Birdland's first night. Hornmen, left to right: Max Kaminsky, Lester Young, Hot Lips Page, Charlie Parker. Cat on piano: Lennie Tristano.

Corbis-Bettman

CHAPTER 109

'ROUND MIDNIGHT
Birdland, 1949

When Parker helped open Birdland, he was only a couple of years removed from electroshock treatments, administered after he was found running naked through Los Angeles. He had fallen asleep in a heroin haze with a lighted cigarette in his hand and had run out to escape the subsequent fire.

A year after Birdland opened, Bird, too, lost his cabaret card, for his habit of showing up in no condition to play — proving that some things hadn't changed just because jazz moved around the corner from Swing Street.

IN THE EARLY years of the century, 52nd St. between Fifth and Sixth Aves. was an affluent stretch of brownstones. Then the speakeasies displaced by the new Rockefeller Center moved in, and when Prohibition ended they stayed in business as late-night music clubs.

Fiorello LaGuardia's vice crackdown of 1934 chased some of the shadiest characters into the background, making the scene exotic but safe, and Swing Street became a hip destination: the Onyx, the Famous Door, the Three Deuces, Leon and Eddie's, Hickory House, Tillie's Chicken Shack, Kelly's Stables, the Downbeat, Jimmy Ryan's, the Orchid.

Swing Street even trumped Jim Crow. Though jazz musicians were always a multi-racial crew, many clubs tried at first to maintain the Cotton Club tradition of keeping the white patrons apart from the black performers. But these were tiny joints, without a dance floor or even much of a stage, and mingling was inevitable. In the summer of 1938, jazz impresario John Hammond helped formally shut down the old policy when he made the Famous Door an offer: He would supply air conditioning if the club would book Count Basie and let his black friends in.

Swing Street boomed through the war, with its endless parade of soldiers and sailors. But the good times also lured back the pimps, drug dealers and hustlers, and postwar crackdowns depleted the ranks of both clientele and musicians. Chano Pozo, whose Afro-Cuban conga rhythms brought down the house at Gillespie's 1947 Carnegie Hall concert, was shot to death a year later when he talked back to his dealer.

By the end of the '40s, most of the jazz clubs on Swing Street had gone dark or become strip joints, even as bebop was getting big enough to need a place of its own.

BOP HAD BEGUN surfacing in the early '40s at musicians' hangouts, and it caught the midtown public's ear with Gillespie's famous gig at the Onyx in early 1944. Gillespie was unable to bring Parker in for that occasion, but Bird staked his own claim in September 1944 with a gig at the Three Deuces.

Around the same time, Morris Levy, a Bronx-born teenager with little formal education but boundless ambition, street smarts and connections, was working hat check in the clubs. Moishe, as everyone knew him, gradually got a piece of this and a piece of that — some said with help from his family, which the feds said was the Genovese family — and he was only 23 when he and eight associates opened Birdland.

Weeks later, George Shearing composed "Lullabye of Birdland" there — in nine minutes, says the legend — and Levy, who recently had learned that a publisher makes money every time a song is played, rode its publishing rights to a six-figure windfall.

Eventually he parlayed that money plus his Birdland profits into a publishing, record label and retail empire. He was indicted regularly for mob-related activities, but he beat everything except a final extortion rap in 1988. By then he was dying of cancer, so he never did get to the big house. When he cashed out in 1990, he was worth $75 million.

CHARLIE PARKER died March 12, 1955, in the Stanhope Hotel, where a wealthy jazz fan had given him shelter; official cause was cirrhosis of the liver. In January 1959, Levy's brother Zachariah was shot to death while working the Birdland bar; the killing went unsolved. In June 1964, Birdland filed a bankruptcy petition listing $103,778 in debts and $7,320 in assets.

By JAY MAEDER
Daily News Staff Writer

AT THIS midcentury the Fourth of July fell on a Tuesday, which meant a four-day holiday weekend under a perfect summer sky, and 2.5 million New Yorkers left the city. There were six-hour backups on the South Jersey highways, miles-long lines at the Delaware ferries, 13,000 kids all bound for summer camp at once out of Grand Central. This didn't even count the 2 million Kokomo Joes incoming from the hinterlands for a taste of the big town. It was 1950, midcentury, and everybody had gasoline and a few extra dollars.

Say, here was prosperity for you: On this weekend, the city's bus and trolley fares went from 7 to 10 cents, and no complaints were heard. New Yorkers seemed almost relieved. Well, it was just easier to plunk down a dime than to count out seven pennies, wasn't it?

G.I.s LANDING IN KOREA AS SOUTH ARMY COLLAPSES, the Daily News headlined Saturday morning the 1st. On this weekend, President Harry Truman had ordered in U.S. ground troops to help President Syngman Rhee's overwhelmed forces repel the northern invaders. At this moment, as New Yorkers headed for the beaches, thousands of soldiers half a world away were getting trucked toward no man's land. Seoul was occupied, and Suwon was falling, and columns of Red tanks were streaming across the Han River.

"How far this Truman gamble will go and who will win is still anybody's guess," The News reflected. "Public opinion in this country appears to go on being in favor of the attempt to stop Communism before it jumps over into Japan or pushes farther south in Asia. Whether that enthusiasm will continue after casualty lists begin coming in remains to be seen."

We are not at war, the President had specified to the nation on Friday, and The News didn't quite know what to make of that. "Where is the dividing line between war and no-war?" the paper's editorial writers wondered. "Or is there such a line these days?" Dutifully American as ever, however, they took Mr. Truman at his word that whatever was happening in South Korea was not a war and thereafter solemnly referred to it as "the whatchamacallit."

At sports editor Jimmy Powers' desk, the Fourth of July was chiefly "that psychologically important date when pennant winners are presumed to jell." Assessing the ball clubs, Powers said of the Yankees: "Biggest disappointment. Most experts now expect the defending world champs to finish fourth." Of the Dodgers: "Not going as well as expected." Of the Giants: "Most pleasant surprise of all." The whole town was looking forward to Tuesday's Dodgers-Giants doubleheader at the Polo Grounds. The Giants, of course, were "still in sixth place in a wobbly league," Powers noted, and he hoped that Eddie Stanky would hold up.

In Union City, N.J., 13-year-old Otto Flaig Jr. could barely sleep. He was going to be at that Polo Grounds doubleheader; his dad's friend Barney Doyle had promised to take him. It was all he could think about.

WE ARE *not* at war, said President Truman. Southward slashed the Red tanks as the Americans fell back 93 miles. Congress moved to extend the draft. In New York, Mayor William O'Dwyer appointed a blue-ribbon civil

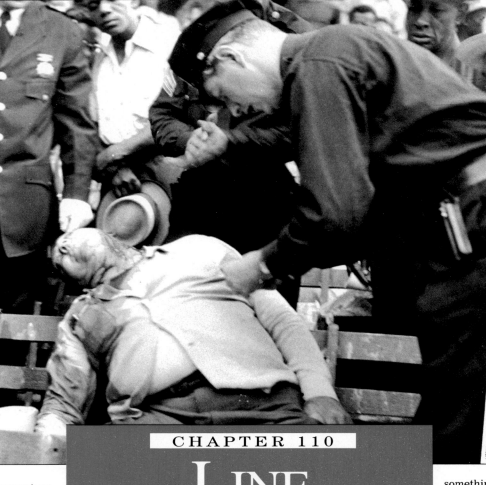

CHAPTER 110

LINE OF FIRE

Independence Day, 1950

defense panel, and hospitals went on full disaster alert in case the Reds showed up on Broadway.

We are not at war, said the President. Record Sunday crowds flooded the parks and beaches. It was still morning when Jones Beach and Jacob Riis and the Rockaways closed their gates. By noon, Nassau police had put up roadblocks across Long Island's highways.

We are not at war, said the President. **TANK-LED TROOPS DRIVING ON G.I.s,** said Monday morning's black headlines. **MARINES ORDERED TO WARFRONT,** said Tuesday's. Dozens of B-29 Superforts were flying out of California. Moscow was demanding immediate U.S. withdrawal from the Korean peninsula. In London, Winston Churchill warned of imminent holocaust. In Valley Forge, Pa., Gen. Dwight Eisenhower addressed a Boy Scout Jamboree and gravely spoke of world enslavement.

"This is not the usual Fourth of July," said a U.S. Navy captain at Tuesday's wreath-laying ceremony at the Shrine of the Eternal Light in Madison Square Park. "Our men are already fighting in the cause of a free people and are suppressing tyranny. We must display that same unity and teamwork developed in the last war in meeting the dangers that oppress free peoples today."

On Tuesday morning, 54-year-old Barney Doyle of Fairfield, N.J., went to church and took Communion, then picked up young Otto Flaig and headed for the Polo Grounds with 49,314 other Giants fans. Heart trouble had recently retired Doyle from Railway Express, and a good Giants game was one of his few remaining pleasures. He never missed one. By noon, he and Otto were in their grandstand seats, upper tier, Row 3, Section

42, between left and center fields. It was a beautiful day for a ballgame.

At the stroke of 12:30, the Dodgers trotted onto the field for their warmup and Doyle turned to say something to the boy.

Then a bullet drilled his forehead, and great fountains of blood cascaded from his nose and ears and mouth, and Barney Doyle was dead before he fell back in his seat.

CHEERING FANS ignored the cops who flooded the park. Young Otto himself complained that the detectives' questions were making him miss the ballfield action. "I've been dreaming about this game for a month," he grumbled. It was soon realized that Doyle must have been killed by a stray Fourth of July shot fired from outside the Polo Grounds, perhaps from the heights, or from the Harlem River Speedway, or from the Macombs Dam Bridge. Officers began going door to door up on Edgecombe Ave.

Standees fought over Doyle's empty seat as medics carried the dead man away. Six hours later, the Giants had won the first game 5-4 and lost the nightcap 5-3. Jackie Robinson had left the field with a leg injury. Fans had been treated to a near-fistfight between Giants manager Leo Durocher and Dodgers outfielder Carl Furillo in a dispute over something or other.

IT WAS WEDNESDAY now, and the holiday weekend was over. The national traffic death toll was a record 466: "It is bitterly ironic that we proclaim our independence from tyranny by a spectacular and tragic confession of our bondage to carelessness and indifference," sighed the president of the National Safety Council.

From South Korea, Gen. Douglas MacArthur declared that the whatchamacallit situation was "not serious in any way." In Washington, Truman expressed confidence that the invaders would soon be driven back, then asked Congress for $260 million to step up atom-bomb production. **REDS CLOSING KOREAN TRAP, SEIZE SUWON,** the papers said. **REDS GAIN IN HUGE DRIVE. RED TANKS KAYO U.S. GUNS.**

At 515 Edgecombe, 1,200 yards away from the Polo Grounds, cops turned up 14-year-old Robert Mario Peebles, who confessed that he had been shooting a .45 automatic into the air from his rooftop. There was a 5-foot parapet; he could not even see the ballpark from where he had stood.

He had ditched the gun in Highbridge Park, he said. It went unfound, but Peebles was too young to be charged with anything but juvenile delinquency anyway. He would spend less than two years in reform school for Barney Doyle's fluke death.

NEWS ITEM: *Washington, July 9 — Congressional leaders today declared the Korean War has launched the dreaded final showdown between the U.S. and Russia and a Republican charged that administration blundering has produced "another grisly Pearl Harbor."*

"The country is closer to World War III than any of us like to admit," said Sen. Wayne Morse (R-Ore).

Shadows gathered now over the first moments of the second half of the 20th century, as if things were suddenly different, as if unthinkably random forces were loose among the fates, as if at any instant a bullet could fall from out of a perfect summer sky.

ARMY CALLS FIRST 20,000 DRAFTEES. 80 TANKS MAUL G.I.s IN SLAUGHTER. POHANG FALLS.

By JAY MAEDER
Daily News Staff Writer

"I tell you, there were times when I truly wanted to jump. You would look out over the city from someplace high above it and you would say to yourself, good Jesus, it's too much for me."
— **William O'Dwyer, afterward**

BY EARLY AUGUST 1950 it was maybe the worst-kept secret in town that Bill O'Dwyer was bailing out. Everybody knew that President Harry Truman was about to throw O'Dwyer the plum ambassadorship to Mexico and get him the hell out of New York City before he brought down the whole Democratic party. "Nothing to it whatever," O'Dwyer growled, but he was lying. Eight months into his second mayoral term, the dams were busting all around him. He could no longer contain things. It was time to start packing.

He had been considered a shoo-in for the Democratic nomination for governor. That prospect vanished on Aug. 15, when he abruptly announced his resignation from City Hall, effective in two weeks. But why? reporters asked him at Penn Station as he returned from Washington with Truman's appointment in his pocket. "That question will have to be answered by the President," he said shortly. Was he really withdrawing from New York politics totally and completely? "Yup." Meanwhile, what did he think about the Brooklyn Grand Jury's report that his many angry charges against District Attorney Miles McDonald's rackets probe were without merit? "I have no further comment."

In his last days in office, he arranged for his own lifetime pension and he rammed through promotions and pay raises for various faithful friends. His personal driver, for example, became a deputy police commissioner. "It's in the best interests of the city," he assured the Board of Estimate.

On Thursday the 31st of August, 60-year-old William O'Dwyer said goodbye to 30,000 New Yorkers in City Hall Park. He stood before them as the essential son of everyone's city, the twinkling-eyed, County Mayo-born lad who had once labored as a longshoreman and coal shoveler, then become a policeman and lawyer and magistrate, then made himself the nationally famous DA who had smashed the Brooklyn rackets and finally been elected mayor of all New York and all its good people. He had inherited Fiorello LaGuardia's financially crippled postwar town and he had built schools and hospitals and housing. New York mayors, he tearfully told the crowd, "are sometimes unavoidably beset by controversies and differences"; his accomplishments, he liked to think, "will live in the public mind long after these differences are forgotten." He hoped he would be remembered as a decent man. "I am willing to accept the judgment of history."

Then the 100th mayor of the City of New York boarded the 20th Century Limited to California and he was gone.

"A lot of people, we think, are going to feel there was very little that was forthright about the whole deal," noted the Daily News. "Rather abrupt, we'd call it."

Mr. and Mrs. O'Dwyer on the train out of town.

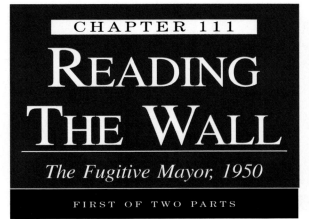

CHAPTER 111

READING THE WALL

The Fugitive Mayor, 1950

FIRST OF TWO PARTS

THE TRUTH WAS that, nine years later, the old smell still clung to Bill O'Dwyer. As Brooklyn DA he had steadfastly refused to pursue charges against mobster Albert Anastasia, and there had never been satisfactory answers to the mysterious 1941 death of his police-protected Murder Inc. witness Abe Reles. A 1945 special grand jury had publicly branded him guilty of gross laxity and maladministration; while he had been able to dismiss that report as an election-year smear and win the mayorship anyway, the ancient unpleasantness had come back to haunt him again in his 1949 reelection bid — *Bill O, The Mob's Man At City Hall* — and the grueling campaign had left him haggard and worn.

Among those who had found his performance as Kings County District Attorney wanting were several of his own assistant prosecutors. One of them, Miles McDonald, was now holding down O'Dwyer's old job himself. At Christmas 1949, the freshly reelected mayor had charmed the city by taking the glamorous 33-year-old socialite model Sloan Simpson as his second wife, and the May-and-December newlyweds had escaped for a storybook honeymoon that made news around the globe. When O'Dwyer returned, he found that the Brooklyn Eagle had published a story connecting the New York Police Department to the city's bookmaking rings and that DA McDonald had just launched the most explosive inquiry into police corruption since the Seabury hearings of 20 years earlier.

McDonald's grand jury steamrolled over the headlines all spring. Cop after cop marched in for grilling; cop after cop fast resigned from the force. Some of the target policemen were O'Dwyer's old friends. He criticized the investigation at every opportunity; it seemed to many that he was working very hard to derail it. "I'm not going to stand by and see the morale of the entire police force shaken," he snapped. "If there are any dishonest cops on the force they should be tossed out, but I'm not going to let the honest ones and their wives and kids suffer." In July, the commander of the Fourth Precinct committed suicide. Ex-cop O'Dwyer led the funeral procession for the dead captain and loudly denounced McDonald's probe as a "witch hunt" that had murdered a good man.

It was, however, entirely apparent that McDonald in fact had the goods on a lot of dirty officers and that matters were soon going to blow up. Democratic Party fixer Boss Ed Flynn went straight to the White House. Mexico City, he suggested to the President, sounded like just the place for Bill O.

TWO WEEKS AFTER O'Dwyer and his bride left town, everything fell apart. On the morning of Sept. 15, Miles McDonald's raiders arrested Brooklyn bookie Harry Gross and announced the breakup of a $20-million-a-year gambling operation that had long enjoyed the friendship of many high-ranking police officials. Gross confessed that he had been paying cops $1 million a year. The sensational disclosures resulted in the most spectacular shakeup in NYPD history, brought Sen. Estes Kefauver's crime committee to town and threw local politics into tumult as Acting Mayor Vincent Impellitteri fast found himself besieged by demands that he throw out the whole bunch of, as one challenger put it, "the gang you inherited from your fugitive mayor."

Sneered a Republican mayoral candidate named Edward Corsi at one point: "Does anyone imagine that *all* the graft went to the police?"

In Albany, Republican Gov. Thomas Dewey openly permitted himself an election-year chuckle; his opponents, he said, "couldn't read." He meant the handwriting on the wall. Explained a Dewey spokesman: "If they hadn't been political illiterates, they wouldn't be running this year. Bill O'Dwyer could read. That's why he got out in time, though Truman was almost too late in throwing him that Mexican lifeline.

"Bill said he was willing to let history be his judge," said Dewey's man. "Well, history hasn't waited long."

BIG TOWN BIG TIME™

By JAY MAEDER
Daily News Staff Writer

ON FRIDAY MORNING the 15th of September 1950, Brooklyn District Attorney Miles McDonald's racket-busters arrested bookie Harry Gross and announced the breakup of a $20 million-a-year gambling operation that had long enjoyed the friendship of many high-ranking police officials. The assistant chief inspector who commanded uniformed cops in Brooklyn and Staten Island instantly put in his retirement papers. Late that night, Police Commissioner William O'Brien and Chief Inspector August Flath, who had spent months scathing McDonald's grand jury as a scandalous waste of taxpayers' money, were summoned by the jury's patron, Kings County Judge Samuel Leibowitz, to listen to wiretap recordings of Harry's boys openly discussing pay-offs to specific officers. In an extraordinary public fracas, the three men had it out in a courthouse hallway, oblivious to reporters standing all around.

"What are you going to do about it?" Leibowitz demanded. "The people have been patient long enough! They don't want mumbo jumbo!"

"I won't stand for anyone besmirching our name," sputtered O'Brien.

"It's the same all over the city!" the judge shouted. "Ice! Ice! Ice! An honest Police Department could stop bookmaking in this city in 24 hours!"

"Show me how to do it! Show me how to do it!" the commissioner shouted back.

Disappearing into Leibowitz' chambers, O'Brien and Flath reemerged at 1 a.m., attitudes adjusted. "We want to congratulate Judge Leibowitz, the district attorney and the grand jury for the excellent work they are doing," O'Brien said stonily. Heads, he pledged, would roll.

HEADS DID. Cracking down vigorously, O'Brien personally busted all of two plainclothesmen back to uniform. This show of stern departmental discipline didn't much impress anyone, considering that word was out all over town that Harry Gross had once gone broke and that his top cop pals had borrowed $100,000 from mobster Joe Adonis to put him back in business. On Sept. 19, Gross met privately with Leibowitz and confessed that he had been paying police $1 million a year — a few bucks a week to harness bulls, more to sergeants, more yet to lieutenants, 10 grand at a time to brass hats. Probably there was going to be a "terrible scandal," Gross sighed.

He wouldn't name names. He couldn't do that, he explained to the judge; he had personal relationships with these men. "I have been with them, been in their homes, been at their graduations," he said. "Gee, I know kids ready to graduate. Another kid about to enter the priesthood. Different things like that."

If the sentimental bookie had imagined this conversation to be confidential, he learned otherwise when Leibowitz gleefully gave the newspapers a full transcript. It didn't matter if Harry clammed up or not; his underlings, the old judge cackled, "are spilling their guts." They certainly were. Suddenly the commander of Times Square's Bright Lights Division went back into uniform. Suddenly whole squads of Manhattan

*Above: Harry Gross. **Below:** Acting Mayor Vincent Impellitteri, Police Commissioner William O'Brien, Brooklyn District Attorney Miles McDonald, Kings County Judge Samuel Leibowitz.*

CHAPTER 112
ICE
Police Story, 1950

SECOND OF TWO PARTS

detectives were walking beats in Canarsie.

MEANWHILE, CITY HALL had fallen into fresh disarray. It had been Boss Ed Flynn's design to throw Acting Mayor Vincent Impellitteri a comfortable judgeship and ease him out, then install elderly Justice Ferdinand Pecora in the mayor's office. This plan was gnarled when Impellitteri decided he liked the job and announced his candidacy as an anti-machine independent in the forthcoming special election. Now, running against Democrat Pecora and the Republican candidate Edward Corsi, Impellitteri — who just happened to be a one-time protege of Judge Leibowitz — divined the wisdom of throwing himself foursquare behind the crusading Miles McDonald and dumping everyone who had ever been associated with recently departed Mayor

William O'Dwyer.

On Sept. 25, 10 days after Gross' arrest, the acting mayor ditched Police Commissioner O'Brien.

"I find my position untenable," announced O'Brien, a 35-year cop. "I find it my regretful duty to turn in my shield." Named at once to replace him was Assistant U.S. Attorney Thomas Murphy, the man who had successfully prosecuted Alger Hiss, and Impellitteri made it plain that Murphy arrived with a large broom and a free hand. On Sept. 26, three hours before their new boss was sworn in, Chief of Detectives William Whalen and Inspector John Flynn of the Confidential Squad put in for retirement.

On Sept. 29, in the biggest single shakeup the department had ever seen, Murphy cleaned out the entire plainclothes division — 336 men.

This occurred after Murphy met with Impellitteri and Republican Gov. Thomas Dewey. "We agreed that no such wholesale corruption could exist unless sponsored and participated in by powerful figures in and out of public office," said ex-prosecutor Dewey, who had declared himself "gravely concerned" about the New York City situation and was now taking a close personal look at things.

The ball now rested with the city's five DAs, Dewey said. Of course he had full confidence in all five? reporters inquired. "I don't know them all," the governor murmured darkly.

AS THE BROOKLYN probe continued, Manhattan District Attorney Frank Hogan was suddenly moved to launch a major investigation of his own. More cops fell. In Washington, Sen. Estes Kefauver announced that his Senate Crime Committee would set up shop in New York to look into alliances between professional gamblers and the Police Department.

In mid-October, on the day before he was to be sworn in as U.S. ambassador to Mexico, Bill O'Dwyer passed through the city, publicly apologized to Miles McDonald for the many unkind things he had once said about him and lauded the "magnificent job" the grand jury had done. "An investigation of this kind is always useful to an honest administration," he said.

Was he surprised that city cops were on the take? a reporter asked him. "No one who has lived in New York as long as I have could be surprised by that," he said.

How did he feel today about New York's rotten cops? he was asked.

"You can machine-gun them for all I care," said the man who might have been governor.

VINCENT IMPELLITTERI *was elected mayor in November. A few months later, Ambassador O'Dwyer returned voluntarily from Mexico to appear before the Kefauver committee and offer an impassioned defense of his public career. The unmoved senators reported in April that O'Dwyer, as DA and mayor, had failed to take "any effective action against the top echelons of the gambling, narcotics, waterfront, murder or bookmaking rackets"; that he "impeded many promising investigations of such rackets"; and that his failures "contributed to the growth of organized crime, racketeering and gangsterism in New York City."*

By the time the Harry Gross affair left the headlines in late 1951, nearly 500 New York police officers had resigned, retired or been sacked.

By JAY MAEDER
Daily News Staff Writer

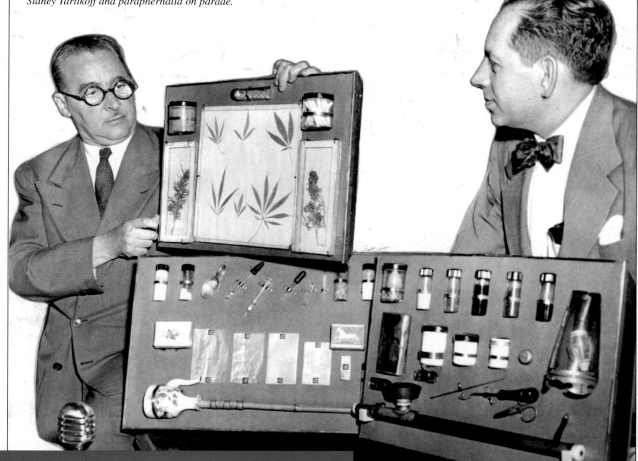

SHOW AND TELL: State Attorney General Nathaniel Goldstein, Assistant Attorney General Sidney Tartikoff and paraphernalia on parade.

NEW YORK OFFICIALLY decided that it had a teenage drug problem in January 1951, when the Domestic Relations Court reported that of 2,263 junior delinquents under court supervision, fully 19 of them were known addicts. This disclosure threw the town into uproars — "The use of narcotics by even one child between the ages of 14 and 16 in New York City warrants the serious attention of the community," thundered Assistant U.S. Attorney Florence Perlow Sheintag — and numerous civic committees were instantly formed to examine causes, treatment and prevention. Cops declared war on street pushers. School teachers were asked to keep an eye out for teaspoons, eyedroppers, safety pins and bottle caps. Superintendent William Jansen ordered principals to report any students who "suddenly begin to associate with new companions" or who, "without satisfactory explanation, begin to wear sporty clothes and expensive neckwear."

Indeed, 252 city teens had been arrested on drug charges in 1950, four times as many as in 1949. Violations, said Police Commissioner Thomas Murphy, historically had been concentrated "in some depressed areas of the city," which mostly meant Harlem, which after World War II had been identified as the dope mobs' primary point of East Coast distribution. But now the problem was spilling over into other communities. At New York Vocational High School on W. 138th St. in the Bronx, a team of undercovers posing as teachers broke up a student peddling ring. Some of the squirts, police said, were pulling in as much as $10 a day. By late February, officials were incorporating drug education into the public school curriculum.

In March, even as Sen. Estes Kefauver's national crime committee named New York bosses Frank Costello and Joe Adonis chiefs of U.S. dope operations for exiled overlord Lucky Luciano, state Attorney General Nathaniel Goldstein announced that 5,000 of the city's 300,000 junior and senior high school students were desperate addicts. Hand-wringing parents got useful daily instruction from the newspapers, which took to printing photos of marijuana plants, in case any were growing in the windowbox, and glossaries of hepcat slang ("Muggles: A marijuana cigarette"), to help them penetrate whatever secret code their kids might be talking in. Goldstein launched a statewide inquiry and called public hearings. In April, he proposed that student vigilante squads patrol school hallways.

THE GOLDSTEIN hearings were a long-awaited sensation when they opened at the State Office Building at 80 Centre St. on Tuesday the 12th of June, broadcast live over WNYC radio. The dope issue was sure to mean long-term political tumult; even the deaf and blind knew that Frank Costello was a big wheel in the city's Democratic machine; Kefauver's famed crime-committee pit bull Rudolph Halley was already running for City Council president on the Liberal ticket. Meanwhile, Jansen had made the mistake of saying that personally he counted only 154 student addicts, not 5,000, which earned him a

CHAPTER 113

THE MONSTER
Teenage Dope Slaves, 1951

public roasting from both Goldstein and Gov. Thomas Dewey. Jansen quickly upped his count to 1,500, but the school system continued to take a flogging for its inattention to a grave matter, particularly after Dorris Clarke, chief probation officer of the Magistrates' Court, testified that she had been trying without success for nearly a year to alert classrooms to the problem.

"We have to fight the monster of drug addiction," Clarke said. "This is a curse spreading through the city."

CITY KIDS DRUG SLAVES, the papers screamed. **GIRL ADDICT DESCRIBES PATH TO PROSTITUTION.** Parades of young cops testified that they had wandered freely through Morris High School in the Bronx, Boys' High in Brooklyn and Galvani Junior High in East Harlem, easily scoring drugs from students. Parades of teens were trotted out by Assistant Attorney General Sidney Tartikoff to describe heroin-sniffing parties in school lunchrooms and lavatories. Yes, they confessed, they stole from their parents, they burgled their neighbors, they pawned their own clothes. Sent to the Youth House of Detention, they snorted their dope there, too.

Some of the youngsters were heard only on tape recordings, their identities protected. One such nameless, faceless 16-year-old Bronx girl broke the town's heart with her lurid page one revelations — "a classic case of child drug addiction," panted the Daily News, "in which the careless use of a marijuana cigarette led with horrid inevitability to heroin and prostitution." If

the lass sounded to some as if she might have been reading from a prepared script — "*My boyfriend injected it into the vein of my arm! I found that it relaxed me! When I tried to stop I got a backache! I knew then that I was addicted! We decided to break into a house! I began to have sexual relationships with older men!*" — well, Tartikoff admitted, it was true that he had helped her marshal her thoughts a little. Still, she was quite electrifying.

By week's end, Goldstein's count of the schools' youthful addicts had increased to 6,000. In Washington, U.S. Narcotics Commissioner Harry Anslinger branded New York the nation's worst drug cesspool. "Social disintegration," he sighed.

THE DOPE MENACE stayed in the headlines through the summer and fall, as state and federal lawmakers imposed harsher penalties and frightened moms and dads regularly turned in their kids to cops. Old-time bootlegger Waxey Gordon had the bad luck to get pinched as a drug racketeer at the height of the fever and swiftly bought 25-to-life. City officials, meanwhile, were mildly mortified when it was found that one ring of peddlers was operating out of Bellevue Hospital.

In November, Dewey and Mayor Vincent Impellitteri announced the joint city-state rehabilitation of the old tuberculosis asylum on North Brother Island into a modern drug rehab facility and pledged that the juvenile narcotics problem would be licked within five years.

As it happened, some officials by now were deciding that perhaps the peril had been overstated anyway. "Most youngsters are not real addicts," ventured Hospitals Commissioner Dr. Marcus Kogel. Agreed a blue-ribbon mayoral commission: "The present situation may not be as alarming as many persons have supposed."

From Italy, Lucky Luciano complained that reports linking him to the traffic were nothing more than attempts to embarrass Dewey. Many observers marveled at the spectacle of the world's No. 1 crime boss rushing to the political defense of the man who had convicted and then pardoned him.

Save These New Air Raid Instructions. If 'Sneak Attack' Comes... ↓ —And →

AT HOME: Hurry beneath bed or table close to wall and away from windows. Cover exposed parts of the body, close eyes.

AT WORK: Get under desk, table or bench. Lie close to wall away from windows or glass doors. Cover body.

WALKING: Take to nearest shelter. If none nearby, fall to ground face downward. Cover exposed parts of body.

IN VEHICLE: Pull to curb, turn off ignition. Shield face and eyes, fall to floor. Follow these rules exactly.

AT SCHOOL: Teachers are trained to meet contingencies. If your child is at school, you stay home, don't phone teacher.

When Advance Warning Siren Sounds, Quickly Observe These Safety Measures:

AT HOME: Draw window drapes, close blinds or shutters. Put out all open flames. Go to basement or designated shelter.

AT WORK: Go to prearranged shelter on your floor. Obey building instructions. Promptly follow guidance by floor warden.

WALKING: Seek nearest public shelter or enter nearest building. Stay near center of building—away from windows.

IN VEHICLE: Park immediately at curb, away from corners and hydrants. Enter nearest building or subway.

AT SCHOOL: Teachers will guide students. Parents are to stay home. Everyone is urged to obey these instructions.

By JAY MAEDER
Daily News Staff Writer

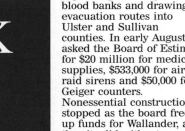
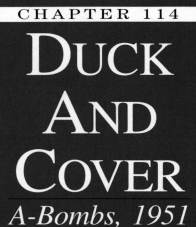

CHAPTER 114

DUCK AND COVER

A-Bombs, 1951

SO FAR AS could be officially determined, only about 100 people died when the atomic bomb fell on New York City on the morning of Thursday the 29th of November 1951. These luckless souls perished on the steps of the New York Public Library when, after they had dutifully bolted from their cabs and buses in midstreet, they found the library doors already locked up tight. "Let me in; let me in," screamed one man who appeared to be taking this exercise very seriously. But the guard inside shook his head. "This is a hell of a situation," grunted Patrolman Matthew Cerick, shepherding the flock across Fifth Ave. to the sanctuary of the Public National Bank. There they were taken in, but of course by that time they had already been vaporized.

Otherwise, New York's first air-raid drill since World War II efficiently hummed along like the finest of sewing machines. After 17 months of planning, there was now near-total order amid near-zero confusion; three minutes after 1,079 sirens began wailing at 10:33 a.m., the city was silent from Chinatown to Harlem and to the Nassau and Westchester borders. A million citizens disappeared into the subways, 35,000 into Rockefeller Center, 90,000 into the Empire State Building, 340,000 into 804 miscellaneous designated shelters, 1,500 into St. Patrick's Cathedral. Fifth Ave. was empty. Penn Station was empty. Times Square was empty. Pushcarts sat abandoned in the Garment District. You could hear the traffic lights click. You could hear the pigeons fly.

All over town, school children climbed under their desks and covered themselves with their coats. On Cortelyou Road in Brooklyn, Mrs. Harold MacKenzie stopped pouring tea for her two guests and the three of them earnestly sat down behind the living room sofa. On Central Ave. in Brooklyn, Mrs. Ernest Garitano locked her dog in the bathroom before taking cover herself.

FORMER POLICE Commissioner Arthur Wallander had gone to work on the city's Civil Defense machinery the minute U.S. ground troops landed in Korea in July 1950. Joe Stalin was going to bomb America any minute, this was simply a fact, and New York was plainly first on the list of target cities; CD Chief Wallander's enormous job included building a control center to which all commands would report, drafting and training

200,000 volunteers, organizing food depots and blood banks and drawing up evacuation routes into Ulster and Sullivan counties. In early August he asked the Board of Estimate for $20 million for medical supplies, $533,000 for air-raid sirens and $50,000 for Geiger counters. Nonessential construction stopped as the board freed up funds for Wallander, and the city did without a new police station and modern traffic lights. At the same time, Wallander banned sirens except for air-raid purposes, and police cars and ambulances all made do with their horns.

New York was going to be bombed. Nuclear hellfires were going to boil the rivers and melt the streets. Fourteen huge underground shelters were proposed, three in Manhattan, seven in Brooklyn, three in Queens, one in the Bronx, each to hold a quarter-million people. After the atomic holocaust, suggested Planning Commissioner Jerry Finkelstein, they could be used as peacetime parking garages. Unfortunately, they would take several years to build. Fortunately, there were already many miles of subway tunnels into which the people could flee, as well as many skyscrapers with thick concrete walls. Ninety havens were designated — the Equitable Building, Met Life, various courthouses — and PUBLIC SHELTER signs were affixed to them.

Eight thousand Welfare Department employees were meanwhile directed to staff 47 smaller shelters in the five boroughs; Welfare Commissioner Raymond Hilliard proudly announced in early September that his people were nearly ready to deal with things in the event, say, two A-bombs fell on Queens. "We are practically out of the planning stage now," he said. The Red Cross organized hundreds of first-aid classes. Thirty-five thousand cabbies were tapped to be ambulance drivers. The Ballantine brewery in Newark offered 1,000 trucks.

Late in September, the state Civil Defense Commission, headed by Gen. Lucius Clay, the man who had directed the Berlin Airlift, began distributing millions of free copies of a 36-page booklet called "You and the Atomic Bomb." Nuclear war was quite survivable, citizens learned, if only they took simple precautions. If indoors: "Draw curtains and blinds. . . . Get under a table and throw a cloth over your head." If outdoors: "Crouch behind a tree." After the blast: "Scrub walls to erase radioactivity." Survivors were advised to drink lots of salt water. The dangers from so-called fallout,

Wallander assured the public, were "greatly exaggerated."

And so New York City waited for World War III.

According to the master plan, a three-minute cry from Wallander's commandeered sirens would mean that an atomic bomb was expected to fall in about eight minutes. A subsequent series of shorter chirps would signal the all-clear, assuming that the nuclear firestorms had not destroyed the sirens.

BY JUNE 1951, when Russia had mysteriously not yet invaded the United States, Congress slashed President Harry Truman's $403 million Civil Defense budget to $31 million. Still, surveys found that one out of two Americans expected war within two years, and in New York, Arthur Wallander remained vigilant. Wallander's volunteer units drilled regularly, and civilian observers were manning plane-spotting stations across the city, breathlessly calling in sightings of commercial airliners. In October, Russia exploded two test A-bombs. It was time, Wallander decided, for a public demonstration of preparedness.

On Wednesday the 14th of November — as armistice talks collapsed in Panmunjom and reports came in that 6,270 U.S. prisoners of war had been slaughtered by their barbaric Red captors — tens of thousands of emergency workers made a trial run. Sirens screamed and flares burned bright as enemy bombers struck at Third Ave. and 149th St. in the Bronx and at Myrtle and Bushwick in Brooklyn. Ambulances careened about in heavy rains. Twenty-nine ferries, barges, tugs and police boats convoyed down the East River, rescuing patients from five hospitals. Myrtle and Bushwick looked like a war zone anyway, as it happened, since the whole area was being leveled to make way for the new Brooklyn-Queens Expressway.

The big show, 15 days later, made a hero out of Wallander, a man who had planned well. It seemed there was only one thing he hadn't thought of, this being horses; deliverymen fleeing their wagons had no idea what to do with their nags except just leave them standing puzzled in the street. The city could be proud of itself, editorialized the Daily News: "You got the impression that if New York ever should be bombed, the survivors would claw the cinders out of their hair, bury the fallen with due respect, make some wisecracks in the New York manner and set forth with cold determination to get their revenge." Old Joe Stalin, the paper mused, should only just watch out.

ANOTHER CITYWIDE *nuclear drill, in December 1952, was somewhat less successful; authorities figured that about a quarter-million New Yorkers died.*

As late as 1958, local and federal officials were talking about building an enormous $2.5 billion public bomb shelter 800 feet beneath Manhattan, large enough to hold 4.5 million people.

By JAY MAEDER
Daily News Staff Writer

TWELVE DAYS BEFORE
Christmas 1951, Private 1st
Class Charles Hunziger of the
Bronx came home to Crotona Ave.
nearly blind. Shrapnel. Heartbreak
Ridge. He'd been a promising
Golden Gloves fighter once, and
now his uncle Joe De Maria
brought him around to the gym on
Bathgate Ave. for old times' sake.
Hunziger took a couple of half-
hearted pokes at the bag, then gave
up. What was the use? He couldn't
even see it. He was 19 years old. "It
sure is tough," murmured Uncle Joe.

A year and a half after U.S. troops landed on
the Korean peninsula, there were now 74,000
broken-bodied Pvt. Hunzigers. There were
another 15,000 dead ones. It sure was tough, but
at least their loved ones could account for them;
another 12,795 American families spent every
aching day not knowing what had become of
their missing-in-action sons, brothers, cousins,
husbands and fathers, some of them unheard
from since July 1950. This miserable thing in
Korea, it was still not yet even formally a war.

Whatever it was, it was not going well at all.
This was not for want of military will to
prosecute. Fumed such organs of popular
national thought as the New York Daily News:
*In Korea, the United States is fighting its first
war under the United Nations flag. Some other
powers are giving token assistance, but we are
carrying about 95% of the UN load. Gen.
Douglas MacArthur was forbidden from the
start to try to win this war. He was at last
dismissed for saying repeatedly that he wanted
to and could win it.*

Even as the Panmunjom truce talks
bogged down, there arrived in Washington
the black tally of 6,270 American prisoners
of war known to have been wantonly
slaughtered by their captors in a direct
affront to the Geneva Conventions. Several
key congressmen were calling for
immediate atomic strikes on the Red
butchers.

*We are learning the pattern of this UN
war,* the Daily News snarled. *It is a war we
are not permitted even to try to win, and in
which we must tamely submit to barbarous
wholesale murders of our captured men. Is
there any guarantee that any future wars
we may fight for the UN will not conform to this
same pattern? No, there is no such guarantee.*

Item 4 on the UN truce agenda at Panmunjom
was a prisoner swap. Given the sickening massacre
reports, U.S. negotiators had no clear idea how
many American troops were alive behind bars in
Korea, but they were hoping to bring them home
for the holidays. The Communists, for their part,
appeared to have little interest in getting back any
of their own 130,000 imprisoned, and weeks of
talks had come to largely nothing.

Finally, the two sides agreed to exchange
prisoner lists. It was a step. The U.S. was
expecting perhaps 6,000 names. In a bitter
disappointment, the Reds turned over 3,182. It was
still a step; for 3,182 American households, there
would be miraculously good news this holiday. For
thousands of others, there would be only more
despair.

On Tuesday evening the 18th of December, on
69th Place in Maspeth, Queens, Mr. and Mrs.
Christian Hansen were among the millions glued
to their parlor radios as announcers read off the
first few hundred names immediately available.
Twenty-year-old Pfc. William Hansen, 2nd Division,
had been MIA since October 1950. The Hansens
had never given up hope. Tonight his name was
13th on the list. Tonight he was in No. 2 camp at
Pyokdong, on the south bank of the Yalu River,
half a world away, seven days before Christmas.

The Hansens rushed to the altar of St.
Stanislaus Kostka Catholic Church and fell to their
knees and stayed there for hours, weeping
gratefully. "My boy, my boy," Eileen Hansen
sobbed.

THAT FIRST NIGHT there were just five
more New Yorkers on the list. *Capt. John
Curtin, India St., Brooklyn. Pfc. Reinol*

CHAPTER 115
SUGARPLUMS
Live From Korea, 1951

Mrs. Norma
Magnant of
the Bronx, and
4-year-old
Leslie.

Gonzales, E. 123rd St., Manhattan. PFC George
Davidson, Midland Beach, S.I. Cpl. Julius De
Benedict, Mariners Harbor, S.I. Cpl. Gerard Brown,
Glen Oaks, Queens.* Through the week the names
came down in agonizing trickles as the
Department of Defense sought first to verify
hometowns; through the week there were prayers
of thanksgiving across a rejoicing city. *Cpl. George
Atkins, Reid Ave., Brooklyn. Pfc. Arthur Bowditch, E.
Tremont Av., Bronx. Sgt. Michael Izzo, Second Ave.,
Brooklyn. Capt. Pastor Oliveras, E. 110th St.,
Manhattan.*

"It's going to be a wonderful Christmas,"
whooped Katherine Seifert of Dupont St. in
Brooklyn after learning that her nephew, Pvt.
Stephen Glowacki, had made the list.

On E. 46th St. in Brooklyn, Louis Giannini had
a grand surprise waiting for Pfc. Michael Giannini,
who had landed at Inchon and been captured in
the Yalu River retreat: 20-year-old Mike, his father
grinned, had a 3-month-old baby brother now. In
Hempstead, L.I., the family of Master Sgt. Montero
Lawrence gazed lovingly at the watch he had made
a point of leaving them; career soldier Lawrence,
who had survived Pearl Harbor and the
Philippines, had feared he would not return from
Korea; now his family knew better.

On Broadway in Brooklyn, teenage Mary
Pereira was aburst with admiration for her
brother, Pfc. Pedro Perira. "Even back in Puerto
Rico, he wanted to be a soldier," she beamed. "He
couldn't wait till he was old enough."

Joy and despair, as day after day more names
appeared on the list and others did not. *Pfc.
Leonard Chiarelli, Bushwick Ave., Brooklyn. Pfc.
Albert Gruaria, Ozone Park, Queens. Lt. Joseph
Magnant, Wadsworth Ave., Bronx. Pvt. Daniel*

*Sugrue, Far Rockaway, Queens.
Pvt. Theodore Thompson, Myrtle Ave., Brooklyn.*

A White House spokesman cautioned against
too-high hopes: "This country has no way of
verifying whether the list is accurate or inaccurate,
true or false, complete or incomplete." In fact, it
was being discovered that many of the names were
those of men whose families had already been
notified of their deaths, whose benefits the Army
already had paid. What was anyone to think? "You
think of the dark side," admitted Louis Giannini,
bouncing his baby son.

*Pfc. Bienvido Acevedo, Broome St., Manhattan.
Sgt. Albert Capozzi, Putnam Ave., Brooklyn. Cpl.
James Gallagher, Menahan St., Brooklyn.* There was
no verification. There was only Christmas. Maybe
the Communists were lying. Maybe all these men
had already long ago been murdered in ditches.
Maybe they were just sweet, fleeting Christmas
dreams, like sugarplums. Maybe no one would ever
see them again.

*Pfc. Thomas Cole, Nassau Ave., Brooklyn. Pfc.
Richard Montanaro, Astoria, Queens. Pfc. Emmanuel
Pantazis, Astoria Queens. Capt. Eugene Shaw, Third
Ave., Brooklyn.*

TWO DAYS AFTER *Christmas, the Communists
announced that there were another 1,058
American POWs they hadn't troubled to list. As
it happened, they said, 571 of them were already
dead anyway.*

*The provisional ceasefire expired that night.
Addressing the Jewish War Veterans in New York
City on Sunday the 30th of December, Secretary of
State Dean Acheson pledged: "We shall not rest until
our men who are being held prisoner are released."*

CHAPTER 116

PUBLIC DUTY
Arnold Schuster, 1952

By JAY MAEDER
Daily News Staff Writer

BROOKLYN-BORN, Hell's Kitchen-reared William Francis Sutton had a signature: He never stayed in the big house for very long. Willie Sutton sawed his way out of Sing Sing. He tunneled his way out of one hard Pennsylvania pen and climbed over the wall of another. By 1950, Willie was America's most famous jailbreaker, even kind of a folk hero, and he remained a hardworking professional bank robber. On Thursday morning the 9th of March, when the Manufacturers Trust Co. on Queens Blvd. in Sunnyside was relieved of $69,933 by five polite bandits, cops knew right away that Willie was on the job again, and they hunted him relentlessly for the next two years, even as he was living quietly the whole time in a furnished room on Dean St. in Brooklyn, three blocks away from Police Headquarters.

Wanted circulars blanketed the town. The fugitive's face decorated the cover of every true-detective magazine. Willie, however, had craftily grown a mustache, and thus he went about his daily affairs unrecognized. Until shortly after noon on Monday the 18th of February 1952, when a 23-year-old Brooklyn clothing salesman named Arnold Schuster boarded a downtown BMT train at Fourth Ave. and 45th St. and took a seat across from a man who looked more and more familiar the more he gazed at him.

Arnold Schuster gulped. *That's Willie Sutton.*

Like a moth to a flame, the fascinated young clothier got up and followed as Sutton left the train at Pacific St. Arnold Schuster now had two and a half weeks left to live.

STAYING HALF A block behind, sleuth Schuster trailed his quarry to a filling station at Third Ave. and Bergen St. — then, as Sutton borrowed a battery to feed a dead car he had sitting around the corner, he ran to a couple of radio patrol cops parked nearby. "You'll probably think I'm crazy, but I just saw Willie Sutton," he breathlessly informed Officers Donald Shea and Joseph McClellan. The policemen shrugged, took a stroll and accosted America's most-wanted bank guy. Are you Willie Sutton? they inquired. Why, no, said Willie Sutton, my name is Gordon. Okay, the cops said, and they left. Watching from a distance, Arnold now felt the fool, had a rueful laugh on himself and went home.

Back at the station, Shea and McClellan related the amusing story of the helpful crime-busting civilian to Detective Louis Wiener, who thought things over and decided it might be a good idea to go have a chat with this Mr. Gordon himself.

That night, Arnold heard on the radio that long-sought fugitive Willie Sutton had been pinched and that hero cops Shea, McClellan and Wiener were all three getting big promotions. There wasn't a word about the citizen who had tipped them off.

ONCE ARNOLD WENT to the newspapers to complain about his exclusion, Police Commissioner George Monaghan revised the official department story, apologized for the oversight and dealt him into the festival of acclaim being enjoyed by Shea, McClellan and Wiener, who now were all first-grade detectives, the radio officers having been jumped four grades. Authorities showered their gratitude upon the young tipster. "I want publicly to commend Arnold Schuster for the great help he gave the police force in ridding the land of one of its most notorious criminals," Monaghan said. "If all citizens would give such help, it would make our burden easier." Arnold got his picture all over the papers and the weekly news magazines. Soon the big TV shows came clamoring for his personal story.

As it turned out, quite surprisingly, there was no reward money on Willie Sutton's head. Arnold ended up making $750 for a couple of TV appearances. It was for this sum that he sold his life.

ON SATURDAY the 8th of March, Arnold left his Borough Park home and went to work at his father's Fifth Ave. store, Mac's Pants. At 8:45 p.m. he locked up for the night. He boarded a 50th St. crosstown bus, rode over to dark Ninth Ave., walked down to darker 45th St. and headed for his front door. It was 9:10. Indoors, kids were listening to the CBS radio program "Gang Busters," which was tonight featuring the thrilling capture of bank robber Willie Sutton.

The killer may have followed him off the bus, may have been waiting in the shadows. Neighbors heard the gunfire and came running. They found Arnold gut-shot and drilled through each eye.

"Very odd," noted Queens District Attorney Vincent Quinn, who had never intended to call Arnold as a witness against Willie Sutton anyway.

In his death, Arnold Schuster became a national emblem. "This murder, above any crime in my memory, was an offense against all the decent people of the City of New York," said Mayor Vincent Impellitteri. "With the possible exception of the Lindbergh baby," agreed former Brooklyn prosecutor Burton Turkus, "no single murder in the past 25 years has so shocked or outraged the American public." Sen. Herbert O'Conor, former chairman of the Senate Crime Committee, praised the dead youth as "a loyal citizen doing his public duty" and called his rubout "a grave challenge to law and order." Fretted City Council President Rudolph Halley: "Honest citizens will be afraid to cooperate with the police."

In his cell, Willie Sutton seemed genuinely grief-stricken, and cops never had reason to suppose he'd had anything to do with the hit. Willie robbed banks, but he didn't hurt people. For a time, he tried to add $10,000 of his own to the growing reward pool. Authorities finally persuaded him that, really, it just wouldn't look right.

The Schusters refused to have anything further to do with reporters. "Publicity has cost us enough already," one relative scolded. "If it weren't for the publicity, Arnold would not be dead." Which was, to be sure, absolutely correct.

THE SCHUSTER FAMILY *sued the city for $1 million, in what was believed to be the first negligence action ever brought against a municipality for failure to assure the well-being of a resident. Several courts ruled that Arnold Schuster was "doing no more than his duty as a member of the general public" and that there was "no duty of special protection owed to him." Eventually the city settled with the Schusters for $41,000.*

There was never an arrest, and the murder remained a mystery until a decade later, when mob turncoat Joseph Valachi revealed that ganglord Albert Anastasia, who was entirely unassociated with Willie Sutton, had watched Arnold on TV one night, roared "I can't stand squealers!" and ordered the hit purely out of personal indignation.

This was a preposterously senseless thing for a ganglord to do, and Lucky Luciano later hinted in his memoirs that Arnold Schuster was one of the reasons Anastasia himself came to an early demise. "Anastasia was really off his rocker," Luciano said. "He was startin' to see himself like some guy in the old gangster movies."

By JAY MAEDER
Daily News Staff Writer

Christine

George

FROM DENMARK one day in June 1952 did there arrive at the Bronx home of Board of Education carpenter George Jorgensen and his wife Florence a letter from 26-year-old George Jr., or Brud, as the family called him, who, several years earlier, following brief service in the United States Army and a term of employment at the New York office of the RKO-Pathe newsreel people, had relocated to Copenhagen to pursue a career as a magazine photographer. Brud's tone suggested that there was something he wished to share.

I am now faced with the problem of writing a letter, one which for two years has been in my mind. The task is a great one . . . . I want you to know that I am healthier and happier than ever. I want you to keep this in mind during the rest of this letter.

The Jorgensens blinked. Whatever could Brud be talking about?

Life is a strange affair . . . . At times it is obvious something has gone wrong . . . . We humans are perhaps the greatest chemical reaction in the world . . . . Among the greatest working parts of our bodies are the glands . . . . An imbalance in the glandular system puts the body under a strain in an effort to adjust . . . . I, along with millions of other people, had such a system imbalance . . . .

Brud seemed to be leading up to something here.

Right from the beginning I realized that I was working toward the release of myself from a life I knew would always be foreign to me . . . . Even as I write these words, I have not yet told you the final outcome of the tests and an operation last September. I do hope that I have built this letter properly, so you already know what I am going to say now.

I am still the same old Brud, but, my dears, nature made the mistake I have had corrected.

And now I am your daughter.

Mr. and Mrs. Jorgensen Sr., understandably thunderstruck, a few months later proceeded to do what anyone would naturally do with such a painfully intimate confessional from a loved one. They handed it over, when he picked up a tip and came knocking, to a reporter from the New York Daily News.

EX-GI BECOMES BLONDE BEAUTY, the News exclusively informed about a gazillion popeyed readers on Monday morning the 1st of December. **BRONX YOUTH IS A HAPPY WOMAN AFTER MEDICATION, 6 OPERATIONS.** It was not strictly correct, as the early popular surmise had it, that the former George Jorgensen Jr. was the world's first surgical transsexual. But he certainly was the first surgical transsexual to suddenly become a page one sensation around the globe.

Two thousand chemical injections. Glandular and psychological transformations. Cosmetic procedures. Tuckaroonies. "The wizardry of medical science!" boomed all the papers. Not unproudly, actually. These *were* remarkable times, weren't they? In her room at the Copenhagen State Hospital, Christine Jorgensen fast got over her initial horror at the great burst of unexpected publicity and welcomed in the world press. Reporters were quite taken with her. "She has beautiful, emotional, feminine hands," burbled one scribe. "She laughed, her blue eyes sparkling and her blonde hair in pretty curls around her broad shoulders." Happily cried Christine: "My miserable masquerade is ended!"

Young George Jorgensen had grown up enduring one of those really awkward childhoods. He preferred hopscotch to football. He liked to play tea party with the neighborhood girls. He liked to play dressup. Mother Nature, he began to divine, had blundered: He wasn't really a boy, and he was never supposed to have been one. There had been a mixup here. Somehow he had drawn the wrong card. In the Bronx of the 1940s, this was not a popular everyday postulation. At Christopher Columbus High School, the regular fellers had been none too kind to George.

At Copenhagen's more progressive Serum Institute, there had been diagnosis and liberation. Now, back home in America — breathlessly sexology-conscious these days in any case, thanks to the researches of Dr. Alfred Kinsey — for weeks on end the public prints were full of sobersidedly clinical explorations of the hermaphroditic and pseudohermaphroditic conditions. "Christine Jorgensen does not walk alone in the mystery land of human sex," one expert wrote. "There are perhaps thousands of Americans living in doubt or ignorance about their true sex. Some are men who really are women. Some are women who really are men . . . . Sometimes the mysterious controls go awry."

"I never realized my son wasn't normal," reflected George Jorgensen Sr. back home on Dudley Ave. in the Bronx. "He'd never been in any trouble."

"Why, my son was in the Army for 16 months," added Christine's mom.

"Did he *like* the Army?" a reporter leered.

"Who likes the Army?" Mother Jorgensen shrugged.

FOR U.S. DOCTORS, the case raised thorny ethical issues. Medically, if they remained silent, they were giving tacit approval; already they were besieged by it seemed like half the homosexuals in America, all demanding the same operation. The Journal of the American Medical Association launched a skeptical inquiry into exactly what had occurred; there were many suggestions that Christine was little more than a hoax. Indeed, in Denmark, surgeons conceded that in fact George Jorgensen Jr. had been neither a hermaphrodite nor a pseudohermaphrodite, merely an extreme queenie. None of this kept Christine from swiftly emerging as the world's No. 1 poster girl for forward-looking sociosexual enlightenment. "Many more persons should

CHAPTER 117
MASQUERADE
Christine Jorgensen, 1952

overcome their shyness and do the same," she proposed.

She played down the personal-bravery part: "Does it take bravery for a person with polio to want to walk?"

ON THURSDAY THE 12th of February 1953, Christine Jorgensen — part solemn medical experiment, part cultural pioneer, part circus freak — came home.

Mobs met her at she got off the plane at International Airport, fashionable and slinky and Tallulah Bankhead-esque. "Look, Ruthie, she used to be a man!" brayed one mom, holding up her small daughter for a better view. Reporters shouted questions as she made her way to a waiting car. "What about marriage?" "Do you still have to shave?" A week later, wrapped in a mink stole, she took a driver's test, and the papers all had a fine time cranking out woman-driver stories. Actually, the examiner said, she drove very well.

By now there was no hope she could ever quietly pursue any career, and Christine Jorgensen resigned herself to making her living being Christine Jorgensen. She wrote the story of her life for the Hearst newspapers' American Weekly magazine. A Hollywood producer announced he was going to make her a movie star. The Hotel Sahara in Las Vegas talked about building a revue around her. Soldiers in Korea voted her Miss Neutral Zone of 1953.

"She's a beautiful girl," her mother had to admit.

BY YEAR'S END *she was making $5,000 a week at the Latin Quarter. First she sang "Getting to Know You," then she made a costume change and did comedy. "Won't it be funny if my child got on my knee and said, 'Mama, tell me about your boyhood!' " she cracked, and audiences just howled. She was hoping someday to do "Anna Christie" in summer stock.*

"We women are getting up in the world," she told the Daily News. "Look how many of us are in government now."

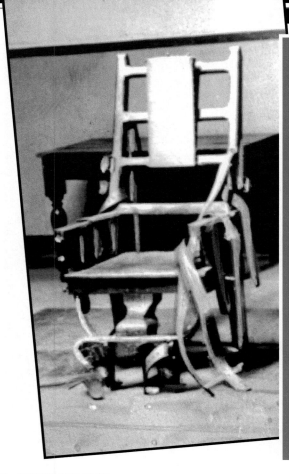

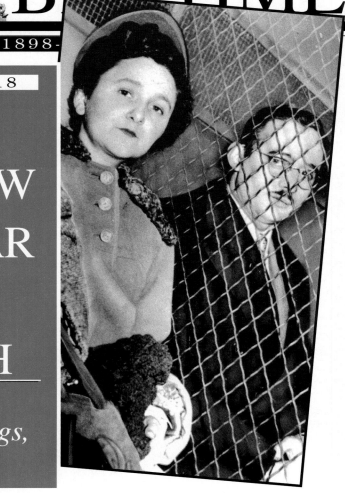

CHAPTER 118

THE SHADOW OF WAR AND DEATH

Burning The Rosenbergs, 1953

By JONATHAN LEWIN
Daily News Staff Writer

FIVE THOUSAND demonstrators gathered in Union Square to offer prayers for the doomed couple. New York police went on citywide alert. Thousands more supporters assembled outside the White House. In Paris, 400 people were arrested in clashes outside the American Embassy.

Julius and Ethel Rosenberg's last hope for life had evaporated that morning, when President Dwight Eisenhower once again refused a plea for executive clemency. "By immeasurably increasing the chances of atomic war, the Rosenbergs may have condemned to death tens of millions of innocent people all over the world," Eisenhower said, and that was the end of it.

Sing Sing, 8 p.m., Friday the 19th of June 1953. The Rosenbergs had been scheduled to die at 11. But their lawyers had protested against the execution taking place during the Jewish Sabbath, and the time had been moved up three hours. This meant that they would have to do without the traditional last meal. They spent their final hours talking together in a visiting-room cubicle. It was the day after their 14th wedding anniversary.

The FBI had set up a prison command post and installed a direct phone line to its New York headquarters. Perhaps, agents figured, one or the other Rosenberg would break down and decide to talk once strapped into the electric chair.

That didn't happen. Julius was the first to enter the death chamber, and he was dead three minutes later, and attendants quickly mopped down the chair with an ammonia solution that masked the stench of burnt flesh. Ethel went harder. After the standard three jolts, she still breathed. The executioner had to give her two more.

In Union Square, the somber crowd quietly dispersed. Outside the White House, anti-Rosenberg pickets eventually outnumbered supporters. Across the land, motorists heard the news on their car radios and blew their horns in celebration.

AMERICANS HAD BEEN stunned when the Soviet Union exploded an atomic bomb of its own in 1949; atom spies must have stolen America's top secrets, many were certain. Indeed, in early 1950, British agents arrested physicist Klaus Fuchs, who confessed he had passed material to Russia while working on the Manhattan Project in 1944 and 1945. That spring, the FBI arrested one Harry Gold of Philadelphia, who admitted being Fuchs' U.S. contact and implicated

one David Greenglass of New York City, a former Army sergeant who in 1945 had worked at the atomic facility in New Mexico. Greenglass quickly gave up one more name — his brother-in-law, Julius Rosenberg, an engineer who lived on Monroe St. in the Knickerbocker Village projects with his wife, Ethel, Greenglass' sister.

The balding, bespectacled, 32-year-old Rosenberg was arrested on July 17, 1950; he was, the FBI said, the man who had recruited Greenglass into the Soviet spy ring. In her home — whose library, reporters noted, included such volumes as "Stalin Must Have Peace" — Ethel Rosenberg denied everything. "I never heard anything like it, it's fantastic," she insisted. The bookshelf notwithstanding, she and her husband were "absolutely not" Communists, she said.

But in fact both had been full members of the local party some years earlier, had indeed often hosted meetings in their home. On Aug. 11, the FBI arrested housewife Ethel Rosenberg as well. Charged with conspiracy to commit espionage, the two of them went to trial in Manhattan Federal Court. "They have committed the most serious crime which could be committed against this country," prosecutor Irving Saypol told the jury.

On April 5, 1951, Judge Irving Kaufman sentenced them to death. Thousands of Americans were dead in Korea because of them, Kaufman said; "Millions more innocent people may pay the price of your treason," he snapped. En route to prison, Ethel Rosenberg sang an aria from "Madame Butterfly." Her husband sang "The Battle Hymn of the Republic."

'WE ARE AN ordinary man and wife," the condemned couple declared in October 1951. "We spoke for peace because we did not want our two little sons to live in the shadow of war and death."

That fall there was formed the National Committee to Secure Justice in the Rosenberg Case, which, by a year later, was a huge international movement built largely on charges of anti-Semitism. The Rosenbergs were Jews "judged by Jews" and "sent to death by other Jews," proclaimed leftist novelist Howard Fast — "exactly the old technique of the Jewish Tribunal employed by Hitler." Paul Robeson threw a Times Square rally that raised thousands of dollars. Trainloads of demonstrators paraded outside Sing Sing. In France — which still remembered the Dreyfus affair of the 1890s, and where the suggestions of anti-Semitism proved especially resonant — there

appeared posters of a grinning President-elect Eisenhower with a mouthful of tiny electric chairs instead of teeth.

Meanwhile, the Rosenbergs waited on Death Row through what would eventually be 22 appeals, visited monthly by their young sons, now being raised by Julius' mother. In February 1953, Eisenhower rejected pleas for clemency, and protest rallies erupted across the U.S. and Europe. The White House got more than 20,000 letters and telegrams urging mercy. The execution date was finally set for June 18.

On June 15, the Supreme Court ended its term by refusing to grant a stay. But two days later — as extra guards were posted outside U.S. embassies in Europe to hold back the shouting crowds — Justice William Douglas granted the stay on his own; citing a technical trial error, he called for the case to go back to district court. An enraged Georgia congressman immediately called for Douglas' impeachment.

That night, without bothering to inform Douglas, Chief Justice Fred Vinson called an extraordinary special session of the remaining justices to respond to their colleague's stay. On Friday morning, they set it aside.

Now a final plea for clemency from Eisenhower was all that was left. The hero general of World War II remained unmoved.

JULIUS AND ETHEL Rosenberg, the first American citizens to be put to death for espionage, were buried Sunday. Outside the I.J. Morris Funeral Home on Church Ave. in Brooklyn, lawyer Emmanuel Bloch told 8,000 mourners: "America today is living under the heels of a military dictatorship dressed in civilian garb."

EVIDENCE THAT surfaced after the breakup of the Soviet Union and the 1995 declassification of Venona, an Army encryption project begun in 1943, suggests that Julius Rosenberg did in fact pass atomic secrets to the Soviet Union. His wife's involvement remains less clear. An FBI memo of June 17, 1953, detailing what questions to ask Julius if he decided to talk, included this one: "Was your wife cognizant of your activities?" Two days before Ethel Rosenberg was executed, the FBI still sought to confirm that she even knew about the crimes for which she was about to die.

It also remains unclear whether or not the material David Greenglass confessed to passing to the Soviets particularly hastened their development of the A-bomb.

The Rev. John Corridan

CHAPTER 119

ON THE WATERFRONT
Longshoremen, 1953

Tough Tony Anastasio

By WILLIAM K. RASHBAUM
Daily News Staff Writer

ON A SUMMER Friday night in 1939, Brooklyn longshoreman Peter Panto told his fiance he had to meet some men to talk union business. He'd be back in an hour, he said, and then he'd help make sandwiches for next day's trip to the beach. And that was the last she saw of him.

Panto had been noisily fighting gangster rule to better working conditions on Brooklyn's piers, and, to the racketeers, he was a grave threat. He fought to the last — struggling fiercely with his killers, biting down to the bone on one of Mendy Weiss' stumpy fingers as the Murder Inc. hit man garroted him in a car.

The crusading 28-year-old leader of Brooklyn's rank-and-file dockworkers was buried in quicklime in New Jersey, one more victim of waterfront czar Albert Anastasia's unforgiving rule.

His was not the only body eventually exhumed from a makeshift Lyndhurst graveyard; Peter Panto's murder was just one of dozens that marked the struggle between workingmen on the waterfront and their long-corrupt union.

It was a struggle that continued for generations, pitting men desperate to feed their families against a well-entrenched gangster combine of dirty unions, crooked pols and dishonest elements of big business. And it played out on the piers, a lawless frontier beyond the reach of cops, judges and legislators.

Albert Anastasia and his brother Tough Tony Anastasio, who controlled six Brooklyn union locals, sneered at the law and lived like kings. On the docks, though, there were few winners and plenty of losers. And, while Peter Panto and others fought their skirmishes and died in the late 1930s and early 1940s, there remained one unlikely

waterfront warlord marshaling forces in the workingman's favor.

PART PHILOSOPHER, part economist, part propagandist and part crusader, the Rev. John Corridan was a socio-industrial critic with a unique perspective. A tall, ruddy, Harlem-born Irishman, policeman's son Corridan came to the waterfront from 15 years of Jesuitical study and contemplation. As executive director of the Xavier Labor School on W. 16th St., just blocks from the Hudson River piers, the priest saw both the desperate poverty that smothered the working longshoreman and the larger economic impact of racketeer unionism on the waterfront economy.

Corridan got to know the port, the roughly 1,800 piers spread across 750 miles of shoreline, where some 10,000 oceangoing ships cleared the harbor each year. They carried a million passengers through a port that each year saw 35,000 longshoremen handle 150 tons of cargo worth between $14 billion and $16 billion.

While the gangsters didn't steal it all, sometimes it seemed like they tried. In one case, they quietly drilled through a warehouse floor and drained the barrels of a valuable French wine shipment as unknowing watchmen stood around the precious casks.

Gangsters padded payrolls, doled out shylocking and bookmaking concessions on the piers to favored hoods and oversaw a thriving traffic in narcotics, illegal aliens and any other contraband on which they could turn a dollar.

And the pernicious hiring system that dominated the piers — the shapeup — left even honest men kicking back a portion of their meager wages to the corrupt hiring bosses, many of whom had long arrest records.

The priest knew more about which mob controlled which union local, which local controlled which pier and which pier controlled which hiring boss than some of the gangsters themselves. His voluminous files filled 16 well-worn cabinets along his office wall at Xavier.

Corridan watched a crippling wildcat dock strike in the fall of 1951 grind freight traffic to a halt in the most costly job action in the harbor's history. The economic repercussions reached around the globe and prompted the New York City Anti-Crime Committee to urge the governors of New York and New Jersey to wipe out gangster control of the International Longshoremen's Association.

By late 1952 and early 1953, it was the 41-year-old priest's understanding of the forces arrayed against him and his driving desire to improve the lot of the workingman that now fueled what had become his personal crusade.

HAVING SPENT six years focused on the harbor, Corridan understood the complex network of corrupt political and business relationships that formed the foundation for racketeer control of the gateway to the nation. And his cassock kept at bay the murderous hoods who had killed Peter Panto and many other men.

The New York State Crime Commission held public hearings from December 1952 to March 1953, when a subcommittee of the U.S. Senate Interstate and Foreign Commerce Committee held hearings on the New York-New Jersey waterfront. Corridan submitted an eight-point reform program to the state commission and later testified on Capitol Hill, where he told senators that maritime unions and industry had no will to rid the docks of crime.

By 1953, the Port of New York had

taken on the look of a police state. The city ultimately brought in some 1,500 cops to guard against expected violence as the struggle between honest longshoremen and their corrupt union heated up.

And when it got hot, Tough Tony Anastasio wasn't shy about playing dirty, leaving bodies floating in the river and smearing his opponents in a birthing new insurgent union as Communists. In November, there was a pitched battle on the Breakwater Pier in Brooklyn's Erie Basin, where workers from the new union ran a gantlet of Anastasio faithfuls. Club-swinging cops broke up the melee, and when it was over, one of Tough Tony's younger brothers, Gerardo (Bang Bang) Anastasia, who held sway in Erie Basin, was behind bars.

Shortly before Christmas, dockworkers were choking the streets in lower Manhattan and in Jersey City, lining up to choose either the old ILA or the new independent union to handle their collective bargaining. Three seamen were stabbed and four badly beaten as the racketeers sought to maintain control over the voting.

Roughly 20,000 dockworkers cast ballots — and the old mob-run ILA kept its grip, by a slim margin of 9,060 to 7,568. For now, gang rule would still prevail on the docks.

Meanwhile, though, the state and federal hearings had resulted in the adoption of the Waterfront Commission Act and Compact, which created a commission that required licensing of stevedoring businesses, pier superintendents, hiring agents and port watchmen.

The commission also required longshoremen to register and could deny those with significant criminal records or organized crime ties. It also eliminated the shapeup system and brought to the docks other reforms the Rev. Corridan had recommended.

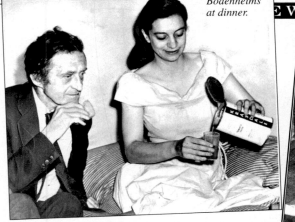

Bodenheims at dinner.

Room 27.

Harold Weinberg.

CHAPTER 120

MATTERS UNANNOUNCED

The Poet, 1954

By JAY MAEDER
Daily News Staff Writer

Death is a black slave, with little silver birds perched in a sleeping wreath upon his head. He will tell me, his voice like jewels dropped into a silver bag, how he has tiptoed after me down the road.

Maxwell Bodenheim

THEIR ROUTINE at the end of things was this: She, 35-ish and not altogether unattractive, would troll the Village bars for younger men until such time as one might suggest she follow him home. Whereupon the sodden older gentleman would stumble forlornly upon them, and she would gasp and explain, *He's a dear old friend, he seems to have fallen on unfortunate times,* and at this point her newfound companion would have to drag along the old coot as well. In this fashion did Mr. and Mrs. Maxwell Bodenheim sometimes secure themselves a night's flop.

Ruth sometimes picked up typing work, and old Bodenheim had his cane and his tin cup and his "I Am Blind" sign, and so the two of them kept body and soul together. So far as that went, Bodenheim could still turn out a comely phrase if so moved, and sometimes he would scribble down a poem on a napkin and trade it for a dollar or a couple of belts of rye whisky. Sometimes at the San Remo some pup would chuckle at the ancient scribbling specter, and his elders would admonish him, *That is Bodenheim,* and point to the backbar, where there hung photographs of Bodenheim taken 30 years earlier, when he had been vital and mesmerizing and an important figure in what had been called after the Great War the New Expressionism, before time had stolen him away and made of him only an apparition.

On the last afternoon of their lives, which was Saturday the 6th of February 1954, Bodenheim and Ruth were seen at the Waldorf cafeteria with a youth she had freshly collected, and before the three of them left, Bodenheim dashed off yet another napkin-poem and sold it. "It's a letter to Jesus," he announced grandly. "It's the last one I'll ever write," he said, and so it was.

BUT HADN'T IT been a time, once, briefly. In the Greenwich Village of the early 1920s, newly arrived from Chicago's avant-garde literary salons, silver-tongued Maxwell Bodenheim had cut quite the swath. He wrote, as the expression had it, "poems of passion." That meant "dirty." Anti-vice crusaders, blanching at his novel "Replenishing Jessica," tried hard to jail him on indecency charges. "The high priest of erotica," he got to be called. "Author of suppressed editions." Some of his more intimate musings went public when a woman named Dorothy Dear was killed in a subway crash and reporters found his letters to her spilled on the tracks; Bodenheim, tabloid readers discovered, was the sort of swain who encouraged his inamoratas to "walk on cobwebs stretched between the horns of the moon" and "wrap themselves in flower silences." In the Greenwich Village of the 1920s, a man could go places with lines like that.

Indeed, at least two other women had taken their own lives for the love of Bodenheim: One Aimee Cortez, known to some as the Mayoress of the Village, had turned on the gas rather than go on without him, and a young cobweb walker named Virginia Drew had hurled herself into the Hudson River after Bodenheim informed her that her poetry was terrible. Drew's very public demise, in July 1928, gave Bodenheim great sorrow, and to salve his pain he took off for Cape Cod with a comforting Brooklyn lass named Gladys Loeb. Gladys, alas, proved to be not of legal years. Chased down by her enraged father, Bodenheim beat it back to New York, Gladys panting lickety-split right behind him, and the newspapers had a wonderful time following the three of them around the Village as Bodenheim ducked in and out of this garret and that, indefatigably chased by both Gladys — "whose sighs could be heard for blocks," the Daily News reported — and the dogged Father Loeb. **SCRIVENING MAGNET OF MISSING MAIDS,** the papers whooped. **PURSUED PASH POET.** Bodenheim was a handsome rascal, it was true.

Hadn't it been a time. Then the Great Depression had suffocated Bodenheim, along with millions more souls. In 1933 he was in Washington Square Park with dozens of other threadbare artists, selling their work for pennies. In 1935 he led a brigade of writers into federal relief offices, declaring that it was the duty of the government to feed such cultural treasures as themselves. For a while he found sustenance with the Federal Writers Project. As late as 1939, he won a prestigious award from Poetry magazine. After that, Maxwell Bodenheim was done.

There was a dollar here and a dollar there. His collected poems were published in 1946, and then the paperback houses rediscovered some of his lurid early stuff. But he and the third wife, Ruth Fagin, were mostly sleeping in basements now, their belongings packed into a single suitcase. Bodenheim had his cup and his cane and his "I Am Blind" sign. She trolled the bars, winking at the fellows.

THE BUILDING was on Third Ave. near 12th St., and Room 27 measured 8 feet by 9 and went for $5 a week. The super found the two bodies Sunday. Ruth Fagin lay on the grubby bed, knifed again and again and again. Bodenheim was on the floor, mouth open, eyes staring, a bullet hole in his chest. In his effects were found a few scribbled crumbs, including this:

*We like to paste a label reading fate
On matters that are always unannounced,
But call it what you will, it is a great
Invisible, sharp stalker, and it pounced
Upon our lives within a rainy night.*

It took cops just a few days to run down the room's fugitive renter of record, Harold Weinberg, a 25-year-old dishwasher who had grown up in Rockland State Hospital and liked to say he was a pearl diver. As Weinberg told it, he and Ruth had been engaged in feverish lovemaking — "She was crazy about me," he boasted — when the whisky-soaked Bodenheim stirred from his stupor and lodged a protest, whereupon there had been nothing to do but shoot him. After that, of course, it was necessary to silence the cringing Ruth. She had been quick work. She was just a little thing.

In court, Weinberg shouted that the deceased had been nothing but a couple of Communist rats anyway. "I did the world a favor and I ought to get a medal," he screamed. Off he went to Bellevue, loudly singing "The Star-Spangled Banner."

CARL SANDBURG called from Chicago and Ben Hecht called from Beverly Hills, and on Wednesday the 10th of February, Maxwell Bodenheim had a proper funeral at Riverside Memorial Chapel uptown.

"There was something unconquerable about him," mourned Rabbi Edward Klein of the Stephen Wise Free Synagogue. "A refusal to compromise, which nothing could destroy. A will that maintained life at all costs. In that perhaps lies a man's true dignity.

"He beat in the air his luminous wings in vain."

After Harold Weinberg's room was cleaned out and Bodenheim's cup and cane and sign were carried to the trash, someone remembered another poem the squandered old man had written once:

*When evenings metaphysically pray
Above the weakening dance of man
They find
That every eye that looks at them is blind.*

William Gaines.

Sens. Thomas Hennings, Estes Kefauver and Robert Hendrickson, with subcommittee investigator Richard Clendenen.

CHAPTER 121

NO HARM IN HORROR

The Federal Comic-Book Inquiry, 1954

By JAY MAEDER
Daily News Staff Writer

THE MODERN NEWSSTAND comic book, an inexpensive pulpwood entertainment in the tradition of the Kit Carson thrillers, Nick Carter astonishers and Weird Tales hair-raisers that had electrified young readers since the War Between the States, was popularized in the spring of 1934 by a New York City entrepreneur named Max Gaines. Exactly 20 years later, his son and successor, William Gaines, sat twitchily in Room 110 of the United States Courthouse on Foley Square, pulling himself together to testify before several U.S. senators convened as the Senate Judiciary Committee's Subcommittee to Investigate Juvenile Delinquency.

In uneasy America on this Wednesday the 21st of April 1954, the Army-McCarthy hearings were roiling toward their conclusion, the Eisenhower administration mulled the imminent fall of the French in Indochina and Vice President Richard Nixon warned again of the Soviet nuclear peril. In this courtroom, the federal matter at hand was comic books, the 100 million or so of them bought every month by an estimated 98% of American children.

The subcommittee's official chairman was Robert Hendrickson, Republican of New Jersey, but its headline-making prosecutor was Sen. Estes Kefauver, Democrat of Tennessee, whose 1951 crime-committee hearings had made him a national figure, one who now aspired to the presidency. As for Bill Gaines, he was an obsessive dieter who relied on prescription amphetamines to get him through his days, and at this moment he was crashing hard.

WHEN MAX GAINES devised the 10-cent monthly magazine called Famous Funnies, his idea had been merely to reprint various of the day's popular newspaper comic strips. Subsequently there arose the concept of original material, notably including yarns that featured a costumed Kryptonian named Superman, and by the early 1940s the comic book was the most stupefyingly successful sensation in all magazine publishing. Beyond the Green Lanterns and Blue Beetles and Cyclones and Whirlwinds and Marvel Mans and the legions of other superpowered heroes who outran automobiles and butted their heads through walls, new genres arose: Western comics, airplane comics, true-crime comics, romances, science fiction, teen comedies, funny-animal cuddlies. Librarians and educators deplored every one of them, maintaining that even the likes of Classics Illustrated fostered rampant subliteracy, which doubtless they did every bit as much as Kit Carson and Nick Carter had done generations earlier.

Reading skills were the least of the alarms; deeper-thinking social scientists in the late '40s were positing a large range of subversions attributable to funny books. Among the fretters was New York psychiatrist Dr. Frederic Wertham, who insisted that Superman was a fascist vigilante who planted into impressionable minds disturbing notions about the appropriate administration of justice. Sheena and Zegra and Tegra and the other scantily clad jungle queens blatantly invited heavy-breathing lads to rip and plunder. Batman was plainly a homosexual dwelling with the fetching Robin in a Batcave paradise of pederasty.

The popular police books, meanwhile, disgracefully hiding behind such pious titles as Crime Does Not Pay and Crime Must Pay the Penalty, were manifestly nothing but how-to manuals for eager student criminals. Studying laboratory groups of behaviorally maladjusted youngsters, Wertham found it telling that *every single one of them read comic books.*

So did every other kid in America — not that this dissuaded Wertham from his theories that juvenile dysfunction was directly linked to the brightly colored 10-cent funny books openly for sale in every corner candy store. Propelled into the public eye by the New York Herald Tribune and the Saturday Review of Literature, which considered the doctor's ideas progressive, Wertham by 1948 was leading a noisy national crusade against the comic-book menace; across the land there erupted public comic-book bonfires sponsored by gravely concerned PTAs and women's clubs and American Legion posts.

Through 1950 and 1951, a New York State joint legislative committee solemnly investigated the question of whether comics publishers should be governmentally licensed. This board initially encouraged publishers to police themselves, but ultimately it sent several regulatory bills to Gov. Thomas Dewey, who kept finding them unlawful and vetoing them.

The uproar never went away. By the time the Senate's juvenile-delinquency subcommittee was formed in 1953, the scope of the comic-book investigations had become federal. In April 1954, a parade of publishers now trooped into Foley Square to defend themselves against charges that their products damaged young minds. Among them was William Gaines, who, as father of the horror genre, was among the anti-comics militants' chief targets in the first place — and who was today dope-addled, bewildered and combative, the personification of the creep publisher perfectly willing to poison the brains of America's children in order to pluck dimes from their fingers.

GAINES STARTED out offering reasoned Jeffersonian arguments, but he lost his way almost at once. Sitting behind him, his business manager, one Lyle Stuart, fleetingly considered trying to slip his boss a couple of furtive pills here in the federal courthouse. But there was nothing to be done. Stuart clapped his head and sank into his chair as Bill Gaines, in one wretched, inarticulate, drug-fogged moment under the hammerings of the crimebusting Estes Kefauver, basically destroyed the comic-book business all by himself.

"This seems to be a man with a bloody ax holding a woman's head up which has been severed from her body," said Kefauver, displaying the cover of a recent Gaines publication. "Do you think that is in good taste?"

"I do, for the cover of a horror comic," Gaines said. "A cover in bad taste, for example, might be defined as holding the head a little higher so that the neck could be seen dripping blood."

"You have blood coming out of her mouth," Kefauver said.

"A little," Gaines admitted.

Gaines the next morning made the front page of The New York Times — **NO HARM IN HORROR, COMICS ISSUER SAYS** — and a good many other newspapers. Amid the hue and cry, his fellow comics publishers didn't even bother to wait for the subcommittee's report; industry leaders immediately formed a self-regulatory group that banned crime and horror books and effectively folded most smaller publishers, within a year reducing the number of titles from the hundreds to the dozens.

Among those forced to give up most of his business was Bill Gaines, who in 1955 played his sole remaining card. He had one title left, a satirical journal called Mad, and he transformed it from a 10-cent comic book into a 25-cent magazine unaccountable to the new industry regulations, and Mad went on to become one of the American century's most cherished and influential cultural institutions, and Bill Gaines made millions of dollars. Estes Kefauver, meanwhile, did not become President.

By JAY MAEDER
Daily News Staff Writer

RIGHT BEFORE Christmas, Ham Fisher had driven over to Jersey to call on his old pal Morris Weiss, who was about the only soul left who could stand him anymore, and by now Weiss' patience was wearing thin too. Fisher was just one of those people: The more the world gave him, the unhappier he got. At 54 years of age, the fabulously successful proprietor of the world-famous "Joe Palooka" newspaper comic strip — creator of beloved prizefighter Joe, cigar-chomping fight manager Knobby Walsh, Ann Howe, Jerry Leemy, Humphrey Pennyworth and Little Max, whose daily adventures were followed by millions of readers around the world — had always been a tormented and self-absorbed man who talked about nothing but his ceaseless persecutions even during the good times. Now that he had been broken and publicly humiliated, he was unendurable.

Weiss had been putting up with Fisher for more than 20 years. Today he had plenty of work stacked up on his own drawing board, and he had no time to listen to much of this, and finally he showed Fisher the door.

"Help me," Fisher begged.

"Help yourself," Weiss said.

There was a long pause.

"I will," Fisher said.

NOW, ON TUESDAY the 27th of December 1955, Fisher's wife was phoning from Manhattan, distraught; she couldn't raise Ham at the studio; *please, would Weiss go find him. Please.* Weiss looked at the pile of work in front of him — these days he was ghosting the old "Mutt and Jeff" strip — and he sighed, and he drove into the city.

It was 9 p.m. At the dark studio on Madison Ave., Weiss found a janitor with a set of keys and had himself let in. On the daybed lay all that was mortal of Hammond Fisher. The pill bottle was empty. The ashtray was full of butts.

Weiss cursed and reached for the phone. There was one final remaining kindness he could perform for his impossible old friend. The first call went to the city desk of the New York Daily Mirror, the "Joe Palooka" flagship from day one, back in April 1930. Fisher would have wanted his paper to get the tip first.

Then Weiss called the cops and the widow.

THE SAD, PETTY business that had brought things to this point had begun in the summer of 1933, when Ham Fisher, who drove a shiny roadster and lived in a grand suite at the Parc Vendome, took on an impoverished young assistant named Alfred Caplin, who, because he was a much better artist than Fisher, was shortly producing most of "Joe Palooka." Fisher felt like the kid's patron, though he paid him practically nothing, and he couldn't believe it when Caplin one day announced that he was leaving his tightwad employ to go start a comic strip of his own.

That feature, in August 1934, turned out to be a hillbilly comedy called "Li'l Abner," and Fisher went purple as he saw that its leading man, Abner Yokum of Dogpatch, bore a remarkable resemblance to one of the "Joe Palooka" supporting characters, a hillbilly named Big Leviticus.

There was some question, actually, as to which one of them, Fisher or Caplin, had been more instrumental in developing Leviticus in the first place. Fisher acknowledged nothing of that; Abner Yokum, so far as he was concerned, was a grand theft of property, and he dedicated the rest of his life to loathing Abner's creator and informing everyone he met what a louse Caplin was. Periodically, whenever Leviticus made a "Palooka" appearance, Fisher would throw in a textblock announcing to his readers that Leviticus was the funny papers' true original hillbilly and that they should not be fooled by imitations.

The bad blood between the cartoonists got only worse as "Li'l Abner" fast became more than just a runaway favorite. Soon it was recognized as a modern satirical masterpiece, and Al Capp, as Alfred Caplin had renamed himself, emerged as

an authentic literary figure. He was all over Time and Newsweek and The New Yorker and Atlantic Monthly; he guest-hosted Drew Pearson's Washington column when Pearson vacationed; his parade of Dogpatch characters — Abner and Daisy Mae, Mammy and Pappy Yokum, Lonesome Polecat, Fearless Fosdick, Available Jones, Marryin' Sam, Joe Btfsplk, the Shmoos — were known to every adult and child in the land; his famous Sadie Hawkins Day mating rite was an annual college campus tradition. Ham Fisher couldn't stand it.

They crossed paths often, in the midtown watering holes and at National Cartoonists Society banquets, and the city's gossip columns were full of their snarling public donnybrooks. Their fellow cartoonists mostly shrugged the feud off; Capp and Fisher were both regarded as loud and unpleasant anyway, and neither was widely liked. This was just a spitting match between a couple of famous rich guys.

One day in 1950, after Capp had written a savage Atlantic piece recalling his impecunious early days as understudy to a dreadful cartoonist who went unnamed to the general reading public but who was entirely recognizable to many New Yorkers, a state legislative committee investigating pernicious influences in comic books received an anonymous package of blown-up photostats of "Abner" panels, doctored to seem semi-pornographic. The legislators were duly shocked. Their committee report specifically identified "Li'l Abner" as a salacious menace to public morals.

Ham Fisher and Joe Palooka.

Al Capp, Milton Caniff and Abner Yokum.

CHAPTER 122

SPITTING ON PICTURES

Funny Papers, 1955

THERE WAS NEVER a question that Fisher was responsible for the outrageous forgeries; everybody knew it. But, called on the carpet by the National Cartoonists Society to account for himself, he denied everything, and after a while the dust settled — until late 1954, when, as Al Capp sought a license for a Boston TV station, the Federal Communications Commission received an anonymous package of what appeared to be lascivious "Abner" drawings.

The resulting brouhaha forced Capp to withdraw his FCC application, and this time he demanded that the Cartoonists Society take formal action to censure the out-of-control Fisher. In February 1955, an NCS ethics committee headed by Milton Caniff, who did "Steve Canyon," and Walt Kelly, who did "Pogo," held hearings. Fisher refused to appear, sending his lawyer instead. In a matter of hours, Fisher was ordered suspended from the Society on grounds of conduct unbecoming a member and a gentleman.

In the circles in which Ham Fisher and Al Capp traveled, this was now the end of the world for Fisher. His 22-year feud with Capp was over. He had lost.

SEVERAL DAYS after Fisher's funeral, Lee Falk, who wrote the scripts for the comic strips "Mandrake the Magician" and "The Phantom," was joined at the bar at Sardi's by Al Capp, and the two comics men talked shop for a while, and eventually the conversation turned to the recent sorry demise of the man who had created "Joe Palooka."

Capp laughed the harsh laugh of the victor. "Ennobled it," he said. "He has ennobled our feud."

Capp turned to address the entire room. "He ennobled it," he brayed. "It is a noble thing he did."

Falk stared into his glass. *My God,* he said to himself. *The man thinks this is Tristan and Isolde.*

By DAVID HINCKLEY
Daily News Staff Writer

IT'S A CITY tradition: Infernal kids make a racket in the street, you poke your head out and tell them to pipe down.

Some music historians say the Teenagers, a singing quintet — Herman Santiago, Frankie Lymon, Jimmy Merchant, Joe Negroni and Sherman Garnes — never trooped up to 165th St. in 1955 to sing outside the apartment of Richard Barrett, a record producer they hoped could help them make a record.

Barrett would always contend that they did — that they even sang his songs, including "Lily Maebelle," a splendid jump tune recorded by Barrett and the Valentines in the hot rhythm and blues vocal group style.

By this account, he auditioned these kids purely to bring peace and quiet to his block.

By other accounts, he found them at Stitt Junior High School, where the Teenagers attended school and Barrett rehearsed the Valentines. By any account, their collaboration sparked more teenage street decibels than any event since World War II ended and newsboys yelled, "Read all about it!"

Barrett thought this rhythm and blues music, rapidly evolving into what was now being called rock 'n' roll, had potential way beyond the colored market. He also heard something in the Teenagers. Himself. Barrett knew his own singing could only go so far. He needed someone whose voice could explode off a vinyl record or out of a radio speaker. Someone from the generation buying that record.

Hello, Teenagers. Thank you, Jesus.

Alan Freed

The Paramount, Brooklyn

CHAPTER 123

YOU MIGHT GET ON THE RADIO

Rock 'n' Roll, 1956

BARRETT BROUGHT the group to George Goldner, a record label owner with an ear that almost, but not quite, kept him ahead of his weakness for the ponies. Goldner recently had been cashing in on the mambo craze and, once he heard that a kid named Santiago sang lead, was very much hoping the Teenagers were a Latin group.

Barrett informed him they weren't, whereupon, by Merchant's account, Goldner decided Herman sounded too Hispanic. But Goldner liked their song "Why Do Birds Sing So Gay?" and he asked who else could sing it.

Twelve-year-old Frankie Lymon didn't have to be asked twice.

So "Birds" was pepped up a little. Garnes, the bass, would kick it off by singing *Doom-bop a doom-bop a doom-bop a doom-bop.* The title was changed to "Why Do Fools Fall In Love?" and it was released on Jan. 10, 1956.

Vocal groups started sprouting up on every other street corner. Having a group was fun, it was cheap and it impressed girls. With the right break, you might get on the radio. The motivation didn't go much deeper than that.

The impact did.

EVER SINCE SINATRA a dozen years earlier, teenagers had been taking over popular music, which meant more songs on teenage love, its innocence and its hormones.

That they were now called rock 'n' roll rather than rhythm and blues made them only marginally less troubling to guardians of cultural and moral tradition — who couldn't hum a single line of "Sixty Minute Man," "Honey Love" or "Work With Me Annie," but knew this so-called jungle music induced teenagers to lose their already tenuous control over their basest urges.

WCBS deejay Bob Hayes called rock 'n' roll "poor music, badly recorded, with lyrics that are at best in poor taste . . . and at worst obscene. . . . This trend in music — and I apologize for calling it 'music' — is affecting the ideas and the lives of our children."

Sinatra himself chimed in: "It fosters almost totally negative and destructive reactions in young people."

Martin Block, who had institutionalized WNEW's "Make Believe Ballroom" 20 years earlier, said he "cringed" every time he had to play new music; current songs, he grumbled, were "abysmal." These kids, they only want a beat.

As if to prove his point, the 1955 movie "Blackboard Jungle" had served up Bill Haley's "Rock Around the Clock" as the martial music for a depraved band of juvenile delinquents who trash a New York high school.

Ironically, "Blackboard Jungle" had not sent nearly so rebellious a message as had 1954's "The Wild One," in which the lead bad guy was an incredibly charismatic Marlon Brando and the beautiful female lead was smothered into despair by idyllic post-war America.

But "Blackboard Jungle" flaunted rock 'n' roll, a clear and present danger. Police had to be summoned to Princeton — Princeton! — when students became disorderly after two undergraduates blasted "Rock Around the Clock" from their windows.

On the other hand, nothing stokes a teenage phenomenon faster than mortified adults, and a vanguard of rhythm and blues records like "Gee" and "Sh-Boom" had already begun seducing white teenagers.

Moreover, these teens could get it just by turning on the radio to the likes of Jocko, Dr. Jive, Doc Wade, Hal Jackson, Ramon Bruce — and Alan Freed.

FREED GOT HIS start in Cleveland in 1951, borrowing style and playlist from black jocks, and in late 1953 he was picked up on tape by WNJR in Newark, which was up to 18 hours of R&B a day.

Freed's first WNJR event, a dance at Newark's Sussex Ave. Armory on May 1, 1954, drew so many kids there was no room to dance. Morever, a quarter of the audience was white, and in September 1954 WINS lured Freed to New York for $75,000 a year — about three times what Mickey Mantle was making.

At Easter 1955, Freed's stage show at the Brooklyn Paramount grossed $107,000, breaking a record set by crooner Russ Colombo in 1932. Freed's end-of-summer show there grossed $178,000, and the crowd's mood, said the trade paper Billboard, "was that of Times Square on New Year's Eve. The kids were screaming and shouting and added to the pandemonium with noisemakers and cowbells."

So when the Teenagers arrived, the stage was set for a bunch of upbeat kids with exuberant voices who made cameras sing and girls swoon.

"Fools" reached No. 6 nationally, stayed on the charts for 21 weeks and made it clear Elvis Presley wasn't the only one who would be entering the rock 'n' roll door.

The Teenagers split up in mid-1957. Frankie Lymon's solo career flopped, and he died of a drug overdose in 1968.

By JAY MAEDER
Daily News Staff Writer

Harry and Bert

Bob and Ray

AS GOOD BEER had been perhaps the single most fundamental bedrock of civilization since the dawn of time, it was entirely to be expected that the Dutch would start building breweries in Nieuw Amsterdam about five minutes after they landed. Indeed, there was very quickly an entire street known as the Brouwer Straat (renamed Stone St. after it occurred to someone to pave it), and, as the generations rolled on, numerous of the city's great beermakers left enduring legacies in the wake of their passage: Cortlandt St. and Van Cortlandt Park, for example, after old Stevenson van Cortlandt the good; Rutgers University across the river after Rutgers Jacobsen van Schoenderwoerdt. William Beekman, in a splendid burst of public-spiritedness, bequeathed his name to not one but two streets ("William" and "Beekman").

Time passed. New Yorkers were chiefly imbibing ales and stouts and porters of the English style until the 1840s, when German braumeisters began to arrive on these shores with the lagers devised by their ingenious Bavarian forebears. Among these Germans were three brothers, Gottfried and Wilhelm and Michael Piel, who in 1883 set up shop in the farmlands of East New York and set about slaking the New World's great thirst.

Time passed, and there came 14 years of Prohibition, at the conclusion of which in March 1933 there were in New York City just 14 beer producers eligible for relicensing: Ruppert, Eicher, Fidelo, Lion and Loewer's Gambrinus in Manhattan; Rubsam & Horrmann on Staten Island; and, in Brooklyn, Schaefer, Hittleman, Interboro, Liebmann, Michael, North American, Trommer and Piel Bros., all companies that had somehow survived the long dry years in the manufacture of soda pops and breakfast cereals. Many other firms had gone under. Others, to be sure, did not win licenses, including Owney Madden's Phoenix Brewery in Manhattan and Dutch Schultz' several enterprises in the Bronx.

Time passed, and now it was 20 years later, and the Big Three, Schlitz and Pabst and Anheuser-Busch, had a solid lock on the national market. In New York there now remained just four of the smaller breweries that had once upon a time heartily sent out foaming pails on wagons to serve the city's needy saloons. There were Schaefer and Ruppert and Liebmann, maker of fine Rheingold. And there was the ever-constant Piels.

Piels was selling about a million barrels a year in the mid-1950s, hardly a major player but still prized across the Northeast as one of those lower-end, "popularly priced" regional brands whose market had always been the working classes. Now, in 1955, Piels was about to revolutionize the uncharted new field of television advertising and give New Yorkers two of their most memorably beloved institutions.

BERT AND HARRY PIEL were invented by a Young & Rubicam copywriter named Ed Graham, who one day took a hard look at the Piels commercials, which were full of stupefyingly solemn numbers demonstrating that Piels was not fattening, and decided that something else might be called for here. In 1955, the flannel-suited wizards of Madison Ave. still knew from pretty much nothing but the traditional hard sell, and Graham's elders shook their heads when he and artist Jack Sidebotham came up with a couple of

CHAPTER 124
SUDS
Bert And Harry Piel, 1956

cartoon characters who did not so much pitch Piels beer as do bits around it. This was, well, creative. This wasn't the way things were done.

Graham persevered. Finally, he got a green light for a test campaign to be run in Harrisburg, Pa., and upstate Binghamton. Now he needed voices. He went straight to a couple of morning-radio pals of his, Bob Elliott and Ray Goulding.

Bob and Ray had arrived from Boston in 1951 with a full repertory company of characters: Bumbling newsman Wally Ballou, daffy nutritionist Mary McGoon, terrible ballroom bandleader Herbie Waitkus, anyone else they felt like making up from one minute to the next and adding to a collection of voices that climbed the full range from booming basso profundo to the more distant falsettos. Bob and Ray lampooned the popular radio dramas ("Mary Backstayge, Noble Wife"; "The Lives And Loves Of Linda Lovely"; "Steel Flint, Interstellar Officer's Candidate") and they skewered commercials ("Do you inhale when you smoke ham?"). Such improv comedy was nothing that most people had ever heard before, and Bob and Ray demolished New York City immediately. Manifestly the two of them had been put here on Earth to do Bert and Harry Piel, and Ed Graham demanded them from the first minute. The elders at Young & Rubicam insisted on auditioning several dozen other voices first, but finally agreed that Graham was probably right.

In the summer of 1955, Bert and Harry tried out in the two burg markets, and Piels sales instantly went through the roof.

BY THE SPRING of 1956, Bert and Harry were seen all over the Northeast and they were the most astonishingly successful salesmen TV advertising had ever known. People stayed home rather than miss their spots. "We

never thought we would see the day that viewers actually enjoyed watching a TV commercial," commented Daily News TV columnist Kay Gardella. Ray Goulding did the bombastic Bert, Bob Elliott the mild little Harry, and hundreds of thousands of people thought the brothers were real. Graham came up with full bios for both of them: Bert had attended Samuel J. Tilden High School and had once been a sales manager for Paige motorcars; Harry was a bachelor chemist who had developed "a colloidal suspension which causes cellulose to congest," this being the trade secret behind that great taste of Piels. They never really tried to sell much beer, mostly just fussed at one another. There were Bert and Harry fan clubs. People wrote them letters. By the end of 1956, when Bert and Harry grumpily presided over a giveaway contest whose grand prize was an actual Bahamian island, Piels sales were up 21%.

Suddenly they were, by themselves, reshaping the nature, the viewpoint and the temperament of TV advertising. "The day could come when TV commercials might be no worse than most of the shows," mused News writer Worth Gatewood.

LATE IN 1960, more than 100 spots later, Young & Rubicam dumped Bert and Harry and launched a new campaign featuring outdoorsy live actors. More than 1.5 million customers wrote irate letters and Piels sales plummeted; two years later, dolefully acknowledging one of the biggest blunders in the history of advertising, Y&R briefly attempted to bring the brothers back.

By now, though, the small brewery was disappearing into history; there were 725 U.S. beermakers in 1934, 440 in 1949, 225 in 1962. Pabst's Blatz, Schlitz' Old Milwaukee and Anheuser-Busch's Busch Bavarian were taking over the lower-end, buck-a-sixpack beer market, and Piels was quietly sold in 1962 to a British conglomerate.

By JAY MAEDER
Daily News Staff Writer

JERSEY LABOR kingpin Joey Fay was out of the big house just two months now, paroled on strict condition that he have nothing further to do with union business, and already he was hard at work pulling strings, and the Daily Mirror's labor man was on the story. Meanwhile, there was still a great stench wafting from International Operating Engineers Local 138 out on Long Island, now that Boss William DeKoning had finished his own prison term for shaking down building-boom contractors, and Victor Riesel was on top of that too. Riesel's column ran in 193 newspapers, and America's labor thugs were blinking in the most unwelcome glare, particularly now that Manhattan U.S. Attorney Paul Williams had mounted two rackets grand juries and Riesel was going to be a star witness before both of them. These probes, Riesel promised his readers, could very well lead to "the Mr. Bigs of the American crime syndicate."

Now it was 12:10 a.m., Thursday the 5th of April 1956. Pinch-hitting for WMCA overnight man Barry Gray, Victor Riesel brought on Peter Batalias and William Wilkens, two Local 138 mavericks who had been beaten up for bucking the DeKoning gang. "It's a tough mob, and it's tied in with the toughest mobs in New York and Chicago," Riesel announced, adding, in a salute to the union rebels: "It's a lot more difficult to be a celebrity when it means taking your life in your hands, when it means that you might come home to your wife and kids with your head batted in." In point of fact, so routinely nervous were Batalias and Wilkens that at 2 a.m., when Riesel concluded the broadcast from Hutton's restaurant at Lexington Ave. and 47th St., they immediately looked under the hood of their car to satisfy themselves that no bomb had been planted while they were on the air.

They were fine. As for Riesel, though, as he and his secretary drove over to Lindy's at Broadway and 51st St., the two of them were quietly followed by a young man carrying a vial of sulphuric acid.

NATHAN RIESEL of the Bronx was active all his life in the embroiderers union and he often took his son along to meetings. In March 1930, the youth found his life's work as he watched grown men weep, jobless, unable to feed their families. Working by day in a hat plant here and a lace factory there, Victor Riesel by night took City College classes in industrial relations for 12 years and along the way began to write for labor publications. By 1940 he was managing editor of The New Leader. By 1942, the same year in which his father was crippled for life by International Ladies Garment Workers Union goons, he was labor columnist for the New York Post.

After the Post dropped him in 1950, Riesel landed at the much larger Daily Mirror and his syndicated "Inside Labor" column became much-quoted in the halls of Congress, particularly as he cranked up the shrillness of his attacks on union Reds. In January 1951, Democratic Rep. Louis Heller of New York waved a Riesel column as he introduced a bill to investigate Communist infiltration of merchant seamen. In 1951 and 1952, Riesel worked with Democratic Nevada Sen. Pat McCarran in a probe of the 35,000-member United Public Workers of America, which the columnist declared was ruled by Moscow and under orders "to capture the government agencies." In 1952, he told the Senate Internal Affairs Subcommittee that New York Local 65 of the Distributive, Processing and Office Workers of America was run by "Kremlin agents" masterminding a "reign of

CHAPTER 125

DARK PLACES
Victor Riesel, 1956

BATTLE TO SAVE RIESEL'S SIGHT

$13,000 Reward for Thug's Arrest

Acid Attacker Hunted

terror," and the Senate demanded that U.S. union officials sign non-Communist affidavits. Red fiends aside, he annoyed plain old hoodlums as well. In 1952, Tough Tony Anastasio of the Brooklyn docks tried to sue Riesel for $1 million after the columnist called him a corrupt mobster. The suit went nowhere, since that's what Tough Tony was.

By the spring of 1956, as the 41-year-old Riesel worked hand-in-hand with federal prosecutor Williams in the most ambitious assault on New York's garment, trucking and other rackets in a couple of decades, this was a man well advised to watch his back. But at 3 a.m. on Thursday the 5th of April, as Riesel and secretary Betty Nevins left Lindy's and walked to Nevins' car, parked in front of the nearby Mark Hellinger Theater, the columnist was paying little attention as a figure suddenly appeared from out of the shadows.

The acid got Riesel squarely in the eyes. "Caught flat-footed," he cursed himself as he was rushed to St. Clare's Hospital, clawing at his face. "I feel like a chump."

THUNDERED U.S. Attorney Williams: "I have now declared all-out war on racketeers, gangsters and hoodlums." Gov. Averill Harriman vowed "to put an end to mob activities and end any intimidation of free speech." Mayor Robert Wagner called summits to address modern industrial racketeering in New York. New York reporters dug into their pockets and put up $14,000 in reward money. Local 138, insisting it had no hand in the attack, added $1,000 of its own: "This is a very embarrassing situation," reckoned William DeKoning Jr., who had succeeded his old man as the local's president. So it was: At this very moment, at the Operating Engineers' national convention in Chicago, Joey Fay was in fact seeking to reestablish himself, and the Riesel

headlines effectively prevented him from doing so.

Detectives meanwhile worried what Riesel's blinding might mean to the rackets inquiry's witnesses. "A beating might have scared off a few," said one. "A shooting might have scared some. But the effects of such attacks would have worn off before too long and some witnesses would still come forth. But the horror of acid in the eyes has such a permanent frightening effect — the probes may collapse."

"The challenge has been laid down flatly and cynically," said the Daily Mirror. "It is a challenge against all men who believe in decency and the rule of law. It is a return of the Al Capone era. It is the simple, bald determination on the part of the underworld to have its own way and maintain its fabulously profitable rackets by terror and death, and in defiance of the law.

"ARE WE TO BE RULED BY THE MOBS OR BY LAW?

"The scum who plotted this cruel attack may rob a man of his eyes — but not of his vision."

Victor Riesel's column, the paper proudly declared, "will be continued without lapse by Mr. Riesel and his staff."

LATE IN JULY, *a nickel-and-dime hood named Abraham Telvi was found shot dead on Mulberry St. Investigators established that Telvi had been paid a few hundred dollars for the acid attack and had subsequently decided it was worth $50,000, thus earning himself his dispatch. Ultimately it was concluded that garment racketeer Johnny Dio, a prime target of Williams' grand juries, had ordered the job, though Dio was never prosecuted.*

Victor Riesel, blinded for life, continued to report on American labor for several more decades.

By DAVID HINCKLEY
Daily News Staff Writer

COME THE LAST week or so of a mediocre season, a baseball player mostly wants to get it over with, to get home and think about next spring, when everyone starts even.

So when the Brooklyn Dodgers were obliged to host the Pittsburgh Pirates for a game of baseball on the chilly evening of Sept. 24, 1957, everyone did so as efficiently as possible. Batters stayed in the box, swung at the first decent pitch and the game was over in two hours and three minutes.

The Dodgers won, 2-0, over a Pirate team notable only for having a young Roberto Clemente in center field. For the home team, Elmer Valo doubled in the first inning to score Junior Gilliam, and Gil Hodges singled in the third to drive in Gino Cimoli.

And those were the last runs ever scored in a major league baseball game in Brooklyn.

PROFESSIONAL ball had been played in Brooklyn since May 9, 1871. That's when the Brooklyn Eckfords took the field at Williamsburg's Union Grounds, America's first enclosed baseball park.

The Eckfords were followed by the Atlantics, the Hartfords, the Bridegrooms and the Brooklyn Wonders of the Players League. The Bridegrooms and the Wonders used Eastern Park, next to Jamaica Bay, and fans had to dodge a fleet of trolleys to reach the entrance, inspiring the term "Trolley Dodgers."

The Bridegrooms joined the National League in 1890 and became the Superbas in 1898, a year before Wee Willie Keeler led them to the championship with a .379 batting average and two years before Iron Man Joe McGinnity led them to a repeat with a 29-9 pitching record.

In 1913, owner Charles Ebbets moved the team from Washington Park, hard by the Gowanus Canal, to a new park in the old Pigtown section.

Ebbets Field was bordered by Montgomery St., Bedford Ave. and McKeever and Sullivan places. It was a park with character, and characters filled it. The Dodger Sym-Phony Band in Section 8, Row 1, playing "Three Blind Mice" for the umpires. Hilda Chester and her cowbells.

On the field, the Dodgers were character-building. No matter how good they were, and starting around 1941 they were very good, they always made one fatal misstep. By the 1950s, the tragedy was downright Shakespearean.

Dem Bums, dey was called, as in "Dem bums blew it again." Brooklyn loved them. Whatever anyone else had, Brooklyn had Dem Bums.

And in 1955, they finally went all the way. Duke Snider hit four home runs, Roy Campanella added a pair,

Walter O'Malley and Horace Stoneham

Johnny Podres pitched two gems and Sandy Amoros somehow ran down Yogi Berra's slicing drive to clinch Game 7.

But now, less than two years later, it was clear that even as the players and fans were still dancing their victory dance, club owner Walter O'Malley was thinking how the words "Los Angeles" would look on the Dodger letterhead.

THE DODGERS and New York City had been talking about a new park since 1947, amid general agreement that old Ebbets was small and rickety and lacked parking. There were also whispers about the state of the neighborhood. So the city would provide new land, and O'Malley would build on it.

The Dodgers designed a 55,000-seat stadium, with a plexiglass dome by Buckminster Fuller. The Dodgers and the Brooklyn Board of Estimate thought this would look swell at Flatbush and Atlantic Aves., near the LIRR.

Unfortunately, one man disagreed,

CHAPTER 126

AULD LANG SYNE

Dem Bums Go West, 1957

The end of Ebbets Field.

and that man was Robert Moses, who basically held veto power over any city project budgeted at more than $250.

Moses, convinced that in the new America everyone would drive everywhere, foresaw only traffic jams in Brooklyn. He wanted a ballpark in Flushing Meadows, Queens, where he was, as usual, building a bunch of parkways.

It was at this point that O'Malley began looking at other sites — like Los Angeles. He sold off Ebbets Field to a developer and in 1956 bought the minor league Los Angeles Angels, giving him a foothold and a park. And he talked Horace Stoneham into moving his Giants to San Francisco so the Dodgers would have company in the Pacific time zone.

Yet, on Tuesday night the 24th of September in 1957, O'Malley was still publicly insisting he had not yet decided what he was going to do with his club.

No one believed him for a minute. His critics — a list that pretty much mirrored the Brooklyn phone book — were sure he had wanted to move at least since 1953, when the Boston Braves bolted for Milwaukee and attendance shot up 50%. In Los Angeles, O'Malley saw rapid-growth virgin turf he didn't want someone else claiming first. He saw a market where he didn't have to put his

games on free TV. He saw 300 acres of downtown land.

The drama had long ago become so depressing, the outcome so bitter, that on Sept. 24, only 6,702 fans showed up for what everyone knew was the last game.

Organist Gladys Goodding played "Am I Blue," "After You're Gone," "Don't Ask Me Why I'm Leaving," "When I Grow Too Old To Dream," "How Can You Say We're Through," "If I Had My Way" and "Que Sera, Sera." As the fans filed out, she played "Auld Lang Syne."

At the same moment, the grounds crew came out, raked the infield dirt smooth and covered the pitcher's mound — all the steps to ready the field for the next game. It was a ghostly ritual, not unlike a convict flossing en route to the electric chair.

ON FRIDAY THE 27th, Brooklyn Chamber of Commerce President Chester Allen appeared before his counterparts in Los Angeles. "The Dodgers were not built by baseball players," he said. "They were built by the people of Brooklyn. The Dodgers are a way of life. If the Dodgers play here, all you have is a bird in a gilded cage. The Dodgers will die in Los Angeles and in any other town outside Brooklyn because they are Brooklyn and belong only in Brooklyn."

On Oct. 9, after the sixth game of the World Series, Walter O'Malley's flack Red Patterson walked into the baseball writers' pressroom and posted a notice that the National League's Brooklyn franchise was being transferred to Los Angeles.

THE NEXT PITCH at Ebbets Field came on Feb. 23, 1960, when a wrecking ball painted with baseball stitches reduced a corner of Brooklyn's soul to landfill. Forty-one years later, the view is still widely held in Brooklyn that the three most evil men of the 20th century have been Adolf Hitler, Joe Stalin and Walter O'Malley.

Frank Costello, nicked

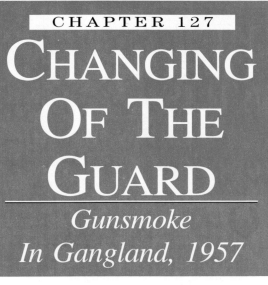

Albert Anastasia, whacked

Vito Genovese, pinched

By JAY MAEDER
Daily News Staff Writer

THE PRIME MINISTER of the Underworld had spent several pleasant hours in a Turkish bath at the Hotel Biltmore, then dined with friends at exclusive L'Aiglon on E. 55th St., then taken a cab back home to the swank Majestic Apartments on Central Park West at 71st St., and he was just letting himself into the lobby when a 300-pound gunman appeared at the top of the foyer steps and fired a single .38 bullet. This, at shortly before 11 p.m. on Thursday the 2nd of May 1957, was the first slug openly fired at a top-level crime boss in a quarter of a century.

End of an era, authorities agreed. *Young Turks rising up against washed-up old men.* These were the guys who had taken out the old Mustache Petes; now it was their turn to go. "A clear underworld signal that a new and brutal power is challenging the old guard of Prohibition mobsters to a finish fight," said the Daily News. Frank Costello, miraculously only grazed, politely insisted to cops that he hadn't seen nothing. "I don't have an enemy in the world," he said. "I must have been mistaken for somebody else." Presently, when one Vincent (The Chin) Gigante was picked up for the bumbled shooting, the Prime Minister found himself unable to make identification.

What authorities did not know was that by now Frank Costello — 65 years old, in failing health and nibbled to death by income tax prosecutions — was already getting out of the rackets voluntarily, that, in fact, the elders of the Unione Sicilione had approved his quiet retirement to his grand home at Sands Point, L.I. It was not known that the Costello hit was not the work of Young Turks but of 60-year-old Don Vito Genovese, who was now making a crazed play for boss-of-bosses supremacy and who deemed Costello, on his way out or not, a visible symbol of Charles (Lucky) Luciano's regime-in-exile. It was not known that, in sunny Italy, Luciano had long been troubled by Genovese's naked ambitions and that, upon learning of his old friend Costello's narrow squeak, had immediately sent word to loyalist Albert Anastasia that perhaps he should exercise some caution as well.

STILL THE much-feared Lord High Executioner, for the record a dressmaker by trade, although one who was believed to have killed 30 men, 55-year-old Albert Anastasia left his elegant Palisades home on Bluff Road in Fort Lee, N.J., on Friday morning the 25th of October, drove into the city and stopped for a haircut at the Park Sheraton Hotel at Seventh Ave. and 55th St. The

CHAPTER 127

CHANGING OF THE GUARD

Gunsmoke In Gangland, 1957

Park Sheraton had once been called the Park Central; kingpin Arnold Rothstein had been shot to death here in 1928. At the barbershop, Anastasia was expecting to be met by a bodyguard, Tony Coppola, but it seemed the bodyguard was running late today.

At 10:30, as Anastasia sat toweled in Chair 4, two black-gloved men strode into the shop and walked straight up to him. The Lord High Executioner got an instant to grasp that he was about to die, and in that instant he was on his feet, fists up. But five bullets were already chopping him down.

Present at the time were two other customers, five barbers, a manicurist and a couple of bootblacks, and every one of them hadn't seen nothing. "I never saw so many blind people in my life," grunted Chief of Detectives James Leggett. Bodyguard Coppola, pulled in, proved to be a man who literally knew how to say, "I don't know nothing" in 19 different languages. Frank Costello refused to talk to police at all.

Many mob experts now decided that Vito Genovese, widely viewed as the apparent inheritor of gangland leadership at this point, was doubtless the next prime target of all these bloodthirsty Young Turks.

ON THURSDAY THE 14th of November, dozens of large black automobiles carrying cigar-smoking, silk-suited men who were discernibly not locals arrived in the tiny western New York community of Apalachin on the

Pennsylvania border and made for the 100-acre estate of Canada Dry bottling czar Joseph Barbara. According to the official State Police story, this startling parade caught the attention of sharp-eyed Sgt. Edgar Croswell, who called in backups. What followed was organized crime's single greatest public humiliation, as Croswell's raiders closed in on Barbara's backyard barbecue and the distinguished leaders of the national crime syndicate threw down their drinks and identity papers and went scrambling pell-mell into the surrounding forests — "like small-town gamblers fleeing a dice game," The News reported — straight into the arms of amused country cops who hauled them all to the jug.

Authorities couldn't believe it. Here in one net were 60-some fish: Joe Bonanno, Joe Profaci, Jerry Catena, Vincent Rao, Carlo Gambino, Paul Castellano, Vito Genovese himself. There was nothing in particular to charge them with, and one by one they were freed, but in Washington, the Senate rackets committee's general counsel, a young prosecutor named Bobby Kennedy, expressed his great interest in the rounded-up parties and announced that all would be hearing from him shortly.

Meanwhile, it was noted that several other key figures — Frank Costello and Meyer Lansky, for example — were quite conspicuously absent from the underworld powwow. Notwithstanding the widely broadcast story of the vigilant Sgt. Croswell, some observers wondered if perhaps some anonymous prankster had picked up a phone and dropped a dime on Vito Genovese.

THE EXACT PURPOSE of the Apalachin Conference was not formally established. If Don Vito had indeed expected to crown himself king, he was shortly disabused of the notion; the nation's mob leaders held him very much accountable for the bungled soiree, and even those who had been inclined to side with his agenda were now not swift to forgive his having made public buffoons out of them, not to mention Senate targets.

A year after the remarkable events of 1957, Genovese was arrested in what by any measure was a cheap drug deal hardly worth the attention of a man of his stature. This was an exquisite setup, personally engineered by Lucky Luciano to rid himself of the Genovese nuisance. Signing off on this brilliant contract, Frank Costello attached a provision that sharpshooter Vincent Gigante should take a fall as well, and this was okay by Charlie Lucky. Both Genovese and Gigante got long prison terms, and Genovese died behind the wall. In the end, a sort of mob justice really did somewhat decently prevail.

Fischer and Tigran Petrosian in Moscow.

CHAPTER 128

THE GENIUS

Bobby Fischer, 1958

By CORKY SIEMASZKO
Daily News Staff Writer

THE BOY WONDER was just 14 years old, a Brooklyn comet streaking across the skies of the rarefied world of chess.

Bobby Fischer's sister had taught him the game when he was 6. By the time he turned 12, he was taking on all comers at the Brooklyn Chess Club. He was the prized pupil of club President Carmine Nigro, who taught his prodigy to play fast by pitting him against the chess hustlers in Washington Square Park and staging exhibition matches where Fischer would take on — and beat — 25 opponents at a time.

At 13, Fischer won the National Junior Chess Championship by besting opponents who were at least five years older than he was. The newspapers took notice. BOY CHESS WIZARD, they called him. REAL KING IN THE REALM OF CHESS. "Gee," Fischer said. "It's just a game. I don't see what everybody is making such a fuss about."

The fuss became a phenomenon Jan. 8, 1958, when Fischer crushed 13 of the nation's top players at the Manhattan Chess Club and won the U.S. chess championship.

Now the papers hailed the Erasmus High School sophomore as a genius, likening his chess feats to a sport more readers understood — baseball — with comparisons to the likes of Duke Snider and Roy Campanella.

"Brooklyn has itself a new triple crown winner," Douglas Sefton of the Daily News crowed.

The American chess world was "aghast with wonder, admiration, envy, an excitement, generated by his result of 13 games played without a loss against the very best players of the nation," wrote chess expert Arthur Bisguier.

"Bobby's victory is simply immense," noted the Chess Review.

Fourteen-year-old Bobby Fischer was now the "player of the century," experts agreed — America's best chance to become a chess superpower on par with the Soviet Union, where masters of the game were treated like movie stars by everyone from the Politburo to the peasantry.

QUITE OBVIOUSLY he was a genius, but on the other hand he was just a kid, and uneasy with his fledgling celebrity. Or, to put it another way, he was a little snot.

The local press played him up as a strange youngster who read nothing but chess books and horror comics, didn't go to the movies, had few friends and didn't seem to want any. He just wanted to play chess. "I'd like to play chess all the time," he said.

With the exceptions of Spanish and science, in which he excelled, he was just an average student who had no interest in going to college. He ate lots of spaghetti and drank lots of Coca-Cola. These mundane details were recorded because Fischer truculently refused to give reporters much of anything else. "I have no objection to being interviewed," he said. "It's just that I don't like what's printed. They do it on purpose to make chess players look like funny people. The more facts I give you, the more they can be twisted."

Accordingly, he would not allow reporters to visit him at the three-room Lincoln Place apartment he shared with his mother, Regina, and older sister, Joan. He had nothing to say about his father, who had abandoned the brood when he was a toddler. He didn't have anything much nice to say about mom and sis, either.

"She doesn't even know the moves," he laughed of his mother. "I've tried to teach her, but no hope.

"Girls can't play," he said. "I don't know, they haven't enough patience."

Nor did he appear particularly grateful to his patron, Nigro. "Sure I beat Mr. Nigro," he chortled.

So he wasn't pleasant. But he sure could play chess.

IN JUNE, the young national champ made an exhibition tour to chess heaven — Moscow. The Soviets proved reluctant to let such a youth play their top-ranking masters and tried instead to match him with some lesser lights, whereupon he angrily stomped out of his scheduled engagements.

It wasn't until he landed in Yugoslavia in September to compete in his first international tournament that he got the reception due an American champion.

Normally circumspect chess fans burst into applause and vaulted over the railings to snag an autograph when the crew-cut teen traipsed out into the playing area to take on some of the world's best players gathered in the Adriatic resort city of Portoroz.

Fischer was ensconced in a suite in one of Belgrade's finest hotels, and chess officials supplied him with two of the country's best players — so he could have somebody with whom he could practice.

"Belgrade is a wonderful city," Fischer said.

He rewarded his hosts with a dazzling display of chess expertise. For hours he sat over the board, pondering at great length before making a move that left aficionados gasping. At other moments, he roamed the hall, cracking his knuckles and biting his fingernails while his befuddled opponents tried to counter him. He finished fifth in this event, good enough to catapult him into the ranks of the international chess masters — the youngest player to make it there.

Afterward, he sent a cable to his mother, instructing her to tell the principal at Erasmus he would not be coming straight home and that he would miss the first week of school.

Grace Corey, an administrative assistant at Erasmus, was much distressed to hear about this. "It will be very difficult to make up the work he lost," she clucked.

As if Bobby Fischer cared. A few days after he turned 16, he quit school.

By DAVID HINCKLEY
Daily News Staff Writer

THERE WERE 390 murders tallied by New York City police in 1959, and the Cape Man did only two of them. But these two shook loose the city's worst nightmares.

Because Salvatore Agron killed two people he didn't know. Because when he was captured, he said he didn't care. Because he was 16 years old. Because he belonged to a street gang. And it didn't help that he was Puerto Rican.

"How do you feel about killing those boys?" a reporter asked when cops gave the press a quick shot at him.

"Like I always feel," the kid said. "Like this."

"Are you sorry?"

"That's for me to know and you to find out."

"Do you feel like a big man?"

"Do *you*?"

"Was it worth killing a kid to be here talking into a mike?"

"I feel like killing you," Agron sneered. "That's how I feel."

Sal Agron started the night of Sunday the 30th of August as a fashion statement: dark blue, red-lined, Dracula-style cape, fancy buckled shoes. He ended it as the city's most wanted man.

When the Cape Man stabbed Robert Young and Anthony (Skinny) Krzesinski a few minutes after midnight in a W. 45th St. playground, he made it impossible to deny a dark secret in the sunny world of the late '50s: America was terrified of its children.

NEW YORKERS WERE especially terrified of other people's children — including the children of the hundreds of thousands of Puerto Ricans who had been arriving by the planeload since the mainland, in a burst of postwar concern for its impoverished island territory, launched *Manos a la Obra,* or Operation Bootstrap.

That program sought to convert Puerto Rico from an agricultural to a light industrial economy, which involved among other things encouraging displaced farmers to come live in American cities, where thriving factories paid more in a day than sugar cane might yield in a month.

The problem was that some new arrivals did not dutifully report to the factory, but to the welfare office. Some of the children, not old enough to work and not comfortable in a big, noisy, new city where they didn't yet speak the language, saw street hustling and gangs as a faster path than schoolwork to yanking up their own bootstraps.

In truth, this didn't distinguish Puerto Ricans from the Irish or Italians of decades earlier. But Puerto Ricans were more visible at the moment: By 1959, the Puerto Rican population of New York was 642,000, more than half of whom had arrived in the previous 10 years.

Moreover, what many people knew about Puerto Ricans came from the gang characters in Leonard Bernstein's hit 1957 Broadway play "West Side Story": One more litter of juvenile

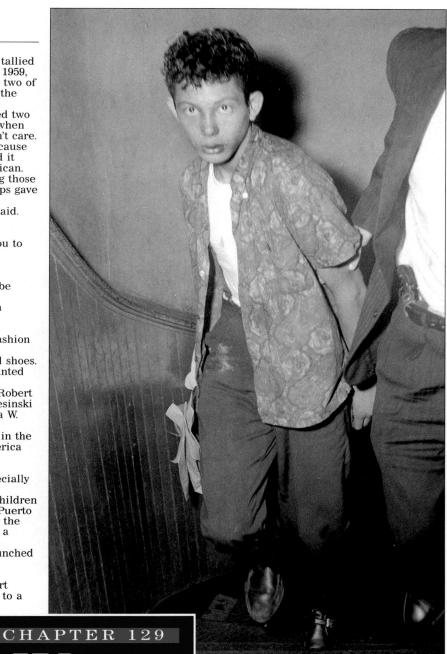

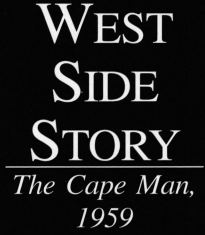

CHAPTER 129

WEST SIDE STORY

The Cape Man, 1959

delinquents.

When police broke down those 390 murders in 1959, they noted that 23 were committed by persons under 16. Another 82 were committed by people between 16 and 20. This sort of statistic was why New York spent $60 million fighting juvenile crime in 1959 — and why, on the day Salvatore Agron was arrested, the Daily News suggested the city was "pouring that money down a rathole rather than getting an adequate return on its investment."

IN FACT, public officials were already vowing to spend smarter. Less than 24 hours after the Cape Man murders, Police Commissioner Stephen Kennedy asked for 1,000 more street cops. Gov. Nelson Rockefeller and Mayor Robert Wagner called a summit to "map an all-out assault" on teen crime and gangs.

The problem with anti-delinquency efforts so far, Wagner suggested, was they had been well-meaning but soft-headed: "When organized gangs invade playgrounds and blindly and wantonly

commit murder, the handling of the matter has passed from the social agencies to the police."

Of course, the problem did have an origin, and the police had no trouble identifying it. The nation's top cop, FBI Director J. Edgar Hoover, traced juvenile delinquency to broken families and a culture that all but gave budding sociopaths an engraved blueprint.

"With regard to the effect of television, movies and other presentations on juvenile delinquency," said Hoover, "I am confident that improperly and unintelligently prepared presentations which recognize no restraint in producing in young minds pictures of torture, fantastic acts of violence and brutality, may have harmful effects."

Material "which makes lawlessness attractive, which ridicules decency and honesty, which depicts the life of a criminal as exciting and glamorous, may influence the susceptible boy or girl," Hoover said.

It was not known exactly what cultural materials Sal Agron had been exposed to. By all accounts, he could barely read. As for the "exciting and glamorous" life of the criminal, cops who caught up with Sal and his buddy Tony (Umbrella Man) Hernandez four days later found them rooting for tomatoes and bakery scraps in a Bronx garbage can.

SAL AND TONY had entered the park around 12:15 a.m. Six white teenagers and one of their kid sisters were already there. "Where's Frenchy?" Sal asked. Told there was no Frenchy around, Sal left — then went back with eight or 10 members of the Young Lords and possibly the Buccaneers, both Puerto Rican gangs.

At that point, one of the white kids, Billy Luken, told police, his group got up to leave and could not: "The guy with the cape says, 'No *gringos* leave the park.' "

Next thing he knew, said Luken, Young and Krzesinski were in a fight. Then he saw blood on their shirts. Luken and his sister bolted while Anthony Woznikaitis and the mortally wounded Young fled for the nearby apartment of John Brody, Woznikaitis' stepfather. A few steps inside, Young fell and died.

The News ran a picture of Brody next to Young's body, captioned, "All the sordidness of New York City's asphalt jungle is laid out before him."

Police first said the confrontation was triggered by friction between whites and Puerto Ricans at the park — that a few nights earlier, Puerto Ricans had been beaten there. Subsequently, they decided that the Cape Man had a beef only with Frenchy, a Puerto Rican who had warned Agron against selling marijuana to his mother, and that the white kids were merely there at the wrong time.

This intensified the nightmare: You could be innocent and uninvolved, and JDs could still snuff you.

It was potent and sordid, a crime magnified by the style in which it was committed.

Less than a week earlier, there had been another gang-related double killing down on the lower East Side. Julio Rosario, 14, was knifed to death by two teens from the rival Sportsmen gang, and Theresa Gee, 15, caught a stray bullet. Now those dead kids were just footnotes — like most of the other 386 people murdered in New York City in 1959.

By DAVID HINCKLEY
Daily News Staff Writer

THE PATHS OF Charles Van Doren and Alan Freed crossed with a brief but spectacular flourish in November 1959, leaving their lives in much the same ruins as America's faith in the nature of things.

Charles Van Doren was one of the most popular contestants and one of the biggest winners in the TV quiz shows to which viewers were briefly devoted in the late 1950s. Alan Freed was the nation's best-known radio disc jockey, Mr. Rock 'n' Roll. Both of them lied to millions of people who believed in them. Both of them paid for that.

'**T**HE $64,000 Question," a CBS program derived from the famous, less pricey radio giveaway shows of the past, premiered on June 7, 1955, and by June 1956 it was the nation's favorite show, bigger than "I Love Lucy." There was the inevitable army of imitators. One of them was NBC's "Twenty-One," which on Nov. 28, 1956, unveiled Van Doren, a $3,600-a-year instructor at Columbia University and son of the Pulitzer Prize-winning poet Mark Van Doren.

Tall and intense, with a commanding academic presence, Charles Van Doren looked good in the isolation booth, where he sweated and grimaced as the nation rooted for him, praying that he would somehow find one more correct answer.

"Some of the most important airplanes used in World War II were the P-40s, the P-47s, the P-51s, the B-24s, the B-25s and the B-26s," began one question Van Doren faced in January 1957. "What were the nicknames the Air Force gave those planes?"

The answers were Warhawks, Thunderbolts, Mustangs, Liberators, Mitchells and Marauders, and sure enough, Van Doren nailed them all, fighting off the challenge of New York textbook writer Ruth Miller and bringing his winnings to $99,000.

On Feb. 18, he named the seven prime ministers of Britain, 1918-1941, to hit $143,000. Then, on March 11, America's heart broke as he named the kings of Denmark, Norway, Sweden, Jordan and Iraq, but somehow couldn't remember Belgium's monarch — and was toppled by New York lawyer Vivienne Nearing, who sent him home with just $129,000.

Others who came after Van Doren struck even bigger jackpots. Elfrida Von Nardroff won $220,500 on "Twenty-One." Robert Strom, an 11-year-old boy genius, hit "The $64,000 Question" for 224 grand, which went into a trust while he attended the Bronx High School of Science. A boxing expert named Joyce Brothers won $134,000.

But the big bucks ultimately couldn't keep quiz shows at the top.

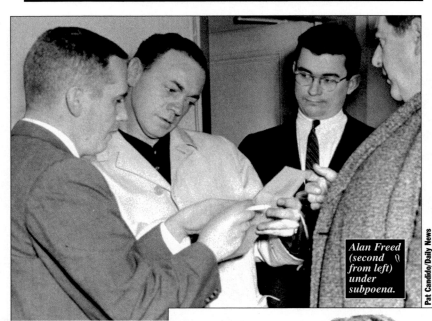

Alan Freed (second from left) under subpoena.

Pat Candido/Daily News

CHAPTER 130

MATTER OF TRUST

Scandals Of The Public Air, 1959

Charles Van Doren confesses to America.

After saturating the market, they began plunging in the ratings, and "Lucy" reclaimed the No. 1 position.

Meanwhile, ugly rumors had been floating that these quiz shows were perhaps not entirely on the up and up.

NATURALLY, NO one wanted to believe that a nice boy like that Charles Van Doren could have been a party to deceit. But in August 1958, a guest on "Dotto" found a scrap of paper left behind by another contestant, containing the day's answers.

This piece of paper was passed to Manhattan District Attorney Frank Hogan, who assigned Assistant DA Joseph Stone to investigate — even though, granted, deceiving TV viewers was a crime nowhere.

Stone grilled more than 100 witnesses. Most contestants, including Van Doren, swore they knew nothing about quiz-show rigging. But several producers sang, and by October, Stone had a scalp. Albert Freedman, the producer of "Dotto" and "Twenty-One," was indicted for perjury.

In June 1959, the grand jury wrote a "presentment," outlining what it basically saw as consumer fraud, and a New York court decided in August to turn over the jury's minutes to Rep. Oren Harris (D-Ark.), whose House subcommittee on legislative oversight planned hearings on the legitimacy of quiz shows.

Harris had been probing "the morals of radio and television programs" since 1952. Worried that the exploding TV industry increasingly felt itself answerable to no one, he now saw the quiz-show scandal as an opportunity to create enough public outrage to sow some regulatory legislation. On Nov. 2, he brought the chastened and humbled Van Doren back to national TV for the last time.

Yes, Van Doren testified, "Twenty-One" had tapped him as the sort of good-looking fellow who could boost the ratings, and he had gone along. He had been "foolish, naive, prideful and avaricious," he admitted.

It was an apology to Congress, but it was also an apology to America.

"I have deceived my friends, and I had millions of them," Van Doren said. "I would give almost anything to reverse the course of my life in the last three years."

So would have millions of viewers, who had just learned the hard lesson that even something they saw with their own eyes might not be true.

NBC, which had hired Van Doren to appear on Dave Garroway's morning "Today" program at $50,000 a year, fired him. And all three networks immediately canceled their remaining quiz shows.

Oren Harris wrapped up his hearing on Nov. 6 with the announcement that he was now going to probe bribery in the selection of records played on the radio. Payola.

WHAT CHARLES VAN Doren was to quiz shows, Alan Freed was to payola — the "principal symbol."

Ever since radio started hit parades and top-40 surveys, there had been the gentle implication that all this sprung from the tastes and wishes of the listener. In fact, those who produced the music often took behind-the-scenes steps to insure it would get in front of that listener in the first place.

Payola was a 100-proof music biz tradition. Irving Berlin had started as a "song plugger," paying singers to perform the songs he was promoting. When radio became the primary means of promotion, record companies provided cash, booze, women, whatever. The system worked.

But by 1959, popular music itself was widely thought to be subverting the morality of America's youth. Psychologist Joost Meerlo published a study that showed rock 'n' roll threw young folks into "prehistoric rhythmic trances . . . that liberate the mind of all reasonable inhibitions. . . . As in drug addiction, a thousand years of civilization fall away in a moment."

The easiest way to stop this was to stop the disc jockey who played it, and the most prominent was Alan Freed of WABC radio and WNEW-TV.

A few days after the Harris announcement, WABC asked all its deejays to swear that they had never received payments for playing music and owned no interest in publishing, recording or merchandising. Freed stalled, and both WABC and WNEW fired him.

"Payola may stink," Freed protested, "but it's here, and I didn't start it."

Unlike Van Doren, Freed felt he had no apologies to make. On his final TV show, Nov. 27, he danced with the kids and vowed: "By no means is this goodbye. I'll be back soon."

CHARLES VAN DOREN *pleaded guilty to perjury, got a suspended sentence and vanished from the public eye. Alan Freed, his career destroyed, worked in radio again only fleetingly, in Miami, and died a broken man in January 1965. In February 1960, the Federal Communications Commission asked Congress to restore public faith in TV and radio by outlawing deception on the public airwaves.*

By KAREN ZAUTYK
Daily News Staff Writer

Sterling Place.

NINE DAYS BEFORE Christmas, Sterling Place in Brooklyn's Park Slope was brightening with the wreaths that had begun to adorn the doorways of the brownstones. Between Sixth and Seventh Aves., two tree sellers were setting out evergreens to offer passersby. Sanitation workers were still shoveling the snow that had fallen over the weekend, and now more flakes were drifting down. Less than a block away, hundreds of children sat in the classrooms of St. Augustine's School, waiting for the holiday break.

Friday morning the 16th of December 1960. Before the noon Angelus rang from St. Augustine's bell tower, Sterling Place would become a scene of devastation and carnage, of twisted metal and smoldering ashes and charred human bodies, and the new snowdrifts would be crimson with blood.

It was shortly after 10:30 a.m. when a teacher supervising a 10th-grade study hall at St. Augustine's, saw that a student staring out the window had suddenly turned ashen. The teacher followed the youth's gaze — and saw the stuff of nightmares: A huge passenger jet, wings perpendicular to the ground, roaring down the narrow street, at shop window level.

Then came the explosion, the shuddering ground, the flames, the screams.

The plane was a United Airlines DC-8 carrying 83 passengers and crew members. One wing sliced through a 16-family apartment building. The nose exploded into the Pillar of Fire Church. The severed tail crashed across Seventh Ave. St. Augustine's was untouched.

On Staten Island 10 miles away, a second airplane, a TWA Lockheed Super Constellation with 44 people aboard, was spiraling toward Earth like, it occurred to one witness, a spinning toy. So slow seemed its descent that police who spotted the stricken ship actually tried to race it to tiny Miller Army Air Field, toward which it was falling.

New Dorp residents who heard the Lockheed's thunder rushed outside — as pieces of metal and leather fell all around them with the snowflakes.

Miller Field looked like a battleground, strewn with bodies and bits of bodies. One corpse hung from a tree on Hylan Blvd. Gaily wrapped Christmas gifts were scattered amid the debris.

ONLY MINUTES BEFORE, the two planes had been completing uneventful flights. United 826 out of Chicago was in a holding pattern over New Jersey, waiting to land at Idlewild International Airport in Queens. TWA 266, originating in Dayton, Ohio, was en route to LaGuardia. The ceiling was just 600 feet, and both planes were flying by instruments.

Groping through the blinding snow 5,000 feet over the eastern edge of Staten Island, they collided.

United 826 apparently rammed TWA 266 broadside, investigators decided later; its right wing slashed through the other plane, instantly breaking it apart. The doomed Constellation, the Daily News reported, "stood straight up on its tail, its four propellers clawing at the sky" — and then plunged down toward Staten Island, taking with it one of the jet's engines. Debris was scattered over 4 square miles; incredibly, no one on the ground was hurt.

In Brooklyn, it was a different story.

CHAPTER 131

RED SNOW

The Brooklyn Air Crash, 1960

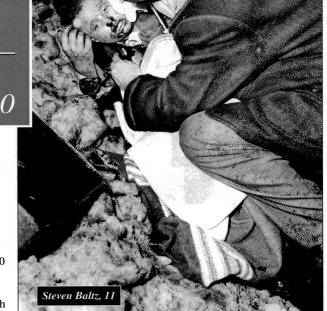

Steven Baltz, 11

The crippled United plane had desperately tried to make LaGuardia. Sterling Place was as far as it got. Now the entire street was ablaze; the homes of 200 families were in flames; the Christmas-tree sellers and a snow-shoveler and a butcher and a dentist and a Pillar of Fire Church caretaker were dead.

Rubble and twisted metal filled the street, 150 feet down toward Sixth Ave. Along with the wreaths, the street was now adorned with pieces of passengers' clothing hanging from fire escapes and trees. An army of 2,500 cops, firefighters, doctors and civil defense volunteers began burrowing through the wreckage in search of survivors.

THERE WAS ONLY one. Instants after the crash, a young boy crawled from the wreckage. Both his legs were shattered and he was hideously burned but he was alive. As he lay in a snowbank, passersby sheltered him with a blanket and an umbrella. "Mommy," he moaned. "Daddy."

At Methodist Hospital, he was identified as 11-year-old Stephen Baltz of Wilmette, Ill. He had been flying alone to New York to join his mother. She had been waiting for him at Idlewild.

As Stephen clung to life, hundreds of callers from around the world jammed the hospital switchboard, offering to donate their blood or their skin for grafts.

He had been looking out the airplane window at the snow falling on New York City, he remembered. "It looked like a picture out of a fairy book," he told a doctor. "It was a beautiful sight."

He suffered for 27 hours, and then, with his parents at his bedside, he died.

SUBSEQUENT INQUIRIES into America's worst air crash indicated that the United pilot had overshot his assigned pattern by nearly 12 miles, and primary blame ultimately was placed on the off-course plane.

But debate raged on for years over whether this was strictly pilot error or errors compounded by glitches in New York's air-traffic control system. In the end, in settling the claims resulting from the disaster, liability was assessed at 61% for United, 24% for the U.S. government, representing the Federal Aviation Administration traffic controllers, and 15% for TWA, which agreed to share responsibility although its pilot had been following controllers' instructions.

By ROGER STARR
Special to The News

ON THE FIRST DAY of January 1954, 8½ years after the end of World War II, Democrat Robert F. Wagner Jr. became, in effect, New York City's first postwar mayor. His two predecessors, William O'Dwyer and Vincent Impellitteri, had been so busy trying to overcome the decay and neglect of 16 years of Depression and war that they had not even identified the municipal problems of the immediate future.

Educated in the Ivy League and at the dinner table of his father, the distinguished liberal United States senator, where he had received a continuing postgraduate course in backroom political realities, Wagner had served as chairman of the city's future-oriented Planning Commission and as Manhattan borough president. As mayor — soft-spoken in manner, lacking the ethnic bravura of previous mayors — he moved so cautiously that he often tended to strain public patience.

But he unleashed two surprises on his first day in office. First was the appointment of Luther Gulick, long-time head of the Institute for Public Administration, to the new post of city administrator. Tammany Hall chief Carmine DeSapio understood at once that such an official would be expected to trim political appointees from well-paid posts that were exempt from Civil Service exam requirements. Such an official also might actually seek to fill vacancies with people who were professionally qualified. DeSapio now undertook to make the rookie mayor understand that excess efficiency makes poor politics.

Second was his reappointment of Robert Moses to a new term on the Planning Commission. Moses was a Republican, and a uniquely effective public-works impresario who for many years had devised and expedited parks, parkways, expressways, bridges, tunnels, beaches, housing developments and bird sanctuaries. His reappointment came amid loud protests from his many critics — people who approved of his products but hated his methods, assuming that some unnamed wizard from somewhere could give them the one without the other.

Behind these two decisions lay the major problems that confronted Robert Wagner as he presided for 12 years over the dramatically changing New York of the 1950s and 1960s.

ONE, HE HAD in his city a critical shortage of legally standard housing.

Two, he had a transit system — crucial to the city's economy and its people's convenience — that lacked an adequate financial base and was governed by short-sighted adherence to an inadequate fare structure that could not provide funds for rehabilitation, replacement and expansion of its capital plant and equipment.

Three, he had a public school system unable even to provide seats and desks as the child population rose cataclysmically. The city desperately needed a system that could provide solutions to emerging urban social and behavioral conditions and a curriculum appropriate to the needs of non-English-speaking pupils.

By 1961, as Robert Wagner sought a third term in office, these matters

CHAPTER 132

MODERN TIMES

The Mayor Of The Future, 1961

were, in his slow and steady fashion, being addressed.

AT THE END of the war, about 1 million New Yorkers were living in tenement houses built in the previous century. With significant financial help from the national and state governments, and the energy of Moses and other advocates of accelerated housing development, 346,000 apartments and free-standing homes were built during Wagner's 12 mayoral years. Wagner got the credit, but Moses took the blame for the often stern spirit with which occupied old homes were demolished to make space for the new.

By the private builders who invested in construction of rental apartments, Wagner was constantly reminded that the rent controls enacted by the federal government in 1943 discouraged investment in new rental housing. Wagner and Planning Commission Chairman James Felt articulated three programs:

For low-income households, federally financed public housing was the principal resource. In 1961, the city's public housing program was simple: "Proceed quickly. Under the law, no state can have more than 15% of the national total of public housing subsidy contracts. Don't let other states get our share if we're late. Better they're late and we get some of their share." Accordingly, Wagner built 123,000 public housing apartments, far more than the nation's other dozen largest cities

combined.

For families whose income disqualified them from public housing, a middle-income program had been devised by the state Legislature. Many such buildings were built for cooperative ownership; apartments were bought with modest down payments. The program produced thousands of new, decent family homes for both blacks and whites, initially those with union sponsors. As both groups found their incomes rising, many bought their own homes, leaving apartments to be purchased by families who had risen economically from public housing.

To stimulate builders to build for the rich, the Wagner administration urged so-called luxury builders to compete with rent-controlled apartment houses by creating more spacious, better designed apartments with modern amenities outclassing the best of those under rent control. Felt engaged architects to develop a new city zoning law that mandated some of these improvements. Despite heavy opposition from lower-end developers, trade unions and many neighborhoods that foresaw changes they did not want, Felt mounted an effective approval campaign, made a few compromises and won press support. Wagner himself mollified builders by giving them a year of grace in which to build under the easier old rules. This key concession in 1961 made New York's new zoning possible.

In transit, meanwhile, Wagner

broke with previous mayors, who had fought to keep the transit lines under strict city ownership, fearing voter criticism if fares rose. To Wagner, it was clear that transit, particularly the subways, served not only local taxpayers but everyone who visited New York, and he took the political risk of urging the state to take over a measure of control and financial support.

Wagner also understood the importance of sound education to the city's future. Construction of schools and colleges took fully a quarter of the capital budget every Wagner year, and the number of teachers increased by more than 1,000 a year. In higher education, the City University was established with a combination of the individual colleges, and five new community colleges were opened.

SLOW AND STEADY Robert Wagner won his third term in November. His patience had made possible his administration's achievements. Great issues, racial ones in particular, remained not easily resolved. In another few years, as emerging social attitudes of the 1960s became incendiary, the new city that Wagner built between the mid-1950s and the mid-1960s would reshape itself into still another one.

Roger Starr was New York City housing commissioner from 1974 to 1976.

By JONATHAN LEWIN
Daily News Staff Writer

"It's the same old story. First the builder picks the property, then he gets the Planning Commission to designate it, then the people get bulldozed out of their homes."

– Jane Jacobs

UNDER TITLE I OF the Federal Housing Act of 1949, federal funds became available to cities for demolition or rehabilitation of blighted areas, and throughout the 1950s, Robert Moses' Slum Clearance Committee lived up to its name, razing entire New York neighborhoods in the name of urban renewal. In 1960, the city's Housing and Redevelopment Board took over those duties, promising to displace residents less brusquely than had been Moses' way. But the city Planning Commission continued to support the basic tenets of urban renewal, believing that New Yorkers would ultimately be much happier in modern, less crowded housing with lots of open spaces.

Jane Jacobs, a 45-year-old editor at Architectural Forum, had another opinion: Urban planners, she believed, were destroying America's cities. She blamed the influence of the Swiss architect Le Corbusier, whose 1920s Utopian visions placed urban residents in skyscrapers surrounded by parkland. This "towers in the park" approach, Jacobs argued, resulted in dangerous housing projects and sterile downtown areas that were deserted at night.

She and her family had been renovating their three-story house on Hudson St. since 1947. Throughout the West Village, many other families had purchased similarly rundown dwellings and restored them. In 1961, the neighborhood was on the rise — interesting, affordable, safe. Jacobs was finishing a book, "The Death and Life of Great American Cities," using the West Village as an example of a successful urban environment, when, on Feb. 20, Mayor Robert Wagner announced the latest New York City neighborhood to be designated as blighted. This was 14 blocks bounded by 11th, Hudson, Christopher, Washington, Morton and West Sts. This was where Jane Jacobs lived.

ON SATURDAY NIGHT the 25th of February, 300 angry people crowded into St. Luke's School at Hudson and Christopher Sts. to form the Committee to Save the West Village. "The aim of the committee is to kill this project entirely," announced co-organizer Jacobs, "because if it goes

CHAPTER 133

CLEARLY NOT SLUM DWELLERS
Jane Jacobs And Urban Renewal, 1961

through, it can mean only the destruction of the community."

By early March, small children were making posters and passing out protest petitions while their parents staffed tables in taverns and coffee shops. This was no slum area, they insisted to the politicians. On March 21, after touring homes and admiring high ceilings, large fireplaces and hand-hewn beams, Manhattan Borough President Edward Dudley agreed with them; West Villagers, he announced, were "clearly not slum dwellers."

But James Felt, chairman of the Planning Commission, insisted that urban renewal would "stabilize and protect neighborhoods, not disrupt or destroy them." Opponents, he said, were "well-meaning" but "misguided" — people "rebelling against our architecture, our technology, our mores and our culture in general [who] have sought to single out urban renewal as the villain."

Jacobs' committee presented Wagner with a petition demanding Felt's ouster, and as the summer wore on, the mayor, who was in the midst of a reelection campaign, began to buckle under the activists' pressure. On Aug. 17, he hailed

Greenwich Village for its "small-town character, its residential qualities, its local color, its rich heritage and its cultural undertones." He pledged that any urban renewal would respect "Village tradition."

Dismissing these promises as "pious platitudes," the committee leaned harder — and on Sept. 6, just before a Democratic primary vote against an opponent, Arthur Levitt, who was on the committee's side, Wagner agreed to ask the Planning Commission to kill the West Village urban renewal project.

To save Felt's face, however, Wagner asked the committee to agree to the "blighted" designation — and in return for this, he said, the project would thereafter be quashed.

Jane Jacobs refused this stipulation.

And so, at City Hall on Oct. 18, the Planning Commission approved urban renewal in the West Village.

ANGRY VILLAGERS, led by Jacobs, rushed the commissioners, charging that secret deals had been made with a builder named David Rose. "This decision will take us back to the dark ages of Robert Moses," declared Assemblyman Louis De Salvio. Felt called police and had the noisiest protesters removed. "A disgraceful demonstration," he said. Cops stood by as the hearing

resumed.

The next day, Jacobs called a press conference to present her evidence of a pre-arranged deal to develop the West Village. The resume of an architect named Barry Benape stated that "as consultant to Rose Associates" he had "prepared sketch plans and perspectives" for "a renewal plan for the West Village." Benape's documents had been typed on the same typewriter that had produced petitions supporting urban renewal that had circulated in the West Village — and they were dated October 1960, months before the renewal plan had been first announced.

Benape tried to explain that the date was a typo, that the resume had actually been prepared in October 1961 — but the thunder built. Louis Lefkowitz, Wagner's Republican opponent in the upcoming election, pronounced the West Village flap "further proof" of Wagner's "fumbling leadership." Days before the election, Wagner declared himself vigorously opposed to the project, and the Housing and Redevelopment Board officially killed it.

For Jacobs, this was just a partial victory: "The next step," she said, "is for the Planning Commission to remove the slum label from our area."

On Jan. 31, 1962, the Planning Commission voted unanimously to do just that.

NO, GUYS, THE FIELD IS THAT WAY: Casey Stengel shows his boys the ropes at spring training.

By DAVID HINCKLEY
Daily News Staff Writer

CHAPTER 134

DON'T MIND THE LOSING
The Amazin' Mets, 1962

ON THE EVE OF the New York Mets' first game, on April 11, 1962, club President George Weiss said he believed "we have a chance of playing .500 ball."

He just didn't say when.

It wasn't in 1962. In 1962, the Mets fell exactly 80 games short of .500 ball, finishing with a 40-120 record that was the worst in 20th century baseball history.

The Amazin' Mets were here.

"You look over there in the Cincinnati dugout and what do you see?" manager Casey Stengel sighed during a game one day. "All mahogany. Then you look at our bench. And all you see is driftwood."

The Mets' regular first baseman was Marv Throneberry, a one-time Yankee hot prospect who was hanging onto the lower rungs of the major leagues when the Mets acquired him from Baltimore early in 1962.

On the sunny afternoon of June 17, Throneberry forgot to get out of the way of a Chicago base runner in the first inning, drawing an interference call and paving the way for four Cubs runs. In the bottom of the first, he strove to compensate by slugging a two-run triple — except that he was called out for failing to touch first base.

Legend has it Stengel started out to protest the call, only to be advised not to bother by first base coach Cookie Lavagetto, who observed that Throneberry had also missed second.

The Cubs won the game by one run, and Marvelous Marv Throneberry became the living symbol of the absolutely terrible 1962 New York Mets.

Two Mets pitchers lost 20 games that season: Roger Craig, 10-24, and Al Jackson, 8-20. Jay Hook was a cinch to make it a trifecta, with an 8-19 record, but Stengel, not eager to become the only manager ever with three 20-game losers on one team, sat Hook down.

There were numerous indications in the spring of what lay ahead. Two days before the season opener, 16 Mets were stuck in an elevator for 20 minutes. Sherman (Roadblock) Jones, scheduled to pitch the home opener, had to postpone when he burned his eye while striking a match.

In the opening game, an 11-4 loss to St. Louis, Craig balked home the first run when he dropped the ball during his delivery. Stengel went to the mound and said, "You're standing on two tons of dirt. Why not rub some on the ball?"

The Mets lost their first nine games and, as it turned out, it *did* take a rocket scientist to figure out a way for them to win. Hook, who had a degree in mechanical engineering from Northwestern, beat the Pirates on April 23, 9-1.

By mid-April, it was clear that this team was so bad it was fun — though that was a realization more endearing to the fans and the press than to the men on the field. Stengel spent the season masking tragedy with a laugh track.

"I got the smartest pitcher in the world," said Stengel about Hook. "Until he goes to the mound."

Stengel's logic proved contagious. "I don't mind the losing," Craig said at one point. "It's not winning that hurts."

THE METS HAD their moments. One night, for reasons that can't be adequately explained, Throneberry wound up coaching first base. In the ninth, with two on and two out, he was sent down the line to pinch-hit. He hit a home run, winning the game.

In early May, Craig Anderson won both ends of a doubleheader against Milwaukee, raising his record to 3-1 before he lost 16 straight to finish 3-17.

The perpetually happy Rod Kanehl, a major leaguer only because of the Mets, beat Don Drysdale of the Dodgers one afternoon with a bases-loaded single in the eighth inning.

Drysdale was otherwise on his way to a league-leading 25 wins, but that wasn't the only reason it was sweet to beat him. The mere existence of the Mets was New York's declaration of independence from the Dodgers, who had pulled out of Brooklyn five years before and taken the Giants with them.

THAT BETRAYAL had left New York with only the Yankees, and while hosting the most successful team in baseball history wasn't a bad consolation prize, that didn't help the fans whose teams had fled.

Dodger and Giant fans, after all, had spent their lives hating the Yankees, who almost always found a way to beat them. For these fans to switch allegiance would have been like a Union soldier suddenly rooting for the Rebs.

Even as the Dodgers were cleaning out their closets, the New York officials who had been unable to stop two teams from leaving vowed to find a new one. There was talk for a while that Cincinnati would move to Brooklyn, but it soon became clear an expansion team was more likely.

Answering this civic outcry for the creation of the city's first new ballclub since 1903 was heiress Joan Payson, sister of the publisher of the New York Herald Tribune and a baseball fan who had been one of those fighting hard to keep the Giants in town back in '57. She financed 80% of the new franchise. And she named stockbroker M. Donald Grant chairman of the board. Their selection of Weiss, a long-time Yankee president, made it evident that the new team intended to embrace its New York past rather than start clean.

Indeed, one of Weiss' first hires was Stengel — a significant coup, because Casey had been Yankee manager in the glory years of the '50s, and his awkward, unceremonious firing after the 1960 World Series had left the Yankees looking even more aloof and coldly corporate than usual.

So New York City's new Mets saw an opening to be warmer and nicer, which they did in part by stocking up on old Dodgers: Gil Hodges, Don Zimmer, Craig, Joe Pignatano, Charlie Neal. Also, they played at the Polo Grounds, long-time home of the Giants.

National League ball was back. And it felt good, even if victory was an elusive cloud on a distant horizon.

CRAIG, WHO lost five 1-0 games during the 1962 season, was asked at one point if he believed in God.

"Yes," he said. "And He wouldn't be a bad guy to have on this team."

MARV THRONEBERRY *was cut early in 1963. In 1964, the Mets moved to the new Shea Stadium in Flushing Meadows, a Robert Moses-approved site that Walter O'Malley had rejected before moving the Dodgers out of town. The Mets had their first winning season in 1969, and they went on to win the World Series. Their manager in 1969 was Hodges, who was also a member of the Brooklyn Dodgers when they won their only World Series in 1955.*

By DAVID HINCKLEY
Daily News Staff Writer

LIVE CHEAP. Meet girls. Save the world. With a job description like that, it's no wonder every bus that arrived in New York in 1962 seemed to carry a kid with a guitar, a dream and a pocketful of folk songs.

True, the folk scene of the early '60s was so contentious that if it were the National Rifle Association, they'd have all shot each other.

But as folk singers, they tended to have a pacifistic strain, and their interest in matters like world peace was one of several convergent reasons why, in 1962, Greenwich Village had become world headquarters for a folk music scene that, to its own occasional shock and horror, was beginning to matter in the music and popular culture biz.

The elements were there. The music industry was between Elvis and the Beatles, and thus poking around for different sounds. The Beat movement of the '50s had left the Village littered with small music venues and hangouts — although, Dave Van Ronk later pointed out, it was a misconception that folkies were just a different strain of Beats. "Beats *hated* folk music," noted Van Ronk. "All these folkniks sitting on the floor singing about the oppressed masses."

But whatever the bloodlines, the folk scene had hit a stretch where talent was flowing over the banks. Bob Dylan released his debut album in 1962, and while its sales receipts could barely buy him a one-way trip on the Staten Island ferry, by the end of the year he had written "Let Me Die in My Footsteps," "Masters of War" and "Blowin' in the Wind." Kid seemed to be on to something.

Musically, what drew the folkies together was an appreciation bordering on reverence for traditional pre-war folk music, which had been resurrected by Harry Smith's "Anthology of American Folk Music," and the "rediscovery" down South of wrinkled old blues singers like Mississippi John Hurt, who could still play like the devil even if they had no idea how these young white kids knew or why they cared.

This not only gave the new folkies common friends, it gave them common enemies — like top 40 radio, the music industry and the Kingston Trio, who had built on the modest success of the Tarriers to become certified top 40 radio stars with upbeat sing-alongs like "Tom Dooley."

What made the Village folk community matter outside its own table, however, was that it had become an important certified subgroup within two larger movements: civil rights and peace.

Both these movements valued a folk-music soundtrack: "We Shall Overcome" on a picket line, "Last Night I Had the Strangest Dream" at a candlelight vigil.

Agitating for peace in 1962 had nothing to do with Vietnam — (*where?*) — and everything to do with heading off World War III. The Cuban missile crisis of 1962 was, to peaceniks, just one more chilling indication that someday some jerk with a red button was going to barbecue the world.

But if the nuclear-war front looked grim, the civil rights scenario offered hope. Even the federal government, now that the rank injustices of Jim Crow had been ripped too wide open to

Suze Rotolo and Jose Feliciano at Folk City.

ignore, seemed to be moving in the right direction.

So folkies got together, often in someone's apartment, to argue strategy, work on songs, swap gossip and at the end of the day, more often than not, get lucky.

"Those were not only the days of good music, those were the days of women," Vince Martin would recall. "It was a rabbit farm."

THE FOLK clubs were often no more than bars or restaurants into which someone had jammed a microphone and a 4-by-6 "stage." The good part was that you and your one cheap drink could usually stay as long as you wanted.

Within five Village blocks, you could find the Purple Onion, the Night Owl Cafe, Cafe Wha?, the Gaslight, the Kettle of Fish, Cafe Figaro, the Bitter End, the Other End — and, the epicenter, a few

blocks away over on Mercer St., Gerde's Folk City.

Folk City was a small joint known for its funky decor, a wide-open door and an audience murmur that lessened rather than stopped during performances. Owner Mike Porco, who had made several earlier stabs at this sort of thing before opening Folk City in June 1960, hosted Dylan's first paid public performance — he opened for John Lee Hooker — on April 11, 1961. Folk City helped launch Peter, Paul and Mary, Judy Collins, Jose Feliciano, Phil Ochs, John Phillips and Lou Gossett Jr., among others.

The scene included honored veterans like Pete Seeger and Sis Cunningham, who had sung with Woody; younger vets like Ed McCurdy or Ramblin' Jack Elliot, who had been singing when it seemed only their friends noticed, and mountain balladeers like Jean Ritchie. Van Ronk was a defector from jazz. Tom Paxton wrote a song every time he drank a cup of coffee. Fred Neil was a Florida troubador who showed up from time to time at the Night Owl. There were the stream of women with the long straight hair, like Carolyn Hester and Joan Baez and Suze Rotolo, and earnest crusaders like Gil Turner, Len Chandler and Ochs.

By February 1962, Cunningham was hearing so many new songs that she started a magazine to publish them, Broadside. The debut issue carried the first printed Dylan song, "Talking John Birch Paranoid Blues."

All was well until the first disturbing signs of success.

FOLKIES HAD sold records before; The Weavers, a decade earlier, sold lushly orchestrated sing-alongs of tunes like "On Top of Old Smoky." Fortunately for their reputation, the Weavers also had been blacklisted during the McCarthy era, which gave them a life-long get-out-of-jail-free card.

Peter, Paul and Mary had no such protection when, in the summer of '62, they had a top 10 hit with "If I Had a Hammer," a bouncy arrangement of a gospel protest tune. They were immediately suspected of harboring commercial ambitions and sellout hearts.

Still, the silent thought balloon now was hovering over the whole Village: *If they can get a deal, I can get a deal.*

There were always stories in counterbalance: folk singers helping each other with music, wine, a warm bed. Arguments? Families always argue.

Besides, there was a feeling in 1962, with assassinations and Vietnam still on the far side of a blind corner, that things just might work out. If you had a guitar and a song, you could find a place to play and sing it, and if you were good, you might make a living at it instead of ever having to work. Love never looked to be more than one introduction away. And, oh yes, you also just might save the world.

CHAPTER 135

NEAR SIDE OF A BLIND CORNER

Village Folkies, 1962

By MARA BOVSUN
Special to The News

JUBILANT CROWDS filled Times Square like it was New Year's Eve. After a bitter four-month strike, New York City's newspapers were publishing again.

The Daily Mirror was the first sheet back on the stands, at 7:30 p.m. on Sunday the 31st of March 1963. **NEW YORK'S ALIVE AGAIN**, said the headline.

Then came the Daily News' page one: **WELL, HELLO THERE! WE HAVE NEWS FOR YOU.**

The banner on the elegant Herald Tribune: **READ ALL ABOUT IT — OH, WHAT A BEAUTIFUL MORNING.**

There were fireworks, and Broadway stars stood on the roof of the Daily News' Art Deco headquarters on E. 42nd St. and sent aloft balloons carrying free-delivery coupons. But the freebies weren't really necessary.

"Every newsstand," The News reported happily, "was the center of an eager crowd that quickly cleaned out the dealer's supply of the papers as fast as the trucks delivered it."

"I never sold papers so fast in my life," said one Bronx newsie. "I was passing them out like a robot."

"My son came home from college, and he was restless the entire week," a Manhattan woman said. "When I asked him what was wrong, he answered, 'How can I sleep without having read a paper?' "

Moaned a Bensonhurst, Brooklyn, man: "I didn't read anything. I felt really ignorant."

NEW YORK HAD always been a newspaper town. There were 14 papers in Manhattan alone in the 1920s, more than twice that when the other boroughs were added. As late as the '60s, when most other cities had just one or two papers remaining, New York boasted seven big dailies.

There were millions of readers — immigrants hungry to learn English, housewives hunting for sales, job seekers, theatergoers, men in gray flannel suits commuting from the suburbs each morning. People hung around newsstands and candy stores, waiting for the trucks. They wanted the sports, the gossip, the stocks, Dick Tracy, Dondi, the daily number. News, too.

So it came as a rude shock on that icy Dec. 8, 1962, when the papers suddenly weren't there anymore.

Nobody knew it at the time, but this was the start of a famine that would starve to death all but three of the city's major dailies.

THE TROUBLE BEGAN when the Big 6 — Local 6 of the International Typographical Union — hit the bricks at 2 a.m., immediately closing The News, The Times, the World-Telegram and The Sun, and the Journal-American.

Five other members of the city's Publishers Association — the Post, the Mirror, the Herald Tribune, The Long Island Star-Journal and the Queens edition of the Long Island Press — closed as well, to show a united front.

Suddenly, 5.7 million papers were gone every working day, 7.5 million on Sundays. Nearly 20,000 workers were out on the street.

Department stores printed flyers, pasted ads on subway doors and hired pretty girls to hold up chalkboards in their windows. A public relations firm sent flacks into the streets with bulletins touting their clients. Merrill Lynch passed out handbills with market prices.

Washington, Boston and Philadelphia papers were imported to fill the void. Some entrepreneurs sold them at double or triple their cover prices.

Even the Santa Claus who sat on a throne in the lobby of the Daily News building was caught on TV with his big red nose stuck in a Middletown, N.Y., paper.

Foreign-language papers started putting out English translations. Life magazine turned out special city editions. Strike papers popped up. Even Waldbaum's supermarkets went into the news business, printing headlines, weather and stocks on their grocery bags.

It didn't help much.

"What do people here in the nation's largest city do without their newspapers?" asked The Wall Street Journal, a nonstriker. "Among other things, they buy less, land fewer jobs, rent fewer apartments, attend fewer funerals, cut theatergoing and scramble frantically for substitute reading matter."

Deprived of reviewers, Broadway shows closed. Not only was funeral attendance down, so were flower sales: "A lot of people just don't know when their friends die," one florist sighed. The Health Department fretted that venereal disease would skyrocket without newspaper campaigns to fight it.

Radio and TV expanded what had been newscasts of no more than 10 minutes. People began walking around with transistor radios pressed to their ears. NBC launched the city's first half-hour TV news program, helmed by Gabe Pressman and Bill Ryan. Other stations quickly followed.

BEHIND CLOSED DOORS, tense negotiations between the publishers and the unions wore on. Money was a central issue; the printers wanted a $20 weekly raise, a 35-hour week and beefed-up benefits. But the real issue was automation. The world was on the brink of a technological revolution, and the printers were fighting to keep the antiquated systems they and their fathers had worked for generations.

It would be progress or bankruptcy, the publishers contended. Indeed, only two New York papers, The Times and The News, consistently made money. The others broke even or were subsidized by wealthy owners.

On the talks dragged, beyond Christmas, into January and February, as Mayor Robert Wagner and labor warrior Theodore Kheel sought to make peace.

On March 31, the final issue was settled with the photoengravers who made pictures for the presses, and the eight unions went back to work. **ENGRAVERS VOTE YES AND THAT'S THAT**, headlined the Daily News.

But that wasn't that, and everybody knew it.

'THIS IS A history of failure," a Publishers Association official said, "the failure of men and machinery, of politics and personalities, of miscalculated maneuvers and misjudged aspirations."

"Nobody won this strike," The News editorialized.

Facing huge strike losses and large settlement costs, The Times and the Herald Tribune immediately doubled in price, returning to the stands at a dime. The Daily News held fast at 5 cents. This meant death for the rival tabloid Mirror, which quietly folded before year's end, still selling 900,000 papers a day.

"How can a paper with the second-largest circulation go out of business?" asked bewildered, out-of-work Mirror columnist Walter Winchell.

TWO YEARS LATER, the papers were at the brink again; the '63 problems, noted Fortune magazine, "were never settled but were, one might say, papered over." Still, the printers refused to let The Times and the Daily News use new hardware. When they hit The Times with a brief walkout in September 1965, most of the other sheets shut down again as well.

By now it was clear that New York simply could not support so many newspapers. When the Herald Tribune, the World-Telegram and The Sun, and the Journal-American tried to make a desperate final survival attempt by merging into The World Journal and Tribune, or "Widget," it was TV reporter Gabe Pressman who broke the story.

And when the Widget died in May 1967, leaving the city with just three major daily papers, most people heard about it first on TV.

CHAPTER 136

STOPPING THE PRESSES

Papers on Strike, 1963

By RICHARD E. MOONEY
Special to The News

WORKERS started tearing down Pennsylvania Station at 9 a.m. on a drizzly Monday the 28th of October 1963. Executives and hardhats beamed for photographers as a crane lifted the first stone eagle down from where it had perched over New York City for 53 years.

In the early 1900s, the Pennsylvania Railroad had been the nation's richest and most powerful transportation company. A half-century later it was struggling to survive, seeking to raise cash from its valuable mid-Manhattan station site. It had given up its air rights for a new Madison Square Garden and office tower. The deal would be a futility: Soon the Pennsy itself would disappear, after a brief and desperate marriage with the New York Central. The Penn Central bankruptcy would be the biggest in history.

Down the old eagles came. "Just another job," shrugged a demolition foreman.

But it wasn't that at all. When somnolent city fathers awoke to what had happened, they enacted a landmarks law that would be hailed as the nation's strongest, a model for preservation laws from coast to coast.

PENN STATION was the work of Pennsy President Alexander Cassatt and architect Charles McKim. Pennsy trains terminated in Jersey City at the turn of the century, and passengers reached Manhattan by ferry. Similarly, passengers on the Long Island Rail Road, which the Pennsy owned, ferried across the East River. Over the years, there had been serious proposals to bridge the Hudson, and disastrous efforts to tunnel beneath it — 20 workers drowned in one attempt.

It was finally Cassatt's heroic vision to tunnel under both rivers, bridge over Hell Gate and raise a colossal terminal in the heart of the city.

McKim began drafting plans for the terminal and the tunnels in 1902. The tunnels were actually the greater feat; at the time, they were the longest underwater tunnels in the world. But the station was the world's largest railroad terminal when it opened in 1910, and what a great, grand place it was.

It filled two city blocks, from 31st St. to 33rd St. between Seventh and Eighth Aves., 7½ acres in all. The main concourse was patterned on the tepidarium — the warming room — of the ancient Baths of Caracalla in Rome, and was sheathed in marble from the same quarries. It was an awesome space, stretching north and south for the full two

CHAPTER 137

IRREVERENCE FOR ANTIQUITY
Penn Station, 1963

blocks — longer than the nave of St. Peter's Basilica in Rome. Lined with columns of pink granite, it soared 138 feet to a vaulted glass ceiling.

In addition to the main waiting room, there were separate waiting rooms for ladies and gentlemen, and a smoking room off the men's. There were private rooms where, for example, funeral parties could pause away from the general hubbub.

Soon after the station opened, it was flanked by two more creations from the architects at McKim, Mead and White — McKim himself having died before the station was completed. The railroad built the Hotel Pennsylvania across Seventh Ave. to accommodate its passengers, and across Eighth Ave. the federal government built the classically colonnaded General Post Office.

For 50 years, Pennsylvania Station served its purpose well. It was busier than ever during World War II. But travel by air and automobile overwhelmed the railroads after the war, and Pennsy officials began to view their icon as an expensive burden. Years before the final destruction, they let it deteriorate. Grime dulled its elegant interior. In the 1950s, they plunked

new ticket counters in the middle of the concourse under a huge canopy, and they milked open floor space for revenue with late-model cars on rotating platforms.

Through Penn Station in its great days, grieved architectural scholar Vincent Scully, "one entered the city like a god. One scuttles in now like a rat."

"Demolition by commercialization," snapped critic Ada Louise Huxtable.

THE RAILROAD was, in fact, thinking demolition outright. It optioned developer William Zeckendorf to acquire the air rights in 1954 and replace the building with a Palace of Progress merchandise mart. The palace never materialized, but in 1960, Pennsy hooked another developer, Irving Felt, who was seeking to remove Madison Square Garden from 8th Ave. and 50th St. and find it a new home.

A small group of architects organized to stop all this, but they were helpless in the face of a zoning law that covered only proposals for new structures; it said nothing about preserving the old. The new Garden needed only city approval for a

22,000-seat arena in a neighborhood zoned for less — and got it.

TENSION BETWEEN preservation and development was certainly nothing new. In 1831, the New-York Mirror had decried the destruction of a 17th century Dutch house on Pearl St., cursing the "irreverence for antiquity which so grievously afflicts the people of this city." In 1941, Robert Moses went after Castle Clinton in Battery Park — "a large red wart with no history worth writing about," he sneered. America's entry into war was the only thing that stopped him.

Unintentionally, Moses strengthened the preservationists with his high-handed sweeping away of old neighborhoods for highways and urban renewal. The city's landmarks law was first proposed during Robert Wagner's mayoral administration in the 1950s and pushed by concerned architects and the Municipal Art Society. It was finally enacted by Mayor John Lindsay in 1966.

New York City's preservation law now protects some 1,000 individual landmarks and 72 historic districts that encompass another 21,000 buildings. Individual landmarks include the Empire State Building, Central Park and the interiors of many theaters and restaurants. The law helped block construction of a tower over Grand Central Terminal in a 1970s test finally settled by the Supreme Court. It might have saved Penn Station, too.

By JAMES S. ROSEN
Special to The News

THE BEATLES *Are Coming!* Everywhere they went in the first week of February 1964, New Yorkers heard this Paul Revere-like warning of a looming British invasion. That was because Capitol Records had shelled out $50,000 to plaster the town with 5 million posters, buttons, bumper stickers and radio ads, all trumpeting the arrival of — the *Whatles?*

"A shrieking, stamping quartet" of young musicians from Liverpool, England, explained the Daily News, pretty much summing up the official grownup point of view. "Dishmop hairdos." "An inescapable, ear-jangling pitch." The photo was of four slender young men, in four black suits and four knit ties, with four Prince Valiant haircuts and four bemused expressions. They seemed largely indistinguishable from one another, but The News helpfully sorted things out: The oldest, 23-year-old Ringo Starr — *Ringo?* — "attacked the drums"; John Lennon was "the chief Beatle, who is married and has a son"; a third one, Paul McCartney, "with Lennon, writes Beatle songs," and the last one, George Harrison, was "the lead guitar."

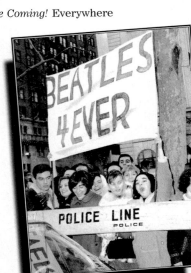

It seemed they had recently taken the UK by storm. "At first, British adults dismissed them, then protested, then succumbed," the paper reported. "Finally, the whole population was swept along." Why, the queen herself had pronounced them "young, fresh and vital." British riot police, though, struggling to control legions of hysterical female fans, appeared to be taking a dimmer view of this "Beatlemania."

Suddenly the four shaggy Britons were exploding across the American popular music charts as well. This week they had two — *two!* — wild songs in the Top 10, rolling over the pleasant likes of Bobby Vinton, Bobby Rydell and the Singing Nun; their first U.S. album was just hitting the stores. Now they were en route to New York to play Ed Sullivan's program and Carnegie Hall. *The Beatles Are Coming!*

Their plane touched down at Kennedy at 1:20 p.m. on Friday the 7th of February. Emblazoned on the side of their Pan Am Yankee Clipper was a single word: DEFIANCE.

THREE THOUSAND screaming fans greeted them. Signs and banners waved aloft. Girls swooned. At first, the Beatles thought the President must be nearby.

"So this is America," mused Ringo Starr. "They all seem out of their minds."

What an ugly race, John Lennon thought.

THOSE WHO couldn't make it out to Kennedy stayed glued to their radios. Beatlemania's prime carrier was 1010 WINS, where deejay Murray (The K) Kaufman was in frenzies. *Triple ripple! Triple play! Three in a row! Without commercial interruption! Here's what's happenin', baby! THE BEATLES!*

She loves you, yeah, yeah, yeah . . .

The New York press corps was waiting to mob the moptops too. *Do you plan to get a haircut at*

all? "I had one yesterday." *What do you think of Beethoven?* "I love him. Especially his poems." *Why does your music excite your fans so much?* "If we knew, we'd form another group and be managers." Jousting done, the four Englishmen were hustled away in Cadillacs to the sedate Plaza hotel on Central Park South, whose managers had not been expecting a singing group and who were now horrified to find police barricades and hundreds of delirious teenagers outside their doors.

Girls charged through the mounted cops, swarmed the arriving cars, pounded on their doors, wept hysterically. Even elderly women ran up and tried to touch the Beatles as the phalanx of guards bore them inside. Kids ran through the hotel corridors, trying to find their idols. "If this keeps up," sniffed a Plaza official, "the Beatles will have to go."

"We sent three cameramen out to Kennedy this afternoon to cover the arrival of a group from

CHAPTER 138

SO THIS IS AMERICA

Meet The Beatles, 1964

England known as the Beatles," said an unimpressed Chet Huntley on the NBC newscast that evening. "However, after surveying the film our men arrived with, and the subject of that film, I feel there is absolutely no need to show any of that film."

GEORGE IMMEDIATELY came down ill, so he stayed in while Murray The K took John, Paul and Ringo out on the town. They hit the Playboy Club and the Peppermint Lounge. Paul found himself a Bunny; Ringo disappeared for hours. John, for his part, was accompanied by his wife, Cynthia. The next day the three of them sat for photo shoots while radio bulletins updated the nation on George's condition.

Ed Sullivan vowed to stand in for the sick Beatle himself if he needed to, but George managed to stagger out of his bed in time for the broadcast. Seventy million people were watching, 60% of American TV viewers.

"The city has never witnessed the excitement stirred by these youngsters from Liverpool," Sullivan announced, rubbing his hands together.

"Ladies and gentlemen, *THE BEATLES!*"

Backstage, a Sullivan studio hand covered his face as screams shook the house. "Good God," he murmured.

By JAY MAEDER
Daily News Staff Writer

SORROWED CITIZENS, not particularly including the souls who had actually watched the thing happen from their windows, would reflect over the years that the incident on Austin St. in Kew Gardens in Queens in the early morning hours of Saturday the 13th of March 1964 rang out with a terrible finality any sense that once upon a time there had been something approximating a compassionate human community in the City of New York. It would be noted that the screaming young woman's savage slaying, literally before the eyes of 38 of her neighbors who watched it for half an hour like it was a television show before anyone could be bothered even to pick up a phone to summon police, was a definable turning point in the city's modern social history. It would be observed around the globe that the City of New York, specifically the community of Kew Gardens in the Borough of Queens, was the metaphor for the numbness that had overtaken the urban condition in the mid-20th century. It would come to be felt that the young woman's death was, really, as one observer put it, "the beginning of the end of decency."

Her name was Catherine Genovese. She managed a tavern called Ev's 11th Hour, over on Jamaica Ave. in Hollis, and she lived above an upholstery shop at 82-70 Austin St. It was her custom to park her car outside the Long Island Rail Road station just a fast walk from her flat. Apparently, shortly after 3 on this chilly Saturday morning, she had realized that she had been followed from the bar — followed from Jamaica Ave. to the Grand Central Parkway to Queens Blvd. to 82nd Road to Austin St., followed into the dark LIRR parking lot — and she had started to run.

She was almost at the safety of her door when the man with the knife caught her.

SHE SCREAMED and she screamed and she screamed, as 38 of her neighbors watched from their windows.

"Leave that girl alone," one of them shouted down.

They watched as the startled attacker fled. They watched as the bloodied woman staggered down the street, stumbled into a doorway and collapsed.

And they watched as, 10 minutes later, her killer sauntered back and, without further interference and altogether at his leisure, finished her off.

SHE WAS JUST another routine homicide at first. **QUEENS BARMAID STABBED, DIES,** reported the Daily News. **QUEENS WOMAN IS STABBED TO DEATH IN FRONT OF HOME,** chronicled The New York Times. It wasn't until a week or so later that police detectives went public with how sick to their stomachs the dreadful residents of Austin St. had made them. Every neighbor they talked to had seen the whole

CHAPTER 139

FOR WHOM THE BELL TOLLS

Kitty Genovese, 1964

thing, and not a one of them had lifted a finger. Some of them, true, rubbing sleep from their eyes, simply hadn't grasped the gravity of the matter. As for the others: "*I didn't want to get involved.*" "*It was none of my business.*" "*I was tired.*" The man who lived just up the stairwell from where Kitty Genovese had fallen had actually peeped out for an instant and seen the knife-flailing assailant cutting her apart, and then he had slammed his door shut so he wouldn't have to think about it.

She was dead on arrival at Queens General Hospital. The first few knife wounds, inflicted out

on the sidewalk, had not been fatal. What killed her were the eight or 10 more she took 15 full minutes after she first shrieked "Help me!" outside her front door. Fifteen full minutes during which the man with the knife had returned to her side and brought his blade out again. Fifteen minutes in which anyone's call to the police would have let 28-year-old Kitty Genovese live another day.

Around the whole world, the mutes of Kew Gardens overnight became the symbols of total indifference, of stone-hearted New York City, of soulless and empty modern times.

THE KILLER, picked up a few days later, was one Winston Moseley, of Sutter Ave. in Richmond Hill, a responsibly employed young family man who, as he matter-of-factly explained to cops, just came down with this urge sometimes to go out cruising for some random woman to cut up. It had been Kitty Genovese's destiny to leave Ev's 11th Hour exactly at the moment he drove past the place, and he had made a U-turn and followed her home. Yes, he said, she had spotted him after she parked her car in the LIRR lot, and she had made a terror-stricken run for her life, but he had been faster.

But, detectives pointed out, there had already been one cry from a window — *Leave that girl alone!* — and he had been forced to sprint away. How could he have come back just minutes later to resume the murderous assault? Had he not supposed that people might be watching?

"Oh, I knew they wouldn't do anything," Winston Moseley said. "People never do. That late at night, they just go back to sleep."

AYEAR LATER, a Journal-American news team quite unsubtly re-created the Kitty Genovese killing on Austin St., and a young woman reporter lay writhing and moaning on the sidewalk for half an hour, and once again not a single person called the law. "I did not call the police then, and I would not call the police now," sniffed one woman who informed the reporters that their questions irritated her. A building super apologetically explained that he had thought about making a call but that his wife hadn't let him.

In October 1965, a Hollywood-handsome Congressman named John Lindsay who was running for mayor on the Republican-Liberal ticket held a campaign rally in the LIRR parking lot and pledged to wipe out crime in the streets with the help of every good citizen of the City of New York.

"We must give to the people of New York faith, so that the double lock will no longer be the symbol of New York," he said. "It will require each citizen willing to be his brother's keeper. It will require citizens to rally to the defense of their neighbors when crime strikes."

John Lindsay stood outside the Kew Gardens station, a fast walk away from the spot where Kitty Genovese had spilled her life's blood, and mourned.

"Something has gone out of the heart and soul of New York City," he said.

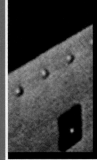

By BRIAN MOSS
Daily News Staff Writer

ON A BREEZY March day in 1964, James Farmer, head of the Congress of Racial Equality, visited Wagner College on Staten Island as featured speaker of the school's 14th annual Faith and Life Week.

Civil rights, the activist told the mostly white students, "is a problem not only for Negroes, but for whites as well. We need white persons in the movement all over the country. If you're a bystander today, you're no longer innocent. You're guilty."

Ten years had passed since the U.S. Supreme Court ruled racial segregation in schools illegal, and frustration was growing among those involved in the movement for civil rights.

The South had been the main battleground. Blacks were staging marches and sit-ins for the simplest of rights — to be served in restaurants, to use public restrooms, to sit anywhere they pleased on public buses and in movie theaters, to vote. By 1964, such demonstrations had become more common in the North as well.

In April, the World's Fair in Flushing Meadows opened under the threat of a "stall-in," a demonstration by mostly black activists designed to snarl traffic on every major roadway to the fairgrounds and disrupt President Lyndon Johnson's keynote address. Though this protest fizzled, the new militancy of the civil rights struggle was apparent.

By this time, Michael Schwerner had already left his Henry St. apartment in Brooklyn Heights to go work in Mississippi. A graduate of Cornell and the Columbia School of Social Work, 24-year-old Mickey Schwerner had been working with children in a lower East Side settlement house, and he had founded a New York City CORE chapter. Now he wanted to do more.

"The Negro in the South has an even more bitter fight ahead of him than in the North," Schwerner wrote on his CORE application, "and I wish to be a part of that fight. I would feel guilty and almost hypocritical if I did not give full time."

When civil rights groups announced plans for a Mississippi civil rights campaign for the summer of 1964, Schwerner, who had worked for several months in Meridian, was an obvious choice to help organize it.

If Andrew Goodman, a 20-year-old junior at Queens College, initially seemed a less likely candidate for Freedom Summer, the one-time theater major from the upper West Side was in 1964 finding passionate moral convictions. Such idealistically awakening young whites were precisely what organizers wanted in Mississippi, to draw attention to the movement in the nation's most racist and backward state.

In Mississippi, newspapers and politicians informed the citizenry that these young whites

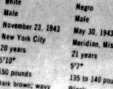

THE FBI IS SEEKING INFORMATION CONCERNING THE DISAPPEARANCE AT PHILADELPHIA, MISSISSIPPI, OF THESE THREE INDIVIDUALS ON JUNE 21, 1964. EXTENSIVE INVESTIGATION IS BEING CONDUCTED TO LOCATE GOODMAN, CHANEY, AND SCHWERNER, WHO ARE DESCRIBED AS FOLLOWS:

ANDREW GOODMAN   **JAMES EARL CHANEY**   **MICHAEL HENRY SCHWERNER**

RACE:	White	Negro	White
SEX:	Male	Male	Male
DOB:	November 23, 1943	May 30, 1943	November 6, 1939
POB:	New York City	Meridian, Mississippi	New York City
AGE:	20 years	21 years	24 years
HEIGHT:	5'10"	5'7"	5'9" to 5'10"
WEIGHT:	150 pounds	135 to 140 pounds	170 to 180 pounds
HAIR:	Dark brown; wavy	Black	Brown
EYES:	Brown	Brown	Brown
TEETH:			

CHAPTER 140

LONG HOT SUMMER

Freedom Riders, 1964

DIRECTOR
FEDERAL BUREAU OF INVESTIGATION
UNITED STATES DEPARTMENT OF JUSTICE

were part of a Northern invasion that would make their home a battleground for hated federal intervention on civil rights issues. One dispatch from Jackson on the eve of Freedom Summer noted matter-of-factly that locals expected "violence and bloodshed."

MICKEY SCHWERNER spent a week in Ohio, training the first group of students who would be going south, and it was there that he befriended Andrew Goodman. On Saturday the 20th of June, Goodman went to Mississippi with Schwerner and another organizer, James Chaney, a black baker from Meridian.

On Sunday, the three of them set out to inspect the ruins of a black church that been torched in Neshoba County. Mindful of local tensions, they told friends before they left that they should check up on them if they weren't back by 4 p.m.

Sometime that afternoon, their blue Ford station wagon, with Chaney driving, was stopped for speeding by Deputy Sheriff Cecil Price. They were jailed — Chaney in one cell, Goodman and Schwerner in another — and several hours later

they put up a $20 bond and were released.

They headed south on Route 19 toward Meridian. Then they disappeared.

"If they're missing," opined Sheriff L.A. Rainey, the chief local law enforcement official, "they just hid somewhere, trying to get a lot of publicity out of it, I figure."

THE U.S. JUSTICE Department figured differently. FBI agents arrived in force to search for the missing trio. The nation started paying attention.

On Wednesday, Goodman's parents and Schwerner's father flew to Washington, where Johnson personally gave them the news he had just received from FBI chief J. Edgar Hoover: The Ford wagon had been found, a burned shell.

Two days later the parents gathered again, this time at the Goodmans' apartment, and begged the mothers and fathers of Mississippi to offer up information on the fate of their missing sons. In Foley Square, marchers picketed around the clock.

Some 400 Navy sailors slogged through snake-infested swamps in search of the three missing men. But there was no trace of them.

Back in New York, there now occurred another event that shifted the city's attention.

ON THE NIGHT of July 16, a black teenager was shot and killed by an off-duty police lieutenant who said the youth had threatened him with a knife. Two days later, a Harlem protest against police brutality turned into a riot. Stores on 125th St. were looted, and bricks and bottles rained on cops from rooftops. Thirty people were arrested.

Violence began erupting almost nightly. Within days, the disorders spread to Bedford-Stuyvesant. When it was all over, one person was dead, 82 civilians and 36 police officers were injured, 202 people had been arrested and 117 stores were damaged in Harlem; in Brooklyn, 10 civilians and 12 cops were hurt, 276 persons were arrested and 556 stores were damaged.

The long, hot summer had come to New York City.

THE MISSISSIPPI manhunt continued to come up empty until Aug. 4, when, acting on a tip, FBI agents found the bodies of Mickey Schwerner, Andrew Goodman and James Chaney entombed in an earthen dam.

Investigators said that after the rights workers were released from jail, they had been chased down by two carloads of men tipped off by Price. Captured, they were taken to an isolated spot, killed in succession and buried.

Nineteen men, including Price, were charged with having denied the dead men their civil rights. Eventually there were seven convictions. No one was ever charged with murder.

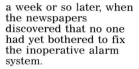
By JAY MAEDER
Daily News Staff Writer

UNLIKE THE fabulously cursed Hope Diamond, which was reputed to visit woe and torment and horrible death and just one thing after another upon anyone who sought to possess it, and apparently did just that on several occasions, the Star of India was an agreeably tempered stone that wished no one harm. Star stones in general, according to the legends of the ancients, were formed in the earth by the sparks from the Star of Bethlehem, and their glowing rays were believed to represent faith and hope and destiny. The Star of India in particular was said to bring joyful good fortune to all its owners. In the chronicles of more than three centuries, the worst thing it ever did was greatly embarrass the directors of New York City's American Museum of Natural History, who were forced to admit, after the Star of India was filched from under their noses, that all the museum's priceless treasures were guarded by a burglar alarm system that hadn't worked for several years.

The burglars were two 27-year-old Miami Beach surf bums named Jack Murphy and Allen Kuhn, who had recently seen Jules Dassin's film "Topkapi," which detailed a gem theft from an Istanbul museum, and been inspired to pull off a caper of their own. When the Star of India and 23 other sparklers were found missing from their display cases in the museum's fourth-floor Morgan Hall of Minerals and Gems on Friday morning the 30th of October 1964, the unbelievable theft immediately became, as the Daily News put it, "a chapter in criminal history that rivals anything in fiction" — the American equivalent of England's Great Train Robbery, a wonderfully glamorous heist whose perpetrators even the cops had to kind of admire.

As international manhunts went, this one rivaled no fiction: Murphy and Kuhn were picked up in Miami Beach a day later. Florida cops knew them as dubious characters, high-living beach boys who managed speedboats and Cadillacs and bevies of babes on no visible means of support, and in fact they'd been under surveillance for a while as suspects in a wave of second-story jobs; when word came down from New York, Murphy and Kuhn were pretty much the first people local officers went to see.

Of the Star of India there was no sign. What could small-timers like Murphy and Kuhn have hoped to do with such a bauble? It was one of the world's most famous rocks, once the property of old J.P. Morgan himself, the largest cut sapphire known to man, 563.35 carats, literally bigger than a golf ball — in short, unfenceable. Several of the other missing gems — the 116.75-carat Midnight

DeLong Ruby, Star of India, Midnight Star.

CHAPTER 141

GENTLEMAN THIEVERY

The Star Of India, 1964

Kuhn and Murphy.

Disenjeweled Gabor shows off boo-boo.

Star, the 100.32-carat DeLong ruby — were nearly equally notorious. They were, well, museum pieces. Suspicion arose that Murphy and Kuhn must have had a deal with some wealthy private patron of the arts. But hard evidence of anything was fairly flimsy.

Free on bond, the bronze-bodied, golden-haired surfer lads — Murphy was known on the beach as Murf the Surf — overnight became celebrities, widely feted as the Raffles-like gentleman thieves who had pulled off one of the world's great heists, yet still free of the nuisance of having the job criminally pinned on them. They announced they were going to open a nightspot called The Star Of India. The waitresses would wear saris.

Back in New York City, the American Museum of Natural History suffered further mortification

a week or so later, when the newspapers discovered that no one had yet bothered to fix the inoperative alarm system.

MURF THE SURF and his buddy Kuhn might have been home scot-free forever, had it not been for actress Eva Gabor, sister of Zsa Zsa, who one day spotted their pictures in the paper, decided that these were the guys who had pistol-whipped her and taken her bracelet a year or so earlier and went to the cops to press a complaint.

Facing this fresh heat, Kuhn in January 1965 cut a deal with Manhattan District Attorney Frank Hogan's office, suggesting that he might be in a position to effect the return of the missing gems in exchange for various considerations. The museum was only too happy to hear about this. There were hints that a $35,000 ransom would be slipped to someone or other. Details were kept under wraps as New York detectives, DA's investigator Maurice Nadjari and beach boy Kuhn galloped around Miami from one mysterious rendezvous point to another, reporters in hot pursuit.

At the end of the trail was a bus-station locker, and inside the locker was a chamois bag, and inside the bag were the Star of India and a few of the other stolen stones.

On Jan. 8, J.P. Morgan's storied sapphire was flown back to New York City and returned to the museum, where it immediately became a prime attraction. Kuhn and Murphy ended up facing simple burglary raps, particularly after Gabor failed to follow through on the Florida charge, and in April the men who had lifted the Star of India drew short prison terms, and the chapter in criminal history that rivaled anything in fiction was now concluded.

Except for the matter of the various other unrecovered gems. The DeLong Ruby remained missing for many more months, finally being found in a Miami phone booth by Daily News reporter Bill Federici and photographer Dan Farrell after a Florida millionaire put up a payoff.

KUHN AND MURPHY *did two years in prison, and Murphy in particular went on to much enjoy his fame as the sleek and classy gent behind one of the world's most romantic jobs. This glamorousness abruptly diminished in 1968, when he was charged with the murders of two young women who were found beaten to death, tied to concrete blocks and dumped into a Florida canal.*

By JAY MAEDER
Daily News Staff Writer

AND HERE were still another couple of emerging pipsqueak nations lately become full voting members of the great world body headquartered at First Ave. and 42nd St. in the City of New York, and today in the chambers of the Security Council the ministers from Guinea and Mali were railing away at the Belgian expeditionary forces that had gone in to rescue white hostages in the seething Congo and Belgium's sputtering envoy was denouncing them both as barbarians. In the General Assembly at this same moment, Maj. Ernesto Guevara, Marxist Cuba's fatigues-clad, cigar-brandishing minister of industry, was sneering at the U.S. push for a denuclearization pact in the Western Hemisphere. It was two weeks before Christmas 1964, and there wasn't much in the way of peace on Earth.

Across First Ave., held back by police, noisy knots of Cubans hurled curses at the mighty glass tower and shook their fists and fervently swung their anti-Castro signs and banners. *El Dictador Fidel! El Asesino! El Monstruo! Communist Murderer! Servant Of Russian Imperialism! Invade Cuba Now!* Again the long-suffering residents of Tudor City and other neighboring apartment buildings cranked shut their windows and wondered why they were living next door to the United Nations.

Police helicopters circled overhead. Police launches prowled the river. Mounted cops blockaded the streets and avenues. Sharpshooters perched on rooftops. On high UN alert, the professionals of the New York Police Department were once more doing the job they had done many times before when dignitaries came to visit.

Among the things they hadn't thought of doing was taking a look directly across the river, just about 900 yards away, to see whether anybody might be sitting there with a World War II-vintage bazooka.

THE SHELL WAS a foot and a half long and it weighed 8 pounds, including the 1.9 pounds of high explosive packed inside it, and it came whistling across the East River straight toward the United Nations at 12:10 p.m. on Friday the 11th of December, and probably it would have killed quite a few people had it not fallen a bit short of the Manhattan riverbank.

The blast rocked the whole building. A great geyser of water shot up from the depths of the river. Diplomats gaped. Cops went for their holsters. From the sea of signs held aloft by the members of the Cuban Student Directorate and the Cuban Workers Committee in Exile and the Cuban Workers Revolutionary Front charged a tiny young woman, straight through the wall of startled cops, across First Ave., over the snow fence, through the shrubbery, toward the majestic citadel of global harmony. As two fast-moving officers tackled her, she went down kicking and screaming and slashing away with the hunting

CHAPTER 142

UNAUTHORIZED ACTIONS

Target United Nations, 1964

knife she had hoped to plunge into the breast of Che Guevara. Informed of this, Guevara serenely blew smoke rings and said, not ungallantly: "It is better to be killed by a woman with a knife than by a man with a gun."

As for the shell, detectives followed the trajectory over to Long Island City, Queens, where, in a weed-strewn lot at the foot of 48th Ave., behind the Adam Metal Supply Co., there sat an abandoned 3.5-mm. bazooka, a Cuban flag proudly waving from it.

NEW YORK HAD always been a haven for every imaginable stripe of political refugee come to lay low and plot — Giuseppe Garibaldi, perhaps most famously, had mapped out the entire Italian campaign from Staten Island — and Cubans had always been among the most volatile of the bunch, not altogether unreasonably, it having been their miserable fortune to have suffered under one butcher or another for generations beyond memory. Unlike the rabble of various other lands, Cuban exiles largely tended to be your better classes, quality folks, professors and poets and generals; Jose Martí himself had lived in the city for many years, dreaming of the day when the Spaniards would be gone, and it was these socially influential New York Cubans whose passionate importunings had moved William Randolph Hearst to beat his drums for the Spanish-American War in 1898.

Nests of them were active again in the 1920s and '30s, indefatigably raising armies and air forces and conspiring to topple first the beast Gerardo Machado and next the bewildering collection of short-lived presidents who followed

in Machado's wake, whichever of them they happened to oppose at the moment. Through the mid-'30s, if it occasionally struck some observers that Cuban presidents seemed to be nothing but the same six or seven people forever overthrowing one another, New York's various exile leaders remained ferociously true to their own particular agendas, and the city's news columns regularly were full of mysterious local assassinations that nobody but the Cubans understood. In September 1934, when the New York-to-Havana liner Morro Castle burned off Atlantic City, the incident seemed to have something to do with clandestine arms traffic. Cuba meanwhile kept getting new presidents. *Norteamericanos* just shrugged and went to Havana pretty much just to drink rum and play the ponies.

Now it was decades later, and tens of thousands of new refugees were dwelling in New York and New Jersey, all factions now united against *El Dictador Fidel*, and the Bay of Pigs horror remained a fresh, raw wound. Credit for the UN blast was immediately claimed by a group called the Black Front — "a Christmas present for the enslaved Cuban people," the communique declared. No extant authority had ever heard of the Black Front, but this was not unusual; the Cuban communities were full of paramilitary outfits consisting of one or two guys with a ditto machine. Three days before Christmas, though, when lawmen arrested teletype repairman Carlos Perez, shoe salesman Ignacio Nova and Jersey doorman Guillermo Nova, the prisoners proved to be aligned with the quite real Cuban Nationalist Movement.

Executive director Felipe Rivero insisted he was mortified by the unauthorized actions of his comrades. "We have made very clear our position not to do anything hostile in this country, anything that would put this country in a difficult position," Rivero said. The Spanish-language El Tiempo newspaper scolded Perez and the brothers Nova for having brought discredit upon the anti-Castro movement, but at the same time announced that they had fired short on purpose, that they had meant only to create an incident, that they had never intended to actually strike the UN building.

Nevertheless, said Assistant District Attorney Edward Herman, "The UN is in the city as a guest, and they have the right not to have bazookas fired at them."

"We are among pirates," grumbled Soviet chief delegate Nikolai Federenko. "How can we work?"

CHARGES AGAINST *Perez and the Novas collapsed on a technicality in June 1965. Noting that their war-surplus weapon had been bought for $35 in an Eighth Ave. shop, Police Commissioner Michael Murphy said that the incident demonstrated "a tremendous need for legislation" to control the sale of bazookas.*

By CLEM RICHARDSON
Daily News Staff Writer

'**L**ET'S COOL *it, brothers.*" That admonition, of course, meant nothing to men with murder on their minds, and there were at least three assassins and possibly more in the Audubon Ballroom at Broadway and 166th St. when it was uttered at 3 p.m. on Sunday the 21st of February 1965.

Malcolm X, the militant yang to the Rev. Martin Luther King Jr.'s pacifist ying, was about to die.

His first words to the crowd of about 400 were "As salaam alaikum (Peace be unto you)." Many replied, "Wa alaikum salaam (And unto you, peace)."

The men who had come to take down Malcolm with shotgun and pistol blasts were young and militant — Black Muslims like himself, only they still loved Black Muslim patriarch The Honorable Elijah Muhammad, whereas Muhammad and Malcolm, formerly the most devoted of Muhammad's disciples, were now mortal enemies.

It was well-planned. A man in an overcoat sitting in the middle of the auditorium stood up and screamed, "Get your hand off my pockets!" to a man sitting next to him. "Let's cool it, brothers," Malcolm said.

CHAPTER 143

WA ALAIKUM SALAAM

Taking Down Malcolm, 1965

MALCOLM AND Muhammad had done much for each other before they fell out.

Born in 1925 in Nebraska to parents who were devout followers of black nationalist Marcus Garvey, Malcolm Little was a pimp, gambler and dope dealer before his family, along with fellow prison inmates, introduced him to Muhammad's Nation of Islam in 1948 while he was doing 10 years for burglary in Massachusetts.

Islam, wrote Malcolm's brother Philbert, was the natural religion for the black man. Another brother, Reginald, brought it all home during a visit, informing him that God had come to America and made himself known to a black man named Elijah.

The man doing the yelling pulled a shotgun from under the flaps of his overcoat. Two men in the front row stood up and pointed pistols at the stage. Someone rolled a smoke bomb across the floor at the rear of the hall.

The Black Muslims had several radical messages: that the white man was the devil, that the devil could not be trusted, that the black man in America who had turned his back on Islam was spiritually and morally dead. But Islam was also puritanical in what it demanded of the faithful: no tobacco, no drugs, no alcohol. Prayer several times a day. Cleanliness. Thrift. Family. Devotion to Elijah Muhammad.

The first volley caught Malcolm with his hands raised as he tried to calm the crowd. The shots slammed him back into a row of folding chairs behind the podium. His head hit the floor with a thud.

Malcolm accepted Islam, began writing Elijah Muhammad every day from his cell and took X as his last name, because Little, he explained, "was just a name some white man gave one of my ancestors."

He went to Chicago to meet and work with Muhammad shortly after he left prison in August 1952, and his rise through the Black Muslim ranks was meteoric. Smart, witty and energetic, he traveled the country and the world lecturing, drawing many thousands of new recruits.

The Nation recruited most heavily among the hopeless: dope fiends, convicts and hustlers who had long ago given up on any of America's promises.

The gunmen, firing wildly, raced for the front and back doors amid the screams of the panicked crowd. A bodyguard shot one of them in the leg. Crowds rushed to Malcolm's aid as he lay sprawled on the floor.

Moved to New York, where he ran the Harlem temple, the tall and photogenic Malcolm X fast became a media darling. "He is, above all else, utterly charming," said Herald Tribune city editor Dick Schaap.

But even as blacks and whites were being beaten and killed in the Deep South through the late 1950s and early '60s, Malcolm declared: "An integrated cup of coffee doesn't pay for 400 years of slave labor." And he excoriated the activists for integration: "The major civil rights leaders have white hearts and white brains, and they wish they had white skins."

Followers tried to minister to Malcolm, who had been struck 16 times. Others beat the wounded gunman, 22-year-old Talmadge Hayer of New Jersey, breaking his leg before cops arrived to rescue him.

Malcolm debated politicians and college professors. He brought reigning heavyweight champion Cassius Clay into the Muslim fold and renamed him Muhammad Ali.

It was at the time of President John F. Kennedy's assassination in late 1963 — "A case of chickens coming to roost," Malcolm termed Kennedy's death — that a growing rift with Elijah Muhammad spilled into the open. Many in Muhammad's inner circle felt that the popular Malcolm took too much spotlight off the leader.

Malcolm was bundled onto a stretcher and wheeled a block to the Vanderbilt Clinic at Columbia-Presbyterian Medical Center. In a third-floor operating room, he was pronounced dead at 3:30 p.m.

Suspended by Muhammad, Malcolm nevertheless still pledged undying loyalty. "Anything that Mr. Muhammad does is all right with me," he told the press. "I believe absolutely in his wisdom and his authority."

But he didn't.

There had been rumors that Elijah Muhammad had fathered several children by several young women, keeping them all on his block-long estate on Chicago's South Side. These rumors were true, and Malcolm did not approve.

By the time his assassins rose to their feet in the Audubon Ballroom, he had renounced the Nation of Islam, gone on a pilgrimage to Mecca, changed his name to El-Hajj Malik El-Shabazz and formed his own group, the Organization of Afro-American Unity.

And, by Feb. 21, 1965, he had suffered months of phone threats against himself and his family. Just a week earlier, his home in East Elmhurst, Queens, had been firebombed as he and his wife, Betty, and their four children slept.

Nation of Islam leaders emphatically denied any involvement in the firebombing or the fatal shooting.

The day after the murder, the Nation's temple at Lenox Ave. and 116th St. was destroyed by arson.

MALCOLM X *lay for several days at the Unity Funeral Home as family and friends tried to find a church that would host the services. More than 22,000 people viewed the body, wrapped in a Muslim funeral shroud beneath a glass-topped coffin, before the funeral at Faith Temple Church of God in Christ.*

Talmadge Hayer and two other men, Norman 3X Butler, 26, and Thomas 15X Johnson, 30, went to prison for the killing.

Malcolm is buried in Ferncliff Cemetery in Hartsdale, Westchester County.

Michael Quill

John Lindsay

By OWEN MORITZ
Daily News Staff Writer

CHAPTER 144

NOTHING TO RIDE

Transit Shutdown, 1966

FOR AS LONG AS anyone could remember, Michael Quill, the fiery, round-faced president and founder of the Transit Workers Union, had threatened mayors, governors and the New York City Transit Authority with a punishing subway and bus strike.

It was a biennial New Year's Eve charade. Every two years, New York's vast riding public would hold its breath as Quill shook his black cane and trotted out his thickest brogue and defiantly announced he wasn't going to negotiate with the Devil incarnate, the "Transit Awtarrity."

Then, at the eleventh hour, he would invariably cut a modest deal, often under the backroom auspices of a Democratic mayor who would then somehow locate the necessary funds or agree to raise fares to pay for the settlement.

On Saturday, the 1st of January, 1966, it was different. This time, the city woke up to find everything standing still.

MIKE QUILL, at 60 years of age perhaps too sick to hold his union post anymore, perhaps feeling heat from union militants, certainly no longer restrained by Democratic mayors, went to war with the city's new chief executive — a photogenic, patrician reform Republican named John Lindsay who, barely in office, was already being touted for President.

No two public figures were more different. County Kerry-born Quill was a one-time ditch digger who, fed up with working 14 hours a day, seven days a week, had formed the Transit Workers Union in 1934. Boisterous, clownish and shrewd, he had spent 12 years as a Laborite city councilman. By 1966, he wanted a four-day, 32-hour work week for his largely Irish union, and he had no use for Lindsay, a Yalie who had been a congressman before becoming elected New York's second Republican mayor of the 20th century.

John Lindsay looked at Quill and he saw the past, wrote columnist Jimmy Breslin. *And Mike Quill looked at John Lindsay and he saw the Church of England.*

Ten minutes after 1965 became 1966, Quill and his bargaining team stormed out of a bargaining session with the Transit Authority, calling its two-year, $25 million offer a "peanut package." As for the incoming mayor, Quill said he had no intention of dealing with a man he openly called a "pipsqueak."

Urged by Lindsay to bargain through the night, Quill said no thanks: "I don't enjoy the midnight shift."

And so, at 5 a.m., Quill's 33,000-member rank and file, along with another 1,800 workers from the Amalgamated Transit Union, walked off their jobs.

Subways, buses, even private bus line shut down. Six million riders had nothing to ride.

"An unlawful strike against the public interest," roared Lindsay. "An act of defiance against 8 million people."

"I don't think there'll be any catastrophe if the strike runs for the next few weeks," Quill replied coolly. "London withstood the blitz."

THE WEEKEND PASSED without incident. As the new work week approached, Lindsay appealed to all nonessential workers to stay home. As few New Yorkers cared to consider themselves nonessential, the 44-year-old Lindsay and his cadre of young advisers had now just misstepped on their new administration's first day.

Still, 1.5 million workers did stay home, and New York survived Monday. Those who did commute to work drove, hitchhiked, walked, biked, roller-skated, rode cabs or made circuitous trips via suburban rail lines. Hotels and armories filled up. Museums shut down; theaters and restaurants suffered from lack of patrons. Business fell off 50% at department stores.

"New York wasn't even a nice place to visit yesterday," the Daily News reported in its Tuesday editions.

BY NOW, QUILL was at war with the courts. When he was served a subpoena ordering his men back to work, the enraged Quill tore it up.

"The judge can drop dead in his black robes," Quill announced. "Personally, I don't care if I rot in jail."

Jailed for civil contempt, the labor leader was taken to jail on W. 37th St. Less than two hours later, he collapsed.

The ambulance taking him across town to Bellevue's emergency room barely made it through the teeming traffic. Doctors said Quill had been overcome by the stress of a strike that was costing the city $100 million a day in lost business.

On Tuesday the 4th, the strike's realities began to hit home. Businessmen camped out in their offices. Modell-Davega on lower Broadway reported its entire stock of blankets and Army cots had been bought by Wall Street banks and insurance companies.

Hotels swarmed with suburbanites. The return to school saw 100,000 high school students absent. In an act of public-spirited generosity, the Circle Line gave workers at seven hospitals free rides on its boats.

But at Pennsylvania Station, four people were injured in the crush of commuters. "We don't have rush hours anymore," a railroad official observed. "We have rush afternoons. Pretty soon we'll have rush days."

The Police Department canceled

leaves and vacations and put officers on 12-hour days. They all were needed. Traffic jams snarled city streets for hours. Commuters were urged not to rush home at the end of their work day. "Stay in town for dinner and then see a show or movie," Lindsay pleaded.

The only good news was the sharp decline in crime.

But New Yorkers were exhausted. On Friday the 7th, eager to get home, workers left their jobs early. Traffic backed up for more than six hours as 850,000 cars tried to exit the city, easily the worst jam in municipal history.

"Be brave and tough," the mayor counseled.

On the street, vendors were selling buttons reading "The Hell with Quill."

NOW A SECOND strike week loomed, and the pressure for a settlement was mounting. Other unions were pressing the Transit Workers Union; after all, their members were losing pay. And Quill's health was worsening. Gov. Nelson Rockefeller hinted that he might call out the National Guard, and his aides suggested that money might be made available for a settlement. President Lyndon Johnson sent his top labor troubleshooters to the city.

"The strike will go on until hell freezes over," union leaders promised. But their vigor was visibly sapped. On Wednesday the 12th, they agreed to a settlement. There were few winners. The 15-cent fare was raised to 20 cents, signaling a new era. Left behind was a disruption The New York Times called "probably the greatest since the Civil War draft riots."

Two weeks later, on Jan. 29, Mike Quill's heart gave out.

THE TRANSIT STRIKE *set the tone for John Lindsay's next four years. He would never gain his stride; militant union leaders would reign, and the late '60s would see momentous sanitation and teachers strikes.*

Central Park.

Charles PAyne / Daily News

Tompkins Square Park

Paul DeMaria / Daily News

169 Avenue B

Dan Farrell / Daily News

By DAVID HINCKLEY
Daily News Staff Writer

AS THE HOUR grew late and working people around Tompkins Square Park began turning out the lights on Memorial Day 1967, police asked several hundred music lovers to turn down the volume of a guitar-and-bongo concert in the park.

The crowd's reply, according to official police reports of the incident, was a barrage of bottles, bricks and fists that left seven officers injured.

Crowd members, conversely, contended that everything was peace and love until the cops waded in with flailing nightsticks.

And thus began the Summer of Love, with 38 arrests and, less than 24 hours later, a prickly debate between Mayor John Lindsay and Police Commissioner Howard Leary on exactly what threat the city's decent people faced from the invasion of this unwashed, indolent, dope-smoking creature known as the hippie.

Allan Katzman, editor of the East Village Other, foresaw 50,000 hippies crashing in the Village for the summer, and Leary warned this could mean no good. Memorial Day represented "a breakdown of law and order," he said. Lindsay, conversely, called the Memorial Day concert "a noisy but generally harmless activity" and suggested the fracas "could have been avoided with a little more tact and diplomacy."

Whatever The Man was thinking, Katzman said The People were working on a two-pronged alternative Welcome Wagon: free mattress space in a network of communes, and a communal bail fund in anticipation of vigorous police enforcement of narcotics statutes.

Optimism tempered with paranoia.

CHAPTER 145

GROOVY

The Summer Of Love, 1967

Welcome to the Counterculture.

HIPPIES WERE themselves a cultural hybrid. Suspicious of the system, they were widely sympathetic to the peace-and-equality agenda of the Left, which was fast piling onto the anti-Vietnam War train. On the other hand, many preferred sex, drugs and rock 'n' roll to speeches, which also gave them spiritual kinship to the 1950s beatniks, whose 1967 remnants included the Fugs singing "Kill for Peace" at the Players Theater by night and lead Fug Ed Sanders running the Peace Eye bookstore on E. 10th St. by day.

While the occasional icon like Allen Ginsberg straddled all counter-culture factions, and while Pravda wrote that hippies might be just the kind of subversives who could overthrow capitalism, much of the Summer of Love crowd was less primed for revolution than just sick of summer jobs, the suburbs or the old man's rules.

These were kids like 17-year-old Linda Fitzpatrick of Greenwich, Conn., who fled to the city for some fun when the semester ended at the stuffy Oldfields School; or 18-year-old Karen Wertheimer of Brooklyn, who turned up at the city's most famous crash pad, 622 E. 11th St.; or James (Groovy) Hutchinson, 21, who came from Central Falls, R.I., carrying not much more than his harmonica.

They joined a crowd composed largely of day trippers or, at most, short-term resident tourists who liked a good toke but ultimately produced less a drug problem than a mild economic boomlet.

By June, downtown had exploded with clothing shops, record shops and head shops selling posters of tigers with stripes that glowed under blacklight. Incense replaced oxygen as the dominant atmospheric element below 14th St., and anyone who wanted a more lasting statement could stop by Underground Uplift Unlimited on St. Marks Place and take home a button ("Bomb LBJ," "Go Both Ways," "1000101," "The Pope Smokes Dope").

Naturally, a few old-time moral guardians found this troubling. Robert Moses, mixing outrage with cultural confusion, told a boy scout rally: "The good scouts will prevail over the shaggy beatniks with their sometimes amusing eccentricities, their sideburns and their tramp girls."

But few in the city saw any percentage in playing the heavy, and the next expression of official municipal concern about hippies came from the Health Department, whose commissioner, Edward O'Rourke, was worried about a VD epidemic from all this free love. "The hippies, the beatniks before them and the Greenwich Village group in general are much more promiscuous and permissive than other parts of the city," O'Rourke declared.

By this time, for reasons unrelated to O'Rourke's speech, both Karen Wertheimer and Linda Fitzpatrick had left.

Linda, at the urging of her family, returned to Greenwich in mid-June, just as Judge Herman Weinkrantz was acquitting the Tompkins Park 38. The cops had arrested people at random rather than for cause, Weinkrantz ruled: "This court will not deny equal protection of the law to the unwashed, unshod, unkempt and uninhibited."

Outside the courtroom, Karen Wertheimer — apparently unaware that her team had won — got arrested for hitting a policeman. It was an accident, she said. Fine, the judge told her. Move back home, or you're doing six months.

Karen thought about that one overnight before deciding okay, she'd go home. She and her father left the courtroom yelling at each other.

And the sun moved through the summer sky, and 500 hippies marched to protest an LSD bust. Some 3,000 people rallied against the war in Central Park. Some 200 hippies marched to protest the rumored arrest of a jazz musician. The rumor proved false, but during the march jazzman Charles Mingus did get arrested, for scuffling with a cop.

Smoke-ins were organized in July and August to protest drug laws, and pictures were taken of genial police officers declining joints. No one was arrested, which annoyed law-and-order folks until the police explained the whole thing was a photo op. No one was smoking dope at all, just tea and herbs.

Those smokers probably still got a better high than did Warren Williams, Philamena Renzie and Catherine Fay, three teenagers arrested naked in Brooklyn while cooking banana peels — whose inside scrapings, legend and song to the contrary, produced nothing more than slightly elevated levels of potassium.

BY SEPTEMBER, the Summer of Love faded into the drumbeat for the October March on Washington, which demonstrators vowed would shut down the Pentagon itself.

As the nights got colder, the streets couldn't compete with that kind of adrenalin-pumping promise, and with most summer visitors having by now returned to school or home, the streets were left with those who wanted a way of life rather than a way to pass time. This smaller band increasingly became prey to more hardened street people who had little use for hippies in the first place and for whom peace and love was never part of the code.

Linda Fitzpatrick came back to the Village after convincing her skeptical parents she could best pursue an art career in the city. Once here, she primarily pursued amphetamines.

Around 10 p.m. on Oct. 7, she and Groovy Hutchinson were seen hanging out on the street, wired and giggling. Three hours later, they were found in the boiler room of an Avenue B tenement, their heads bashed in with bricks. The killers, found and convicted two years later, never offered a coherent motive.

Following the double murder, the NYPD formed a special unit to protect defenseless hippies.

By BRIAN MOSS
Daily News Staff Writer

'**WHAT IN** hell's the matter with him?" a pol had complained to Daily News City Hall columnist Edward O'Neill in 1962, speaking of 73-year-old World's Fair President Robert Moses, who was quarreling with city Traffic Commissioner Henry Barnes over whether buses should be allowed on New York's parkways.

"We gave him a big new World's Fair to play with and keep him busy. All he had to do was mind the store and slide out gradually in a blaze of glory.

"But no, he has to make headlines as an irascible old guy who can't be disagreed with."

In fact, that's exactly what Robert Moses was, and but for the word "old," what he always was. But the difference at this point was that "Big Bob," as The News liked to call him, was no longer the powerful parks commissioner of New York City. Or head of slum clearance. Or city construction coordinator.

And the many other state jobs he held — including state parks council chairman, Long Island State Park Commission president, state power authority chairman, for example — were at the sufferance of Gov. Nelson Rockefeller, who kept him on by waiving the state's mandatory retirement clause.

"At the hint of slippage," wrote O'Neill, "Moses is finding the wolves move in fast."

The old man held them off for six more years. In the end, though, it wasn't wolves that finally did him in. It was Robert Moses himself.

THE DISPUTE between Moses and Barnes perfectly symbolized why Moses found himself in difficulty by the early 1960s, after nearly 40 years spent building highways, housing and parks for the public. Barnes favored mass transit to slow the city's growing traffic snarls. Moses, who was chauffeured everywhere because he never learned to drive himself and whose notions of motoring had been shaped early in the century, thought parkways should be for pleasure trips. Traffic jams a problem? Build more roads. Crowded, dirty mass transit, starving for lack of funds? Too bad.

Though neither an architect nor an engineer, Moses carved out a powerful role for himself in New York life, and beginning in the 1920s, in the administration of Gov. Al Smith, there were few parts of either city or state untouched by his ideas.

He was responsible for 12 bridges, 35 highways, 658 playgrounds and more than 2 million acres of parks. Among his major achievements were Jones Beach, Orchard Beach, Riverside Park, Lincoln Center, and New York City's interconnecting bridge, tunnel and road system that for all the traffic still kept the city a vital and growing metropolis.

Any one of those projects would have been a

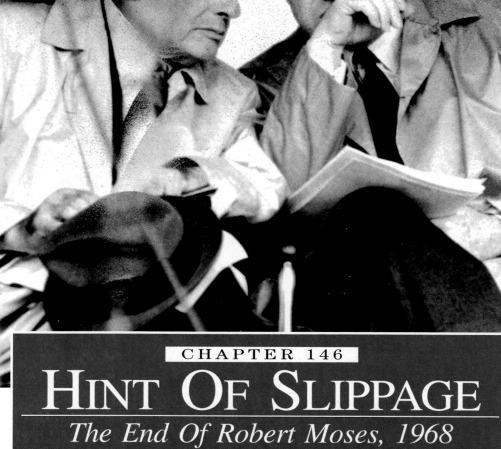
Moses and Rockefeller.

CHAPTER 146
HINT OF SLIPPAGE
The End Of Robert Moses, 1968

monumental achievement. That Moses managed to build them all was testimony to his remarkable combination of intelligence, vision and ability to acquire and use personal authority, sometimes brutally.

He created that authority himself, through clever legislation he guided through Albany and through his ability to ingratiate himself to union leaders and politicians who were glad to have someone make politically impossible decisions for them. Though he had occasional defeats and setbacks over his long career, his methods worked exceedingly well until the 1950s, when, slowly but inexorably, his web of power began to unravel.

THE FIRST LOOSENING came in Moses' effort to build a parking lot for Tavern on the Green in Central Park, by the builder's standards a small bulldozing job. But its location in the middle of Manhattan, adjacent to one of its tonier neighborhoods, made it a cause celebre for the residents who opposed it and for the city's newspapers, which, having championed him many times over the years, now depicted Moses as a tree-killing villain. When it turned out that Tavern's owners had a sweetheart deal with Moses, one that allowed them to get rich while the city saw little benefit, the public view of Moses at last began to sour.

In the wake of the Central Park debacle — Moses eventually caved in and put up a playground instead of a parking lot — more and more public doubts were raised about Moses' stewardship of his many city positions.

His role as Slum Clearance Committee chairman, in which he was essentially able to condemn property and then steer it to political friends for development — sometimes at ridiculously low prices — came under particular press scrutiny. He was actually relieved to give that job up, along with his other city posts, in exchange for becoming head of the 1964-65 World's Fair.

But he still held his state jobs, and he was still a man to be reckoned with.

So too, in 1962, was Nelson Rockefeller.

UNLIKE OTHER politicians with whom Moses had worked in city and state government over four decades, the wealthy Republican whose patrician personality was as outsized as Moses' didn't particularly need him.

Now Rockefeller wanted Moses to give up his parks commission chairmanship so his brother Laurance could take over. Moses balked. And, in trying to keep his post, he used a tactic that always had worked before with lesser politicians: He imperiously threatened to resign all of his positions. Surely no governor would permit the vital Robert Moses to walk off his jobs. But that's exactly what Rockefeller did.

'**N.Y. STATE** Loses a Big Man," the Daily News editorialized, but noted that Moses still headed the World's Fair, which would keep him occupied through 1965, and still coordinated all city highway construction. And he remained the unassailable czar of the Triborough Bridge and Tunnel Authority, which controlled millions of dollars in toll money — millions, for the most part, that Moses could spend as he pleased on projects he liked. He still had the power of the purse.

Those who coveted that money included Mayor John Lindsay, who watched helplessly as the city's vast subway system sputtered for lack of funding, and Gov. Rockefeller, a visionary builder in his own right, who needed money to proceed with some of his own grand plans.

Moses was not about to give it up, and he let both officials know it.

Lindsay, in 1966, tried and failed to legislate Moses and the TBTA out of business. A year later, Rockefeller employed a different strategy. Knowing he could not legally push Moses from office, he instead led the old man to believe he would be an important part of his new Metropolitan Transportation Authority, the regional transportation system that would absorb the TBTA — and its revenue stream.

Moses, now 79 and beginning to recognize that the winds were shifting, took Rockefeller at his word and agreed not to fight the MTA proposal. What he got in exchange was an MTA consultancy, which let him keep his chauffeur, an office staff and the trappings of power, but no real power itself.

This was not what he had expected, but it was all he would get, and he accepted. And on March 1, 1968, the TBTA became part of the MTA, and Robert Moses' career became part of history.

JAMES GARRETT DAILY NEWS

By JAY MAEDER
Daily News Staff Writer

HE HAD LEFT Bimini at 7 a.m. and flown to Miami and Washington and Newark, and now, shortly before midnight Friday the 22nd of March 1968, outside the E. 90th St. apartment of state Supreme Court Justice Arthur Markewich, he formally surrendered to New York Sheriff John McCloskey, then, affably puffing on a good cigar, sat with the judge and accepted the terms of his previously negotiated parole.

Then uptown he went, grinning broadly. Screaming supporters mobbed him at the Renaissance Ballroom at Seventh Ave. and 138th St. Women flung themselves deliriously upon him. *Daddy's home! Daddy's home!* "Keep the faith," he instructed them one by one.

So it was that 60-year-old Adam Clayton Powell Jr., Democratic U.S. representative, 18th Congressional District, a man at war with the entire Congress, a duly elected representative of the people who had dared not set foot in his own district for fear of arrest and jail, returned to the City of New York for the first time in nearly 18 months.

IT WAS TRUE, of course, that America's highest-ranking black man of the past quarter-century had brought his difficulties pretty much upon himself. For eight years one of his own constituents had dogged him through the courts, and for a year and a half he had been hiding out in the tropics, defying subpoenas. "Adam was a terrific congressman until a few years ago," said the Harlem grandmother who had sought to unseat him in 1967. "Then his personal and legal problems caught up with him, and he hasn't done his job since."

Son of a Baptist minister and heir to his church, Powell came to political manhood as the Great Depression devastated Harlem, organizing marches, demanding fair employment practices, establishing himself as the voice of the disenfranchised. The Rev. Adam Clayton Powell Jr. was the single reason New York's black workers made entry into the transit systems, the Post Office, hospitals, schools, the

CHAPTER 147

FAITH

Daddy Comes Home, 1968

phone company, and years later even his harshest critics would grant him that: "He taught them how to ask and work for what they needed, and what, it may be added, was due them," said Roy Wilkins of the NAACP, no close friend of the abrasive Powell's at all.

In 1941, he was elected New York's first black City Council member. Two years later he went to Congress, genuine evidence to many that America's institutions were capable of fundamental change.

If he was openly manipulative of his constituents, Harlem didn't much mind, and Harlem kept reelecting him by whopping majorities for the next two decades as he continued to fight noisily for black rights in America. He was Daddy, pastor of the great Abyssinian Baptist Church, and he could not be dislodged: The national Democrats tried to dump him in 1956 when he bolted the party and endorsed Dwight Eisenhower for President; the local Tammany machine sought to bounce him in 1958, all to no avail.

"I know that you are going to vote for me till the day I die," he grandly announced at every rally and the crowds roared all the louder: *Daddy! Daddy! Daddy! Keep the faith, Daddy!*

One March night in 1960, he collided with Esther James.

ESTHER JAMES was an elderly Harlem domestic who, while discussing New York police corruption on a public-affairs TV show one night, Rep. Adam Clayton Powell Jr. of the 18th Congressional District matter-of-factly called a "bag woman" for on-the-take cops.

She demanded a public apology, but Powell didn't apologize even to fellow congressmen, and he wasn't

about to apologize to a maid. So she sued him for defamation. And she won. In April 1963, he was ordered to pay $211,500 in compensatory and punitive damages. Several appeals later, when the case came back to trial, he failed to appear. Half a dozen subpoenas were issued, ordering him into court; sunning himself in the Bahamas, he paid no attention to any of them.

Finally, he was found guilty of civil contempt of court. In November 1966, he was found guilty of criminal contempt as well. This meant that he was immediately subject to arrest the next time he came to New York.

By now, House Democrats, already long annoyed by a colleague who spent little time in Washington in the first place and insulted them to their faces when he did, were looking into other troubling allegations: a no-show job for his wife, private travel paid for with public funds. On Jan. 9, 1967, he was deposed as chairman of the House Education and Labor Committee, the first congressman so stripped in 160 years. On March 1, the full House voted 307 to 116 to deny him his seat in the 90th Congress altogether.

Sipping Scotch and milk at the End of the World bar in Bimini, Powell was asked by reporters whether he would seek to reclaim his seat in the forthcoming special election. "Why, I'll do anything my good people want me to do," he said. "I wouldn't deny my good people."

THERE WAS NOW, in 1967 America, an immediate racial flash point as blacks saw the political castration of a powerful force. In fact, House leaders had fought desperately to contain the anti-Powell vote, urging mere censure rather than exclusion. But the prevailing mood on the Hill had been summed up by Florida Rep. Sam Gibbons: "If just once Adam had come in and said, 'I made a mistake,' things might have turned out differently. Instead he called us all hypocrites and went off to Bimini." In 1967 America, Adam Clayton Powell Jr. had now been effectively martyred.

"A slap in the face to every black man in this country," said Floyd McKissick, national chairman of the Congress of Racial Equality. "A

mockery of democracy without precedent," said A. Philip Randolph, vice president of the AFL-CIO. "The fact that stands out is that members of the House have denied the right of another member's electorate to their own representation in Congress," said the Rev. Martin Luther King Jr. "In the end, it is meaningless," concluded civil rights elder Bayard Rustin, "because the people of Harlem will elect him again and again and again."

They certainly did. New York Republicans briefly sought to field as their candidate for Powell's seat James Meredith, who in 1962 had been the first black student admitted to the University of Mississippi and who remained a figure of some stature in the civil rights movement. But Meredith quickly withdrew from the race after Powell supporters took him out back and gave him a talking-to. In the April 11 special election, Powell — without campaigning at all, without once showing his face in the city — won 86% of the vote, flattening his closest challenger 7 to 1.

On Bimini, the newly elected Powell went out fishing again and never once even tried to take his seat in Congress.

AND NOW IT was March 1968, eight years after he had offended Esther James, and he had paid the old woman $56,000 and arranged with the courts to permit his return to the city, and he was home. *Daddy! Daddy!* the crowds screamed.

On Sunday the 24th, he took his Abyssinian Baptist pulpit for the first time in 18 months. "You thought I was gone, baby, but I'm back!" he shouted, and the church exploded in cheers.

This time he was flanked by black nationalist bodyguards he introduced as "the wave of the future." Nonviolent revolution was no longer possible, he declared, and America faced "a new civil war." Then he ordered that a stained-glass image of a white Christ be torn from a window and replaced by a black one.

Outside, reporters asked if he expected to play an active role in the new civil war. "Who, me?" he said. "I'm just the old man of the sea, that's all."

By JAY MAEDER
Daily News Staff Writer

GOD, HERE SHE was again, Valerie or Valeria or whatever she was calling herself this week, up the clanking old elevator, into the big sixth-floor studio, back again with the silly screenplay she wanted Andy to film. And Andy was on the phone with his actress superstar Viva, and he motioned to Valerie or Valeria and bade her wait a few minutes while he finished up. Really, Andy should have blown the chick off long ago, everyone told him that, but he was too sweet a guy to be hard about it, he didn't want to hurt her feelings, he couldn't just clap his hands and send her on her way. So he motioned at her to wait and turned back to the phone, and that's when she shot him.

Andy crumpled as the slugs boinged around inside him and tore apart his spleen and stomach and liver and esophagus and both his lungs. The magazine editor visiting from London galloped to a storeroom and locked himself in. One of Andy's associates got up from his desk and fell to his knees begging for his life as Valerie briefly put the gun to his head. Then she reconsidered, walked back to the elevator and went clanking back down again to Union Square.

Three hours later, at 7:30 p.m. on Monday the 3rd of June 1968, 28-year-old Valerie Solanas walked up to a rookie traffic cop at Seventh Ave. and 47th St., handed over two guns and surrendered. "I am a flower child," she informed the startled young officer. "He had too much control over my life."

Andy Warhol, the pop artist and avant-garde film maker, was still undergoing emergency surgery, given no better than 50-50. "There are many involved reasons," Solanas explained in the din of the E. 21st St. stationhouse as police and reporters pushed and shoved and flashbulbs popped. "I have written a manifesto of who I am and what I stand for." And calmly she began to hand copies of a 31-page mimeographed document to everyone around.

FRANK RUSSO DAILY NEWS

CHAPTER 148

THE WOMAN THING

Shooting Andy Warhol, 1968

SHE'D BEEN A familiar Village figure for several years, a surly, pinch-faced, hard-eyed, starved-looking girl who panhandled in the streets and prowled the bookshops trying to sell copies of her manifesto for small change. Her organization, of which she was the only known member, was called the Society for Cutting Up Men, or SCUM, and she preached that males were "not ethically entitled to live"; women everywhere, she cried, must rise up to "eliminate through sabotage all aspects of society not relevant to women (everything), bring about the complete female takeover, eliminate the male sex and begin to create a swinging, groovy, out-of-sight female world."

The SCUM founder seemed to believe that women could "learn to reproduce without benefit of men and bring forth only females." Acquaintances agreed that she was quite serious.

Even TV talk-show host Alan Burke, who specialized in deranged guests, threw her off his program in mid-taping. When she rented a hall for a SCUM rally, nobody showed up. Grove Press didn't care to publish either her manifesto or the play she'd now also written. Neither, after she moved into the Chelsea Hotel on 23rd St. and became his neighbor, did Maurice Girodias, the elder-statesman eroticist who had issued Vladimir Nabokov's "Lolita" and Henry Miller's "Tropic of Capricorn" — although he did advance her $600 to try to turn the play into a novel, which she never did.

One night Girodias took her to the ballet and was dumbfounded to note that for once she had put on a dress and done up her hair. "Don't you think I'm a good-looking girl?" she fluttered at him. But he still wouldn't publish her, and after that she started writing him violent letters.

At some point in late 1966 or early 1967, Valerie Solanas pushed her way into the nether world inhabited by the ever so fashionably bizarre Andy Warhol, and Warhol, who was always happy to meet such fabulously interesting people, took her in.

ANDY WARHOL was by now several years past his soap-pads-and-soup-cans period that had briefly made him a glittering, if bewildering, gossip-column celebrity, and he had turned his attention almost exclusively to low-budget moviemaking, grinding out dozens after dozens of formless, pointless, unwatchable films: methedrine soaked explorations of downtown decadence, 45 minutes of a man eating a mushroom, six hours of a man sleeping, eight full hours of the Empire State Building doing nothing.

If there remained a body of Warhol admirers forever determinedly discussing his "refutation of abstract expressionism" and so on and so forth, there was also a growing critical suspicion that, emperorwise, Warhol was not necessarily wearing all that many clothes.

To his faithful posse of freaks and geeks and zombies, he was still God Himself, and here was certainly the man who would film Valerie Solanas' play, and she managed to insinuate herself into the outer fringes of his circle. Warhol had a habit of adopting fragile young women — "wounded starlings," one observer called them — and he had taken several of them into his repertory company and made fleeting underground film stars out of them. In 1967, Valerie, as Valeria, had a small part in his production "I, A Man," for which she was paid $20.

This was the beginning and end of her screen career. As for her play, which was something about a woman who strangled her son and which, one of the Warhol women later said, was "so vile and filthy it turned my stomach," the film maker had no interest in it, and he politely kept trying to tell her so, over and over, as she kept coming back to see him again and again.

Just blow her off, everyone told him. But, really, he was just too sweet a guy. He couldn't hurt her feelings.

IN COURT, charged with attempted murder, Valerie or Valeria refused legal counsel. "I didn't do it for nothing!" she shouted. "I was right in what I did! He's a liar and a cheat! I have nothing to regret! I feel sorry for nothing!" Ordered held without bail pending psychiatric evaluation, she was applauded and cheered and proclaimed a "revolutionary heroine" by Ti-Grace Atkinson's New York chapter of the National Organization for Women as she was hauled away.

"She is one of the most important spokeswomen of the feminist movement," said lawyer Florynce Kennedy, who immediately went to state Supreme Court to complain that Solanas "has not been taken seriously" and was being subjected to jail because she was a woman.

A new day was dawning, Kennedy triumphantly announced: "The woman thing is going to be like the campus thing," she predicted. "Women may be the third force to link up with youth and black people."

VALERIE SOLANAS spent several years in and out of mental institutions. Andy Warhol, recovered from his wounds, returned to work in September. Reflecting on things at the time, a one-time associate expressed some sadness about the "sick sorority house" over which the artist presided: "From the beginning, he surrounded himself with these emotional basket cases and Bellevue outpatients who develop a dependence upon him. Andy's their pop papa, their Peter Pan. They're like little kids waiting for him to tell what game they'll play next. . . . He takes them in like homeless waifs, he uses them as props in his films and they're all expendable.

"What happens to them? They just disappear, as mysteriously as they materialize."

By OWEN MORITZ
Daily News Staff Writer

"According to history, over 100 years ago a man named Albert Shanker got hold of a nuclear warhead."

— **A character in Woody Allen's "Sleeper," explaining how the world was destroyed**

THE REST OF America may not have grasped that gag, but New York did.

Albert Shanker was the president of the United Federation of Teachers, the man who shut down New York City's schools for two months in the fall of 1968 over the issue of community control.

The shutdown — actually three separate strikes — idled more than 50,000 teachers and 1.1 million kids.

The kids sat home watching early morning civics courses on TV and went out for makeshift classes at churches, libraries and museums. Their dismayed parents scurried around to private schools and suburban districts in hopes, usually in vain, of finding open seats somewhere. A report-card period was missed. Regents exams were postponed. Deadlines for college admissions came and went.

And when the strike was finally settled Nov. 18, students found themselves required to make up lost time by staying in school each day for an additional 45 minutes — and then attending classes right through the Christmas vacation.

It was a divisive and disruptive moment in city history, and it tore the racially fragile town apart.

All because of a stand-off at a junior high school in the Brownsville-Ocean Hill section of Brooklyn.

BY THE LATE 1960s, all across America, minority parents were pressing for better urban schools. Lagging academic performances by ghetto students and growing dissatisfaction with sluggish educational bureaucracies led parents to demand more control over inner-city classrooms.

As 1968 arrived and state legislators began debating a plan to carve the city's elephantine school system into 32 decentralized districts, Brooklyn's largely black Brownsville-Ocean Hill neighborhood, with eight schools and 8,000 students, became the focal point of the nationally spotlighted experiment in decentralization.

The Ford Foundation poured in money. The UFT was even an early partner. A governing board that included local parents was organized. Rhody McCoy, a seasoned school administrator, was named the district's chief.

McCoy soon became a familiar face on TV as cities across the nation monitored the Ocean Hill demonstration project and its ground-breaking concept of letting urban parents have a say in the running of local schools.

But no one had drawn up ground rules. Ocean Hill was a civics lesson for all New York.

On May 9, citing "a loss of confidence by the community," restless activists on the governing

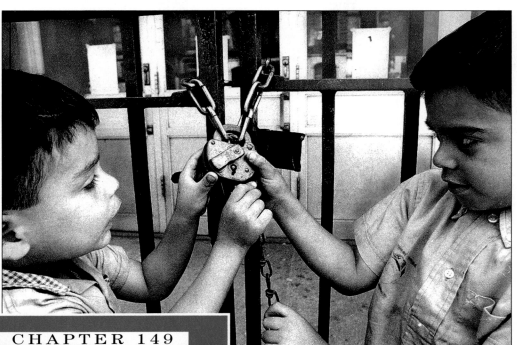

CHAPTER 149

NO MORE PENCILS, NO MORE BOOKS

Schools On Strike, 1968

board ordered the ouster of 19 teachers, administrators and principals — 18 of them white — from Junior High 271.

The charges were never specified, though at times the 19 were accused of everything from sabotage to insubordination to indifference. Then, the local board on its own replaced three principals with three acting principals drawn from other schools.

On this most passionate of issues, where community idealism confronted unionism, the battle lines were drawn.

ON THE morning of May 14, angry black parents blockaded JHS 271's front doors. Police approached, escorting the ousted teachers, now ordered back into the school by Superintendent Bernard Donovan. Nearby, teachers sympathetic to the governing board hissed and jeered. The parents stood their ground, vowing no entrance. After several tense minutes and fearing a bloody confrontation, police retreated with their charges. Two days later, authorities ordered JHS 271 "closed until further notice."

Tensions did not ease over the summer. *They're our schools,* said neighborhood activists. *Let us get teachers and administrators who care.* This, countered the teachers union, was an open invitation to favoritism and intimidation. What about job security and due process? What about collective bargaining agreements?

As Sept. 9 approached, the first day of school, Albert Shanker and his union brain trust made a fateful decision.

They could have localized an action to the Ocean Hill district at issue. Instead, illegally, they resolved to close the entire school system until the ousted teachers were reinstated — or, failing that, the state took over the recalcitrant district.

"We are the strongest organization in this fight," Shanker said.

THE UNION STRUCK on opening day. Two days later, there was a tentative agreement. Several days after that, the agreement fell through, and Shanker's teachers struck again. Another return-to-work agreement collapsed when

parents clashed with police as officers escorted the disputed teachers back into the reopened JHS 271. Nine people were arrested, 10 cops injured.

Now both sides hunkered down for what evidently was going to be a prolonged battle.

And extremists moved in to fan the flames.

As a union, the UFT was 90% white, mostly Jewish; the neighborhood was predominantly black and Hispanic. Perhaps it was inevitable that cross-charges of racism and anti-Semitism would begin to fly. When a black teacher, Leslie Campbell, went on radio to recite a student poem that contained a Jewish slur, the union made sure the city heard about it. Critics accused Shanker's people of seizing on even marginal slights to gain popular support.

Meanwhile, the Black Panthers patrolled JHS 271's corridors in a show of force. Career rabble-rouser Sonny Carson became a local symbol of black militancy. In Queens, equally militant Rabbi Meir Kahane announced the creation of the Jewish Defense League to combat what it called "black and white anti-Semitism."

In the end, at a huge cost to the city's equilibrium, the union prevailed. Courts had already thrown out Ocean Hill's attempt to replace principals with those of its own choosing; a state trustee now was put in charge, and the teachers were reinstated.

The controversial McCoy, whose suspension had been a condition of the striking teachers, was returned as administrator under state supervision. Then, with the state's blessing, McCoy announced a nongraded school experiment.

"We're not going to be allowed to run our schools," grieved the Rev. C. Herbert Oliver, president of the Ocean Hill governing board. "The agreement cuts out the heart of community control."

When the schools reopened on Nov. 19, 38 of the first 45 days of classes had been lost to the strike.

And there was a deep split between blacks and Jews, formerly liberal allies in the civil rights struggle. Albert Shanker had once marched in Selma, Ala., himself.

THE LONGEST SUMMER, headlined the Daily News at strike's end. It was a very long year as well.

ON DEC. 14, *a month after the bitter strike was settled, the Board of Education proposed to shift operating powers to 32 community districts that could hire their own superintendents. The Legislature adopted a whittled-down version of this plan.*

Twenty-eight years after the ugly war for control of the city's schools — 28 years marked by widespread abuses in patronage and management and little evidence of improved scores — the Legislature repealed the decentralization law over only minor protests.

Albert Shanker

By OWEN MORITZ
Daily News Staff Writer

THE TV WEATHER forecasters were brimming with confidence: rain, wind and sleet, they said, just a chance of snow. A typical weather pattern, they assured viewers in the second week of February 1969.

But snow it was, and once it started falling that Sunday the 9th, it didn't stop. Ten inches by 7 p.m. By midnight, 15 inches in Central Park, 20 inches at Kennedy Airport. The entire Northeast was paralyzed under mountains of snow.

Hundreds of motorists were trapped on the Tappan Zee Bridge, thousands more on the New York State Thruway as the blizzard shut down the road between New York City and Newburgh.

Most of the 2,000 motorists caught in deep drifts at Kennedy fared fairly well: Rescue crews lifted them to safety after many had spent up to eight hours in their cars. But a Bronx mailman and his wife and a friend weren't so lucky: Bound for a Florida vacation, they were found dead in their stalled car in the National Airlines parking lot, apparently victims of carbon monoxide poisoning.

Inside the airport, 4,000 stranded travelers were entertained by Soupy Sales and Goldie Hawn. Parked planes were turned into overnight lodgings. One man said it was better than a lot of hotels he had stayed in.

Walloped by the howling storm, New York awoke Monday frozen in time and place. Schools closed; commuter and elevated subway lines shut down. Weddings were postponed, sporting events canceled, theaters locked. Go to work? Forget about it.

And at City Hall, it wasn't a good day either.

THROWN OFF BY the weather report, sanitation officials hadn't called out snow-clearing crews until Sunday night, and they hadn't even thought yet about recruiting private contractors. The bureaucrat with the emergency powers to call out the sanit troops had been inaccessible for 12 hours. Sunday overtime was frowned upon anyway.

But this was the worst storm in 18 years. Red-faced National Weather Service officials admitted they had underestimated a low-pressure front racing up the East Coast while a storm was rolling in from the Ohio Valley. The mix was potent, and it seemed the worst of the storm's fury was reserved for eastern and central Queens. Forty-two people died, half of them in Queens, and the city was disrupted for days.

More than anything, the killer blizzard of February 1969 turned into a political storm for New York's high-profile mayor, John Lindsay. Lindsay's Snowstorm, it was called, much to the Presidentially minded mayor's chagrin.

While Manhattan and other parts of the city were recovering by Wednesday the 12th — schools were reopened, though pupils were asked to bring their own lunches, and mass transit was back in service, if only sporadically — the borough of Queens lay prone.

Residents stranded in their homes. Impassable streets. Abandoned cars everywhere. No mail, no services, limited food supplies amid reports of price

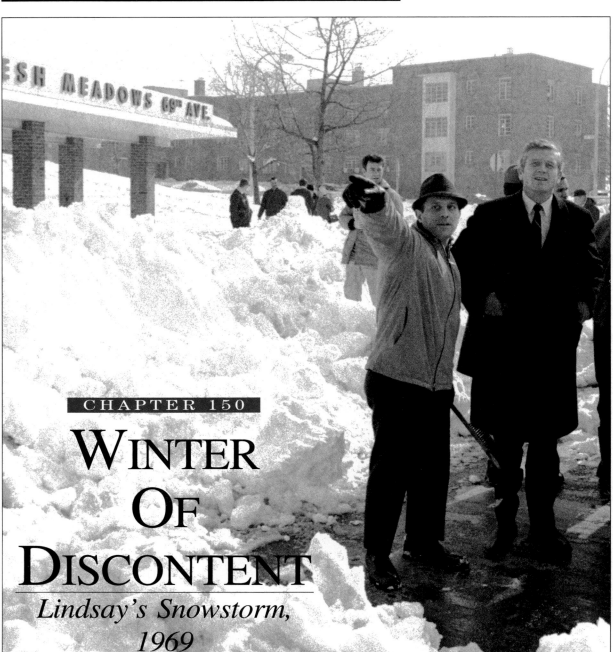

CHAPTER 150

WINTER OF DISCONTENT

Lindsay's Snowstorm, 1969

gouging. And the borough's residents asked: Where were the snowplows?

"As a snowbound resident of Kew Gardens, Queens, where I have been a homeowner on Grosvenor Road for 17 years, I urgently appeal to you," went one desperate wire to the mayor of New York from the United Nations' No. 2 man, Undersecretary General Ralph Bunche. "In all those years, we have never experienced such neglect in snow removal as now."

Bunche went on: "The snowstorm came on Sunday. This message is sent Wednesday morning. In all that period no snowplow has appeared on our street or in our vicinity. There are no buses, no taxis, no mail, newspaper or other deliveries, and there have been no trash or garbage collection since last Friday. The shelves of our neighborhood grocer are empty. As far as getting to the United Nations is concerned, I may as well be in the Alps."

That day, Lindsay ventured out to the Alps of Queens.

HIS LIMO, followed by a caravan of newsmen, got as far as Rego Park. There, the entire party switched to four-wheel-drive trucks. Still impossible going. The trucks could not negotiate several snow-blocked streets.

At Main St. in Kew Gardens, Lindsay got out of his truck — and was openly booed by the locals.

"You should be ashamed of yourself," a woman yelled. "In the 23 years I've lived here, this is the first time the streets have been unplowed. It's disgusting."

Things didn't get better. In Fresh Meadows, a woman called Lindsay a bum. A doctor informed the mayor he couldn't treat patients because his car was mired in a snowbank. On Horace Harding Blvd., the mayor went into a pharmacy to call City Hall. When he came out, 200 persons were waiting to fling catcalls at him.

Back at City Hall, a chastened Lindsay ordered "all available manpower and apparatus" sent to the borough for snow removal. Meanwhile, mayoral aides let it be known that there were many causes of the snow snafu — including suspected sabotage and foot-dragging by the sanitation workers' union, with whom Lindsay was often at odds. The union denied the charges.

Lindsay was months from a reelection campaign, and this was now the lowest point of a difficult term.

THE QUEENS snowstorm was a watershed in the history of municipal services. The failure for a week to extricate the borough from a 20-inch snowfall exposed the sorry state of the city's snow-fighting equipment and the poor communication among agency heads. Things would change.

Indeed, each new threat of snow for the rest of the winter prompted the mayor to order sanitation workers by the hundreds into the borough, even before the first snowflake fell.

LATER IN 1969, *with the delivery of municipal services at issue, the damaged Lindsay lost the Republican primary to Sen. John Marchi of Staten Island. This was a break in disguise, however; running as an independent, Lindsay won reelection in a stunning upset because his Democratic and Republican opponents ended up splitting the vote between them.*

By JONATHAN LEWIN
Daily News Staff Writer

"If I'm elected, at least the bad news will be couched in elegant language."

– Norman Mailer

THEY HAD TO be kidding. They weren't really serious. Were they? Norman Mailer running for mayor of New York? Jimmy Breslin campaigning for City Council president alongside him? Accused of entering the mayoral race purely to get material for a book, Mailer snapped: "I've proved that I can write books without working this hard." Added Breslin: "Anyone who runs for office in this city, with the shape this city is in, and takes it as a joke is committing a mortal sin."

The Odd Couple, the Daily News called them. Mailer, Harvard-educated novelist and essayist, had been a darling of the literati for years. Reporter Breslin, a self-described "unlettered bum," had little use for the sort of literature favored by Mailer's circle. ("'Portnoy's Complaint'? I don't read nothin' that ain't written in English.") But Breslin was known and respected by everybody in town; it was Gloria Steinem who suggested that he would give Mailer's ticket some, as she put it, "street smarts." (Steinem, meanwhile, had decided not to run with them for controller, fearing her candidacy would turn the ticket into a "campy literary exercise.")

On May 1, 1969, Norman Mailer and James (no longer Jimmy) Breslin officially entered the race. Mailer conceded that a victory would be a miracle but pledged that the two of them would run a "serious campaign." Breslin showed up an hour late, eyes sunken, voice hoarse. He dismissed the other candidates as "bums and nuts" and predicted an easy victory. Asked if he thought going into politics would damage his credibility as a writer, he said: "It didn't hurt Winston Churchill."

THEIR PLATFORM seemed, well, reasonable enough. They called for New York City to become a 51st U.S. state, with individual neighborhoods controlling their own education, housing, sanitation, police. "It's insanity that we let a bunch of lobster fishermen from Montauk and a bunch of jerks from Niagara Falls tell us how to run our schools," declared Breslin. And they wanted to ban automobiles from Manhattan; Mailer proposed a monorail running around the island, augmented by electric jitneys going up and down First and Ninth Aves. and across 32nd and 59th Sts. The Mailer Rail briefly became quite a popular idea. Greenwich Village Rep. Ed Koch read the proposal into the Congressional Record.

Mailer said he would outlaw the birth control pill if he could: "Part of the slime that overlays civilization." And he opposed legalizing marijuana: "The cigarette companies would take it over and put vitamins in it."

CHAPTER 151

VOTE THE RASCALS IN

The Mailer-Breslin Ticket, 1969

NEWS REPORTS that Life magazine was paying Mailer $1 million to write about the upcoming moon landing tended to discourage large campaign contributions, and Mailer and Breslin ended up having to sink their own funds into the campaign, starting with the $1,000 Mailer received in early May when he won the Pulitzer Prize for "The Armies of the Night."

They did raise a few dollars through the sale of Mailer-Breslin campaign buttons bearing the slogans VOTE THE RASCALS IN and NO MORE BULLSHIT. At one whistle stop, Mailer slipped a 10-year-old boy one of the latter specimens, advising him, "Tell your parents you stole it."

Quite a few of the Mailer-Breslin stunts caught the public fancy, particularly a flyer handed out at Aqueduct Race Track, handicapping the candidates as if the campaign were an actual horse race. Former three-term Mayor Robert Wagner, now seeking to make a comeback and unseat John Lindsay, was described as a "12-year-old gelding."

Meanwhile, there were several disasters. At one fundraiser at the Village Gate, Mailer, whisky glass in hand, spewed out a profane speech announcing that he was running to "free Huey Newton and end fluoridation," then turned on his audience, informing them that they were "a bunch of pigs." Even Breslin quickly fled that scene. "I knew *I* was crazy," he told campaign adviser Jack Newfield, "but you got me running with Ezra Pound."

"If you and Breslin go ape on the same evening, who will run the city?" Mailer was asked at one point. Mailer replied that probably this wouldn't happen on the same night.

MAILER FINISHED next to last in the June primary, with 41,136 votes — just 5%. Conservative winner Mario Procaccino defeated Wagner by 31,000 and Herman Badillo by 37,000. Some analysts wondered whether Badillo would have won had it not been for Mailer, since they were competing for the same liberal votes. With conservative John Marchi defeating the incumbent Lindsay in the Republican primary, the stage was set for Lindsay, running on the Liberal line, to defeat his two conservative opponents in November with only 42% of the vote. Had the liberal Badillo been the Democratic nominee, the results might well have been different.

Breslin actually got more votes than Mailer — 75,480 — but also finished next to last. The only candidate he bettered was a little-known Harlem assemblyman named Charles Rangel.

Asked if he would ever run for anything again, Mailer replied: "That's like saying would I try love again. Yes, sure, but the next time I expect to be wooed a little."

Asked if he would ever run for anything again, Breslin replied: "I am mortified to have taken part in a process that required the bars to be closed."

By MARA BOVSUN
Special to The News

FLAGS FLEW AT half-staff over Fire Island. Thousands of mourners stood for hours outside the Frank E. Campbell funeral home on Madison Ave. It was Friday the 27th of June 1969, and Judy Garland was dead at 47, victim of pills, booze and misery. On record players and radios all across New York, she still yearned to be in the wonderful faraway place where troubles melt like lemon drops.

It went on into the night, Judy's song, over and over, in a little red brick bar at 53 Christopher St., where the walls were painted black, go-go boys bounced on countertops and powdered men danced with each other under flashing gel lamps, then sat quietly nursing drinks and thinking of Judy.

If happy little bluebirds fly beyond the rainbow, why, oh why, can't I?

Minutes after midnight, there was a flash of bright white light at the door.

The cops were raiding the Stonewall Inn.

"Oh, no," said one high-heeled, black-clad queen. "Not tonight."

COPS RAIDED gay bars all the time. There was nothing surprising about it. Gay bars were easy targets, mostly controlled by the mob and filled with patrons likely to be doing things that were against the law, like dancing stubbly cheek to cheek or wearing a dress. Indeed, the Stonewall had been hit just a few weeks before. Homosexuals generally did not protest overmuch. They might be arrested. Their names might appear in the papers. They might lose their jobs, their friends, their families.

Tonight it was just business as usual as far as the cops were concerned. They weren't there to roust the patrons; they had come to seize booze. The Stonewall was an unlicensed private club. It could not legally sell a drink. At the bar, officers pulled the IDs of 200 customers, then released them one by one, permitting them, as they regularly did, to slip away into the night.

Tonight they didn't slip away.

Spontaneously, one by one, they assembled in tiny Sheridan Square Park across the street.

It was not clear what specifically triggered the Revolt of the Queens. By several accounts, it may have been a police nightstick. In just minutes, the park exploded.

HOMO NEST RAIDED, QUEEN BEES ARE STINGING MAD, the Daily News reported the next morning: "Queen power exploded with all the fury of a gay atomic bomb. Queens, princesses and ladies-in-waiting began hurling anything they could get their polished, manicured fingers on. Bobby pins, compacts, curlers, lipstick tubes and other femme fatale missiles were flying in the direction of the cops."

Cries of "Pigs!" and "Faggot cops!" rang out, and soon the crowd was throwing rocks, bricks, bottles, garbage and plate glass. Bonfires erupted. One handcuffed drag queen beat a policeman to the ground with her stiletto shoe, snatched his keys and freed herself and another damsel-in-chains. Others ripped off their wigs and began whipping cops with them. A group of queens

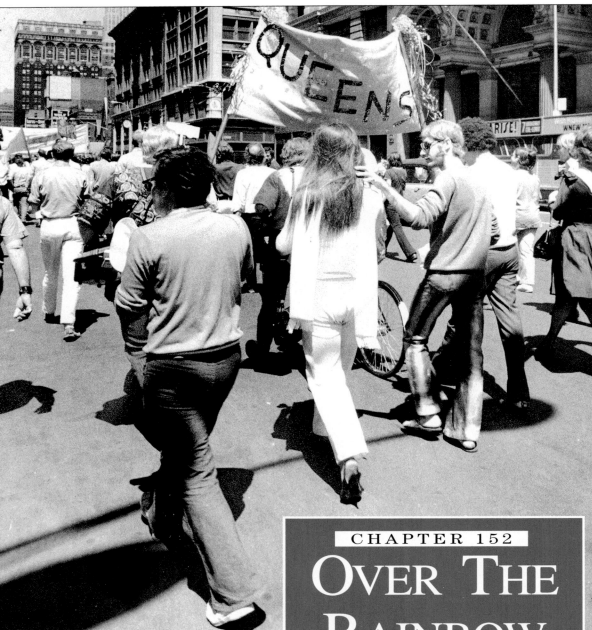

CHAPTER 152

OVER THE RAINBOW
Stonewall, 1969

formed a kickline and, to the tune of "It's Howdy Doody Time," began serenading the world:

We are the Stonewall girls
We wear our hair in curls
We wear our dungarees
Above our nelly knees . . .

Police ran for cover inside the Stonewall. A trash barrel crashed against the door. Then someone ripped out a parking meter to use as a battering ram. Someone squirted lighter fluid through the bar's smashed window, threw in matches and started several small fires. When police reinforcements arrived, there were nearly 1,000 rioters on Christopher St.

The melee lasted two hours. There were 13 arrests. Four policemen were injured, including one who slipped and broke his wrist. That sent snickers through the city's gay communities: *limp-wristed cop.*

DISTURBANCES continued all day Saturday. Thousands flocked to Sheridan Square. Graffiti appeared on the Stonewall's boarded-up windows and everywhere else: "Legalize Gay Bars"; "Gay prohibition corupts (sic)

cop$ and feed$ Mafia."

A new rallying cry swept through the streets: "Gay Power!" On Saturday night, Tactical Patrol Force officers linked arms and marched through the Village, clubbing at least two persons and periodically breaking ranks and charging into the crowds. Rioting went on in fits and starts for five days.

"The police are sure of one thing," The News said. "They haven't heard the last from the Girls of Christopher St."

Homosexual beat poet Allen Ginsberg came to survey the scene. Gays, he noted, had "lost that wounded look that fags all had 10 years ago."

THE GAY BOSTON Tea Party, it all came to be called. Gays started acting in a way unthinkable just a week earlier. They were bitchy, they were loud, they were in your face and they weren't afraid of getting their names in the newspaper.

DO YOU THINK

HOMOSEXUALS ARE REVOLTING? broadsided the militant, newly formed Gay Liberation Front. **YOU BET YOUR SWEET ASS WE ARE.**

Before Stonewall, there had been just a handful of activist groups: the Mattachine Society, the Daughters of Bilitis. Suddenly there were hundreds. A movement had been born.

ONE YEAR LATER, *the anniversary of Judy Garland's death and the Stonewall riots was designated Gay Pride Week. Again, thousands gathered near the Stonewall Inn, this time to march in the first Gay Pride Parade. "For the first time in history, we are together as the Homosexual Community," a Gay Liberation flyer declared.*

"Out of the closets, into the streets," the crowds chanted as they marched up Sixth Ave. to the Sheep Meadow. For part of the march, the new movement was led by a man dressed like Glinda, the Good Witch of the North.

CHAPTER 153

TEAR DOWN THE WALLS
Weathermen, 1970

By WENDELL JAMIESON
Daily News Staff Writer

THE BLASTS shattered windows throughout Greenwich Village, showering the streets with glass and blowing a gaping hole in of one of W. 11th St.'s Greek revival townhouses. Dustin Hoffman lived next door, and he emerged into the soggy afternoon carrying paintings and a lamp, venturing back and forth through the curling smoke until he was stopped by cops who said it was too dangerous to go back inside.

A fire captain proclaimed the conflagration a probable gas leak as gallons of water were poured on the ruin.

The mangled body of a young man was found on the first floor. Two women, alive, were also found — one nude, one only in jeans, their faces covered in soot, their skin cut and bloodied. A neighbor took them in, gave them clothes, turned on the shower and went back to the scene. When she returned to her house, the women were gone.

This, on Friday the 6th of March 1970, was the first puzzle in a parade of mysteries that slowly unraveled as investigators sifted through the rubble of what had been 18 W. 11th St.

Soon the world would learn of a bomb factory on one of Manhattan's most picturesque streets, run by some of the city's wealthiest children, their anger inflamed by the Vietnam War, their name inspired by a line from Bob Dylan's "Subterranean Homesick Blues."

You don't need a weatherman to know which way the wind blows.

BY THE TIME 18 W. 11th St. was blown apart, opposition to the Vietnam War had boiled across the country for years. Student riots and marches paralyzed college campuses starting in the spring of 1966 and cast an angry pall over the 1968 Democratic Convention in Chicago. In New York, opposition to the war was one of several reasons student protesters closed down the Columbia University campus in the spring of 1968, taking over five buildings before they were driven out in a pre-dawn police raid.

The Columbia takeover was organized by the campus chapter of the national group Students for a Democratic Society. Among the architects was a frenetic, red-haired 21-year-old honors student named Theodore Gold — who shortly quit SDS to become a leader in a more radical breakaway group, called the Weathermen.

Never numbering more than a few hundred, the Weathermen intended to bring down American capitalism by provoking the government to institute oppressive measures. They ran wild in one Brooklyn high school, distributing leaflets and gagging and tying up two teachers. They seized a cop's gun in a Brooklyn luncheonette, then lectured the terrified patrons about their struggle.

Their best-known exploits occurred in Chicago during what they called the "Days of Rage" in the summer of 1969. A group of 70 Weatherman women, wearing helmets and carrying clubs, gathered in Grant Park and announced they were going to march upon an armed forces induction center and destroy it.

They never got there. Twelve of the women were grabbed by cops; the rest were allowed to leave after laying down their weapons. Those arrested included Cathlyn Pratt Wilkerson, 24, a graduate of elite prep schools and Swarthmore College, whose father, James Wilkerson, owned a string of radio stations in the Midwest and lived with his new wife at 18 W. 11th St. in Manhattan.

In March 1970, James Wilkerson and his bride headed for a vacation in St. Kitts.

TWO DAYS AFTER after the Wilkerson townhouse was blown to bits, police identified the body found in the rubble. It was Theodore Gold.

That same day, police precincts were told to be on the lookout for Cathlyn Wilkerson, now identified as one of the mystery women who had fled following the blast. The other was thought to be one Kathy Boudin, another member of the Weathermen, daughter of a Manhattan attorney.

By now, cops were pretty sure a gas leak had nothing to do with the blasts — neighbors had counted three — that destroyed the house. On March 10, they got their answer: Down in the basement, under piles of bricks and several feet of water, they stumbled onto a cache of terror — 60 sticks of dynamite, blasting caps, pipes wrapped in tape and nails.

They also found another body, or part of one.

The dead woman was identified as a 28-year-old student radical named Diana Oughton.

Buildings on the south side of W. 11th St. were evacuated. People living across the street were told to stay away from their front windows. The FBI was called in.

James Wilkerson rushed back to New York, surveyed his blackened home and made an emotional plea for his daughter to come forward. Wherever she was, he told her, he loved her and he would support her. But the world needed to know: How many people were inside the Weatherman bomb factory when it blew up? Every day, firefighters were risking their lives, picking through the rubble. She should contact him, somehow, he said, and let him know what perils awaited authorities as they continued their dangerous search.

She never did.

On March 12, the echo of explosions rang out through Manhattan. Within 29 minutes, three bombs went off in midtown skyscrapers, blowing out walls, windows and plumbing, further terrorizing an already jittery city but injuring no one. By day's end, bomb scares had evacuated 15 more buildings. The Weathermen were striking back for their dead comrades.

Two days later, a third body, mutilated beyond recognition, was pulled from the 11th St. wreckage. This dead man was never identified, and he was assumed to be, like the others, a violent underground activist whose politics were intense but who really wasn't very good at building bombs.

THE WEATHERMEN *became the Weather Underground, fading from view after the 11th St. incident as the anti-war movement continued to tear at the nation.*

And then the war ended for the United States, and Richard Nixon resigned the presidency, and fugitives Cathlyn Wilkerson and Kathy Boudin became lesser priorities as the 1970s moved along.

In July 1980, Wilkerson walked into Manhattan District Attorney Robert Morgenthau's office, surrendered and became front-page news again — a radical relic from another era. Her politics remained unchanged, she announced, and she gave a clenched-fist salute as she went to prison for three years on a weapons conviction.

In October 1981, Boudin was one of a gang of machine-gunners who held up an armored car in Nyack, Rockland County, killing two cops and a guard. She went to prison for 20 years.

By JAMES S. ROSEN
Special to The News

MIDWAY THROUGH, Muhammad Ali shouted five words at Joe Frazier and, with each word, swung at Frazier's head.
DON'T — YOU — KNOW — I'M — GOD?
"Well, God," Frazier said, "you gonna get whupped tonight."

MADISON SQUARE Garden, the 8th of March 1971. "The biggest event of all time," boasted promoter Jerry Perenchio. "There has never been anything like it before," agreed the Daily News' Phil Pepe. "And there doesn't figure to be anything like it again."

The Ali-Frazier fight was unprecedented: Two unbeaten heavyweight champions squaring off. Making more money for a single performance than any athlete in history, an outrageous $2.5 million each. Drawing a record-setting Garden crowd of 20,455 and a record-setting worldwide closed-circuit TV audience of 300 million.

Also clear and present, noted The News' Bill Gallo, was "a good guy-bad guy aspect, depending on your political views." Frazier's ascension to the heavyweight title in 1968, and the entire emotional appeal of that night's event, stemmed from Ali's forced 43-month absence from the ring, an exile imposed upon the former Cassius Clay by the nation's boxing and criminal justice establishments after he refused military induction on religious grounds during the Vietnam War.

If you opposed the war, you cheered for Ali — "because of the poetic justice," explained James Earl Jones, "not in beating Frazier, but in being champion again and beating the system."

If you viewed Ali's conscientious-objector claim as a betrayal of country, you backed Frazier. "During that 43-month span," wrote The News' Gene Ward, "when Frazier

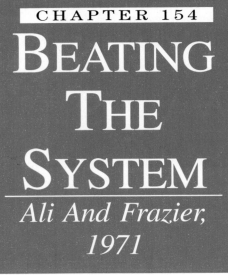

CHAPTER 154

BEATING THE SYSTEM

Ali And Frazier, 1971

was thinking only of fighting, Ali was engaged in legal maneuvering to beat the draft and in vilifying his country, at $1,500 per speech, on the college campuses."

Added Dick Young: "Whites of the middle-aged generation, those who served in wars gone past, and those with sons or nephews in this one . . . are the whites who think with hate in their hearts, and who root for Joe Frazier."

Ali fueled the fires: "Uncle Tom," he sneered at Frazier. "The white man's champion."

"He ought to be ashamed of himself," replied Smokin' Joe. "This country gave him everything he's got, and he don't want to fight for it. He don't help blacks. He hurts them. He ain't no leader of the blacks. He's just full of con."

Politics and social meaning entirely aside, the Ali-Frazier fight also represented a crystalline moment in heavyweight boxing history. Would Ali dance? *Could* he still dance? Could Frazier connect with Ali's jaw? Would he need to? "Kill the body, and the head will die," said Frazier, predicting that the fight would be over inside 10 rounds.

Both men weighed in at their heaviest: Frazier, the slight betting favorite, at 205½, Ali at 215. Frazier waited in seclusion till fight time. Ali recited poetry in the lobby of the Hotel New Yorker:
Joe's gonna come out smokin'
And I ain't gonna be jokin'
I'll be peckin' and a-pokin' . . .

FRANK SINATRA took ringside photographs for Life magazine. Burt Lancaster gave color commentary on closed-circuit. "The most glittering night in the history of the Garden," proclaimed Howard Cosell. Frazier fans included Flip Wilson, Yogi Berra and Brenda Vaccaro. In Ali's corner were Glen Campbell, Tom Seaver and Zsa Zsa Gabor. "Dahling, I had a lot of fights with all my husbands and I never got $2.5 million," Zsa Zsa said.

The two fighters rushed each other when the bell sounded, then started circling. Ali landed the first decent punches, an odd left-right combination that sent a ripple of alarm through the crowd. Then Frazier landed a solid left hook, and Ali shook his head, *no*.

It stayed that way for several rounds: Ali picking his spots, taunting Frazier from the corner, rope-a-doping. By Round 3, the ref ordered them to start fighting, and they did: Ali with stiff left jabs and quick right crosses that snapped Frazier's head back, Smokin' Joe with whooshing left and right hooks that drove Ali around the ring. Scorecards split: The two of them were *too* evenly matched.

Round 11 found Ali on the ropes. Frazier bade him return to center ring. Ali beckoned with his glove: *Come back to the corner*, and Frazier obliged him. He scored a solid left hook to Ali's jaw, then another to the belly. "Only the rope keeps him from going down," Dick Young jotted.

Dazed, Ali made faces. Frazier missed with a roundhouse left. Ali stumbled across the ring on automatic pilot, in serious trouble, weaving blindly, his hands hanging

like lead weights. The bell sounded. Ali could barely stand.

Round 15. Now Ali danced and jabbed as the crowd cheered, feigned two lefts, pushed Joe away. As Frazier moved in, Ali started a right uppercut. But Smokin' Joe was already connecting with the greatest left hook of his career.

Muhammad Ali spent a full second flat on his back. To some, the promise of an era died in that instant.

ALI WILLED HIMSELF up at the count of four. There was more punishment to take — and give. When the last bell sounded, Smokin' Joe was spitting blood — but Ali, Phil Pepe wrote, had "lost his first fight as a professional, his claim to the heavyweight championship and much of his mystique."

The next day, Ali acknowledged Frazier to be "a great slugger, a great street fighter."

He looked like he'd been beaten with a rolling pin. "When a great man loses," he said, "it helps other people face their own defeats."

SAID HUNTER THOMPSON: "A *very painful experience in every way, a proper end to the '60s . . . Joe Frazier, like Nixon, had prevailed for reasons that people like me refused to understand." Agreed Abbie Hoffman: "When Ali got beat, that became a symbol for me of the death of our kind of heroes. Now we're gonna see Nixon heroes."*

Ali and Frazier fought again in 1974, when neither was champion. Ali took a 12-round unanimous decision at the Garden with no knockdowns; fight buffs still debate whether the ref saved Frazier from a Round 2 knockout.

The "Thrilla in Manila," a year after that, often tops lists as the greatest heavyweight title fight in history; Ali retained his crown when Frazier, after 14 savage rounds, failed to answer the bell. Ali said later that the Thrilla felt like death. Many fans wish it had been his last fight.

New York City Off-Track Betting Corporation

CHAPTER 155

OUT OF THE GATE

OTB, 1971

By DICK SHERIDAN
Daily News Staff Writer

AT MIDMORNING on Thursday the 8th of April 1971, the cavernous main concourse of Grand Central Terminal was uncharacteristically at a standstill.

Not that things were quiet. Balloons soared everywhere. Young women in lemon-and-lime jockey outfits passed out buttons proclaiming "There's A New Game In Town." And a four-piece band played "Camptown Races."

The thousands filling the massive station were not train riders. They were horseplayers.

Some were lifelong gamblers. Others had never placed a wager before. But all were eager to be numbered among the first Americans to put down legal off-track bets on a race.

It was inauguration day for the New York City Off-Track Betting Corp., the nation's first government-run bookie operation.

THE HORSES had been an exciting and vibrant part of New York's social life ever since 1665, one year after the staid Dutch ceded the colony of Nieuw Netherland to the more sports-loving English. The royal governor, Richard Nicholls, established Newmarket Track on Salisbury Plain, in what became Hempstead, L.I. Meanwhile, Church Farm Course became the first track to be laid out within the boundaries of present-day New York City; located by most accounts in lower Manhattan, it conducted racing from about 1725 to 1750.

Racing, with deep English roots, fell out of favor with patriotic New Yorkers around the time of the Revolutionary War, but, as the years passed and memories of occupation faded, it revived in popularity. As the 19th century progressed, a total of 11 tracks with names like Union Course, Morris Park and Empire City arose in the city.

Most of these courses were thoroughbred tracks, where saddled horses ridden by jockeys were the contestants. But on the city's streets and surrounding country lanes another type of racing — standardbred — was emerging out of the friendly but spirited contests between owners of horse-drawn buggies and carriages.

As the 19th century progressed, this new style of racing, relying on horses who paced or trotted while harnessed to a light rig instead of galloping freely, rapidly became a distinctively American sport.

Whether thoroughbred or standardbred, both forms of horse racing shared a common attraction: Gambling.

BOOKMAKERS, AT FIRST operating legally, long thrived both on track and off. Their various questionable practices — such as using leg-breakers as collection agents and charging usurious interest rates — eventually led to reforms that prohibited wagering away from the track itself. By the 1940s, the only bet permitted under New York State law was so-called pari-mutuel betting, in which wagers were pooled and winnings distributed out of the pool.

A legally mandated percentage of the betting pool was not distributed back to the winners. It was retained by the race operator to pay his costs, taxes and make a profit. In 1971, that percentage, called the takeout, was fixed at 17%.

But the demand for expanding social services had been putting a strain on New York City's budget through the turbulent 1960s. In 1963, under Mayor Robert Wagner, city voters had approved a measure to raise revenue through off-track betting.

It was left to Gov. Nelson Rockefeller to push through a change in the state betting laws that allowed counties and large municipalities to conduct off-track betting as a means of generating revenues without raising taxes.

Subsequently, Mayor John Lindsay tapped Rochester businessman and aspiring politician Howard Samuels to head up New York City's betting operation — OTB, as the municipality's public-benefit corporation became known.

In upstate Democratic circles, Samuels was known as "The Man with The Plan." Wisecracking off-track bettors down in the city had their own moniker for him — "Howie the Horse."

In 1971, only Aqueduct Racetrack, which had opened in Queens in 1894, still conducted thoroughbred racing within the city limits, operated by the nonprofit New York Racing Association, which also ran Belmont Park in Nassau County and upstate Saratoga. NYRA officials bitterly opposed any off-track betting scheme and refused to cooperate with the fledgling corporation.

OTB had better luck with standardbred tracks at nearby Yonkers Raceway in Westchester County and Roosevelt Raceway on Long Island. Management at these tracks agreed, although reluctantly, to allow OTB to handle bets on their races.

Insiders touted OTB as a longshot to finish in the money. The pressure on Samuels to prove his corporation could be a money-earner was intense. With no extensive branch-office network in place throughout the five boroughs, with no computerized system set up to handle bets, Howie the Horse now guided his corporation out of the gate.

AT 10:40 A.M. in Grand Central, with thousands of his fellow punters behind him, retired postal worker Philip Gross of Bensonhurst, a self-described "loser" who had camped out on line since the previous day, placed the first bet — a $2 wager on the nose of Adora's Nicki in the first race at Roosevelt Raceway.

Mayor Lindsay, who had surrendered his honorary first-in-line spot to Gross, then stepped up to the first of 10 windows in operation and put $2 on a pacer named Money Wise in Roosevelt's seventh.

By just an hour later, $10,000 had been bet at Grand Central's 10 windows, a sum that Samuels had hoped might be the entire day's handle.

Despite two-hour waits and limits on the number of bets a customer could make, a total of $66,098 in off-track bets was wagered over the next five hours at Grand Central, a second OTB office on Queens Blvd. in Forest Hills and by phone.

UNDER SAMUELS, *OTB continued to amaze. By the end of its first full fiscal year of operation, in June 1972, the corporation had computerized its betting operation, opened a total of 80 branch offices in the five boroughs and was taking in and paying out a total of $3 million in bets and winnings on an average day. After just 17 months in business OTB had earned more than $17 million in revenues for city and state coffers.*

Samuels left OTB in 1974 to seek the Democratic gubernatorial nomination, and over the years the corporation fell into less professional hands. In 1994, under the sticky-fingered maladministration of Hazel Dukes, OTB suffered a net loss of $5.3 million, the only bookie in the world to lose money. More recent belt-tightening has resulted in some upturn of OTB fortunes.

Samuels, Lindsay, Gross.

By JAY MAEDER
Daily News Staff Writer

SINCE AT THIS point every other aggrieved special-interest group in the firmament was glomming onto the emerging politics of victimization, a dodge that quite usefully absolved everybody of everything, it occurred in the spring of 1970 to 47-year-old Joseph Colombo, boss of what had once been the Profaci crime family and was by now the Colombo crime family, that perhaps he might grab a piece of this action himself. *The Mafia. La Cosa Nostra.* What the hell was it with all that stuff? Why, there was no such thing as the Mafia. It was just something the FBI had made up. It was just a dirty slur against all the good, honest, hardworking Italian-American people, that's what it was. Joe Colombo wasn't going to stand for it.

How come everybody the FBI arrested had Italian names? Therefore, all Italians were mobsters, was that it? Was that what the FBI was imputing? This was like arguing that all Italians were New York mayors, since Fiorello LaGuardia had been one once, but legions of pols immediately rushed in to join the crusade all the same. "Stigmatizing an entire ethnic group!" roared Bronx Rep. Mario Biaggi. "A psychological burden on all of us!" The FBI couldn't believe its ears. Mobsters were complaining now that they were being *discriminated* against?

The freshly minted Italian-American Civil Rights League got to work in April, coincidentally enough just minutes after one of Colombo's three sons, 23-year-old Joseph Jr., was charged with melting down coins for resale as silver ingots. Suddenly there were hundreds of picketers outside FBI headquarters at Third Ave. and 69th St., protesting the federal persecution of all Italians everywhere. This extraordinary spectacle went on for weeks. Neighborhood residents finally went to court to demand some peace and quiet.

Now, all at once, the league was chartering chapters all over the Northeast. On June 29, nearly 100,000 people rallied in Columbus Circle to hear chest-thumping speeches from Biaggi, longshoreman boss Tony Scotto and hoodlum Vincent Gigante's priest brother Louis. Shortly, U.S. Attorney General John Mitchell deemed it enlightened to ban such words as "Mafia" from Justice Department communications: "There is nothing to be gained by using these terms," Mitchell ordered, "except to give gratuitous offense" to "many good Americans of Italian-American descent."

In Albany, Gov. Nelson Rockefeller directed the state police to amend its vocabulary as well. Ford Motor Co. chief Lee Iacocca pledged that the offending words would no longer be heard on the Ford-sponsored TV series "The FBI." Producers of the forthcoming film "The Godfather" agreed to drop them from the script. In November, 5,000 guests at a black-tie league event at the Felt Forum ponied up a half million dollars in contributions as Frank Sinatra, Jerry Vale, Connie Francis and Vic Damone entertained.

Joe Colombo had discovered something. In 1970s America, all you had to do was cry out *Ethnic bias!* and everybody around you would cave in on the spot.

It was really quite brilliant. Considering that Joe Colombo was, after all, a Mafia boss.

AND NOT EVEN much of one at that. Joe's fellow bosses just rolled their eyes. Hands-down the most featherweight boss the mob had ever known, Joe had spent his life running craps games until fortune beckoned in the early '60s, when Joe Bonanno handed him a contract to whack Carlo Gambino and the up-and-coming Colombo realized it was in his better interests to tip off his target instead and then accept his

CHAPTER 156
STAIRWAY TO HEAVEN
Joe Colombo's Great Civil Rights Crusade, 1971

gratitude after Bonanno was deposed. Just a cheesy little bust-out guy, that's all Colombo had ever been, and now his new patron Gambino was throwing him a whole family. Nobody could believe it.

And now, for God's sake, he was also the loudest and most headline-happy boss the mob had ever known. Like so many populist demagogues before him, Joe Colombo was finding that he quite enjoyed the attention. On the night of March 22, 1971, he threw himself a testimonial banquet, and more than 1,400 supporters assembled at the Huntington Town House in Huntington, L.I., to hail him as "the guiding spirit of Italian-American unity" and to salute him for "restoring dignity, pride and recognition to every Italian."

Comic Tom Poston emceed. Enzo Stuarti sang. "We are building a stairway to heaven!" the feted Colombo cried out. "Peace and brotherhood, that is all I seek! There is a conspiracy against all Italian-Americans!" As it happened, he was due in court the next day on a perjury matter. "My conscience is clear!" he bellowed. The silver-ingot case against Joe Jr., meanwhile, had recently collapsed, by reason of a key witness' abrupt inability to remember anything about anything.

Through the spring the juggernaut noisily rolled on under the stewardship of 26-year-old Anthony Colombo, who liked to denounce "self-loathing Italians" such as state Sen. John Marchi, who regularly informed the public that the league was plainly nothing but a con. "Italian-Americans have been had," Marchi sighed.

Anthony also sued WCBS-TV for $1 million for reporting that he was a "reputed Mafia chief." Quite a glib fellow, he suffered only one small embarrassment, when the federals seized what they said were loansharking records and he angrily replied that in fact they were lists of benefit-ticket buyers, then had to try to explain why an anti-defamation group would identify one of those individuals as "Johnny the Wop."

In May, the Colombos announced they were joining forces with Rabbi Meir Kahane and the Jewish Defense League, and that they would all be fellow freedom fighters together.

John Marchi was not the only New York

Italian deeply troubled by the league. Another was Don Carlo Gambino, who was becoming increasingly unhappy with his one-time protege Joe Colombo. What was Don Carlo supposed to do with a crime boss who kept holding press conferences?

ON MONDAY MORNING the 28th of June, there were just 3,000 supporters at the second annual unity rally in Columbus Circle, but it was early yet. Presiding over events, Joe Colombo at 11:15 a.m. was striking poses for photographers when one of them pulled a gun and pumped three slugs point-blank into his head and neck, whereupon he himself was instantly gunned down by other parties who then instantly vanished.

Mob war, cops agreed. The dead shooter was one Jerome Johnson, a black ex-con presumably linked to the recently disimprisoned Crazy Joey Gallo. Everybody knew Crazy Joe had been openly plotting to move in on the Colombo Brooklyn rackets with his newly built black army. This was something Carlo Gambino could easily have stopped if he'd felt like intervening.

Anthony Colombo, for one, found this law-enforcement theory distasteful, since its premise was that there were rival Italian crime families in the first place and was therefore defamatory to Italian-Americans. His own position was that his grievously wounded father had been cut down by shadowy historical forces, like President John F. Kennedy had been.

"They need patsies," he suggested darkly.

"The CIA has done this before," nodded the Rev. Louis Gigante.

COMATOSE JOSEPH Colombo lingered on for several more years. So did the Italian-American Civil Rights League, under new management, the younger Colombos having promptly abandoned the group after the shooting.

Crazy Joey Gallo was rubbed out in Little Italy in April 1972.

The three Colombo sons pleaded guilty in 1986 to federal racketeering charges and went to prison. "I have not admitted that I am a member of organized crime," Anthony Colombo declared.

By JAMES S. ROSEN
Special to The News

'**I**'M SO DAMNED** mad!" fumed Martha Mitchell to a United Press International reporter at the other end of the line. It was 3 a.m., Sunday the 26th of August 1973, and once again she was bouncing off the walls of her Fifth Ave. apartment. "I asked them to let me speak to the President. They told me, *Tell it to UPI.*"

White House operators knew Martha Mitchell all too well. And in the summer of 1973, amid the nation's long national Watergate nightmare, so did most other Americans. "Outspoken wife of Attorney General John Mitchell," the papers usually called her. They could say that again. There was practically no getting away from the woman.

MODERN AMERICAN** politics had seldom known an official wife less circumspect than 54-year-old Mrs. John Mitchell — and this in a cabinet notable for its colorlessness. Richard Nixon's vice president was the rock-ribbed Spiro Agnew; his national security adviser, the Machiavellian Henry Kissinger; his attorney general, the stern-visaged, pipe-puffing John Mitchell — privately a genial enough man but publicly the Nixonian symbol of law and order in an uneasy era of lawlessness. It was Mitchell who would stop the assassins and the druglords. It was Mitchell who would crack down on the protests and the riots. It was Mitchell who would crush "the Movement."

He was married to a loon.

Second wife Martha Beall Jennings of Pine Bluff, Ark., had never been careful with her tongue. Once upon a time, as a Wall Street lawyer's wife, her Southern-butterfly eccentricities had proved merely entertaining to the Mitchell guests in their swank Rye home.

But now John Mitchell was attorney general of the United States, a cabinet man whose every private thought his wife did not hesitate to broadcast to anyone who would listen.

"Some of the liberals in this country, he'd like to take them and exchange them for the Russian Communists," she informed CBS after an anti-war rally; her husband, she confided, "has said many times" that was what he'd like to do. And after Sen. William Fulbright, a Democrat from her home state, voted against Nixon-Mitchell Supreme Court nominee G. Harrold Carswell, she called the Arkansas Gazette at 2 in the morning and ordered the paper: "I want you to crucify Fulbright!" (Drily allowed Fulbright: "She is a little unrestrained in the way she expresses herself.")

This was not altogether unrefreshing at first, and Martha Mitchell's celebrity swelled. Every feature writer, style editor and gossip columnist in the country dispensed daily doses of her wit and wisdom; by late 1970, she was, The New York Times reported, "a household word for three-quarters of the nation's adult population." Her flag-pin views were always populist, and since they largely accorded with the President's own, Nixon cheered her on publicly, urging her to "give 'em hell."

Privately, he and many other senior Republicans worried about her volatility. It was not only that Martha Mitchell frequently outshone the President; the mere fact that a cabinet wife spoke so plainly and freely at all made her a heroine among groups hostile to the Nixon White House, including feminists. She was the GOP's top fund-raising draw. And she made party elders very nervous.

THOUGH SHE** initially backed the White House's conduct of the Vietnam War — the Cambodian incursion was "100% wonderful," she assured America — her position changed after

CHAPTER 157

DEFENDER OF AMERICA
Martha Mitchell, 1973

her son from a previous marriage wound up in uniform. "The Vietnam War stinks," she informed reporters one day aboard Air Force One. The startled scribes asked John Mitchell if he wanted to hear his wife's remarks. "Heavens, no," he blanched. "I might jump out of the window."

On it went, and it began to be recognized in more and more quarters that the grand lady was really quite ignorant. On blacks: "I can't get over saying 'colored.' I said it all my life. All the Negroes seem to resent it, and I don't know why." On the Supreme Court's ruling on school busing: "Nine old men should not overturn the tradition of America." On feminism: "Equal rights. We don't need that. It's silly." On Communism: "There's a difference in Communists — one is Marx and one is Lenin, and I don't know which is which."

She held a special dislike for New York Mayor John Lindsay, a "political opportunist" who "should be expelled from the Republican Party," she said. In 1971, when the Daily News published ballots asking readers whether the liberal-minded mayor should switch parties, Martha Mitchell — listing her occupation as "Defender of America" — mailed in a yes vote. "He would be more fun to defeat!!" she scrawled.

Then, on June 17, 1972, came the Watergate arrests.

Here was a problem. What was the dependably loose-lipped Martha Mitchell likely to say now?

MARTHA SOBS: I'M A PRISONER,** read the Daily News headline after reporter

Marcia Kramer found Mrs. John Mitchell in seclusion at the Westchester Country Club. When Watergate broke, a bodyguard seeking to keep her in a news blackout had ripped her phone from the wall. There had been a bruising struggle: Her hand went through a window; a doctor was summoned, an injection forcibly applied.

By this time, John Mitchell had already resigned from the Justice Department to lead Nixon's reelection effort. Now he got a public ultimatum from his wife: "*I'm not going to stand for all those dirty things that go on.*" Square in the middle of the burgeoning scandal, Mitchell quickly quit the Nixon campaign and devoted himself to attempting to keep his wife quiet. They moved back to New York, where Martha announced she might enter local politics and knock off Lindsay.

But the Watergate noose was tightening, and there were more and more drinks and pills, and there was no keeping Martha Mitchell away from her telephone, and her public utterances grew darker. "Mr. President should resign immediately," she told UPI in May 1973. John Mitchell finally exploded. "Martha's late-night telephone calls have been good fun and games in the past," he snapped. "However, this is a serious issue."

As her husband's legal problems deepened, the Defender of America stepped up her personal assaults on the President of the United States. "He bleeds people," she told UPI. "He draws every drop of blood and then drops them from a cliff." John Mitchell, she announced, was a fool, "like he has always been in trying to protect the President. . . . We need a new government."

Now she began to hold visibly unhinged daily sessions with reporters camped outside her Fifth Ave. building. At one point, she slugged one of them. One day a WCBS-TV crew watched in stunned silence as she and her daughter had a sidewalk argument so stormy that nuns had to pull them apart.

IN SEPTEMBER** 1973, John Mitchell walked out on his wife and moved into the Essex House. In the bitter divorce proceedings that followed, she set fire to his cherished hockey mementoes and war medals.

"It could have been worse," Mitchell said after his conviction in the Watergate coverup trial Jan. 1, 1975. "They could have sentenced me to spend the rest of my life with Martha Mitchell."

A NEW YORK EPIC: 1898-1998

By JONATHAN LEWIN
Daily News Staff Writer

"The underprivileged are beating our brains out. You know what I say? Stick 'em in concentration camps."

— **Dialogue from "Death Wish"**

IN JANUARY 1974, for the first time in years, more New Yorkers described themselves as conservatives than as liberals. Widespread fear of crime was hardening attitudes on issues from welfare to the death penalty. Two out of three New Yorkers cited "crime, danger in the streets or law and order" as the worst problem facing the city.

The second-worst problem was drugs, which made street crime more random and more violent. Nearly three-quarters of those surveyed said they were afraid to walk outside alone at night. And 56% had no confidence that a captured criminal would end up behind bars. Everybody knew that New York was the most dangerous city in the United States.

Actually, New York had less crime per capita than most other large American cities. But the statistics were still grim enough: Murders had risen from 681 in 1965 to 1,607 in 1974, rapes from 1,154 to 4,054, robberies from 8,904 to 77,940. And the crime wave was spilling into areas that previously seemed immune.

"Five years ago, you never heard the term 'block association' on the East Side," said the founder of one such group. "Everyone thought this was the safe Silk Stocking District." Now there were 17 East Side methadone clinics between 59th and 96th Sts. Cops called 86th St. "the Times Square of the East."

On the West Side, meanwhile, in the first nine months of 1974, 207 crimes were reported on the premises of two large single-room-occupancy hotels along Broadway in the 70s. Community activists railed against the neighborhood's armies of addicts, hookers and pimps, as well as the former mental patients the state had turned out into the streets. An occasional tenant of an SRO at 50 W. 77th St. was charged with murdering eight of that hotel's elderly tenants.

The criminal justice system was overwhelmed, increasingly unable to protect the populace. When a Barnard College sophomore was raped in Morningside Park, Columbia's chief of security declared the park "unpoliceable" and advised students never to go there at any time. On College Walk, the university's main campus thoroughfare, even a large varsity football player was mugged. On the night of April 25, Mayor Abraham Beame strolled through the lower East Side, calling out through a bullhorn: "Walk the streets and do not be afraid." This was the first of several "Walk and Talk" excursions designed to comfort the citizens of the City of New York. But in 1974, millions of them knew all too well the wisdom of locking themselves securely into their homes.

Amid this fear and resignation, on the 25th of July, a film called "Death Wish" opened.

PUTTING FORTH the proposition that what New York City really needed was a locked-and-loaded vigilante, "Death

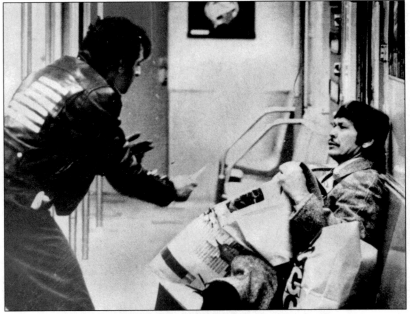

CHAPTER 158

THE TOILET
Fear In The Streets, 1974

Charles Bronson in "Death Wish."

Wish" was greeted rather more enthusiastically than Beame's walks and talks.

The film told the story of one Paul Kersey, a typical New York liberal until the day his wife was beaten to death and his daughter raped into a state of catatonia in their own home, whereupon Kersey turned into a ruthless avenger, stalking and gunning down

miscreants of all races, creeds and colors in alleys, parks and subway trains. Muggings quickly dropped, in this film, from 950 to 470 a week, and the police were no little pleased by that. Somewhat cynically, when they caught Kersey, they allowed him to leave town quietly, unprosecuted for his killing spree.

New York audiences broke box-office records cheering on Charles

Bronson every time he blew away another dirtbag.

But some recoiled at this startling public bloodlust. Perhaps, they feared, fed-up New Yorkers would be inspired to start taking the law into their own hands. Indeed, said one theater manager, he had overheard many exiting patrons discussing the possibility of a gun purchase. "It was mostly said in jest," he said. "I think."

IF 'DEATH WISH' was perhaps never intended to be a serious social statement, the fact was that it resonated with a number of critics. Asked the Daily News' Rex Reed: "Who can deny the grim picture 'Death Wish' paints of New York City as an 'uninhabitable toilet' in which dope addicts and freaked-out hoods are driving away the white urban middle class with spray paint cans, zip guns and switchblade knives?"

Not everyone thought the depiction of the city as an urban hell crawling with drug-crazed criminals was entirely fair. Nowhere was safe, not even Kersey's spacious apartment in a doorman building on Riverside Drive. The city's defenders saw the film as the view of paranoid tourists: Executive producer Dino Di Laurentiis was an Italian, director Michael Winner was an Englishman and screenwriter Wendell Mayes lived in California. What did they know about New York City?

But, argued Winner: "Any art mirrors the society of its time. I talked to people at a New York police station. They told me that what they need is an execution squad."

As controversy swirled around the film, city officials were grudgingly drawn into the debate. Said a police spokesman: "It's senseless to speculate on whether vigilante action might reduce the crime rate." Said an aide to Beame: "I don't know why we should dignify this movie by making a comment. New York City is the greatest city in the world."

ON THE DAY "Death Wish" opened, a 20-year-old addict was arrested for the May 13 mugging of 13-year-old John F. Kennedy Jr. in Central Park in broad daylight.

A few days later, a man riding a Brooklyn subway train at 9 p.m. was shot to death for no apparent reason as his wife looked on. Beame immediately ordered subways running between 8 p.m. and 4 a.m. to close off half their cars so that transit cops would have less ground to cover.

BIG TOWN BIG TIME™

By RICHARD E. MOONEY
Special to The News

YEARS OF FISCAL fakery finally pushed New York City to the brink of bankruptcy in 1975. City Hall needed $43 million it didn't have to meet its payroll on Friday the 6th of June, and there was an additional $800 million of bills to pay the week after that. With the city already in the hole for more than $11 billion, borrowing more in the bond market was out of the question.

Disaster was avoided with a quick fix, but not for long.

Budgetary smoke and mirrors crafted by three mayors, three governors and legions of state legislators had led the big town to this disgraceful pass. Not that the politicians had wrecked the place all by themselves: Not a peep had been heard from Wall Street's banks and investment houses as they pocketed their profits from peddling New York's mounting debt, and the credit-rating agencies, Moody's and Standard & Poor's, hadn't troubled to blow any whistles, either.

The whole country was struggling through a recession in any case. This weakened tax collections at the same time it pushed up welfare costs. The fires of inflation were raging, so prices for everything the city bought were up as well. And Great Society programs were no longer the fountains of federal aid they had been in the 1960s.

A lot of things were going broke. Penn Central, Lockheed and the Franklin National Bank had collapsed. And the Urban Development Corp., one of Gov. Nelson Rockefeller's bricks-and-mortar creations, had just defaulted on a $105 million issue of notes.

But an entire city?

Urban economist Robert Poole subsequently assessed matters: "New York City spent and spent, creating a vast city hospital system, a city university open to all at no charge, the highest welfare benefits in the country and a civil service system unparalleled in its solicitude toward employees — all without concern for its increasingly hard-pressed taxpayers."

CHAPTER 159
RUNNING ON EMPTY
Tap City, 1975

THE PATH TO near-bankruptcy had been laid in the early 1960s, on Mayor Robert Wagner's watch. His sins were trifling compared to those of his successors, but one of his gimmicks in particular set a poisonous precedent: slipping ordinary expenses into the capital budget, then borrowing to pay for them.

The city issues bonds and notes to pay for its capital budget items on the time-honored principle that these items have long, productive lives — schools, hospitals, infrastructure. Ordinary expenses — salaries, social programs, paper clips — go into the operations budget and are paid out of tax collections. The state constitution requires that this budget be balanced every year. Sneaking expense items out of the operations budget and into the capital budget makes the balancing act much easier. Although fraudulent.

By 1974 — Mayor Abraham Beame's first year after John Lindsay's eight — more than half the capital budget was expense items that didn't belong there.

BORROWING HAD driven the city's debt above $11 billion. "Wall Street is only 10 blocks from City Hall," explained Sen. Daniel Patrick Moynihan, noting that the city "was, in effect, printing money" — by borrowing.

Added the Securities and Exchange Commission in a subsequent report: "The city employed budgetary, accounting and financial practices which it knew distorted its true financial condition."

In 1974, Wall Street started to get anxious.

In October, an advisory group of bankers cautioned city Controller Harrison Goldin that there might soon be no bidders for new issues of city notes and bonds. Soon turned out to be just four months later, when a sale of notes had to be canceled because it attracted no bids.

Stopgap help from Wall Street and Albany got the city over the immediate hump. Meanwhile, Gov. Hugh Carey asked a four-man panel to find a better answer. Those men — lawyer Simon Rifkind, Wall Street's Felix Rohatyn, Richard Shinn of Metropolitan Life and Donald Smiley of Macy's — devised the Municipal Assistance Corp., a state agency that would borrow money for the city, with the guarantee that its bonds would be backed by revenue from the city sales tax. MAC opened for business on June 10, 1975, just four days after City Hall's payroll crunch.

By now, the need for real belt-tightening was obvious. Some of the tightening was serious. Much of it was fictitious. Despite double-digit inflation, the city's labor unions accepted a one-year freeze on employees earning over a certain amount and relinquished some fringe benefits. Taxes and the transit fare went up. Tuition fees were imposed at City University. But lay-offs were announced and then not executed; some "lay-offs" were merely transfers off one payroll account onto another. And the city continued the old dodge of budgeting for tax collections that never would materialize.

In August, MAC Chairman William Ellinghaus told Carey that City Hall wasn't fooling anyone. Its efforts at reform were "not credible," he said. "Emergency action of a new and decisive kind is necessary . . . if default is to be avoided." Whereupon the Emergency Financial Control Board was created not only to oversee but also to enforce strict budgeting.

The governor would chair the board. Mayor Beame, cornered, had only one vote.

BEAME AND CAREY had turned to Washington for help in May with no success. For months, President Gerald Ford had made no secret of his feeling that New York had created its own problems and that it was up to New York to solve them. On one occasion he even repeated these sentiments to the Mayor of Belgrade.

On Oct. 29, Ford made a speech on the subject to the National Press Club, and suggested that the city would do well to declare bankruptcy.

Whereupon the Daily News issued a page one headline that explained the President's position fairly straightforwardly:
FORD TO CITY: DROP DEAD

The political backlash — from the nation's mayors, from concerned members of Congress, from Democrats warming up for the 1976 elections — was immediate. The administration quickly entered into face-saving negotiations. A few weeks later, the government extended $2.3 billion in loans. More money became available after that. MAC bond sales netted the city $1.5 billion in the crisis summer of 1975, and nearly $10 billion all told in the 10 years MAC was in the business of raising new money.

It is not entirely the case that financial finagling is a thing of the past in New York City. But it is markedly less flagrant than in those golden days a quarter of a century ago, when no one would face the music.

FORD TO CITY: DROP DEAD — Vows He'll Veto Any Bail-Out — Abe, Carey Rip Stand — Stocks Skid, Dow Down 12

By BILL BELL
Daily News Staff Writer

THERE'S NOTHING like a swell party to make New Yorkers forget their troubles, and in the summer of 1976 the city was in plenty of trouble.

A financial crisis had left the town staggering on the edge of bankruptcy, with painful cuts in everything from library hours to subway service, and the confidence of its inhabitants was in depressed free fall. Only months before, President Gerald Ford had flatly refused to come to the city's financial rescue. There was considerable doubt that New York could even afford to join the rest of the nation in celebrating America's 200th birthday.

And indeed, the grand, gaudy, loud, proud, star-spangled blast that the dispirited city managed to stage on the Fourth of July weekend almost didn't happen at all.

A PRIVATE GROUP, New York City Bicentennial Corp., had been set up by the City Council in 1973 to organize the party. This was a huge, complex and expensive project and it fast ran into difficulties. A full year before the celebration, the city cut off funding, unpaid bills piled up and staffers were laid off.

The city's own fiscal crisis was just one reason for this. Another was the charge by the borough presidents that the bicentennial's master plan was vague and amateurish. The boroughs wanted to run their own celebrations, which they said would cost far less than the millions the Bicentennial Corp. proposed to spend.

But, argued Deputy Mayor Stanley Friedman: "The spirit of '76 is something New York cannot afford to lose." And so the badly strapped city okayed another $500,000 and the corporation pressed ahead.

The original idea of a national party stretching from sea to shining sea had been endorsed by President Richard Nixon long before the Watergate scandal forced him to resign in 1974. A national advisory body, the American Revolution Bicentennial Commission, was set up to coordinate the 65,000 individual projects saluting the 200th birthday of the adoption of the Declaration of Independence. Several cities nominated themselves as the national host for these galas: Philadelphia because, after all, the

JAMES HUGHES DAILY NEWS

CHAPTER 160

YANKEE DOODLE DANDY

Bicentennial, 1976

Declaration of Independence was signed there and it had the Liberty Bell. Boston, because of Bunker Hill, Paul Revere, the Tea Party. Washington, because, well, it was the capital.

But Philadelphia's plan to combine its bicentennial party with a world's fair fell into financial and organizational disarray, and the national commission finally nixed the whole idea. Washington, meanwhile, had been damaged and divided by rioting in 1968. It fell, finally, to New York City to throw the biggest celebration of all.

This was not illogical. It was in City Hall Park that the declaration was read to George Washington's troops. The first battle between colonial and British forces had taken place in what was now Brooklyn's Prospect Park. The first U.S. capital building had stood at what was now 26 Wall St.; it was there that George Washington had taken the oath of office as the nation's first President. He had bade his officers farewell at Fraunces Tavern when he left New York to take up his federal duties.

Besides, New York had the Statue of Liberty.

THE centerpiece of New York's many bicentennial celebrations was Operation Sail '76, initially a private citizen's modest idea, subsequently the awesome, spectacular symbol of the entire anniversary festival.

The citizen was Frank Braynard, a writer and illustrator who loved ships and had previously organized a small Operation Sail — with 24 sailing vessels from 12 countries — during the 1964 World's Fair in Queens.

For Op Sail '76, Braynard organized a private committee headed by America's Cup yachtsman Emil Mosbecher. Five years of hard work resulted in a thrilling spectacle: 228 sailing ships, 53 naval vessels and uncounted hundreds of yachts, tugs, fireboats, yawls and punts from more than 40 countries, including two tall-masters from the Soviet Union.

Sixteen tall-masted square-riggers and windjammers, including a British schooner crewed by women, passed in review up the Hudson as hundreds of thousands cheered wildly from the shore. Among the midshipmen aboard a Spanish naval vessel was Christopher Columbus, a descendent of the Florentine explorer. The astounding array electrified the country.

By that time, the city had been spruced up a bit. Near the South Street Seaport, nine blocks of 18th- and 19th-century buildings had been restored to their long-ago glory.

There were dozens of small, significant moments. New York City's oldest Jewish congregation, Shearith Israel, displayed the blood-stained Torah scroll that was thrown into the street when rowdy redcoats had burst in and fired at the cantor 200 years earlier. (They had missed.)

Many of the tall ships riding the East River were open to visitors, and tens of thousands pushed into the Seaport for a look, so many that police had to close it.

Hundreds of thousands more merrymakers filled parks and shorelines along the Hudson to see the great flotilla anchored there. At Pier 88 alone, police put the crowd at 150,000.

The Queen of England visited. So did Princess Grace of Monaco.

On the last day of the formal celebration, July 6, fireworks lit the skies over Battery Park and Riverside Park, and about 2,000 sailors, accompanied by five brass bands blaring patriotic melodies, marched up Broadway to City Hall under a blizzard of ticker tape.

When it was all over, revelers had left 1,772 tons of debris in lower Manhattan. Snowplows were brought in to clear it all away.

It was a week later before the last of the ships sailed away. Someone said that sailors hadn't been this popular in New York since Gene Kelly and Frank Sinatra danced in "On the Town."

By KIERAN O'LEARY
Daily News Staff Writer

CHAPTER 161

FRENZY
Son Of Sam, 1977

THEY ONLY HAD eyes for each other, and that gave their killer all the time he needed. Stepping from the darkness that shrouded the Hutchinson River Parkway service road, he thrust a .44-caliber revolver through the parked car's passenger window and fired five times. Alexander Esau, 20, and Valentina Suriani, 17, never had a chance.

As the two sweethearts lay dying, the gunman put down a letter on the bloody front seat between them.

I am a monster, he had written. *I am the Son of Sam.*

This, on the night of April 17, 1977, was the coming-out missive of a maniac, addressed to Capt. Joseph Borelli, the police detective heading the manhunt for the gunman who was targeting young women with long, dark hair.

I love to hunt. Prowling the streets looking for fair game — tasty meat.

He had struck five times already. Three women were dead, four other people wounded. The papers had dubbed him "The .44 Caliber Killer."

Now he had given himself a name.

Son of Sam.

I'll be back. I'll be back.

Across the city, frightened young women began cutting off their hair, or hiding it under a hat, or dyeing it blonde. Young couples started avoiding lovers' lanes. Anxious parents swept their kids in from the streets as soon as the sun went down. The Son of Sam had put into motion a frenzy of fear unparalleled in the history of New York.

THE KILLING HAD started the previous summer on a quiet street in the east Bronx. Eighteen-year-old Donna Lauria was the first to die.

She and her friend Jody Valenti had gone dancing in New Rochelle, then driven back to Donna's home on Buhre Ave. at about 1 a.m. Enjoying the warm night, the two young women lingered in Valenti's blue Cutlass to chat. Then a stranger approached.

"Now who is this?" said Lauria.

An instant later she was dead. Valenti, 19, was wounded.

There were three more shootings before police connected them:

Oct. 23, 1976: Carl Denaro, 20, wounded as he sat in a car with Rosemary Keenan, 21, on 160th St. in Flushing, Queens. Denaro wore his hair to his shoulders; the gunman apparently mistook him for a woman.

Nov. 27, 1976: Donna DiMasi, 17, and Joanne Lomino, 18, wounded as they sat outside the Lomino home on 262nd St. in Floral Park, Queens.

Jan. 29, 1977: Christine Freund, 26, shot dead near the Forest Hills, Queens, railroad station as she sat in a car with John Diel, 30.

A police task force was quietly assembled. Then, on March 8, there was another shooting, just a half-block from where Freund had died. The 19-year-old victim was Columbia University student Virginia Voskerichian. Eye to eye with her killer, she had reflexively raised a textbook to her face. The bullet tore through it.

Three days later, Mayor Abe Beame and Police Commissioner Michael Codd publicly acknowledged that a serial killer was on the loose.

But, in a city that had seen 1,622 murders the year before, the news caused little more than a ripple of alarm.

THAT CHANGED when Esau and Suriani died — and cops read their slayer's letter. Under the direction of Inspector Timothy Dowd, 75 detectives and 225 officers checked out the 400 New Yorkers who had permits for .44-caliber revolvers, even attempted to trace all 28,000 Bulldogs manufactured by the Charter Arms Co. They consulted with psychics and astrologers. And they issued an unprecedented public plea for Son of Sam's surrender.

"We know you are not a woman hater," police said. "We know how much you have suffered. Please let us help you."

Sam liked the attention. In early June, he wrote to Daily News columnist Jimmy Breslin.

Hello from the gutters of New York.

Don't think because you haven't heard from me

for a while that I went to sleep.

I am still here. Like a spirit roaming the night. Thirsty, hungry, seldom stopping to rest. Anxious to please.

On June 26, he shot Sal Lupo, 20, and Judy Placido, 17, as they sat in a car outside a Bayside disco. Both lived.

The fear spread. A police tip line started ringing off the hook as neighbors and co-workers reported each other, mothers tearfully turned in their sons, women handed over their husbands and lovers.

Son of Sam, said the T-shirts hawked in Central Park. *Get Him Before He Gets You.*

HE KILLED AGAIN on July 31, now in Brooklyn. Robert Violante and Stacy Moscowitz, on their first date, had gone to the movies, then driven to Shore Parkway and Bay 17th St. Under the light of a full moon, they walked hand in hand across a footbridge to the edge of Gravesend Bay — then quickly returned to the car when Violante spotted a man watching them.

The stranger was faster. He dropped into a crouch and shot them both. Moscowitz was killed, Violante badly wounded.

Now there was mounting panic. Moscowitz wasn't even a brunette. Now Sam was shooting anyone.

Meanwhile, he had made a mistake.

Unable to find a parking space on the Bath Beach streets as he stalked Moscowitz and Violante, he had left his Ford Galaxie at a fire hydrant on Bay 17th St. For months he had

craftily eluded the biggest manhunt in NYPD history. Now he had a parking ticket.

THAT TICKET SWIFTLY led to 24-year-old David Berkowitz of Pine St. in Yonkers. Examining the car parked outside his apartment, police spotted a rifle inside — and waited.

Fifteen cops drew on Berkowitz when he showed up several hours later. He was carrying a manila envelope. Inside it was a .44, the gun that had killed six people and wounded seven.

"Okay," he said. "You got me."

The reign of terror was over.

THE FACE OF evil belonged to a pudgy postal worker who worked a 4-to-midnight shift sorting mail in the Bronx.

He told court-appointed psychiatrists that the killing spree had been ordered by his neighbor's dog. The neighbor, Sam Carr, had lived 6,000 years ago, Berkowitz explained.

After shooting Violante and Moscowitz, he said, he had gone home and dutifully written a $35 check to pay the parking ticket: "It's the law."

Doctors differed over his sanity. A judge finally ruled him competent to stand trial, and he pleaded guilty. On June 12, 1978, he was sentenced to 547 years in prison.

"I know a lot of victims' parents and stuff, you know, they always say 'Why?'" mused David Berkowitz.

"I hate to disappoint all these people. They're not going to find out."

By WENDELL JAMIESON
Daily News Staff Writer

WINDOW WASHER Jack Forbes thought right away there was something strange about the bearded, kerchief-wearing, determined-looking man with the harness on his back, walking purposefully toward the World Trade Center. Say, where did he think he was going? The man didn't answer, although he could have, with just one word:

Up.

Forbes watched curiously, at 6:30 a.m. on Thursday the 26th of May 1977, as George Willig, a 27-year-old Queens toymaker who liked to climb mountains, approached the complex's south tower with a group of pals. They looked around for guards — and then got to work.

At the 110-story building's northeast corner, Willig pulled some tools out of his bag, tools that included a set of odd-looking metal blocks attached to nylon cords. His friends took snapshots as he pushed one of the blocks into a window-washing groove and locked it into place with a twist. Then he stepped onto the nylon sling, pushed a second block into the groove a little higher up, locked that one and stepped up. He then reached down, untwisted the first block and repeated the process, pulling himself up by the harness secured to a block above his head.

George Willig had now traveled the first few feet of a 1,350-foot, 3½-hour climb up the silvery sheer facade of the newest symbol of New York City, an epic ascent that would transfix and thrill a crime-battered, debt-ridden metropolis badly in need of a distraction.

Realizing that something was going on here, Forbes ordered the climbing figure to come down immediately.

But Willig was 10 feet up, just out of reach. He didn't answer. He just pulled out the lower block, swung it up, twisted it into place and took another step.

A couple of Port Authority cops were on the scene by now, waving and shouting. But there wasn't anything they could do either.

George Willig was on his way.

WITHIN 30 MINUTES, scores of cops were flooding the plaza, inflating a huge red-and-white air bag beneath the climber, although few thought it would do any good if he dropped from above the 10th floor. "He'd go through that thing like it wasn't even there," mused one officer.

Work-bound commuters, who had watched the Trade Center's floor-by-floor construction through the late 1960s, looked up to see Willig shrink into a tinier and tinier speck. Crowds gathered. Everyone instantly dubbed him The Human Fly.

"What's holding him up?" asked one onlooker.

"A lot of guts," a cop replied.

This was not the first daredevil spectacle at the World Trade Center. On Aug. 7, 1974, French acrobat Phillipe Petit had walked across a 130-foot cable between the towers. On July 22, 1975, Owen James Quinn, an unemployed construction worker, had strapped on a parachute and jumped from the top, floating straight down into the waiting arms of police.

But those feats took mere minutes. Willig's climb was going to take hours. The city had all morning to boil into a frenzy.

Six news helicopters were soon circling, capturing the climb for TV and the papers. A seventh chopper, representing the Police Department, tried to chase them away.

Willig kept inching up.

Having failed to stop him from below, the NYPD decided to stop him from above. Two cops were lowered from the roof in a window-washer's bucket. Officer DeWitt Allen, who had once scaled the George Washington Bridge to talk down a suicidal jumper, and Port Authority cop Glenn Kildare, who didn't like heights, met Willig outside the 55th floor.

"We have to stop meeting like this," Allen said.

The police officers politely invited him to step into the bucket with them. Willig politely declined. "I'd like to climb to the top," he explained.

Willig then pulled out one of his blocks, switched it to another window-washer's groove farther away from the two cops and stepped over. Then he continued upward.

Considering the possibility that he had a crazy man on his hands, Allen asked him a couple of questions designed to determine his state of mind.

"Every response he gave me was reasonable," Allen reported. "The only thing that was unreasonable about it was that he was on the outside of the building."

GIVING UP, Allen and Kildare went along for the ride, slowly ascending a few feet from Willig, making small talk, giving him water.

As the ground got further away, city lawyers combed their books, trying to determine what to charge Willig with.

The crowds in the plaza and surrounding streets got bigger and bigger. At 10:05 a.m., when Willig reached the top, pulled himself through a 30-inch hatch and turned and waved, a great roar of applause filled the New York sky.

He was promptly handcuffed and placed under arrest, charged with criminal trespass, reckless endangerment and disorderly conduct.

That afternoon, as more than 100 reporters waited outside the 1st Precinct stationhouse for Willig's release, Corporation Counsel representative Edwin Lieberman used a bullhorn to announce that the city intended to sue Willig for $250,000, the cost of police overtime and the fuel for the NYPD helicopter.

He was soundly booed.

The climber emerged from the stationhouse as the city's newest celebrity. He said he'd been planning the stunt for a year, that he'd practiced on the grooves several times under cover of darkness, that his shoulder was sore from the harness and that he'd been in scarier situations, like at Yosemite National Park.

Why had he done it?

"I wanted to get to the top," he said.

MAYOR ABRAHAM BEAME, *a man not widely known for his public-relations talents, was ultimately persuaded that a $250,000 suit against George Willig was not a brilliant idea. The figure was reduced to $1.10 — a penny for each Trade Center floor The Human Fly had climbed, lifting the city's spirits with him.*

MICHAEL LIPACK DAILY NEWS

CHAPTER 162

EIGHT MILES HIGH

The Human Fly, 1977

CHAPTER 163

PAYDAY

The Blackout, 1977

DAILY NEWS

By WENDELL JAMIESON
Daily News Staff Writer

THREE LIGHTNING bolts. All at exactly 8:28 p.m. on the 13th of July 1977, striking from a line of sodden black thunderclouds rolling across northern Westchester County. Absolutely a one-in-a-million coincidence, the electrical engineers would agree.

Three lightning bolts that plunged the sprawling metropolis into a Wednesday night of darkness and fear, lighted only by the flames raging in storefronts and leaping from garbage cans in the streets.

The bolts severed three power lines, two connecting nuclear plants in Westchester with plants in Rockland and Orange counties, one running to the Con Ed substation at Pleasant Valley. That station quickly became overloaded. Within minutes, the other lines shut off, tripped by safety switches designed to prevent them from burning out.

New York City, cooled this sweaty night by thousands of whirring air conditioners and using a lot of juice, suddenly lost 1,200 megawatts of the electricity that had always dependably streamed down from Canada and upstate.

WORRIED ENGINEERS at the New York Power Pool's brick building in Schenectady cut city voltage, first by 5%, then 8%. They dimmed the lights in Mount Vernon, then in Elmsford.

But it was too late. The city sucked power from Long Island and New Jersey. The whole system — even the entire Northeast — could go dark, just as it had in 1965. At 9:21 p.m., the Long Island Lighting Co. cut itself off from the five boroughs, fearing a burnout of Con Ed-LILCO cables under the Sound. A few minutes later, New Jersey did the same.

At 9:30, Big Allis, the massive generator in Ravenswood, Queens, shut herself down automatically to prevent damage.

Lights flickered. Televisions sputtered. Air conditioners rattled.

And then the skyline was gone.

FOR A FEW minutes, there was revelry in the sudden, fascinating disappearance of the 20th century. Many saw the blackness as a test of their New York ingenuity: They lit candles, dug flashlights out of closets, walked into intersections to help direct traffic. In bars, knowing the beer would soon go warm, they ordered extra rounds.

"It's going to be a beautiful night," someone said in the warm candle-light of Snooky's Pub on Seventh Ave. in Park Slope, Brooklyn.

"Fantastic!" someone shouted on the street. "It's the whole city! It's the whole goddamned world!"

That included Broadway. At "Beatlemania," the mop-topped actors discarded their electric guitars and, illuminated by flashlights, finished the show acoustically.

In the Daily News' E. 42nd St. city room, night editors got out the edition using generator-powered klieg lights borrowed from the film crew shooting "Superman" downstairs in the lobby.

People trapped in subway cars were led through sweltering, pitch-black tunnels to safety. Those in elevators crawled through hatches or waited. And waited.

Many found themselves recalling the Great Blackout of 12 years earlier, when few cared that the whole Northeast went powerless — they were having too much fun. That dark night, just 59 people were arrested, fewer than the daily average. It became a New York legend — never proved, never really discounted — that there was a boomlet of babies nine months later.

But this was 1977, not 1965. And it was a muggy July, not a cool, crisp November. A few hours went by, and the laughter died down. And everyone began to feel that something palpably awful was happening.

A FEW BLOCKS from Snooky's, somebody rolled garbage cans into the street and set them ablaze. The flames lit the faces of soon-to-be criminals fast realizing that the city — and every unaffordable item behind every plate glass window, everything they ever wanted and ever needed — was free for the taking.

Someone smashed a drugstore window. A squad car, red lights giving the street an eerie glow, edged up to the growing crowd. Two cops stepped out, looked around — and quickly left. The crowd chuckled. They could do anything they wanted.

In the past 12 years, too many neighborhoods had become too poor. Now, in the dark, store owners who had been friends became leeches, driving in from the suburbs to greedily take money from their stricken customers.

They were the first ones to get hit.

"You take everything you can get," openly boasted an 18-year-old named Cherryl Ross. "Look, dungarees are $17.99 and sneakers are $24. Who wants to buy sneakers for $24? [President Jimmy] Carter is not giving us what we want. He ain't giving us nothing. So we have to take it."

In Fort Greene, Flatbush and downtown Brooklyn, in the South Bronx and along the Grand Concourse, in Jamaica, Queens, in upper Manhattan and especially in Bushwick, Brooklyn — a neighborhood that tonight would be permanently scarred — armies formed. They tied storefront grates to car bumpers and yanked them down. They played tag with outnumbered cops.

And they took. They grabbed groceries from supermarkets. They carted off instruments and stereos from music stores. They stole 50 Pontiacs from a Queens showroom. They took diapers and radios and televisions and shirts and shoes and toasters and records and boxes of cereal and baseball gloves and pots and pans. They carried $100,000 worth of sofas, chairs and tables from Furniture By Alec Zanders on the Grand Concourse, leaving behind only a parking meter that had been ripped up from the street and thrown through the Zanders window.

Soon it wasn't just the outsiders' stores that were targeted. Two men who were raised on the upper West Side and had opened a furniture store with a small business loan watched as their life's work was savaged. What the looters couldn't carry away, they destroyed, smashing a glass chandelier and plunging knives into leather sofas.

And they set fires. Bushwick and Flatbush and the South Bronx were bathed in orange. The Fire Department was overwhelmed; most of the blazes raged on. In Brooklyn, a knot of firefighters turned their hose away from a burning building and used it to scatter looters pillaging a store across the street.

The National Guard was notified and waited to be called in, but Mayor Abe Beame decided against it, relying instead on the 25,000-member NYPD. For the cops, there was no such thing as finishing a shift.

WHEN THE LIGHT of another muggy morning finally came, it revealed a new city, a smoky war zone of broken glass, shattered neighborhoods, debris-strewn streets — and the murmured voices of store owners saying they were closing down and never coming back. There had been 3,400 arrested, 558 cops injured, 851 fires, $1 billion in damage.

Con Ed didn't get all the lights back on until about 10:30 p.m., leaving much of the jittery city to wonder as night came again whether the looting armies would regroup.

But in the ravaged, soot-covered neighborhoods where the marauders won the night before, most were confident the horror would not be repeated.

There just wasn't much left to take.

By CORKY SIEMASZKO
Daily News Staff Writer

THEY DIDN'T recognize the shoeless man lying unconscious on the floor of the posh Manhattan townhouse. The blonde trying to resuscitate him was frightened and out of breath.

"How long has he been out?" one of the paramedics asked.

"Five minutes," she gasped.

His body was warm, but they couldn't find a pulse. Now they began administering oxygen and injecting powerful drugs into the shoeless man's veins to jump-start his heart.

Six minutes later the electrocardiogram line gave a wiggle. But as paramedic William McCabe radioed nearby St. Clare's Hospital that the squad was ready to roll, he got inexplicable orders to head for farther-away Lenox Hill Hospital instead.

At Lenox Hill a few minutes later, the ambulance was met by Dr. Ernest Esakof.

"All right," Esakof announced to the crew. "Let's not talk about this."

At 12:20 a.m. on Saturday the 26th of January 1979, 70-year-old Nelson Aldrich Rockefeller, former four-term governor of the State of New York and former vice president of the United States of America, was declared dead, apparently of a heart attack.

Forty minutes later, Rockefeller family spokesman Hugh Morrow began unspooling the official story of the great man's last moments.

But matters were already spinning out of control.

THE SCION OF the family that oversaw America's most famous fortune, Nelson Rockefeller lusted his entire life for that which even his millions could not buy — the presidency.

An aristocrat who treated his wives to new Rolls-Royces each year, he had nonetheless always been a hit with the masses. "Rocky" worked hard at being a regular guy, throwing out a jaunty "Hiya, fella!" as he glad-handed voters en route to his four terms in Albany.

But he was often at odds with his own Republican Party, and in the twilight of his career he'd had to settle for a truncated two-year stint as vice president to Gerald Ford, a man the otherwise populist Rockefeller considered his distinct inferior.

In the summer of 1975, the unhappy veep had met a 22-year-old wire-service reporter named Megan Marshack, who seemed to have won his interest by plying him with cookies. When he left Washington the following year, Marshack came back to New York with him as his $60,000-a-year assistant — moving into a luxurious co-op at 25 W. 54th St., a few doors from the townhouse Rockefeller kept in the city.

The first press reports of Rockefeller's death paid moving tribute to the hardworking GOP elder who had died at his desk while working on a book about modern art.

Solemnly, Morrow told reporters Rockefeller had suffered a heart attack at 10:15 Friday night in his office at 30 Rockefeller Plaza and that a security aide, the only other person present, had tried to revive him and failed. The stricken man

CHAPTER 164
SPIN
R.I.P. Nelson Rockefeller, 1979

Megan Marshack

had been admitted to Lenox Hill at 11:15, he said, and widow Happy Rockefeller had arrived at 12:25 a.m., 10 minutes too late. Of the frightened blonde, Morrow made no mention.

The following day, Morrow admitted he'd gotten one or two details wrong. Actually, Rockefeller had died at his 54th St. townhouse, he said. A chauffeur also had been there at the time. Of the blonde, there was still no mention.

But there she was in the police reports, and now the press wanted to know about her.

Well, yes, Morrow acknowledged, he had just learned that Nelson Rockefeller's young assistant also had been present when his heart gave out.

IN HIS DEATH, the distinguished Nelson Aldrich Rockefeller now became a lurid tabloid astonisher.

None of the story held up. He'd been stricken at 10:15, he arrived at the hospital at 11:15 — why, the press wondered, had it taken an hour to get Rockefeller to the hospital? No, the Rockefeller camp said, the heart attack had actually occurred minutes before 11:15 and the time originally given out had been incorrect. "It was simply a case of people under pressure making a mistake," said spokesman George Taylor. As for Marshack, said Morrow, she had called 911, and that was the sole extent of her involvement.

But it wasn't Marshack who had called 911 at all, it quickly developed. That call had been made by TV personality Ponchitta Pierce, who lived in Marshack's building and who had departed the scene before cops arrived.

Marshack was gone now too — visiting friends in the country, Morrow said, he didn't know where. That story collapsed when it was learned that The Associated Press had reached Marshack by phone four hours after Rockefeller's heart stopped beating, and that she'd told the AP that Morrow was with her.

Morrow clammed up altogether at this point. By now the questions were too large to contain. Why hadn't there been an autopsy? Why had Rockefeller been so quickly cremated? And who exactly was this Miss Marshack, anyway?

MEGAN MARSHACK had several acquaintances quite willing to dish to the papers. Quickly there came revelations that Rockefeller had helped her buy her plush apartment, furnished it with antiques and art from his personal collection, provided for riding lessons at his Pocantico Hills estate in Westchester. Marshack's neighbors said Rockefeller, stooped though he was by worsening health, was a frequent visitor and always brought flowers for his comely assistant. Former co-workers made it plain they regarded Marshack as a gold-digger, a woman who talked openly of snaring a man with money.

Manhattan District Attorney Robert Morgenthau made an "informal" inquiry into the events surrounding Rockefeller's death — then declined to reveal what he'd turned up. "I don't want to get into questions like that," he said.

In an America still uncertainly coming to terms with the notion of seeing the names and reputations of its devoted public servants sullied, social observers fretted that the line between news and gossip was perhaps becoming blurred, not to mention the line between privacy and public interest. But it wasn't long before Johnny Carson could start drawing laughs merely by uttering the words "Megan Marshack."

EIGHTEEN-YEAR-OLD Steven Rockefeller, the dead man's grandson, finally broke the family's silence. He was satisfied, he said, that Marshack and everyone else had done everything they could to save his grandfather.

"I don't know what Megan's role was exactly," he said, "but if she was involved with Grandaddy, I hope she did the best she could and that she was instrumental in some of his success."

Asked what he would say to Megan Marshack, the young Rockefeller said: "I would tell her, 'I hope you made my grandfather happy.'"

LATER IN 1979, *Mayor Edward Koch fired chief medical examiner Michael Baden after the M.E.'s office dropped hints that Nelson Rockefeller had died while having sex.*

ROBERT ROSAMILIO DAILY NEWS

By BILL BELL
Daily News Staff Writer

HE arrived at 9:01 a.m. on Tuesday the 2nd of October 1979, 14 minutes ahead of schedule, aboard a chartered Aer Lingus jetliner temporarily named "Shepherd I," and as he stood on a soggy red carpet at the Marine Air Terminal at LaGuardia Airport, the rain that had followed him from earlier stops in Ireland and Boston still pelted down.

Now, with one hand, he held his white skullcap tightly in place as the sharp, chill wind whipped his red cape around his burly shoulders. With the other hand, he grasped a welcoming floral spray shyly extended by Yolanda Zawisny, a 6-year-old Staten Islander wearing a traditional Polish folk costume.

And so Pope John Paul II, ruler of the world's tiniest sovereign state, began a hectic, tumultuous visit to New York, capital city of the world.

As he passed along the line of dignitaries, one grasped his hand. "I am the mayor of New York," said Edward Koch.

John Paul grinned. "I will try to be a good citizen," he said.

THIS WAS NOT the first papal visit to the city. Paul VI had spent a day here in 1965, addressing the United Nations. But he lacked the robust charismatic appeal of John Paul, a singular celebrity and, for many, a still mysterious newcomer.

John Paul had ruled for less than a year. He was Polish, the first non-Italian pope since the 16th century, and, at 58, he was the youngest pope this century. As a young man he had played soccer, skiied, climbed mountains, acted, wrote poetry and plays and argued philosophy — an irresistible package of energy and intellect.

Even the Italians who regarded the papacy as their own liked him. For one thing, he spoke their language, plus several others, including English, which he spoke with a pronounced Slavic accent.

"I have looked forward to this moment," The Pope Of Peace told the VIPs at LaGuardia before stepping into a limo that took him directly to the UN and his first major speech.

That address was the official reason for his visit. Unofficially, he was here to make a pastoral call on his New York flock — about a third of the city's population.

WHEN HE ARRIVED at the UN, he found about 4,000 people braving the rain, pushing against security barriers, hoping for a glimpse and maybe a blessing. They got both.

Inside, he talked about human rights for more than an hour and received a warm, standing ovation that lasted nearly two minutes. After shaking a few hundred hands, and already 35 minutes behind schedule, he was gently hustled onto his next stop, St. Patrick's Cathedral, to greet nuns and priests.

Thousands more New Yorkers waited in the

CHAPTER 165

NEW YORK KIND OF GUY

John Paul II, 1979

rain outside St. Pat's, and as the Pope left, headed for Harlem's Church of St. Charles Borromeo, he clasped his hands together and shook them above his head like a boxer. The crowd went nuts.

Some 12,000 uniformed officers guarded the route, the heaviest security any visitor had ever received. Sharpshooters were assigned to rooftops. Security was so tight that manhole covers were welded shut and garbage cans removed from streets.

When John Paul climbed onto a wooden platform in the street outside the Harlem church, a choir burst into a jubilant rendition of the black Baptist hymn, "Wade in the Water." The Pope congratulated the singers. "You ain't heard nothing yet, Mr. Pope," somebody boomed.

The next stop was a vacant, muddy three-acre lot in the South Bronx, the site of a promised project to build 100 homes for low-income families. It had taken a week to clean up the corner, and by the time the Pope arrived, many of the people who hoped to live in the new houses were surrounding the lot, waving flags and chanting greetings.

Speaking in English, Spanish and Italian, the Pope blessed the crowd, the vacant lot and the entire South Bronx.

The last stop was Yankee Stadium, rented by the archdiocese for $20,000, the standard price, for an outdoor Mass. As the white Popemobile, a special steel-reinforced vehicle with a raised portable throne in the back, rolled slowly into the Stadium from the right field bullpen, the crowd — officially set at 72,545 — erupted in pandemonium.

In keeping with his penchant for blunt, straight talk, the Pope told the hushed throng it was immoral for Americans to consume so much of the world's dwindling resources when so many were hungry and poor.

He spent the night in the official Madison Ave. residence of his host, Terence Cardinal Cooke, but before he turned in, there was one more wave and blessing for a singing, cheering

crowd that had waited outside for hours.

THE second day began at 8 a.m. with prayers at St. Patrick's, then he went on to a youth rally at Madison Square Garden. There, 20,000 kids feted him like a rock star, starting with a nine-minute-long earsplitting din of a welcome.

John Paul brushed away an aide who complained the kids were wrecking the schedule. "We will destroy the schedule," he said, to more cheers. He was presented some decidedly nonpapal gifts — blue jeans, a Big Apple T-shirt, a guitar. Reportedly, he could play a few chords, a talent dating back to his student years, but he did not risk a riot at the Garden by proving it.

At Battery Park, against the backdrop of Ellis Island and the Statue of Liberty, he greeted leaders of the Jewish community by shouting, "Shalom!"

He said he was there to deliver a message that New Yorkers knew well — about welcoming the stranger and extending a helping hand. "I appeal to all who love freedom and justice to give a chance to all in need, to the poor and the powerless," he said.

There was the traditional ticker-tape parade, too; the city figured that about 100 tons of confetti — mostly waterlogged computer cards and shredded paper — had rained down on the papal motorcade. This was far below the record, and officials blamed the bad weather. But other observers wondered if it wasn't because New Yorkers might think it was not polite to throw things at a Pope.

JOHN PAUL'S 28½-hour visit was winding down now. There was a brief stop at the St. James Cathedral in Brooklyn for prayers and greetings there with clergy, and then an ecumenical service at Shea Stadium (the rent was $15,000).

Then, by early afternoon, it was into the limo and back to LaGuardia. The papal tour would go on to four more cities, with riotous receptions in all of them, before ending in Washington with a handshake with President Jimmy Carter.

The reviews in New York were uniformly glowing. John Paul had lived up to his billing, they said. The spontaneous ad libs had made him a New York kind of guy, and his sermons and speeches had made him a champion of the little guy.

Cooke said the visit had revitalized the Church and that the Pope told him he would like to come back sometime.

*J*OHN PAUL II *returned to New York in 1994, this time for four days, and it rained again. The reception was a little more restrained, but the cheering, singing multitudes turned out by the tens of thousands for Masses at Belmont Raceway, Giants Stadium and Central Park. He was 75 now, and in frail health, and many of the faithful made a point of seeing him because, they said, perhaps he would not visit again.*

By JERE HESTER
Daily News Staff Writer

THERE WAS NEVER a cop around when you needed one, especially in the subways, where these grim days they were needed more than they had ever been needed since, it seemed, the IRT opened for business in 1904. With the transit police force sliced from 3,600 to 2,200 in the wake of the mid-1970s fiscal crisis, the city's main mode of public transportation had become a festering Petri dish breeding violent young punks looking for quick cash and cheap kicks.

You could tuck the gold chain in your shirt, but you couldn't hide the swell $60 Pumas, which were like magnets for packs of teenagers carrying switchblades or worse. Fifty cents was the price of admission for a potential hell ride, an underground horror story waiting to be written in blood and graffiti.

Tasting the fear and seeing opportunity in this sorry state of affairs was a tough-talking Brooklyn kid with a sense of civic duty that was surpassed only by a talent for self-promotion. Cross Jimmy Cagney with Leo Gorcey, add a heap of P.T. Barnum — and you had Curtis Sliwa.

EARLY IN 1979, Sliwa, a 24-year-old high school dropout, formed the Magnificent 13, a volunteer patrol that rode the IRT at night — particularly the No. 4 train, known to cops and riders alike as the Mugger's Express.

Before year's end, the Magnificents' numbers had swelled far past 13, having drawn scores of mostly minority teenagers who were as fed up with the crime around them as anyone else. Sliwa — Rock, he liked to call himself in those days — rechristened his group the Guardian Angels and articulated what fast became a very popular philosophy as New York City's murder rate approached a frightening record 1,800.

"I have a very simple outlook toward problems," Rock mused. "Every problem can be attacked simply, without complex thinking. You are either right or wrong. If you're ripping someone off, you've got to be stopped."

And straphangers were only too happy to have the Guardian Angels riding with them — karate-trained youths, fanning out through the night, anywhere from 12 to 40 eight-Angel patrols at a time. Mostly they were just deterrents to the bad guys and reassuring presences to frightened riders. But they fast jumped into action when they needed to — chasing away predators, pulling to safety people who had been pushed onto the tracks, at one point even coming to the rescue of a policeman who was being beaten with his own nightstick.

The papers were full of their exploits. **ANGEL ROUTS 3 MUGGERS. ANGEL AIDS COP IN BMT ARREST. NAB 2 AFTER SCUFFLE WITH ANGELS. RIDERS HAVE ANGELS LOOKING OVER THEM.** Every day was another chapter in the thrilling adventures of the multi-racial band of protectors in red berets and red-and-white T-shirts, making the subways safe for the people of the City of New York.

"I was born in this city many years ago," said 67-year-old John

CHAPTER 166

EITHER RIGHT OR WRONG

Angels On Patrol, 1980

Caserno of Queens in a typical accolade. "Things have become almost impossible to deal with. But they help."

"God bless you," one elderly man told a band of Angels patrolling the No. 3 train early one winter's morning. "The mayor should give you a medal."

Mayor Edward Koch wasn't so sure about that.

AS CURTIS SLIWA and the Guardian Angels began grabbing headlines faster than a speeding A train, there were those who had misgivings about what was, after all, a private army. "Paramilitaries," Koch denounced them, suggesting they should join the police force if they wanted to fight crime. But cops also were suspicious of them: the Angels had clashed several times with rank-and-file officers, and police brass and union officials did not welcome their help.

"We don't need 'em and we don't want 'em," said Capt. Gerald McClaughin, commander of the Central Park Precinct. "Historically, these groups have always turned bad. I think they'll probably assault somebody."

If City Hall was a little slow to grasp the social phenomenon that was the Guardian Angels, Lt. Gov. Mario Cuomo got it more readily. Still smarting from a 1977 mayoral primary loss to Koch and eyeing bigger and better things, Cuomo became the Angels' most eloquent champion. "They are a better expression of morality than our city deserves," he said.

Confronting the largely unspoken issue that these Angels were 80%

black or Hispanic, he added: "If they were sons and daughters of doctors from Great Neck, would people be calling them vigilantes? Everyone would be giving them medals." New York City should be proud of the Angels, he said, kids who had been "born in troubled areas" and had "survived the test."

Sliwa himself missed no opportunity to make that same point: "We are taking kids who might have been committing the crimes and giving them an outlet to fight it. Before, while they were watching Superman and Batman on TV, they had no outlets for their good impulses to fight crime."

City Hall eventually started negotiations to work with the Angels but remained wary. "I don't know everything about the Guardian Angels," Koch said. "I do know they love publicity."

HE WAS RIGHT, of course. Curtis Sliwa apparently had been born with built-in media radar. At 16, he had pulled several people out of a burning Brooklyn building one morning while on his Daily News delivery route; that earned him Newsboy of the Year honors and a photo op with President Richard Nixon, who presented him with a tie clip and a pen. In 1978, he won notice for starting an anti-litter campaign in the Bronx. That same year, he got some publicity returning a lost wallet packed with $300.

But with the Guardian Angels, Sliwa took a geometric leap into the big time — and played it to the hilt. He did Tom Snyder. He did "Nightline." He was followed around by reporters from Japan and

Norway and France.

There was talk about a movie of his life — and he was adding to the script each day, with hair-raising tales of his narrow escapes from death. There were the three guys claiming to be transit cops who took him for a little ride and told him to disband the Angels — or else. There was the gunman who opened fire at him and missed. There were the thugs who kidnapped him and tossed him in the river. You didn't have to be Ed Koch to be dubious about some of these stories.

Meanwhile, as if New York weren't already a big enough stage, Sliwa, a one-time McDonald's manager, started franchising. Child killer in Atlanta? The Angels were there. Trouble in Detroit? Los Angeles? San Juan? You could count on the Angels.

By the end of 1980, some 700 Guardian Angels were roaming the New York subways, regularly racking up dozens of citizens arrests. The city, overwhelmed by a relentless publicity juggernaut, began moving toward an agreement under which the Angels would remain autonomous but would get police-issued ID cards and a modicum of police cooperation.

Koch sounded almost conciliatory: "It's like chicken soup," he said. "Have they hurt? No. Have they helped? Yes."

"The badges make the New York Times crowd feel good," Sliwa told the Daily News. "The people on the subways in Brooklyn never needed to see a badge. They were always happy enough just to see us get on the train."

By JAMES S. ROSEN
Special to The News

JOHN LENNON had lived in New York since 1971, since shortly after he stopped being a Beatle, and he had been a little fearful of the city once, but now he had conquered that. "When I started walking out, I was worried that people might want to speak to me or jump on me," he said Dec. 7, 1980, the day before he died. "Now they might ask for an autograph, but people don't bug you."

For the first few years, he and his avant-garde artist wife, Yoko Ono, had lived in the Village, oddball millionaires who dabbled in radical politics, fought to prevent Lennon's deportation over a minor British drug conviction and released albums of sporadic brilliance; Lennon made his last live performance in the city, at Madison Square Garden in 1974. Now, in 1980, he and Ono and their small son, Sean, had lived in seclusion for five years at the Dakota, the old Gothic fortress at 1 W. 72nd St. And now, in 1980, he was emerging from his retirement and being seen again.

From his first studio recordings since 1975, he had released a new single, "(Just Like) Starting Over"; a new album followed, "Double Fantasy," a big two-record set. At long last, John Lennon was back.

In Honolulu, pudgy, 25-year-old Mark David Chapman gazed fixedly at the album's jacket photos.

I became enraged at him. . . . Pictures of him smiling on the sumptuous roof of the Dakota building; the decadent bastard, the phony bastard, who had lied to children, who had used his music to mislead a generation of people who desperately needed to believe in love. . . .

He told us to imagine no possessions, and there he was, with millions of dollars and yachts and farms and country estates, laughing at people like me who had believed the lies and bought the records and built a big part of our lives around his music. . . . I remember the exact moment that I thought about killing Mr. Lennon.

'IS THAT okay? Is that what you want?" John Lennon asked his killer outside the Dakota on Dec. 8. Frozen with awe, Mark David Chapman had just handed over his copy of "Double Fantasy" for Lennon to sign. JOHN LENNON, DECEMBER 1980. There were always crowds of fans outside the Dakota. Then Lennon and Ono tumbled into a waiting limo and headed back to the recording studio for an evening's work. "John Lennon signed my album," Chapman mumbled. "Nobody in Hawaii is going to believe me."

Later, Sean Lennon's nanny walked by with the little boy in tow. Chapman clasped his hand and told him it was an honor to meet him. Sean just sneezed. "You'd better take care of that runny nose!" Chapman told him. "You wouldn't want to miss Christmas!"

"Why are you still hanging around here?" an elevator operator asked him.

JOHN AND YOKO had made dinner plans, but after leaving the studio they impulsively canceled them and headed home instead, and

CHAPTER 167

DEAD SILENCE

Incident At The Dakota, 1980

at 10:45 p.m. they stepped out of the limo and strode toward the Dakota gate and the crowd of fans.

I stood up and I said, "This is it, this is it." . . . There was no anger. There was nothing. It was dead silence in my brain. Dead, cold quiet, until he walked up. He looked at me. . . . The man was going to be dead in less than five minutes, and he looked at me and I looked at him and he walked past me and then I heard it in my head. It said, "Do it, do it, do it," over and over again. "Do it, do it, do it," like that.

EARLIER IN THE day, Lennon had granted an interview, in which he gave "thanks to God, or whatever it is up there, that we all survived. We all survived Vietnam or Watergate or the tremendous upheaval of the whole world. . . .

DAILY NEWS

"I am going into an unknown future, but we're all still here. We're still wild about life. There's hope."

I WALKED A *few feet, turned, pulled the gun out of my pocket . . . I aimed at his back. I pulled the trigger five times. And all hell broke loose in my mind. It was like everything had been stripped away then. It wasn't a make-believe world anymore. The movie strip broke. . . .*

OFFICER TONY PALMA, sitting in his patrol car at Columbus Ave. and 82nd St., got the call: "Man shot, 1 W. 72nd St." He and partner Herb Frauenberger found Lennon facedown on the ground, bleeding from the mouth, his red shirt soaked with blood. The two cops loaded him into a patrol car driven by Officer Jim Moran. Racing toward Roosevelt Hospital, Moran looked into the back seat and asked: "Are you John Lennon?" Lennon groaned and nodded.

Shortly after 11:07, Dr. Stephan Lynn, Roosevelt's director of emergency service, informed Yoko Ono that her husband was dead.

MARK CHAPMAN had thrown down his gun, sat curbside and quietly read from "The Catcher in the Rye," and doorman Jose Perdomo had kicked away the .38 revolver and screamed, "Do you know what you just did?"

"I just shot John Lennon," Chapman said.

As Officer Stephen Spiro spread-eagled him, Chapman whimpered, "Don't hurt me, I'm unarmed."

By 4 a.m., more than 500 weeping fans stood outside the Dakota, lining police barricades yards from the murder scene, beginning a flower-strewn vigil that would go on for four days.

By 6:20 a.m., prisoners at the Manhattan Criminal Court Building had found out who their new housemate was. Sitting in his 6-by-8 cell, Chapman could hear another inmate serenading him with "Yellow Submarine."

And our friends are all aboard Many more of them live next door...

DAILY NEWS

By JAY MAEDER
Daily News Staff Writer

"We'll forget that Abbott had something of a reputation as a jailhouse writer and that he had some fancy friends. We'll remember that he should have been behind bars on the night that he murdered Richard Adan. We'll forget that our judges have some nice-nelly notions about overcrowding our prisons with criminals. We'll remember that our streets are overcrowded with criminals."

— Editorial,
New York Daily News

Abbott.

AS THE UTAH killer Gary Gilmore awaited the firing squad and it became known that the New York author Norman Mailer was completing a rhapsody to Gilmore's penal journey, another swaggering Utah con named Jack Henry Abbott wrote to Mailer, assuring him that there was no way such a city slicker as he could know much of anything about the brutal realities of The Life, and offering to give him a useful crash course. The hard-case Abbott had spent years in solitary, and his letters raged with raw animal pain, and in this damaged man Mailer imagined he had found an epically American frontiersman outlaw saint: *I felt all the awe one knows before a phenomenon. Abbott had his own voice. I had heard no other like it . . . Not only the worst of the young are sent to prison but the best — that is, the proudest, the bravest, the most daring, the most enterprising, and the most undefeated of the poor.* In 1980, the thoroughly infatuated Mailer persuaded the New York Review of Books to publish a selection of Abbott's prison letters. These were spotted by an editor at Random House, who proceeded to envision a soulful book-length collection of authentic screams from the abyss. The prisoner's-wounded-cry genre, of course, was marketable enough. Eldridge Cleaver and George Jackson had both done well with it, not to mention Charles Colson.

At this same time, Jack Henry Abbott was coming up for parole, and Norman Mailer stood for him. There was not inconsiderable literary precedent for such sponsorship; Genet, indeed, had been a protégé of Sartre himself. In June 1981, as Abbott's "In the Belly of the Beast" approached publication to what it was understood were going to be warm reviews, Mailer brought Abbott to New York, settled him into a Bowery halfway house, engaged him as a $150-a-week research assistant and introduced him around to the quality folks. There were network TV appearances. There was a spread in People magazine. There were champagne toasts from New York City's leading literary lights. Abbott, 37 years old, a man who had been behind bars since age 12, was an overnight star.

All the fancies and nellies and swells had forgotten one fundamental thing about Jack Henry Abbott. He was a junkyard dog.

AWESOME, THE reviewers agreed. Brilliant. Fiercely visionary. Less dazzled readers perhaps found typical Abbott to be quite

CHAPTER 168

THE WORTH OF CULTURE

Jack Henry Abbott, 1981

Mailer.

flabbergastingly puerile ("I have been twisted by justice the way other men can be twisted by love . . . I can never be happy with the petty desires this bourgeois society has branded into my flesh, my sensuous being"), but the reviewers were all charmed to find themselves a major new writer. Several of them were sure that they, too, felt all his primal anguishes. "If, finally, his genius as a writer does depend upon anger and rage, that need not be a problem," one essayed. "There is much to be angry about."

Mailer and Random House's Scott Meredith fussed over their noble savage. Both were "touched by his childlike sense of wonder," they happily told everyone; he didn't even know how to buy toothpaste at the drugstore. After a few weeks, he was worldly enough to enjoy occasional furloughs from the halfway house and to go out spending the $15,000 Random House had advanced him. Late on the night of Saturday the 18th of July, he had two women on his arm and they were drinking in a Second Ave. bar called the Binibon, and here did Jack Henry Abbott collide with Richard Adan.

Adan was one of that legion of young New York actors who waited tables between breaks. He was 22 years old, newly married, full of promise; he had recently toured Spain with the Miriam Colon Puerto Rican Traveling Theater and he had just finished writing a play he hoped

would be staged by the La Mama experimental troupe. The quarrel with tonight's gaunt, walrus-mustached customer was a small one, having to do with whether or not the Binibon's washroom was available to patrons or strictly to employees, but in the end both combatants agreed to take it outside. Abbott was the one with a knife in his waistband, and Adan was dead on the sidewalk a few minutes later.

By the next day Abbott had fled the city.

Adan.

KILLING CLOUDS EX-CONVICT WRITER'S NEW LIFE, clucked The New York Times. "Norman and I are stunned and distressed," sighed Scott Meredith.

"Many people are carrying a heavy burden," snarled Detective William Majewski of the 9th Precinct.

"I guess there's some residual regret on everyone's part," Meredith conceded.

THE writer Jerzy Kosinski could not stop flagellating himself. "Both Mailer and I believe in the purgatory power of art," he mourned. "We pretended he had always been a writer. It was a fraud. It was like the '60s, when we embraced the Black Panthers in that moment of radical chic without understanding their experience.

"I blame myself again for becoming part of radical chic," Kosinski grieved. "I went to welcome a writer, to celebrate his intellectual birth. But I should have been welcoming a just-freed prisoner, a man from another planet."

"Jack Abbott is a loaded gun," stormed Richard Adan's father-in-law. "You don't put him out on the street. You don't take somebody with 25 years in a garbage camp and suddenly throw him in the streets. Take him off the street and take him off forever. Don't experiment with our lives."

"Sometimes culture is worth the risk," reflected Norman Mailer, quite solemnly, as if he really thought everyone was going to nod and murmur.

WHILE THE intellectual journals mulled over what it all meant, Abbott remained at large for two months before New York detectives caught up with him, on a hooker's tip-off, near New Orleans. Returned to the city in manacles, he was visibly pleased to learn that "In the Belly of the Beast" was selling well.

At trial, he at first claimed self-defense, insisting that it was Adan who had pulled the knife; after that argument was demolished, he contended that Adan had basically impaled himself on the blade. On Jan. 21, 1982, he was found guilty of manslaughter. In April, he was sentenced to 15 years. By that time, he had contracted with a movie company for the story of his life.

"I don't really think I'm going to be in prison long," boasted the major new writer.

DEFENDING HIMSELF *in 1990 against a damage suit brought by Richard Adan's widow, Abbott confidently maintained that there was no evidence Adan had been sufficiently talented to guarantee a successful future and that therefore his life was worth nothing financially. Apparently startled by the jury's rejection of this odious argument, he was returned to prison, complaining that he was the victim of a conspiracy to keep him from writing.*

By MARY ANN GIORDANO
Daily News Staff Writer

'**TWAS BEAUTY** killed the beast the first time King Kong made it to the top of the Empire State Building, back in 1933.

Fifty years later, all it took was some bad weather, and before you knew it, the beast was a goner, dangling from the needle-topped tower like a rubber sack.

Back when "King Kong" had debuted at the New Roxy Theater and Radio City Music Hall, the slim, glimmering 102-story Empire State was less than two years old, the tallest building on the planet, a world wonder. From its peak had the great Kong plunged, blitzed by airplanes and done in by love, dragged in chains from Skull Island only to die in a heap on 34th St.

And for the next 50 years after that, nobody could ever gaze upon the skyscraper without seeing Kong atop, shrieking Fay Wray clutched tight in his hairy ape hand.

By 1983, though, time had taken some of the glamor off the Empire State. Past its prime, run down, no longer the biggest kid around, it needed something to zest up its image. Something to remind people of what it once had been.

Like a reunion.

BUT NOT JUST a movieland reunion, with some foot-tall ape model perched on some scale-size tower. This had to be big. New York big. A stunt to top all stunts.

It started with a letter from a Brooklyn man, Dick Cuffari, reminding the Empire State Building people of the film's forthcoming 50th anniversary, which, frankly, was nothing that had ever occurred to them.

Good idea, though, they decided. A plaque. A cake. A press conference. Something to get the building on the TV news and the Associated Press wire.

But now Robert Keith Vicino, president of Robert Keith & Co. of San Diego, had another idea.

His firm specialized in making big vinyl-coated fabric things — "cold air giant inflatable advertising displays," as they were called in the trade. Vicino's firm did $10 million a year in king-size beer bottles and soda cans. But he had always dreamed of putting King Kong back on top of the world again.

In a letter to the Empire State Building people, he offered to mount a Kong-size Kong above the Observation Deck. He would foot the $100,000 bill for building the thing. All they had to do was pick up the affixing costs — something like 10 hours of labor, to cost no more than $50,000, he estimated.

On April 6, 1983, King Kong returned in a crate to the Empire State Building. All New York had to do was carry him upstairs, blow him up and fasten him to the side of the building.

And such a lot of beast there was to fasten.

KING KONG stood 10 stories high. When inflated with 600 pounds of cold,

compressor-driven air, he weighed a ton and a half. His raised arm alone was 12 feet long. Supposedly, he had been built to withstand 80-mph winds. The plan was to keep him spectacularly on display high over the city for 10 days.

But on April 7, the morning of his scheduled debut, as citizens converged upon the Empire State Building for the big show, there remained nothing to see. Kong had strained backs, broken a few windows and kicked loose some debris, but he was still just a vinyl sack. There had been twisted riggings, misplaced armatures, blowouts in his armpits and shoulders, repair jobs. But the gala parties had already been scheduled.

Harry and Leona Helmsley, principal owners of the Empire State Building, poured champagne as workers continued to try to get Kong into place. Two hired bi-planes made flybys, regardless of the fact that there was no beast to buzz.

"It is so American," said a Tokyo TV newsman in town to cover the festivities. "It is big. It is, if I may say, crazy. And it doesn't work."

Beastmaker Vicino, for his part, thought everything was a thrilling success. "We have been trying to tell the world about the power of the medium," he declared. "The exposure we're receiving here, you can't buy that."

And Fay Wray sent a letter noting the "graceful destiny" that had brought building and beast together once again.

The troubles hadn't even started yet.

MORE ROPES. More armatures. More tears, including a great 7-foot gash in King Kong's neck.

And then, as workers struggled for a fifth day, heavy winds and barrels of rains, nearly 4 inches, a downpour that shattered the daily precipitation record for April.

Finally, on the eighth day, Kong went up.

And briefly he was every inch the Kong of yore. New Yorkers gawked, pointed, laughed, pointed long lenses out windows, fed quarters to enterprising kids who were renting binoculars on the street.

Then the winds picked up again, and Kong suffered a 16-foot rip in his right shoulder that everybody decided was too much trouble to fix.

At 6 a.m. on April 15, King Kong was hanging limply from the side of the Empire State Building.

With as many as 22 riggers on duty around the clock for a week, some making $45 an hour on overtime, costs had now gone past $650,000, which was more than it had cost to make the 1933 film.

Vicino didn't care. Neither did Helmsley publicist Howard Rubenstein. "Nobody says it wasn't worth it," he said. "I can't recall a stunt that has gotten this attention. We challenge anyone to top this."

Added Vicino employee Carlos Alvarado: "New Yorkers are famous for not looking up because they don't want to be taken for tourists. But we got them to look up."

KING KONG, repaired, rested for a while on Central Park's Great Lawn, then went off on world tour.

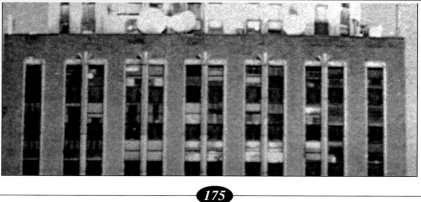

CHAPTER 169
GRACEFUL DESTINY
The Return Of King Kong, 1983

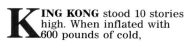

By BRIAN MOSS
Daily News Staff Writer

FRIDAY THE 13th of July 1984 was supposed to be a great day for Rep. Geraldine Ferraro and a great day for New York.

Front pages everywhere trumpeted the news that Walter Mondale had named the Queens congresswoman to be his vice presidential running mate for the November elections — the first woman at the top of a national ticket, and a hometown Italian-American at that.

"Gerry has excelled in everything she's tried," the Democratic standard-bearer declared, "from law school at night to being a tough prosecutor to winning a difficult election to winning positions of leadership and respect in the Congress."

Geraldine Ferraro, Mondale said, was "really the story of a classic American dream."

To wildly cheering delegates at the Democratic convention in San Francisco a week later, where Ferraro had family near Naples.

But within days, her campaign would be in tatters, never to fully recover. Her candidacy would drag down Mondale as well and send her political career into a permanent tailspin.

It seemed that the Democratic candidate for vice president of the United States had a spouse problem.

HER LIFE STORY, as she liked to tell it: She started out as a legal secretary, put herself through Fordham Law School by night while teaching elementary school by day, stayed at home until the youngest of her three children went to school, then worked as an assistant district attorney in Queens for her prosecutor cousin before being elected to Congress in 1978 under her maiden name.

This overlooked the matter of her husband's money. John Zaccaro had real estate firms that did business mostly in Little Italy, Chinatown and SoHo. In post-Watergate America, political candidates were expected to make public their financial records, and indeed, Ferraro pledged to do that.

Perhaps she had not consulted with Zaccaro on the matter. Two weeks after her nomination, Ferraro announced that her husband would not permit her to release his business records.

Campaigning with a grim smile, Ferraro joked that women married to Italian men "know what it is like."

This fell quite flat. The public wondered: What exactly was it that Zaccaro didn't want known?

BECAUSE FERRARO had listed herself on her congressional financial-disclosure form as secretary-treasurer of her husband's

Campaigning in Forest Hills.

ASSOCIATED PRESS

firms, the family business was fair game for inquiry whether Zaccaro liked it or not.

Reporters began searching building records for code violations, failed inspections, unusual tenants. They looked into Zaccaro's business dealings and associates. It happened that they found nothing particularly amiss — but Ferraro's continued refusal to provide information kept raising more and more questions daily, and by early August the din was so great that she found herself unable to campaign effectively. Finally, she was forced to announce that she would indeed make full financial disclosure.

Before she got around to doing that, though, the media discovered that Zaccaro had used money from an elderly widow's estate he was protecting as a court-ordered conservator for a real estate deal. This was a flat illegality on his part — and suddenly it raised new questions about Ferraro's judicial connections in Queens.

ON AUG. 20, she released records going back six years and said she hoped this disclosure would put an end to things. It

CHAPTER 170

BECAUSE OUR CAUSE IS JUST

Geraldine Ferraro, 1984

did not. The documents, in fact, established that Ferraro and Zaccaro had underpaid taxes in 1978, forcing Ferraro to ante up more than $50,000 in arrears and interest to the IRS. Conspicuously absent from the pile, meanwhile, were the tax returns of her husband's real estate companies.

The next day, she made history again, becoming the first candidate for national office to submit to two hours of televised questioning by reporters over personal finances.

"The supposition was that we had something to hide, and obviously we don't," she said defiantly. "I expect we will answer all of your questions today and get this out of the way today."

That was not the case either. For one thing, Ferraro's carefully constructed persona as the hardworking neighborhood housewife who happened to be a congresswoman dissolved with the revelation that she and her husband shared a net worth of $3.8 million.

Things got only worse after that. One of Zaccaro's long-time tenants was a pornographer, the papers said; one of Ferraro's fund-raisers and contributors was a union racketeer. The New York Post earned Ferraro's particular wrath when it reported that her parents long ago had been indicted for numbers running upstate; a child at the time, Ferraro had never known about that.

Not unpredictably, she played the obvious cards: "Would they have done it if I were male?" she demanded. "Would they have done it if I were not Italian-American?" Asked by TV host Phil Donahue if she had wept over that story, she replied piously: "There are certain things, Phil, that are personal."

Personal or not, the damage was devastating. In New York State alone, a Daily News poll found that 17% of voters were more likely to vote for the Mondale-Ferraro ticket because of Ferraro, but 15% were less likely to.

She went down fighting. In the final whirlwind of the campaign, she made lofty attempts to link her vice presidential run to the destinies of women everywhere, moving audiences to tears with invocations of Susan B. Anthony: *"Because our cause is just, we cannot fail."* On Election Day, Tuesday the 6th of November, the Mondale-Ferraro ticket lost to Ronald Reagan and George Bush by the second-largest margin in presidential election history. In Ferraro's 9th Congressional District, the Democrat candidates won 40% of the vote.

"You did so much for women," comedian Rita Rudner told Ferraro. "You didn't do so much for the Democrats."

JOHN ZACCARO *pleaded guilty in 1985 to a misdemeanor count of falsifying business documents.*

By BOB KAPPSTATTER
Daily News Staff Writer

IT WAS AN unseasonably mild and sunny winter's Saturday, the temperature hitting 60 as shoppers thronged the streets three days before Christmas. Sidewalk Santas rang their bells and carols filled the afternoon, and you could almost forget for a minute that in a town like New York City it was good to maintain a healthy quotient of everyday paranoia.

At 1:44 p.m., it would all snap back into sharp focus as the cracks of five rounds from a silver-plated, snub-nosed .38 Smith & Wesson inside a graffiti-scarred subway car reverberated across the city and the nation and around the world. Car No. 7657, seventh in a 10-car southbound IRT Seventh Ave. Express train, would become the symbol of everything that everyday law-abiding citizens felt about everyday urban thugs, all the rage, all the disgust, all the impotence — all the fear.

Aboard No. 7657, a bespectacled, mild-seeming white man found himself surrounded and intimidated by four black youths who asked him first for the time, then for a match and finally for $5.

"Yes," he said. "I have $5 for each of you."

Then he stood up, pulled the unlicensed .38 from the waistband of his jeans and started firing.

As more than a dozen other passengers gasped, his four tormentors went down.

With the sounds of the shots still ringing off the car's metal walls and the smell of cordite rising in the air, the gunman walked over to one of the fallen young men.

Citizen Goetz accepts award from Jerry Preiser of the New York State Rifle and Pistol Clubs (1988).

CHAPTER 171

YOU DON'T LOOK SO BAD

The Subway Vigilante, 1984

"You don't look so bad," he mused, then calmly shot him again.

As the train lurched to a stop in the Chambers St. station, the gunman leaped onto the tracks and fled into the tunnel.

It would be nine days before the world knew the shooter's name, and it would be more than a decade before Bernhard Goetz would manage to slide back into obscurity.

On this holiday weekend, as the subway shootings hit the news, the incident aboard No. 7657 galvanized a city long fed up with living in fear of crime.

Was the shooter a frightened citizen carrying a weapon for his personal protection? Or was he a serial exterminator, a real-life, in-the-flesh version of Charles Bronson's "Death Wish" character, an avenger riding the night in search of human garbage? Cops didn't know, but much of the town at large immediately voted — hopefully — for the latter.

And so, in the City of New York, three days before Christmas 1984, there arrived the legend of The Subway Vigilante.

CERTAINLY THE Vigilante's victims handily fit every thug stereotype. They were Darryl Cabey, 19; Troy Canty, 19; Barry Allen, 18; and James Ramseur, 18: four buddies from the Bronx, all possessing arrest records. Aboard the speeding train, three of them were carrying screwdrivers. Witnesses to the shootings told police they had been a boisterous bunch before they encountered the mild-seeming man with the .38.

By Monday, a police telephone hotline had received just a handful of tips — but more than 500 calls from New Yorkers who desired to congratulate The Subway Vigilante. Several of them offered to pay his legal expenses when he was arrested. A World War II veteran named Fred Pollizi called the Daily News to offer the gunman his Bronze Star.

"It's scary on those trains," Pollizi said. "Did you ever have a punk ask you for money on a train?"

Mayor Edward Koch quickly condemned the shootings. "Vigilantism will not be tolerated in this city," he said. "We are not going to have instant justice meted out by anybody." Koch now ordered 1,350 street cops to join transit police in patrolling the subway system, which, in 1984, had logged nearly 12,000 felonies.

The mounting public enthusiasm for the vigilante's actions, fretted Gov. Mario Cuomo, was "dangerous and wrong." One Australian newspaper, meanwhile, observing from afar, called the city's jubilation "a sign of moral health."

NINE DAYS LATER, on the last day of the year, 38-year-old Bernhard Goetz walked into the state police barracks in Concord, N.H., and surrendered himself as New York City's subway gunman.

If the public had been entertaining some Charles Bronsonesque fantasy, Bernie Goetz was something of a letdown. An electronics technician who lived on 14th St., Goetz had been mugged several years earlier, then applied for a city pistol permit and been turned down, then went to Florida and bought a gun there, and it was this gun he was carrying when he was accosted by Cabey, Ramseur, Canty and Allen.

Critics sought to paint a picture of a man who couldn't wait for a chance to use his new weapon, a trigger-happy stalker who rode the trains hoping someone would hit him up sooner or later. Goetz denied this. He had been minding his own

business, he said. The kids were manifestly about to rob him, he said. "I'm sorry," he said, "but it had to be done."

The case took 2½ years to wind through the legal system, as Bernie Goetz meanwhile became a symbol of both the put-upon Everyman defending himself against predators and of armed evil prowling the night for meat. There were those who never conceded that the four youths were bandits. There were those who felt that even if they were, shooting them was perhaps too severe a punishment. There were, of course, even those who contended they had every right to rob him in the first place, considering they were poor and underprivileged.

As all this thoughtful public debate raged on, a Manhattan grand jury declined to indict Goetz for anything but gun possession. An attempted-murder charge was subsequently filed, then thrown out, then refiled; a jury finally acquitted him of that charge but found him guilty on a weapons count, for which he ended up serving eight months in prison.

"He's a pathetic man," said jury foreman Michael Axelrod. "His life is ruined."

BARRY ALLEN and James Ramseur both subsequently went to prison on unrelated matters, Ramseur for a brutal rape that sent him up for many years. Troy Canty shortly landed in a drug treatment program. Darryl Cabey had no further brushes with the law, but then, he was in a wheelchair, paralyzed for life.

IT'S DO OR DIE FOR GIANTS TODAY
Stories in Sports section
SEE THE GAME ON CHANNEL 2 AT 3:30 P.M.

DAILY NEWS
NEW YORK'S PICTURE NEWSPAPER
December 23, 1984. Sunny, Chilly, High 42. Details p. 2

FEARS MUGGING, SHOOTS 4 ON IRT

CHAPTER 172

SURVIVAL OF THE FITTEST

The End Of Westway, 1985

By OWEN MORITZ
Daily News Staff Writer

SHE WAS the Soot Lady. He was a no-nonsense federal judge. And along with the two of them were the striped bass that mated in the Hudson River.

Together they took on and defeated the grandest, costliest, most ambitious public-works project ever proposed for New York.

It was called Westway — a $2 billion highway and waterfront development earmarked for Manhattan's lower West Side.

Never had a project of this magnitude enjoyed such a well-oiled bandwagon. The big wheels of labor endorsed it for the jobs. Powerful business interests backed it for the benefits to the economy. And the politicians loved it because here was the ultimate pork barrel — the federal government had agreed to pay $1.7 billion of the cost.

Who could find fault with a sleek, covered, 4.2-mile, six-lane highway between W. 42nd St. and the Battery?

Who could disagree with the idea of housing and commercial development atop the highway's roof, plus the magnificent waterfront park that would replace the rotting Hudson piers?

Who could object when construction would involve no relocation — and the existing 12th Ave. roadway was falling apart anyway?

Who could oppose a project that the state's senior senator, Daniel Moynihan, said would do for the 20th century what Central Park had done for the 19th?

The Soot Lady, the federal judge and their fishy friends, that's who. And in the end, they prevailed.

WEST SIDE TRAFFIC in Manhattan had always been gridlocked. The Miller Highway, a rickety viaduct over 12th Ave., was the main north-south waterfront route. But almost from the day it opened in 1931, experts worried that it would be only a matter of time before the elevated structure gave out.

That happened Dec. 15, 1973, when a loaded dump truck plunged through a pothole near the Gansevoort Market. The highway was promptly shut south of 42nd St., and demolition of the elevated structure began in 1976.

By that time, Westway was coming together. State officials had begun exploring plans for a new road project on Hudson River pilings in August 1971. Full planning got under way in April 1974. In January 1977, President Jimmy Carter's Department of Transportation approved the project.

And in 1981, after repeated delays — but days after the Army Corps of Engineers gave preliminary approval — President Ronald Reagan rushed to the city with a symbolic $85 million check for the purchase of right of way.

"The Westway project begins today," Reagan announced.

Not quite.

WESTWAY'S VAST array of supporters had not bargained on Marcy Benstock, a Buffalo-reared Radcliffe graduate who had become a one-woman crusade against auto emissions. By the early '80s she was celebrated as the West Side's Soot Lady who had led locals in a campaign against the polluted air that she blamed for the excessive soot in her apartment. Her Clean Air Campaign, peopled by scores of volunteers and lawyers, soon targeted the new Westway project.

Foes called her an obsessive zealot, an anti-development fanatic who somehow seemed to believe that Westway's builders actually intended to pave over the Hudson River. Her reply: "Every year that the critical Hudson River is left in its natural state is another year for this extraordinary East Coast ecosystem."

Still, while Benstock and the anti-Westway coalition could delay the big project with legal roadblocks, they couldn't stop it.

Then they discovered an improbable ally: striped bass, which spawned under the decrepit old piers and thus would be endangered by the acres of landfill Westway's builders needed to pump into the river.

And the bass, which happened to be critical players in the Atlantic Ocean's food chain, found, in turn, an odd champion in U.S. Judge Thomas Griesa.

The Army Corps of Engineers, while granting a landfill permit for the project, had conceded that the dredging and landfill would do significant damage to the bass spawning grounds.

That was enough for Griesa in 1982 to void the landfill permit and order the corps to go back and conduct another review.

When the agency came back with a study that contended the project would not harm the fish after all — but could not reconcile that conclusion with its earlier warnings of significant damage — the stern-faced Griesa blew his top.

"Incredible," said the judge. He ordered an extraordinary nonjury trial in his courtroom — a trial that literally hinged on the meaning of the single word "significant."

On August 7, 1985, Griesa ruled that the corps had botched the environmental study. As Westway's supporters gasped in disbelief, he permanently barred the corps from granting a landfill permit and for good measure ordered the Federal Highway Administration to cut off funds.

"An inquisition," said state officials of Griesa's ruling. "He set out to find fault," growled Sen. Alfonse D'Amato, "and he did exactly that."

APPEALS WERE VOWED — but by now the tide had turned. By 1985, Congress was filled with New York-hating fiscal conservatives who were all too ready to doom the project.

Nor did it help New York that behind the scenes, Congress' New Jerseyans — who feared that development on the New York bank would harm their own Hudson waterfront development — were circulating stories that the project's true cost was $4 billion.

The city's political community, facing a deadline for the trade-in of Westway funds for mass-transit aid, realized things were finished. On Sept. 19, 1985, 14 years after Westway was proposed and after $200 million in federal funds had been spent on planning and land acquisition, a humbled Gov. Mario Cuomo, Mayor Edward Koch and the state's two senators gathered in Washington to announce Westway's abandonment. The biggest-ever highway and development project had been killed by a small band of environmental activists, mass-transit advocates and friends of the striped bass.

"It's dead," grumbled Koch. "I believe those who are responsible for its death carry a heavy burden."

Exulted Marcy Benstock: "A glorious day for transit riders, taxpayers, the environment and everyone who loves New York."

It was either the last hurrah for militant environmentalism in New York or the last hurrah for big, start-from-scratch urban development in New York, and probably it was both.

By KIERAN O'LEARY
Daily News Staff Writer

THE FORD LTD swerved erratically as it left the Grand Central Parkway and rolled to a stop near Shea Stadium.

Behind the wheel was one of New York's most powerful politicians. And at 1:50 a.m. on Jan. 10, 1986, he was bleeding to death all over the front seat.

The driver was Donald Manes — Queens borough president, man on the fast track to one day be mayor. Now a secret life had driven him to desperation in the wee hours of a winter's morn.

TWO COPS who had followed Manes off the parkway found him bleeding badly from deep wounds on his left wrist and left ankle. Mystery mounted as, for three days at Booth Memorial Hospital, he refused to discuss what had happened to him. Then, finally, he spun a startling yarn: He had been kidnapped by two men outside Borough Hall in Kew Gardens.

The story didn't add up at all, but Manes stuck to it. Mayor Edward Koch went to the bedside of his friend "Donny," and assured him the public would forgive him even if he had been with a prostitute.

On Jan. 16, Chief of Detectives Richard Nicastro announced that police were convinced Manes' wounds were self-inflicted. And on the 24th, clad in a bathrobe, propped up by pillows in his hospital bed, Manes admitted that he had tried to take his own life.

"There were no assailants and no one but me is to blame," he said. Then he declared that he no longer intended to talk about "these personal things."

But it wasn't going to be that easy.

For one thing, if Manes wasn't talking, a man named Geoffrey Lindenauer was. To the feds.

IN THE CORRIDORS of power, Donny Manes and Geoffrey Lindenauer were unlikely chums. Manes, boss of the Queens Democratic machine, was courted by big shots in government and business; Lindenauer ran a psychotherapy institute based on two phony doctoral degrees he'd bought from a diploma mill. In 1976, Manes prevailed upon his friend Stanley Friedman, the Bronx Democratic chairman, to find Lindenauer a position in the city's Addiction Services Agency.

Lindenauer wasn't much good at that job and he soon got fired. So Friedman found him a new post, with a raise in salary, as assistant director of the Parking Violations Bureau.

In May 1978, at Manes' urging, one Lester Shafran was named PVB director. Two months later, at Manes' urging, Lindenauer became Shafran's deputy. The PVB was now controlled by the Queens Democratic machine.

Even as in the grand old days of Boss Tweed's Forty Thieves, this gang of brigands now quite merrily began helping itself to pretty much anything that didn't appear to be nailed down.

LINDENAUER AND Manes took their first bribe in November 1979. Michael Lazar, a former city transportation official, was now a consultant for Datacom, a company that dunned parking-ticket scofflaws and which was entirely willing to make a few payoffs in order to get more PVB contracts. Lazar gave Lindenauer $500 in cash and promised to deliver an envelope every month.

Manes and Lindenauer soon jacked up the price. By 1982, the payments were $2,500 a month, split 50-50 by the two of them.

Meanwhile, in 1980, Lindenauer had been approached by another collection company, Systematic Recovery Systems. Its owner, Bernard

DAILY NEWS

FEEDING THE METER

Donny Manes And The Public Trough, 1986

Sandow, agreed that SRS would pay a bribe of 5% of all commissions it earned. Over the next four years, that came to more than $300,000.

Bronx boss Stanley Friedman, for his part, had in 1982 discovered a wonderful new invention: A hand-held computer that traffic agents could use to print out parking tickets.

This gizmo was the brainchild of a company called Citisource. All Friedman had to do was rig the bidding process so Citisource could get a fat city contract. In exchange, Citisource would go public. Friedman, Manes and Lindenauer would each secretly get 57,500 shares of Citisource stock, initially worth $5 a share.

Everybody was going to get rich on this one. Alas, the scheme fell apart when Citisource found itself unable to actually produce the computer. But by now Friedman was more closely associated with

collection companies, including Datacom. He worked out a deal to get Datacom still more PVB work, taking in return a cut of the bribes the company paid.

Through 1985, the cash was just rolling in.

UNFORTUNATELY FOR everyone, it happened that Sandow had been paying bribes in Chicago too. And in late December, news came that Sandow was a key target in a major corruption probe in that city.

Donny Manes was paralyzed with fear. Sandow would certainly also talk about the SRS dealings in New York if the feds squeezed him hard enough. He ordered Lindenauer to stop collecting bribes immediately.

But on Dec. 27, Sandow did indeed make a pact with prosecutors.

The first day of January 1986 was brisk and clear. At City Hall, Edward Koch was sworn in to a third term. In places of honor at the ceremony were Manes and Friedman. "Public service is the noblest of professions if it's done honestly and well," Koch intoned as the machine's borough bosses looked on.

Also present was U.S. Attorney Rudolph Giuliani, who, with Sandow as an informant, was already probing the Parking Violations Bureau. He was not sure yet how far upstairs the venality went.

Donny Manes' suicide attempt answered that question.

MANES WAS barely in the hospital before Geoffrey Lindenauer agreed to cooperate with prosecutors.

And on Jan. 23, Daily News columnist Jimmy Breslin brought down the Queens political boss after one Michael Dowd, a partner in a collection agency called Computrace, confessed to him that he had paid Manes $36,000 in bribes over an 18-month period.

Mayor Koch declared himself betrayed and publicly branded his old friend Donny a crook. On Feb. 11, Manes resigned in disgrace.

A month later, Lindenauer admitted in Manhattan Federal Court that he had been Manes' bagman and pleaded guilty to taking $410,000 in bribes from PVB contractors.

At 9:52 p.m. on the 13th of March, Donald Manes opened a kitchen drawer in his Jamaica Estates home, took out an Ekko stainless steel knife and plunged it into his heart.

Once again he was rushed to Booth Memorial. This time, he died there.

IN MARCH AND April, a raft of federal indictments came down, against Friedman, Lazar, Shafran and others involved in the PVB racketeering enterprise. Manhattan District Attorney Robert Morgenthau, who had jousted with Giuliani for a state piece of the high-profile case, indicted Friedman as well. At federal trial, which Giuliani personally prosecuted, Friedman denied any wrongdoing, as meanwhile, Lindenauer for seven days spelled out every detail of the racket.

Disgusted by businessmen who matter-of-factly handed out bribes and by public officials eager to pocket them, the jurors in November convicted the whole sorry bunch.

THE PLUNDERING OF *the PVB was just one of numerous scandals to hit the city in 1986. Throughout the year, probes were launched into towing and cable TV contracts, the Taxi and Limousine Commission, an assortment of judges. A special Commission on Public Integrity concluded that City Hall had missed, or ignored, obvious evidences of corruption.*

By BILL BELL
Daily News Staff Writer

THE NEW YORK Mets had played lousy before and they would certainly play lousy again, but in 1986 they were the guys to beat. Even as the season opened, manager Davey Johnson was openly predicting a World Series triumph.

And why not? The Mets had Tom Seaver, Dwight Gooden, Gary Carter and Howard Johnson, Darryl Strawberry and Lenny Dykstra, Ray Knight and Keith Hernandez. And behind them, plenty more talent.

The Amazin's — this their derisive nickname won over the numerous sad-sack seasons — had finished runnerup in the National League East for two consecutive years and had won 98 games in 1985, second only in club history to the 100 wins by the '69 Miracle Mets.

But it wasn't simply that the Mets were deep in pitching and hitting. The team also was blessed with guys with the right mix of instincts and reactions that separate also-rans from champions. And they got along, no small thing in an era of highly-paid, ego-driven stars.

All the pieces fit, all the chemistry worked. The Mets ended the regular season with 108 victories, a feat the rival Yankees had achieved only twice up to then (in 1927, when they won 110 games and in 1961, when they won 109). They won the East Division crown by an astounding 21 1/2 games.

It wasn't the first champagne moment for the Mets. They had won National League pennants in 1969 and 1973, and they had won the World Series in '69 by defeating Baltimore four games to one. (One of history's little ironies: Davey Johnson, then an Orioles second baseman, flied out to left to end the last game).

The season of seasons had been '73, when the Mets, dead last in the East Division in late August, went on a tear that had all New York chanting, along with ace relief pitcher Tug McGraw, "You gotta believe!"

The Mets won the division title on the final day, Oct. 1, by beating Chicago. They finished with a won-lost percentage of .509, the lowest winning average for a title-winner in baseball history.

They did win the National League pennant by knocking off the Cincinnati Reds' celebrated "Big Red Machine" in five games, but lost in the Series, four games to three, to the defending champ Oakland A's.

(Still, it was enough for comedian George Burns, playing the deity in the 1977 film "Oh, God!," to sum the season up in one memorable line: "My last miracle was the New York Mets.")

BUT THE 1986 season was one for the scrapbook. It was the club's silver anniversary — 25 years earlier, the then quite dreadful Mets had brought National League ball back to New York after the departure of both the Dodgers for Los Angeles and the Giants for San Francisco.

By the All-Star break, the Mets had blown everybody away, and had the East Division title virtually wrapped up. They ruled New York; the Yankees didn't seem nearly as exciting or entertaining.

Jesse Orosco.

In the National League playoff, the Mets topped the Houston Astros four games to two, taking their first pennant in 13 years, and set the stage for one of the most dramatic — and costly — bobbles in World Series history.

The Boston Red Sox, usually the luckless rivals of the Yankees, had won the American League title. In the far, far past, they also had won two World Series titles over New York teams — the Giants in 1912, and four years later, the Dodgers.

This time, they weren't given a chance against the Mets, but, playing in front of a boisterous, delirious, sellout Shea Stadium crowd, the Sox started like a house afire. Bruce Hurst limited the Mets to four hits in a 1-0 victory in Game 1. The Sox then took a two-game lead by hammering Gooden for six runs.

But the Mets bounced back in Boston, spraying 25 hits around Fenway Park in back-to-back wins that knotted the Series at two games each. Hurst won his second game, 4-2, by outdueling Gooden, and Boston returned to New York needing one victory for its first world championship since 1918.

Then came The Moment.

BOSTON HAD the Series all but wrapped up. They led 5-3 going into the last of the 10th inning. The bases were empty and the Mets were down to one out.

Then Carter, outfielder Kevin Mitchell and Knight singled to make it 5-4, and a wild pitch brought in the tying run.

The next batter, Mookie Wilson, a long-time fan favorite, tapped a grounder to first baseman Bill Buckner, who forever became a Red Sox goat by letting the ball roll under his glove as Knight raced home with the run that made the Mets 6-5 winners and squared the Series at three games each.

In the deciding game, the Sox and Hurst held a 3-0 lead going into the sixth inning, when the Mets rallied to tie it on singles by pinch hitter Lee Mazzilli and Wilson, a walk to Tim Teufel and a looping single by Hernandez.

The Mets scored three more the next inning, and Strawberry slammed a home run in the eighth that crushed the Sox, made the Mets champions, and touched off some of the wildest celebrations since World War II.

The next day, the Mets rode up Broadway for a ticker-tape salute that drew an officially estimated crowd of 2.2 million, one of the biggest ticker-tape celebrations in city history.

Mets maniacs were jammed 20 deep along the parade route to City Hall, where Mayor Koch handed the players keys to the city. The fans booed so lustily and loudly when Koch and other politicians tried to speak that they tossed their speeches and settled for shouts of "Let's go, Mets!"

TWO YEARS *later, in 1988, the Mets again won the Eastern Division title, winning 100 games and finishing 15 games ahead of Pittsburgh, but fell four games to three to the Dodgers for the National League championship.*

Since then, the team has finished as high as second in the East and as low as sixth. But there's always next year.

CHAPTER 174

GOTTA BELIEVE

World Series, 1986

By PETER GRANT
Daily News Staff Writer

IT WAS THE 17th of September 1986, and the curtain was now coming down on the greed-is-good Wall Street boom.

On the surface, nothing seemed much different in the high-flying world of leveraged buyouts, corporate raiders, junk bonds and suspendered yuppies chasing dizzying amounts of money.

But behind the scenes, one of the icons of this era was cutting a deal with federal agents and an ambitious U.S. Attorney named Rudolph Giuliani in the biggest insider-trading investigation in history.

Ivan Boesky, the mega-rich and super-arrogant 49-year-old king of the arbitragers, was agreeing to sing like a platinum canary to get off with a relatively light sentence for his role in the scandal.

Boesky's cooperation gave investigators the weapons to crush a Wall St. conspiracy that involved illegal information-swapping among titans of finance, manipulation of huge corporate takeovers and suitcases full of cash being passed on street corners. It was the biggest scandal on The Street since 1938, when Richard Whitney, the aristocratic president of the New York Stock Exchange, had gone to Sing Sing for grand larceny, wearing a three piece suit.

By the time all the gold dust settled, Boesky would agree to pay a $100 million fine and spend 22 months in jail. The great junk bond firm Drexel Burnham Lambert would be bankrupt. And Drexel's junk-bond guru, Michael Milken, would be behind bars.

But it was not just the mega-rich that would be hurt as the roaring 1980s came to an end. The wild bull stock market that had served as a backdrop to the scandal would also fall victim to greed and overreach.

Thirteen months after Boesky's plea-bargain deal, the stock market crashed even more catastrophically than it had done in 1929. In a single day, the Dow Jones industrial average plummeted 508 points, or 22% of its value.

The crash, together with the insider trading scandal, ended an era of decadence and opulence that New York had not seen since the Roaring Twenties.

WITH RONALD REAGAN in the White House preaching deregulation and supply-side economics, corporate America went on an orgy of spending and growth through the 1980s, with Wall St. as its caterer.

Corporate raiders like T. Boone Pickens and Carl Icahn bought huge companies, saddled them with immense amounts of debt and then fired thousands of workers so that they could afford to pay it back. Wall St. loved it, but hundreds of company towns across the country suffered mightily from layoffs.

In New York, fortunes were made as the stock market roared and salaries and bonuses skyrocketed in the city's brokerage houses, investment banks and white shoe law firms. Almost overnight, it seemed, the city was packed with business school graduates in their 20s and 30s, spending lavishly on cocaine, clubs and condos.

And Ivan Boesky was their overlord, a man who made hundreds of millions of dollars in a business known as risk arbitrage, which involves trading on the huge stock swings that result from corporate takeovers.

Boesky's line of work depended on information. His Fifth Ave. offices had 300 telephone lines, his limousine three. He worked them all incessantly, digging up data on mergers and acquisitions, and he always seemed to be one step ahead of the market.

DAILY NEWS

CHAPTER 175

FEELING GOOD ABOUT YOURSELF

Ivan Boesky And The Street, 1986

The son of a Russian immigrant, Boesky lived on a 200-acre estate in Westchester County with his heiress wife Seema Silberstein. He spent money lavishly. At the glitzy Cafe des Artistes one day, he decided on a whim to order every entree on the menu just to taste each one.

Boesky also attained distinction for a 1985 speech in which he unashamedly provided the philosophical justification for the Gimme Decade. "Greed is all right," he said. "Greed is healthy. You can be greedy and still feel good about yourself."

THOUSANDS followed his advice, including a 33-year-old investment banker named Dennis Levine, who put federal investigators on the trail to Boesky and Milken after he was arrested for insider trading in May 1986.

The first of his Queens family to attend college, Levine seemed the embodiment of the American dream. With brains and drive, he worked his way up to a high-level job in the mergers and acquisitions department at Drexel Burnham. His compensation was over $1 million a year.

But that wasn't enough in the Gimme Decade. Levine opened offshore bank accounts from which he began playing the market with inside information he got from his job and Wall St. contacts. He would learn of mergers, acquisitions, buyouts and other transactions before anybody else and make millions by buying and selling stock in these companies before the news hit.

It seemed like a perfect scheme. Yet it suffered a fatal flaw: Levine forgot that others were just as venal as he was.

His world began to unravel in 1985, when an anonymous tipster notified Merrill Lynch's headquarters that two of its executives in Caracas were getting rich in an unusual way. The two had recognized that one of their customers, whom they knew only by a secret bank account number, always seemed to pick the right stocks to buy. They simply mimicked all of his trades.

Merrill Lynch called in the Securities and Exchange Commission. After a few months they were able to determine who owned the account: Levine.

Confronted by the evidence investigators had against him, Levine agreed to cooperate. He gave up enough evidence for them to arrest four young lawyers and investment bankers working for the top firms on The Street. And he also helped them begin to make a case against Ivan Boesky.

EACH ARREST shook Wall St.'s conviction that the go-go years would last forever. On Nov. 14, 1986, the day the government announced Boesky's plea-bargain deal, takeover stocks were clobbered.

Ironically, Boesky's own stock portfolio was not hurt by that plunge. Under the terms of the deal, he had been permitted to sell most of his holdings.

With the sanction of the federal government, Boesky conducted his last insider trade. He sold stock on the basis of inside information that he was about to plead guilty to insider trading.

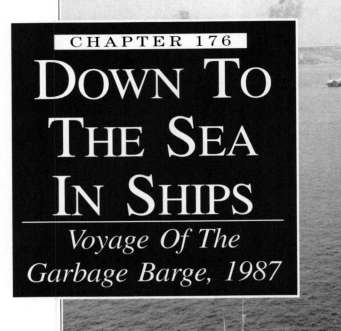

CHAPTER 176

DOWN TO THE SEA IN SHIPS

Voyage Of The Garbage Barge, 1987

ROBERT ROSAMILIO DAILY NEWS

By DICK SHERIDAN
Daily News Staff Writer

THE TUGBOAT Break of Dawn was one of hundreds of modest working vessels that plied the waters off the U.S. East Coast during the year 1987, and this was just another job: hauling a 230-foot-long bargeload of 18-foot-high commercial garbage from New York to North Carolina.

Every day, New York City routinely exported 25,000 tons of garbage that its landfills no longer had room for. Most of it was trucked overland hundreds of miles to landfills in Pennsylvania, West Virginia and other places. Whenever costs and location came together to make a sea voyage feasible, the stuff went out on a barge like this one, the Mobro. Skippered by Capt. Duffy St. Pierre, the Break of Dawn left the pier at Long Island City in Queens on March 22.

Down in Morehead City, N.C., trash hauler Lowell Harrelson was waiting to offload the Mobro's cargo for burial in Jones County.

Then North Carolina's environmental watchdogs thought to ask the City of New York to certify that this load of trash contained no toxic wastes or other harmful materials.

The truth was that city officials had no idea. Only some of the garbage came from the city itself. Most of it had originated in Islip, L.I., having been turned away from that town's nearly overflowing landfill. Pressed on the matter, about all that state Environmental Conservation Commissioner Henry Williams could say was that he doubted the load contained anything dangerous. Probably most of it was construction and demolition debris, he said. Probably.

This response did not suit North Carolina, which instructed the Jones County landfill not to accept the load of New York trash. Then officials went to court and got an order prohibiting the Mobro from unloading anywhere in their state at all.

Like a rejected suitor, St. Pierre put out of Morehead City on April 6, bound for — well, Louisiana, he thought.

IT WAS 1,400 miles around Florida and across the Gulf of Mexico to Avondale, not far from New Orleans, and even as the Break of Dawn steadily sailed on, the ruckus raised by North Carolina was wafting westward toward the Mississippi River.

Now the Avondale landfill operators got a letter from the Louisiana Department of Environmental Quality, informing them that accepting this load of uncertified and no doubt suspicious New York garbage would constitute a violation of their state operating permit. Mississippi, Alabama and Texas then joined Louisiana in deciding to deny the Break of Dawn entry.

Where was the garbage going to go? Just in case the Break of Dawn figured it could perhaps slip into Mexico, the Mexican government dispatched two naval vessels and a number of aircraft to keep an eye on the tug's course. The military of the Central American nation of Belize was ordered to put the barge and its cargo under surveillance too. The Bahamas also said no.

Officials in the sleepy Florida resort community of Key West briefly considered accepting the trash for the island's incinerator. Hearing about that, Florida Gov. Bob Martinez mobilized state agencies to block any such thing.

Suddenly, the New York City Garbage Barge was banned by six states and two foreign nations.

IN EARLY MAY, trashman Harrelson instructed the Break of Dawn to anchor 5 miles off Key West so the barge's cargo could be inspected by the federal Environmental Protection Agency and he could ponder his next move.

Federal agents in protective suits and breathing gear swarmed aboard the Mobro, swatted aside the flies and began to root through the bales in search of leakage, toxics, corrosives or combustibles. "It's ordinary garbage," sighed Break of Dawn first mate David Soto. That's certainly what it appeared to be, reporters verified: old clothes, carpet scraps, magazines, foam rubber, car tires. "It didn't smell as bad as our local landfill," said one Key West scribe.

Certified toxic-free, the garbage barge now headed back north again. But by now nobody wanted it anyway. Even New Jersey wouldn't take it at this point. "We will not accept the spoiling of a beautiful area or a beautiful river," Sen. Frank Lautenberg told the Coast Guard after he heard that the Mobro was to be anchored on the Jersey side of the Hudson River. "We don't want anyone's garbage, especially New York's," said Fort Lee Mayor Nicholas Corbiscello, noting that city trash passed through his community via the George Washington Bridge every day: "Now it's sneaking up the river."

The Break of Dawn's anchorage was shifted to Upper New York Bay about 2 miles from the Statue of Liberty. Tug and barge arrived May 16.

Meanwhile, environmentalists, politicians and bureaucrats squabbled as lawyers tried to hammer out a resolution in Long Island state Supreme Court.

Islip Town Supervisor Frank Jones refused to take any of the trash back. "They can haul the garbage to Gracie Mansion and compost it on the front lawn along with the rest of the garbage that visits," he said.

"It's Islip's garbage," snapped Mayor Ed Koch. "I don't think we [in the city] should have to deal with it."

And the garbage barge sat anchored for another two months.

FINALLY, ON July 10, newly named Environmental Conservation Commissioner Thomas Jorling announced that the barge's rotting cargo would be unloaded and burned at the Southwest Incinerator at Bay 41st St. in the Bensonhurst section of Brooklyn.

From there, officials said, the resulting 400 tons of ash would be trucked by private carrier to the Islip municipal landfill in Hauppauge.

With the exception of Brooklyn Borough President Howard Golden, who objected to his borough's becoming a dumping ground, and his Queens counterpart, Claire Shulman, who stll worried that the trash might be toxic, New York City and Islip town officials hailed the compromise.

On Aug. 24, after state Supreme Court Justice Dominic Ladato of Brooklyn cleared the last legal challenge to the state-city-town plan, the Mobro finally docked in Brooklyn.

"That's one small barge for New York City, one giant bale of garbage for mankind," said city Sanitation Commissioner Brendan Sexton as he watched the Mobro being towed to the incinerator pier.

The unloading began Sept. 1. Ten days later, the ashes were transported to Hauppauge and buried in the Islip town dump.

Harrelson refused to say how much the Mobro's 6,000-mile voyage to nowhere had cost him. The price tag was believed to be nearly $1 million.

But the trip of the Mobro did focus America's attention on the growing national problem of solid waste management, encouraged an expansion of recycling programs and brought pressure on Congress to the pass the 1990 Clean Air/Clean Water Act.

POLICE ARE WATCHING THIS CRACK BLOCK

HARRY HAMBURG DAILY NEWS

CHAPTER 177

FEVER

The Crack Scourge, 1988

By GENE MUSTAIN
Daily News Staff Writer

CRACK MADE Leslie Torres feel like God. At the same time, he explained to the jury at his murder trial, he saw the Devil every time he looked in the mirror. So pushed and pulled by the deities, he was willing to do anything to get more cash to cop more crack. It was the only reason he had for wasting five people and wounding six others early in 1988.

He'd never been in trouble before. He was only 17 years old.

His rampage had begun on New Year's Day and ended eight days later when police cornered him on an East Harlem rooftop. In an extraordinarily bad year for crime, this remained the city's worst single killing spree. And it was the definitive example of what crack — a smokable derivative of powdered cocaine — was doing to the City of New York.

"I was anxious to get crack," Torres said. "It made me get blind."

THE DRUG that made its users blind with desperation for more and more and ever more of it had arrived in the city in 1985, from Los Angeles, where cocaine dealers had perfected a way to turn expensive powdered coke into inexpensive small rocks. They did this by adding baking soda and water to the cocaine, then boiling the mixture into pellets that gave off a cracking sound when smoked. This enabled them to transform a $1,000 ounce of powder into 280 100-milligram vials of crack that could be peddled for, say, $10 apiece — or $2,800. For the first time, cocaine, previously a pleasure of the affluent, became affordable to the lesser economic orders. It was, some expert later told Congress, as if McDonald's had invented the opium den.

Perversely, crack packed an even bigger wallop than cocaine — and caused the typical user to become addicted much faster. Crack vapor got to the brain in about five seconds. The euphoric rush would last just about 10 minutes, and then the user would be overwhelmed by a depression erasable only by another hit on the crack pipe. Very quickly,

crack users became like dogs chasing mechanical rabbits in endless circles.

Meanwhile, chronic use produced intense paranoia. "Everybody becomes a user's potential enemies," another expert explained. "He strikes first before they can get him."

Leslie Torres, who was spending $500 a day on crack, never even gave his last victim a chance to turn over his cash. He walked into Jesus Rivera's little bodega, put down a bottle of Yoo-Hoo on the counter and immediately shot Rivera in the head.

Confessing this to police, Torres remembered: "He opened his eyes like he was surprised."

LESLIE TORRES was a terrible harbinger of things to come in 1988, when marauding crack addicts swarmed across the whole town. Thousands of citizens were robbed. Dozens were killed, including cops and witnesses. Nineteen people died simply because they happened to walk into the crossfire as warring dealers opened up on one another.

By several measures, the city was brought to its knees. It was the worst year ever for murder; nearly 40% of the 1,896 homicides were drug-related, meaning mainly crack-related. It was the worst year ever for total violent crimes — murder, plus robbery and assault. The violent-crime total, 152,600, meant that New York had as many victims as Syracuse had people.

Though no part of the city was safe from an addict in thrall, the worst peril was in the poorest neighborhoods. In the South Bronx, for instance, violent crime was 44% higher in 1988 than in 1985. "Crack crime in poor neighborhoods is at such levels that if the same were true in wealthy neighborhoods, we would be under martial law," Citizens Crime Commission President Thomas Reppetto told the Daily News.

Crack ripped apart families the same way it did neighborhoods. Domestic violence reports increased 24% in 1988 — and were up 150%

since 1985, the dawn of crack. Child abuse and neglect petitions shot up 19% — and were up 156% since 1985. Some kids never got a chance to be rescued; a record 133 died of abuse and neglect. More than 5,000 were born with severe ailments caused by their crack-pipe mothers.

The young abused the old as well. Attacks against the elderly by youthful relatives shot up 44%. By midyear, said Kevin Smiley, the city's probation boss, crack had "wiped out certain ethics" that even criminals once had. "Crack," he said, "is a scourge, a curse — and it's now pandemic."

People lucky enough to escape the violence paid in other ways. Car theft increased 25%. Burglary went up only 6%, but many theft victims weren't bothering to file police reports anymore, believing — quite accurately — that crime-swamped police didn't have time to deal with small property matters.

In fact, the system was arresting, indicting, trying, convicting and jailing more people than ever. The boss of the cops' anti-crack unit, which had opened for business in May 1986, kept a chart of crack-dealer arrests on his office wall, and in June 1988 it showed that his unit had arrested 13,200 sellers — an average of one every 85 minutes for 25 months.

But those sellers were so easily replaced that police finally gave up the citywide fight against street-level operations and instead adopted a new strategy of driving sellers and users out of specific neighborhoods. Large chunks of some of these target neighborhoods were controlled by a wanton new breed of gangster — the crack boss — and these czars were not happy with the police interference. In South Jamaica, Queens, in a crime that rocked the city, crack bosses ordered the murder of Edward Byrne, a rookie policeman sitting by himself in a squad car, guarding the home of a witness in a case involving $30

worth of crack. One of the two assassins was high on crack.

The most notorious of the crack gangsters was Baby Sam Edmondson, who lorded over Brownsville and East New York, in Brooklyn, the old stomping grounds of Murder, Inc. At least nine people were murdered by Edmondson and his men in an 18-month reign of terror aimed at protecting his crack empire.

And what an operation it was. Employing separate specialists for cooking, cutting, packaging and selling crack, Edmondson averaged $100,000 a day in grosses. Police said that Baby Sam, who wore a $40,000 pendant with the words WORLD IS MINE spelled out in diamonds, made more money than the entire Gambino organized crime family did with its unions and construction companies.

In April 1988, shortly after Edward Byrne's execution in Queens, Baby Sam's men gunned down a housing officer, Anthony McLean, and this new cop killing now galvanized the law enforcement community and marked the beginning of the end for Edmondson and the other crack gangsters. It would take a couple of years yet, but they would be brought to justice and made to pay with life sentences — as had been one of their customers, young Leslie Torres.

MEANWHILE, THE mayhem unleashed by crack led the city to hire thousands more cops and moved legislators to pass stiffer laws against drug sellers. Things would remain bad through 1989 and 1990 — but not so bad as they had been in 1988. The tide turned.

It turned because society fought back. But it also turned because crack simply burned itself out. In many neighborhoods, rare was the family that had not somehow suffered. Increasing numbers of young people began to think of crackheads as losers.

Almost as quickly as it had become fashionable, crack became uncool. The fever was broken.

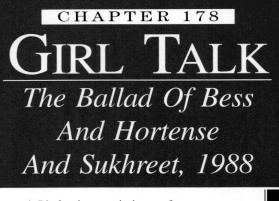

Former Commissioner Myerson.

MISHA ERWITT DAILY NEWS

Sukhreet and Mother Gabel.

CHAPTER 178

GIRL TALK

The Ballad Of Bess And Hortense And Sukhreet, 1988

By KAREN ZAUTYK
Daily News Staff Writer

BESS & CO. NOT GUILTY, the Daily News headlined two days before Christmas 1988, and at long last the city's favorite interminable real-life courtroom saga — the Bess Mess, this was called — had played itself out.

The Bess in the mess was Myerson, noted ex-beauty queen and one-time cultural affairs commissioner for Mayor Edward Koch. Bobbling around with her in the sordid legal stew were: 1) her much younger lover, a ditch digger-turned-sewer contractor; 2) a frail and nearly blind 75-year-old former state Supreme Court justice, and 3) the judge's clinically depressed and spectacularly attention-starved daughter, who, as a flamboyant witness for the prosecution, at one point had been ordered not to appear in court wearing any clothes with animals on them, which deprived her of showing off any more of her self-created wardrobe of zebra prints and leopard prints and at least one outfit with little papier-mache creatures dangling from it.

But we get ahead of our story.

DEEP INTO HER middle years, Bess Myerson, once described as "the best-looking broad on the city scene," remained strikingly attractive. Miss America 1945 had aged well. Indeed, she had captured the eye and heart of one Carl (Andy) Capasso, who had been born in the year Myerson strolled down the runway in Atlantic City in bathing suit and high heels.

Capasso, not only 21 years younger but also a full head shorter than his 5-foot-10 inamorata, nevertheless had much to recommend him. The ex-laborer had done good. He had seven cars. He had five homes, including a Long Island estate. He had a net worth of something between $12 million and $15 million. He also had a wife, Nancy.

Myerson, of course, could hardly be accused of gold-digging. After two failed marriages, she was the very picture of the successful, independent, single career woman. She had been a TV game show hostess. She had been a TV journalist. She had cultivated a wondrous ego. "I have a special quality," she informed New York magazine. "I am larger than life."

Indeed, she had carved out a little special-quality niche in the world of politics, serving as Mayor John

Lindsay's commissioner of consumer affairs and subsequently as commissioner of cultural affairs for Koch, whose social escort she had often been during his mayoral campaign. Between those two city stints, in 1980, she had sought, unsuccessfully, a seat in the U.S. Senate.

That had been a low point. "After the Senate race," she told People magazine, "I was dogmeat. I couldn't even find a man to take me to the movies."

Enter Andy Capasso, full of youth and the charm of the petite, who began showering her with phone calls and flowers and gems. It was love, Bess Myerson cooed. It was also the beginning of the end.

WHILE THE lovebirds billed and twittered in secret rendezvouses around Manhattan, an increasingly suspicious Nancy Capasso steamed at home. When she finally got the truth, she threw her husband out of the house and went to divorce court, where, in June 1983, after rejecting a $2 million settlement, she was awarded $1,850 a week in child support and maintenance.

In charge of the Capasso divorce case was one Hortense Gabel, a judge with an unblemished reputation and an unemployable daughter, originally named Julie Bess but now self-renamed Sukhreet following a spiritual awakening she had experienced at the Indian pavilion of the 1965 New York World's Fair. This was not even close to the oddest thing about her.

Hortense Gabel and Bess Myerson had known each other socially for a couple of decades, but the judge later insisted she'd had no knowledge of the Myerson-Capasso affair when she heard Nancy Capasso's divorce suit.

What she did have was Sukhreet, who, despite fluency in five languages and despite being thisclose to a Ph.D. in sociology and despite having sent out 300 resumes and gone on 150 to 200 interviews in just one year, just couldn't find a soul who wanted to hire her to do anything. There she was, just hanging around the house, day in, day out.

"Poor child," Bess Myerson

clucked. Well, Sukhreet did have a few problems. She had undergone electroshock therapy at one point. And she was gulping anti-depressants. But then who wasn't? Myerson met Sukhreet in June 1983, and soon they were going to Shakespeare in the Park together and having chatty little girltalk dinners. On Aug. 29, Myerson took her on as a $19,000-a-year personal assistant.

On that very same day, Hortense Gabel heard an appeal in state Supreme Court from Andy Capasso's lawyers and ordered Nancy Capasso's weekly support payments reduced to $680.

NOTWITHSTANDING HER credentials, Sukhreet Gabel did not last more than a few months in her friend Bess Myerson's warm employ, finally being asked to resign.

Over the next couple of years, the city's Department of Investigation began to get anonymous letters about a mysterious Hortense/Sukhreet/Bess connection. When the Daily News in 1986 printed a story about the alimony reduction, Myerson took time out from her civic missions ("promoting the city's cultural life and heritage") to visit Sukhreet for a heart-to-heart. Andy Capasso, meanwhile, had by this time developed tax problems, to the degree that he required four years of treatment in a federal prison.

Then, with new city scandals breaking all around him by the hour, Koch turned on the TV news one night to discover that yet another dear friend, Bess Myerson, had stepped deep in the doo-doo. She had refused to cooperate with the Capasso-taxes grand jury. The mayor now authorized his own probe, headed by former judge Harold Tyler, whose subsequent report led to Myerson's abrupt resignation from her $78,800-a-year city post.

Koch sealed the report, but then somebody leaked it to The Village

Voice, instantly altering the average New Yorker's admiring perception of the self-described "Queen of the Jews."

In September 1988, Bess Myerson, Andy Capasso and the now-retired Hortense Gabel all went on trial in Manhattan Federal Court on charges they had conspired to rig Nancy Capasso's divorce settlement. The star witness for U.S. Attorney Rudolph Giuliani's prosecutors was Sukhreet Gabel, who happily spent nine days on the stand testifying against her own mother.

The witness for the prosecution had even taped two phone conversations she'd had with mom, though Giuliani insisted he was shocked to learn about that. "I told her not to," he said, "but she inadvertently pressed the wrong button."

The recordings themselves turned out to be less than sensational, with mom for the most part murmuring things like "Okay" and "I know" and "Okey-doke" while Sukhreet rattled on about truth and justice and how "grievously wronged" she felt herself to be. Still, they catapulted the witness into the headlines, and hordes of fans followed her around daily. Being on the stand, she chirped, was like "being buoyed up on a cloud."

The standing-room-only trial went on for more than three months. At the end, the jury took four days to decide there was no evidence of quid pro quo between the divorce settlement and Sukhreet Gabel's job. Everybody was acquitted on all counts, and off they trotted into obscurity.

Except for Sukhreet, who parlayed her few minutes of fame into a few minutes more. She launched a line of greeting cards, did a photo spread for a fashion magazine (wearing animal prints) and attempted a fling as a cabaret performer, appearing at King Tut's Wah Wah Hut, where she warbled "Sometimes I Feel Like a Motherless Child."

By JAMES S. ROSEN
Special to The News

'**I**T WAS one romantic night. There were roses and champagne and everything.''

It was March 1989, and Alison Gertz was remembering a storybook evening from seven years earlier, when she had been 16 years old.

"That was it," she said. "I only slept with him once."

That was the night Alison Gertz, a white child of wealth and privilege, got AIDS.

AIDS HAD BEEN a dark specter through the 1980s; in New York City there had been 26,000 reported cases. It was perceived that there were, frankly, certain kinds of people who got AIDS and certain kinds who did not. "The common wisdom," said researcher Dr. Jody Robinson, is "that AIDS is really the gay plague, and disease of intravenous drug users . . . [that] the warning on heterosexual spread was a false alarm."

Alison Gertz almost single-handedly changed the common wisdom.

She was an unpromiscuous heterosexual woman, a responsible, sober and affluent product of Park Ave. Her grandfather had founded the Gertz department store chain, her father was a real estate executive, her mother had started the fashion chain Tennis Lady. Gertz attended Horace Mann and the New York Tutorial School and studied art at Manhattan's Parsons School of Design. She was a talented illustrator, and after an artist's agent signed her up and she decided that life was just beginning, she quit smoking and joined a health club.

In the summer of 1988, six years after the unprotected sex that had doomed her, she got sick.

Probably just a bug, her physician was sure. But she wasn't getting any better. Into Lenox Hill Hospital she went for tests, and AIDS was deemed so unlikely a diagnosis that it was three weeks before doctors even thought to look for it.

"*Oh, my God*," she thought at once. "*I'm going to die.*"

'**A**LISON GERTZ wasn't supposed to get AIDS,'' wrote The New York Times when she decided that perhaps she could diminish other human suffering if she publicized her own tragedy. "It's a dreadful disease, but it's also a gift," she said. "If I die, I would like to have left something, to make the world a little bit better before I go, to help people sick like me, and prevent others from getting this. It would make it all worthwhile."

After The Times story ran (**UNLIKELY AIDS SUFFERER'S MESSAGE: EVEN YOU CAN GET IT**), she got hundreds of calls and letters: words of encouragement from other HIV-positive women, a poem from a California prison inmate, a note in Portuguese from a Brazilian who praised the healing power of macrobiotic diets. AIDS hotlines lit up nationwide. Lobbying in Albany for the Gay Men's Health Crisis, the state's largest private AIDS service organization, activists found that Alison Gertz had given legislators a new awareness.

"Her case changed a lot of minds," said Dr. Nicholas Rango, director of the state's AIDS Institute.

Stylish and articulate, she appeared on the 'Joan Rivers' and "Sally Jessy Raphael" programs, on "Good Morning America," on "20/20." People magazine put her on its cover. Esquire named her Woman of the Year. She made a film for the World Health Organization. She and her parents founded AIDS groups. One of them, Concerned Parents and Friends for AIDS Research, raised more than $75,000 with a single dinner-dance at the Copacabana.

But at the end of every day of missionary fervor, there remained a dying 23-year-old woman who could only hope that AZT, Ganciclovir and Bactrim would help her stay alive until a cure was discovered.

"I've made a conscious

CHAPTER 179

THE GIFT
Alison Gertz, 1989

decision not to cry in front of people," she said. "But I do give myself a certain amount of time each month to be miserable."

AS A DIRECT result of the Alison Gertz case, HIV-positive women got new attention from AIDS researchers. *How did the virus enter a woman's bloodstream during sex? Why did men and women develop different symptoms? Why did diagnosed women die faster than men?* In 1989, all this remained unknown.

By summer, the Daily News reported, AIDS was "the biggest killer of New York City women between the ages of 25 and 34." Women represented 13% of the city's reported AIDS cases, 2,631 of them, "the fastest growing group. . . . State health officials say their numbers will double by 1993."

AS TIME WENT by, others picked up the torch and shared their painful stories. Elizabeth Glaser, wife of TV actor Paul Michael Glaser, addressed the 1992 Democratic National Convention about her battle with AIDS. Speaking before the Republicans was HIV-positive Mary Fisher, a one-time aide to President Gerald Ford.

In March 1992, as the Gertz family's fund-raising neared the $1 million mark, ABC broadcast a two-hour TV movie, "Something To Live For: The Alison Gertz Story." Within 24 hours, the federal AIDS hotline received a record 189,251 calls.

On Aug. 8, 1992, Alison Gertz died at her family's summer home in Westhampton Beach, L.I. Said a friend who was at her deathbed: "I think she knew that we were all going to be all right, and decided it was okay to go."

NICOLE BENGIVENO DAILY NEWS

CHAPTER 180

LOVE STORY
The Happy Land Horror, 1990

By MARA BOVSUN
Special to The News

WHAT STARTED IT, as they start so many things, was just another matter of the heart on a cold Saturday night in the city.

Heartsick 36-year-old Julio Gonzalez went to the Happy Land social club, at 1959 Southern Blvd. in the Bronx, to plead with Lydia Feliciano to let him come home to the East Tremont apartment they had shared for eight years and from whose warm comforts she had pitched him five weeks earlier. Feliciano, who checked coats at the unlicensed club, told him to get lost. She had lots of boyfriends. What did she need him for?

They argued. Bouncers appeared. About 3:30 on Sunday morning the 25th of March 1990, Julio Gonzalez was shown the door.

Enraged, stomping off into the icy early morning, he shouted back at Feliciano, "You won't be here tomorrow!" He was wrong about that. She did live to see another day. But 87 other people didn't.

INITIALLY HE considered just squealing to the cops about the illegal club and getting it shut down. The Happy Land was supposedly out of business, supposedly closed two years earlier during a crackdown that followed a killer fire at a Bronx social club called El Hoyo. Despite the vacate order, though, the place was still operating. So Julio Gonzalez thought about letting the law know about that.

But the point was, he was very angry.

"The devil got to me," he explained to cops later.

The devil made him pick up an empty plastic jug from the street. The devil made him walk to a nearby filling station and buy a dollar's worth of gasoline.

Then the devil made him run back to the club, where the drinks were flowing and dancers moved to the beats of salsa and reggae and *samonango teleno* from Honduras, which was the Central American country that most of the Happy Land patrons called home, and then the devil

made him pour the gasoline around the front door, which was the place's only point of entrance and exit, and throw in two lighted matches.

ENGINE COMPANY 45 was just two blocks away. But by the time firefighters got to the roaring inferno a mere instant later, the screams already had been silenced.

Some 200 firefighters put out the blaze in five minutes. Then they crept into the smoldering ruin, and right away there were 19 charred bodies. They weren't even on the second floor yet.

"Just layers of bodies," firefighter Dennis Devlin told the Daily News. "Intertwined, contorted, fused together from the heat. We had to untangle them. You could reach up and there was always another body."

Minutes earlier, the crowd of young Honduran immigrants had been celebrating birthdays, new jobs, soccer-league victories or just the weekend. They were mostly illegals who had fled the grinding poverty of their homeland to work in El Norte as housekeepers and day laborers. On a Saturday night, Happy Land was their Rainbow Room. They were all wearing their party best. In death, some were holding one another tight. Some were slumped in their chairs, drinks still in their hands. Some had sought to somehow save themselves by hiding under tables.

There were no sprinklers, no windows, no way out except through the flames that had blasted the front door off its hinges. Just six people got out alive, including Lydia Feliciano. For 61 men and 26 women, the American dream was over.

EMERGENCY MEDICAL Service crews ran out of body bags before daybreak, and they were just stacking up the corpses like cordwood under a tarp as word fast spread

among the 6,000 Hondurans and other Latinos in East Tremont and hundreds of anguished people raced to the torched social club to stand in the icy drizzle and wait to identify husbands, wives, mothers, sweethearts. Whole families had been wiped out. It was the city's worst fire toll since the Triangle Shirtwaist Factory blaze of March 25, 1911, 79 years earlier to the day.

The Triangle fire had been a terrible accident. This was arson. Julio Gonzalez, a Cuban Army deserter who had come to the U.S. in the 1980 Mariel boatlift, was now the worst mass murderer in the nation's history.

COPS FOUND HIM sleeping in his small rented room on Buchanan Place, still smelling of gasoline 12 hours later. He readily confessed and was charged with 174 counts of murder, two for each victim. When he went to trial in the summer of 1991, it took the prosecutor five minutes to read the names of the dead.

Gonzalez pleaded temporary insanity. He had been very angry. The devil got to him. The jury didn't buy that, and he got the max, 25 to life.

"There are many to be blamed," said Judge Burton Roberts now, directing the court's ire at Happy Land's wealthy landlords — real estate tycoon Alexander DiLorenzo and club leaseowner Jay Weiss, husband of actress Kathleen Turner, who at the time of the Happy Land fire had been starring on Broadway in "Cat on a Hot Tin Roof." DiLorenzo and Weiss were later fined for building code violations — no sprinklers, for example — and their insurance companies settled up with the victims' families for $15.8 million.

City officials repented having allowed their 1988 crackdown on illegal social clubs to run out of steam, and they launched a new crusade against such establishments. This continued in force for about a year, after which the illegal club scene once again returned to normal in the poorer immigrant neighborhoods of the City of New York.

By TOM ROBBINS
Daily News Staff Writer

THE FIERY RABBI, his familiar beard now gone gray, spoke as fervently as ever to some 60 of his followers gathered in the big second-floor ballroom.

The topic was the threat to Israel posed by the recent Iraqi invasion of Kuwait. The place was the old Halloran House hotel on Lexington Ave., grandiosely renamed the New York Marriott East Side.

It was the 5th of November 1990, and the meeting was billed as the founding conference of a new group, the Zionist Emergency Evacuation Rescue Operation. But the hook for the crowd wasn't the group, but the speaker. For more than two decades, Meir Kahane had loomed as a key figure in local and international Jewish affairs, a lightning rod for the controversy that he seemed to delight in arousing.

Every Jew a .22 had been his 1960s battle cry in the tame streets of Brooklyn's Borough Park, when, after being fired by his Howard Beach, Queens, congregation, he formed the Jewish Defense League — a group of self-described former "nice Jewish boys" who now practiced martial arts, conducted rifle practice and mimicked the tactics of the Black Panthers. But if some of its antics were juvenile, the JDL's other motto — "Never Again" — resonated deeply with many post-Holocaust Jews.

The enemy then had been the Soviet Union, which denied Jews the right to emigrate, and JDL members threw stink bombs into Lincoln Center to disrupt Russian ballet performances. They also were linked to a real bomb tossed into the office of a theatrical producer who handled the Bolshoi Ballet. One person died in that blast, and 13 were injured.

Moving to Israel in the 1970s, Kahane referred to Arabs as "dogs" and demanded their removal from Israel. So extreme was he considered by Israeli authorities that he was barred in 1988 from running for reelection to the Knesset.

But, at age 58, Kahane remained a force to be reckoned with in Israeli politics, largely because of his still-strong base among right-wing New York Jews and his potent fund-raising abilities. He had publicly announced that he intended to be Israel's prime minister someday.

Tonight his remarks were warmly received, and when he took his seat shortly after 9 p.m., well-wishers pressed forward to be closer to him.

Among them was a solidly built man with black hair and Middle Eastern features. El Sayed Al Nosair, a 34-year-old Egyptian, had been viewed with some initial suspicion by the guards as he entered the meeting. But he was, after all, wearing a yarmulke.

NOSAIR SAT patiently through the rabbi's long speech, then joined the group advancing toward him. He wore, one person in the audience noted, a strange smile.

An instant later, a pistol shot exploded in the room and a high-caliber bullet plunged into the left side of Meir Kahane's neck and ripped outward from his right cheek.

Pandemonium erupted as Kahane slumped to the floor, bleeding profusely. Nosair, waving a large silver gun, fled toward the door. There he

CHAPTER 181

NO IMMEDIATE LINKS

The Assassination Of Meir Kahane, 1990

Kahane

ran into Irving Franklin, a 73-year old Jewish activist who had been selling pamphlets outside the room. Franklin threw a body block at the fleeing man and was shot in the leg.

Nosair bolted down a flight of stairs, raced through the hotel's high-ceilinged marble lobby and burst through the revolving doors onto the east side of Lexington Ave. at 48th St. There, he jumped into a yellow cab and, at gunpoint, ordered driver Frank Garcia to speed away.

The terrified Garcia did as instructed, then — a law-abiding New York City cab driver — slammed on the brakes when the light turned red at the next corner. Panicked, Nosair jumped out of the cab, gun in hand, and was immediately spotted by Postal Service Police Officer Carlos Acosta, who drew his own pistol and ordered Nosair to freeze.

Both fired at once. Acosta, wearing a bulletproof vest, was struck in the chest. Nosair, hit in the chin, fell to the street, his .357 Ruger revolver skittering around alongside him.

Upstairs, in the hotel ballroom, an Emergency Medical Services team was working feverishly to save the life of Meir Kahane as JDL members crowded around their fallen leader.

But, rushed to Bellevue Hospital, Kahane was declared dead at 9:57 p.m.

WITHIN AN HOUR, dozens of mourners were gathered outside Bellevue, weeping and waving Israeli flags. At one point they began arguing violently over who would lead a prayer service.

Inside, gunman Nosair wasn't talking. A devout Muslim and member of a mosque, he had emigrated from Egypt in 1981 and become a U.S. citizen in 1989. He lived quietly in Cliffside Park, N.J., with his wife and two children and worked as a boiler maintenance man for the City of New York, having used a false Brooklyn address to get the job. At his home, detectives found 1,400

Nosair
SAID ELATAB MIDDLE EAST PHOTO

ANTHONY PESCATORE DAILY NEWS

rounds of automatic rifle ammunition and bomb-making manuals.

In his address book, Nosair had written the names of several Jewish officials, including two judges who recently had extradited an Arab terrorist. But they found no immediate links to any co-conspirators.

"I am strongly convinced he acted alone," said Chief of Detectives Joseph Borrelli.

At Nosair's trial a year later, Muslims and Jews daily squared off against each other like a tiny microcosm of the Mideast. "Filthy murderer," shouted the Jews. "Allah is great," responded the Muslims.

In an astounding verdict, the jury acquitted Nosair of murder but convicted him of assault and possession of the death gun. Some jurors said they'd had to give credence to the theory advanced by Nosair's attorney, William Kunstler, that one of Kahane's followers had shot the rabbi in an argument over money and then somehow planted the gun on Nosair.

A furious Judge Alvin Schlesinger sentenced the prisoner to the maximum, 7 1/3 to 22 years in prison.

For Kahane's adherents, the slaying and the verdict became new rallying cries. To honor him, they formed a new political organization called Kahane Chai — Hebrew for long life.

IT WASN'T *until three years later that federal law enforcement officials investigating the terrorists behind the deadly February 1993 World Trade Center bombing learned that the conspiracy to kill Kahane had been hatched as part of the same terrorist agenda.*

Convicted with nine others in the Trade Center blast — including some of his staunchest supporters at his first trial — Nosair was sentenced to life.

By MARA BOVSUN
Special to The News

THE WORLD'S tallest building? So what. The Statue of Liberty? Big deal. The Great White Way? Eh. For decades, *the* spot in New York City was the Automat.

It was more than a place where you could plunk a nickel into a slot and get a cup of the city's best coffee poured through a spigot shaped like a dolphin. People were born there, met and got married there, brought the whole family there for Thanksgiving. Some even died there. Princes and movie stars and huddled masses alike were mesmerized by the ornate, cathedral-like restaurants and the 5-cent crocks of baked beans and macaroni and cheese.

At their peak, there were 45 Automats in New York, and more than 350,000 people patronized them every day.

By 1991, the glory had given way to decline and only one was left, at Third Ave. and 42nd St. Finally, the company that had built the Automat empire decided to go into the mail-order catalogue business instead.

On the 9th of April, the last Automat served its last cup of coffee.

"Closed for Renovations," said the signs outside. But inside, crews had already started taking the place apart. Soon it would become a Gap.

"It was equivalent to the Woolworth Building and Macy's windows as the most public place in town," mourned Parks Commissioner Henry Stern. "It was everything."

FROM THE 1920s through the 1960s, the famous Automats were among the first places any new tourist in the big city went.

Joe Horn and Frank Hardart, who had opened their first coin-operated restaurant in Philadelphia in 1902, brought the idea to Broadway in July 1912 and built their first shop, a white, two-story terra cotta palace, in the heart of Times Square, forever linking the Automat name to the glamor of the Great White Way.

Inside was a food museum — row upon row of glass-front compartments neatly organized under illuminated signs: PIES, BREAD & ROLLS, SANDWICHES, ICE CREAM. You put in your nickel, you turned the knob, you opened the shining metal door. For New York, it was love at first bite. On opening day, customers dropped nearly 9,000 nickels.

From then on, the Automat was a Broadway sensation, feeding theatergoers, actors, playwrights, chorus girls and comics. Hollywood stars were regularly photographed there for years. W.C. Fields declared that he ate at the Automat and picked his teeth in front of the Astor.

Hordes of immigrants went there too, just off the boat, unable to order a meal from a waiter and practically penniless anyway. Thousands of people streamed in and out from early morning till late at night, drinking coffee and reading books and arguing politics and literature in a babel of languages. At the next table there might be Jean Harlow or the maharanee of Baroda, enjoying a piece of lemon meringue pie.

Then came the Crash of '29, and for the Automats, while fortunes faded everywhere else, things got even better.

FOR A NICKEL, you had always been able to sit in the Automat for as long as you pleased. Now the world was full of down-and-outers who had no appointments to keep, and the Automat was where they all went. The food was cheap and the food was good. Not fancy, but good. It was all prepared in the six-story Horn & Hardart commissary on W. 50th St. Taking their lead from Henry Ford's assembly line, H&H "flivverized" production, then whisked the food around town in a fleet of electric trucks. H&H quality-control executives sampled everything daily, making sure the cooks did their jobs properly.

Even for those without a lot of nickels to rub together, there was always free Automat lemonade, made with the free lemons and ice put out near the iced tea dispensers, and free Automat tomato soup, made with the free hot water and ketchup and salt. Despite the poverty, the sheer number of customers gave the Automats their best years ever all through the Depression.

And the Automats remained hugely popular through World War II, when they were always filled with soldiers and sailors.

With peace, they began to fade. People moved to the suburbs. Emerging fast-food restaurants cut into business.

The Horn & Hardart people tried to keep things afloat with new specials and gimmicks: rock concerts, roller-skating waitresses, cocktail parties, formal dances. But none of this ever really caught on. One by one, the Automats closed, and finally there was just one of them left, the one at Third and 42nd.

By then, the wonderful old Automat food had gone pretty dreadful anyway.

ON A SCALE of 0 to 30, Zagat's rated the Automat at an 8 in 1991: "The memories are better than the cafeteria-style food at this last remaining Automat. . . . All the charm of eating in a subway."

Eulogized Daily News restaurant critic Arthur Schwartz: "To attract a new crowd, they brought in David's Cookies and put in a salad bar. Some nights, in the kind of last-chance gesture that often compromises the dignity of the dying, they gussied up the old girl with balloons and rented her out for parties.

"It's better that she rests in peace."

CHAPTER 182

DIGNITY OF THE DYING

The Last Automat, 1991

CHAPTER 183

BIG PROBLEM
Crown Heights, 1991

JOHN ROCA DAILY NEWS

By STEPHEN McFARLAND
Daily News Staff Writer

IT WASN'T THE worst uprising the city had ever seen, but its intensity turned Crown Heights into a national symbol of hair-trigger racial animosity.

At 8:20 p.m. on Monday the 19th of August 1991, a 1984 Mercury Grand Marquis station wagon traveling west on President St. in Brooklyn collided with a 1981 Chevrolet Malibu headed north on Utica Ave.

The Mercury was driven by a young Orthodox Jewish man named Yosef Lifsh, a member of the Lubavitcher Hasidic community that made its world headquarters nearby on Eastern Parkway.

He was bringing up the rear of a three-car motorcade carrying the spiritual leader of the Lubavitchers, Rabbi Menachem Schneerson, home from a police-escorted visit to the Queens gravesites of his wife and her father.

As the rabbi and the police continued along President St., apparently unaware of the crash behind them, the station wagon careened out of control onto the sidewalk — where two black children, cousins Gavin and Angela Cato, were playing outside their homes in the summer twilight.

Both 7-year-olds were crushed beneath the big wagon's wheels. Within minutes, an ambulance from the Hasidic-run Hatzolah ambulance service and two from the city's Emergency Medical Service arrived and began ministering to the grievously injured children.

And, in many other neighborhoods, that might have been the end of the story for everyone not directly involved.

But this was Crown Heights.

THIS CENTRAL Brooklyn neighborhood of 207,000 or so people had been through the standard post-World War II story of white flight and shifting populations. By 1991, it was about 80% African and Caribbean-American and about 8% white — almost all of these Hasidim.

The two groups lived side by side in a wary state of mutual incomprehension and mistrust broken by occasional physical eruptions. Historically, Deputy Mayor Bill Lynch explained to the rest of the city, "you have two groups who feel they have a grievance. The Hasidim believe they are faced with deep-seated anti-Jewish

feeling and that they can't move safely through their community. The African-Americans feel the Hasidim get preferential treatment. They feel the Hasidim get too much in the way of police protection."

In that atmosphere, an angry crowd quickly assembled at the crash site, and the first police officers on the scene called for help, reporting that the driver and passengers from the station wagon were being assaulted.

Officer Nona Capace later told investigators that when she arrived in response to the call, she ordered the Hatzolah ambulance to remove the black-coated Hasidic men from the scene.

The children were taken in separate city ambulances to Kings County Hospital. Gavin Cato was pronounced dead; his cousin survived. A rumor quickly spread that the Hatzolah ambulance crew had ignored the dying black child to minister to their co-religionists from the station wagon. Ignited by the false story, resentments exploded into violence.

LESS THAN AN hour after the crash, 911 operators were flooded with reports of a riot at President and Utica, as blacks and Hasidim shouted at one another and fought. Groups of young black men threw rocks, bottles and debris at police, residents and homes.

By 11 p.m., a large crowd of blacks, mainly young men, was surging down President St., breaking into smaller groups that rampaged around the neighborhood attacking people and property.

"Big problem," Robert Brennan of City Hall's Community Assistance Unit reported to the superiors who had dispatched him to the scene.

At 11:20, Yankel Rosenbaum, a 29-year-old Hasid visiting Crown Heights from Australia, was attacked by a dozen or more black youths at President St. and Brooklyn Ave., five blocks from the scene of the crash.

He was stabbed four times. Cops quickly collared Lemrick Nelson, 16, who was identified by Rosenbaum as his attacker.

Rosenbaum was expected to recover despite the multiple wounds, and he was even visited in the hospital by Mayor David Dinkins, New York's first black mayor, who had gone to Kings County to meet with the families of Gavin and Angela Cato.

By 2:30 Tuesday morning, Rosenbaum was

dead, apparently because one of his knife wounds had inexplicably been overlooked by the Kings County staff and gone untreated.

That was the end of the loss of life in the Crown Heights rioting. But the street violence continued for days, as crowds of angry blacks and angry Hasidim went on confronting one another across a blue wall of police.

For three days, the Police Department emphasized a policy of restraint, concentrating on attempts to keep the warring sides away from one another.

On Thursday, the force was beefed up and the tactics were changed. The order of the day: "Take back the streets." Crowds were dispersed and mass arrests were made for unlawful assembly. Order was restored.

Forty-three civilians and 152 police officers had been injured in the four-day disturbance that had sprawled over a 94-block area. Six businesses on Utica Ave. had suffered extensive property damage.

David Dinkins fast became a lightning rod for all subsequent controversy. The Hasidim accused him of having allowed the violence to go on too long unchecked by police. Meanwhile, when he came into the neighborhood for a community meeting, unruly black youths shouted "White nigger!" at the Mayor of the City of New York, and threw bottles at him.

THOUGH A STATE *investigative panel found no evidence that Dinkins or anyone in his administration had muzzled police during the disturbances, the Crown Heights affair was a significant factor in his failure to win reelection in 1993.*

Lemrick Nelson was acquitted in state court of Yankel Rosenbaum's murder, then later convicted of federal civil rights-violation charges and sentenced to 19½ years in prison.

In 1997, the city agreed to pay a total of $1.1 million to 29 plaintiffs in a federal lawsuit brought by mainly Jewish residents of Crown Heights for injury or loss in the riots.

A wrongful death suit brought by Rosenbaum's family against Kings County Hospital was still pending in late 1998.

A grand jury declined to bring criminal charges against Lifsh, the driver of the station wagon that killed Gavin Cato, and he later left the U.S.

By CORKY SIEMASZKO
Daily News Staff Writer

THE STRANGER was barefoot and muttering to himself when he first appeared on W. 96th St.

He was big. He was bad. He was crazy.

The chief feeling that Larry Hogue initially inspired in the good residents of 96th St. was pity — not fear. When they spotted him pawing through their garbage, they started leaving milk, crackers and cheese out on the curb for him. When they found him shivering on a subway grate, they covered him with blankets. Nobody tried to chase him away.

Not yet.

THE HOMELESS had been part of everyday New York City life for some few years by now, an army of unfortunates sent packing into the streets when the state began shuttering its mental asylums. Many were just a prescription away from madness. Hundreds of them bedded down every night in refrigerator boxes, on subway gratings, on benches in the Port Authority Bus Terminal, in the hidden recesses along the train tracks at Grand Central. They begged on every corner. By 1992, there were an estimated 100,000 of them — 40% of them substance abusers, a third of them mentally ill.

Any municipal attempt to regard these souls as problems to be dealt with ran afoul, instantly, of pious civil libertarians. An emblematic case was that of Joyce Brown, better known as Billie Boggs, who lived at Second Ave. and 65th St., often cursing at the top of her lungs and usually defecating where she pleased. When social workers tried to commit her, the New York Civil Liberties Union fought them in court, won, then cleaned Billie up and proudly trotted her out on the talk-show circuit. She was back on the streets a few weeks later.

Two high-profile murders committed by deranged homeless men further eroded public sympathies:

Steven Smith, a 23-year-old ex-con who openly roamed Bellevue Hospital dressed as a doctor, a stolen stethoscope draped around his neck, was charged in January 1989 with raping and murdering five-months-pregnant Dr. Kathryn Hinnant as she worked late one night in a hospital lab.

Two years later, a young dancer named Alexis Fichs Welsh was attacked as she walked her cocker spaniels near W. 69th St. Six witnesses identified the man who hacked her to death with an 11-inch butcher knife as a crack-addicted homeless man named Kevin McKiever.

Upper West Siders, however, viewed themselves as a tolerant bunch, and they were less put off by the raggedy legions at their doorsteps than were residents of many other neighborhoods. This, after all, was still the bastion of the liberal left, where the anti-war movement had been strongest, where the rich and poor and middle classes of many races and creeds lived side by side in relative harmony.

Larry Hogue would test them sorely.

THE MANHATTAN Spirit newspaper, writing about Larry Hogue's case in early 1992, naturally made the old point that there is no more devout a conservative than the liberal who has just been mugged.

Hogue had been mugging the whole neighborhood. Authentic fear gripped 96th St. as the public behavior of its resident homeless fixture careened from the mildly bizarre to the bent, a change that appeared to coincide with the arrival in the late 1980s of a new urban plague — crack cocaine.

Overnight, the pitiful wretch became a raving lunatic who snapped mirrors off cars and heaved rocks through the stained-glass windows of a local church. He menaced children with nail-studded clubs. He stalked senior citizens and threatened to roast and eat their dogs.

The police would arrest Hogue and take him to the psycho ward. Cut off from his crack supply, Hogue's demons would disappear. And, after a few weeks, to 96th St. he'd return.

Then he slugged a 16-year-old girl and pushed her into the path of an oncoming Con Edison truck. She escaped unhurt, and an angry mob of bystanders held her assailant for arriving cops. Doctors said Hogue, a North Carolinian whose brain damage appeared to be the result of a head injury suffered in the Army as well as of his crack addiction, needed to be in a hospital. The courts thought otherwise, found him guilty of reckless endangerment and gave him 12 months in jail.

Then he went straight back to 96th St. again.

For four years, Hogue held the street hostage as the revolving legal door kept spinning. Doctors couldn't keep him hospitalized. Cops couldn't keep him behind bars.

Then, on Jan. 5, 1992, Hogue hurled a stone slab through the windshield of local activist Lisa Lehr's Oldsmobile so hard it bent the car frame.

First Lehr went to the police. Then she went to the Manhattan Spirit, which put the 48-year-old Hogue on the front page and turned him into a public debate.

Politicians now vowed to crack down on the Larry Hogues everywhere. Mental-health experts pondered the adequacy of state laws to commit problem people like Hogue. Liberals clashed again with city officials over civil rights. "How can a society get itself in a position where all you can do is wait for a fellow to commit a more serious crime?" demanded Paul Shechtman, the prosecutor assigned to Hogue's case. "He seems to have fallen through every crack in the system."

And while everyone blathered on, Hogue quietly bailed himself out of jail.

In August, following him around, detectives made a remarkable discovery: He had money. The man who spent his days begging at subway entrances and scrounging for food was getting about $36,000 a year from the Veterans Administration. Most of it he blew on crack.

After cops caught him slashing a parked car with a long knife and hauled him off to the Creedmoor Psychiatric Center in Queens, a battery of state psychiatrists concluded what 96th St. residents had known for a long time — Larry Hogue was "a disaster waiting to happen."

The ensuing legal battle became another test of whether people like Hogue could be committed to state hospitals. The civil libertarians branded Hogue's aggrieved upper West Sider neighbors a bunch of elitists insensitive to the needs of the poor. Hogue made it an explicitly racial matter, declaring the people who had once covered him with blankets "the 96th St. Ku Klux Klan."

In December, he was ordered committed at last. He was out six months later. By that point, though, he had found Bridgeport, Conn., more to his liking, and he resettled there. Whatever else did or did not lie ahead for him, he wasn't 96th St.'s problem anymore.

CHAPTER 184

No Place Like Home

The Wild Man Of 96th St., 1992

Gotti in dock, Gravano on stand.

CHRISTINE CORNELL SPECIAL TO THE NEWS

CHAPTER 185

CURTAINS
The Dapper Don Goes Over, 1992

By GENE MUSTAIN
Daily News Staff Writer

THE MOST PREGNANT pause in Mafia history occurred on March 2, 1992.

This was the four electric moments that elapsed between the time Salvatore Gravano was called to the witness stand in a Brooklyn federal courtroom and the time he actually sat down and began burying John Gotti.

Gotti, the most flamboyant gang boss since Al Capone, waited out the delay with a scowl. Gravano, once his faithful underboss, now the biggest underworld informer since Joe Valachi three decades earlier, was fretting in a room off the judge's chambers. He was nervous, and his new government friends were giving him a pep talk.

The courtroom, filled with Gotti acolytes and FBI agents, stayed as quiet as a confessional. In the annals of the New York mob, No. 2 had never betrayed No. 1. And until the moment Gravano finally entered, some Gotti stalwarts were banking on a loss of nerve.

That possibility evaporated a few minutes into Gravano's testimony.

"John barked, and I bit," the witness said. For all practical purposes, all that was left of the John Gotti trial was the final curtain.

'THIS WAS THE greatest theater you can possibly see," the actor Anthony Quinn would say a few days later, after taking in a morning's testimony.

Quinn was one of many celebrities who went to court to show Gotti support and say so to reporters, and it was hard to fault his review.

The trial did have all the elements of great drama — strong characters locked in conflict; a plot rife with suspense and surprise; rich, original dialogue — plus a compelling back story built on ambition, betrayal and murder.

It was Gotti's fourth time in the dock since he became a household name in December 1985. He was the hoodlum cops and agents most wanted to interrogate after Gambino family boss Paul Castellano was

assassinated on a midtown Manhattan street heavy with Christmas shoppers.

New Yorkers hadn't seen such a bold and stylish Mafia hit since Albert Anastasia got his in a hotel barbershop in 1957. And Gotti, a Queens capo who had immediately succeeded Castellano, played dumb rather charmingly.

"I am the boss of my family — my wife and kids," Gotti quipped when an unrelated appointment in court gave the press a chance to grab a quote from the reputed new don.

It was the start of seven noisy years in gangland. Gotti, who looked and sounded like everyone's idea of a Mafia boss, beat three cases the authorities threw at him — once by intimidating a witness into imagining himself on a meat hook, twice by seeming to win jurors over. With each victory, his legend grew. The Teflon Don, the papers called him, the silky Dapper Don, the boss who couldn't be beat.

He rose as all the city's other Mafia chiefs fell. They, a doddering lot compared to him, were one by one chopped down by racketeering laws that made gangsters pay for lives spent in crime with lives spent behind bars. And, as they were hauled off to Marion, the hard-time prison in Illinois, Gotti cavorted in nightclubs and pretended to ignore cover stories in Time and People.

His notoriety — and in some quarters, unabashed popularity — propelled the authorities to keep going after him. And, unknown to him, the law enforcement people on the flip side of his most famous victory — his acquittal in a federal trial in Brooklyn in 1987 — had started another case the very day he strutted out the courthouse, wagging his finger and saying, "Shame on them!"

It took FBI agents and lawyers for Brooklyn U.S. Attorney Andrew Maloney five years to put it together. The team included the earnest young assistant U.S. attorney who second-seated the first trial, John Gleeson; he had since become a top prosecutor with a drawerful of scalps belonging to lesser Gambino hoods, and this time he'd occupy the first seat at the government table.

The second federal trial — the

one that brought Quinn to Brooklyn — began late in January 1992 and lasted nine weeks. It began with a demonstration and ended in a riot; in between, anonymous callers threatened to blow up the courthouse and kill the judge. It included hysterical outbursts by relatives of Mafia victims, running commentaries by gangsters posing as public relations men and, as time wore on, an increasingly agitated lead defendant.

UNLIKE IN the 1987 case, the government this time came loaded for bear. In one of the FBI's greatest black-bag jobs, agents had sneaked into Gotti's secret meeting place — an elderly widow's apartment above the Gambino playhouse on Mulberry St. in Little Italy — and planted listening devices that caught him blabbing away about murder.

One particularly devastating day, Gotti was overheard approving the demise of three men, all Gambinos accused of violating the family rules, including the one about absolute obedience to the boss, John Gotti.

"Louie DiBono," Gotti was overheard to growl to an associate. "You know why he's dying? He's gonna die because he refused to come in when I called."

That excerpt, plus others on the so-called apartment tapes, strung a noose around Gotti's neck. And the noose had grown tighter a few weeks before trial, when Gravano — one of two co-defendants in the case — went over to the government side.

Gravano had sized up the evidence and decided there was no point in going to jail with Gotti for life; he agreed to become John Gleeson's main witness.

The witness came with wicked baggage — the 19 murders he admitted under his plea deal with the government. But Gleeson bet that jurors would find Gravano credible, if loathsome, and welcomed him aboard.

Pivotally and poetically, Gravano also related an insider's account of the murder of Paul Castellano.

"I was there," Gravano told Gleeson. "John was there. We were in a car on the street. I was a backup, in case the shooters

missed."

The one-two punch of the apartment tapes and Gravano made the case against Gotti virtually unbeatable. About the only defense Gotti had was the one Gleeson had privately dubbed the "I'm guilty, so what?" defense, which Gotti — with his swagger and wit — had been planting in the public mind for years.

The jury, for the first time in Brooklyn federal court history, was both anonymous and sequestered — meaning that, among many inconveniences, the jurors' media access was controlled. Even so, Gotti hoped to get his so-what message through, somehow. After the trial began, he began popping off to reporters, making vows and jokes sure to make headlines.

"We're going to beat this," he told a Daily News reporter during one pause. "This guy," he added, referring to Gleeson and an alleged Gotti-busting obsession, "You know what he says to his wife when he gets up in the morning? 'Hiya, John.' "

His men also tried to augment the "I'm guilty, so what?" defense. That's why they brought in Quinn — and actor Mickey Rourke, as well as others — and furiously worked the courthouse hallways, telling reporters Gotti was joking on the tapes and that Gravano was a bum they were lucky to be rid of.

It was all for naught, and near the end — after the tapes were played and Gravano took the stand — Gotti knew it. At the defense table, he swore and gestured angrily.

The jury dropped the curtain swiftly, sorting through a complex indictment and, on April 2, coming to its guilty-on-all-counts decision after only 14 hours. Gotti winced, then smiled wryly, but kept quiet.

Two months later, he returned for sentencing. Outside, 3,000 faithful rioted. Inside, the flashiest boss since Capone still had nothing to say.

After the judge handed down the mandatory life sentence, Gotti was escorted out and made to trade in his double-breasted finery for an orange jumpsuit. In a few hours more, he was hustled aboard a government plane and flown to a high-security cell in Marion, the boss who finally had been beaten.

CHAPTER 186

SHE'S LEAVING HOME

The Woody And Soon-Yi And Mia Show, 1992

By DAVID HINCKLEY
Daily News Staff Writer

OKAY, SO Woody-and-Mia was a relationship that from the beginning had seemed to be composed entirely of quirks. But until that sunny day in August 1992, they always looked like harmless and charming quirks.

Woody Allen was a well-regarded film maker best known for endless variations on the theme of neuroses, most prominently his own. He didn't like to drive, and he wouldn't take elevators. He joked that he took his temperature every two hours. He invited a casual friend to dinner every few months because he didn't know how to change his typewriter ribbon. On an out-of-town movie shoot, he ordered the same dinner every night for six months (soup, sole, boiled potato, asparagus vinaigrette, creme caramel).

It was said he would not use a shower if the drain was in the middle. He wouldn't enter lakes or the ocean because fish lived there. When a scene in "A Midsummer Night's Sex Comedy" called for his character to fall into the lake, a double did the plunge and Allen poured bottles of Evian water on his head to look wet.

Allen saw none of this as especially odd. In his mind, he was a regular guy who worked days and liked a Knicks game at night. He also saw no need to publicize anything about his life except his movies.

Mia Farrow was best known in 1992 for having starred in a dozen of Allen's films, but she had grown up in showbiz, first coming to public attention as Allison McKenzie in the '60s TV soap "Peyton Place." In her youth she visited the maharishi, and at 19 she married Frank Sinatra, then 50. But her real love was collecting children. By 1992, she had four of her own, three by second husband Andre Previn and one by Allen, and she had adopted seven more.

The family included one child with a physical handicap and three Asian orphans: Daisy and Lark from Vietnam, and Soon-Yi from Korea. Farrow's idea of a good day was to walk all the children to a museum, and a good evening was to let the children invite over a quota of friends and order pizza and ice cream all around.

She was just a natural mother and homebody, she said. Besides the kids, her apartment had dogs, cats, fish, turtles, guinea pigs, chinchillas and birds. On the wall she hung a needlepoint commemorating her first date with Woody, Aug. 17, 1980. For their first several months of dating, he had his secretary make the arrangements because he felt uncomfortable speaking on the phone. Mia said she didn't find this odd.

They never lived together, he keeping his Fifth Ave. penthouse and she living across the park on the West Side. They were simply opposites, Allen would say: She hated air conditioning and loved the country. He loved air conditioning and hated the country. He also never had much time for kids, but when she said in 1989 that she couldn't imagine not being the mother of nine, Allen said he was getting to like the little critters better himself and added,

"Mia has a talent for mothering the way some people have a green thumb or a talent for medicine."

He sounded less impressed Aug. 13, 1992, when he filed a sealed motion in Manhattan Supreme Court calling Farrow an unfit mother and asking for custody of Satchel, 4, their biological child, as well as Dylan and Moses Farrow, 7 and 14, whom he and Farrow had jointly adopted.

WHILE THERE WERE rumors for some months that things had passed the billing-and-cooing stage for Allen and Farrow, it was rather a bolt out of the blue to accuse the poster girl for motherhood of being a fraud.

Asked what lay behind the filing, Allen spokeswoman Leslee Dart replied, "The documents speak for themselves. Mr. Allen has never discussed his private life in public and does not wish to begin doing so now."

That was no doubt true. White Star Line officials hadn't wanted to comment on the sinking of the Titanic, either.

But that became less of an option the next day, when the scorned Farrow dropped the bombshell announcement that the poster boy for harmless eccentricity, who incidentally was 56, was having an affair with 19-year-old Soon-Yi Previn. That was something Soon-Yi's 46-year-old adoptive mom learned when she found some snapshots Allen left lying around and saw they featured Soon-Yi with no clothes on.

Allen shrugged off the photos and added that he didn't see the affair as a big deal. "Happily, it's true," he said in a press statement.

Less happily, Connecticut officials had already begun to investigate, at Farrow's urging, the rather more shocking charge that Allen also sexually molested little Dylan in an attic.

Absurd, Allen shot back; he was far too claustrophobic to ever set foot in an attic. But the scandalous allegation had already turned the world's eye everywhere Allen never wanted it to go. In 72 hours, all privacy had imploded into a black hole.

ON AUG. 19, Mia Farrow filed a counter-motion for custody, asking that Woody Allen be allowed, at most, brief supervised visits

with any of the children. Farrow's mother, actress Maureen O'Sullivan, branded Allen a disgrace. "Soon-Yi used to be such a nice girl," she sighed.

Allen responded to that by informing Time magazine that his affair with Soon-Yi began long after Farrow told him their relationship was over, and that it had never occurred to him there were any issues beyond two consenting adults falling in love.

In October, Vanity Fair quoted friends of Farrow as saying Allen was "dangerously obsessed" with little Dylan and reported details from a home video tape on which the child, at Farrow's encouragement, talked about Allen touching her.

For Thanksgiving, Woody went on "60 Minutes" to say Mia had harassed him for months with crazed late-night phone calls in which she threatened his life and called him "the Devil incarnate." For Christmas, he said, Mia removed the notes he had put on his presents to the kids.

Mia, meanwhile, signed a $3 million book deal.

Somewhere in there, young Moses sent Allen a letter saying he hoped Woody was so humiliated he would kill himself. And Farrow's attorney charged that Woody and Soon-Yi had sex in front of Dylan. Allen complained that during his supervised visits with the kids, they would now wipe off his kisses, saying Mommy told them they couldn't love him.

In this conciliatory atmosphere, the custody case barreled into court.

Allen's side said Farrow was an "uneven" mother and suicidal besides, given to taking anti-depressants and red wine in large quantities. Farrow's Connecticut housekeeper, reversing previous testimony, said that after Mia made the Dylan tape she had commented: "Everything's set now." Farrow's side argued that Allen's self-absorbed attitude made him barely fit to keep custody of his clarinet.

Allen testified that his affair with Soon-Yi had begun when she came home from college for Christmas vacation 1991. It apparently moved on the fast track, because Farrow found the nude pictures a few weeks later.

One or two few details did seem to meet the standard of privacy. When Farrow was asked on the witness stand if one of her former husbands had threatened to break Allen's legs, she replied yes, but she had been told by Judge Elliot Wilk not to reveal which one.

IN JUNE 1993, *Wilk gave Mia Farrow custody of the three disputed children, saying he had seen nothing to indicate Allen had any parenting skills.*

In September, a Connecticut prosecutor said there was "probable cause" to believe a child molestation had occurred, but said he was dropping the case anyway, basically on grounds that everybody was sick of hearing about it by now.

A month later, a New York court replied that no, in fact there was "no credible evidence" of molestation at all, and at this point things came to an end, and the various players began to drift back home to the movies, the kids and mercifully private lives.

By TOM ROBBINS
Daily News Staff Writer

IN A CERTAIN light they look like trees, the largest in the forest, towering over lower Manhattan. Like trees, at 110 stories, the twin towers sway in the wind. They draw a daily stream of tourists and school kids who ride the swift elevators to the observatory where, on clear days, they see Connecticut. The towers are the work place of 50,000 people, a symbol of economic might. They have a grand name to match their size and prominence: The *World* Trade Center.

They are something else, however, to a group of Middle Eastern immigrants with a twisted plan to teach America a painful lesson about the casual violence and cruelty that has marked decades of Mideast conflict.

They are the perfect target.

The lesson begins shortly after noon on Friday the 26th of February 1993. Skies are cloudy and overcast; snow is predicted. A rented yellow Ford Econoline van is riding suspiciously low as it rolls into the public garage beneath the Vista International Hotel, but nobody really notices that. Now the van parks illegally on the ramp of the B-2 level at the base of the south wall of Tower One and a passenger leave quickly in a red car that has followed them into the subterranean garage.

Locked inside the parked Econoline is a terrible cargo: 1,500 pounds of explosive nitrate compounds packed in cardboard boxes, three tanks of compressed hydrogen gas, four containers of nitroglycerin. The murderous stew has been mixed in a Jersey City apartment whose walls have been turned blue by the fumes of the chemicals.

Four 20-foot long fuses are sputtering at the rate of 1½ inches per second toward one of the deadliest bombs built in modern American history.

JUST A FEW feet away, on the other side of the wall, several employees of the buildings' landlord, the Port Authority of New York and New Jersey, are working or beginning their lunch break. They include Bob Kirkpatrick, 61, a locksmith; Monica Smith, 34, a secretary who is five months pregnant with her first child; Steven Knapp, 48; and Bill Macko, 57, who runs the buildings' heating and ventilation systems.

In the garage near the van, John DiGiovanni, 45, a dental equipment salesman, is parking his car, on his way to call on a customer. Wilfredo Mercado, 37, a purchasing agent for the Windows on the World restaurant on the 107th floor, is sitting down to take a break at a loading dock.

At 17 minutes and 37 seconds after noon, the explosives ignite with enough force to blow a five-story-high, 180-foot-wide hole in the base of the tower. Like a tornado in a small space, it shreds automobiles like paper in a fraction of second and reduces 2-foot-thick concrete floors into powder.

There is an unbearable roar of wind. Then there is thunder, darkness, smoke and choking dust. This is what terrorism feels like.

THE FOUR PORT Authority workers are killed outright by chunks of pipe and concrete that are flung at them like bullets. DiGiovanni is smashed to the ground, soon to die of a heart attack and smoke inhalation. Mercado, still in his chair, is pitched headlong into the bottom of the crater that has opened beneath him and instantly buried beneath a ton of rubble.

Everywhere there is panic and chaos. One floor up, Port Authority Police Lt. Herman Gabora is smacked to the ground by falling concrete. Building mechanic Fred Ferby, working nearby, is hurled across the room and buried in debris. Maintenance man Vito Delea is knocked down, a

bloody gash in his head. The blast knocks over and deafens Hector Donascimiento as he prepares food for a concourse restaurant.

On the upper floors, the building rocks and shakes. The rumble of the explosion is heard, but there are no alarms, no explanation. Some imagine a plane or a helicopter has struck the towers. The explosion knocks out electrical systems and cripples ventilation ducts that would have sucked out the smoke that now billows up the elevator shafts and spreads out onto the floors, choking and terrifying.

The city's television stations, which have their transmitters located on the roof of the Trade Center, are knocked off the air. Only Channel 2, which keeps a backup transmitter at the Empire State Building, is able to continue broadcasting. Telephone beeper systems are similarly immobilized.

Everything is darkness and smoke. On the 57th floor, where the governor of the state has his office, there is what sounds like the crack of lightning, then the lights go out as smoke fills the suite.

It is the same on the 105th floor, where brokerage workers feel the building shake and are then plunged into the dark. With the elevators blocked, they head for the stairwells and grope their way down in darkness. It is nearly a quarter-mile from the top floor to the ground. For many, the exit is blocked halfway down where the smoke is too thick to continue. They can't go back up and they can't go down. Some try to smash windows with fire extinguishers to let in air.

Outside, at the instant of the explosion, the blast blows out windows of cars passing by on West St. Across from the towers, at Liberty and Greenwich Sts., firefighters at Engine Co. 10 feel the ground beneath them tremble. Then they answer the biggest fire alarm in city history.

People are tumbling out the doors, covered in black soot, weeping, bleeding. Within minutes, the streets are a tangle of fire trucks and emergency vehicles. Ambulances, taxis and police cars will ferry 228 people to hospitals. Another 474 will be treated on the scene for smoke inhalation. All told, there are more than 1,000 people injured.

High above, on the observatory floor, there are

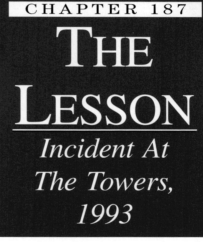

KEN MURRAY DAILY NEWS

CHAPTER 187

THE LESSON
Incident At The Towers, 1993

200 school kids who have chosen this day to visit. Some are trapped outside in freezing temperatures. About 70 are wedged into a single elevator that dangles hundreds of feet above the street. Many are kindergartners. They remain there for more than five hours awaiting rescue. Their teacher has them sing the "Barney" song: *"I love you, You love me, We're a happy family."*

THERE ARE MANY heroes. Bill Lavin, who had excused himself from the Port Authority lunchroom moments before the blast to get some air, hears his co-workers call for help on his walkie-talkie and rushes back inside. He finds six people trapped under rubble, a few feet from where a fire is beginning to rage. Lavin picks and punches his way through the debris to free them.

Food service worker Victor Castillo pulls out a small flashlight after he and friends are buried. He forms his friends into a single line, each holding the shoulder of the person in front like a contingent of the blind, and leads them to safety.

Firefighter Kevin Shea is one of the first into the bomb crater area searching for victims. In the pitch-black smoke he falls 35 feet into the chasm, shattering his knee. A lowered plastic bucket is used to haul him out.

AND THERE ARE many ghouls, eager to claim authorship of this horror. Within 75 minutes of the blast, police receive 19 phone calls claiming credit, the first of them from someone claiming to be part of a Serb terrorist group. It is a lie, but it's ample proof for newspaper headlines the next day.

The real culprits also have sent messages bragging of their deed, but theirs are lost for a time in the avalanche of pretenders.

But on Sunday, federal investigators find a twisted piece of metal with a vehicle identification number that is traced to a New Jersey truck rental office. Four days later, a man named Mohammed Salameh, a 25-year-old Palestinian, decides to press his luck by showing up at the rental office to get his $400 deposit back. The FBI is waiting.

SIX MEN *were convicted of the World Trade Center bombing, all of them sentenced to life in prison plus 240 years.*

By DAVID HINCKLEY
Daily News Staff Writer

IN JUNE OF 1912, the Alaskan volcano Mount Katmai exploded with such force and mass that it left a residual haze floating across much of the North American sky for the remainder of the summer — blocking enough of the sun's rays that temperatures dropped an average of 13 degrees, and those on the ground below ever after referred to 1912 as the year without a summer.

The baseball strike of 1994 had a very similar effect.

At 12:45 a.m. on the 12th of August, the moment the Seattle Mariners wrapped up an 8-1 victory over the Oakland A's, both teams walked off the field and the unthinkable became the truth: Baseball ended.

The rest of the 1994 regular season, 668 games, was never played. The playoffs were not held. The World Series, an annual national event every autumn since 1905, was canceled. It was as if "north" had fallen off the American compass.

"This is bad for New York," Mayor Rudolph Giuliani said one day into the strike, "and it's bad for America."

THE YANKEES AND Mets played on Aug. 11, and both games went into extra innings, as if some external force wanted to squeeze in every last possible moment of baseball. In the end both teams lost, as if by that point it much mattered.

Adding to the frustration for New York fans, the Yankees led their division on Aug. 11, seemingly poised to win their first championship since 1981. That would have been particularly gratifying insofar as Don Mattingly, the team's much-admired captain, had never played in a Series and his deteriorating back made it problematic how many more seasons he could play beyond 1994.

The Mets also were rebounding from several grim seasons, and baseball interest generally had been running high. Tony Gwynn of the San Diego Padres was hitting .394 on Aug. 11, giving him a legitimate chance to become the first player to hit .400 since Ted Williams in 1941.

Come the strike, then, the local teams had to refund hundreds of thousands of pre-sold tickets, which was only the beginning of the strike's cost. The lost-revenue estimate would eventually reach $20 million for the Yankees, $16 million for the Mets.

The players forfeited millions in lost salaries, and in a sport where the average career lasts less than five years and a new kid wants your job every spring, giving up two months of prime showtime is a gamble.

The biggest cost, however, came in the loyalty of the fans whose ticket and hot dog dollars underwrite the whole enterprise. At a point when football was nipping at baseball's heels as the National Pastime, and more kids wanted to be Michael Jordan than Cal Ripken, it was an act of sheer insanity for baseball to tell the fans forget it, it's over, we're taking our ball and going home.

But that's what baseball did, and fans howled with fury to talk shows,

DAN FARRELL DAILY NEWS

CHAPTER 188

THE FINGER

Baseball Goes Home, 1994

letters columns and anyone who would listen at the local sports bar, where the TV was now turned to Australian-rules thumb wrestling.

Baseball, to which fans gave their hearts each summer, had given fans the finger.

BASEBALL HAD KNOWN strikes and lockouts before — seven since the ballplayers unionized in 1966. A nasty 50-day strike in the middle of the 1981 season split that season in half.

But there had always been the sense in 1981 that both sides would settle. In mid-August 1994, as Don Mattingly headed home to Ohio and Steve Howe to Montana and Wade Boggs to the Florida Keys, the wind blew no such scent.

And how did it get to this point? Money, of course.

What had for much of the century been a small group of family-owned teams, operating on annual budgets of a few million dollars and worth about that in resale value, now were big business. Annual budgets were moving toward $50 million, with

revenue growing apace, and a team like the Yankees, for which George Steinbrenner and his partners paid $10 million in 1973, was now probably worth $200 million-$300 million.

A healthy chunk of this new money was also flowing to the players, thanks to the mid-'70s Andy Messersmith decision that turned all players into free agents at the end of their contracts rather than binding them to one team forever through the "reserve clause."

It wasn't until the late 1950s that any player made $100,000 a year, and until well into the '60s, most players held off-season jobs.

By 1994, that was less necessary. The average salary had risen to more than $1 million, which was commensurate with the general revenue growth in the game, but which still far outstripped the average fan's ability to absorb such a number.

A player who could hit .260 in the major leagues ranked in the elite 1% of all professional baseball players. But to the fan, who only compared

him to other major leaguers, he was just average, and the idea that he could pull down $1.4 million a year seemed testimony to a sports world gone mad.

At the very least, these economics insured that neither owners nor players had much public support. Daily News baseball columnist Bill Madden summed up local fan reaction by comparing it to Henry Kissinger's reported crack about the Iran-Iraq war: It was a shame they couldn't both lose.

MILLIONAIRE PLAYERS fighting with billionaire owners over how to divide up the fan's $10 bill. No, there was little sympathy for the participants. Only for the sport they had seemingly left for dead.

Technically, the strike was triggered by the owners' demand for a "hard" salary cap — an absolute limit prohibiting a team from spending more than 50% of its revenue on player salaries. That was the only way, the owners argued, to save the sport from the fiscal ruin of astronomic salary escalation — and they were counting on that public resentment of those high salaries to put pressure on the players to give in.

The owners seemed to forget the public had little use for *them*, either — because the owners paid those salaries, meaning the "cap" was a request that the players save the owners from themselves.

In any case, the players, now getting about 58% of total revenues, were not about to vote themselves a pay cut — and as much as they looked like spoiled millionaires to the average fan, they were also in the rare labor situation where they could call the shots. These employees, unlike assembly line workers at Caterpillar, had unique skills and name recognition that could not be replaced. They also wouldn't have to sell pencils if they missed a few paychecks.

So periodically there would be a meeting between the owners' representative, the helpless Richard Ravitch, and the players' representative, the humorless Donald Fehr. Nothing would be accomplished, and as weeks went by, the owners incrementally canceled the rest of the season, then the playoffs, then the World Series.

Fans, whose reaction swung between anger and a vow of disinterest, had a final irrational burst of hope in early September — the sense that okay, guys, you really had us going there, but you wouldn't really blow off the World Series, would you?

Yes, they would.

In January, WQEW radio host Jonathan Schwartz canceled his annual Super Bowl Sunday salute to baseball, saying that this year there was nothing to salute.

THE STRIKE *was settled in the spring of 1995, two months after both sides rejected President Clinton's plea that it be settled by Feb. 5, the 100th anniversary of Babe Ruth's birthday. The owners did not get a hard salary cap and Don Mattingly, who retired after the 1995 season, never played in a World Series. Major league attendance, which had been 69 million in 1993, dropped to 50 million in 1995.*

By DAVID HINCKLEY
Daily News Staff Writer

BEING THAT the whole point of being a club kid was that you were way cooler than everyone else because you acknowledged no limits and recognized no rules and nothing really mattered and thus everything you did in your every waking moment was a work of art, it is perhaps mildly ironic that when club-kid gurus Michael Alig and Robert Riggs finally got around to murdering someone in March 1996, they did it like a couple of dimwit busted-nose mobsters.

The murder, they didn't much care about. But the style — ah, in the club world, style was everything.

Michael Alig ran a network of trendy downtown clubs for moneyman Peter Gatien and, while he was something less than the household word he imagined himself to be, he had achieved a certain notoriety in the modest loop of clubs and the media that cover them, a

ROSARIO ESPOSITO

CHAPTER 189

FABULOUS
Club Kids, 1996

circle that since the beginning of Manhattan nightlife has always made everyone feel famous and important.

Alig's specific job, in fact, was to become and stay famous, because that was how he kept the fickle public eye from wandering away to clubs other than the ones he ran, like Danceteria and Dance 2000.

In this pursuit, Alig one night led some 80 club kids into the Times Square Burger King and ordered Whoppers all around. Sensing BK was BYO, the kids arrived with their own vodka, which they drank out of paper cups before Alig climbed onto a table and gyrated wildly as his kids pelted him with paper, trash and half-eaten burgers.

He was dressed at the time in silver lamé stockings. Just silver lamé stockings.

Moments like this — or the one where he urinated off a balcony onto a bartender — illustrated a basic lesson of club dynamics: A few crazy people are necessary to insure a club gets a buzz. Ideally this draws a few famous people whose presence accelerates that buzz. This in turn draws the people who actually pay the bills — young adults out for a good time, single professionals with some money to burn, the bridge and tunnel crowd from the boroughs and Jersey. Those ordinary people are not-so-secretly scorned, because of course they are not nearly fabulous enough. But their presence is tolerated because it underwrites the glamor crowd and spins a profit for the owner.

As a promoter, Alig was good. As early as 1988, when he was 22 and not long off the train from South Bend, Ind., he promoted himself onto the cover of New York magazine, for a story on club kids and their glittery world.

Living for the decadent revelry of the night was hardly a pastime invented in the '80s, of course. Back through hip-hop clubs, Studio 54, the

Peppermint Lounge, 52nd Street, the Cotton Club and the speakeasies of the '20s, not to mention a citywide honeycomb of neighborhood "social clubs," New Yorkers had long cherished shadowy places where the more annoying rules were not tightly enforced.

Furthermore, each successive generation brought its own style to the scene, changing the fashion, the music and the drugs of choice. In the case of club kids of the '90s at Limelight, the Tunnel, Danceteria, Nell's, Dance 2000 and dozens of other joints that opened and closed as if someone were surfing with a remote control, the drugs took a harsh turn.

From the "poppers" of Studio 54 and the relatively modest stimulant Ecstasy, hard-core club patrons of the '90s increasingly turned to crack cocaine, heroin and Special K, the street name for ketamine. Developed as an anesthetic in the '60s, ketamine in high doses created intense hallucinations, not to mention the potential loss of all neural sensation.

Some saw this as a recipe for disaster. Alig saw it as an opportunity. A heavy user himself, he saw as his role in these drug supermarkets the guy who got on the figurative PA system, encouraging shoppers to buy more.

In March 1995, he threw himself a 30th birthday party at Limelight, the former church on Sixth Ave. and 19th St. He called it Bloodfeast and the invitation showed Alig dead on the floor, his skull demolished with a hammer and a popular club kid named Genitalia enjoying a forkful of his brains. "Melting in a bloodbath," the invitation promised. "Legs cut off!"

By this time, Alig was getting

many of his own drugs from one Andre (Angel) Melendez, who had arrived from Colombia in the '70s and whose signature club outfit was a pair of feather-covered wings.

Melendez said he wanted to make $100,000 dealing drugs and then start making movies. By early 1996 he had $20,000, which he stashed in Alig's

Michael Alig

apartment at Riverbank West.

Alas, Alig and Angel had an edgy relationship, held together more by supply and demand than genuine affection. Early in 1996, by the account of friends, Angel found Alig had "borrowed" one or two thousand dollars from his stash, and demanded repayment. Alig said he should count the money as his contribution to the rent, and an argument ensued in which Angel threatened to tell the cops about the backstage drug action at Gatien's clubs.

At this point Alig's friend Riggs, also known as Freeze, entered the room and attempted to mediate by smashing Angel on the head with a hammer. Angel dropped to the floor in convulsions and then, according to statements given to police, Alig poured Drano into his mouth and taped it shut.

Angel died of asphyxiation and Alig and Freeze put him in the bathtub. A week or so later, inconvenienced by their inability to take a shower as well as by Angel's increasingly unavoidable odor, they hacked off his legs, wrapped them in garbage bags and threw them in the river. Then they packed the rest of the body into a cardboard box, flagged down a cab to drive them back to the river and gave the rest of

Angel the opportunity to go meet up with his legs.

POSSIBLY NO ONE else would have missed Angel much, but he did have a brother, who started tacking up missing-person posters. A Village Voice story asked where Angel had gone and hinted vaguely that someone out there had been talking about the murder a great deal. That was Alig, who could never resist telling a good story to impress the other club kids.

Publicly, however, Alig insisted he didn't know anything, and soon he took Angel's remaining $18,000 and went off to spend some time in the Midwest.

When he came back later in the year, figuring the coast would be clear, he found that Peter Gatien had filled his job. By all accounts, this upset him much more than Angel's disappearance ever did.

Meanwhile, Angel's body had long ago washed up on Staten Island. Now, in November, he was finally identified through dental records. Police busted Alig's Manhattan roommate on a cocaine rap and, to beat hard time, she gave him up. In December, cops arrested Alig with his New Jersey roommate at a motel in Toms River.

Once behind bars, Alig complained that he was regularly being abused by the other inmates, but bravely added that he had turned his time into a fabulous party at which the inmates held drag fashion shows with the guards as judges.

He regularly called his old friends in the media and kept up-to-date on all his press clips. He enjoyed a TV documentary on his club years, called "Party Monster." In September 1997, Alig and Freeze pleaded to manslaughter and got 10 to 20 years each.

In early 1998, Peter Gatien was tried on charges of allowing his clubs to become drug distribution centers, and while Alig's information had been pivotal in assembling these charges, he was considered too morally tainted to be an effective witness. Gatien, acquitted, immediately announced plans to reinvigorate his club empire.

By WENDELL JAMIESON
Daily News Staff Writer

THE QUEEN OF The Skies, it was called, and at 8:18 p.m. on July 17, 1996, the Boeing 747 jumbo, TWA Flight 800, Kennedy to Paris, eased away from its gate carrying 230 souls who would be dead in less than 30 minutes.

The cockpit voice recorder captured the crew going through the mundane details of take-off and ascent. They chatted about an erratic fuel gauge as they brought the plane to 13,000 feet. On the port side, window-seated passengers could see all of Long Island stretching into the Atlantic, swathed in orange. The "Fasten Seat Belt" signs were still on.

The humming engines revved higher as the liner got clearance to climb to 15,000.

At 13,700, a thundering blast ripped the jet apart. The cockpit sheared off whole and dropped downward into the night. Now the headless fuselage, wings engulfed in flaming jet fuel, lurched onward as seats, floorboards, wiring, baggage, shoes and passengers sprayed out into the dark, and the fiery carcass hurtled forward for another 2½ miles before it slammed into the water.

The medical examiner would later reassure grieving relatives that their loved ones had not suffered. The blast, he said, had created such sledgehammer-like force that it instantly broke everyone's neck.

ALONG Westhampton Beach, on the fishing docks of East Moriches and other towns near Long Island's Shinnecock Canal, many watched the strange fireworks show out at sea and heard distant thunder. Several thought they had seen a tiny red dot streaking upward, into the sky, seconds before the shattering blast.

Then they watched as two giant pieces of airplane spiraled, flaming, into the sea.

Fishermen and boaters ran to their docks, revved engines and headed outward with blankets and bottles of water for any survivors.

Of course, there were none. There was nothing but fire across the dark waters as far as they could see.

WITH FIRST LIGHT, there was silence. As the sun rose in the blue-green morning, it glinted off the calm ocean and made rainbows in the sheets of jet fuel coating the sea. Across a debris field half the size of Manhattan, rescuers-turned-salvagers picked up pieces of airplane and shreds of bodies and the bobbling possessions of those who had been aboard Flight 800.

A pair of blue jeans, neatly folded. A nylon shaving kit. A bottle of cologne. A double-decker bus ticket stub. A New York guidebook.

BILL TURNBULL DAILY NEWS

CHAPTER 190

HOMESICK ANGEL
Flight 800, 1996

Underwear. Passports. A bottle of Nivea cream. A paperback novel, the last-read page marked. Sneakers. A crushed jewelry box. Two baseball caps tucked inside each other. A photograph of a little girl standing on a beach.

FAST BEHIND the rescuers came the investigators. James Kallstrom, the head of the New York office of the FBI, and Robert Francis of the National Transportation Safety Board held a joint press conference the afternoon after the crash. Kallstrom would head up the criminal probe, to determine whether TWA 800 had been brought down by terrorists; Francis and his team would investigate the possibility of catastrophic airplane malfunction.

It had to be terrorists, everyone was certain. Surely it was unthinkable, Kallstrom hinted, that a Boeing 747, the workhorse of the sky, thousands of them taking off and landing every day, could just blow apart on its own. And he confirmed that investigators were eying one particularly harrowing scenario: a missile, shot from below to bring down TWA 800.

Indeed, many ground witnesses were sure they had seen something shooting toward the doomed jet. And radar tapes seemed to show a small dot zipping through the sky. Investigators fanned out along the docks of Long Island's South Shore, questioning boaters. They contacted the Navy and the National Guard, both of which had warships, helicopters and aircraft in the area at the time of the blast: *Had Flight 800 been accidentally shot down by the military?*

Kallstrom promised quick answers as engineers began putting the jet back together, piece by salvaged piece, in a hangar in Calverton, L.I.

But as the summer dragged on, and as the papers reported each daily tally of bodies freshly recovered from the sea, there were no answers, just raised hopes quickly dashed.

The Boeing's engines, investigators said, could solve the puzzle. But each was recovered and found to be intact.

The cockpit voice recorder, they said, would surely contain the key. But there was nothing on it, besides a comment from Capt. Ralph Kevorkian remarking that the plane was "flying like a homesick angel" — pilot slang for going too fast — and a split-second noise just before it abruptly cut off.

Several shadowy terrorist organizations claimed responsibility, but the claims were quickly discarded as braggadocio.

Investigators flew to Greece, from which the jet had flown into New York just before it took off for Paris, but nothing turned up. Everyone who had ever come into contact with the liner was questioned.

Nothing.

The case seemed to break open when traces of explosives were found on several seat cushions. But this apparent strong lead dissolved as well when it was learned that explosives had been hidden on the jet months earlier to test bomb-shiffing dogs.

FLIGHT 800, the investigators finally theorized, had indeed just blown up in midair. Fuel fumes in the nearly empty center tank had ignited, they decided, cleaving the jet in two and setting the full wing tanks ablaze. The FBI dropped out of the case, the bomb and missile theories discounted. And the NTSB forged ahead, finding that the most likely culprit was a faulty probe in the tank designed to check the fuel level: Somehow, a microscopic spark had arced between the probe and a frayed wire and ignited the fumes.

BUT THE *absence of any truly conclusive findings allowed Flight 800 to enter the great conspiracy annals, and many are convinced to this day that the plane was destroyed by a missile accidentally fired by a Navy cruiser and that officialdom, all the way up to the highest levels of government, has covered that up.*

By TOM ROBBINS
Daily News Staff Writer

BY RIGHTS, at the close of the 20th century, the nation that conquered the Depression and built the world's strongest economy, helped defeat worldwide fascism and won the Cold War should have been able to step back and take a breath. Maybe even a bow.

Instead, in the wake of the World Trade Center and Oklahoma City explosions, it found itself daily afraid of small men with twisted minds and recipes for bombs — vermin who lived somewhere in the mazes and the warrens of the big city, faceless little guys wandering around thinking unthinkable things.

Guys like Gazi Ibrahim Abu Mezer.

A 23-year-old Palestinian from Israel's West Bank, traveling on a Jordanian passport, Abu Mezer arrived in New York in the late spring of 1997 and took to the city like a pigeon to the park. Together with another footloose young Palestinian, 22-year-old Lafi Khalil, Abu Mezer took a cheap rathole on the fringe of trendy Park Slope near Brooklyn's Arab neighborhood. They put tea and rice in the pantry, plugged in a second-hand TV, tossed a couple of mattresses on the floor and called it home.

Sometimes they picked up a bit of money sweeping floors. Most of the time they just watched the TV soccer games, studied the girlie magazines at the corner newsstand and slickly called out "hey, baby!" to women on the street.

This was certainly paradise compared to the grinding poverty and daily perils of the West Bank, where Abu Mezer had once been arrested for stoning Israeli troops. And here in paradise he had grand plans.

At a neighborhood hardware store, he bought batteries, wires, nails. Along with a bit of gunpowder, those materials became several crude but very deadly devices, entirely capable of killing all living things within 25 feet.

WHAT HE WAS going to do, he boasted to his visitor Abdul Rahman Mossabah on the night of the 30th of July, was carry his homemade pipe bombs in a knapsack a few blocks north on Fourth Ave. to the bustling Atlantic Ave. subway station, where thousands of Brooklynites using many subway lines merged with commuters from the adjoining Long Island Rail Road station.

A lot of the people he would kill certainly would be Jews, he said, and he would be as great an Islamic warrior as the bombers who recently had killed 15 persons and wounded 150 in a Jerusalem market. He was very angry at the paradise America now in any case, for he had been nabbed for jumping a subway turnstile; Gazi Ibrahim Abu Mezer would avenge himself.

If he himself were to perish in this great explosion, he would be a martyred Muslim. Were he to live, he would become a proud soldier of the prestigious Islamic Jihad.

"I will burn them like this!" he cried gleefully, detonating a tiny pile of gunpowder on the grimy apartment floor.

Mossabah was dubious. A recent arrival from Egypt, where he had won a U.S. visa in an immigration lottery, 31-year-old Mossabah had always thought that Islam counseled against wanton mass murder. Personally, he liked America. He hoped to bring over the rest of his family somehow.

Troubled in his soul, he took a long walk in the Brooklyn night.

And when he found two Long Island Rail Road police officers, he knew he must unburden himself of his terrible secret. He could speak almost no English. Flailing his arms, desperate to

MIKE ALBANS DAILY NEWS

CHAPTER 191

BOOM BOOM BOOM

Faceless In Paradise, 1997

make himself understood, he fell back on sounds that, in the late 20th century, were recognized the world over.

"Boom," he said. "Boom boom boom."

The cops understood.

JUST BEFORE DAWN, an army of police and SWAT troops moved into the streets around Abu Mezer's building, crept across his litter-strewn courtyard and smashed through his door. One of the two men in the back bedroom lunged for the nearest pipe bomb, and the cops opened fire. Khalil was hit five times, Abu Mezer twice.

As they were arraigned in their Kings County Hospital beds and charged with plotting murder and mayhem, police and FBI agents searched the grubby apartment and found not only five bombs filled with big 16-penny nails, but also a long, rambling letter that threatened suicide bombings, demanded the release of jailed Islamic militants and claimed credit for the 1996 midair explosion of TWA Flight 800 off Long Island.

Abu Mezer wasn't good with English either. *"We are ready by our soul-blood boombes bombs to deines our gouls goals,"* his manifesto vowed.

Notwithstanding all that, there appeared to be no real connection between the two suspects and

Hamas or any other radical terrorist group. Indeed, the more investigators dug into the backgrounds of their men, the less they came up with *mujahedeen* warriors and the more they came up with just a couple of politically infatuated morons.

But it remained the case that the bombs were deadly real. Replicas assembled and exploded by the FBI at the Marine Corps base at Quantico, Va., fragmented into deadly shards of metal and nails that were hurled for yards with flesh-puncturing velocity. Had Gazi Ibrahim Abu Mezer set them off inside the Atlantic Ave. subway station, they certainly would have killed or maimed hundreds of human beings.

AWAITING TRIAL, Abu Mezer kept his guards busy. He made two escape attempts, once leaping atop a courtroom table right in front of marshals who quickly tackled him, another time crawling into an air duct, where he fast became stuck.

During a trial recess, he turned on co-defendant Khalil, beating him in a holding pen near the courtroom in Brooklyn Federal Court. Khalil was treated for his injuries and then kept apart from his comrade for the remainder of the trial.

Lawyers for Abu Mezer said the real crime was attempted blackmail, not attempted murder. The bombs, they said, were merely props to shore up a scheme in which Abu Mezer intended to defraud the government by exposing a phony terror campaign.

But the young Palestinian didn't help himself when he took the witness stand and triumphantly announced that he had once attempted to assassinate President Clinton.

As Lafi Khalil's fingerprints were not found on the bombs or the letter, the jury acquitted him of the bomb plot. But they did convict him of immigration fraud. Gazi Ibrahim Abu Mezer was found guilty of conspiracy, weapons possession and threatening to use a weapon.

And off they went to serve many years in prison, as, in the City of New York in the frightened final moments of the American 20th century, the mazes and the warrens continued to swarm with faceless little guys just like them.

By DAVID HINCKLEY
Daily News Staff Writer

WHAT THEY never grasped, the bleeding hearts and the do-gooders, was how *annoying* the squeegee men were.

Nobody thought the squeegee men were making any money out of their racket, no more than enough to buy a couple of 40s and a sandwich. But here you were just trying to get out of town, make it through some tunnel or over some bridge, staggering to the finish line of another hardworking day, and they were, frankly, just one more thing you didn't need.

It happens right about the time you hit the 30-minute backup. Even when the light changes you're not moving, and suddenly, *splat!* The dirty water hits your windshield and some guy is pushing it around with a rag and you're yelling *No! No! No!* and maybe you even turn the wiper blades on, but all that does is spray more dirty water around and by then he's finished anyway and you've got to slam your window shut before he knocks on it and says, "C'mon, man, I'm trying to make it, not take it."

So he stands there, and you're not going anywhere, and finally you fish out 50 cents and pass it through as small a crack as you can make in the window, and when you finally crawl away, you feel like you got fleeced for a week's pay at three-card monte.

Whatever other perceptions were held by Rudolph Giuliani, a Brooklyn kid from a family of tavern owners, firemen and cops, he understood that this was annoying.

CHAPTER 192
QUALITY OF LIFE
The Mayor Who Understood, 1998

EVY MAGES DAILY NEWS

EVEN BEFORE he was elected the 107th mayor of the City of New York in November 1993, Rudy Giuliani insisted that if the city took care of little things, like squeegee men, big things wouldn't seem so insurmountable anymore.

The quality-of-life campaign, he called it, and he had plucked the right chord for a population whose concerns in the last 40 or so years had downshifted from being toasted by Soviet nuclear warheads to tripping over the homeless.

So before the mayor's first term was over, he declared war on street vendors, aggressive beggars, jaywalkers, protruding newsstands, subway singers, hookers, rude cabbies and, of course, porno shops.

A Republican squeezed into office by an anorexic 44,000 votes in a Democratic town, Rudy Giuliani knew New York's favorite mayors have been political Frank Sinatras — tender tough guys who at 10:15 deliver impassioned sermons on the importance of teaching civility and respect to children, and then at 10:25 suggest New York's slogan should be "Our city can kick your city's ass."

New York City, proudly marching into the next millennium with its humility intact.

TRUE, MANY New Yorkers would not have chosen Rudy for their dad. Much of the black media called him Ghouliani, or worse. But there was a fairly broad consensus in many other communities that in contrast to his much-too-nice predecessor David Dinkins, Giuliani was making the city a better place to live in.

Not because he said he kicked the mob out of the Fulton Fish Market — how were you going to prove that, ask the fish? — but because even if he couldn't make all cab drivers civil or send all the rude beggars to Jersey, he understood that the average citizen, while sympathetic in theory to the plight of the less fortunate, might be ready for a break.

It's okay to think about the quality of your own life, Mayor Giuliani told that citizen, and when reelection time rolled around in 1997, he was swept back into office by a margin more commonly associated with Chinese balloting under Chairman Mao.

While Giuliani had pushed hard on bigger issues, like putting welfare recipients to work and upgrading the schools, his victory was a clear endorsement of the quality-of-life campaign. In

1998 he celebrated with a further crackdown on vice, a campaign to keep the Yankees in town by moving the Bronx Bombers to the West Side of Manhattan and the suggestion that perhaps police should start ticketing people who drop gum on the sidewalks.

He conceded the gum suggestion was not an official declaration of war, but added that he still expected to take some jibes from the press — which, when it came to quality-of-life, still did not get it.

In reality, the quality-of-life campaign did better in the voting booth than on the actual scorecard anyhow.

The squeegee men were a big win, and so were the street vendors of 125th St., whom Giuliani swept to 116th St.

When he targeted porn shops and topless bars in 1997, the First Amendment folks huffed and puffed. But in 1998 the courts approved Giuliani's plan to exile those places to the far side of nowhere.

Of course, the porn shops were a gimme with voters. No big demographic has ever gone to the wall for the rights of dirty old men in raincoats.

Less acclaimed was Giuliani's campaign to kick food vendors off midtown streets, on the grounds they clogged pedestrian traffic. They probably did. But they also provided cheap lunches for hundreds of thousands of midtown office workers, who did form a significant voting demographic. That plan was withdrawn for further study.

An equally long overreach was the crackdown on jaywalking, a daily activity that most New Yorkers have always regarded as a solution, not a problem. Ordering the police to stop New Yorkers from jaywalking was like sending them into Kissena Park with orders to stop the grass from growing.

The most interesting aspect of the jaywalking campaign was Giuliani's eagerness to announce and defend it. To his supporters, it showed he was fearless. To his detractors, it showed he was clinically megalomaniacal.

The latter argument gained momentum when New York magazine unveiled a bus ad proclaiming itself "The Only Good Thing in New York Rudy Hasn't Taken Credit For." The mayor, widely viewed as somewhat thin of skin at best, took his incensed complaint against this ad all the way to the U.S. Supreme Court, which in 1998 told him to

sit down and be quiet.

The man did have his confrontational moments, it was true. Giuliani fought with teachers, firefighters, black activists and police unions. He forced a schools chancellor and a police commissioner to leave. He was so infuriated by a brief spat with the head of the Grammys in 1998 that he did everything but have a severed horse's head sent to the awards ceremony, which he did not attend.

There was periodic concern this aggressive attitude might be trickling down in the wrong ways — like to the wrong police officers. In 1994, a football thrown by a Bronx man named Anthony Baez glanced off Officer Francis Livoti's squad car. An argument ensued, Livoti placed a choke hold on Baez and he died. In 1997, citizen Abner Louima required surgery from severe injuries apparently sustained in a stationhouse after he was arrested on a minor charge.

Even the mayor departed from his usual benefit-of-the-doubt support for the police in the Louima case, making a major show before the 1997 election of appointing a commission to study police brutality. But when the report was delivered in 1998, calling for several reforms, the mayor tossed it in the circular file.

THE THING WAS, drivers never really disliked most squeegee men, personally. They just wanted to get home without having to case every street corner like a combat patrol looking for snipers.

The mayor knew that. He knew a wise leader always understood what people complained about over dinner. Whether or not Rudy Giuliani could guarantee every child a good education and put every welfare recipient to work, he could show concern over pebbles in the path of daily life.

In contrast to Soviet warheads, squeegee men were something a mayor could do something about. In the battle for the quality of life in the World's Greatest City, Rudolph Giuliani fought The Good War early, and as the five boroughs celebrated a century together, they seemed quite happy to have a mayor who realized that through every crazy flash point, every apocalyptic crisis, every inexplicable news bulletin and every bizarre character of those hundred years, the one practice that hardly ever failed any leader was giving the people what they wanted.